2022 EDITION
BUSINESS MANAGEMENT
COURSE COMPANION

Loykie Lominé
Martin Muchena
Robert A. Pierce

OXFORD
UNIVERSITY PRESS

![Oxford University Press logo]

Great Clarendon Street, Oxford, OX2 6DP, United Kingdom

Oxford University Press is a department of the University of Oxford. It furthers the University's objective of excellence in research, scholarship, and education by publishing worldwide. Oxford is a registered trade mark of Oxford University Press in the UK and in certain other countries

© Oxford University Press 2022

The moral rights of the authors have been asserted

First published in 2022

All rights reserved. No part of this publication may be reproduced, stored in a retrieval system, or transmitted, in any form or by any means, without the prior permission in writing of Oxford University Press, or as expressly permitted by law, by licence or under terms agreed with the appropriate reprographics rights organization. Enquiries concerning reproduction outside the scope of the above should be sent to the Rights Department, Oxford University Press, at the address above.

You must not circulate this work in any other form and you must impose this same condition on any acquirer

British Library Cataloguing in Publication Data
Data available

978-1-38-201683-4 (print)
10 9 8 7 6 5 4 3 2 1

978-1-38-201687-2 (ebook)
10 9 8 7 6 5 4 3 2 1

Paper used in the production of this book is a natural, recyclable product made from wood grown in sustainable forests. The manufacturing process conforms to the environmental regulations of the country of origin.

Printed in China by Golden Cup

Acknowledgements

The publisher would like to thank the following for permission to use their photographs and artworks:

Cover: Selina Yau/Getty Images

Artworks: QBS Learning

Photos: pvii: LightField Studios/Shutterstock; **pxii:** pongimages/Shutterstock; **p1:** Travel mania/Shutterstock; **p5:** Alexandros Michailidis/Shutterstock; **p6:** Split Second Stock/Shutterstock; **p10:** ESB Professional/Shutterstock; **p16:** marvent/Shutterstock; **p19:** E.J. Baumeister Jr./Alamy Stock Photo; **p20:** fotomak/Shutterstock; **p23:** ST House Studio/Shutterstock; **p25:** create jobs 51/Shutterstock; **p28:** Franck Chapolard/Shutterstock; **p31:** Lenscap Photography/Shutterstock; **p38:** zieusin/Shutterstock; **p41:** David Grossman/Alamy Stock Photo; **p42:** kickers/iStock/Getty Images; **p43:** Geography Photos/Universal Images Group/Getty Images; **p45:** COLOR PHOTO/Shutterstock; **p53:** Martin Priestley/Alamy Stock Photo; **p61:** MOZCO Mateusz Szymanski/Shutterstock; **p67:** Greg Epperson/Shutterstock; **p70:** Iakov Filimonov/Shutterstock; **p71:** PHILIPPE HUGUEN/AFP/Getty Images; **p73:** TungCheung/Shutterstock, **p80:** pinkbadger/123RF.com; **p82:** Vadym Pastukh/Shutterstock; **p86:** MikeDotta/Shutterstock; **p87:** Benny Marty/Shutterstock; **p104:** OMONIYI AYEDUN OLUBUNMI/Alamy Stock Photo; **p106:** NakoPhotography/Shutterstock; **p115:** VGstockstudio/Shutterstock; **p117:** Drazen/Getty Images; **p121:** Monkey Business Images/Shutterstock; **p126:** Serghei Starus/Shutterstock; **p135:** fizkes/Shutterstock; **p140:** Greanlnw studio/Shutterstock; **p145:** Jim West/Alamy Stock Photo; **p149:** katjen/Shutterstock; **p154:** Pat Behnke/Alamy Stock Photo; **p156:** Casimiro PT/Shutterstock; **p157:** Neil Cooper/Alamy Stock Photo; **p159:** MEE KO DONG/Shutterstock; **p163:** Daniel Irungu/EPA/Shutterstock; **p167 (T):** Marina Usik/Shutterstock; **p167 (B):** alice-photo/Shutterstock; **p172:** Kuznechik/Shutterstock; **p181:** Rawpixel.com/Shutterstock; **p195 (T):** Drazen/Getty Images; **p195 (B):** RZUK_Images/Alamy Stock Photo; **p202:** Jonathan Austin Daniels/Getty Images; **p216:** Space-kraft/Shutterstock; **p219 (T):** Bjoern Wylezich/Shutterstock; **p219 (B):** MT.PHOTOSTOCK/Shutterstock; **p227:** jax10289/123RF; **p229 (T):** AngieYeoh/Shutterstock; **p229 (B):** DenPhotos/Shutterstock; **p231:** monticello/Shutterstock; **p232:** JeanLucIchard/Shutterstock; **p237:** Altrendo Images/Shutterstock; **p239:** Girts Ragelis/Shutterstock; **p241:** Andrew Kemp/Alamy Stock Photo; **p242:** Jeremy Moeller/Getty Images; **p243:** Freebird7977/Shutterstock; **p248:** Sorbis/Shutterstock; **p257:** Kenishirotie/Shutterstock; **p261:** ispyfriend/Getty Images; **p263:** dpa picture alliance archive/Alamy Stock Photo; **p267:** Kalki/Alamy Stock Photo; **p273:** incamerastock/Alamy Stock Photo; **p281:** Ned Snowman/Shutterstock; **p282:** Geopix/Alamy Stock Photo; **p285:** Tupungato/Shutterstock; **p292:** Mick Buston/Alamy Stock Photo; **p294:** GoodLifeStudio/Getty Images; **p299:** Peter_Fleming/Shutterstock; **p303:** Nick Beer/Shutterstock; **p309:** economic images/Alamy Stock Photo; **p315:** sirtravelalot/Shutterstock; **p316:** shutter_o/Shutterstock; **p319:** Jason Mintzer/Shutterstock; **p322 (T):** Tetra Images, LLC/Alamy Stock Photo; **p322 (M):** Marco Crupi/Shutterstock; **p322 (B):** Nordroden / Shutterstock; **p328:** Cum Okolo/Alamy Stock Photo; **p329:** Don Pablo/Shutterstock; **p334:** Hadrian/Shutterstock; **p336:** Olivier Le Moal/Alamy Stock Photo; **p340:** MDart10/Shutterstock; **p343:** Bernsten/Shutterstock; **p354:** Vitaly Titov/Shutterstock; **p363 (L):** Frederic Neema/Sygma/Getty Images; **p363 (R):** Corbis/VCG/Getty Images; **p366:** Sunshine Seeds/Shutterstock; **p371:** balajisrinivasan/Shutterstock; **p375:** vichie81/Shutterstock; **p380:** Gorodenkoff/Shutterstock; **p388:** Monkey Business Images/Shutterstock; **p389:** kornnphoto/Shutterstock; **p393:** Proxima Studio/Shutterstock; **p405:** Jasmin Merdan/Getty Images; **p406:** Iakov Filimonov/Shutterstock; **p401:** Oleksii Didok/Getty Images; **p313:** Jenson/Shutterstock;

The publisher and authors are grateful to those who have given permission to reproduce the following extracts and adaptations of copyright material:

Adapted from the article 'Coffee recycling' published by bio-bean Limited. Used with permission from bio-bean Limited.

Adapted from the blog 'The story of microfinance in India' by Jhanvi Sonakia, published by Bridge India on 25 March 2020. Used with permission by Bridge India.

Extract from the article 'How Kenya created the world's most successful mobile-payments service' by Andrea Esther Barry, published by HBS digital initiative. Reprinted by permission of the Author.

Adapted from the article 'What is Accounting Ethics?', published by Corporate Finance Institute (https://corporatefinanceinstitute.com/resources/knowledge/accounting/accounting-ethics/). Used with permission of CFI Education, Inc.

Extract from the article 'Future of Residents and Staff Secured as Care Home is Sold Out of Liquidation', published by Real Business Rescue.

Adapted from article 'Overview of sustainable finance', published by European Commission'. © European Union, 1995-2021. Used under CC-BY-4.0.

Adapted from article 'How Niche Brands Create Social Media Sales In China' by Amber Ran BI, pubblished by Jing Daily (4 September 2020). Used with permission of Jing Daily.

Adapted from article '13 Amazing Differentiation Strategy Examples (in 2021)' by Ani Miteva, published in mktoolboxsuite.com. Used with permission of the Author.

Adapted from article 'How 5 Massive Companies Changed Using Market Research' by Survey Police, published by SurveyPolice Blog (21 March 2015). Used with permission of Survey Police.

Adapted from article 'Apple's seven Ps marketing mix' by Kevin Vejo. Used with permission of Author.

Adapted from article 'The circular economy giant you've never heard of is planning a major expansion' by Madeleine Cuff, published by GreenBiz. Used with permission of GreenBiz.

Adapted from article 'Robots have already taken over our work, but they're made of flesh and bone' by Brett Frischmann and Evan Selinger. Copyright Guardian News & Media Ltd 2021. Used with permission of guardian News & Media Ltd.

Although we have made every effort to trace and contact all copyright holders before publication this has not been possible in all cases. If notified, the publisher will rectify any errors or omissions at the earliest opportunity.

a la memoria de Gisela

Contents

Introduction iv

Introduction to concepts v

Introduction to the Business Management toolkit vii

Introduction to Theory of Knowledge (TOK) x

Introduction to inquiry xii

Unit 1: Introduction to business management
1.1 What is a business? 1
1.2 Types of business entities 14
1.3 Business objectives 34
1.4 Stakeholders 52
1.5 Growth and evolution 59
1.6 Multinational companies (MNCs) 76

Unit 2: Human resource management
2.1 Introduction to human resource management 80
2.2 Organizational structure 94
2.3 Leadership and management 102
2.4 Motivation and demotivation 111
2.5 Organizational (corporate) culture **(HL only)** 131
2.6 Communication 139
2.7 Industrial/employee relations **(HL only)** 144

Unit 3: Finance and accounts
3.1 Introduction to finance 149
3.2 Sources of finance 152
3.3 Costs and revenues 166
3.4 Final accounts 170
3.5 Profitability and liquidity ratio analysis 187
3.6 Debt/equity ratio analysis **(HL only)** 194
3.7 Cash flow 202
3.8 Investment appraisal 210
3.9 Budgets **(HL only)** 219

Unit 4: Marketing
4.1 Introduction to marketing 227
4.2 Marketing planning 235
4.3 Sales forecasting **(HL only)** 251
4.4 Market research 256
4.5 The seven Ps of the marketing mix 270
4.6 International marketing **(HL only)** 308

Unit 5: Operations management
5.1 Introduction to operations management 313
5.2 Operations methods 320
5.3 Lean production and quality management **(HL only)** 327
5.4 Location 338
5.5 Break-even analysis 349
5.6 Production planning **(HL only)** 362
5.7 Crisis management and contingency planning **(HL only)** 374
5.8 Research and development **(HL only)** 378
5.9 Management information systems **(HL only)** 385

Unit 6: Assessment
External Assessment 396
Internal Assessment 403

Index 407

Access your support website for the answers to the student workpoints, toolkits and practice questions here:
www.oxfordsecondary.com/9781382016834

INTRODUCTION

This book is a companion for students of Business Management in the International Baccalaureate Diploma Programme (IB DP). It rigorously follows the *DP Business Management Guide* published by the IB, regarding not only the syllabus (the curriculum **content**) and the assessment strategy, but also the IB educational philosophy (the IB Learner Profile) and pedagogy (the IB approaches to teaching and learning, especially regarding the importance of **concepts** and **contexts**).

As IB educators, we wrote this book to help you study business management, and also to inspire you to become a lifelong learner, giving you the keys to make sense of the dynamic business world around you.

During your course, you will study a diverse range of organizations, both for-profit (commercial) ones and not-for-profit ones, and you will learn about many topics, from marketing to finance, and from human resources to operations. You will discover how the concepts of change, creativity, ethics and sustainability can help us understand the world of business management as it is today, and as it will develop tomorrow. Regarding contexts, you will explore local, national and international examples and case studies of business organizations, and how they adapt to their environments.

Some of the questions and activities in the book will challenge you and you will want to learn more. This book can act as a foundational resource if you plan to study business management at university, or if you want to set up your own business. It also gives you the skills necessary to work in an organization and understand its structure, functions and operations. Even if you do not plan to study business management at university or set up your own business, this book and your IB DP Business Management course will help you to better understand the world around you and give you valuable knowledge and skills applicable to whatever vocation calls you.

In this book we also make many links to theory of knowledge (TOK), which is at the core of the Diploma Programme. TOK can help you understand Business Management (for example, the sources of knowledge we have in our subject), and in turn Business Management can help you better understand what TOK aims to achieve in terms of critical thinking.

This book will help you as you study IB DP Business Management, at standard level or at higher level, and it will also help you become an even better IB learner!

The authors

The "In cooperation with IB" logo signifies the content in this textbook has been reviewed by the IB to ensure it fully aligns with current IB curriculum and offers high quality guidance and support for IB teaching and learning.

INTRODUCTION TO CONCEPTS

Concepts can be defined as big ideas that reach beyond the boundaries of a specific subject. For example, topics such as "social media marketing" (Chapter 4.5) and "benchmarking" (Chapter 5.3) are subject-specific: they belong exclusively to Business Management. However, big ideas such as ethics and creativity are not specific to Business Management: they are "concepts".

IB DP Business Management has four key concepts: change, creativity, ethics and sustainability.

Defining the four key concepts

There is no universally accepted definition of these terms, but the table below gives you a solid starting point. You are not expected to memorize the definitions; what matters is that you understand these four key concepts, both in general and in Business Management.

Concepts	Initial definitions
Change	**Change** refers to modification or transformation from one form, state or value to another, over time or across places. In Business Management, change is usually the result of internal or external influences. For example, externally, new competitors and new trends in consumer behaviour may lead an organization to adapt its objectives and operations; internally, the arrival of a new CEO may lead to a shift in the priorities of the organization's strategic plan.
Creativity	**Creativity** refers to the process of generating new ideas and considering existing ideas from new perspectives. It includes the ability to recognize the value of ideas when developing innovative responses to problems. In Business Management, creativity may lead to the incremental or radical improvement of a business idea, of a product or of a process, in order to be more successful or more competitive. For many organizations, a key challenge is bringing innovation and managing the process of improvement in a sustainable way that does not create conflict.
Ethics	**Ethics** refer to the moral principles and values that form the basis of how a person or an organization conducts their activities. In Business Management, it is important to realize that every decision may have moral implications, impacting on internal and external stakeholders and the natural environment. Ethics is present throughout the organization, from marketing communication to operations, and from recruitment of new staff to accounting practices.
Sustainability	**Sustainability** refers to the ability of the present generation to meet its needs without compromising the ability of future generations to meet their own needs. It can be enhanced by conserving resources, finding more efficient ways to produce or discovering new resources. In Business Management, decisions should consider the triple bottom line of people, planet and profit, and their resulting impact, taking into account not only financial aspects, but also communities and the natural environment.

Why learn about the four key concepts?

There are several reasons why it is important to learn about the four key concepts.

1. The four key concepts enable you to **gain a better understanding of Business Management as a whole** by realizing how the different topics relate to one another. For example, creativity connects research and development, product development, and promotional activities. You could otherwise have the impression that the elements constituting the course are disconnected, but they are not: the concepts enable us to make these links!

> **As IB learners we strive to be:**
> **KNOWLEDGEABLE**
>
> We develop and use conceptual understanding, exploring knowledge across a range of disciplines. We engage with issues and ideas that have local and global significance.
>
> Source: *IB Learner Profile*

2. The four key concepts will help you **make connections to other IB subjects**. For example, ethics is one of the four components of the knowledge framework in TOK, and creativity is at the heart of all literature and artistic endeavour. Thinking through concepts can help you learn across disciplines, which is a key aspect of the "knowledgeable" attribute of the IB Learner Profile.

3. Your conceptual understanding is **assessed in your internal assessment** (IA), where you write about an organization from a conceptual viewpoint, ie from the perspective of one of the four key concepts. The way you connect your chosen concept and your chosen organization is assessed through criterion A, worth up to 5 marks (one fifth of your total IA score!).

4. Your ability to **think and reason conceptually** will also help you with your exams, even in the absence of a direct question about the concepts themselves. For example, Paper 3 has a social entrepreneurship focus; social enterprise is about ethics, creativity, change and sustainability, so the four key concepts give you a framework to analyse the scenario of the exam paper.

The four key concepts in this book

The four key concepts are not "extra topics" that would be added to the rest of the syllabus. Therefore there is no specific chapter about them; they are present throughout. In many cases, you will see boxes drawing your attention to important conceptual links, like the example in the margin.

> **Concept**
>
> **CHANGE**
>
> Due to changes in their external environment (such as new competitors) and changes in their internal environment (such as restructuring), organizations may need to modify their objectives and strategies.
>
> Do some research to find examples of such changes in objectives or strategies.

However, these boxes are not the only instances where you can link the concepts and the contents of the syllabus. As you progress through the book, and you learn more about Business Management, you should keep making links between the contents and the four key concepts. Likewise, as you discover new examples and case studies, and as you learn about business issues in their context, you should keep identifying links to the key concepts. This will help you to understand the concepts ... and the contents! Ultimately, the three aspects are linked (**concepts**, **contents**, **contexts**), as shown by this diagram.

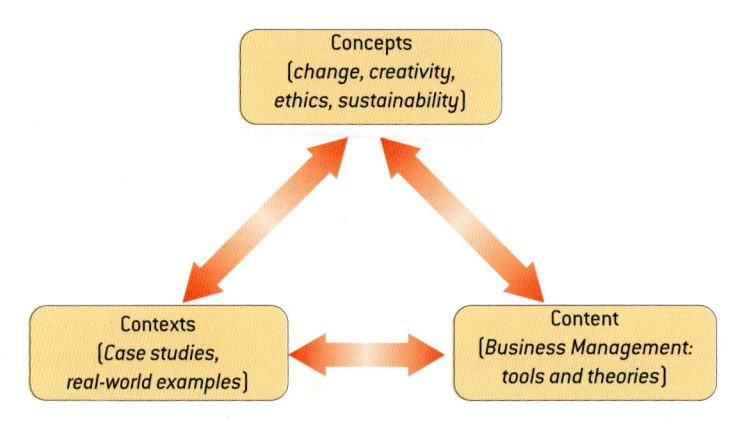

```
              Concepts
        (change, creativity,
         ethics, sustainability)
           ↗           ↘
          ↙             ↖
    Contexts   ←→    Content
   (Case studies,   (Business Management:
  real-world examples)  tools and theories)
```

INTRODUCTION TO THE BUSINESS MANAGEMENT TOOLKIT

The Business Management (BM) toolkit is a collection of tools designed to help in the analysis and evaluation of the course. These tools can be broadly categorized as either situational, planning or decision-making tools.

- **Situational tools** assist in examining the internal and external factors affecting a business.
- **Planning tools** review the action steps that businesses need to take while implementing their projects.
- **Decision-making tools** assess the possible alternatives facing a business before a decision is made.

Despite this categorization, the tools provided in this BM toolkit do have overlapping applications. They should be used to help you learn about the course content, concepts and contexts. Each unit in this book contains toolkit boxes that provide suggestions about how the BM tools are integrated throughout the course, like the one below.

> **BCG matrix**
>
> The BCG matrix is a planning and decision-making tool that uses graphical representations of a firm's goods or services in order to help the firm to decide what to keep, sell or invest more in.
>
> How can the knowledge of this tool help businesses to improve their financial decision-making?

The tables on the next two pages show the BM tools used in the course as well as their brief definitions.

Table 1 The Business Management toolkit (SL and HL)

Business management tools	Brief definition
Ansoff matrix (pages 48, 297)	The Ansoff matrix is a tool that provides a business with a framework to analyse and plan its growth strategies. The four growth strategies it includes are: market penetration, market development, product development, and diversification.
Boston Consulting Group (BCG) matrix (pages 215, 276–79)	The BCG matrix is a tool that evaluates an organization's portfolio potential based on relative market share and industry growth rate factors. It helps in long-term strategic planning and decision-making with regard to what the organization should invest in, discontinue or develop in the future. It is a four-square matrix that uses graphical representations to plot the organization's offerings.
Business plan (pages 10, 301, 324)	A business plan is a road map that provides a detailed account of a business's goals and how it plans to achieve those goals. It is a guide that lays out a business's functions from finance, human resources and marketing to operations and other elements essential to its success. It can be used to attract investment for the business as well as keep it on track.
Circular business models (pages 42, 275, 318, 331, 391)	Circular business models signify the diverse ways in which goods and services are produced and consumed. These models explore how organizations create, offer and deliver value to their stakeholders while reducing environmental pressure and social costs resulting from economic activity. In this BM course the following circular business models will be studied: • Circular supply models • Resource recovery models • Product life extension models • Sharing models • Product service system models
Decision trees (pages 68, 342)	A decision tree is a graphical tool that uses a branching model to demonstrate every possible outcome of an organization's decision. These tree-like branches represent various choices facing the organization, including costs, results, probabilities or risks. Businesses use decision trees to determine specific courses of action.
Descriptive statistics (pages 91, 98, 121, 126, 168, 369)	Descriptive statistics are quantitative means that are used to summarize a given set of data. It is a process of using and analysing given statistical data. Descriptive statistics help to present a large amount of quantitative data in a simplified or manageable form. They are broken down into measures of central tendency and measures of variability. In this BM course the following measures will be used: • Mean • Pie charts • Mode • Infographics • Median • Quartiles • Bar charts • Standard deviation
STEEPLE analysis (pages 59–62)	STEEPLE stands for Social, Technological, Economic, Environmental, Political, Legal and Ethical. STEEPLE analysis is a useful tool for a business that aims to study its external environment. It provides a detailed overview of or insight into the various external factors influencing an organization.
SWOT analysis (pages 45–48, 83, 192, 303)	SWOT stands for Strengths, Weaknesses, Opportunities and Threats. Strengths and weaknesses are internal aspects influencing an organization, while opportunities and threats are external factors affecting an organization. In conducting a SWOT analysis, a business must examine all of these elements as they all have the potential to impact its success or failure.

Table 2 The Business Management toolkit **(HL only)**

Business management tools	Brief definition
Contribution (pages 168, 349–50)	Contribution in this context refers to a set of tools that are used to aid decision-making in a business after analysing and evaluating its given revenue and cost situations. Businesses need to pay particular attention to the decisions they make due to their direct impact on their financial performance. The contribution tools studied in this case are: • Make or buy analysis • Contribution costing • Absorption costing
Critical path analysis (page 367)	Critical path analysis is a tool that helps a business to schedule and manage complex and time-sensitive projects. It is used to map out all important tasks that are essential to complete a project. It helps to set realistic deadlines for a project and monitor the achievement of project goals, providing remedial action where required. In this BM course the following will be required: • Completion and analyses of a critical path diagram (drawing of the diagram is not expected) • Identification of the critical path • Calculation of free and total float
Force field analysis (page 347)	Force field analysis is a tool used by businesses to analyse the forces for and against change to inform decision-making. It is useful when organizations are planning and implementing programmes on change management. The force field analysis diagram provides a comprehensive overview by illustrating the driving and restraining forces influencing a given situation.
Gantt chart (page 372)	A Gantt chart is a graphical tool that helps to plan and schedule project tasks. It shows a given project schedule, including how the tasks or activities are performed over a set period of time. It is useful in breaking down complex projects into a simpler display that is easy to understand. In addition, where large teams of stakeholders are involved, it helps to keep tasks on track.
Hofstede's cultural dimensions (pages 109, 311)	Hofstede's cultural dimensions is a tool aimed at understanding the cultural similarities and differences across countries and determining the various ways that business can be conducted in these cultures. It is a framework that compares the different national cultures and their dimensions as well as examining their impact on a given business setting. Countries can be classified according to six cultural dimensions: power distance, individualism/collectivism, masculinity/femininity, uncertainty avoidance, long-term/short-term orientation, and indulgence/restraint.
Porter's generic strategies (page 246)	Porter's generic strategies explore how a business can obtain a competitive advantage over other similar businesses across its specified market scope. These strategies help a business to determine its direction as well as how to beat its competition. The generic strategies include: cost leadership (producing at a low cost); differentiation (offering uniquely different and value-added quality products); and focus (selling its product to specialized market segments). Focus is further subdivided into cost focus and differentiation focus.
Simple linear regression (pages 253, 254, 351)	Simple linear regression includes a set of tools that describe or predict the relationship between two variables. They estimate how changes in an independent variable (the variable used to predict the value) may affect changes in the dependent variable (the variable being predicted). The simple linear regression models explored in the BM course are: • Scatter diagrams • Line of best fit • Correlation/extrapolation

INTRODUCTION TO THEORY OF KNOWLEDGE (TOK)

Every Diploma Programme (DP) student must complete the DP course called **Theory of Knowledge** (TOK), which is unique to the IB. TOK is about critical thinking and inquiry into the process of knowing. It is not about learning a new body of knowledge. Instead it explores the nature of knowledge and how we know what we claim to know.

TOK is taught in two ways:

- Through 100 hours of tuition (compared to 150 hours for a subject at standard level and 240 hours for a subject at higher level).
- Through the DP subjects themselves, as they all give students the opportunity to ask questions that contribute to their overall understanding of TOK.

TOK links

1. To what extent does knowing help us in predicting?
2. How do we know that our sales predictions are reliable?
3. Is it ethical to knowingly overpredict?

TOK in this book

As TOK encourages students to analyse knowledge claims and explore how knowledge is constructed, each chapter in this book suggests relevant TOK knowledge questions. They are meant to illustrate TOK and ignite classroom discussion, giving opportunities to explore the nature of knowledge and TOK connections to Business Management.

How is TOK assessed?

TOK is assessed in two ways:

- Through an essay (on one of the six prescribed titles issued by the IB for each examination session, and submitted at the end of the second year of DP for external assessment).
- Through an exhibition (normally organized in the first year of DP, internally marked by the teacher and externally moderated by the IB).

For the exhibition, students explore how TOK manifests in the world around us. You will select three specific objects (or images of objects) that connect to one of the 35 "internal assessment (IA) prompts" listed in the TOK guide. Some of those prompts have a direct relevance for Business Management; for example, "Who owns knowledge?" (number 29) conjures up images of copyright agreements and patents (see Chapter 5.8) or of data centres (see Chapter 5.9).

Links between TOK and Business Management

Name of TOK element	Brief definition	Possible links and applications to Business Management
Core theme: "Knowledge and the knower"	The core theme encourages students to reflect on themselves as "knowers", on what shapes their views and perspectives, where their values come from, and how they make sense of the world around them.	This core theme can be addressed by discussing what counts (or not) as knowledge in Business Management; where (and how) we can gain knowledge in this subject; and who created this knowledge, for what purposes, with which authority. Notions of values and communities are important, with regard to both the subject knowledge and the students themselves, within their own sociocultural and economic context.
Optional themes	Those themes all have a significant impact on the world today and play a key role in shaping people's perspectives and identities. You will explore two from a list of five: • Knowledge and technology • Knowledge and language • Knowledge and politics • Knowledge and religion • Knowledge and indigenous societies	The theme "knowledge and technology" is particularly relevant to Business Management. For example, Chapter 5.9 considers how advanced computer technologies (enabling data mining and data analytics) and innovations (such as artificial intelligence) may impact decision-making processes in business organizations, and raise ethical issues, for example about data anonymity and privacy. The theme "knowledge and language" is relevant to Business Management as some models (such as the seven Ps of the marketing mix (HL only) or the five Vs of big data) were coined in English. When translating them into other languages, we lose the consistency of the initial letters and therefore the overall coherence of the model. This shows that this knowledge about the marketing mix and about big data was constructed through the English language and is linked to that specific language.
Areas of knowledge	The five areas of knowledge (AOK) are specific branches of knowledge, with their own nature and methods for producing knowledge: • History • Human sciences • Natural sciences • Mathematics • The arts	As Business Management is one of the human sciences, it is interesting to explore how research methods such as questionnaires are trusted as reliable ways to gain knowledge (eg about a market, a product or a business), given the challenges around neutral language, leading questions, or sampling and selection effect. Market research is often undertaken to help companies increase their profits, so it could also be worth examining the purpose and context within which knowledge is pursued in the human sciences in general, and in Business Management specifically.
Knowledge framework	This tool helps to explore the themes and the AOK. It is composed of four elements: • Scope • Perspectives • Methods and tools • Ethics	**Ethics** is particularly relevant as it is one of the four key concepts underpinning the DP Business Management curriculum. The first aim of the course is *"to develop ... confident, creative and compassionate business leaders, entrepreneurs, social entrepreneurs, and ... change agents"*. Ethical decision-making is relevant in all areas of the curriculum, from the moral objectives of social enterprises to privacy issues relating to big data and consumer profiling. From a TOK viewpoint, the focus should be on ethics concerning knowledge, for example about criteria used to make judgements, who decides, and based on which values. **Perspectives** is also relevant, especially as the topic of stakeholders is recurrent in Business Management, regarding their differing viewpoints, conflicting objectives, and how they are affected by change. It is helpful to consider the differing perspectives of stakeholder groups in order to gain a greater understanding of issues as diverse as financial accounts and workforce participation.

INTRODUCTION TO INQUIRY

> **As IB learners we strive to be:**
> **INQUIRERS**
> We nurture our curiosity, developing skills for inquiry and research. We know how to learn independently and with others. We learn with enthusiasm and sustain our love of learning throughout life.
>
> Source: *IB Learner Profile*

Inquiry is a key aspect of the IB approaches to teaching (ATT) and approaches to learning (ATL): the principles that, according to the IB, can help you be a successful IB learner. Being an inquirer is the first of the ten attributes of the IB learner profile.

In Business Management, learning through inquiry can take different forms, especially:

- Inquiry through research
- Inquiry through "inquiry questions"
- Inquiry through problem-based learning (PBL)

Inquiry through research

Inquiry and research go together. This book covers the syllabus of the IB DP Business Management, but for your studies you will also need to carry out your own research to find contemporary examples of business issues around you, locally, regionally, nationally and internationally. For instance, after learning about franchising (Chapter 1.5) or about crowdfunding (Chapter 3.2), you should do research to learn about examples of franchises near you, or about recent crowdfunding campaigns on topics that interest you. This will also help you to link the contents of the course to the world around you, and appreciate the relevance of our subject to business news in the media.

Your internal assessment (IA) is a research project. The task has specific requirements regarding research activities, but research will also be necessary throughout the course to help you contextualize your theoretical learning.

Inquiry through "inquiry questions"

These open questions can help you to link the **content** of this textbook, the key **concepts** (sustainability, ethics, change, creativity) and the **contexts** (of the examples that you will find through your research). Formulating such questions is a good exercise in itself, as it makes you create links. Answering them will also help you to develop your thinking skills and your writing skills.

The table below gives you some examples of such inquiry questions.

Unit in this textbook	Examples of inquiry questions
Unit 1 Introduction to business management	• How can change lead to conflicts between stakeholders? • Is the impact of multinational corporations on host countries always ethical?
Unit 2 Human resource management	• How can a democratic style of leadership encourage creativity in a business? • Can fringe payments sometimes be regarded as not fair and thus not ethical?
Unit 3 Finance and accounts	• Why could final accounts analysis be essential in changing stakeholder perspectives? • In some countries, the state subsidizes many organizations in the creative industries. Does that mean that they do not need to be financially sustainable?
Unit 4 Marketing	• How can social media change an organization's marketing strategies? • Are all pricing strategies ethical?
Unit 5 Operations management	• Is intellectual property protection only about ethics and creativity? • How has digital technology enabled new business models to flourish?

Inquiry through problem-based learning (PBL)

PBL is about analysing a real-world problem faced by an organization and proposing solutions to it, using your knowledge of business management tools, theories and techniques. Comparing different investment options (Chapter 3.8) or different pricing strategies (Chapter 4.5) will help you appreciate the applied nature of our subject. Beyond the Business Management subject itself, this can also help you to improve other skills such as evaluation, reasoning, critical thinking, communication skills and even teamwork, if you collaborate with other students.

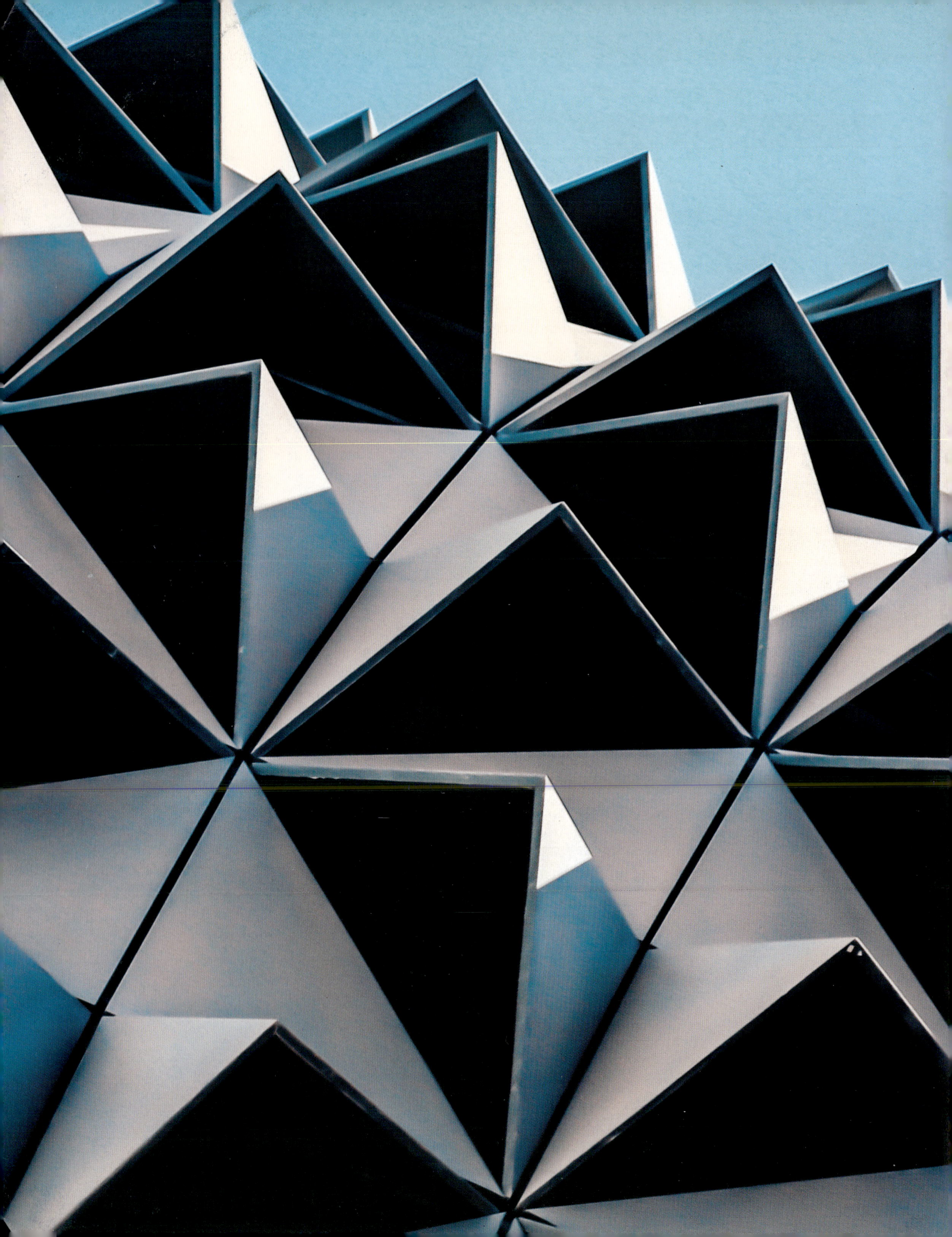

1 INTRODUCTION TO BUSINESS MANAGEMENT

1.1 What is a business?

> **By the end of this chapter, you should be able to:**
> → Explain the **nature of businesses** and how they combine human, physical and financial resources to create goods and services
> → Define **primary**, **secondary**, **tertiary** and **quaternary sectors**
> → Outline the **nature of business activity** in each sector and the **impact of sectoral change on business activity**
> → Examine **challenges and opportunities** for starting up a business

The nature of business

A business aims to meet the needs and wants of individuals or organizations through any of the following activities:

- Producing crops or extracting raw materials from the earth
- Creating a product
- Providing a service

Some businesses focus on one activity. For example, a business may grow olives or manufacture transistors. Other businesses engage in multiple activities. For example, a farm that grows olives may convert the olives into olive oil for sale under its own label. Sometimes a business will cluster several related activities or sometimes even engage in activities that are completely different from each other.

1 Introduction to business management

All of these businesses input resources and process them to generate the desired output. This is how the business adds value (sometimes referred to as "added value") to the inputs. It is rewarded by gaining revenue (sales) and/or recognition for satisfying a want or a need.

Many activities or organizations that most people would not consider to be "a business" operate under various business principles. All organizations must have human, physical, and financial resources. Thus, many charities, religious organizations (churches, mosques or synagogues, for example) and other types of organizations (such as clubs) are in a sense a business.

Needs and wants are different. To survive, we all need the basics – food and water, clothing and shelter – and many businesses provide for our basic needs. Other businesses provide for our wants. Religious organizations, charities, clubs and so on all provide services or products that people need or want, and in that sense they are businesses.

Business activity is summarized in the flow chart shown in Figure 1.1.1.

```
human ─┐
physical ─┤
financial ─┼──► production ──► goods
enterprise ─┘               └──► services
```

Resource inputs → Processes to add value → Product outputs

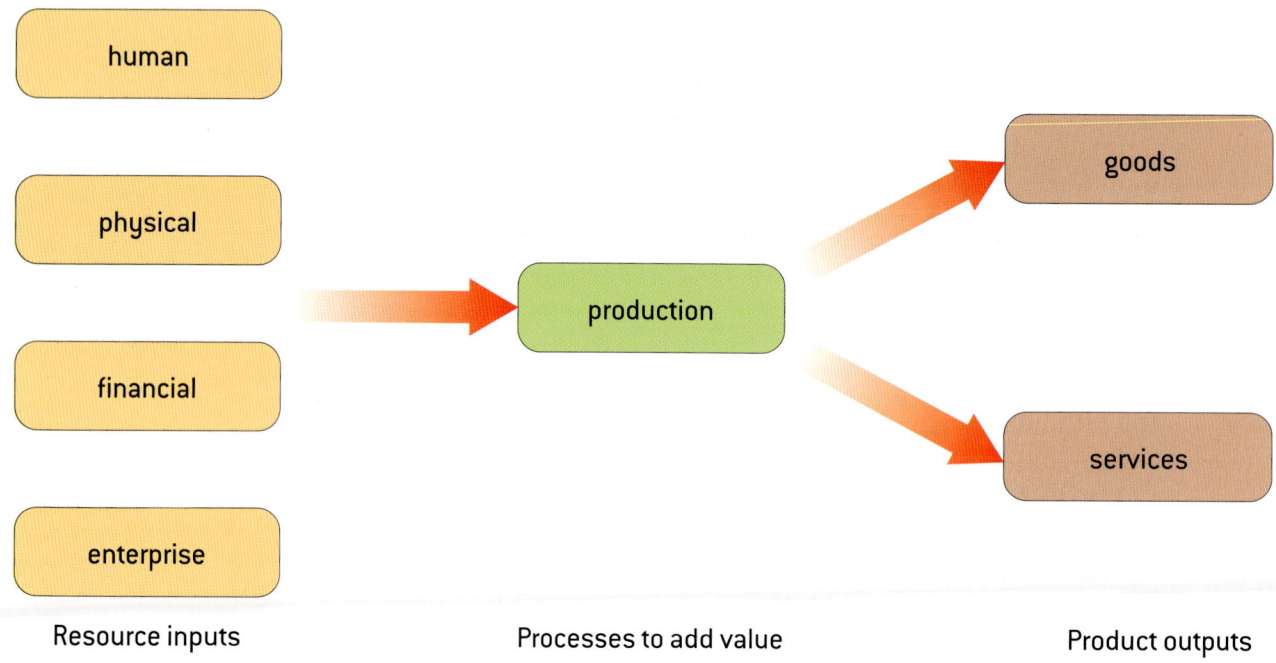

Figure 1.1.1 Summary of business activity

The **resource inputs** can be categorized as follows:

- **Human** – the right quality and quantity of people required to make the product or provide the service. All businesses, even highly automated ones, still require human input – even if it is only one person. Others require many individuals, often with different skillsets.

- **Physical** – the right quality and quantity of materials, machinery, and land space required to make the product or service. Even internet businesses require some office space and a computer.

- **Financial** – the right quantity of cash and other forms of finance required to make the product or service.

- **Enterprise** – the least tangible input but crucially important for business. It is the business idea and the determination to turn that idea into a functioning and, ideally, thriving business. Enterprise is sometimes referred to as "entrepreneurship", which is a term often associated with high-tech and cutting-edge businesses dealing with computers, smartphones, social media, etc. But enterprise exists in all types of business, including the everyday (such as lawn-mowing services, laundry services or brick manufacturing).

Production processes to add value can take many forms:

- **Capital-intensive** processes use a large proportion of land or machinery relative to other inputs, especially labour. Sometimes the land or machinery may have proprietary or special qualities (land rich in a resource, or specialized equipment with unique features), or the land and the machinery simply cost a great deal due to the scale of the operation (a car factory, for example).
- **Labour-intensive** processes use a large proportion of labour relative to other inputs, especially in relation to land or machinery. Labour-intensive operations may involve fairly low-skilled workers but can also involve highly skilled employees.

Product outputs can be categorized as follows:

- **Goods** – these are tangible products that we can physically take home. They might be items produced in the primary sector, such as agricultural products or other items extracted from the environment, or they might be things made in the secondary (manufacturing) sector, such as an iPad or a car.
- **Services** – these are intangible and the buyer does not physically take them home. They include, for example, a karate class, a medical examination, and the international delivery of a package. Retail sales are a service: the retailer provides the service of having an array of products for consumers to purchase.

Business functions

All businesses, from small start-ups to huge conglomerates, are organized along the same lines, by function – what is to be done. There are four key functions:

- Human resources (HR)
- Marketing
- Finance and accounts
- Operations management or production

The only difference between small businesses and large ones is that the owners of smaller businesses have to deal with these functions themselves, whereas a larger business can afford to hire specialized managers to carry out the functions in separate departments.

1 Introduction to business management

A small business

A large business

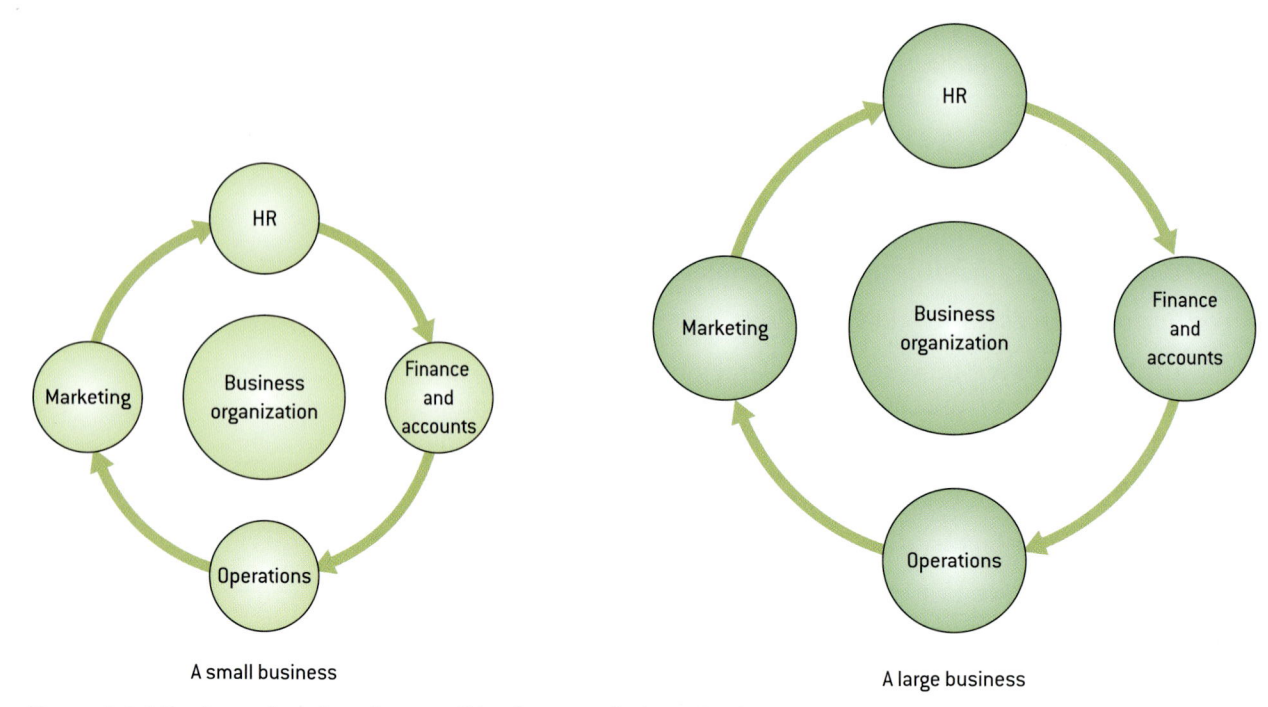

Figure 1.1.2 Business functions in a small business and a large business

The role of business departments

In larger businesses, "specialized" managers will focus only on their function and in doing so help the business to achieve its overall objectives. Some examples are set out below.

Table 1.1.1 Business functions

Function	Role
HR	Ensuring that appropriate people are employed to make the product or service and that they are suitably rewarded for doing so. To accomplish these goals, the HR department must recruit people, train them, at times dismiss them, and determine appropriate compensation.
Finance and accounts	Ensuring that appropriate funds are made available to make the product or service. To accomplish this goal, the finance and accounts department must forecast requirements, keep accurate records, procure financial resources from various providers, and ensure proper payment for goods and services acquired to operate the business.
Marketing	Ensuring that the business offers a product or service that is desired by a sufficient number of people or businesses for profitable operations. To accomplish this goal, the marketing department must use appropriate strategies to promote, price, package, and distribute the product or service.
Operations management or production	Ensuring that appropriate processes are used in order to make the product or service, and that the product or service is of the desired quality. To accomplish this goal, the operations management or production department must control the quantity and flow of stock, determine appropriate methods of production, and, in today's competitive world, look for ways to produce the good or service more efficiently.

All of these functions are interdependent. For example, if the marketing department determines that a product needs to be made differently as a result of changes in consumer taste, the operations management or production function must redesign its processes, at least to some degree. That redesign may require financial resources, which the finance department must procure. The redesign may influence the number and type of people working in the business, which would have to be coordinated with the HR function.

The character of the interdependence can change over time. Initially, businesses typically focus on survival, with HR, finance and accounts, marketing, and operations management or production all geared towards that end. Once a business is established in the marketplace, its priorities may change. For example, a business may plan to diversify (produce other goods or services), which places new requirements on each of the four business departments. If a business is very successful, then growth and even control of the market might become a priority, which could require significant modifications to the different business departments.

The strength of a particular business depends on how successfully aligned the four functions are. Is the business producing a desired good or service for the market it is targeting? Are the right people producing the good or service, and are those people rewarded appropriately (financially and non-financially)?

Small businesses often have an advantage in that they can respond quickly to changes in the marketplace. On the other hand, large businesses generally have greater resources, wider reach, and more name recognition. However, even a business dominating a market must remain vigilant. If they become complacent, large businesses can fail.

Case study

Thomas Cook

For 178 years, Thomas Cook provided travel agency services for the British. The company arranged individual and group travel first within the UK, and then to Europe and eventually to the entire world. However, when the internet became widely available, traditional travel agency services were severely threatened. Companies offering travel services (like Expedia, Kayak, and Travelocity) reduced the need for traditional travel agents.

By the beginning of the 21st century, Thomas Cook was experiencing significant competition from these new online booking services. A poorly conceived merger in 2007 with MyTravel added to Thomas Cook's problems. Though the company tried a number of tactical moves to retain its viability, none of them seemed to work. According to *The Guardian*, on the eve of Thomas Cook's collapse, only one in seven Brits used traditional travel agency services. Finally, in 2019, the venerable company that had created the phenomenon of mass tourism began laying off 22,000 employees, liquidating its assets, and leaving 150,000 travellers stranded overseas.

1 Introduction to business management

Key terms

Primary sector
the part of the economy engaged in extraction (such as of minerals or oil) or production of raw materials (farming, fishing, forestry, raising livestock, and quarrying)

Secondary sector
the part of the economy engaged in the production of finished goods (ie the manufacturing sector of the economy)

Tertiary sector
the part of the economy engaged in the delivery of services, such as banking, healthcare and restaurants

Quaternary sector
the part of the economy engaged in the production, processing and transmission of information. Whereas some consider the quaternary sector a subset of the tertiary sector, others emphasize that quaternary sector activities are based on advanced knowledge and include information technology services, consultancy, and research and development.

Primary, secondary, tertiary, and quaternary sectors

Traditionally, economists have grouped business activity into different sectors, as set out in Table 1.1.2, and this activity can take place in different geographic areas.

Table 1.1.2 Sectors of business activity

Goods	Primary	All raw materials are acquired in the primary sector. This can be by extraction, mining, farming, fishing, hunting, or even trapping. Today, because of the scarce nature of many resources in the primary sector or because of the potential to damage fragile environments, governments closely monitor activities in the primary sector.
	Secondary	In the secondary sector raw materials are processed, usually by manufacturing. Goods from the secondary sector can take many forms, such as consumer durables, non-durable consumer goods, and capital goods. For most of the 19th and 20th centuries, much secondary sector production occurred in what are referred to today as "developed" countries. Since the 1970s, however, manufacturers in developed countries have been facing increasing competition from manufacturing firms located in "developing" countries and "emerging markets".
Services	Tertiary	All services are provided in the tertiary sector, sometimes using manufactured products. These services can be financial, leisure, healthcare, education, transport, security, and many others. As manufacturing (the secondary sector) has shifted to developing countries, the tertiary sector has grown in importance in developed countries. Services such as banking, insurance, transportation, retail and wholesale, and consultancy have become especially important.
	Quaternary	This sector, a subgroup of the tertiary sector, provides services that are focused on knowledge. Generally speaking, various types of e-services and those involving IT, the media, and web-based services are considered quaternary. This sector is typical of "post-industrial" economies and, thus, many businesses in the developed world engage in quaternary activities.

The four sectors are typically linked in what is referred to as the **production chain** or **chain of production**. A chain of production is the steps through the different sectors that have to occur in order to turn raw materials into a consumer good that is marketed.

Fishing is an example of an industry in the primary sector

For example, many types of raw material (metals, rubber, materials to make plastic and glass, etc) are extracted (primary sector) and processed into the materials (secondary sector) that manufacturers turn into car parts (secondary sector). The car parts are then used on an assembly line to make cars (secondary sector). The cars are shipped (tertiary sector) to car dealerships, which sell the cars to consumers (tertiary sector). Car dealers also typically provide after-sale services (oil changes, tune-ups, and even major repairs), also in the tertiary sector. Sometimes, before consumers buy cars, they read magazines or online reports about car features and service records. Sometimes this information is free and provided by the government, but in other cases this type of information is produced by for-profit companies that sell information. This type of business is in the quaternary sector.

Sectoral change

The size of each sector of the economy may change because, just as individuals or businesses grow and develop, so too will countries. Economists usually measure the size of each sector in terms of the number of people employed by the industries in that sector. The traditional pattern is set out in Figure 1.1.3.

Closely related to changing economies are the complexities of social contexts. The more advanced sectors require more complex social contexts for businesses to thrive. Thus, whereas raw material extraction is often possible with relatively few skilled workers and large numbers of low-skilled workers, the quaternary sector relies both on highly skilled workers (producers and managers of information) and consumers – people and businesses that want and have the ability to make use of advanced information. Thus, more developed economies typically see social technologies and economies advance in tandem: as the economy develops, social technologies improve; as social technologies improve, economies develop.

However, developments are not linear. Technological innovation in one area (for example computerized word processors) and its related workers (individuals knowledgeable about operating word processors) can make other technologies and occupations obsolete, such as typewriters and typists. Thus, while some occupations become obsolete, new ones emerge (which are often perceived as "high skill").

Businesses that can anticipate or adapt to the changing environment can do well, even in industries that are perceived as "in decline". In general, developed economies have moved away from the primary sector. In both Canada and Australia, however, two primary sector industries have done remarkably well: organic farming in Canada and wine production in Australia. Another example is Germany: as one of the most developed economies of the world, it has a strong quaternary sector. However, German businesses have retained two of their long-standing strengths: high-quality engineering and a strong secondary sector.

> **Student workpoint 1.1**
>
> *Be a thinker*
>
> Think of some everyday products that you use and imagine their production chain. Consider:
>
> - A cherry pie you purchase
> - A skateboard
> - A smartphone
>
> What primary, secondary, tertiary, and quaternary businesses are involved in the production, distribution, and marketing of these products?

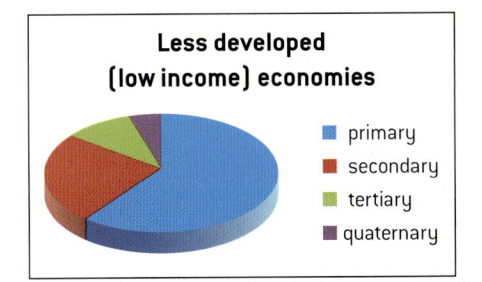

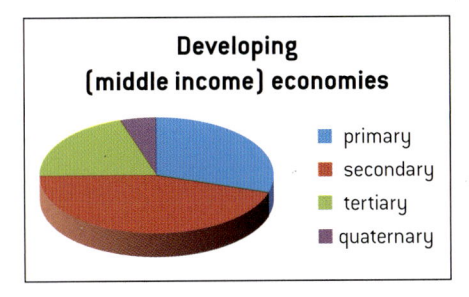

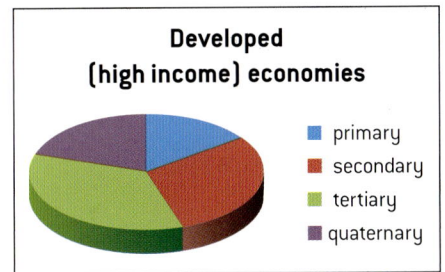

Figure 1.1.3 Size of sectors

1 Introduction to business management

The process of shifting from one proportional weighting of sectors in an economy to a different weighting (shifting from an economy based on the primary sector to an economy based on the secondary sector, for example) can produce strains on resources, such as human resources. Secondary sector businesses may require specialist skills that may be in short supply. Financial resources, too, will be diverted from one sector to another. Finally, an economy based mainly in the tertiary or quaternary sectors will require fewer physical resources (they will not be needed as much in the production of intangible services as for tangible goods).

Other strains can occur as well. As an economy shifts to the secondary sector, legislation and other protections against environmental damage are often weak, and manufacturing firms in developing countries often do more damage to the environment than manufacturing in developed economies.

Challenges and opportunities for starting up a business

Reasons for starting up a business or enterprise

People start businesses for many reasons, as summarized in Table 1.1.3. Each of these reasons presents an opportunity.

Table 1.1.3 Reasons to start a business

Rewards	Working for someone else means that you do not get to keep all the rewards yourself. Although some criticize this aspect of capitalism, one central element is that those who put their capital at risk (the business owners) get the rewards, whereas those who do not put their capital at risk (employees) receive wages or salaries that are typically less than the return on capital is to the owners. Many millionaires own "boring" small businesses.
Independence	Working for yourself means that you are your own boss and not following someone else's rules. Individuals with an entrepreneurial spirit sometimes feel constrained by bosses, policies, and procedures in large organizations. Starting your own business means that you can set and change the policies and procedures as you see fit.
Necessity	Sometimes businesses are started by individuals whose positions were made redundant or who could not find work. The necessity of having an income leads them to start a small business.
Challenge	Some people just want to see whether they can "make it" themselves. Starting a small business typically requires one person to perform all functions of the business (HR, marketing, accounts and finance, and operations management or production). Over time, if the business is a success, the business owner then has to learn new skills as his or her role changes to accommodate a larger and more complex operation.

Interest	Many interesting businesses are set up by people with a passion for something who want to just keep doing what they enjoy doing. The business producing Hawaiian Tropic suntan lotion was started by a high-school chemistry teacher who liked spending time at the beach. Many specialty shops – guitar stores, lamp stores, ballet clothing stores, rare books stores, etc – allow their owners to work in an area for which they have a passion.
Finding a gap	Businesses may see or find an untapped opportunity in order to achieve "first-mover advantage". Sometimes businesses, large or small, stumble into opportunities that they were not looking for. The idea of Post-its, one of the most successful products of the 3M Company and which revolutionized interoffice communications, was stumbled across by accident by Dr Spender Silver, a scientist working at 3M.
Sharing an idea	If you really believe in something, you may want to sell the idea to others. Yoga studios, for example, are typically owned by people who themselves do yoga and want to spread the idea that yoga enhances quality of life. Marketing the idea helps their business, but often the original motivation to open a yoga studio is to spread the idea.

> **Concept**
>
> **CREATIVITY**
>
> Creativity can be defined as the process of generating new ideas, or of considering existing ideas from new perspectives. Setting up a business involves creativity in numerous ways. For example, entrepreneurs must be creative, with the initial business idea itself, and also to prepare a business model with limited resources, to get the initial finance for their start-up costs, or even to invent the name of the business.
>
> Can you think of other areas where creativity is a key element of entrepreneurship? This may give you ideas for your IA.

The process of starting up a business

Two features are common to all successful start-ups:

- The business idea
- Planning

The **business idea** refers to the fundamental activity that the business will do, whether it is something basic (such as a house-cleaning service) or something more sophisticated (such as manufacturing). The business idea can be market-driven – that is, determined by the needs of the market or product – or service-driven, which means that in some sense the entrepreneur or business must convince others that the product or service is worth purchasing.

Regardless of whether the new business is basic or sophisticated, market- or product-driven, the entrepreneur must have a basic business idea. Then the entrepreneur should carefully plan the business in order to reduce the many risks associated with starting up a business.

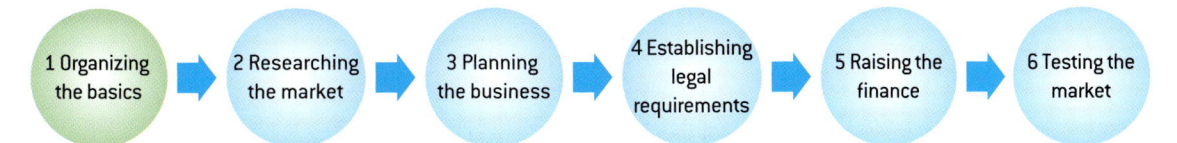

1 Organizing the basics → 2 Researching the market → 3 Planning the business → 4 Establishing legal requirements → 5 Raising the finance → 6 Testing the market

Figure 1.1.4 Steps for start-ups

1. **Organizing the basics.** The entrepreneur starting a new business must address several basic questions: Where is the business going to be based? What will the entrepreneur call the business? What will be its legal structure? What will be its operational structure? Is there a sufficient business infrastructure to make the business feasible – suppliers, potential customers, and government services?

1 Introduction to business management

2. **Refining the business idea through market research.** Once the entrepreneur has determined that, in broad outline, the business concept is feasible, they should do market research to determine how the business will distinguish itself from others in the market. Rarely is a gap in the market obvious. If that were the case, it would be easy to start a successful business. However, new businesses have very high failure rates. While precise rates of failure are difficult to determine, as many business are so small and so short-lived that they elude detection in surveys, failure rates in the United States, for example, are between 50 and 80% in the first four years of operation; 25% fail in the first year alone.[1] In Europe, another developed economy, failure rates are also high.

   Thus, once the basic business idea is determined, the business must then do market research to determine the precise market segment it will target, and the entrepreneur must answer some basic questions: How will they conduct market research? Who will be the target market? Can the new business test its concept? What will be its "unique selling proposition" (USP)? How will the business communicate with the market?

   Let's consider the example of the entrepreneur who wants to enter the grocery business. The idea is very attractive. After all, food is one of the basic necessities of human existence. However, market research may be very revealing. A market may have too many competitors, or a segment of the grocery market (high volume, low cost, for example) may be saturated. Market research might reveal that a small niche market (such as for organic products or specialized meats) is where there is a gap in the market. Thus, researching the market has narrowed and refined the basic business idea (a grocery store) to a significantly more precise idea: a speciality grocery store that offers either organic products and/or specialized meats.

   Market research could lead an entrepreneur to sell only local, organic groceries

3. **Planning the business.** Once the concept has been narrowed, the entrepreneur should write a business plan, which is a document that addresses all the issues that need to be planned before operations begin. The business plan will be of use to multiple stakeholders, especially potential owners of the business and financial institutions (banks, lending companies) that may provide capital.

Student workpoint 1.2

Be a researcher

Imagine that you are an entrepreneur seeking to start a for-profit social enterprise. Develop a basic business plan for a business with which you could make a profit and fulfil a social purpose.

---

[1] http://www.statisticbrain.com/startup-failure-by-industry/

The composition of the business plan requires the entrepreneur or people starting the business to think through most of the specific elements of how the business will operate. For investors and financiers, the business plan can provide some confidence as it indicates that the business has foreseen potential issues and is trying to address them.

4. **Establishing legal requirements.** All businesses operate in countries that have laws that can influence the legal organization of the business, its labour practices, and its operational practices, as well as determine tax obligations. In most countries, businesses must be registered, even if they are sole traders (which are not legally separate entities from the operator of the business). Other types of business – corporations, for example – are legal entities that must be established in accordance with the laws of the host country. In many countries, businesses must have specific licences and/or pass certain inspections before they can operate. These legal requirements can be extensive and costly.

   Finally, the business must investigate the tax requirements of the country. These taxes would include not only income taxes, but also various sorts of payroll tax that must be paid, such as for employees' pensions from the government, unemployment and sickness benefits, or even medical insurance.

5. **Raising the finance.** Once the basic business idea has been refined, a business plan written, and legal requirements met, the business must then raise finance – money – to get the business started and to support the business until it can sustain operations from profits, which can often take years. (Even if the business is profitable from the beginning, its cash requirements may be greater than the profits.) Any investor or lender must have confidence in the accounting and auditing procedures of the business. Who will prepare accounts in the business and who, external to the business, will verify that they are accurate?

   The business must attract start-up monies. Some or all may come from the entrepreneur, or other investors may be required. When someone provides equity capital, it means that person is a partial owner of the business. Most entrepreneurs who start up a business do not want to lose control of the business, so some of the capital will be in the form of investment – selling shares – but some of the capital may be loans to the business. Who will the lenders be? What kind of terms will they want?

6. **Testing the market.** The final stage is the launch of the business. How will that occur? Will the business begin on a small scale (a "pilot") to test consumer reaction? What will the criteria for success of the pilot be? In some types of business, especially capital-intensive manufacturing, the initial launch is extremely expensive and the firm can respond to market reactions in only a limited and slow way. Other types of business – restaurants, for example – can often respond quickly and easily, by changing the menu, changing recipes, or changing other aspects of the business.

   The purpose of testing the market is to verify that the business idea will be received well enough by consumers to suggest that the business has a reasonable chance of success.

Student workpoint 1.3

Be a thinker

Choose one of the following businesses:

- Local delicatessen and café
- Manufacturer of a new energy drink
- Travelling hairdresser and beautician
- After-school sports club

Work in groups to discuss the challenges and opportunities that you would face when opening up such a business. Write down at least five challenges and five opportunities.

1 Introduction to business management

Challenges that a new business may face

Even when the six steps outlined above are followed, start-ups still have a high probability of failure. Businesses that fail often do so because of what they did before the business even opened. For example, the business had problems in basic organization, its products or services were based on insufficient or poor-quality market research, planning was poor, it was unable to convince investors or lenders, legal requirements were not properly satisfied, accounts were poorly kept and/or the business had insufficient funds to operate, or the launch was unsuccessful and sales did not materialize. All of these problems can cause a business to fail.

If a start-up has a good business idea and develops a strong business plan, the business may still fail. Sometimes failure results from a lack of recognition of the business name in the marketplace. Other times failure stems from the inability to recruit labour with the right skills. In other cases, it is because the business cannot accurately anticipate the reactions of competitors (and certainly a start-up cannot control the actions of its competitors). New businesses generally have less capital to rely on if the economy weakens. When a business is put under stress, often problems between managers or executives surface which would not be present if the business were operating successfully. Therefore, many things outside a business's control can cause it to fail.

Table 1.1.4 Reasons why start-ups fail

Organization	• The location of the business was inappropriate. • The structure of the business did not work. • Supplies were unreliable.
Market research	• The market research was poor. • The target market wasn't appropriate. • The test was too optimistic. • Channels of communication were weak.
Business plan	• The business plan did not convince. • Goals were too vague or contradictory.
Legal requirements	• Labour laws were not addressed. • Registration was too difficult. • Tax obligations were not addressed.
Finance	• The accounts were not kept properly – cash flow, in particular, was a problem. • Raising start-up capital was too difficult. • Raising medium-term to long-term finance was difficult.
The market	• The launch failed. • The pilot was inconclusive. • Success was limited – the product failed to inspire.

Student workpoint 1.4

Be an inquirer

Go to Kiva or one of the other microfinance lending sites. Find three businesses that you find interesting and compelling. What is it about these businesses that interests you? Why do you think they could be successful? Would you consider making a small donation to one of these businesses?

TOK discussion

1. Is business management an art or is it a science?
2. As a business can operate in more than one sector, why do we need the categories called "sectors" (primary sector, secondary sector, etc)?
3. To what extent can entrepreneurs know in advance the challenges they may encounter when starting up a business?

1.1 What is a business?

Revision checklist

- ✓ Businesses combine human, physical and financial resources to produce goods and services.
- ✓ Human resources are the people needed to carry out the aims of the organization. Physical resources include buildings, machinery and raw materials. Financial resources include the money needed to make the product or service.
- ✓ Business activity is categorized into one of four main sectors:
    - ✓ The primary sector generally involves the acquisition of raw materials.
    - ✓ The secondary sector involves processing raw materials, usually to create a product.
    - ✓ The tertiary sector is where most service businesses sit.
    - ✓ The quaternary sector provides services that focus on knowledge.
- ✓ Business offers many opportunities, which is why so many people start businesses. Steps involved in starting up a business include researching the market, planning the new business, establishing legal requirements, raising finance, and testing the market.
- ✓ A new business might face challenges at each stage. The business will be able to control some of the challenges but not all of them.

Practice question

To answer the question below effectively, see Unit 6 pages 398–402.

Starbucks

Starbucks, a large coffee store chain with its headquarters in the United States, has been profitable for years and thus has considerable cash and other resources. Starbucks wants to open coffee shops in India, which has a large population and is a potentially large market. The laws of India regarding foreign businesses operating in the country present an obstacle to Starbucks.

To get around this legal obstacle, Starbucks is considering working with Tata Coffee, a major Indian company that has its own coffee shops and is involved in aspects of the coffee business besides retail.

In addition to coffee shops, Tata Coffee also owns coffee farms where coffee is grown. Its labour force on these farms is trained and knowledgeable.

a) With reference to Starbucks and Tata Coffee, explain the role of businesses in combining two of the following: human resources, physical resources, or financial resources to create goods and services. [4 marks]

1.2 Types of business entities

By the end of this chapter, you should be able to:

→ Distinguish between **the private and the public sectors**

→ Outline the main features of the following types of organizations:
- **sole traders**
- **partnerships**
- **privately held companies**
- **publicly held companies**

→ Outline the main features of the following types of for-profit social enterprises:
- **private sector companies**
- **public sector companies**
- **cooperatives**

→ Outline the main features of the following type of non-profit social enterprise:
- **non-governmental organizations (NGOs)**

Key terms

Private sector

the portion of an economy not controlled or owned by the government

Public sector

those portions of the economy owned or controlled by the government, such as government services, public schools, and state-owned corporations

Sole trader

a business owned and operated by one person. No legal distinction exists between the business and the owner. Thus, the owner has unlimited liability for the liabilities of the business, and the business ceases to exist when the owner dies.

Partnership

a business owned and operated by two or more people. No legal distinction exists between the business and the partners, each of whom are legally responsible for 100% of the liabilities of the partnership.

Difference between the private and public sectors

Public sector refers to those parts of the economy controlled by the government. The term "public sector" can be used in a broad sense, meaning any type of activity (including the military, police, and public education) that is run by the government and has meaningful economic implications. However, in business, "public sector" generally has a narrower usage. A public sector company is one that the government owns. Common types of public sector companies include utilities, telecommunications companies, and public transport.

Private sector refers to those parts of the economy not controlled by the government. The private sector is managed by individuals and companies that are not owned by the government. Most private sector businesses are for-profit.

Main features of the most common types of profit-based (commercial) organizations

Profit-making businesses come in various types of legal organization, but the most common are:

- Sole traders
- Partnerships

1.2 Types of business entities

- Privately held companies or corporations
- Publicly held companies or corporations

One of the main aims of all of these types of business is to generate profit. The profits a business receives can be shown using the following formula:

$$\text{Profits} = \text{total revenues} - \text{total costs}$$

Total revenues, often called "sales" or "sales revenue", are all the income received by the business in a specified period of time. Total costs are all the costs incurred by that business in the same period of time. (The way that revenue and expenses are measured is actually more complex than this simple formula suggests, but for now the simple form is enough.)

Sole trader

Most people starting their own business typically begin with a limited budget and a simple organization. Facing these constraints, they often choose to operate as a sole trader (sometimes called a sole proprietor), which is the simplest form of business to organize.

Being a sole trader fulfills many of the reasons why people start a business: being their own boss, seeing a gap in the market and wanting to respond quickly, creating their own product, serving the community, or just living their dream.

The main features of a sole trader business include the following:

- **The sole trader owns and runs the business.** Sole traders may employ other people, including those empowered to make some of the decisions, but the sole traders themselves make management decisions and have ultimate responsibility for the business.

- **No legal distinction exists between the business and the sole trader.** The sole trader *is* the business and, thus, is liable for all the debts of the business or other claims (such as the outcome of a lawsuit). In other words, sole traders have "unlimited liability".

- **The finance is usually limited.** Here, finance refers to the money that the business has available for use. It can come from the personal savings of the sole trader or from other sources, such as a loan from family and friends or from a bank. Regardless, sole traders typically have limited finance, either because their personal savings are limited or because family, friends, banks, and other financial institutions may be reluctant to lend the sole trader money because of the high failure rate of start-up businesses.

- **The business is often geographically close to the customer.** A sole trader is usually a small business that allows the sole trader to interact with each customer. Sole traders get to know their customers on an individual basis, which allows them to provide a more personalized service than larger businesses.

- **The sole trader has privacy and limited accountability.** Most of the time, sole traders do not have to declare their finances to anyone except the tax authorities, which want to know how much profit the business has made for tax purposes. Sometimes sole traders borrow

Monique owns and runs her own café business – she is a sole trader

money or enter into a financial contract (such as a lease), and lenders or lessors may need to see financial statements. In general, however, sole traders have a high degree of privacy.

- **Registering the business is generally relatively easy and inexpensive – and quick.** Although laws vary from country to country, starting and operating as a sole trader is generally simpler than for other types of legal organizations. Sole traders usually have less legal paperwork to fill out and file. Sole traders make all decisions themselves and therefore do not have to devote time to discussion and to building consensus for decisions.

Advantages of sole traders

One of the greatest advantages of being a sole trader is that all profits from the business belong to the sole trader, as no legal distinction separates the owner from the business. Other advantages of operating as a sole trader include the following:

- Complete control over all the important decisions.
- Flexibility in terms of working hours, products and services, and changes to operations.
- Privacy, as sole traders generally do not need to divulge information.
- Minimal legal formalities.
- Close ties to customers, which can give a competitive advantage.

Disadvantages of sole traders

The success of businesses operating as sole traders depends on the drive, enthusiasm, and health of the sole traders themselves. Any of these can falter. Sole traders also have other disadvantages, which include the following:

- Competing against established businesses all by yourself can be a daunting challenge.
- There may be stress and potential ineffectiveness because the sole trader makes all the decisions, often with limited time to make them and limited opportunity to seek advice from others.
- There will be a lack of continuity in the event of a serious accident or the owner's death – the business itself may not continue.
- There may be limited scope for expansion as the owner spends all their time running the business.
- Generally there will be limited capital, which may also create a burden on the business. The focus will be more on having sufficient cash for day-to-day operations than on looking to the future.
- There is unlimited liability of the owner for any faults, debts, or mistakes made.

Most sole traders remain small businesses and typically the business comes to an end when the sole trader retires or dies. Sometimes, sole traders want to stay small, which allows them to make a decent living and not have to manage and worry about the many complexities of operating on a larger scale. Sole traders often have a niche in the market and see no need to expand.

When sole traders want to expand, the challenges are sometimes too great. Their profits are not large enough to support growth, or the risks of growth are too great. Just surviving may be the chief goal of a sole trader: many sole traders give up or fail within the first few years of existence.

Partnerships

An alternative type of business is that of a partnership. This type of business is formed by two or more people. They could be friends, associates, or people with similar or related skills. Partnerships are popular with professional people who have related qualifications, such as doctors, lawyers, accountants, or even business consultancy firms.

The main features of a partnership business include the following:

- **Decisions are made jointly by the partners**, who own and run the business together. Partners may employ other people, but they make all the management decisions. Partners also own the business, each partner having a percentage ownership.

- **The business is owned and managed by more than one person.** Although the number of partners is technically unlimited, getting agreement is more difficult as the number of partners increases. Most partnerships have between 2 to 20 partners.

- **No legal distinction exists between the business and the partners**, who are liable for all of the partnership's debts and other obligations. Partners have unlimited liability and legally can be called upon to pay for 100% of the partnership's debts, even if a partner owns only a small percentage of the business.

- **Finance is usually more available than for a sole trader business.** All partners contribute some capital to start up the business or to "buy into" the business, which usually means there is more capital than if provided by only one person. Also, banks and other financial institutions are usually more willing to provide finance to a partnership than to a sole trader, as a partnership is considered more stable than a sole trader.

- **Some partners may be "sleeping partners"**, which means that they provide some finance (their investment in the partnership) and expect a share of the profit. A sleeping partner performs no other role in the business.

- **The business operated as a partnership can often offer a more varied service than a sole trader.** Different partners may bring different expertise, and the product or service offerings of the business can vary. This situation is especially true in the case of partnerships of professionals such as lawyers or doctors. For example, a law firm could have lawyers specializing in criminal law, commercial law, international law, and civil law.

- **Partnerships typically have a greater degree of accountability than a sole trader.** Although in most countries partnerships are not legally required to draw up a deed of partnership, partnerships often do.

Having a deed of partnership makes good business sense because it is a legally binding document that sets out the rights and duties of the partners. It includes information about:

- responsibilities
- financing
- division of profits
- liabilities
- procedures for changing circumstances.

With a deed of partnership, partners know their rights and responsibilities within the partnership, and the likelihood of a major disagreement between the partners reduces.

- **Partnerships are typically more stable than sole traders and have a higher likelihood of continuity.** Drawing up a deed of partnership will slow down the registering of the business, but it will help the organization in the long term.
- **Partners do not necessarily share all of the profits equally.** Usually, profits are allocated and paid out according to each partner's percentage ownership of the business. If one partner has provided a substantial amount of finance, then that person may expect a greater proportion of profits than the other partners are allocated. In addition, in partnerships with "sleeping partners", the active partners may get agreed-upon salaries or drawings that are considered expenses for the purpose of determining the partnership's profit. Then, after the profit is determined, the profits are allocated to partners according to their percentage ownership.

Advantages of partnerships

Partnerships have certain advantages compared to sole traders:

- As partners often bring different skills and qualities, partnerships may have more efficient production as a result of the specialization and the division of labour.
- In general, partners bring more expertise to a business than one person can.
- As partnerships are perceived as having greater stability and lower risk, they generally have access to more finance.
- Partners can help in emergencies or when others are ill or on holiday.
- Partnerships have more chance of continuity as the business will not necessarily end if one partner dies.

Disadvantages of partnerships

Partnerships also have certain disadvantages:

- Each partner has unlimited liability, which means that each partner is legally responsible for all of the business's debts or the actions of any other partner. The one exception to this liability is when, in the deed of partnership, a partner or certain partners are declared "limited partners". Although the laws vary according to country, in general, limited partners have limited liability but also limited control (both specified in the deed of partnership).

- Compared to businesses that operate as companies (corporations), partnerships usually have less access to loans from banks and other financial institutions. Limited finance can often prevent a business from expanding or maximizing opportunities for making profits.

- An individual partner does not have complete control over the business and has to rely on the work and goodwill of others.

- Profits must be shared among the partners.

- Partners may disagree, which in the worst case could lead to the break-up of the partnership.

In summary, partnerships are safer than sole traders but they are more complex organizations. As multiple partners can typically raise more finance than sole traders, and because of the greater inherent stability, partnerships have a greater chance of surviving changing market conditions and have more chance to expand if the conditions are right.

Case study: Brown Brothers Harriman

Brown Brothers Harriman (BBH) is one of the largest and oldest private banks in the United States. Unusually, the bank operates as a partnership. Businesses legally organized as a partnership are usually relatively small, but BBH, headquartered in New York City, has approximately 6,000 employees and offices around the world. Founded in 1931, the bank has grown and has revenue in excess of $1.3 billion. Despite this growth and size, the owners of the business have decided to remain a partnership.

Companies or corporations

The main categories of companies (also called "corporations" in North America) are privately held companies and publicly held companies. Their similarities and differences are examined below.

You can recognize a company as it may have the following abbreviations after its logo:

- INC – Incorporated (USA/Canada)
- LLC – Limited Liability Company (USA)
- PLC – Private or Public Limited Company (UK)
- LTD – Limited Company (various)
- SA – Sociedad Anónima (Latin America except Brazil and Mexico)
- SA – Sociedades Anônimas (Brazil, Portugal)

- SpA – Società per Azioni (Italy)
- AB – Aktiebolag (Finland, Sweden)
- Bhd – Berhad (Malaysia, Brunei)
- GIE – Groupement d'Intérêt Economique (France)
- GmbH – Gesellschaft mit beschraenkter Haftung (Austria, Germany, Switzerland)

Other countries have other designations and abbreviations. Whichever is used, this type of designation means the same thing: that the business is a limited liability company. This type of business is the only one that can be called a "company" (corporation) to distinguish it from the other types of business.

A business can become a company by a simple but very powerful process – the business and the owners of the business are legally separated and the liability of the company is distinct from the liability of those who own it. Another feature of a company is that, typically, it has multiple owners, each owning a fraction of the company in the form of shares (shares of stock or equity shares) in the company.

The business – the company – has legal existence in its own right. The company employs executives to manage the business and workers who handle the day-to-day operations.

Just like sole traders and partnerships, a company has certain responsibilities in the community: it must obey the laws of the land and pay taxes. Unlike sole traders and partnerships, companies keep the profits from their business activities – unless the owners (also called shareholders) decide to pay all or a portion of profits (past or present) to the shareholders in the form of dividends.

Shareholders receive a proportion of the profits as dividends at the discretion of the company, and their proportion of the dividends is determined by their proportion of the shares of stock. For example, if a company makes a profit of €1,000,000 and decides to pay total dividends of €600,000, the total payout (€600,000) will be divided by the number of shares of stock issued and outstanding. If that figure was 100,000, the owner of each share of stock would receive a dividend of €6 for each share the person owned. If one person owned 20,000 of the issued and outstanding shares, that person would receive €120,000.

Often individual shareholders own only a part of the business. When that is the case, in theory individual shareholders do not control the business unless they own a majority of the shares. In practice, sometimes a shareholder who owns a smaller percentage can still have a deciding say in the decisions of the company and can, therefore, control it.

In the case of very large companies, it is rare for one person to own all or a majority of the shares. With smaller companies, it is not uncommon for one person to own 100% of the shares, or for a small group of family members or friends to own 100% of the shares.

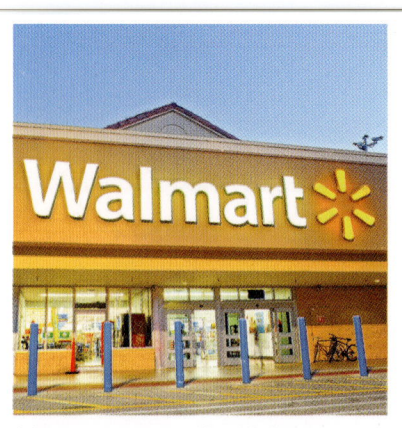

A large company like Walmart might have hundreds of thousands of shareholders

1.2 Types of business entities

Advantages of being a shareholder

Shareholders are rewarded for investing in a company in three ways:

- **The price of the share(s) they hold may increase in value if the company is performing well.** In theory (though not always in practice), the value of a company is based on its profits. As profits increase, so too should the total value of its shares. Therefore, individual shares of stock in the company should increase in value at the same rate.

- **The company issues a portion of the company profits as dividends.** The amount of money each shareholder receives depends on the number of shares they own. With small or new companies, dividends are often not paid or are relatively small. With large, established companies, dividends are often paid regularly – once every three months (quarterly) – and individuals invest in the company partly because they want the regular dividend income that comes with share ownership in that particular company.

- **The shareholder has limited liability**, which is one of the single most important features and benefits of owning stock in a company. Unlike sole proprietors or partners in a partnership, shareholders in a company are not responsible in any way for the company's debts. If the business fails, then all the shareholders can lose is their investment in the company, but no more.

  For example, if a company goes into receivership (bankruptcy) owing millions to individuals, banks, and other companies, the shareholders do not have to pay any of those debts. The shareholders' liability is limited to their investment. (However, in the event of liquidation of a company, the shareholders are the last party to receive any monies from the sale of the assets of a business; all debts will be paid first).

Disadvantages of being a shareholder

The costs to the shareholders of investing in a company are as follows:

- **The price of the share(s) they hold may decrease in value if the company is not performing well.** As noted above, in theory the value of a company is based on its profits. If profit declines, so too (typically) will the value of individual shares.

- **The company may choose not to issues dividends if it does not have to.** Businesses need funds for many reasons. Companies that are doing poorly may not have sufficient cash on hand to be able to pay dividends. Businesses that are growing rapidly also need money to support the growth (to pay for more investment in equipment and working capital). As a result, many companies rarely or never pay dividends. The entire measurement of the value of the investment is based upon the rise or fall in the stock value.

- As "owners" often own only a fraction of the shares of the company, **owning shares in a firm may not mean that an individual shareholder has any meaningful say in decisions about the business.** In April 2021, Mitsubishi Corporation (MC) in Japan had more than 2.14 billion issued and outstanding shares of stock.

1 Introduction to business management

An individual investor owning 100 shares would, practically speaking, have no say at all in a giant company such as MC. To own even 1% of the company (and thus have a 1% say in who the executives are) would require an investment of approximately $606 million dollars.

Typically, businesses initially choose to become a company because the owners of the business want the business to have a separate legal existence from them personally, thus giving the owners, as shareholders rather than as a sole trader or partners, limited liability.

There are also other reasons for becoming a company:

- The enhanced status of being a company is generally recognition that the business has been successful.
- Selling shares is a good source of finance for a business, especially one with growing working-capital requirements.
- Being a company increases the stability of the business, as a company has a legal existence separate from its owners. If a shareholder or shareholders die, the business continues. In the case of small businesses, the death of a major shareholder (if that person is also an active executive in the firm) can cause some disruption. Nevertheless, the business does continue.
- Companies typically have improved chances of gaining further finance, especially loans, from financial institutions and governments.

Achieving company status is often a turning point in the evolution of a business. Up until the point that a business becomes a company, some questions exist about the survival of the business and its continuity and growth.

As with any legal organization of a business, the choice to become a company has advantages and disadvantages. To take full advantage of becoming a company, a business will have multiple investors and thus a major infusion of capital. However, when this occurs, the original business owner loses some control over the business and could even lose personal involvement in the company. When a business becomes a company, its new owners (the shareholders) may hire executives to make all major decisions. The original business owner (as sole trader or partner) may now be merely an investor.

Privately held companies and publicly held companies

When a business reorganizes as a company, it can choose to become either of these types of organization:

- Privately held company
- Publicly held company

The main difference between the two forms of company is that the **privately held company** can only sell shares in the company privately: to people known to the owners (such as friends, family, and associates). Although the number of shareholders permitted in a privately held company varies from country to country, generally it is low (around 20). As a result, becoming a privately held company limits the amount of finance available but allows more control to be maintained.

> **Key terms**
>
> **Privately held company**
>
> an incorporated business offering limited liability to the owners. Owners' liability is limited to their investment in the company. In most countries, shareholders of privately held companies cannot sell their shares unless they have first been offered to existing shareholders; the shares cannot be traded on a stock exchange; and there are limits on the number of shareholders.
>
> **Publicly held company**
>
> an incorporated business offering limited liability to the owners. Owners' liability is limited to their investment in the company. The shares of the company are traded on some public exchanges, and publicly held companies must disclose or make public considerable information about the company, including audited financial information.

1.2 Types of business entities

Another difference is that, in most countries, privately held companies have less onerous disclosure and reporting requirements than publicly held companies. For example, publicly held companies must produce audited financial statements once a year, whereas in many countries privately held companies do not have to.

If the business decides to become a **publicly held company** (and the phrase typically used is "the company is going public"), then it has to offer its shares in a public place, such as a stock exchange in one of the major financial centres (London, New York, Frankfurt, Tokyo, Shanghai or Singapore), or online. For example, the FTSE, Wall Street, the Nasdaq, the Nikkei.

Going public opens up the possibility of securing large sums of capital. In 2012, for example, Facebook acquired $16 billion from its "initial public offering" (IPO), or first sale of shares to the public. More recently in 2020, for example, Airbnb acquired $3.51 billion from its "initial public offering" (IPO), or its first sale of shares to the public.

When a company goes public, it does lose some privacy. Publicly held companies have to allow potential investors to see their accounts, which become open to everyone. Further, the business itself has no control over who buys their shares.

The main features of a company include the following:

- **The shareholders own but do not necessarily run the business.** Their purchase of shares provides finance, but otherwise the shareholders have little input into the day-to-day running of the business (unless they are very small privately traded companies with a small number of shareholders who also serve as managers). Instead, professional managers are normally employed to make all the management decisions.

- **The business and the owners are legally separate entities.** The shareholders are not liable for any of the debts of the business. The shareholders' liability is limited to their investment in the company. As the business and the owners (shareholders) are legally distinct, the owners can change. A person owning shares in the company can decide to sell the shares for any reason whatsoever.

- **The details of the company's formation are legally recorded and are matters of public record.** To form a company, owners of the business must have two documents drawn up and registered with the appropriate government agency, which varies in name from country to country (as do the names of the documents):

  - **Memorandum of association** – this document records the key characteristics and the external activities of the company being created. For example, the memorandum will provide basic information on the objectives of the business and record the share capital initially required.

  - **Articles of association** – this document specifies how the company will be regulated internally. For example, it will explain the initial organization of the executives of the company, with their titles and areas of responsibilities (chief executive officer, chief financial officer, etc), and the rights and responsibilities of each shareholder.

The shares of a publicly held company can be bought by anyone through a stock exchange or "over the counter", via a dealer network

Assessment advice

Do not confuse the term "public sector" with "publicly held company", or "private sector" with "privately held company".

- **Greater finance is generally available.** The initial offering of shares represents a one-time injection of capital to the business. Once the business sells its shares, it receives the price paid at the IPO. Thereafter, the initial shares and any future gains (or losses) in price are to the benefit (or cost) of the shareholders only, unless the company issues and sells additional shares to raise more capital.

- **A company is held to a high degree of accountability.** The owners and the company are separate entities, so from time to time the company must provide information to the shareholders so that they can understand the condition of their investment, and so that the company and its management are seen as being held accountable. Information on a company is generally provided by:
    - published, audited annual company reports (and in some countries, unaudited quarterly reports)
    - an annual general meeting (AGM) open to all shareholders
    - an extraordinary general meeting (EGM) if called by the shareholders.

- **Compared to other forms of business organizations, companies have greater stability and a higher chance of continuity.** When a shareholder dies or sells shares, the company continues to operate. The death of a shareholder or the sale of shares has no direct impact on the company. All that happens is that one partial owner of the business is replaced by another partial owner. A company can theoretically last for ever because it is independent of the shareholders.

The oldest company in the world is a Japanese construction company, Kongo Gumi, which was founded in 578 CE and began operations by building a Buddhist temple. In 2006, the Takamatsu Construction Group acquired the shares of Kongo Gumi, which nonetheless continues to operate.

Advantages of companies

Advantages of operating a business as a company include the following:

- **Finance is more readily available than for sole traders and partnerships.** Companies are perceived as having greater stability and lower risk than sole traders and partnerships. Individuals and institutions are more likely to invest, and banks and financial institutions are more likely to make loans to companies.

- **The investor has limited liability.** Investors can lose only the value of the shares and nothing else. By owning small numbers of shares in many different companies, investors can build up relatively safe investment portfolios. Each individual investment is limited, and thus their risks are spread out among many companies.

The companies also benefit from this. Many companies have a huge number of "small" investors (individuals or institutions that own a very small number of shares). However, the sum of the investment of all those small investors can add up to a large amount of finance.

- **There is continuity.** The business will not necessarily end if a shareholder dies or sells their shares, or if any of the directors leave. Companies can go bankrupt and be liquidated (with all the assets sold off to pay off the liabilities), thus terminating their operations. However, companies have a greater chance of continuity than a sole trader or partnership.

- **There are possibilities for expansion.** Companies have more opportunity to expand because generally they last longer and have more access to finance. For a business to grow, it often needs to invest money in equipment, marketing efforts, or new activities. With fewer opportunities for finance, many small businesses, including sole traders and partnerships, cannot take advantage of business opportunities to expand. Often companies can.

- **An established organizational structure exists.** Managers and workers do not have to change every time a shareholder sells shares. This stability can help the business develop long-term relationships with customers and suppliers alike. It can also allow the business to hire individuals with expertise for individual positions who will enhance the performance of the business.

Disadvantages of companies

Disadvantages of operating as a company include the following:

- **Setting up a company can take time and cost a great deal of money to fulfil the necessary legal requirements.** Whether reorganizing into a company or starting a business as a company, the owners must retain lawyers, have legally required paperwork filled out, and file papers with the appropriate government agencies.

- **Selling shares, especially if the company "goes public", does not guarantee that the desired or intended amount of finance will be raised.** Sometimes IPOs are unsuccessful, and a business has sold itself for relatively little cash. Thus, reorganizing a business as a company or starting up a company involves risk.

- **Owners risk partial or entire loss of control of the business.** If a business decides to become a company, especially for a publicly held company, the owners must give up some control of their business. Even if, during incorporation, former owners still retain 51% of the shares, they must still answer to the new owners (other shareholders). In the case of public companies, loss of control can be significant. Original owners can have a very small percentage of the shares after the firm has gone public.

- **There is a loss of privacy**. A publicly held company is required to fulfil a number of legal obligations, including publishing its accounts publicly. Many business people unaccustomed to sharing information with others dislike publishing their accounts. Further, if the company's performance has been weak – sales are down or profits are negative – the future performance can be further jeopardized. Some customers may not want to purchase from or do business with a weak company, a situation that can be particularly damaging to those businesses that offer product warranties or after-sales service on products.

A publicly held company's accounts can be scrutinised by those outside the business

- **A company has no control over the stock market.** Share prices may fall, which can damage the image of the company. Such a loss of share value can sometimes occur not because the business has done anything wrong, but simply because of an external factor: an election, negative news about another business in the same industry, a downturn in the economy, or a natural disaster.

- **A company has limited control over who buys its shares.** For example, a competitor may want to take over the business. If the shareholders are willing to sell their shares, the company cannot prevent a takeover. Companies are especially vulnerable to being taken over if their share price falls, which, as noted above, sometimes occurs through no fault of the business itself.

In general, privately held companies are smaller than publicly held companies. However, many small public companies exist, and some privately held companies are huge. Mars, Incorporated – which manufactures many different types of sweets, food and petcare – is a privately held company with annual revenues in the billions of dollars. Mars is a multinational enterprise and one of the larger companies headquartered in the United States.

> **Concept**
>
> **CHANGE**
>
> Business entities sometimes change the legal status of their business. The common examples are a sole trader who decides to register as a privately held company, or a privately held company that "goes public" (becomes a publicly held company and sells its shares in a public place, like a stock exchange).
>
> Do some research to find examples of such changes of legal status – in the case of sole traders and privately held companies, it may be businesses around you.

Case study: Tsuen Tea

Tsuen Tea in Kyoto, Japan, is the thirteenth oldest company in Japan. Founded in 1160 CE, Tsuen Tea is over 800 years old. Though the building it operates in is not the original, the location is, just east of the Uji Bridge. Currently, Yusuke Tsuen manages the business. He is the twenty-fourth generation of the Tsuen family to run the shop and tea house. The business is organized as a private company, one feature of which is legal continuity.

For-profit social enterprises

The term "social enterprise" has a slightly different meaning or legal standing in different countries. Scholars and business people have not settled on a universally agreed definition. In general, the term "social enterprise" refers to a form of business that has a social purpose. "Social purpose" generally means that the organization aims to improve human, social, or environmental well-being.

Although social enterprises should and typically do operate to a professional standard (regarding legal existence, proper accounts, management structure, reporting procedures, etc), the social aim nevertheless takes priority over any other aim – such as growth, maximizing sales, or making profits, which are typical objectives of for-profit organizations.

For-profit social enterprises aim to make a profit. However, they do not want to maximize profits if doing so compromises their social purpose.

Private sector companies

Social enterprises vary in their legal organization. Some take the form of one of the three models examined above (sole trader, partnership, or company). Some for-profit social enterprises operate in the private sector.

One example of a for-profit social enterprise organized as a company and operating in the private sector is TOMs. For every pair of shoes that TOMs sells, the company donates one pair of shoes to underprivileged children in developing countries and emerging markets.

Public sector companies

Some social enterprises, typically organized as companies, operate in the public sector. Examples are for-profit companies that make meals and deliver them to older people who for financial or physical reasons are unable to prepare their own meals. Such for-profit social enterprises bid for contracts with local or regional governments.

Another common area where for-profit social enterprises operate in the public sector is services related to recycling.

Cooperatives

Some social enterprises are organized as cooperatives. A cooperative is a form of partnership where the business is owned and run by all the "members". Unlike partnerships, which in most countries have limits on the number of partners, cooperatives typically have many members. Each member participates actively in the running of the business.

Cooperatives can take many forms:

- A **financial cooperative** is a financial institution with ethical and social aims that take precedence over profits. Sometimes, for example in the case of credit unions, the social aims might mean lending money at lower rates of interest or providing non-lending services at a lower cost than banks or other financial institutions. Or a financial cooperative may provide finance (loans) to its members who otherwise might not be able to borrow money.

- A **housing cooperative** is run to provide housing for its members (as opposed to providing rent for private landlords). A common activity of a housing cooperative is owning an apartment building in which each "member" is entitled to one housing unit in the building. The members, through the cooperative, own the building, and surpluses are reinvested in the building and its operation, so costs to individual members are lower.

  In addition, housing cooperatives typically have control over who can become a member, thereby ensuring that all members agree to rules and conditions and thus increase the likelihood of social harmony in the building.

- A **workers' cooperative** is a business that is owned and operated by the workers themselves, and the wages of the managers and the workers are similar. Providing employment to workers is a priority. Often, a workers' cooperative emerges when a business is about to fail. Workers, fearful of losing their jobs, take over the business, sack the

Key terms

Social enterprise

a business that advances a social purpose in a financially sustainable way. While aiming to do social good, social enterprises rely on business models, have sales revenue, and reinvest what profits they make in the business. Social enterprises generally do not depend on philanthropy.

For-profit social enterprise

an organization with many similarities to a normal social enterprise, except that it often earns a profit, some of which might be distributed to owners. The primary aim of a for-profit social enterprise is to provide a social service.

Cooperative

business organization owned and operated by its members, who share any profits. Cooperatives exist in many industries but are common in agriculture.

managers (or drastically reduce their pay), and reinvest all of the profits in the business (rather than paying them out as dividends).

- A **producer cooperative** is where groups of producers collaborate in certain stages of production. Producer cooperatives are particularly common in agriculture, such as grape farmers having a cooperative wine-production facility, or olive producers having a cooperatively owned press to produce oil.

With producer cooperatives, often the aim is to maximize the utilization of an expensive piece of equipment that individual members by themselves could not afford. At other times, cost efficiencies can only be achieved when a stage of the production process is carried out on a large scale. Thus, many producers pool their resources to obtain the cost efficiencies.

- A **consumer cooperative** provides a service to its consumers who are also part owners of the business. In Europe and the United States, a common type of consumer cooperative involves certain grocery stores. Individual consumers become "members", which entitles them to purchase groceries at the cooperative, often at lower prices than for-profit grocery stores.

Grape farmers and wine producers can form a producer cooperative together

In many cases, the cooperative's priority is not to make profit. Rather, the cooperative sells or offers its products or services typically at as close to cost price as possible, thereby lowering the costs to members. However, if its prices are too low, the cooperative runs the risk of failure by not reinvesting in the business (and thus not updating its products or services), or not having a significant financial cushion to weather a difficult period or an unexpected expense. Thus, cooperatives generally aim to make some profit, but maximizing profit is not their main aim.

The main common features of for-profit social enterprises include the following:

- **Profit is important but not the priority – social aims take precedence.** These aims may vary, and for-profit social enterprises need to generate profits to ensure the survival and growth of the business. The aim, however, is not to maximize profits but to earn profits sufficient to sustain the business.

- **A high degree of collaboration between the business and the local community exists.** For-profit social enterprises usually signify a desire for cooperation between the business community and government because both recognize a need being met by ordinary business activity or by government.

- **Cooperatives are more democratic than other typical for-profit companies or organizations.** In for-profit social enterprises, decision-making tends to be more consultative and transparent. This style of governance reflects the spirit of social enterprises, which is typically to do good and not devise aggressive business strategies (such as to take market share from competitors or to maximize profits).

This style of governance also stems from the nature of social enterprises, which often rely on support or aid from others (such as workers willing to work for lower wages, or landlords willing to lease properties at discounted rates). Consultation and transparency convey the social spirit and generate greater willingness on the part of stakeholders to be supportive.

- **The business operates the same functions as any other business.** For-profit social enterprises are businesses, and must attend to production, marketing, HR, and finance decisions, just as in any other business. In some respects, areas of the business have to be run with more care than other businesses, which often have greater profits and profitability.

Advantages of for-profit social enterprises

Advantages of for-profit social enterprises compared to traditional sole traders, partnerships, and companies include the following:

- **A favourable legal status is achieved.** Anyone can engage in activities that are good for humans, society, or the environment. The legal structure of a for-profit social enterprise allows individuals to engage in those activities without being personally liable or accountable to shareholders with traditional business interests (maximizing profits).

- **A strong communal identity exists.** For-profit social enterprises often have highly motivated employees and other stakeholders working together with a common sense of purpose. Employees often report a high degree of satisfaction, knowing that they are doing something positive for society.

- **The stakeholder community benefits.** For-profit social enterprises help many stakeholders, including the direct beneficiaries of their products and services. They may help the government more, because for-profit social enterprises typically tackle human, social, or environmental problems that a government is not addressing, and so help reduce problems in the community.

Disadvantages of for-profit social enterprises

Disadvantages of for-profit social enterprises compared to traditional sole traders, partnerships, and companies include these:

- **Decision-making is complex and time-consuming.** In being consultative and transparent, for-profit social enterprises often take a long time to make decisions. If many parties are involved with the decision, which is often the case, this extended decision-making time can limit the effectiveness of the business.

- **Capital may be insufficient for growth.** The business model for a for-profit social enterprise may not be sufficient in the long term. Most businesses rely on healthy profit margins and profits, much of which are retained, for investment in property, plant, and equipment, and to provide working capital as working capital requirements increase with the size of the business. Without large profits, for-profit social enterprises may struggle to survive and expand.

- **Capital may be insufficient for financial strength.** For-profit social enterprises tend to have lower profit margins and profits than traditional for-profit businesses because they often try to make their

1 Introduction to business management

products and services as inexpensive as possible. As a result, for-profit social enterprises tend not to have a financial strength that can help them to survive a recession or times when finance is less available.

Non-profit social enterprises

The main features of non-profit-based (commercial) organizations (NPOs) are as follows:

- Some businesses operating in the private sector do not aim to make profits at all. These businesses are also social enterprises – that is, their main aim is for a social purpose – but they are different from for-profit social enterprises in that they do not aim to make any profits whatsoever.

- Though these social enterprises are run as businesses, they generate (or aim to generate) surpluses rather than profits. A **surplus (sometimes referred to as surplus revenue)** is, conceptually, very similar to a profit. However, rather than being distributed to the owners of the business, the surplus is used to advance the social purpose for which the business was set up.

A surplus is any extra revenue generated after subtracting an NPO's costs. A surplus is calculated as follows:

$$\text{surplus} = \text{total revenues} - \text{total costs}$$

Many non-profit social enterprises are very large: United Way, Red Cross and Red Crescent, the Mohammed bin Rashid Al Maktoum Knowledge Foundation, and the Calouste Gulbenkian Foundation are just a few examples. These organizations, and many other large NPOs, are bigger than most traditional businesses.

Social enterprises can take many possible forms, and the differences between them can be subtle (and confusing). Nevertheless, two broad categories of non-profit social enterprises exist: non-governmental organizations (NGOs) and charities.

Non-governmental organizations (NGOs)

"NGO" was a term first used by the United Nations, and it has since become a common way to describe a variety of social enterprises. The aim of these various social enterprises is to support a cause that is considered socially desirable.

Some of these NGOs are concerned with a single issue (such as Save the Whales); others with a broader spectrum (such as Greenpeace). Some have no political affiliation or agenda (such as the Aga Khan Development Network), while others have political aims (such as the National Rifle Association). A common element of all these NGOs is that they are not organized or run by any government.

Charities

Charities are a specific form of NGO whose aim is to provide as much relief as possible for those in need. Charities differ from other NGOs in that their focus is on philanthropy and a desire to help those who cannot help themselves.

Some charities are single-event charities that provide, for example, emergency aid for specific natural disasters or wars (such as Saba Relief).

Key terms

Non-profit social enterprise

an organization with many similarities to a normal social enterprise, except that it is less willing to (and often does not) earn a profit or surplus. The primary aim of a non-profit social enterprise is to provide a social service.

Non-governmental organization (NGO)

non-profit organizations, often with a humanitarian or social purpose. NGOs are independent of government, but they often receive government grants or funding and cooperate with government.

Student workpoint 1.5

Be a researcher

Look at the websites for two NGOs – one local and one international. Make notes about when they were established, the work they do, and any recent news articles about them. Can you find any information about their funding and organization?

What are the main similarities and differences between the two NGOs?

Other charities focus on a single issue (such as Save the Children). As with regular NGOs, charities may have no interest in politics (such as the International Red Cross and Red Crescent Movement). Others can have strong political ties or particular preferences (such as Catholic Charities USA). With all of these charities, the idea is that the business is not run by any government and that it operates in the private sector of the economy.

Finally, one clear distinction between NGOs and charities exists: charities, because of their charitable status and philanthropy, are exempt from paying taxes. NGOs, as with all other businesses, are not exempt from taxes.

Common features of non-profit social enterprises

In addition to the common features of social enterprises mentioned above, common features of non-profit social enterprises include the following:

- **Profits are not generated** – instead, these businesses generate surpluses and surpluses are used to advance the social purpose of the business. Sometimes non-profit social enterprises retain surpluses, in a fashion similar to retaining profits, for the capital requirements of the organization. Typically, the surpluses are used directly to provide the goods and services for which the non-profit social enterprise was created.

- **Donations are important** – these businesses cannot rely on government funding or other forms of income, so a large part of their revenues comes from voluntary donations from individuals. In some cases (the Novo Nordisk Foundation, for example), the organization has endowments and the proceeds from the endowment provide reliable ongoing revenues. Nevertheless, virtually all non-profits want to do more – provide more goods and services for those in need – and welcome large and small donations from individuals and organizations.

- **There is unclear ownership and control.** Who owns these organizations? Who should decide who sits on the board of directors? Who selects new board members? Should individuals who contribute large amounts of money have a larger say in the operation than others? How are managers selected? What is appropriate compensation?

    The issue of compensation is especially contentious when the organization is huge, and its management requires the skills of executive officers of major, for-profit companies. Should the head of a multinational NGO or charity be paid the same amount as the CEO of a multinational company? To attract executives of the necessary calibre and skillset, are for-profit corporate salaries necessary?

    These kinds of questions routinely plague non-profit organizations of all kinds, and can be the source of discontent among stakeholders if not handled effectively.

Advantages of non-profit social enterprises

Non-profit social enterprises have a number of advantages compared to any of the businesses discussed above. These include:

- **They help people or causes in need.** Individuals, organizations, and governments rarely have sufficient resources to solve all the needs of local people and/or communities. Non-profit social enterprises cannot

The surplus generated from a charity's business activities, such as this second-hand clothes shop, is used to advance the social purposes of the organization

address all the needs either. Nevertheless, for the specific groups or causes that are supported, the work of non-profit social enterprises is crucially important and valuable.

- **They can foster a philanthropic spirit in the community.** People may feel good about helping others, which can foster socially constructive views in general. In turn, positive attitudes in a community can make it a better place to live and can improve the general business climate.

- **They can foster informed discussions in the community about allocation of resources.** As noted above, individuals, organizations, and governments rarely have sufficient resources to solve all the needs of local people and/or communities. The actions of non-profit social enterprises and the individuals working for and contributing to them can lead to better information about local and distant problems, issues, and causes. With better information, individuals and organizations, including various government agencies, can carry out more informed decision-making.

- **They can innovate.** Employees or members are often "forced" to be creative – to try new ideas and tactics to address problems and find solutions – because non-profit social enterprises often do not generate surpluses and therefore do not have funds for reinvestment.

Disadvantages of non-profit social enterprises

Non-profit social enterprises have a number of disadvantages compared to any of the businesses discussed above. These include the following:

- **Intense lobbying from non-profit social enterprises can lead to socially undesirable goods.** For example, High North Alliance in Norway lobbies for Arctic coastal communities and seeks to protect the rights of whalers. In effect, it supports consumption of whale meat.[1] Two non-profit lobbying groups in the United States, the National Rifle Association and Gun Owners of America, are powerful enough to effectively lobby state and national legislatures to prevent meaningful restrictions on gun ownership, including the possession of hand guns and assault weapons. Both gun ownership and gun-related deaths are far higher in the United States than in other industrial countries.[2]

- **Sometimes the employees of non-profit social enterprises have a passion and zeal that ill serve the organization or its cause.** Greenpeace employees, for example, have at times taken direct action, acting as pirates by boarding whaling ships, which is illegal and can lead to loss of support for the organization or business.

- **Funding can be irregular.** Non-profit social enterprises are generally very reliant on donations, which can be a problem in economic recessions.

> **TOK links**
>
> 1. As non-profit organizations can make a profit (called "surplus") and profit-making organizations can operate at a loss (not making any profit), what is the point of the notion of "profit"?
>
> 2. As different countries have different legal frameworks, how useful is it to create a universal classification of types of organizations?
>
> 3. Is the term "social enterprise" an oxymoron?

---

[1] Doyle, A. March 2008. "Eat whale and save the planet". *Reuters*; Bjørnseth, S. September 2020. "Demand for whale meat in Norway rising after years of decline". *The Guardian*.

[2] Aizenman, N and Silver, M. August 2019. "How the US compares with other countries in deaths from gun violence". *NPR*.

Revision checklist

✓ Businesses in the private sector are owned and controlled by individuals or groups of individuals.

✓ Businesses in the public sector are owned and controlled by governmental authorities.

✓ Sole trader businesses are owned and managed by a single person. The individual is liable for any debts the business might incur. Registering a business as a sole trader is relatively quick and easy.

✓ A partnership is a business owned and managed by more than one person. Decisions should be made jointly, and all partners are equally liable. Multiple partners can bring different kinds of expertise and may also bring extra sources of finance.

✓ Companies and corporations have multiple owners – usually shareholders. When a business has registered as a company or corporation, the owners themselves are legally separate from the business, so they are no longer liable for debts.

✓ For-profit social enterprises have a social mission, but they still aim to make a profit.

✓ A social mission is the main aim of non-profit social enterprises. Any money made is called surplus. Most NGOs and charities fall into this category.

Practice question

To answer the question below effectively, see Unit 6 pages 398–402.

Off2SchoolSupplies

Off2SchoolSupplies (O2S) is an office supply company that for years sold exclusively to small, privately held companies located in the region where *O2S* was located and with which *O2S* had strong relationships. *O2S* never tried to sell to state schools, the government, or large publicly held companies. *O2S's* approached worked. The company saw its sales revenue grow year on year for two decades.

With the arrival of the internet, however, *O2S* has experienced slowing sales revenue growth. More and more small companies now purchase their office supplies from online sellers. To generate additional sales revenue to offset the slowing growth in the private sector, *O2S* has started trying to reach public sector organizations.

a) With reference to *O2S*, distinguish between the private and the public sectors. [4 marks]

1.3 Business objectives

> **By the end of this chapter, you should be able to:**
> → Explain the definitions and roles of **vision statements** and **mission statements**
> → Examine common business objectives, including **growth**, **profit**, **protecting shareholder value** and **ethical objectives**
> → Explain **strategic** and **tactical objectives**
> → Describe **corporate social responsibility (CSR)**

Vision and mission statements

Successful businesses have a clear identity, shared values, and a sense of purpose that all stakeholders identify with. To create or reinforce this identity, communicate these values, and maintain focus on the purpose, many businesses produce mission and vision statements. Some businesses will have one of these, others both. When done properly, both types of statement can help a business to reach its loftiest aims and stay focused day to day.

Mission and vision statements are sometimes confused, but they have different purposes. The vision statement is more forward looking and speaks to the long-term aims and highest aspirations of a business. A mission statement is more grounded in the aim of accomplishing objectives to achieve the mission: an intermediate step on the way to the vision.

The two statements should complement each other, with the vision statement being produced first. Less specific than a mission statement, the vision statement serves as a guiding principle or principles.

> **Key terms**
>
> **Vision statement**
> a philosophy, vision or set of principles which steers the direction and behaviour of an organization
>
> **Mission statement**
> states a company's purpose and explains why the business exists. A mission statement generally includes the business's aims and, whether expressly stated or implied, indicates its most important values.

Table 1.3.1 Comparison of vision and mission statements

	Vision	**Mission**
Concept	What do we want?	Why are we doing what we are doing?
Purpose	A vision statement points to the future. It is what the business would like to see itself as.	A mission statement, based upon where the business is now, communicates what needs to be done in order to achieve the vision.
Audience	To internal stakeholders, the vision statement inspires and motivates employees. For external stakeholders, the vision statement binds them to the business by giving a sense of shared beliefs.	To internal stakeholders, the mission statement provides a means for accountability by defining key performance indicators. For external stakeholders, the mission statement measures how successful the business is at achieving its vision.
Change	As an expression of the business's core values, the vision should *never* change.	A mission statement may change: in a world of dynamically changing external environments, a mission statement *may* need to be modified to meet new circumstances.

1.3 Business objectives

Here are two examples of the vision statements of major corporations that you probably know (and whose products you might use):

- Microsoft: "A personal computer in every home running Microsoft software."
- Toyota USA: "To be the most successful and respected car company in America."

In both cases, the vision statements are brief and express aspirations that are high and long term. They are inspirational. Both statements convey a sense of confidence in their purpose. They also convey the sense that if the companies are not at this lofty place yet (Microsoft running software in every home or Toyota USA being the most successful and respected car company in America), they will not give up until they have reached their aspiration.

Student workpoint 1.6

Be reflective

Here are the vision statements of two large organizations:

Oxfam: "A just world without poverty."

Amazon: "Our vision is to be earth's most customer centric company; to build a place where people can come to find and discover anything they might want to buy online."

What do the statements reveal about the aims and attitudes of the organization? Look carefully at the words that each statement uses – what affect do they have on you?

Aims, objectives, strategies, and tactics

Businesses may distinguish between aims and objectives and between strategies and tactics. All of these concepts are interdependent and all of these terms (including vision and mission too) are linked in some way or another. Figure 1.3.1 attempts to show their relationship with each other.

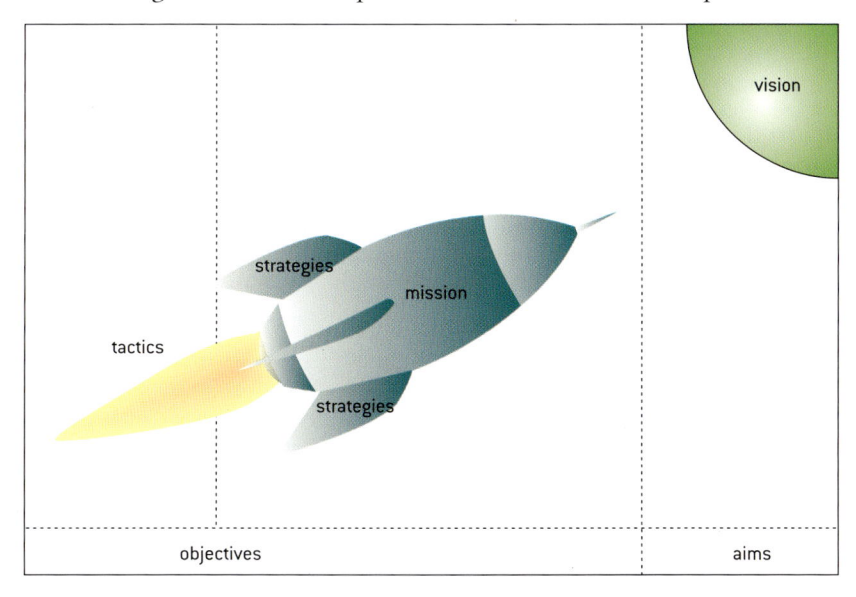

Figure 1.3.1 The vision and mission statements – relationship between aims, objectives, strategies, and tactics

Key terms

Business objectives

the articulated, measurable targets that a business must meet to achieve the aims or long-term goals of the business. It is critical that objectives are specific and measurable.

Strategic objectives

the long-term goals of a business that indicate how the business intends to fulfil its mission. Strategic objectives usually include performance goals, such as increasing market share or improving profitability.

Tactical objectives

short- to medium-term targets that, if consistently met, will help a business reach its strategic goals. Whereas strategic objectives are typically set by the board of directors with top executive management, tactical objectives are usually set by executive management working with middle-level management.

1 Introduction to business management

> **Student workpoint 1.7**
>
> **Be reflective**
>
> Think about your long-term life goals. Write a personal vision statement, and a personal mission statement, linked to these life goals.

The **aims** of a business are its long-term goals – what it wants to achieve in the future. An example of an aim might be: "We want to be profitable every year through the production of tasty, high-quality meat products." Another aim might be more focused on the delivery of the service: "We aim to deliver consistently high-quality plant and garden products through a helpful sales staff." The **vision statement** is a summary of these aims (sometimes literally the sum of these aims, at other times with modified wording).

In contrast to aims, **objectives** are the medium- to short-term goals that clarify how the business will achieve its aims and reach its vision. A **mission statement** summarizes these objectives.

Common business objectives

Business objectives vary according to organization. For some organizations, their most important aim is to grow. The board of directors and corporate leadership believe that growing the organization, gaining market share and increasing sales will, in the long run, enhance profits. Other organizations focus on profits or profitability, where the board and the corporate leadership are more focused on profits in the immediate future. A middle path aims to protect shareholder value by making profits now but looking sufficiently to the future to ensure shareholder value is there in the long run.

Businesses often establish a different category of objectives: ethical objectives. These are goals based on established codes of behaviour that, when met, allow the business to provide some social or environmental benefit, or at least not to hurt society or the environment in the process of making a profit.

For example, a business might aim for all of its employees to be treated without discrimination, harassment, or even favouritism. Another ethical objective might be to treat customers with respect and honesty. Ethical objectives can cover a whole range of activities and many businesses set them.

Business objectives come in three types:

- **Strategic objectives** – sometimes referred to as "global objectives" – are the medium- to long-term objectives set by senior managers to guide the company in the right direction to achieve its aims.
- **Tactical objectives** are the medium- to short-term objectives set by middle managers to achieve the strategic objectives.
- **Operational objectives** are the day-to-day objectives set by floor managers (and sometimes workers themselves) so that the company can reach its tactical objectives.

Table 1.3.2 Vision and the three types of objective

Vision (summary of aims)	Strategic objectives	Tactical objectives	Operational objectives
Long-term and highest aspiration	Long-term goals	Medium or short-term goals	Day-to-day goals

1.3 Business objectives

Strategic and tactical objectives

Businesses use the term "hierarchy of objectives" to describe the relationship between all of their goals. At the top of the hierarchy are the **aims**, which are few in number and set by the entrepreneur or the chief executive officer (CEO). The aims are (and should be) rather general.

How the business achieves these aims is through the next level of managers – the senior managers (directors or executives). These **strategic objectives** will be greater in number and concrete in nature. Ideally, these objectives will also be SMART (see below for details). With SMART objectives, the entrepreneur or CEO has some fair and measurable way to assess the performance of the executives and their divisions. If SMART objectives are not met, the CEO must ask: Were the objectives properly set, or did the directors or executives not perform properly in meeting the objectives? If the directors or executives vastly exceed the objectives, the CEO may decide to set more ambitious objectives the following year.

Businesses achieve their strategic objectives through the next tier of objectives: those that are tactical. **Tactical objectives** tend to be greater in number than strategic objectives and are usually set by the next level of managers – the middle managers (heads of department or supervisors).

At the lowest level, **operational objectives** will be set: floor managers will determine specific objectives that, in sum, ensure that the tactical objectives will be met.

Consider the hierarchy of objectives shown in Table 1.3.3.

Table 1.3.3 The hierarchy of objectives

Aim	Strategic objective	Tactical objective	Operational objective
To be the most successful car dealership in the city.	To have the highest market share of car dealerships in the city.	To hire and retain enough salespeople so that the dealership has sufficient salespeople to serve customers at all times.	To have the average amount of time that a customer waits to be greeted by a salesperson to be less than two minutes.

In the example in Table 1.3.3:

- The CEO sets the aim that a particular car dealership should be the most successful in the city.
- The head of sales determines that the best way to measure success is by having the highest market share of any car dealership in the city.
- The sales managers realize that to have the highest market share within a specified time frame means having more qualified sales staff to serve customers.
- The salespeople, realizing that their chance of making a sale increases the sooner they greet the customer, agree as a group that no customer will go more than two minutes without being greeted and offered service by a salesperson – even if it means that salespeople will not finish their coffee during their break.

1 Introduction to business management

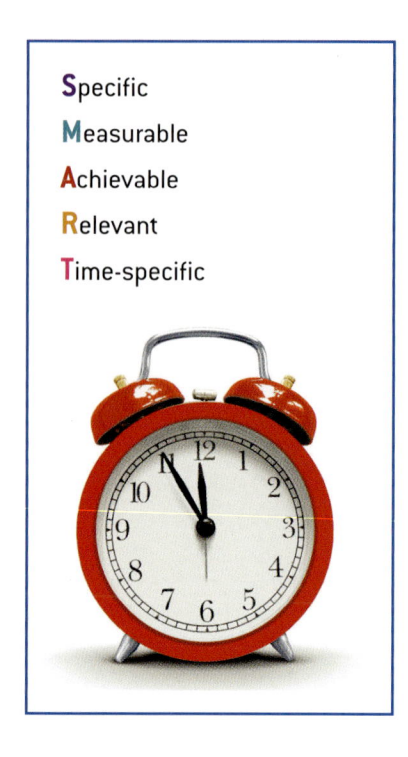

An important difference between aims and objectives is that objectives are concrete and can be translated into something specific and measurable. A vision such as "To be the most successful and respected car company in America" is motivating, but it is also (purposely) vague. This vagueness allows almost everyone to feel connected to it, but vagueness and abstractness are not qualities that employees can act on in unison.

SMART objectives

Specific
Measurable
Achievable
Relevant
Time-specific

Businesses are effective when they take their vision and transform it into specific objectives. The best business objectives are SMART. SMART objectives are as follows:

- **Specific** – is the objective clear and well defined? Objectives should relate to the nature of the business and be unambiguous. Rather than set an objective that the business "should grow", a smart objective would clarify that it wants to "increase its membership" or "increase the number of units sold" or "increase market share".

- **Measurable** – can the objective be measured to see whether it has been achieved or not? Not only should the objective be specific, it should also be measurable, as each of the above examples are (number of members, number of units sold, size of market share).

- **Achievable** – can the objective be achieved (is it realistic)? When objectives are achievable, they can be motivational. Objectives that are beyond the reasonable reach of a business or its employees can have the opposite effect, with employees giving up because they think or fear that they cannot reach the objective. Achievable goals also reduce dissonance and distractions (when employees or managers wonder how other aspects of the business are going to support these objectives).

- **Relevant** – is the objective actually of any use? Businesses can set objectives that are distractions from the main purpose of the company or, more commonly, set objectives for specific employees that are not relevant to the employees' area of responsibility. At a school, telling a member of the custodial staff that the objectives are for students to achieve high IB scores is not particularly relevant. Telling the custodial staff that, to lower expenses, they need to reduce the amount of cleaning supplies by 7% is relevant.

- **Time-specific** – has a sufficient time frame been set? If objectives do not have a time frame or deadline, they are not meaningful. For a car dealership to tell the sales staff that the number of cars sold per salesperson must increase by 5% is meaningless unless the sales staff is told the date by which the new sales target is to be met.

Business strategies

A **business strategy** is a plan to achieve a strategic objective in order to work towards the aims of the business. This strategy will be medium to long term and will require senior managers to make the decisions approved by the owners and/or the CEO.

1.3 Business objectives

Strategies are not unplanned or spur of the moment. They involve:

- Careful analysis of where the business is.
- The development of a plan (strategy) for how to get to where the business wants to be (aims).
- Careful consideration of how to implement the strategy.
- A periodic evaluation process to determine whether the plan is working or, after a specific period of time, has worked.

A **business tactic** is a plan to achieve a tactical objective to work towards the strategies of the business, which themselves are the path to reaching the aims of the business. This tactic will be short-term and will require middle managers to make the decisions approved by the senior managers. Tactics are easier to change. They are less closely tied to the long-term health of the firm, instead focusing on how to achieve measurable targets within the strategy.

A business can have a sound strategy but a poor tactical plan. A strategic objective, for example, might be offering food that is perceived by restaurant customers to be of the highest quality of its type in a market area. One tactic for determining customers' satisfaction might be customer count or observing customers' reactions as they eat the food. A better tactic might be to obtain a more direct form of customer feedback on food quality (but it might not be a better form if the direct feedback does not otherwise fit with the marketing mix of the restaurant).

The need for organizations to change objectives

Businesses often need to change objectives. Sometimes this requires changing strategic objectives. More commonly, it involves changing tactical objectives and, day to day, floor managers and supervisors change operational objectives. Regardless of the level, objectives change because of changes in either of these environments:

- The internal environment, which refers to changes in the conditions within the business.
- The external environment, which refers to anything outside the business that nonetheless has a bearing on its operation or performance.

Changes in the internal environment

Changes in the internal environment might include the following:

- **Leadership** – a change of leadership often can lead to a change in aims and objectives. A famous example is when, in 1996, Steve Jobs returned to Apple. Sometimes new leaders brought into a company will have a different leadership style from their predecessors, which can require significant changes to objectives.
- **HR** – the term "human resources" covers a vast array of elements of a business. Conditions related to HR can change and can alter objectives all the way down the hierarchy. Industrial action, which refers to actions taken by unions or other forms of organized labour, can often precipitate change in an organization.

> **Concept**
>
> **CHANGE**
>
> Due to changes in their external environment (such as new competitors) and changes in their internal environment (such as restructuring), organizations may need to modify their objectives and strategies.
>
> Do some research to find examples of such changes in objectives or strategies.

- **Organization** – business organizations change. A merger or acquisition, such as when Kraft took over Cadbury, can have a ripple effect through an organization, causing the new organization to rethink many of its objectives. In other instances, some internal pressures may cause an organization to modify one aspect of its business. However, given the interconnectedness of all the business functions, changes in one area can require changes in another, including changes to strategic or tactical objectives.

- **Product** – products are sold in a marketplace. Sometimes, the performance of the product in the marketplace may require changes in either the product or even an entire product line. In the 1980s, for example, Lucozade reoriented itself as a sports drink because of market pressures, and sales tripled. With this change in the branded identity of the product, from an illness-curing beverage to an energy-providing sports drink, many different aspects of Lucozade's strategic and tactical objectives had to change (which led to an even greater number of changes in operational objectives).

- **Finance** – all business activity must be financed. When the circumstances of finance change, especially when sources of finance become fewer and the amount of finance decreases, organizations have to modify their strategies or change the emphasis of their business. For example, in 2009, FIFA introduced the "Financial Fair Play" rule, which modified how much money football teams could spend on players, and teams had to respond.

  Many other sets of circumstances can change finance. After the world recession began in 2008, for example, many banks raised lending standards and businesses had to make adjustments because they had more limited access to capital to finance activity.

- **Operations** – ideally, most businesses are innovating constantly, not just by offering new products but also by developing better methods for producing or delivering their core service or product – that is, by innovating their operations. Sometimes changes in operations occur for more everyday reasons, such as relocating a factory. Either way, changes in operations can necessitate other changes in objectives.

If any of the above internal factors are altered, then the business may well have to respond or even pre-empt them by changing its objectives.

Changes in the external environment

Usually, a business has limited or no control over the external environment, but often objectives have to change in response to changes in the external environment. A "STEEPLE" framework is commonly used to frame issues related to the external environment. Steeple factors are as follows:

- **Social** – this refers to changes in society or culture, such as demographic change (social) or cultural change (such as an increased preference for expensive coffees, like those supplied by Starbucks or Coffee Aroma). Social changes such as these may force the business to reappraise its objectives.

  One example is the business of education. More women are attending university and obtaining degrees than they did a few decades ago and, as a result, universities are modifying many of their objectives, from course offerings to residential practices, to suit the greater number of women.

- **Technological** – today is an era of rapid technological change, which can change the environment for business in any number of ways. A product a business offers can be rendered obsolete or uncompetitive because of technological innovation (think how quickly Blackberry went from being a "hot" product to one that struggles to compete with new smartphones). Technological innovation can force changes in production techniques if a competitor develops new methods for producing products more cheaply than other businesses.

  Technological changes can also force a business to change for "softer" reasons. All businesses need to be more aware of their environment and their actions in it because information technologies allow communication in ways previously unknown. Today, for example, Nike would have a harder time manufacturing shoes in low-income economies and using child labour compared to several decades ago, when companies could often follow those tactics without being discovered.

- **Economic** – changes in the market conditions (such as the presence of new competitors), or simply changes in the economy (such as the global financial crisis) can have a profound influence on businesses and force them to change strategic and tactical objectives.

  For example, interest rates on loans can increase because of changing economic conditions, raising the cost of capital for businesses and preventing capital investment. If a company sells a product the demand for which is income elastic (see more on this in Chapter 4.5), sales may fall in an economic downturn. For many reasons, changing economic conditions can force a business to change.

- **Ethical** – sometimes quickly, sometimes slowly, the values of a society can change. Changes in ethical values in a society encourage or even force a business to change its practices. Fifty years ago, relatively few businesses were deeply concerned about sustainable business practices – Paul Hawken's concept of "natural capitalism" was unheard of. Today, even if the owners or executives of a business are not genuinely concerned about sustainable practices, external stakeholders will almost certainly expect their business to not harm the environment, or at least to minimize that harm.

  In a host of other ways – such as ethics in lending, diversity in hiring, attentiveness to sexual harassment, and product safety – changes in society's values have led to changes in many businesses' objectives.

- **Political** – change to the political system very often forces business to change its approach. Multinational businesses plan for this possibility and will often carry out a "country risk assessment" before investing in a particular country. A country risk assessment attempts to determine the likelihood that drastic political change in a country could put at risk the investment or operations of a business there.

Consumer demand for ethical products has increased greatly recently

1 Introduction to business management

Political risk, however, can also occur at home. For example, if the outcome of a political election determines that the legislature of a country changes from centre-left to centre-right, the business environment can change. Sometimes, though, political change can occur unexpectedly and not from the results of an election. Legislatures can decide to take action because of a scandal, a crime, or even an accident, that in turn affects the business environment.

- **Legal** – when responsibility for legislation changes from one party to the other, or one coalition to another, changes in the legal environment often occur. Regulation, taxes, and a host of other factors can be changed merely by statute, and businesses have to respond.

In the 1980s in the United States, for example, many individuals across the country grew tired of the number of fatal or traumatic injuries occurring to young people due to excessive alcohol consumption. One by one, most state legislatures raised the minimum drinking age in the United States from 18 to 21 years. Many taverns, bars, and clubs that targeted customers in the 18–20-year-old age range had to modify their business strategies.

- **Ecological** – growing environmental awareness and the "green" revolution have had a significant effect on many businesses, for example with the emergence of hybrid cars. Ecological factors can affect businesses in ways other than the now-dominant focus on sustainability. Ecological depletion, such as from fisheries off the coast of Canada, or through some types of mining, can force a business to change strategies. Large oil companies, sometimes notorious for their ecological disasters such as huge oil spills, are nonetheless highly innovative in their search for new sources of clean energy, in anticipation of rising demand and declining traditional sources of energy (such as oil).

> **Resource recovery models**
>
> Resource recovery models help to recycle waste into secondary raw materials, thus reducing the final disposal of waste and reducing the extraction and processing of virgin natural resources. The case study below gives an example of an organization using a resource recovery model.

Case study

Bio-bean

Bio-bean is the UK's largest recycler of coffee grounds and works with other companies in the country to transform coffee waste into valuable products at an industrial scale.

They provide a solution to the approximate half a million tonnes of waste coffee grounds produced annually in the UK, helping businesses to save money while achieving greater sustainability.

Heavy, wet coffee grounds weigh down whichever waste stream they enter, typically increasing the collection fees for most businesses that produce coffee. Bio-bean works with logistics and waste management infrastructure across the UK by taking segregated spent coffee grounds from these businesses, reducing the weight of their waste and in turn the costs associated with disposal.

Bio-bean recycles spent coffee grounds from businesses at every scale: from coffee shops, cafes and restaurants to office blocks, transport hubs, universities and instant coffee factories. Segregated spent grounds are collected and delivered to their factory in Cambridgeshire, where their innovative proprietary processes condition and dry the grounds, renewing them for reuse in valuable products to benefit both people and planet.

Source: Adapted from https://www.bio-bean.com/renewals/coffee-recycling/

Corporate social responsibility

Corporate social responsibility (CSR) is an idea that has gained much attention since the 1960s. Part of this attention was in reaction to the many companies which, in focusing on maximizing shareholder value, either exacerbated existing problems (such as environmental degradation) or created new problems (such as the elimination of defined benefit pension plans).

The main thrust of CSR is that companies should do more than merely make money for their shareholders, and more than just consider the perspectives of all relevant stakeholders when making decisions. Corporations should instead do positive good for society.

Companies can operationalize a commitment to CSR in many ways, including philanthropy, generous salaries and wages, meaningful benefits such as flexitime for working parents, or by doing more for the environment than the minimum legal compliance required by government regulations.

Some would argue that the roots of CSR are much older than the 1960s and that there have always been some companies that have acted in ways which were good for society. Regardless of when exactly the idea emerged, today CSR is a powerful force in companies all over the world.

Why organizations set ethical objectives

Businesses may set themselves ethical objectives for some very good commercial reasons, including these:

- **Building up customer loyalty** – repeat customers are vital to most businesses. Customers are more likely to return to a business they trust and respect, and ethical objectives and ethical action foster this.

- **Creating a positive image** – both existing and potential customers are likely to shop at businesses with good reputations. The opposite is also true: customers will avoid businesses with reputations for being untrustworthy.

- **Developing a positive work environment** – businesses that have well-motivated staff who enjoy working for the business have a competitive advantage. Businesses with strong ethical objectives can be attractive to many potential employees and serve to improve morale and motivation.

- **Reducing the risk of legal redress** – being unethical can cost a company money, both from dissatisfied customers not returning and from the bad word-of-mouth reports generated by unethical behaviour. Sometimes unethical behaviour can lead to legal redress by the government, by other businesses or by the customers themselves. Even if a business "wins" in court, the process can be expensive and cause significant damage to the firm's reputation.

- **Satisfying customers' ever-higher expectations for ethical behaviour** – with improved ICT and the internet, business decisions and actions are more visible than ever before. Today, consumers are aware of what is considered ethical and unethical behaviour. They often "punish" unethical behaviours by not patronizing certain businesses. Few businesses can disregard public opinion.

> **Key term**
>
> **Corporate social responsibility (CSR)**
>
> CSR is the view that businesses, rather than focusing solely on increasing shareholder value, should contribute to the economic, social, and environmental well-being of society

> **Student workpoint 1.8**
>
> *Be a thinker*
>
> Many businesses set ethical objectives. What are the three or four most important ethical principles that you would want in any organization that you work for or start up yourself?

This poster from the clothing company Matalan clearly states the business's ethical policy

- **Increasing profits** – opportunities for businesses to behave ethically are growing. Often banks will not lend to dubious businesses, clothes manufacturers will not use "sweatshop" workers, and coffee houses use "fair trade" coffee. Many people seek out and purchase from businesses that behave ethically, which can lead to higher profits.

The impact of implementing ethical objectives

When a business implements ethical objectives, many areas of the business environment will be affected. The effects may be on the following:

- **The business itself** – although in the long run, the business may experience benefits from implementing ethical objectives, in the short term, costs are likely to rise, and employees who are accustomed to certain norms and practices may resist change.
- **Competitors** – in order to maintain their market position, competitors may have to respond.
- **Suppliers** – if the business implementing ethical objectives includes the policy of buying only from other ethical businesses, suppliers may have to respond in order to protect their orders.
- **Customers** – they are likely to trust the business more and develop a strong brand loyalty.
- **The local community** – businesses that have and follow ethical objectives generally see an improvement in their relationship with the local community, which can benefit them in terms of employment and goodwill.
- **Government** – feeling pressure from voters and other stakeholders, local, regional, and national levels of government are increasingly recognizing businesses with ethical objectives, overall creating a government–business environment fostering ethical objectives.

How ethical objectives are linked to CSR

Ethical objectives are closely related to corporate social responsibility. Ethical objectives are specific goals that a business may set for itself based on established codes of behaviour. CSR is the concept that a business has an obligation to operate in a way that will have a positive impact on society.

As part of its CSR policy, a business would want to assess its actions. As a result of such an assessment, the business may wish to implement a particular ethical objective. For example, a business might open a crèche facility (an early childhood day-care centre) for its employees.

CSR is broader and less specific than ethical objectives. A company committed to CSR is intending to act as a good "corporate citizen": acting responsibly and in a manner that benefits society as a whole in all matters. A business committed to CSR not only obeys laws but also interacts responsibly and honestly with customers, and reduces its impact on the environment.

By recognizing its CSR, a business is more than likely to have a sustainable business model. By building strong links with society and the environment, the business is more likely to be a valued part of the society.

1.3 Business objectives

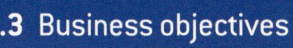

Case study: Timberland

Timberland is an American company founded in 1928 that manufactures outdoor wear, especially shoes. The company has long had a commitment to doing social good and does so through of a variety of ways, some of which are encapsulated in the quote below, taken from the company's webpage:

"We are committed to the work of building a more inclusive company and being a force for social and environmental good.

- Build an inclusive workspace
- Strengthen communities of color
- Invest in design education
- Support black entrepreneurs"

Every quarter, Timberland publishes a CSR report, which is made available to the public through its website. In this report, Timberland provides details about its manufacturing processes, the materials used in its products, its resource efficiency, and its community service initiatives. By providing metrics on these aspects of its corporate social responsibility programme, anyone can see what environmental and social impacts Timberland is making and its improvements in various areas quarter on quarter and year on year.

These efforts at transparency suggest that Timberland is not merely engaging in "greenwashing" (the process where a company tries to create the impression that it is "green" when in reality it is not), but rather that Timberland is genuinely committed to reducing its environmental impact and creating a better world.

Source: Adapted from https://www.timberland.com/responsibility.html

Concept: ETHICS

Corporate social responsibility and ethics are closely related. Many organizations publish a "CSR policy" or a "CSR strategy" on their website, where they show and communicate their ethical objectives. For example, the case study here describes how Timberland publishes a CSR report every quarter.

Do some research on the internet to find examples of such documents.

Many businesses, and increasingly big businesses, want to position themselves as role models – as leading citizens – setting the standard for everyone for responsible behaviour. In an international context this might be more difficult because of different opinions about ethical values, but with globalization and the greater integration of the world's economies through the actions of multinational companies, this can still be possible.

Although many businesses do not reach their highest aspirations for CSR, since around 1980 the movement towards CSR has been significant and has led to dramatic changes in the attitudes and practices of businesses.

SWOT analysis

SMART objectives are part of a coherent strategic plan. In the 1960s, a business tool called the SWOT analysis was developed to help businesses set these objectives. Although use of this tool has not been without criticism, in general many businesses rely on SWOT analyses for planning purposes.

Student workpoint 1.9

Be reflective

Read the article "Corporate social responsibility is shifting as a result of 2020's triple crisis" by Carolyn Berkowitz (you can find this online on the 3BL CSRwire website).

What important themes and ideas from Chapter 1.3 are evident in this article?

SWOT analysis

"SWOT" stands for strengths, weaknesses, opportunities, and threats. Organizations often use this tool themselves during a strategic planning process. Anyone else trying to understand an organization may also want to do a SWOT analysis of it.

The focus of the tool is on the organization and its contexts. Those involved in the strategic planning process think about their organization and identify its current strengths and weaknesses, which are internal to the company. The planners then look externally and determine the opportunities and threats that the organization faces.

These four categories of items are then put into a table, often with the format below:

Strengths	Weaknesses
Opportunities	Threats

SWOT analysis is meant to be the first stage in the planning process. It helps managers to brainstorm the perceived strengths, weaknesses, opportunities, and threats facing the business. These elements are combined in a matrix as shown in Table 1.3.4.

Table 1.3.4 The SWOT matrix

	Positive factors	Negative factors
Internal to the business	Strengths	Weaknesses
External to the business	Opportunities	Threats

The SWOT matrix is based on perceptions. The wider the sources and the more reliable the data, the stronger will be the analysis of the SWOT factors. The opposite is also true. If a SWOT analysis is done in a poor, sloppy, or uninformed fashion, it can actually mislead a business. Like any business tool, it is useful only when thoughtfully and properly applied.

A SWOT analysis for a given organization

Table 1.3.5 shows an example of a SWOT matrix for Apple Inc (as of January 2021).

Table 1.3.5 SWOT matrix for Apple Inc

Strengths	Weaknesses
• Well recognized among most consumers. • Largest percentage of global market share in the global cellphone market (23.4%, fourth quarter 2020). • Strong brand image provides an edge over competitors. • Very profitable – $90 billion cash and marketable securities. • Focused research and development creating stylish products. • Provides integrated operating systems, hardware, application software and service to its customers. • Major increase in share value over the last 5 years. • Tablet sales remain solid.	• Apple products lack compatibility with much non-Apple software. • Limited distribution network. • Very dependent on Chinese suppliers. • Price – other similar products are more affordable.
Opportunities	**Threats**
• Strong growth in smartphone markets. • Strong growth in tablet markets. • Mobile advertising market is forecast to reach approximately $240 billion by 2022. • Increased scope in the educational market. • Development of new products and product lines in online services.	• Aggressive competition from major firms like Samsung and Amazon. • Many low-cost firms imitate Apple's products. • Rising labour costs in China. • The Covid-19 pandemic has compromised supply chains.

Note that the purpose of a SWOT analysis is not to brainstorm the strengths and weaknesses of a business strategy itself; it is the first part of developing the strategy by identifying the different strengths and weaknesses of the business. Once these are known, the SWOT matrix can be analysed and so a strategy can be formulated.

SWOT analysis and market position

Use of the SWOT matrix can be strengthened by "pairing" key factors from each quadrant and then adopting a relevant strategy, as shown in Table 1.3.6.

Table 1.3.6 Pairing key factors to determine the relevant strategy

	Strengths	**Weaknesses**
Opportunities	S–O **Growth** strategies	W–O **Re-orientation** strategies
Threats	S–T **Defusing** strategies	W–T **Defensive** strategies

- **Growth strategies** are best achieved by combining the strengths of a business with the market opportunities, which produces the most positive short-term strategy available from the matrix. The business should pursue growth strategies when it is confident that it has no big issues in any other area.
- **Defensive strategies** are adopted when a business is at its most vulnerable. When threats and weakness exist in combination, the business needs to act defensively and quickly. Defensive strategies are the most "negative" short-term strategies, but they may be necessary to help the business survive.
- **Re-orientation strategies** are adopted when a business focuses on addressing its weaknesses in order to use them for the opportunities available in the market. Re-orientation strategies are positive and long term. Their adoption assumes that the business will first address its weaknesses, then can re-orientate itself in a new direction.
- **Defusing strategies** are designed to eliminate threats in the market by focusing on the strengths of a business. Defusing strategies assume that the business does not need to look for new market opportunities but can simply defuse the threats through a focus on core strengths. This is a neutral and medium- to short-term strategy.

The Ansoff matrix

Another business tool to help businesses plan and set objectives is the Ansoff matrix, which was designed by Igor Ansoff in 1957. Many businesses use the Ansoff matrix to help plan their growth strategies.

The Ansoff matrix

The Ansoff matrix looks at the growth potential of a business in terms of the market and product. It considers both the existing markets and products, and new markets and products:

	Product Existing	**Product** New
Market Existing	Market penetration	Product development
Market New	Market development	Diversification

Figure 1.3.2 The Ansoff matrix

There are four possible growth strategies: market penetration, market development, product development and diversification. These are explored below.

Market penetration

Market penetration occurs when a business grows by increasing its market share, selling more of its existing products in the same market. Market penetration is considered the safest option for growth, but opportunities for increasing market share may be limited by the competitors in the market.

Market penetration relies heavily on promoting brand loyalty in order to encourage repeat customers, and on promotion in general to lure customers away from the competition. For example, Netflix has used series like *The Crown* and *The Queen's Gambit* to develop great brand loyalty to its streaming services.

Key factors to increase the chance of success are:

- The growth potential of the market
- The strength of customer loyalty
- The power and ability of competitors

Market development

Market development expands the market by looking for new markets or for new market segments in the existing market. Market development is a riskier strategy than market penetration, as the business may not understand the new markets.

For example, Starbucks was unsuccessful when it initially opened coffee stores in Australia. Walmart was also unsuccessful when it expanded into Germany. Walmart had underestimated the loyalty of the German public to existing (German) superstores.

Successful market development requires different approaches from market penetration.

Key factors to reduce the risks of market development are:

- Effective market research
- Having local knowledge on the ground
- Having an effective distribution channel

Product development

Product development is the development of new products for the existing market. Sometimes it may be a genuinely and wholly new product. Often, however, so-called "new" products are upgrades of existing products (such as the iPad, iPad 2, iPad 3, iPad mini and all the different variations). At other times, a "new product" is a variation on an existing product. For example, this was the case when Singapore Airlines introduced their budget airline "Scoot" to fight off competition from Australian budget airlines.

Product development is riskier than market penetration, with much depending on how loyal customers are to the original products. Key factors to reduce the risks of product development are:

- Effective market research
- Having a strong research and development system
- Having first-mover advantage

TOK discussion

1. If the effects of mission statements and vision statements cannot be measured, does this mean that they are worthless?
2. Should all businesses have ethical objectives?
3. Does the notion of "corporate social responsibility" change over time?

Diversification

Diversification is the riskiest growth strategy a business can pursue. When diversifying – introducing a new product into a new market – a business combines two elements of risk:

- Lack of familiarity and experience in the new market
- The fact that the new product is untested

When Apple moved away from home computing and entered the digital music market and then the handphone market, it successfully diversified. Many attempts at diversification, however, have failed. For example, Microsoft bought the telephone company Nokia in 2013, but by 2015 Nokia had failed and Microsoft had to write-off $7.3 billion.

Key factors to reduce the risks of diversification are:

- Effective market research
- Due diligence testing to determine:
    - the attractiveness of the market
    - the cost of entering the market
- Recognition of the existing business
- Possible tie-ups with other businesses with the necessary experience

Revision checklist

✓ A vision statement should encapsulate what the business hopes to be in the future. It should remain constant.

✓ A mission statement describes what the business is doing now. It might need to be modified as time passes.

✓ Aims are long-term goals.

✓ Objectives are short- or medium-term goals which allow a business to meet its aims. Objectives should be SMART (specific, measurable, achievable, relevant and time-specific).

✓ A business strategy is an overarching plan of objectives which will enable aims to be met.

✓ Business tactics are the actions and objectives which allow a business to implement strategy.

✓ Ethical objectives are goals that a business sets for itself based on established codes of behaviour.

✓ Corporate social responsibility (CSR) is the concept that all businesses have an obligation to operate in a way that will have a positive impact on society.

✓ A SWOT analysis is a tool used in business planning. It involves analysing strengths, weaknesses, opportunities and threats, both inside a business and externally.

✓ The Ansoff matrix is used to plan business growth. It considers new and existing products and new and existing markets to identify opportunities. It allows a business to identify areas of market penetration, market development, product development and diversification.

1.3 Business objectives

Practice question

To answer the question below effectively, see Unit 6 pages 398–402.

Route 11 Chips

Route 11 Chips is a privately held company that is located in the Shenandoah Valley of Virginia, USA, which manufactures potato chips (or "crisps" in UK English). The business began as an outgrowth of the Tabard Inn, a restaurant located in nearby Washington, DC. The owner of the Tabard Inn also owned a certified organic farm in the Shenandoah Valley.

Through a combination of luck and an interest in sustainability and locally sourced food, the owners of the Tabard Inn began making potato chips. A farmer approached the owners of the Tabard Inn. He had a huge surplus of potatoes and was trying to sell them. The farmer and the owner of the Tabard Inn decided to make potato chips.

At the time, the business had no real factory, no distribution network, and no name recognition other than, perhaps, some limited awareness of the Tabard Inn. However, the business was able to buy equipment from a small chip manufacturer that was going out of business and, in 1992, it opened a factory on Route 11 in the Shenandoah Valley. The business adopted the name Route 11 Chips.

In 2008, the company built its current factory and all aspects of the new factory followed green principles. Among other sustainable features, Route 11 Chips uses:

- certified organic sweet potatoes
- locally produced regular potatoes whenever possible
- 100% renewable hydroelectric power to run its factory and offices
- waste potato peelings and reject chips to feed cows in the area.

In addition to selling chips, Route 11 Chips sells a range of products designed to encourage brand recognition and loyalty: T-shirts, fridge magnets, hats, and other items.

Posted on its website is an offer to hear charity requests: "Route 11 Chips is committed to supporting a healthy community and environment. We enjoy having opportunities to give. We review our charity requests once per month, generally on or around the 5th of the month, and make a decision on one or more opportunities to support generally on or before the 15th of the month."

a) State **two** features of a privately held company. [2 marks]

b) Explain **two** ways that Route 11 Chips practises corporate social responsibility. [4 marks]

c) Explain **one** challenge and **one** opportunity that the owners of Route 11 Chips faced when starting their potato chip business. [4 marks]

1.4 Stakeholders

By the end of this chapter, you should be able to:
- Outline the interests of **internal stakeholders**
- Outline the interests of **external stakeholders**
- Discuss possible **areas of conflict** between stakeholders' interests

Stakeholders are any individual or groups of individuals who have a direct interest in a business because the actions of the business will affect them directly. They are called "stakeholders" because they have a stake or interest in the business. Sometimes the stake is directly financial (they are shareholders, lenders, suppliers, or employees), and at other times it is less direct, such as the community in which a business operates. Nevertheless, all stakeholders have an interest in the business.

Internal and external stakeholders

There are several different ways to categorize stakeholders. One is to separate them into **market** and **non-market stakeholders**. Market stakeholders are those that the organization has a commercial relationship with (that is, "money changes hands"). Market stakeholders include groups such as customers, suppliers, and lenders.

Non-market stakeholders are stakeholders with which money does not change hands, like the media or the community.

Another common distinction is between **primary** and **secondary stakeholders**. Primary stakeholders are those directly affected by or affecting the organization, whereas secondary stakeholders have an indirect relationship with the organization. Common examples of secondary stakeholders include the media, government, or NGOs.

There is also a third common way to categorize stakeholder:

- **Internal stakeholders** are individuals or groups that work within the business.
- **External stakeholders** are individuals or groups that are outside the business.

In practice, grey areas exist between internal and external stakeholders:

- Employees of a business live in the community where the business is located. As employees, they are internal stakeholders; as residents of the community, they are external stakeholders.
- In democratic societies, employees (internal stakeholders) are voting citizens and thus in some ways they are external stakeholders, as voting citizens have some claim on the government.

Key terms

Stakeholder

a person or organization that affects or is affected by a business. Stakeholders are often classified as internal versus external, market versus non-market, or primary versus secondary.

Internal stakeholder

a stakeholder who is internal to (inside) the business, such as an employee, a manager, or shareholders

External stakeholder

a stakeholder who is external to (outside) the business or organization, such as suppliers, customers, government, media, or the community

1.4 Stakeholders

- Consultants to a business, such as financial planners, are external to the business. They are brought in because of their expertise in a particular area. However, once hired, in some fashion they have an internal position.
- Small shareholders in large publicly traded companies are considered internal stakeholders, even if they own a tiny fraction of the company. However, someone who owns a small stake of a large publicly traded company has virtually no ability to influence the business and in most respects is external to the business.

In addition, in other instances individuals have multiple stakeholder interests: employees who own shares, and managers who are part of the management team, have multiple stakeholder interests.

The interests of internal stakeholders

- Shareholders focus on returns on their investments.
- The CEO or managing director focuses on coordinating the business strategy and delivering profits and returns that satisfy the shareholders.
- Senior managers focus on the strategic objectives for their functional areas.
- Middle managers focus on the tactical objectives for their functional areas.
- Foremen and supervisors focus on organizing tactical objectives and formulating operational objectives.
- Employees and their unions focus on protecting their rights and working conditions.

The interests of external stakeholders

- Government (at all levels) focuses on how the business operates in the business environment.
- Suppliers focus on maintaining a stable relationship.
- Customers and consumers focus on the best product that meets their needs.
- People in the local community focus on the impact of the business in the local area.
- Financiers focus on returns on their investments.
- Pressure groups focus on how the business has impact on their area of concern.
- The media focuses on the impact of the business in terms of news stories.

External stakeholders include the local community living near a business (if some of these residents are also employees of the business, then they are also internal stakeholders)

Competitors are considered to be stakeholders because they can affect the operation of the business. Consider the following example. On 9 April 2017, David Dao Duy Anh, an American medical doctor, had taken his seat on a United Airlines flight from Chicago, IL, to Louisville, KY. Before the plane began to taxi for take-off, United Airlines personnel asked him to exit the plane. His seat was being given to a United Airlines employee.

1 Introduction to business management

Dr Dao objected, saying that a patient was scheduled to see him the following morning. United Airlines personnel called security personnel, who forcibly removed Dr Dao from the airplane and, in the process, injured him.

This incident was reported to the media, and the story quickly affected the entire airline industry. Many members of Congress (the legislative branch of the government of the United States) demanded that the matter be investigated and that new regulations regarding the treatment of passengers be set for the entire airline industry. This impacted on all airlines, which were therefore all affected by the actions of one of their competitors (United Airlines).

Conflict between stakeholders' interests

Groups of people with a common interest, such as a business, may also have differences of opinion. This situation makes sense: although all stakeholders have a "stake" in the business, their focuses are different.

Consider the example of a pay rise for employees. Shareholders may object to the idea, as it could reduce profits and therefore reduce their return on investment. At the other end of the spectrum are the employees themselves, who would favour pay rises which could give them a higher standard of living. In between these two positions there will be various stakeholders who will have different opinions.

- The CEO and senior managers would in principle probably support paying higher wages, as this would make the employees happier. However, the CEO and senior managers are responsible for ensuring profit targets and return on investment ratios are met, so they would also be worried that pay rises would reduce profits.

- Managers may also be concerned that by reinforcing the use of extrinsic motivating factors, a pay rise might undermine their efforts to foster a culture of intrinsic motivation. Extrinsic motivating factors are types of external rewards, such as pay increases or bonuses. Intrinsic motivation occurs when people do things because they find that doing so is rewarding. Often the use of extrinsic motivating strategies weakens intrinsic motivation.

- Those in the local community would in principle favour higher wages for employees, as it would mean that employees would have more money to spend in the local community – at restaurants and shops, for example. However, if the pay rises in any way threatened the existence of the business, the community would probably not favour the idea.

Thus, any decision of importance, such as a general pay rise at the business, will elicit different reactions from different stakeholders. In this situation, friction may result and alliances may be formed as each stakeholder group tries to achieve their desired outcome.

One feature of successful businesses is that the interests of stakeholders are sufficiently satisfied most of the time. In some instances, managing stakeholders' interests is not particularly complicated. An individual running a small shop as a sole trader typically has relatively few internal stakeholders: the sole trader and perhaps an employee or two. While in theory the business would have several external stakeholders, such as the community, the government, financiers and suppliers, these external stakeholders typically (though not always) have such a small stake in the business that the decisions of the shop are relatively inconsequential.

Thus, for this type of business, satisfying the interests of stakeholders is not complicated. The main requirement is for the business to be profitable enough to pay for expenses and provide the sole trader with an income, and to be in compliance with laws and government regulations and with community standards.

For other types of business, especially large ones, coordinating the interests of stakeholders is a much more formidable challenge. When a large business operates a factory in a small city or in a town, the factory may be the most important employer in the area. In this instance, the various stakeholders have a major stake in the success of the business.

For example, in the case of a factory that is the main employer in a town, a 20% reduction in the workforce might lead to reduced expenses for the business. It might also make the retained workers more productive if they were pressured into working harder to make up for the smaller workforce. Shareholders might be happy with this outcome, as might the CEO and senior managers (who may receive greater year-end bonuses).

The workers, however, would be dissatisfied. Those losing their jobs would be unhappy. Even those keeping their jobs would not like seeing their co-workers go. Even if the business was not pressuring the remaining workers to work harder to make up for the lost work of those retrenched, a general sense of fear – of more job cuts – would affect the workers.

Many other stakeholders would be affected as well. Here are just a few of the implications for the local community and the local government.

- Many employees could struggle to find new jobs, in which case government expenses (support for the unemployed persons) would increase.
- People might move away from the town, selling houses or moving out of rental properties, thus depressing the real estate market.
- When families move away, the number of children in the schools may reduce, thus leading to lay-offs of teachers in those schools.
- Local businesses would suffer, as fewer employees at the factory would mean fewer people with the resources to spend money in local shops and restaurants.

Stakeholder analysis

Large businesses or those businesses that have complicated stakeholder interests often perform a stakeholder analysis. The first step is to prioritize or rank the interests of various stakeholders. One conceptual approach to this step is to determine how "close" each stakeholder is to decision-making in the business. This is shown in Figure 1.4.1.

> **Concept**
>
> **SUSTAINABILITY**
>
> Sustainable development may be a cause of conflict between stakeholders, when some are focused more on short-term profit maximization, while others are concerned about long-term social and environmental impacts.
>
> Can you find an example of such a stakeholder conflict around sustainability? This could be a starting point for your IA research project.

1 Introduction to business management

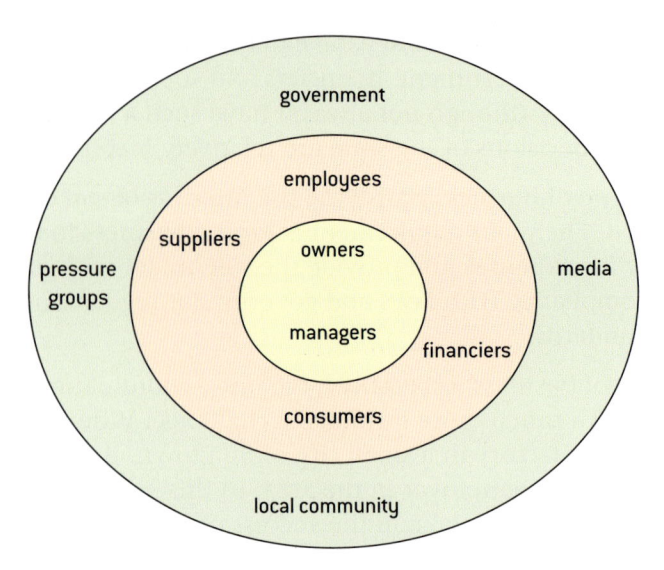

Figure 1.4.1 The comparative closeness of stakeholders to decision-making

Under this approach, owners and managers are central to decision-making, while suppliers, employees, financiers, and consumers are further removed. Most distant are government, pressure groups, the media and the local community. Decision-makers try to satisfy those stakeholders closest to the centre.

Another conceptual approach involves a tool called **stakeholder mapping**. Numerous models for mapping stakeholders exist. One particularly valued model was formulated by Johnson and Scholes and is called the power–interest model.

Figure 1.4.2 The power–interest model (Johnson and Scholes)

By placing each stakeholder group in the matrix, a business can decide on likely strategies.

- **Stakeholders in group A.** These stakeholders, who have minimal interest in the business and have limited power over it, are rarely a problem for the business. Owners and managers can fairly safely ignore these stakeholders, or at least devote limited energy and attention to satisfying their interests.

- **Stakeholders in group B.** For owners and managers, making this group feel included is important. Newsletters, events, and other ways of conveying a sense of belonging are important.

- **Stakeholders in group C.** This pivotal group of stakeholders must be kept satisfied. They have the power to influence other groups. The business must find ways to flatter the self-esteem of members of this group to make them feel important.

- **Stakeholders in group D.** These stakeholders are the most important. The business must not merely communicate with them; it must also consult with them before any major decisions are made. The business should focus on their needs in preference to the others. Failure to involve and satisfy these stakeholders can have very negative consequences for the business.

Student workpoint 1.10

Be reflective

One theory for running a business is that management should focus solely on legally making profits and increasing shareholder value. Another theory, which emerged in the 1980s, argues that when making major decisions, management should communicate with all of the relevant stakeholders and consider their interests.

Which of these two theories makes most sense to you and why?

TOK discussion

1. Is it possible to be both an "internal stakeholder" and an "external stakeholder" of an organization at the same time?

2. Are all stakeholders equally important? If not, who decides on their relative importance? Which criteria are used?

3. If anyone can potentially be considered a stakeholder, how useful is the notion of "stakeholder"?

Revision checklist

✓ Stakeholders are individuals or groups who have a direct interest in the business.

✓ Internal stakeholders are individuals or groups that work within the business, such as employees and managers.

✓ External stakeholders are individuals or groups outside the business, such as customers and suppliers.

✓ The interests of the various stakeholders will differ. Interests might include return on investment, the impact on the local area, working conditions, and the quality of the product produced.

1 Introduction to business management

Practice question

To answer the question below effectively, see Unit 6 pages 398–402.

Ecosoluciones

Ecosoluciones is a non-profit research organization located in Madrid, Spain. One of their objectives is to try to introduce non-polluting sources of electricity in developing countries.

One successful application of their research was the Alumbre Project. This provided electricity created by wind generators to the remote village of Alumbre, Peru, which previously had no electricity.

In Alumbre, wind generators were installed by Ecosoluciones to supply electricity for the first time to a textile factory: one of the few firms in the area operating in the secondary sector. Ecosoluciones also agreed to maintain and repair the generators. There was a complete transformation in the production process. The factory was able to buy new machinery. Productivity increased dramatically. New jobs were created.

Ecosoluciones also promised, in partnership with Peru Telecom and the Peruvian government, to help fund the improvements in communication between Alumbre and the rest of Peru. This also allowed regional trade to develop. The entire community experienced significant improvements in their quality of life. The Peruvian government saw this as a practical solution to develop other depressed areas of the country.

Unfortunately, in 2008 a severe financial crisis hit Europe and the Spanish government suspended part of its funding for research organizations such as Ecosoluciones. As a direct result, the management of Ecosoluciones felt it may no longer be able to maintain Alumbre's wind generators.

a) Identify **one** internal stakeholder and **three** external stakeholders mentioned in the above case study. *[4 marks]*

b) Discuss **two** possible areas of conflict between stakeholders in the Alumbre Project. *[10 marks]*

1.5 Growth and evolution

> **By the end of this chapter, you should be able to:**
> → Define the terms **economies** and **diseconomies of scale**
> → Explain reasons for **businesses to grow**
> → Explain reasons for **businesses to remain small**
> → Outline the difference between **internal** and **external growth**
> → Explain the following **external growth methods**:
> - mergers and acquisitions (M&As)
> - takeovers
> - joint ventures
> - strategic alliances
> - franchising

The impact of the external environment on a business

All businesses, no matter how small or big, operate in an environment. In business, "environment" does not have the narrower meaning of "ecology", as the word usually means or implies. Rather, it refers to various conditions (including ecological ones) external to the business. Even when a business manages to control its internal environment – and that challenge alone can be difficult – elements external to a business will still affect its growth and evolution. The environment may also require a business to evolve.

Businesses have only limited means to influence the elements of the external environment. They can, however, prepare and make contingency plans in order to have greater control over their plans for growth and expansion.

One common tool for this type of planning process begins with a STEEPLE analysis, which highlights and focuses on these external elements. Earlier versions of the STEEPLE analysis included a PEST or PESTLE analysis. All elements of those analyses were incorporated in the STEEPLE framework, shown in Figure 1.5.1.

What is the difference between PEST, PESTLE and STEEPLE analyses?

- **PEST** – Political, Economic, Social and Technological
- **PESTLE** – Political, Economic, Social, Technological, **Legal** and **Ecological**

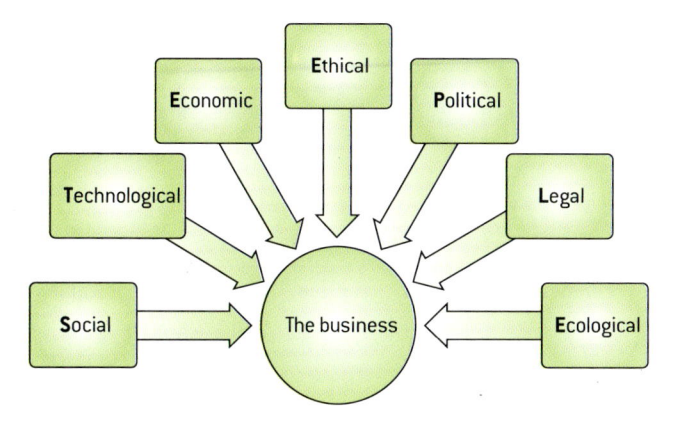

Figure 1.5.1 The STEEPLE framework

- **STEEPLE** – Sociocultural, Technological, Economic, Environmental (also known as Ecological), Political, Legal and **Ethical**.

The addition of the extra elements (first "legal" and "ecological", and then "ethical") reflect an evolution in business practices and thinking since 1967, when the idea of PEST first emerged.

As businesses have grown larger, many have become multinational and even global. They have had to consider the different legal frameworks in which they operate. A similar transformation has occurred with the addition of environmental and ethical. Whereas in the 1960s and 1970s many businesses focused only on making profits, today most businesses have broader concerns, including striving towards sustainable practices and treating all stakeholders ethically.

The impact on growth of changes in any of the STEEPLE factors

If any of the STEEPLE factors change, this will have an impact on the objectives, strategy and ultimately the growth and evolution of a business.

In a STEEPLE analysis, a business first considers particular influences of each element on the business. (Common influences are listed in Table 1.5.1.) Then the business conducts an analysis to determine the most important influences. Once the most important influences are isolated, the business can develop a strategy to take them into account.

Table 1.5.1 Common influences in a STEEPLE analysis

Sociocultural influences	• lifestyles • social mobility • demographics	• education • fashions or tastes
Technological influences	• technological improvements • new technology transfer • infrastructure	• ICT • research and development costs
Economic influences	• the economic or business cycle • the rate of economic growth • the rate of inflation	• the rate of unemployment • the exchange rate • interest rates
Ethical influences	• corruption • codes of business behaviour	• transparency • fair trade
Political influences	• political stability • trade policies	• regional policies • lobbying or electioneering
Legal influences	• regulations • employment laws	• health and safety legislation • competition laws
Environmental influences	• depletion of renewable resources • global warming	• organic farming • carbon footprints

Not all businesses react to the influences or changes shown in Table 1.5.1 with the same degree of energy or purpose. Often, a business might not need to be concerned with changes in particular laws (if they are not relevant to the business) or to changes in fashion or tastes (if its product or service is not determined by fashion or tastes). How the business will react to (or try to pre-empt) these influences will depend on their relevance to its current strategy and objectives.

Businesses that are flexible and can adapt to change will be more successful than businesses that are inflexible and do not adapt. Being an early adaptor and having first-mover advantage can be very useful for businesses that move fast enough. Planning based on STEEPLE elements often allows a business to determine changes to environmental factors, which may give it the opportunity to respond and perhaps even to have a first-mover advantage.

> **Assessment advice**
>
> Remember that when you cite numbers such as GNI per capita in a report, the numbers have limited meaning unless you include some comparative data. For example, if you say New Zealand has a GNI per capita of $42,760, that figure does not tell your readers very much. The figure takes on much more meaning if, by way of comparison, you point out that the GNI per capita of Denmark is $63,950 and of Morocco is $3,190.
>
> Another way to make a comparison is to provide historical data, such as New Zealand's GNI per capita in 2010, 2015, and 2020.

STEEPLE analysis

A STEEPLE analysis is a way to examine external factors that influence or have the potential to influence a company. A STEEPLE analysis is often used by companies before entering foreign markets, as it is a systematic way to consider how the following factors in the foreign market will influence the company:

- **S**ociocultural
- **T**echnological
- **E**conomic
- **E**nvironmental
- **P**olitical
- **L**egal
- **E**thical

A STEEPLE analysis can also be an effective tool for companies that take a proactive approach to addressing issues in their home country. Periodic analysis of these factors in a company's home country can alert the company to changing contexts that the business operates in.

A STEEPLE analysis requires research into each of the seven factors listed above. When researching these factors, what types of information might you gather? As an example, the case study below lists some of the questions that the company Uber might consider before entering a foreign market.

Case study: Uber

Uber is the car-sharing app that has threatened traditional taxi and car rental companies. Founded as UberCab in 2009, by 2012 Uber's main business had taken the form for which it has become famous.

Customers use an app to arrange an Uber driver to pick them up. When the business opened in the United States, Uber drivers used their own cars and Uber considered them independent contractors rather than employees, thus allowing Uber to avoid many of the costs associated with employees. The drivers could work when they wanted to and as much or as little as they wanted to.

1 Introduction to business management

> Uber's business model allows customers to have transport in a service similar to traditional taxi services, but at a much lower price. However, the business model does not work everywhere. In France, for example, Uber must classify its drivers as employees and Uber bears all the responsibilities of an employer.
>
> As Uber expands into foreign markets, performance of a STEEPLE analysis of those markets could help the company identify possible problems:
>
> - **Social:** Do people in this market frequently use taxi services, or are they more like to use other forms of public transport like buses and trams? How would people feel about getting into a car driven by someone without a proper taxi licence?
>
> - **Technological:** Do many people in this market own cars – enough so that drivers could be recruited? Is there widespread use of smartphones and credit cards, both necessary for the Uber business model to work?
>
> - **Economic:** Would people pay for Uber rides? Though cheaper than traditional taxis, an Uber ride is nonetheless more expensive than catching the bus. Will people be willing to pay for such a service?
>
> - **Ethical:** What impact will the presence of Uber's service have on the traditional taxi industry in the country? What impact will it have on the employment of these traditional taxi drivers?
>
> - **Political:** How will the government of the country react to Uber's disruptive influence? Are traditional taxi drivers unionized? Does their union have much influence within the political system?
>
> - **Legal:** Is it legal to operate a service like Uber in the country? Some countries require taxi drivers to be professionally trained and licensed. Will Uber be able to legally operate in the country? Is any legislation being considered that could constrain Uber or prevent it from operating according to its current business model? What are the insurance and liability laws in the country?
>
> - **Ecological:** In general, the presence of Uber increases the use of cars, as people are more willing to use Uber than a traditional taxi service. What impact will this increase in the use of cars have on the local environment, in the narrow environmental sense but also in a broader sense (noise pollution, traffic congestion, etc)?

Assessment advice ✓

When doing a STEEPLE analysis, remember that the analysis is of external factors (ie factors external to the company), not internal ones. A common mistake in STEEPLE analyses is that, when considering technological and environmental factors, students focus on internal conditions of the company, such as the technological capabilities of the company or the degree to which it is a green company.

Key terms

Economy of scale

the decrease in per unit production cost as output or activity increases

Diseconomy of scale

the increase in per unit production cost as output or activity increases

Economies and diseconomies of scale

Businesses that expand or increase their scale of operations can often use the larger scale to become more efficient. "Scale of operations" refers to the size or volume of output.

When a business increases its scale of operations, it produces more or in greater volume. When a business increases its scale of operations and in the process becomes more efficient, the business has achieved **economies of scale**. The term "economies of scale" refers to the reduction in average unit cost as a business increases in size.

1.5 Growth and evolution

However, sometimes a business experiences inefficiencies as it becomes larger. When this situation occurs, the business has achieved **diseconomies of scale**, which refers to an increase in average unit cost as the business increases in size.

Efficiency is measured in terms of **costs of production per unit**. For a more complete explanation of the different types of cost of production, refer to Unit 5. For now, think of costs of production in terms of the following formula:

$$\text{total cost} = \text{fixed cost} + \text{variable cost}$$

Using the abbreviations TC for total cost, FC for fixed cost and VC for variable cost, the formula is:

$$TC = FC + VC$$

Fixed costs are costs that do not change as production changes. For example, if a business operates in a rented (leased) factory, the monthly rent payments are the same regardless of the quantity of production of the business.

Variable costs are costs that vary as production changes. For example, if a furniture manufacturer expands production, then it will require more raw materials (wood, metal springs, cloth, leather, etc).

Further costs are known as **average costs** (or **unit costs** or **average unit costs**). All three refer to **total cost per unit**, which can be calculated with the following formula:

$$\text{Average cost} = \frac{\text{total cost}}{\text{quantity produced}}$$

And if AC is average cost (unit costs or average unit costs) and Q is quantity produced, the formula becomes:

$$AC = \frac{TC}{Q}$$

As we saw above, TC refers to total cost, derived from adding FC and VC. Thus, average cost can also be calculated with the following formula:

$$AC = \frac{FC + VC}{Q}$$

Expressing the formula in this way helps to explain the concepts of economies and diseconomies of scale. First, as the business expands by producing a greater quantity, variable costs increase. However, the fixed costs are spread over a greater quantity of units produced. As a result, the average costs go down. Thus, the business becomes more efficient. It has achieved economies of scale.

Sometimes, when a business expands, it starts to experience inefficiencies that increase average unit costs. This situation refers to diseconomies of scale.

> **Assessment advice** ✓
>
> When defining the term "economies of scale" or "diseconomies of scale", be sure to include the phrase "per unit" or "per average unit cost" in your definition.

> **Key terms**
>
> **Fixed costs**
> costs which do not change according to the amount of goods or services produced by the business
>
> **Variable costs**
> costs which increase or decrease according to the amount of goods or services produced

For example, imagine that a business expands production year on year. As it does, it initially achieves economies of scale. One reason for this is that the fixed cost of rent is being spread out over a larger number of units produced. However, at some point in time (if growth continues), the business will be at its maximum production level for the size of its factory. It will be at 100% capacity utilization (see Unit 5). The business will have to acquire different or additional space to expand production.

In this scenario, remember that the business is expanding year on year. When acquiring different or additional space – another factory or a larger factory, for example – the business should probably acquire a significantly greater amount of space rather than just enough space for the next year or two. That way, the business can grow for years to come without having the cost and disruption of changing locations frequently.

When a business doubles its factory size, its capacity utilization will go down (initially) and its rent will increase. In our example, in the old factory or old space, the business had 100% capacity utilization. When the space is doubled but production remains the same (initially), capacity utilization will decrease from 100% to 50%. The business's rent expense will increase significantly (it could double). The higher rent will now be spread over the same (or a slightly higher) number of units produced. With the higher rent, the business will initially have a higher average unit cost. Thus, it will have achieved diseconomies of scale.

Figure 1.5.2 shows this progression.

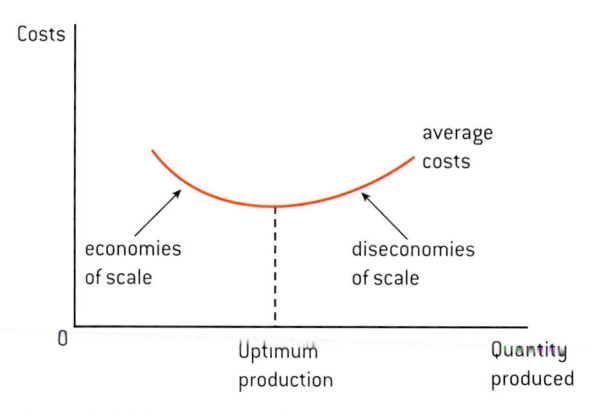

Figure 1.5.2 Progression from economies of scale to diseconomies of scale

As the business grows, it produces more output and initially the average costs go down. The business becomes more efficient.

At the point of lowest average costs, the business is at "optimum production". In our example using rent as the chief fixed cost, optimum production would also be the point where the business is at 100% capacity utilization. Then as the business continues to expand, it starts to become more inefficient. Average costs start to rise.

The minimum point of the average cost curve is the optimum level of production. At that point, average costs are at the lowest and profits are at their maximum.

Efficiency is not related to production alone. A business can become more efficient if it can lower average unit costs, regardless of the area of the business in which the savings per unit occur.

Internal and external economies of scale

Table 1.5.2 Internal economies of scale (efficiencies that the business itself can make)

Type	Explanation	Example
Technical	Bigger units of production can reduce costs because of the **law of variable proportions** – the increase in variable costs spread against a set of fixed costs.	Operating a container ship with one crew, one fuel bill and one berthing fee is cheaper than running two or more smaller vessels. Similarly, some new large planes will be cheaper to operate than two traditional long-haul aircraft; an articulated lorry will be cheaper to operate than two or three smaller vehicles.
Managerial	A bigger business can afford to have managers **specializing** in one job as opposed to trying to do everything.	Managers specializing by function (such as production, marketing, finance, and HR), as opposed to having a "general" manager, can typically work with greater efficiency.
Financial	Bigger businesses are **less risky** than smaller businesses.	Banks and other financial institutions charge lower rates of interest on loans or overdrafts to businesses they consider financially stable.
Marketing	Bigger businesses can **run more effective marketing campaigns**.	Only large businesses can afford to sponsor major sporting events such as the Olympic Games, the Super Bowl or the FIFA World Cup, which are higher yielding promotions per dollar, pound or euro.
Purchasing	Big businesses can gain discounts by **bulk buying** – buying in large quantities.	Supermarkets such as Lotus or Lotte Mart buy large quantities of food at very low prices from farmers.
Risk bearing	Big businesses can afford to produce a bigger range of products and in doing so spread the risk of one product failing – **hedging their bets**.	PepsiCo owns a number of different brands such as Pepsi, Gatorade, Tropicana, Lipton's Teas, Quaker Foods, and Lay's.

Table 1.5.3 External economies of scale (efficiencies that the business achieves because someone else has expanded)

Type	Explanation	Example
Consumers	A shopping mall increases the number of potential of customers, as more people go to the mall compared to an independent shop because of the ease of one-stop shopping. So, a whole range of other businesses benefit from someone else building the infrastructure.	A shopping mall, an international airport, and a business park or zone all require servicing and maintenance as well as their core business.
Employees	Labour concentrations occur when some cities or geographic areas concentrate on certain industries or sectors. Individual businesses located in those areas and operating in the industry that has the concentration can often benefit from lower recruiting and training costs.	Hollywood is famous for having many actors and others skilled in various aspects of film and television production. London is a major banking centre, where numerous professionals in financial services live and work.

Introduction to business management

Internal and external diseconomies of scale

As we noted above, if a business expands too much then it can achieve diseconomies of scale.

Table 1.5.4 Internal diseconomies of scale (inefficiencies that the business itself can make)

Type	Example
Technical	A container ship can be too big to berth in a harbour, an airplane can be too big to land at smaller airports, or a lorry may be too large to drive on minor roads.
Managerial	Businesses may have "over-specialized" managers who cannot (or will not) work outside their area of expertise or for everyone's benefit. This often occurs in the investment and commercial banking sectors.
Financial	Sometimes big businesses with large amounts of "surplus" cash make poor investments. Poor decisions occur because the businesses do not think through the consequences of investment choices. For example, in 2012, Alphabet purchased Motorola for $12.5 billion to develop premiere mobile devices. Two years later, Alphabet sold Motorola to Lenovo for $2.9 billion.
Marketing	Sometimes big businesses can make big marketing mistakes. In the 1990s, Hoover offered free flights to anyone who spent more than US$150 on a vacuum cleaner. Hoover did not realize that, for many people, an expensive vacuum cleaner was worth buying if it included a free flight anywhere in the world! When Hoover refused to honour the deal, the courts ordered the company to pay US$50 million in compensation to customers. Weakened by this expense, Hoover was acquired by a competitor, Candy.
Purchasing	Large businesses often buy too much stock, which can be costly if the cost of the capital funds used to purchase the stock is greater than the cost savings from buying in large quantities. Stock can also become spoilt, obsolete or unfashionable. The first stock market crash was as a result of too many tulips being bought by Dutch traders in the 17th century.
Risk bearing	Risk bearing is the sharing of responsibility for accepting losses if projects go wrong. Some risk exists in all economic activities. In 2005, eBay bought Skype in the hope of broadening its range, but in 2011 sold it to Microsoft. In 2008, Bank of America bought Countrywide, a mortgage lender, just as the housing market in the United States started to decline. The acquisition eventually cost Bank of America $50 billion.

Table 1.5.5 External diseconomies of scale (inefficiencies that the business achieves because someone else has expanded)

Type	Example
Employees	If one geographic region becomes too concentrated on one economic activity, typically a shortage of skilled workers in the industry will occur. For an individual business, this relative shortage of skilled workers means that the business will have to pay higher wages than before to attract and retain skilled workers.

Reasons for businesses to grow or stay small

Reasons for businesses to grow

Big businesses have some advantages:

- **Survival** – large firms have a greater chance of surviving. They are less likely to fail and less likely to be taken over by another firm.
- **Economies of scale** – large firms typically enjoy economies of scale, which translate into greater profits, higher returns, and a healthier balance sheet.

1.5 Growth and evolution

- **Higher status** – large firms have greater status than smaller ones. However fashionable some clothing brands may be, working for a larger firm such as Abercrombie & Fitch or Benetton can provide status and motivation to employees.

- **Market leader status** – McDonald's is the market leader in fast-food restaurants in most of the industrial world. All by itself, McDonald's can shape market habits, giving it a competitive advantage.

- **Increased market share** – large companies that have a large market share can control the market by determining prices and deciding which services will be the industry standard.

Reasons for businesses to stay small

Not all businesses want to expand. Many businesses simply prefer to remain small. Some business owners do not want the added complications of growing their business or managing a large business.

Many service businesses and businesses offering high-quality, specialized products prefer to align closely with their markets and their clients. For example, among the many tent manufacturers, only a few make "portaledges", which are portable hanging tents used by rock climbers when climbing big walls. Serving this niche market means that the manufacturers stay close to their small pool of customers and remain entrenched in the culture of big-wall climbing.

Many professional firms also prefer to stay small. In the legal sector, some law firms are large multinational companies, but around the world many small practices exist, their lawyers preferring to serve a small group of familiar clients. In accountancy, four major firms serve clients around the world – the so-called Big Four. However, countless small accounting firms serve the needs of small businesses around the world.

Advantages of being a small business include:

- **Greater focus** – because customers do not expect small businesses to know everything and be able to help everyone, small businesses can focus investments where they want and where they believe the greatest profitability lies. They may have lower profits than larger businesses, but often they have greater profitability and higher returns on investment.

- **Greater prestige** – small businesses sometimes have a greater sense of exclusiveness than larger businesses. As a result, some small businesses are able to charge more for their goods and services, leading to higher profit margins.

- **Greater motivation** – having more prestige can motivate managers and other employees. Often employees are also motivated by the idea that they matter to the business. Very large businesses sometimes find it difficult to convey the sense that all employees matter.

- **Competitive advantage** – being small, providing a more personalized service, and being flexible can give a competitive advantage.

- **Less competition** – sometimes a market is so small (a true niche market) that big businesses do not want to consider getting involved. This situation often means a market with limited competition.

This "portaledge" tent is an example of a niche market product

1 Introduction to business management

Decision trees

One way a business can decide whether to grow or to stay small is to use a decision tree. This is a planning tool designed to help simplify complex decisions.

Decision trees follow certain conventions:

- Where a decision must be made, the decision is represented by a square "node" with possible choices as lines stemming from the node.
- When multiple outcomes are possible, they are represented by a round node with lines stemming from that node and the outcome written above the line.

The nodes are numbered to help identify them.

Here is an example decision tree based on three choices and the data given in the table below:

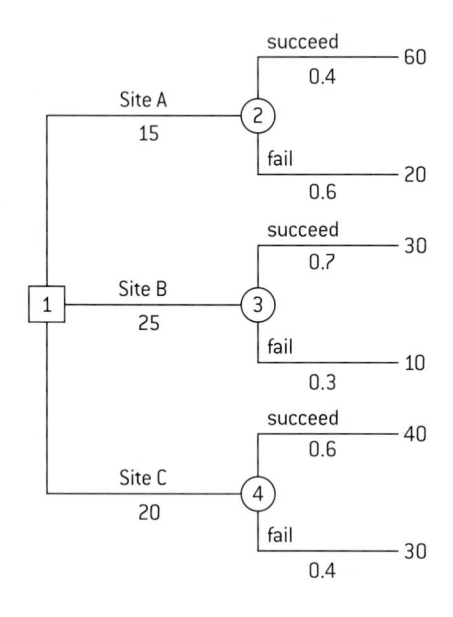

```
                           succeed
                           ─────── 60
                             0.4
         Site A    ╭───╮
         ─────────(  2 )
            15     ╰───╯
                           fail
                           ─────── 20
                             0.6

                           succeed
                           ─────── 30
                             0.7
┌───┐    Site B    ╭───╮
│ 1 │────────────(  3 )
└───┘      25      ╰───╯
                           fail
                           ─────── 10
                             0.3

                           succeed
                           ─────── 40
                             0.6
         Site C    ╭───╮
         ─────────(  4 )
            20     ╰───╯
                           fail
                           ─────── 30
                             0.4
```

Choice	Outcome	Probability	Returns (US$m)	Cost (US$m)
A	succeed	40%	60	15
	fail	60%	20	
B	succeed	70%	30	25
	fail	30%	10	
C	succeed	60%	40	20
	fail	40%	30	

In this decision tree:

- The **costs** of the choices being considered are written under the respective choice lines (under "Site A", "Site B" and "Site C" here).
- The **probability** that a choice will succeed or fail is written below the line for a particular outcome (under "succeed" and "fail" for each choice here).
- The **values** of each outcome actually happening are written at the end of each outcome line.

In this scenario, which option should the manager choose?

1.5 Growth and evolution

The difference between internal and external growth

Businesses with growth as a strategy have two broad options to choose from:

- Internal (organic) growth
- External (fast-track) growth

Internal growth is often known as "organic growth" because it happens slowly and steadily, and grows out of the existing operations of the business. Although it may take a long time, a business can grow this way without taking too many risks. The business expands by simply selling more products or by developing its product range.

Although most businesses that are growing internally still have to borrow some money from banks for major capital outlays – such as to update or expand property, plant, and equipment – most of the expansion from internal growth is self-financed using retained profits.

External growth is a quicker and riskier method of growth than internal growth. Instead of selling more of its own products itself, the business expands by entering into some type of arrangement to work with another business, such as a:

- merger and acquisition (M&A)
- takeover
- joint venture
- strategic alliance
- franchise.

External growth usually requires significant external financing. Although the risks are greater, the potential rewards are that the business can increase market share and decrease competition very quickly.

External growth methods

The most common forms of external growth are as follows.

Mergers and acquisitions (M&As) and takeovers

This type of expansion occurs when two business become integrated, either by joining together and forming a bigger combined business – a merger – or by one business taking over the other – an acquisition.

When the acquisition is unwanted by the company being acquired, the term typically used is "takeover" or "hostile takeover". Only publicly held companies can be taken over, as the shareholders in a privately held company do not have to sell their shares if another company wants to buy them. Public companies, whose shares sell in public forums, can be taken over.

The result of a merger, acquisition, or takeover is the same: one bigger business.

Key terms

Internal growth
sometimes referred to as organic growth, this occurs when a business grows by relying on its own resources and capabilities: investment in new products, or new sales channels, or more stores etc to increase sales

External growth
occurs when a business expands with the aid of resources and capabilities not developed internally by the company itself. Instead, the company obtains these new resources and capabilities by acquiring another company or forming some type of relationship, like a joint venture, with another organization.

Merger
occurs when two companies that are theoretically "equal" legally become one company

Acquisition
when one company purchases a majority or all the shares of another company

Takeover
when one company acquires a majority or all the shares in another company. When the word "takeover" is used, the situation usually means that the company being acquired does not welcome the transaction.

However, the underlying business reason for the integration can vary. In general, integration occurs in one of the following ways, although the processes are very different.

- **Horizontal integration** occurs when the two businesses being integrated are not merely in the same broad industry, but are actually in the same line of business and in the same chain of production (for example, when two airlines merge or when one chain of grocery stores purchases another).

  When horizontal integration occurs, the new business (the combination of the two that merged or were involved in the acquisition) will have increased market share and market power. Often it can take advantage of economies of scale. In 2018, Vodafone merged with Idea Cellular and became the largest telecom company in India.

- **Vertical integration** occurs when one business integrates with another at a different stage in the chain of production, or when a business begins operations in an earlier stage through internal growth. Vertical integration occurs for various reasons, including to ensure reliable supply, avoid government regulation (such as price controls or taxes), reduce transaction costs, and eliminate the market power of other businesses.

    - If a business becomes involved in an earlier stage in the chain of production (either through integration or internal growth), this process is called **backwards vertical integration**. This usually occurs when a business wants to protect its supply chain. The upstream stage can treat the "downstream" stage as a preferred customer in terms of quantity, availability, and price. In 2018, for example, Apple bought chip maker Dialog Semiconductor, to make sure the German supplier would continue to sell to Apple.

    - **Forwards vertical integration** occurs when one business integrates further forward (to a later stage) in the chain of production. For example, a farm producing organic crops and meats might open a retail store or a restaurant that sells the organic food and meats produced on the farm.

      Forward vertical integration usually occurs when a business wants to ensure a secure outlet for its products. In 2017, Amazon bought Whole Foods and immediately gained almost 500 bricks-and-mortar stores. Because Amazon was already selling groceries (albeit on a small scale), this acquisition had a horizontal element to it. Nevertheless, the acquisition was mostly vertical, as it gave Amazon a physical store presence it previously lacked.

- **Conglomeration** occurs when two businesses in unrelated lines of business integrate. This type of integration is also known as **diversification**. It occurs for many reasons but mainly to reduce overall corporate risk. For example, the Indian company Tata Group has among its many businesses Tata Chemicals, Tata Steel, Tata Teleservices, Tata Motors and Indian Hotels Company. If any one of the businesses (such as the chemical business or the steel business) were to fail, Tata Group would still have successful businesses in other industries.

A furniture maker acquiring a wood mill would be an example of backwards vertical integration

Another reason that a business may diversify is to have complementary seasonal activity. If a business that does most of its sales in the summer months purchased a business that had most of its sales in the winter months, then the new, combined enterprise would not have long periods of inactivity.

Integration has many advantages for businesses, including economies of scale, complementary activities, and control up or down the chain of production. However, M&As can be costly. In addition to the cost of the business being acquired, typically there are high legal and consulting fees. Sometimes when one company acquires or combines with another company, especially if the takeover is hostile, a culture clash occurs. Employees from the two companies do not work well together.

In addition, the profitability of integration can change over time. At first, a company may achieve cost savings or other benefits from backwards vertical integration, but later determine, because of changes in the market, that outsourcing this process is more cost-effective. Thus, sometimes a business will integrate vertically only to divest upstream and downstream stages at another time.

Joint ventures

Joint ventures occur when two businesses agree to combine resources for a specific goal and over a finite period of time. As a result, a separate business is created with funding by the two "parent" businesses. After the defined time period is over, the new business is either dissolved or incorporated into one of the parent businesses, or the two parent firms extend the time frame.

Although a joint venture may be temporary in nature and open up new areas of business, considerable transfer of specialist skills can occur. This transfer of skills, knowledge, and expertise could benefit either party in the future. Sometimes in a joint venture one of the partners begins to play a dominant role and then buys out the other.

Examples of joint ventures include Uber–Volvo (formed in 2016), Sony–Ericsson (2001–2012), Channel Tunnel Group–France-Manche (1985–1994), New Zealand Post–DHL (2004–2012), and BMW–Brilliance (formed in 2003).

Joint ventures have the advantage that the two firms typically enjoy greater sales, but neither loses its legal existence or its identity. Joint ventures also have the advantage that the two businesses forming the joint venture can bring different areas of expertise, amalgamating to create a powerful combination.

However, sometimes joint ventures do not produce the desired outcome, or a company realizes that it could have accomplished what the joint venture is doing without having to share the profits with the other company. At least conceptually (though not always legally), a joint venture is a partnership. All partnerships run the risk that a disagreement between partners will occur. Sometimes a disagreement may be so severe that the effectiveness of the partnership is compromised or the partnership (or joint venture) breaks up.

Assessment advice ✓

When people use the word "takeover", they are communicating that the takeover is not wanted. Because publicly held companies are sold on an exchange, only publicly held companies can be subject to a takeover. If the owners of privately held companies do not want to sell their shares, they do not have to.

Key term

Joint venture

an organization created, owned, and operated by two or more other organizations. The joint venture is legally distinct from the organizations that created it.

The Channel Tunnel, which links the UK and France, was built as part of a joint venture

Assessment advice ✓

Remember that, unlike a strategic venture, a joint venture involves the creation of a legally distinct new organization owned by the companies forming the joint venture.

1 Introduction to business management

> **Key terms**
>
> **Strategic alliance**
>
> occurs when two or more businesses cooperate in some legal way that enhances the value for all parties. Members of the alliance retain their independence. A strategic alliance is less binding than a joint venture, as no new organization is created.
>
> **Franchising**
>
> a method of distributing products or services, where the franchisor develops products or services and its brand and then sells the right to use the brand and its products or services to franchisees. The franchisee pays a fee and typically some percentage of revenue or profits to the franchisor.

Strategic alliances

Strategic alliances are similar to joint ventures because they involve businesses collaborating for a specified goal. However, strategic alliances differ from joint ventures in several fundamental ways:

- **More than two businesses may be part of the alliance.** Strategic alliances often, though not always, involve more than two businesses. In the airline industry, the Star Alliance has 26 airlines in the alliance, including Singapore Airlines, Lufthansa, South African Airways and United Airlines.
- **No new business is created.** No new legal entity comes into existence; instead, a strategic alliance is typically an agreement to work together for mutual benefit.
- **Individual businesses in the alliance remain independent.** The existing businesses may agree to share resources but they remain independent and often otherwise compete against each other.
- **Strategic alliances are more fluid than joint ventures.** In a strategic alliance, membership can change without destroying the alliance.

All of these strengths are also weaknesses. The more businesses that are involved in a strategic alliance, the more challenging coordination and agreement becomes. Without legal existence, the alliance has less force than an enterprise that exists in law. Individual businesses may benefit from the alliance, but remaining independent means that they do not get the capital strength of legal merger with other enterprises, nor do they enjoy economies of scale that other forms of external growth provide. Lastly, greater fluidity of members also means that the alliance lacks stability.

Franchises

Franchising, another form of external growth, is becoming increasingly popular for businesses that want to expand globally. Franchising involves the following:

- An original business, known as the **franchisor**, that developed the business concept and product or service, then sells to other businesses the right to offer the concept and sell the product or service.
- Businesses, known as the **franchisees**, buy the right to offer the concept and sell the product or service. In other words, the franchisee sells the products/services developed originally by the franchisor. The franchisee usually also has to be consistent with, and in some instances identical to, the original business concept developed by the franchisor.

A business that starts to franchise is the franchisor. Franchising is often a rapid form of growth because the franchisor does not actually have to produce anything new. Instead, the business (the franchisor) sells that right to other businesses (the franchisees). Franchisees can be individuals, partnerships, or companies.

Franchising is proving particularly attractive as a means to grow globally. The franchisor has a host or home country. The franchisor can then sell to other businesses in the other places where it wants to expand – as long as it finds buyers of the concept of the enterprise. The franchisees typically have knowledge of local markets, local conditions, and local cultures. Franchisees also know local languages, which is particularly helpful if the franchisor wants to grow in different countries around the world.

There are many examples of franchises in lots of different areas of business, including:

- McDonalds – fast food
- Budget – car hire
- Hilton – hotels
- Kumon – education
- Wokinabox – fast food
- Spar – food stores
- Benetton – clothes
- Body Shop – cosmetics.

An outlet of the Body Shop in Hong Kong

The cost of the franchise has two parts. First, the franchisee must pay for the franchise itself – essentially a right to operate a business offering the franchisor's concept and product or service. Then the franchisee must typically pay royalties – a percentage of sales or a flat fee – which go to the franchisor.

Both the franchisor and the franchisee have specific responsibilities in their relationship. These responsibilities vary somewhat according to individual business concepts and industries. For example, McDonald's franchisee agreements would not be exactly the same as those of Yum! Brands (KFC, Taco Bell, and other restaurants), nor exactly the same as the franchise agreement for Enterprise Rental Cars. However, in general, the division of responsibilities between franchisor and franchisee are as follows.

The **franchisor** will provide:

- The stock
- The fittings
- The uniforms
- Staff training
- Legal and financial help
- Global advertising
- Global promotions

The **franchisee** will:

- Employ staff
- Set prices and wages
- Pay an agreed royalty on sales
- Create local promotions
- Sell only the products of the franchisor
- Advertise locally

Which party provides the outlet and which party provides the start-up costs can vary considerably according to the strength of the brand. Some brands, such as McDonald's, are especially strong. Rarely does a McDonald's restaurant close. A new McDonald's restaurant is almost certain to immediately have strong name recognition and high sales, so the franchisor is in a strong position to dictate the terms of owning a McDonald's franchise. Other brands have less market power. In those circumstances, the franchisor may have less bargaining strength when setting the rights and responsibilities of the franchisor and franchisee.

For businesses (regardless of legal organization), acquiring a franchise has many advantages and disadvantages compared to developing their own business model.

Advantages to the franchisee

- The product exists and is usually well known.
- The format for selling the product is established.
- The set-up costs are reduced.
- The franchisee has a secure supply of stock.
- The franchisor can provide legal, financial, managerial, and technical help.

Disadvantages to the franchisee

The franchisee:

- has unlimited liability for the franchise
- has to pay royalties to the franchisor
- has no control over what to sell
- has no control over supplies.

Franchisors also have advantages and disadvantages.

Advantages to the franchisor

The franchisor:

- gains quick access to wider markets
- makes use of local knowledge and expertise
- does not assume the risks and liability of running the franchise
- gains more profits and the sign-up fees
- makes all of the global decisions.

Disadvantages to the franchisor

The franchisor:

- loses some control in the day-to-day running of the business
- can see its image suffer if a franchise fails or does not perform properly.

Do some franchisees eventually become tired of the control of the parent company? Perhaps, but by then the operators of the franchise may have enough expertise to start their own independent business. On the other hand, many franchisees, even if tired of the control of the franchisor, enjoy the great profitability that can come with a successful franchise. Regardless, for the franchisor, selling franchises is an easy and fast way to break into new markets with a minimum of difficulty and risk, and it is a way to gain an advantage over its competitors.

> **TOK links**
>
> 1. For a business deciding to grow (or to stay small), is "big" or "small" just a matter of perspective?
> 2. Can we state that economies of scale are always good?
> 3. To what degree are businesses limited in how much they can know about their market and other factors outside of the business that influence it?

1.5 Growth and evolution

Revision checklist

- ✓ A STEEPLE analysis is a way of evaluating all the external factors which might influence the success of a business. The factors are: social, technological, economic, ethical, political, legal and ecological. If any of the factors change, a business may need to adapt its strategy.

- ✓ As companies grow, they often experience economies of scale but also, at times, diseconomies of scale. These can be internal or external.

- ✓ Companies can grow either internally (organically) by expansion of existing operations or externally (inorganically) by forming some types of relationship with an external organization.

- ✓ Many reasons exist for businesses to grow, including to increase market share, increase market dominance, and increase profits.

- ✓ Many companies choose not to grow and find advantages from remaining small.

- ✓ External growth can happen through mergers, acquisitions, takeovers, joint ventures, strategic alliances, and franchising.

Practice question

To answer the question below effectively, see Unit 6 pages 398–402.

Statson Inc

Statson Inc (SI) manufactures faucets (taps). Five years ago, the company acquired another faucet manufacturer, *FlowForm Ltd (FF)*, which continued to operate independently but under the name *SI*.

The combined companies were able to eliminate many of the expenses, such as promotional costs, associated with having two different names. *SI's* name recognition improved, and sales grew rapidly. However, as sales and production grew, delivery times increased and some customers complained that service seemed less personal.

SI's management anticipated that many economies of scale would result from the acquisition. However, in the first two years after the acquisition, *SI* found that it was experiencing several diseconomies of scale. *SI's* management conducted a thorough analysis of the situation. This analysis revealed that the combined companies were experiencing:

- Communication problems between *SI* and the company formerly known as *FF*.
- The ability to negotiate more favourable purchase prices from suppliers.

SI's management was convinced that, in time, the advantages of the acquisition would outweigh the disadvantages.

a) State **two** features of an acquisition. [2 marks]

b) With reference to *SI*, distinguish between economies of scale and diseconomies of scale. [4 marks]

c) Explain **one** reason why *SI* grew and **one** reason why it perhaps should have remained small. [4 marks]

1.6 Multinational companies (MNCs)

By the end of this chapter, you should be able to:
→ Evaluate the **impact of MNCs** on the host countries

Globalization

Globalization has had a significant impact on businesses' growth and evolution. Globalization is the process by which the world's regional economies are becoming one integrated global unit. The process is not wholly new. The Roman Empire, the Silk Road, the Age of Exploration, the British Empire and other historical examples and periods saw some degree of economic global interdependence. Nevertheless, since the Second World War, the phenomenon known as "globalization" has changed from earlier forms of interdependence.

First, just in terms of the intensity, scale, speed, and economic value of goods and services being exchanged, global interdependence today is on a completely different scale from that seen in earlier periods or circumstances.

Second, current globalization is being characterized by a relatively small number of extremely large "post-national" businesses. Post-national means that, although these companies have a home of record (the "home" office is legally registered in one country), the businesses are otherwise transnational; apart from the legal home of record, these businesses consider no place their home (or every place their home). They will do business wherever they can make a profit. Loyalties are to the company itself and to its profits, and not to any country.

Globalization can have a significant impact on the growth of domestic businesses for the following reasons:

- **Increased competition** – large foreign businesses can force domestic producers to become more efficient as the domestic consumer has more choice. "Greater efficiency" can mean lower-cost goods and services for consumers. However, one way that businesses become more efficient is by slowing the growth in wages of its workers and extracting greater productivity from them.

- **Greater brand awareness** – domestic producers have to compete with big brand names and so they need to create their own unique selling point (USP). Sometimes they do this by emphasizing the local or national origins of their products compared to the "foreign" products sold by multinationals and global firms. Creating a USP can make many businesses more competitive and efficient.

> **Student workpoint 1.11**
>
> *Be knowledgeable*
>
> Different people have posed different arguments about when globalization began. Was it during the Roman Empire or the Silk Road? Was it the Age of Exploration or when the British Empire was at its peak? Was it during the Second World War or the Pax Americana? Was it the era of container shipping or the internet?
>
> Learn about these different arguments to develop a nuanced understanding of globalization.

- **Skills transfer** – foreign businesses, no matter how big, must use some local knowledge: at least some of their workforce must be local, which will lead to a two-way transfer of knowledge and skills. The multinational or global firm will learn from the workers hired in particular countries, while those workers can learn new approaches and develop new skills.
- **Closer collaboration** – whether through joint ventures, franchises, or strategic alliances, domestic producers can create new business opportunities.

Reasons for the growth of multinational companies

A multinational company is a business that operates in more than one country or is legally registered in more than one country. The word "multinational" suggests that a company is global or operating in many countries, but that is not always the case. For example, a small company operating in the small countries of Luxembourg and Belgium is a multinational.

However, multinational companies are typically the biggest type of business and in fact they often generate more revenues than the country they operate in. For example, Table 1.6.1 shows a comparison of the world's leading countries and businesses in terms of GDP and sales revenues.

> **Key term**
>
> **Multinational corporation (MNC)**
>
> a company that operates in two or more countries. It is generally a very large company, but it does not have to be. MNCs are also sometimes referred to as a multinational enterprises (MNEs).

Table 1.6.1 The world's leading countries and businesses – GDP and sales revenues

Rank	Country	GDP (in millions USD)	Rank	Company	Revenue (in millions USD)
1	United States	21,433,226	1	Walmart	514,405
2	China	14,342,903	2	Sinopec Group	414,649
3	Japan	5,081,770	3	Royal Dutch Shell	396,556
4	Germany	3,861,124	4	China National Petroleum	392,976
5	India	2,868,929	5	State Grid	387,056
6	United Kingdom	2,829,108	6	Saudi Aramco	355,905
7	France	2,715,518	7	BP	303,738
8	Italy	2,003,576	8	Exxon Mobil	290,212
9	Brazil	1,839,758	9	Volkswagen	278,341
10	Canada	1,736,426	10	Toyota Motor	272,612

Source: Adapted from World Bank & Fortune Global 500, 2019

Four factors have allowed multinational companies to grow rapidly:

- **Improved communications** – not only ICT, but also transport and distribution networks.
- **Dismantling of trade barriers** – allowing easier movement of raw materials, components and finished products.
- **Deregulation of the world's financial markets** – allowing for easier transfer of funds, as well as tax avoidance.
- **Increasing economic and political power of the multinational companies** – this can be of enormous benefit, especially in middle- and low-income countries.

The impact of multinational companies on the host countries

Multinational companies can have both positive and negative impacts on the host (domestic) countries in which they operate.

Advantages for the host country include:

- **Economic growth** – multinational companies can boost the domestic economy by providing employment, developing a local network of suppliers, and paying taxes and providing capital injections.
- **New ideas** – multinational companies may introduce new ways of doing business and new ways of interacting socially.
- **Skills transfer** – multinational companies may help develop the skills of local employees. Domestic businesses can benefit from starting their own business with the skills learned.
- **Greater choice of products** – the domestic market will benefit as the variety of products will increase.
- **Short-term infrastructure projects** – multinational companies often help to build infrastructure (for example roads to the factory, schools for workers' children).

Disadvantages for the host country include:

- **Profits being repatriated** – the multinational companies may pay into the local tax system, but the bulk of their profits will be rerouted away from the host country.
- **Loss of cultural identity** – the appeal of domestic products, ways of doing business, and even cultural norms may suffer. This is especially important for the younger generations who are more likely to buy global brands.
- **Brain drain** – many highly skilled employees may look to work for the multinational company in another country.
- **Loss of market share** – as multinational companies take over more of the domestic market, domestic producers may suffer.
- **Short-term plans** – multinational companies may not intend to stay for a long time – if lower-cost producers can be found elsewhere, they may move out at short notice.

Revision checklist

✓ Multinational companies (MNCs) operate in more than one country.

✓ MNCs can have both positive and negative effects on the countries in which they operate.

TOK links

1. As businesses grow internationally and become multinational, how do their methods of knowing change (knowing their customers, knowing their markets, knowing their business environment, knowing their competitors)?
2. How can we know about the different impacts that MNCs may have on their host countries?
3. Are the terms "international", "multinational" and "global" interchangeable? If there is a difference between them, who should give the ultimate, authoritative definition?

1.6 Multinational companies (MNCs)

Practice question

To answer the question below effectively, see Unit 6 pages 398–402.

Khumalo Pottery (KP)

Lungile Khumalo owns a small company called *Khumalo Pottery (KP)* in Johannesburg, South Africa. *KP* manufactures plates and bowls that are sold to small shops. *KP* has a unique selling point (USP) based on traditional African designs and patterns decorating the pottery. *KP* does not pay its workers high wages and has never made anyone redundant, even during difficult economic times. Lungile always repeated to his workers that beauty was more important than quantity. Workers at *KP* could take time to produce beautiful pottery. They also developed great pride in the company and in their work.

Across the Atlantic, in the United States, pottery with African designs was becoming increasingly popular. As a result, several large American pottery manufacturers, operating on a very large scale, began to mass produce pottery with African-looking patterns. Thanks to their economies of scale, these American manufacturers sold their products at a very low price.

In 2013, one large American company opened a highly automated factory in Johannesburg. The aim was to produce and sell African-looking pottery to large retailers across sub-Saharan Africa. If successful, the American company would employ up to 150 South Africans. These jobs would not require much creativity: the pottery would not be hand-made, but the company would offer good wages with fringe payments (benefits).

The American company used penetration pricing in South Africa, and large retailers eagerly stocked their shelves with the pottery. *KP's* sales started to decline almost immediately, as the small shops selling *KP's* pottery were losing customers to the large retailers who had lower prices.

a) Evaluate the impact on South Africa of the American company opening a factory in Johannesburg. [10 marks]

Source: Adapted from IB examination paper, May 2014

2 HUMAN RESOURCE MANAGEMENT

2.1 Introduction to human resource management

> **By the end of this chapter, you should be able to:**
> → Explain the role of **human resource management**
> → Explain internal and external factors that influence **human resource planning**
> → Explain reasons for **resistance to change** in the workplace
> → Discuss **human resource strategies** for reducing the impact of change and resistance to change

Role of human resource (HR) management

Human resources are critical for any business. The issue of human resources is especially important for businesses operating in the tertiary and quaternary sectors. Nevertheless, all businesses must ensure that they have the right types of employee and that those employees are working effectively.

Successful businesses are likely to have a clear framework for how to get the best from their human resources. HR management and planning are continuous processes. Businesses strive to make sure their employees are in jobs for which they are properly trained and properly suited. At the same time, as part of HR planning, a business estimates its future HR needs

2.1 Introduction to human resource management

(the correct type and number of employees), so that the business does not have too many employees (which increases costs) or too few employees (which can hurt productivity).

This framework for getting the most from a business's human resources is the process of HR. With large businesses, the various elements of the HR process are written down and are known as the HR plan. With smaller businesses, the HR plan might not be written down, but the director of HR or the owner of the small business will decide HR issues and have a plan in mind.

The internal and external factors that influence HR planning

Many factors can influence an organization's HR plan. Even before a business employs someone, some external factors can have an effect on the pool of labour available for potential employment. Also, the business itself may change and internal factors may influence the HR plan that is already in place. This is shown in Figure 2.1.1.

> ### Key terms
>
> **Human resource management**
>
> how an organization manages its human resources; includes recruitment and retention, setting compensation and benefits, and specifying job responsibilities
>
> **Demographic changes**
>
> shifts in demographic factors, such as birth rates, death rates, education levels, religion, ethnicity, age, etc
>
> **Labour mobility**
>
> the ability of workers to move occupationally or geographically (within countries or internationally). Ie how easily workers can change their place or type of work.

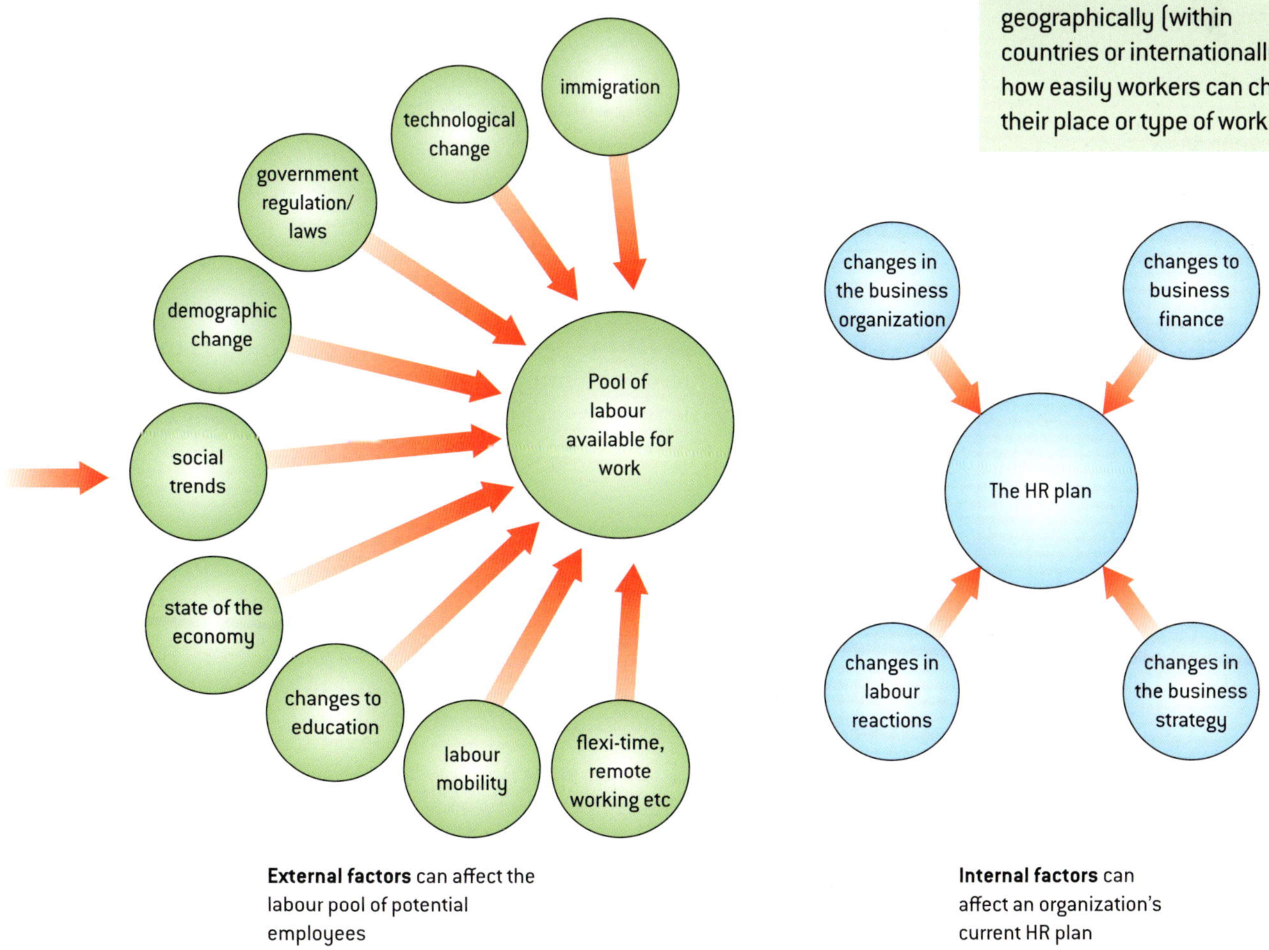

External factors can affect the labour pool of potential employees

Internal factors can affect an organization's current HR plan

Figure 2.1.1 External and internal factors affecting the HR plan

2 Human resource management

> **Key terms**
>
> **Immigration**
>
> the international movement of people into countries where they are not citizens. People who are temporarily in a foreign country, like tourists or students, are not considered to be immigrants; rather immigrants are those who seek permanent residency in the new country.
>
> **Flexi-time**
>
> a flexible work schedule that allows workers to adjust the starting and finishing times of their work day, giving them flexibility to meet other demands (such as childcare requirements)
>
> **Gig economy**
>
> an economy where many positions are temporary and organizations hire independent workers for short-term commitments

Technological change has made it easier for people in certain sectors to work from home

External factors

External factors have an impact on the size and availability of the pool of potential employees for the business, and include the following:

- **Technological change** – improvements in ICT can lead to more teleworking and working from home. Infrastructure improvements, such as new roads or other transport links, can make employing someone who lives further away easier than before.

- **Government regulations** – changes in laws or government regulations regarding health and safety issues can influence a potential workforce. Laws or government regulations can affect maximum weekly working hours or contractual issues, such as equality in the workplace irrespective of age, gender, ethnicity, or disability. Laws generally determine obligations such as pension provisions or retirement age.

- **Demographic change** – an aging population, reduced fertility rates, or changes in immigration and emigration patterns are just some of the demographic changes that can have an impact on the potential employees available and their specific requirements to work.

- **Social trends** – changes in society, such as the role of women in society, a rise in the number of single-parent families, or the importance of leisure in the "work–life balance" can all have significant impacts on the labour pool.

- **The state of the economy** – an economic boom will lead to a strain on the pool of labour available and consequently lead to increased wages; a recession will have the opposite effect, as more unemployed workers are available and so they may accept lower wages.

- **Changes in education** – some would consider changes in levels of education a factor of demography. Regardless, rising or falling education levels can have a direct impact on the suitability of labour for employment. Also relevant is the range and type of courses available to students.

- **Labour mobility** – many factors can influence labour mobility, which can refer either to occupational mobility (changing occupations) or geographical mobility (changing locations). In either case, the mobility of the workforce significantly affects the labour pool.

- **Immigration** – a shift in immigration can result in new workers being available or a change in the skillset of newly arrived workers.

- Changes such as flexi-time, remote working, or gig-economy contracts can also influence how people work.

Internal factors

Internal factors stem from within the business itself and will have an impact on the current HR plan, which may have to change as a result of the following:

- **Changes in business organization** – businesses change the way they are organized to better meet their strategic objectives. Any reorganization can affect the current HR plan. Organizational changes affecting the HR plan can also occur when a business acquires another business or is itself acquired.

- **Changes in labour relations** – labour relations can have a significant impact on workforce planning. If the labour force chooses to unionize, for example, the business will have to contend with the work requirements of the union. If the power of a union decreases, on the other hand, the business may have more flexibility with workers. Either way, the long-term labour circumstances will change.

- **Changes in business strategy** – whether in response to changes in circumstances in the market or to the business re-orienting itself, changes in business strategy may lead to amendments to the HR plan.

- **Changes in business finance** – the financial situation of a business will have a bearing on the HR plan. A business that has limited resources may not be able to pay the highest wages and salaries, which can affect recruitment and retention. Other financial factors can have an impact as well. For example, unfunded pension liabilities can influence available resources for the current workforce, or a significant increase in profitability may allow for a greater number of staff.

> ## SWOT analysis
>
> Companies often use a SWOT analysis as part of their strategic planning process (see Chapter 1.3). However, SWOT analyses can also be used for narrower purposes.
>
> Consider, for example, a company planning on opening a new factory in a different region of their home country. The HR manager must recruit qualified new employees to work in the factory. They could do a SWOT analysis with a narrow focus on the strengths, weaknesses, opportunities, and threats that they will face as they look for staff for the new factory.
>
> How would the SWOT analysis of one function, such as recruitment of new employees to work at the new factory, be different compared to a SWOT analysis for strategic planning purposes?

Changes in work patterns, practices, and preferences

Since the 1970s, many changes that affect employers and employees have occurred in work patterns, practices, and preferences. Some of these changes have stemmed from external factors affecting the pool of labour. For example, social trends have led many employees to want a better work–life balance, and many businesses are trying to respond to the desires of these employees. Other social trends have stemmed from internal factors affecting businesses, which can benefit from some of the new work practices.

2 Human resource management

> **Case study**
>
> ## Work–life balance and the "right to disconnect"
>
> In 2000, the French government reduced the statutory working week from 39 to 35 hours. Then in 2017, the French government introduced the "right to disconnect". This new law prohibited companies with more than 50 employees from sending or replying to emails when not at work. The aim of the legislation was to protect workers from having to do additional work from home, for which they were not being compensated.
>
> In 2018, Spain adopted a similar right to allow employees to disconnect. The right to disconnect is spreading. The Philippines, Belgium, the Netherlands, Luxembourg, India, Québec, and the federal government of Canada are considering or have proposed adopting the right to disconnect. Even the "city that does not sleep", New York City, is considering adopting a right to disconnect legislation.

Some of the factors changing the working environment include:

- Privatization and the move away from public-sector to private-sector employment.
- Increased migration of potential employees in a country or region and across the globe.
- Increasing participation of females in the workforce.
- Changing educational opportunities.
- Increasing urbanization and the consequent rise in stress levels.
- An aging population and increasing average age of the workforce.

Changes in work patterns

One change has been in the patterns of work – the types of jobs required by businesses, as well as the types of jobs people want.

Table 2.1.1 shows the top 10 jobs that employers around the world were trying to fill in 2020, according to LinkedIn. Table 2.1.2 shows the 10 fastest-declining occupations in the United States (forecast for 2019–2029).

Table 2.1.1 Top 10 sought-after jobs in 2020

1	Software developer
2	Sales representative
3	Project manager
4	IT administrator
5	Customer service specialist
6	Digital marketer
7	IT support/help desk
8	Data analyst
9	Financial analyst
10	Graphic designer

Source: https://www.cnbc.com/2020/07/02/linkedin-the-worlds-10-most-in-demand-jobs-that-dont-need-a-degree.html

Table 2.1.2 Ten fastest-declining occupations in the United States, forecast for 2019–2029

Occupation	Employment in 2019 (000s)	Employment in 2029 (000s)	Percentage change (%)
Word processors and typists	52.7	33.5	−36.4
Parking enforcement workers	8.1	5.2	−36.2
Nuclear power reactor operators	5.3	3.4	−35.7
Watch and clock repairers	3.2	2.1	−32.3
Cutters and trimmers, hand	9.8	6.9	−29.9
Telephone operators	5.0	3.6	−27.9
Travel agents	82.0	60.8	−25.9
Data entry keyers	172.4	130.0	−24.6

Occupation	Employment in 2019 (000s)	Employment in 2029 (000s)	Percentage change (%)
Electronic equipment installers and repairers, motor vehicles	10.4	8.0	−23.2
Switchboard operators, including answering service	69.9	54.1	−22.5

Source: Adapted from https://www.bls.gov/emp/tables/fastest-declining-occupations.htm

One significant change that has happened, especially with the improvements in ICT, has been an increase in **occupational and geographical mobility**.

Today it is fairly easy to determine which occupations will experience an expanding number of positions and which will experience a contracting number. For example, email, electronic banking and online bill payment services are reducing the need for traditional mail services. Letter carriers, or other individuals in contracting professions, can easily work out which occupations are growing and then seek to acquire the necessary skills for those positions. Thus, occupational mobility is more common than previously.

Similarly, ICT also provides opportunities to match people seeking positions with countries or regions that have shortages of people with certain skills. Prior to the Covid-19 pandemic, the United Kingdom and Belgium, for example, had shortages of both nurses and chefs. Many countries have shortages of pharmacists and ICT professionals.

Before the ICT revolution, matching skilled people to places where they were needed was vastly more challenging than it is today. ICT allows for faster processing of data (who has what skills and what skills are needed in particular geographic regions). Then, ICT allows for easier dissemination of that information. For example, Skills Panorama, a website run by the European Commission, offers *data* and *information* on where mismatches exist between skills needed and jobs available in different countries.

Changes in work practices

Not only have the types of jobs changed. The nature of work routines has also changed as businesses have responded to greater demands for more flexible working practices.

Work practices in decline

- **Full-time work** – when employees work the maximum hours per week accepted by law (for example, working 35 hours a week in Europe).
- **Permanent contracts** – when employees are hired for positions without a predetermined time limit.

Work practices on the increase

- **Part-time work** – when employees work less than the full-time weekly maximum hours.

> **Student workpoint 2.1**
>
> *Be reflective*
>
> Look at the jobs listed in tables 2.1.1 and 2.1.2. Do any of the results surprise you?

- **Temporary work** – work that is on a fixed-term contract, usually of a temporary nature (for example, to cover maternity leave). The employee would normally sign up to an agency who finds them work.

- **Freelancing** – when someone who is self-employed works for several different employers at the same time.

- **Teleworking** – work taking place from home or a telecommunication centre. Usually, the employee would have a core number of hours they have to work at the office, and the remainder would be from home.

- **Homeworking** – when an employee works from home. Usually, the employee would have a core number of hours they have to work at the office, and the remainder would be from home.

- **Flexi-time** – work involving a set number of hours of an employee's own choosing. Usually, the employee would have a core number of hours they have to work at the office; the rest is up to the employee.

- **Casual Fridays** – when an employee is allowed to wear less formal dress on a Friday so that it is easier to go away at the weekend.

- **Three-day weekend** – instead of working, say, five eight-hour days, the employee works four ten-hour days and so has a three-day weekend.

- **The gig economy** – where organizations hire independent workers for short-term commitments. Some people laud the gig economy for its flexibility for both employers and employees, while other criticize it as it typically means workers are not receiving most of the benefits of full-time employment, such as sick leave or paid vacation.

Companies like Deliveroo and Uber have benefited from the gig economy

Case study

The future of working from home

The impact of the Covid-19 pandemic on work practices will be studied for years to come. Already, some changes in work practices are evident. More professional-level workers will work from home (WFH) than ever before. WFH may vary from always working from home, or WFH may mean employees work two to three days a week from home and go into their offices for two to three days.

The impact could become even greater if workers only come into their office once every two weeks or even once a month and participate in virtual meetings most of the time. If this situation becomes the norm (and at the time of writing the situation is still unclear), employment and population centres like London, New York, or San Francisco, where real-estate prices for both commercial and residential properties are extraordinarily high, may lose some of their lustre.

However, not all jobs will be done remotely. This statement is true for most service sector employees, such as those who work in restaurants or who clean houses or repair cars. Even many professional-level employees will continue to "go to the office".

> Jamie Dimon, Chairman and CEO of J.P. Morgan, has encouraged young bankers to return to working in the bank's offices. According to Dimon, young employees need to learn the culture of organizations, which will only happen when they come into work. Dimon also argued that considerable creativity occurs not from formal meetings but the kind of informal exchanges and small gatherings that occur when people are not working from home.
>
> Thus, the WFH trend may not be as powerful as it seems now, at the peak of the pandemic. Hybrid models, variations by industry, and employees' stage of career may all be factors that determine WFH practices in the future.

Changes in work preferences

Instead of working continuously for 20 to 30 years for the same business, many employees are now adapting their work routines to suit changing lifestyles. Common methods to adapt work routines include:

- **Career breaks** – an employee decides to stop working for a time, usually a year or more, before returning to work in the same career. Sometimes the employer formalizes this and agrees to take the employee back after the break – this is known as a "sabbatical".
- **Job share** – two or more employees decide to share a job in order to free up more time for other activities.
- **Downshifting** – an employee gives up a senior position or highly paid employment in order to change career into a different lower-paid field or area of interest.
- **Study leave** – an employee is granted time off work to acquire a new qualification, such as an MBA.

The impact of innovation, ethical considerations, and cultural differences

Innovation, ethical considerations, and cross-cultural differences can also have an impact on HR processes.

Innovation

Innovation or its opposite – inertia – can have a major impact on HR processes. A business committed to being innovative must have a greater strategic focus on HR than any other business function. Innovations come from people. The business will not be successfully innovative unless it recruits and retains the right people. Developing a supportive and stimulating business environment – a vital part of HR planning – will help the creative process.

Ethical considerations

A strong connection has always existed between HR planning and ethical behaviour. HR processes are based on relationships, which are reflected in the way that the business treats its employees. Today most stakeholders rightly insist that businesses should treat their employees ethically.

Google prides itself on being innovative and employing creative individuals; this approach is reflected in its offices

2 Human resource management

The internet enables people to send and receive information. Social network sites, in particular, can be places where employees can tell others how they have been treated. As a result, businesses must be careful to act in an ethical manner – or at the least to create that appearance.

Ethical issues that might be addressed through the HR plan can be seen in Figure 2.1.2.

Figure 2.1.2 Ethical issues in the HR plan

One example of how an improved information flow has intersected with ethical considerations involves executive compensation in the banking sector. Through the news and other forms of ICT, a perception emerged after the global financial crisis that some executives were awarding themselves excessive salaries and other forms of financial rewards not matched by their performance. Many stakeholders in the banking sector got very angry about this situation. As a result, there were changes in the financial packages of executives at several banks.

Cultural differences

Cultural differences can also have a significant effect on the HR plan for any business that employs a multicultural workforce. Such businesses would naturally include multinational businesses operating in different countries. Many domestic businesses also employ migrant workers.

The citizens of many countries are becoming increasingly diverse as children of migrant workers grow up as citizens in their parents' adopted country. Businesses that adapt their HR plan to suit a more varied cultural

2.1 Introduction to human resource management

workforce are more likely to be successful with a diverse workforce, especially if their markets are as diverse as their workforce.

In the HR context, Figure 2.1.3 highlights some of the factors that might affect the cultural expectations of a business's employees.

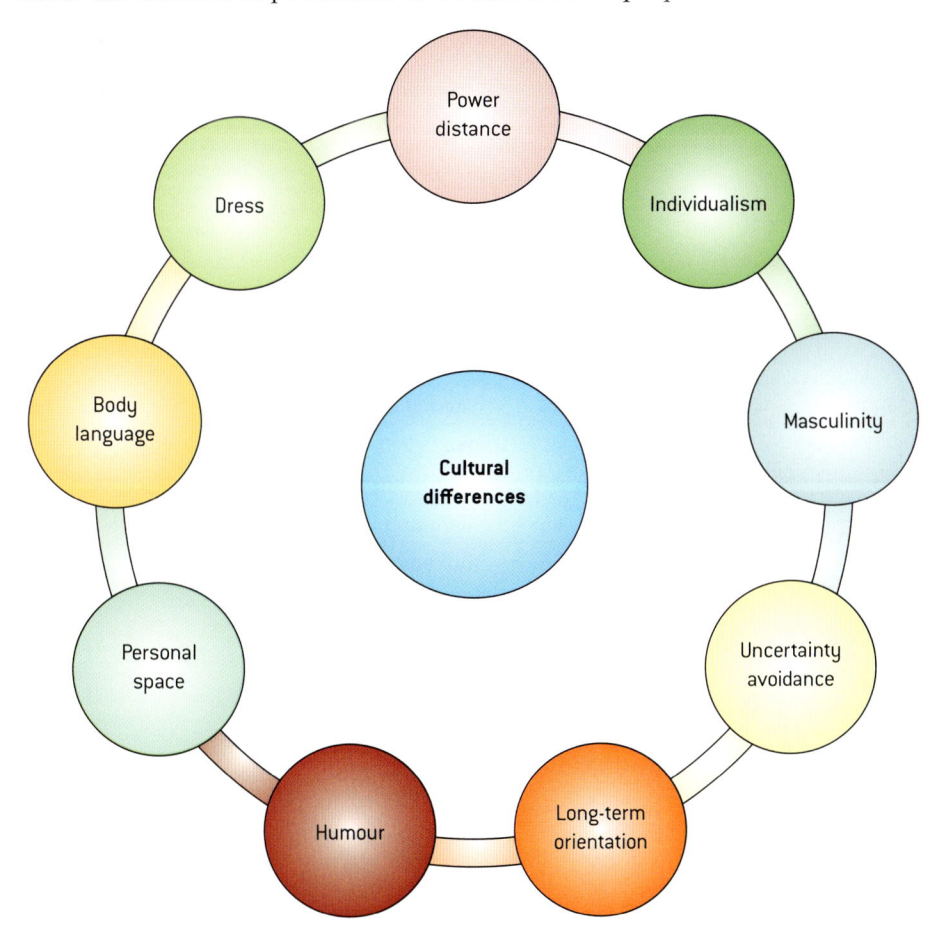

Figure 2.1.3 Cultural differences in the HR plan

The concept of "power distance" was developed by Geert Hofstede to indicate the acceptance by society of inequality. Power distance refers to the extent to which people in a particular society or organization accept that power is not distributed equally. Inequality is a fact, not a problem, and all members of the culture accept this fact.

Some example scores from Hofstede's power distance index (PDI) are shown in Table 2.1.3. According to Hofstede, employees from a society with a high level of power distance would not expect to be consulted and included in decision-making. They are more accepting of authority. Employees from countries with a low score would expect the opposite.

As the power distance index shows, people from different parts of the world and from different cultures have different expectations. Training people to work in diverse workforces can reduce potential misunderstanding and friction that can emerge from cultural differences.

Such training can also help businesses to take advantage of one of the most important benefits of a diverse workforce: increased innovation and creativity. Innovation occurs when people see a problem and solve it. When people from different backgrounds are gathered together to solve problems,

2 Human resource management

the diversity of perspectives increases the likelihood that a successful and novel solution will be found.

Table 2.1.3 PDI scores for selected countries

Country	PDI	Country	PDI
Malaysia	100	Spain	57
Panama	95	Pakistan	55
Saudi Arabia	95	Japan	54
Philippines	94	Italy	50
Mexico	81	Argentina	49
China	80	South Africa	49
Ecuador	78	United States	40
Indonesia	78	Hungary	46
India	77	Netherlands	38
Singapore	74	Australia	38
Egypt	70	Costa Rica	35
Brazil	69	South Africa	49
France	68	Germany	35
Hong Kong	68	United Kingdom	35
Thailand	64	Switzerland	34
Chile	63	Finland	33
Portugal	63	Sweden	31
Uruguay	61	Norway	31
Zambia	60	Ireland	28
Greece	60	New Zealand	22
South Korea	60	Denmark	18
Iran	58	Israel	13
Taiwan	58	Austria	11

Source: https://www.hofstede-insights.com/product/compare-countries

> **Student workpoint 2.2**
>
> **Be an inquirer**
>
> Go to the webpage https://www.hofstede-insights.com/product/compare-countries/, where you can compare countries along the six dimensions of culture that Hofstede uses. What countries have cultures similar to your home country and in which countries is the cultural difference greater?

Reasons for resistance to change in the workplace

For many reasons, employees may resist change in the workplace. Change is typically "forced" on them by managers because of changes in the internal or external environments. Whereas managers typically view change as desirable (or necessary) for the health of the organization and for profitability, workers are often threatened by change.

Specific reasons that workers and employees may resist change include:

- **Discomfort** – employees are often happy with the current situation and want to maintain the status quo.
- **Fear** – changes often makes employees afraid simply because they do not know what will happen.
- **Insufficient reward** – employees often perceive that implementing the change requires them to do more work without an increase in compensation.
- **Lack of job skills** – employees may not have the skills necessary to perform in the changed work environment.

- **Loss of control** – when managers insist on change, employees feel that they do not have control over their lives.
- **Mistrust** – employees sometimes do not trust managers.
- **Poor communication** – employees do not know why the business needs to change.
- **Poor timing** – change is brought about for the needs of the organization but might occur at a time that, for either professional or personal reasons, may fit poorly with the needs of employees.
- **Prior experience** – an employee may have had a bad experience with change in another organization, or at an earlier time with their current employer.
- **Social support** – an employee who works with a group of people who resist change may choose to resist for the sake of maintaining social relationships.

HR strategies to reduce the impact of change and resistance to it

Good organizations do not blindly move forward with change; they lead and manage employees through a change process. When effectively done, a change process helps to reduce the resistance and transitions the organization to its new and desired set of circumstances.

Organizations and managers can reduce the impact of change through various steps. The first is simply assessing the potential impact of the change, assessing employees' possible reactions to it, and determining the degree to which managers can control the change process. Thereafter, the management team should take the following steps:

1. Develop a vision for the change process and the desired outcomes. If necessary, the business may have to realign its largest aims and vision for the organization.
2. Forecast and allocate the necessary resources to implement the change.
3. Involve employees in the change process from the outset so they are not surprised and so they do not feel powerless.
4. Regularly communicate to all appropriate stakeholders how the change process is unfolding. Managers should not be afraid to report problems or implementation dips. Pretending that problems in the process are not occurring when they clearly are will weaken employees' confidence. On the other hand, managers should report successes in the change process to inspire confidence.
5. Train employees in advance of those changes that affect them directly, which should allow them to see the benefits of change immediately. If employees are not properly trained, the fears of lack of competence will be heightened.
6. Routinely communicate the benefits of the changes.
7. Be aware of the stress that change can cause and support employees as much as possible before, during, and after change.

> **Concept**
>
> **CHANGE**
>
> In many ways, human resources management and workforce planning are about adapting to change: changes in work patterns, work practices or work preferences, resistance to change, strategies to reduce the impact of change, etc.
>
> Research recent examples of changes in HR that have had a positive impact, and others that have had a negative impact. This could also give you ideas for your IA.

> **Bar chart**
>
> A bar chart presents data with rectangular-shaped bars, plotted vertically or horizontally, proportional in length to their values. It compares different categories and is a powerful way to show data visually, as illustrated in the case study on the next page.

2 Human resource management

Case study

Managing change

One of the major challenges for executive management is managing change. A major study by Towers Watson, based on a survey of 276 large and midsize organizations around the world, found that three out of four change management initiatives fail.

Often the failure of change initiatives is blamed on employees, who, for many reasons, frequently resist change. The Towers Watson study, however, found that most of the problems stemmed from management itself.

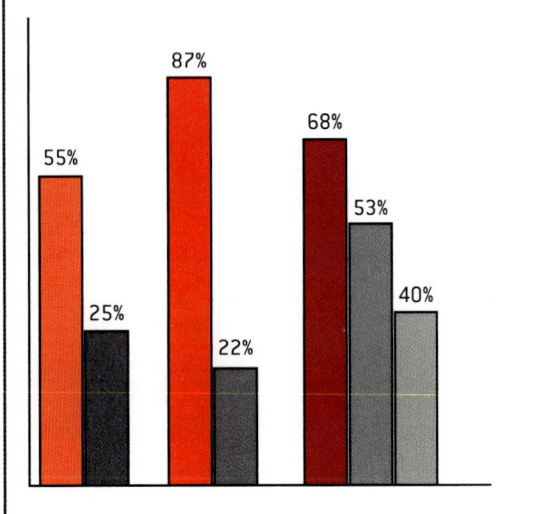

- Employers felt 55% of change management initiatives met initial objectives, but only 25% felt gains were sustained over time.
- 87% of respondents trained their managers to "manage change," but only (a dismal) 22% felt the training was actually effective.
- 68% of senior managers said they're "getting the message" about reasons for major organizational changes, but that figure falls to 53% for middle managers and 40% for front-line supervisors.

Figure 2.1.4 Change management and why it often fails

TOK links

1. Is it possible to identify all the factors, internal and external, that influence workforce planning?
2. As the future cannot be precisely predicted, is workforce planning a futile task?
3. Are there as many reasons for resistance to change in a workplace as there are employees?

Revision checklist

✓ Human resource processes are designed and planned to ensure that employees are selected, used and developed in the most effective way.

✓ Both internal and external factors can influence human resource planning.

✓ There are many reasons employees often resist change.

✓ Effective organizations plan and manage change, which, when done well, reduces resistance to change and helps the organization through the transition.

✓ As working practices and patterns have changed, businesses have had to adapt their HR strategies.

2.1 Introduction to human resource management

Practice question

To answer the question below effectively, see Unit 6 pages 398–402.

Premium Fruit Drinks

Premium Fruit Drinks (PFD) is a small manufacturing company that makes healthy, low-sugar fruit drinks. Over the last decade, *PFD's* sales and revenue have grown considerably. *PFD* hopes that this growth will continue, though the management worries about obtaining appropriate sources of finance and filling future human resources needs.

PFD is located in an industrial park out the outskirts of Kuala Lumpur, the capital city of Malaysia. The city has grown significantly in the last 30 years and is now a modern city, with a growing high-tech sector and an increasing number of technical schools and universities producing an ever-growing number of graduates.

Some of the human resource needs at *PFD* will be for relatively low-skilled workers, which are easy to find. However, the company needs two types of specialist employees: industrial engineers to manage the factory, and nutritionists who can develop new healthy drinks. Traditionally, both of these types of specialized employees were hard to find and had to be paid high salaries.

The head of the workforce planning team believes that *PFD* can take advantage of several factors in the labour market to find new specialist employees. Improvements in *PFD's* IT infrastructure allows professional-level employees to work from home at least 50% of the time, which employees prefer. Working from home also fits well with flexi-time, which many employees also prefer (especially those with small children). Finally, with careful planning, certain tasks (the development of new drinks, for example) can be subcontracted out to independent contractors working in the gig economy.

a) Define the term *gig economy*. [2 marks]

b) With reference to *PFD*, explain **two** roles of human resource management. [4 marks]

c) Explain **one** internal and **one** external factor that will influence *PFD's* human resource planning. [4 marks]

2.2 Organizational structure

> **By the end of this chapter, you should be able to:**
>
> → Explain the following terminology to facilitate understanding of different types of **organizational structures**:
> - delegation
> - span of control
> - levels of hierarchy
> - chain of command
> - bureaucracy
> - centralization
> - decentralization
> - delayering
> - matrix structure
>
> → Explain and draw the following types of **organization charts**:
> - flat/horizontal
> - tall/vertical
> - by product or by function or by region
>
> → Evaluate the **appropriateness of different organizational structures** given a change in external factors
>
> → Evaluate **changes in organizational structures** (such as project-based organization, Handy's "Shamrock Organization") **(HL only)**

Even the most chaotic of start-ups with more than one owner must have some sense of organization, roles, and responsibilities if the business is to survive. When a business succeeds and grows, then it must develop a formal plan clearly outlining the structure of the organization. An organizational structure formally represents the roles and responsibilities of a business, as well as the reporting lines between individuals in the business.

Organizational charts

The most common way to present the structure of an organization is through an organizational chart – a diagram that outlines the formal roles, responsibilities, and reporting lines. Figure 2.2.1 shows a typical organizational chart for a business.

> **Key term**
>
> **Organizational chart** depicts the reporting relationships within an organization. All levels of the organization are depicted and the chart shows who reports to whom down to the least senior level of employees in the organization.

2.2 Organizational structure

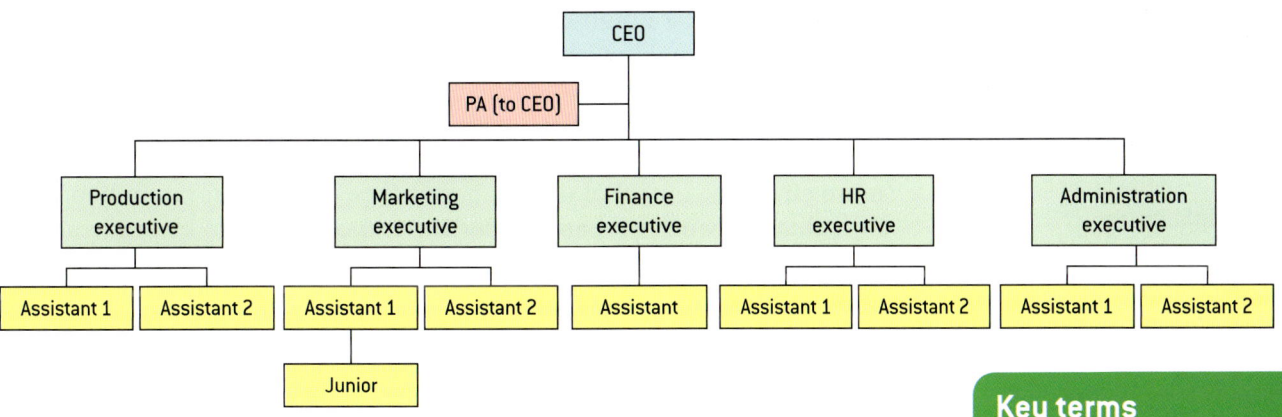

Figure 2.2.1 An organizational chart for a business

A few terms help to describe the organizational structure in an organizational chart:

- **Levels of hierarchy** – this term refers to how many levels of responsibility are in a business. Each level indicates a level of seniority in the business. In this case, four levels range from most senior (the "CEO") to the most junior (the "Junior" working in the marketing department).

    Each level of hierarchy indicates **line managers** – people who have the authority to make decisions and who bear responsibility for the outcomes of those decisions.

    Note that the Personal Assistant (PA) to the CEO is not included in the levels of hierarchy in Figure 2.2.1. This employee is known as a **staff manager** – someone with the authority to communicate a decision made by the CEO without the responsibility for that decision. Other types of staff managers could be secretarial and administrative staff.

- **Chain of command** – this term refers to the formal route by which a decision must travel through the organization. Traditionally, decisions travel from the top of the organization downwards and are therefore often referred to as "commands". In this case, if the CEO wants to communicate with the Junior in the marketing department, then the message will pass through the chain: from the CEO (typically through the PA) to the Marketing Executive, to Assistant 1, and finally to the Junior.

- **Span of control** – this refers to how many subordinates are directly under the authority of a manager, for whom managers are responsible. In this case, the span of control of the CEO is five. Note that the various assistants and the Junior are not included in the span of control, and any staff manager such as the PA would not be included either.

The following terms are relevant to how an organization is structured (though not necessarily to an organizational chart):

- **Delegation** – this occurs when a manager assigns to a subordinate authority for a particular decision, but not the responsibility for the outcome of that decision. That remains with the manager. Delegation is more likely when the span of control is wide. A manager who has a narrow span of control usually keeps a tighter control on all decisions.

Key terms

Hierarchy

a system organizing or ranking people according to power or importance

Chain of command

the official hierarchy in an organization. The chain of command indicates who reports to which manager and which manager has authority over specific employees.

Span of control

the number of people reporting to a specific manager. A wide span of control means many people reporting to the manager; a narrow span of control means a small number of people reporting to the manager.

Delegation

assigning authority or responsibility over specific tasks from one person, a manager, to someone lower on the organizational chart. The manager remains accountable for the successful completion of the delegated tasks.

Bureaucracy

refers to any organization with multiple layers of authority. Because bureaucracies often have complex approval processes, decision-making is typically slower than in small organizations.

2 Human resource management

> ### Key terms
>
> **Centralization**
> when personnel at the main or central office of the business have the authority for decision-making. Personnel not in the central office implement the decisions made by it. Centralization can also occur at one location, when senior management retain all key decision-making functions for themselves and delegate little or no decision-making authority to others.
>
> **Decentralization**
> the opposite of centralization; decision-making authority is delegated out to offices from the main or central office. Managers in regional or outlying offices have authority for making many types of tactical and operational decisions.
>
> **Delayering**
> the process of removing levels (layers) of hierarchy in an organization. The aim of delayering is usually to improve an organization's efficiency by making it less bureaucratic.
>
> **Matrix structure**
> typically exist in contexts where projects and project completion require involvement from people with different expertise from different areas of the organization (such as HR, marketing, operations, etc). In a matrix structure, people work in teams and report to these people with different expertise. Thus, they report to more than one person when doing their job.

- **Centralization** – a high degree of centralization indicates that all major decision-making is maintained within a small group of managers operating close to the head of the business. This type of organizational structure is usually associated with businesses that have many levels of hierarchy and narrow spans of control – so that key managers can keep more effective control of their subordinates. Delegation rarely happens in such an organization and leadership is more likely to be autocratic.

- **Decentralization** – this is the opposite of centralization. In a decentralized organization, senior managers may maintain core strategic decisions, but other decision-making authority is delegated to middle managers. This type of organizational structure is usually associated with businesses that have fewer levels of hierarchy and wider spans of control – so that key managers allow greater freedoms to their subordinates. Delegation is more likely to happen in such an organization and leadership is more likely to be democratic.

- **Bureaucracy** – originally a term referring to non-elected officials serving in government, today this term means any administrative system. In business, the term indicates the relative importance of rules and procedures. An organization that is "bureaucratic" has many rules and procedures and set ways of doing things. Personal initiative, flexible thinking and delegation are not expected.

  This type of organizational structure is usually associated with businesses that are well established and have been operating for many years. As such, they are more likely to have many levels of hierarchy. Typically, such organizations require paperwork to get tasks accomplished and have "red tape" (rules and checks) to show that procedures have been correctly followed. Delegation is not likely.

- **Delayering** – this is a process that occurs when a business reduces the levels of hierarchy by removing layers of management. This business strategy is usually associated with businesses that are well established and have been operating for many years. As such, they are more likely to have built up many levels of hierarchy. Delayering is intended to reduce bureaucracy and increase the decision-making capability of middle managers. It typically reduces costs as the business does not have to employ as many levels of managers.

- **Matrix structure** – a matrix structure combines two different types of organizational structures: typically organization by function (design, operations, finance, marketing, etc) with organization by product or, more typically, by project. For example, a team managed by a product manager moves a project forward by getting input (and often approval) from individuals from functional areas.

  Matrix organization is complex and can be ambiguous, as people on the team effectively have multiple bosses (such as the project manager and individuals from the functional areas).

Types of organization chart

Many different types of organizational structure exist. The most common are described below.

Tall or vertical organizational structure

A tall organizational structure is the traditional organizational form of a business and it is common in well-established businesses. It has the following features:

- Many levels of hierarchy
- Narrow spans of control
- Centralized decision-making
- Long chains of command
- Autocratic leadership
- Limited delegation

Flat or horizontal organizational structure

A flat organizational structure is a modification of the more traditional structure, and has become popular with businesses set up since the 1960s or with those attempting to reinvent themselves. Flat organizations have the following features:

- Few levels of hierarchy
- Wider spans of control
- Decentralized decision-making
- Shorter (though more diffuse) chains of command
- Democratic leadership
- Increased delegation

Organizational structure by hierarchy

Another way to show an organizational structure is by showing hierarchy. Individuals at the top have more authority than those below them. This is the traditional way of presenting an organizational structure and is shown in Figure 2.2.2.

Organizational structure by function

An organizational structure can be presented by function – indicating what employees do. Employees are grouped by department (see Figure 2.2.3). They will then be organized by seniority.

> **Assessment advice**
>
> With delegation, a manager passes authority or responsibility over specific assignments *down* the organization, to someone lower down the hierarchy, but the person doing the delegation is ultimately responsible for the outcome of those delegated assignments.

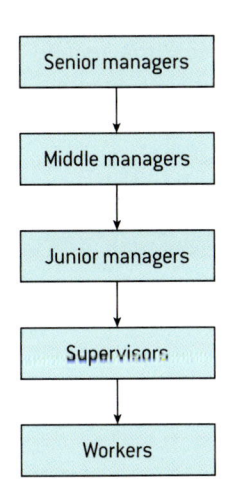

Figure 2.2.2 Organizational structure by hierarchy

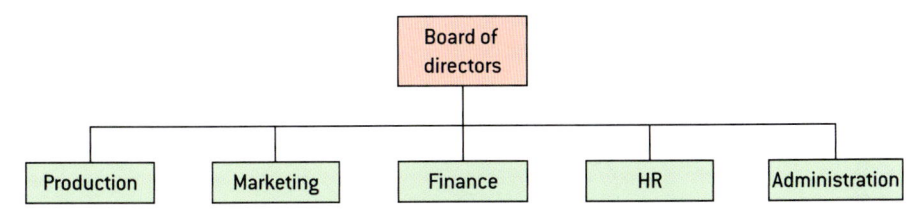

Senior managers → Middle managers → Junior managers → Supervisors → Workers

Figure 2.2.3 Organizational structure by function

Board of directors → Production, Marketing, Finance, HR, Administration

Organizational structure by product

Another typical way of presenting an organizational structure is by what the business produces. For example, Figure 2.2.4 shows a publisher organized according to the types of books it produces.

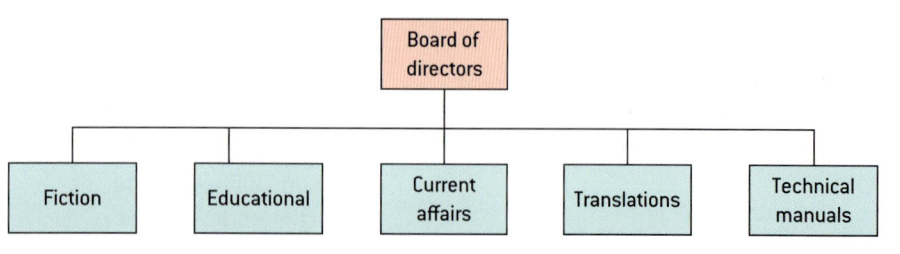

Figure 2.2.4 Organizational structure by product

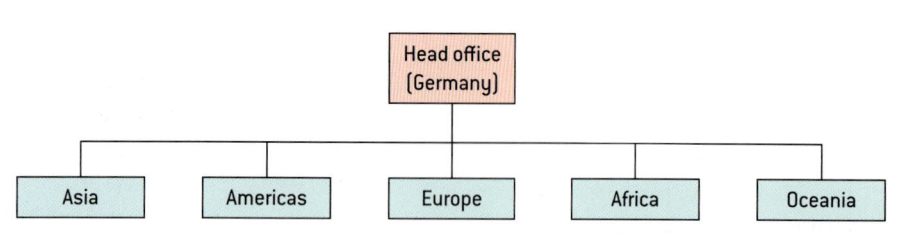

```
Board of directors
├── Fiction
├── Educational
├── Current affairs
├── Translations
└── Technical manuals
```

Organizational structure by region

A further typical way of presenting an organizational structure is according to where the business operations are. Figure 2.2.5 shows an example structure for a multinational corporation.

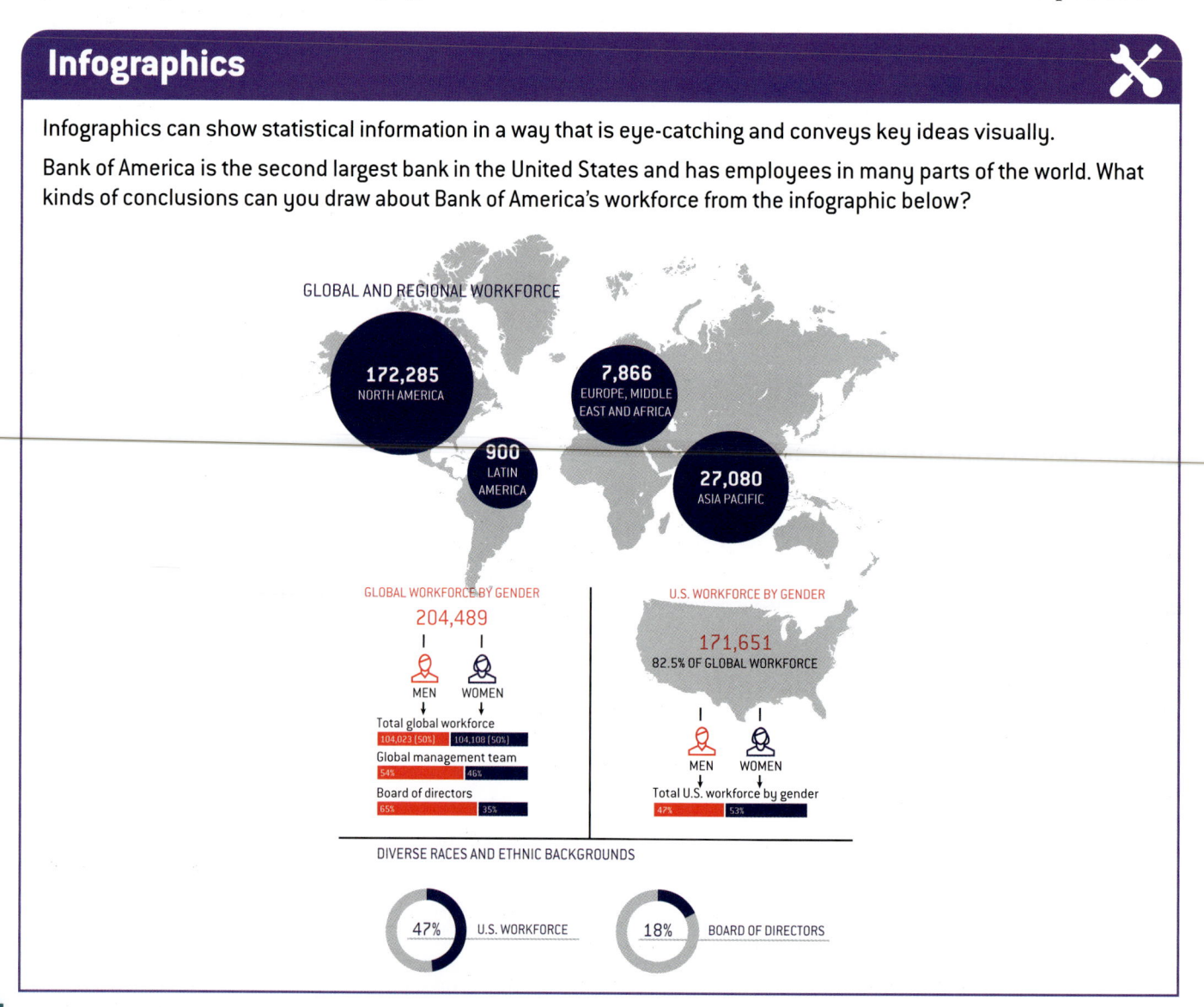

Figure 2.2.5 Organizational structure by region

```
Head office (Germany)
├── Asia
├── Americas
├── Europe
├── Africa
└── Oceania
```

Infographics

Infographics can show statistical information in a way that is eye-catching and conveys key ideas visually.

Bank of America is the second largest bank in the United States and has employees in many parts of the world. What kinds of conclusions can you draw about Bank of America's workforce from the infographic below?

GLOBAL AND REGIONAL WORKFORCE

- 172,285 NORTH AMERICA
- 7,866 EUROPE, MIDDLE EAST AND AFRICA
- 900 LATIN AMERICA
- 27,080 ASIA PACIFIC

GLOBAL WORKFORCE BY GENDER
204,489
MEN / WOMEN

Total global workforce
- 104,023 (50%) / 104,108 (50%)

Global management team
- 54% / 46%

Board of directors
- 65% / 35%

U.S. WORKFORCE BY GENDER
171,651
82.5% OF GLOBAL WORKFORCE

MEN / WOMEN

Total U.S. workforce by gender
- 47% / 53%

DIVERSE RACES AND ETHNIC BACKGROUNDS

- 47% U.S. WORKFORCE
- 18% BOARD OF DIRECTORS

2.2 Organizational structure

Changes in organizational structures (HL only)

As well as the standard types of organizational structure described above, some businesses have attempted to adapt their structure to take account of changes in the business environment. Two examples of this are:

- Project-based organization
- Shamrock organization

Project-based organization

Project-based organization is designed to be more flexible and responsive to market demands. Project-based organizations have project managers who run teams of employees focusing on individual projects. After the project is completed, the team is split up and reassembled to begin another project.

Typically, many teams operate at once, but they do not need to interact with each other because each team is focused on completing its own project. Each team "borrows" members of different departments to complete the project, such as accountants, operations managers and marketing specialists.

This type of business structure is common in construction and IT, where businesses are often under contract to run a number of different projects at the same time. It is also known as a matrix structure as often the organizational teams are shown as a matrix (see Table 2.2.1).

> **Key terms**
>
> **Project-based organization**
>
> an organizational form, often similar to a matrix structure, that organizes work into projects. Thus, project-based organizations create temporary systems for carrying out different projects.
>
> **Shamrock organization**
>
> An organizational structure based upon the work of human-resources expert Charles Handy, who modelled the structure on the shamrock (a clover-like plant). A shamrock organization has three types of employees: the full-time professional core, a flexible labour force, and a contractual (outsourced) group.

Table 2.2.1 Matrix of organizational teams

	Operations management	Finance	Marketing	HR	Administration
Project 1 manager	4 employees	2 employees	1 employee	1 employee	1 employee
Project 2 manager	3 employees	2 employees	2 employees	2 employees	1 employee
Project 3 manager	3 employees	2 employees	1 employee	1 employee	1 employee

Shamrock organizations

This type of organization is based on a model suggested by the Irish management theorist Charles Handy. Handy argued that businesses can be more flexible by taking advantage of the changes in the external environment and its impact on workforce planning. His idea uses the national symbol of Ireland – the shamrock – which is a type of clover that has three leaves on each stem.

The model suggests that businesses can reduce costs, gain competitive advantage and increase response time by trimming their workforce to retain only a multiskilled core, which is concerned with the creation or delivery of a product or service. All other supporting, non-central functions are outsourced wherever possible to the periphery:

- The first leaf of the shamrock represents the core managers, technicians and employees essential to the business.
- The second leaf Handy calls the "contractual fringe", because non-core activities are subcontracted out to specialist businesses.
- The third leaf consists of a flexible workforce made up of part-time, temporary, and seasonal workers.

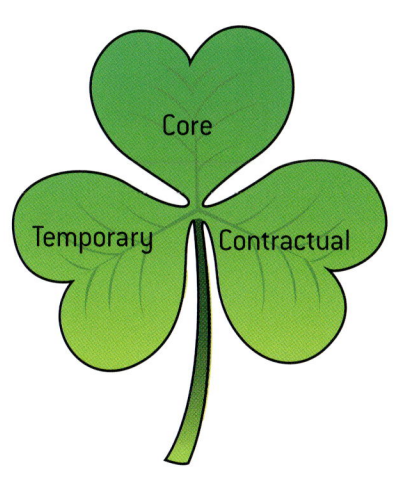

Figure 2.2.6 The shamrock model

2 Human resource management

> **Student workpoint 2.3**
>
> *Be a thinker*
>
> Consider the various types of organization structures discussed in this chapter. In what ways does each of the organizational structures affect individual employees? In what ways does each organizational structure potentially affect employees' work–life balance?

> **TOK links**
>
> 1. How useful are the images and metaphors used to talk about organizational structure (for example: chains, layers, vertical, horizontal, matrix, shamrock)?
> 2. Why can organizational charts be misleading?
> 3. How are our values reflected in the language we use to describe the structure of organizations (for example: bureaucracy, centralization, delayering)?

Appropriateness of different organizational structures

No one "correct" form of organizational structure exists. When organizations are formed or as they grow, executives structure their organizations in the way that they think will maximize the objectives of the business. Large chains of grocery stores are often organized by region. Manufacturing firms are often organized by function or by product, depending on the nature of their markets.

As objectives change or external conditions change, executives often rethink how they have organized their business and they restructure. Many large bureaucratic firms periodically delayer in order to make the business leaner, ie less bureaucratic and more responsive to market pressures.

Many high-tech start-ups often have flat organizational structures and, as they grow, management sees the need to bring more order and starts to add levels of hierarchy. Thus, when thinking about organizational structure the question is not "What is the best structure?" but rather "What are the consequences (advantages and disadvantages) of any potential organizational structure that is selected?"

Revision checklist

- ✓ Delegation occurs when a manager gives authority for a particular decision to someone else. The manager still has responsibility for the outcome of that decision.
- ✓ The span of control is how many employees are directly under the authority of a particular manager.
- ✓ A level of hierarchy is a level of responsibility within a business.
- ✓ The chain of command is the formal route through which a decision must travel. Usually, decisions are made at the highest level and are communicated down.
- ✓ Bureaucracy refers to rules and procedures within an organization.
- ✓ Centralization occurs when the majority of decisions are made by a small group of individuals in a senior position within the business. Decentralization is found where decisions are made by middle managers. Senior management is likely to retain control of key strategic decisions.
- ✓ Delayering occurs when a business reduces the levels of hierarchy by removing layers of management.
- ✓ A flat organizational structure has few levels of hierarchy and tends to have a wide span of control. Decision-making is decentralized.
- ✓ A tall structure has many levels of hierarchy and narrow spans of control. Leadership tends to be autocratic and decision-making is centralized.
- ✓ Organizational structures can be organized by hierarchy, by function, by product or by region.
- ✓ Some organizational structures, like Handy's shamrock model and project-based organization, are dynamic and change rapidly according to needs and circumstances. **(HL only)**

2.2 Organizational structure

Practice question

To answer the question below effectively, see Unit 6 pages 398–402.

ABC plc

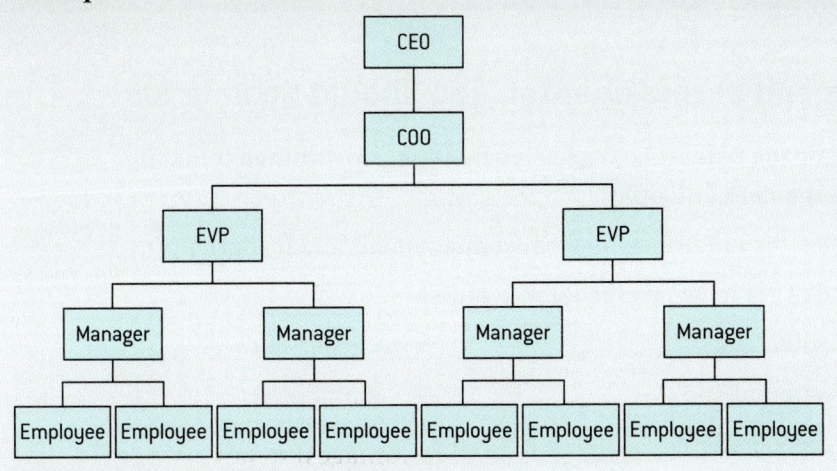

```
                    CEO
                     |
                    COO
                   /    \
                 EVP    EVP
                / \    /   \
          Manager Manager Manager Manager
           / \   / \    / \    / \
         Emp Emp Emp Emp Emp Emp Emp Emp
```

Chart 1 Current organizational chart for ABC plc

ABC plc has decided that the company is too bureaucratic and needs to delayer.

a) Define the term *delegation*. [2 marks]

b) Explain what type of organizational chart is shown in Chart 1. [2 marks]

c) Draw a new organizational chart for ABC plc after a process of delayering. [2 marks]

d) With reference to ABC plc, explain **two** advantages of delayering. [4 marks]

101

2.3 Leadership and management

> **By the end of this chapter, you should be able to:**
> → Explain the difference between **scientific** and **intuitive thinking/management (HL only)**
> → Explain the difference between **management** and **leadership**
> → Discuss the following **leadership styles**:
> - autocratic
> - paternalistic
> - democratic
> - laissez-faire
> - situational

Introduction to management

Management is made up of the people in organizations charged with making sure tasks, whether large or small, are accomplished. They are not the people who do the work of the organizations. Rather, they are the people with a special set of responsibilities who ensure that the work of the company is performed.

For example, in a television manufacturing company, those in management roles are not actually making the televisions on the shop floor. Rather, they have some supervisory role to make sure televisions are made according to company standards.

Management covers a range of levels. Top management includes the CEO and the various people in charge of each of the major business functions (HR, accounting and finance, marketing, and operations management). Other levels of management exist, all the way down to the floor or the office supervisors. To some degree, even they are part of management.

In *Administration Industrielle et Générale* (1916), Henri Fayol outlined five major functions of management based upon his experiences as a manager at a large French coal mine:

- **Planning** – managers must plan. They must set strategic objectives, tactical objectives, and even operational objectives, all of which have implications throughout the organization.
- **Organizing** – managers must then make sure that the business has sufficient resources to achieve its objectives. This process requires careful organization, as too many resources tie up too much capital; too few mean that the organization's objectives cannot be met.
- **Commanding** – managers must make sure that all individuals know which duties they are to perform. If necessary, managers must also make sure that employees receive instruction in how they are to perform their tasks.

> **Key terms**
>
> **Management**
> the ongoing process of planning, decision-making, organizing, leading, motivating and controlling the financial, human, physical, and information resources of a business or organization, with the aim of efficiently and effectively reaching the goals of the business or organization
>
> **Leadership**
> a process of motivating a group or team of people to work towards the goals of a business or organization. Unlike management, which is generally considered a science, much of leadership is an "art": an intangible ability to inspire, lead, coerce, or charm through charisma and other affective and intellectual qualities.

- **Coordinating** – managers must bring together the various resources to achieve objectives. In many types of business, various different activities are going on, with each activity contributing to the output of the businesses. Managers must coordinate these activities, making sure that each activity is done when and where it is supposed to be.

- **Controlling** – managers control. They have power over a given situation to achieve objectives. They have power to test (or "control for") quality so that processes can be changed if necessary. They also have power to expand or reduce the scale of operations as conditions require.

Fayol argued that these functions were universal and could therefore be applied to any organization.

> ### Case study
> ### Charles Clinton Spaulding (1874–1952)
>
> When scholars write about the history of management, they usually include the Frenchman Henri Fayol (1841–1925), whose *Administration Industrielle et Générale* (1916) is considered a groundbreaking work.
>
> Another name should get some attention too: Charles Clinton Spaulding. An African American living in North Carolina at a time when Black people faced terrible hostility and complete segregation, Spaulding built what was then the largest Black-owned business in the United States, the North Carolina Mutual Life Insurance Company, which he ran for over 50 years.
>
> Traditionally, an important cultural practice among African-Americans is the "homegoing": a formal funeral service and burial ceremony. In the first half of the 20th century, few African Americans could afford these elaborate celebrations of life. One way to surmount this obstacle was to buy life insurance, which many low-income African Americans were willing to do. Spaulding filled this market opportunity with policies offered by the North Carolina Mutual Life Insurance Company.
>
> In 1927, Spaulding wrote a short article, published in two editions of the *Pittsburg Courier*, entitled "The Administration of Big Business". In this article, Spaulding actually articulated many of the same concepts as Fayol, whose work was not available in English until 1949. The *Pittsburg Courier* was a weekly newspaper serving the African American community and probably had limited readership, if any, among Whites.
>
> Probably for this reason, and because Spaulding was African American, and because his two-piece article was rather brief compared to Fayol's 150-page book, Spaulding's ideas rarely get mentioned, though they should. He encountered many obstacles, socially, culturally, economically and politically, yet he was able to formulate pioneering ideas about management as a science.
>
> To what degree does prejudice still prevent marginalized people from starting and growing businesses even today?
>
> To what degree do academic and practical business literature still exclude improbable voices such as Charles Clinton Spaulding?
>
> How do the concepts of creativity, change, ethics and sustainability illuminate the story of Charles Clinton Spaulding?

The difference between scientific and intuitive thinking/management (HL only)

Managers and leaders can approach their responsibilities in several ways. One simple categorization divides managers into those who use **deliberative thinking processes**, also known as "scientific thinking", and others who follow their **intuition**. In reality, most managers use a combination of both approaches according to the specific circumstances at the time they make their decisions.

Sometimes evidence suggests that a manager should make a decision a certain way. Following the evidence in this way would be a form of scientific management. At other times, managers will see evidence and choose to disregard it. The manager is acting on a feeling: a "hunch", or what their "gut" tells them. In this latter case, the manager is broadening in an unsystematic way all the evidence that they are considering.

Management versus leadership

A manager is responsible for planning and overseeing the work of a group, monitoring the group's progress, and ensuring that the plan is put into effect. A manager therefore deals with complexity.

Many would argue that a **manager** is **task-orientated** (that is, a manager is focused on getting tasks accomplished in a timely manner rather than on leading people). To get tasks accomplished, managers:

- instruct and coordinate people
- help subordinates to resolve problems
- generally, have technical expertise and bring that technical expertise to bear (by setting strict schedules and giving precise instructions)
- have authority by virtue of their position in the organization
- generally like to make the organization function (and therefore tend not to challenge the organization).

In contrast, a **leader's** role is more emotional, since a great leader will have the ability to inspire people to follow them voluntarily. A leader spends a great deal of time and energy building relationships and is therefore **relationship-orientated**. Leaders:

- motivate and inspire with their personal qualities
- often rely on instincts even in the face of evidence that they are choosing the less safe option
- have vision – and others follow them because of that vision
- often have the vision that the organization should be doing things in a totally different way, and can inspire the confidence needed to bring about systemic change and innovation.

Aliko Dangote, founder of The Dangote Group

Case study

The Dangote Group

The Dangote Group was founded in the late 1970s when Aliko Dangote, with the help of a $3,000 loan from his uncle, began a business that traded sugar and consumer goods. Over time, the business began trading other commodities. The Dangote Group has experienced considerable growth over subsequent decades. Today, the business continues to trade commodities, but it is also engaged in textile manufacturing and has interests in cement, sugar, flour, salt, seasoning, pasta, beverages and real estate. The Dangote Group also has investments in fertilizer, natural gas, steel, and telecommunications.

The number of employees has grown from one (Aliko Dangote) to over 30,000. One study found that the company's leadership, its organizational culture, its training and development programme, and financial rewards schemes have all improved employee performance.

Mr Dangote has built one of the largest businesses in Africa in part because of his company's effective human resources management. Today, Mr Dangote is also a major philanthropist with a special concern in the area of public health.

2.3 Leadership and management

Leadership styles

Leadership styles can be categorized as follows.

Autocratic

Autocratic leaders hold on to as much power and decision-making authority as they possibly can. They tend not to consult (or only consult minimally) with employees when making a decision. Their orders should be obeyed, and employees should welcome the structured environment.

This style of leadership is most likely to be used when subordinates are unskilled, not trusted, and their ideas are not valued. It is also more likely in an organization that focuses on results and has to make urgent decisions that depend highly on the manager. Many in the military rely on an autocratic style, which is often accompanied by very detailed instructions and close supervision. In some situations, subordinates may expect, and like, to be told what to do.

Autocratic leadership will probably be unsuccessful when employees have the opposite characteristics to those just described. Highly skilled individuals who have experienced democratic systems and who like to do things their own way are unlikely to tolerate an autocratic manager.

A benefit of autocratic leadership is that lines of authority are clear, and decisions can be made quickly. What the leader communicates is what is to be followed. Employees come to depend on the guidance but also to execute instructions precisely.

The major negative aspect of an autocratic leadership style is that employees tend not to develop the ability to manage on their own or to make decisions. And rarely, in any business, can the leader make all the decisions.

Paternalistic

Paternalistic leadership shares some features with autocratic leadership in that the leader has considerable authority over employees. Unlike autocratic leaders, however, a paternalistic leader views the employees as "family" – a figurative family, certainly, but a family all the same. "Paternalistic" derives from the Latin word for "father", which is at the heart of the paternalistic style. Paternalistic leaders have great concern for the business's employees.

Paternalistic leaders are like parents. They provide employees with a sense of safety. The employees come to believe that, no matter what, the business will stand by them. As a result, paternalistic leaders often get total loyalty and even blind trust from employees. If employees like this style of leadership, they will probably remain at the business for a long time and become totally committed to it, the leader, and the leader's aims.

A positive aspect of paternalistic leadership is that employees take great pride in the organization and do whatever is necessary to make it successful. They take some (figurative) "ownership" of the business, in part because they do not want to let the leader down.

> **Key terms**
>
> **Autocratic leadership**
> occurs when the leader concentrates all or most decision-making in their own hands. Autocratic leaders typically do not seek input from others and are confident in their own decision-making.
>
> **Paternalistic leadership**
> occurs when the head of an organization treats employees like they are part of their family. A paternalistic leader is typically warm and protective of employees but also expects loyalty and obedience.

However, paternalistic leaders place great importance on loyalty, which may mean that they do not have a fully objective, critical eye when evaluating employees' performance. Thus, paternalistic leaders may come across as having favourites or favouring certain employees. In addition, knowing that they are part of a "family", employees may at times take advantage of the leader and the leader's loyalty to them.

Democratic

The democratic leader involves employees in decision-making and informs them about issues that affect them. Democratic leadership can occur across a spectrum. At one end is the truly democratic leader, who facilitates the democratic process and honours it as much as is possible and practical. Truly democratic leadership is rare in business or any organization, as ultimately one role of a leader is to make decisions. Thus, a more common type of democratic leader is one who consults employees regularly. However, as a practical matter and because the leader is ultimately responsible for the decisions of the team, the leader will have the final say.

Democratic leadership is probably the most popular style among employees, possibly because for most people the word "democracy" has positive emotional connotations. They also like being involved in the decision-making process, especially when the decisions have a major impact on them. The democratic leader can produce results since many employees like the trust, cooperation, and sense of belonging that go with it. Employees feel as though they have a voice.

The democratic leadership style may not always work out. It is likely to be most effective when used with skilled, free-thinking, and experienced subordinates who enjoy the relationships and chaos that can result from belonging to a highly effective team. However, the democratic process may slow down decision-making and may prove too costly. The style also requires a positive "chemistry" in the team. If this characteristic is absent, no amount of democracy can make the style work.

Laissez-faire

Laissez-faire means "to leave alone". In this leadership style, the manager gives employees considerable freedom in how they do their work. Employees can set their own goals, make their own decisions, and resolve problems as they see fit.

This management style may be appropriate when employees can be trusted to do their job because they are motivated, skilled, and educated. Universities tend to be laissez-faire, as university lecturers, researchers and professors, who are generally world experts in their field, resist being told what to do. In other professions too, individual practitioners demand considerable freedom. It may be appropriate when working with a culture based around the individual and where people can work successfully on their own.

The benefit of a laissez-faire style is that many employees enjoy the freedom it provides, and it can foster creativity and innovations. However, the individual interests of the employees may diverge too far from the focus of the organization, and the organization can veer away from its vision and aims.

Democratic leadership involves employees in the decision-making process

Key terms

Democratic leadership

occurs when the leader regularly seeks input from employees and involves them in decision-making

Laissez-faire leadership

occurs when the leader of an organization gives employees considerable freedom to make decisions on their own

From an employee's perspective, a laissez-faire leadership style may be unnerving, as this type of leader does not give much guidance and may not provide much feedback. Precise instructions and a watchful eye can give comfort to employees, whereas a laissez-faire style requires confident and disciplined employees. In instances where a leader adopts a laissez-faire style and the employees are not disposed to be successful under it, the results can be disastrous.

Situational

Situational leadership rests on the notion that different situations require different styles of leadership. Thus, no one style of leadership would ever be deemed "the best". Sometimes, the nature of the employees (for example, unskilled workers versus highly trained professionals) will determine which leadership style fits the situation. At other times, the nature of the circumstances will determine the most appropriate style.

In emergency situations, even highly democratic leaders will often become autocratic in order to lead the employees and the organization quickly and efficiently through the emergency. Sometimes, in situations where the outcome of the decision is not altogether consequential for the organization as a whole but may influence employee morale, even autocratic leaders may allow democracy and let the employees decide.

The benefit of situational leadership is that leaders match their style to the circumstances at hand. However, a leader may too frequently change styles or may change styles when the circumstances of the situation determining the switch are not clear to employees. In either of these scenarios, the leader may come across as unpredictable or arbitrary, which may demotivate employees.

In summary, the style of leadership is likely to be influenced by:

- the **subordinates** (subordinates' skills, age, education, expectations, and motivation)
- the **decision** (whether urgent, important, or consequential)
- the **leader** (the leader's character, values, experience, and expectations)
- the **environment** (whether creative, standardized, repressive, democratic, or compliant).

Ethical considerations and cultural differences

Ethical considerations and cultural differences may influence leadership and management styles in an organization.

Ethical considerations

Ethical considerations can influence both leadership styles and management styles, though in somewhat different ways. Leaders, as opposed to managers, focus on "doing the right thing" with respect to their people, whereas managers tend to do the right thing with respect to their organizations.

> **Key term**
>
> **Situational leadership**
>
> Situational leadership occurs when leaders in an organization adapt their leadership style to (1) the nature of the situation, task, or work and (2) the ability and expectations of the people in the organization

> **Assessment advice**
>
> Do not assume that one type of leadership is "good" or necessarily preferred over another type of leadership. Each of the leadership styles have advantages and disadvantages and you should know what these are.

> **Student workpoint 2.4**
>
> *Be reflective*
>
> Draw a table showing the advantages and disadvantages of the five leadership styles discussed here.

Leaders and ethical considerations

Leaders are focused on people. As a result, they focus on building relationships and on inspiring employees. To accomplish these objectives, leaders have to do more than merely say that they care about "their people". They must actually demonstrate that care when circumstances require.

Leaders guide organizations towards ethical ends. In the military, for example, leaders are those who risk their own lives to protect the lives of their subordinates. In business, leaders are willing, if necessary, to take the blame for bad outcomes if it means serving their employees by protecting them from excessive or unwarranted criticism.

A leader might, for example, intervene when a manager wants to sack a young employee who made an error of judgment, on the grounds that the employee was inexperienced. The leader might argue that the right thing to do is to give the employee a second chance. In this instance, the leader is taking a personal risk – responsibility not only for the employee's error of judgment but, arguably, for any future errors of judgment the employee might make.

Another example of ethical considerations is when a leader adopts ethical objectives for the organization, even when some stakeholders object (typically because ethical objectives have a financial cost). So central is ethical behaviour to leadership that many would argue that an unethical leader is not a leader at all.

Managers and ethical considerations

On the issue of ethical considerations, managers are often criticized. They are criticized as being bureaucratic "rule followers", and for putting their own positions and rewards ahead of their employees. Most of the time, this criticism of managers is somewhat unfair.

Managers, in contrast to leaders, see their ethical obligations more to the organization or business than to the employees. For example, the manager supervising a young employee who has made a major error in judgment sees the employee as a liability to the business. From this perspective, the manager believes that the right thing to do is to sack the employee to prevent further errors in judgment, which could cost the business money.

However, if a manager is too hasty in sacking an employee or is not giving the individual due process and fair consideration, the manager deserves the type of criticism mentioned above. If, to protect themselves from criticism, managers are too hasty in sacking an employee, they are not focusing on the interests of their organization but rather on their own career.

In summary, most leaders and managers are influenced by ethical considerations. With leaders, ethical considerations are centred on people, whereas with managers, ethical considerations are centred on the organization. When people in these roles behave unethically, whether they are leaders or managers, they really are not leading people or managing an organization. They are, unethically, putting their own interests ahead of others.

Cultural differences

Cultural differences can also influence leadership and management. The most famous treatment of this concept is the work of Geert Hofstede, who over his business and academic career developed and refined his cultural dimensions theory. According to Hofstede, cultural influences relevant to business have six dimensions:

- Power distance
- Individualism
- Uncertainty avoidance
- Masculinity
- Long-term orientation
- Indulgence

Different cultures value individualism (Anglo-American cultures), for example, whereas others (such as the Japanese culture) value group cohesion. The style of leadership or management that an individual adopts will be influenced by the culture from which they originate, and should also be influenced by the cultures of the people they lead or manage.

Employees from cultures with great power distance prefer (and arguably function better, at least initially) in organizations with autocratic leaders. On the other hand, employees from countries or cultures with low power distance might resent an autocratic leader and would probably perform better under democratic leadership.

TOK links

1. To what degree is it misleading to claim that a manager and a leader are different? How helpful is this terminology?
2. Is the difference between scientific management and intuitive management the same as the difference between natural sciences and human sciences?
3. Is being knowledgeable an essential quality in a manager, or are other traits and characteristics more important?

Hofstede's cultural dimensions (HL only)

Hofstede's country comparison tool, which you can find at https://www.hofstede-insights.com/product/compare-countries/, allows users to compare cultures in different countries according to different socio-cultural measures.

With this tool, a CEO could make a judgment about which country might be better for their company to expand into, and determine the degree of intercultural competency training their employees may need.

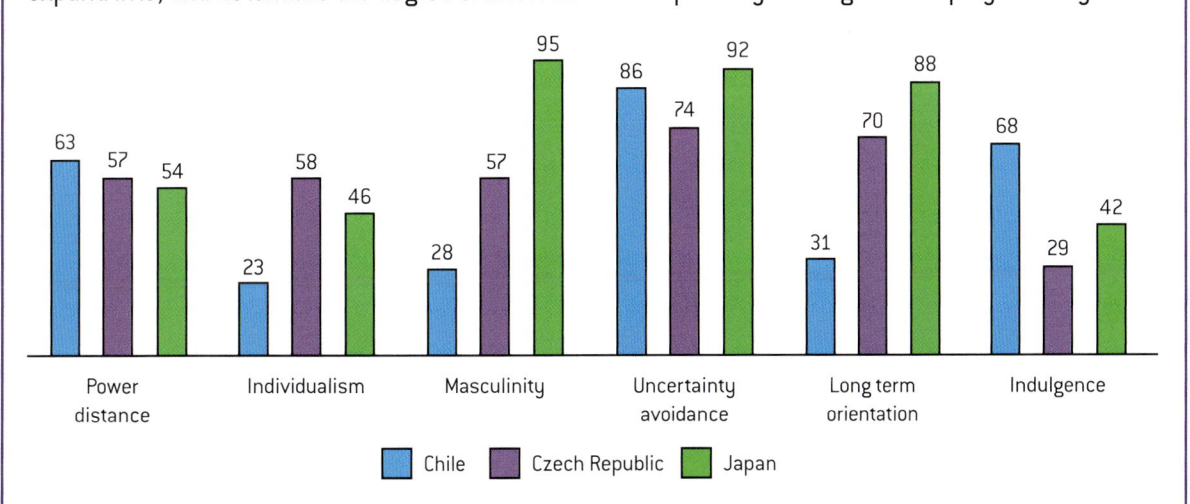

Dimension	Chile	Czech Republic	Japan
Power distance	63	57	54
Individualism	23	58	46
Masculinity	28	57	95
Uncertainty avoidance	86	74	92
Long term orientation	31	70	88
Indulgence	68	29	42

If you ran a Chilean company and were considering opening an office in either the Czech Republic or Japan, which country would be most culturally aligned with yours?

2 Human resource management

Revision checklist

✓ The key functions of management are to plan, to organize, to command, to coordinate and to control.

✓ A manager's role is to plan and oversee the work of a group. In contrast, a leader's role is to motivate and inspire.

✓ Autocratic leaders hold onto as much power as they can. They make all decisions, and their instructions should be obeyed.

✓ Paternalistic leaders also have a lot of decision-making power. They have concern for their employees and instil trust and loyalty.

✓ A laissez-faire leadership style allows employees much freedom. Employees can set their own goals and manage problems as they see fit.

✓ A democratic leader will involve employees in decision-making and inform them of issues which will affect them.

✓ Cultural and ethical considerations can and should influence leadership styles.

Practice question

To answer the question below effectively, see Unit 6 pages 398–402.

Rox and Inclusive Music (IM)

Rox was a music band managed by Michel Mbappe. The band enjoyed considerable commercial success thanks to Michel's autocratic leadership style. He personally made all decisions. *Rox* gave generously to local schools and other non-profit organizations. The band received many awards for their acts of corporate social responsibility. Their last CD, *Action Not Words*, brought them considerable fame.

In June 2020, Michel was asked to help the start-up of a new non-profit social enterprise, a music school called "Inclusive Music" (IM). IM's aim was to support young musicians from low-income families. At first, Michel was very enthusiastic and prepared a business plan. Unfortunately, he realized that *Rox* could not afford to finance IM fully.

In June 2021, IM opened with the mission statement "Action not words". To support its mission, it offered free lessons and allowed students to borrow musical instruments. Michel asked a popular former singer, Louis Marsaud, to be the school's director. Louis adopted a laissez-faire leadership style, hoping it would allow creativity among students.

Initial student attendance was lower than expected and quickly worsened. Within three months, many instruments had gone missing, and many students were no longer attending music lessons.

Michel took action and organized a concert by *Rox* to promote IM. Without consulting anyone, he dismissed Louis. In the music media, Michel received much criticism for dismissing Louis.

a) State **two** features of a non-profit social enterprise. [2 marks]

b) Define the term *corporate social responsibility*. [2 marks]

c) With reference to IM, distinguish between an autocratic leadership style and a laissez-faire leadership style. [4 marks]

2.4 Motivation and demotivation

By the end of this chapter, you should be able to:

→ Describe the following **motivation theories**:
- Taylor
- Maslow
- Herzberg (motivation–hygiene theory)
- McClelland's acquired needs theory **(HL only)**
- Deci & Ryan's self-determination theory **(HL only)**
- equity and expectancy theory **(HL only)**

→ Explain **labour turnover (HL only)**

→ Explain the following **types of appraisal (HL only)**:
- formative
- summative
- 360-degree feedback
- self-appraisal

→ Explain **methods of recruitment (HL only)**

→ Evaluate **internal** and **external recruitment (HL only)**

→ Explain the following types of **financial rewards**:
- salary
- wages (time and piece rates)
- commission
- performance-related pay (PRP)
- profit-related pay
- employee share-ownership schemes
- fringe payments (perks)

→ Explain the following types of **non-financial rewards**:
- job enrichment
- job rotation
- job enlargement
- empowerment
- purpose/the opportunity to make a difference
- teamwork

→ Explain the following types of **training**:
- induction
- on the job
- off the job

2 Human resource management

> **Key terms**
>
> **Intrinsic motivation**
> motivation which comes from the satisfaction of carrying out a particular activity (no external reward is required)
>
> **Extrinsic motivation**
> motivation that is derived from external factors (in a business context, typically money)

Intrinsic and extrinsic motivation

This chapter studies the factors that influence a person to work. If managers can motivate employees, it is more likely that those managers will achieve their goals.

Intrinsic motivation occurs when someone gets satisfaction from the activity itself without threats or rewards from outside. Employees are more likely to be intrinsically motivated if they are in the following work situations:

- They can see that their success is a result of something they have done. If they put in more work, they will achieve more positive outcomes.
- They have some control over their results – they are given a degree of freedom.
- They are interested in the work they are doing.

Rewards are **extrinsic motivators** – motivators that come from outside the individual. In the workplace, pay is an obvious example. Extrinsic motivators provide satisfaction that the job itself may not provide, and may compensate workers for the "pain" or dissatisfaction that they experience at work.

Motivation theories

Frederick Winslow Taylor

Taylor was a mechanical engineer who observed the phenomenal contribution science had made to agriculture and the Industrial Revolution, and wanted to apply scientific methods to management to achieve similar results. He published research between 1894 and 1912 and is often referred to as the founder of scientific management, since his ideas on management attempted to apply scientific methods of measurement under controlled circumstances to maximize output.

Taylor believed that **standardization of work methods** and **enforced adoption of the best ways of working** were how to ensure that output would be maximized in the shortest possible time. Taylor's ideas were adopted when many poorly educated Americans were leaving agriculture and starting to work in factories. Many managers in these factories took a hands-on style in decision-making. The introduction of Taylor's ideas and methods was often resented by workers and provoked numerous strikes.

Taylor is most famous for his time-and-motion studies, which involved breaking a job down into its component parts and measuring how long it took to perform each task. One of his most famous studies involved shovels, but consider a different example. If you watch how a hamburger is prepared in a large and busy fast-food restaurant, then you will get some idea of the huge benefits that can arise if each "bit" of the system is managed precisely.

The burger is cooked at a given temperature, for a precise amount of time on each side. The fries are also cooked at a given temperature for a precise amount of time. Each worker will have a specific role and will not move far from their position to minimize time wasted in movement. The result of all this coordinated effort is consistent fast food, cooked quickly and efficiently at low cost. Skill has been largely removed from the system, so employees can be employed at low cost and with little training.

Abraham Maslow

Maslow is most famous for proposing a **hierarchy of human needs** to explain motivation. He argued that people have a number of needs and arranged these in terms of their importance.

Self-actualization — morality, creativity, spontaneity, problem solving, lack of prejudice, acceptance of facts

Esteem — self-esteem, confidence, achievement, respect of others, respect by others

Love/belonging — friendship, family, sexual intimacy

Safety needs — security of: body, employment resources, morality, the family, health, property

Basic needs — food, warmth, shelter

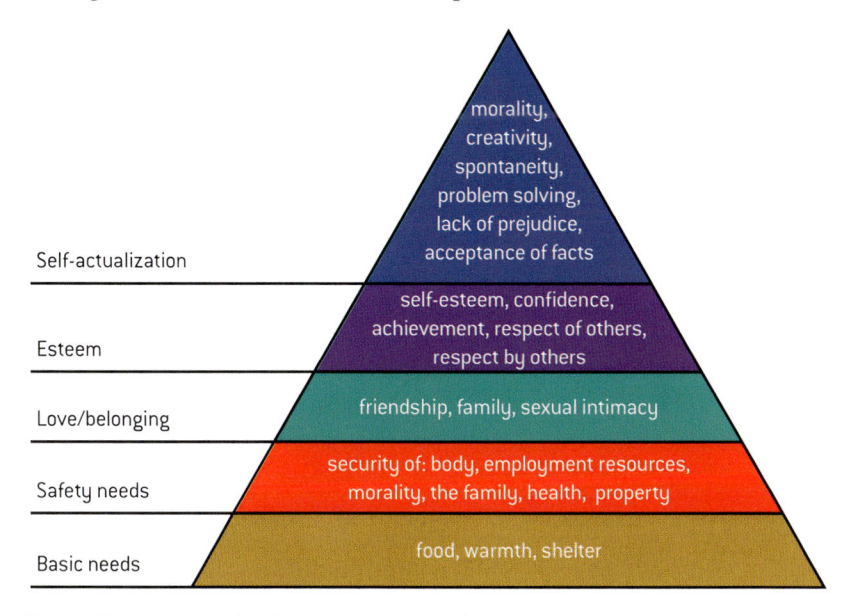

Figure 2.4.1 Maslow's hierarchy of needs[1]

The basic needs at the bottom of the diagram are most important and an individual will suffer anxiety if they are not met. The first four levels are considered "basic needs". Once these needs are met, they "go away" or no longer cause anxiety.

The remaining needs are "growth needs". Once these needs are initially fulfilled, they do not "go away". In fact, the individual will strive to find new ways to satisfy these needs. These needs involve people fulfilling their potential: being the best they can be in as many areas as possible.

One of the key issues for managers is that once a need is satisfied, providing more of the same will not motivate a worker. So, in Taylor's factories, workers will have initially been motivated by the need for food, warmth, and shelter, but the failure of his factories to satisfy higher-level needs may explain why his methods often resulted in labour unrest.

Frederick Herzberg

Herzberg developed a two-factor theory of motivation based on **hygiene needs** and **motivational needs**. Hygiene needs are those factors that provide dissatisfaction at work if they are not attended to. At school you will probably be demotivated if the classrooms are not clean, or if the heating is not working properly. If these things are satisfactory, however, it is unlikely to lead to motivation. Hygiene factors are the things that are necessary for you to get started, but they do not drive you to succeed.

Motivators are the things that get you working because you get some intrinsic reward from them. For example, if you play in a football team,

---

[1] "Hierarchy of needs", developed 1943–54 and published in Maslow, A. (1954) *Motivation and Personality*, Harper & Row, New York

you will probably be motivated by the successes you have notched up and the recognition you get for playing as part of the team.

Herzberg's "hygiene needs" are:

- Company policy and administration
- Relationship with supervisor
- Work conditions
- Salary
- Company car
- Status
- Security
- Relationship with subordinates
- Personal life

Herzberg's research identified that true "motivators" were other completely different factors:

- Achievement
- Recognition
- The work itself
- Responsibility
- Advancement

He argued that people have a number of needs and arranged these in order of their importance.

McClelland's acquired needs theory (HL only)

David McClelland was an American psychologist who focused on human needs, and he theorized, based upon extensive academic research, that employees have three needs: achievement, affiliation, and power. These needs influence employees' motivation.

- **Achievement** motivates some employees. They want to work on tasks where their success is determined by their mastery and hard work.
- **Affiliation** – the creation and maintenance of social relationships – motivates other employees. These types of employees like being part of the group. For this reason, they often do not make the best managers as they worry too much about what others think of them.
- Finally, **power** motivates some employees. They want to encourage, influence, or teach others. Power-motivated employees tend to think in terms of winning and losing, and they want to win or to gain power.

McClelland did not say that each employee neatly fits into one of these three categories. On the contrary, all employees have some measure of each of these needs. The power-motivated employee still wants achievement and to be liked, or at least not disliked. The affiliation-motivated employee wants to feel loved and accepted, but they also want achievement and may well want some power, uncomfortable though that may make them feel at times. The achievement-motivated employee also wants to be liked, though gaining professional recognition for mastery is more important than whether the group likes them or whether they get power.

According to McClelland, when managers understand each employee's needs, the managers can better create a motivational approach for each employee.

Deci and Ryan's self-determination theory (HL only)

Deci and Ryan were two American psychologists who collaborated in their research with psychologists all over the world. In their self-determination theory, Deci and Ryan argued that two types of motivation exist: autonomous and controlled.

Autonomous motivation occurs when an individual has a full sense of volition and choice in what they are doing. **Controlled** motivation is when an individual is doing something in order to get a reward or avoid a punishment.

Deci and Ryan further argued that all humans have three sets of needs that relate to motivation:

- **Competence:** when individuals feel competent in a particular domain, they get a reward (self-satisfaction) for doing something well and develop the confidence to take on new challenges. Managers can help build a sense of competence by avoiding putting employees in situations where they are likely to fail. They should nurture competence by giving employees suitably more challenging tasks as the employees become more competent.

- **Relatedness:** individuals have the need to feel connected to others – both to care for and be cared for by others. When individuals feel connected to others in the workplace, this important psychological need is met. Managers can enhance feelings of relatedness by fostering a sense of team spirit, encouraging collaboration, and building a culture of mutual support.

- **Autonomy:** individuals do better when they feel that they have some sense of control over what they are doing. Whenever possible, managers should give employees control over what they do. Rarely can a business give employees complete autonomy, but managers can, when possible within organizational constraints, give employees choice on which assignments to take on and how to approach solutions.

Deci and Ryan argued that feeling connected to others in the workplace can increase motivation

When these three psychological needs are met, employees' sense of autonomous motivation will increase.

Intrinsic and extrinsic motivation do not necessarily conflict, according to Deci and Ryan. Sometimes employees internalize the extrinsic forms of motivation in a way that actually then bolsters their sense of autonomous motivation.

If employees are just doing things because of controlled motivation, their sense of purpose and their motivation will be less strong than if their motivation is autonomous. When the controlled motivations are properly set and align with the autonomous motivation that has developed, highly productive people will then internalize the extrinsic motivators and work more effectively towards the organization's aims.

Equity theory and expectancy theory (HL only)

The theorist John Adams developed a theory called the **equity theory** based upon the concepts of "inputs", "outputs", and "equity". His theory is that employees will be motivated when they perceive that a balance, or equity, exists between their inputs into the business and their outputs from it.

Inputs are those affective and cognitive qualities that an employee brings to a business or organization. Inputs include:

- Ability
- Adaptability
- Attitude
- Dedication
- Determination
- Effort
- Flexibility
- Hard work
- Knowledge
- Loyalty
- Personal sacrifice
- Skill
- Support from co-workers and colleagues
- Time
- Tolerance
- Trust in superiors

Outputs are what an employee receives from working at the organization. Outputs can be negative and thus in some sense subtract from the positive outcomes (though Adams did not believe that inputs and outputs could be quantified). Typically, outputs are positive and include:

- Fringe benefits
- Job security
- Praise
- Recognition
- Reputation
- Responsibility
- Reward
- Sense of achievement
- Stimuli
- Thanks

When employees believe that their outputs are greater than their inputs, they will be motivated. If, however, employees are giving more (inputs) to an organization than they receive (outputs), they will be demotivated. Employees want some degree of equity between what they give to the organization and what they receive. Motivation, according to this theory, is based upon a perception of fairness.

The sense of fairness is not restricted solely by the employee's relationship to the organization. Employees also compare their "ratio" of inputs to outputs and compare it to that of other employees. If employee A perceives that employee B has a more favourable input-to-output ratio, employee A will suffer a loss of motivation.

Closely related to equity theory is **expectancy theory**, developed by Victor Vroom. Expectancy theory holds that employees are motivated when they believe that their efforts will lead to good performance, for which they will be rewarded, and that the rewards will be worthwhile (ie the rewards are desirable).

Student workpoint 2.5

Be an inquirer

Nobody has ever come up with a motivational theory that seems to fit all people in all circumstances.

Ask 10 different people you know, from a variety of backgrounds and ages, what motivates them. Compare their responses.

Which of the motivational theories above seem to fit best with their responses?

Three key terms in expectancy theory are **expectancy** (will the effort lead to good performance?), **instrumentality** (will the performance produce the expected outcomes?), and **valence** (are the outcomes desirable to the employee?). When all three of these elements align, employees will be motivated.

Labour turnover (HL only)

Labour turnover refers to the movement of employees into and out of a business in a given time period (usually a year) and is an indicator of how stable a business is.

Labour turnover is usually measured by the following formula:

$$\text{labour turnover} = \frac{\text{number of staff leaving over a year}}{\text{average number of staff employed in a year}} \times 100$$

A high labour turnover rate suggests that the business has labour problems. For some reason or reasons, employees do not stay for a long period of time. By itself, high labour turnover suggests that workers are dissatisfied by some aspect of their employment situation. This source of dissatisfaction may also affect workers who remain at the business and may lead to lower productivity.

When a business has high labour turnover, it must frequently hire new labour, which can cause problems for the business. Recruitment and training can be expensive. New workers are often less productive than those who are established in the business.

High turnover can affect employees' motivation, as it leads to some interruption in work practices and routines. In addition, high turnover communicates to employees that the business has a problem with some aspect of employment there. Even if workers are otherwise satisfied in their jobs, high labour turnover may lead them to believe that they should be dissatisfied.

Businesses can anticipate certain circumstances when labour turnover will be higher than others. In a booming economy, employees tend to look for new opportunities since jobs are plentiful. In addition, younger employees tend to change jobs more often than middle-aged employees.

Finally, some labour turnover can be good for a business. A low turnover rate may indicate a stable business, but stability can lead to complacency and lack of progress. New employees tend to bring energy and new ideas, especially if they have just left college or have been retrained and/or reskilled. Sometimes, a business has employees who are less productive or who make minimal contributions to the business but otherwise provide no basis for separation (being fired or sacked). When a worker such as this leaves a business, managers may actually be happy.

The HR plan should be designed to make sure that the labour turnover rate is kept at an acceptable level, which will vary according to the industry and the skill and experience requirements for each position. A grocery store chain might expect fairly high labour turnover among its cashiers (even if it did not want it), but a law firm would not want to see high turnover among its experienced lawyers. Managers pay close attention to any significant changes in the labour turnover rate.

> **Key term**
>
> **Labour turnover**
>
> the percentage of employees who leave a company during a fixed period of time, typically one year. The percentage is calculated by the ratio of the number of an organization's employees who leave (whether because of attrition, dismissal or resignation) to the total number of employees during that period.

Grocery stores and supermarkets are likely to have a high labour turnover among their cashiers and staff on the store floor

2 Human resource management

Labour turnover can get higher quickly as a result of a significant change in circumstances either in or outside the business. By tracking the labour turnover rate, the business can try to correct internal factors or mitigate against external factors.

Methods of recruitment (HL only)

There are three parts to recruitment:

1. Identification
2. Application
3. Selection

The identification processes

Identification	The business realizes that it needs a new employee because of a change in its internal factors.
Job description	This gives details about the job, such as: • the job title • what the employee will have to do • the employee's responsibilities.
Person specification	This gives details about the type of person required to do the job, such as: • the skills required to do the job • the qualifications necessary • what experience is necessary.
Internal or external recruitment	The business has to weigh up the advantages of recruiting internally by promotion (or redeployment), such as it being: • cheaper • quicker • more efficient, as the person would know how the business works. It then has to weigh up the advantages against the disadvantages. For example, recruiting internally: • limits the pool of potential candidates • may cause resentment • causes the "domino" effect as the person promoted would leave a vacancy to be filled, and so on down the hierarchy. Searching externally would be the reverse of all of the above.

> **Concept**
> ### ETHICS
> Some organizations deliberately recruit employees from socio-demographic groups that are underrepresented in their workforce, in order to ensure more diversity. For some social enterprises, this can be a direct part of their mission, ethical objectives and CSR strategy.
>
> Find some examples of HR practices that relate to recruitment and diversity.

> **Key terms**
>
> **Internal recruitment**
> occurs when a position becomes available at an organization, and the organization recruits someone who is already working there to take on the new position
>
> **External recruitment**
> when an organization recruits employees who are not presently employees of the organization

The application processes

Application	The business has to decide how to find the best applicants for the job.
Job advert	The business will need to consider: • where to place the advert so it is seen by the right people • what should be included in the advert, so the applicants have sufficient information • the legal requirements that have to be met.
Application form or résumé (CV)	What is the most appropriate tool to process the applications? Every tool should include the same elements (eg personal details, skills and qualifications, work experience, interests and hobbies, and references). Application forms are: • standardized (so they are useful for jobs with lots of possible applicants) • designed specifically to match the job requirements • focused on the issues that the business wants • legally binding. However, a résumé (CV): • is better for jobs with limited applicants (such as senior posts) • is more personal and can reveal more about the applicant • can be more flexible • can be quicker for applicants to submit as it can be prepared beforehand.
Internal or external agency	The business has to weigh up the advantages of finding the best applicants internally using its HR department, such as it being: • cheaper • quicker • more efficient, as the HR department will know precisely what the business requires. It then has to weigh up the advantages against the disadvantages. For example, using its HR department: • limits the pool of potential candidates; agencies may have plenty more applicants in their databases • may cause a lack of focus in other areas • may not cater for specialist skills, in contrast with an agency that specializes in administrative vacancies, for example.

> **Student workpoint 2.6**
>
> *Be a thinker*
>
> A new restaurant is opening in your local town. It will sell expensive food cooked by a highly trained and well-known chef. The restaurant is advertising for waiters and waitresses. Draw up a job description of this role, including a detailed person specification.
>
> One you have finished, think about how you'd change the job description to suit a busy fast-food restaurant.

2 Human resource management

The selection processes

Selection	The final part of the process of recruitment is the selection of the best applicant for the job.
Shortlisting	The business will have to discard many applicants on the basis of: • their overall quality • how many are required for interview • any legal requirements that have to be taken into account.
Testing	Many businesses like to subject the shortlisted applicants to some form of test, to be used as a complement to the final interview. These tests can be: • aptitude (task-orientated activities, designed to test understanding and application of theories or concepts) • psychometric (personality questionnaires, designed to test reasoning skills and personality traits) • team-based (exercises designed to focus on the qualities necessary for working in project teams).
Interviews	The interview is the final part of the recruitment process and there is no one best style of interview. It will depend on circumstances but may include the following: • face to face (one to one) • panel (with more than one person) • video conference (or telephone) • multi-stage (one interview leads to another) • multi-day (conducted over a number of days).

Training

Training can help an employee's professional development. It can keep the employee up to date with the latest ideas and technologies. It may lead to the employee finding a new career path as a result of being reskilled. Training might even prevent the employee from losing a skill that they had learned previously (deskilling).

However, training is also important for a business. It can:

- improve the quality of the work
- lead to greater productivity
- motivate the employee
- reduce labour turnover.

In some countries, a full-time worker has the right to be allowed to take time off to train.

Training can take many forms, including the following:

- **Induction** – training that focuses on making a new employee familiar with the way the business functions and with lines of authority (who to report to, for example). A good induction programme helps to ensure

> **Key terms**
>
> **Induction**
> the introduction of new employees to an organization. The process aims to increase the likelihood that new employees can successfully do their new job.
>
> **On-the-job training**
> involves training employees at their place of employment during their normal working hours
>
> **Off-the-job training**
> involves employees receiving training not at their place of employment but offsite. The employee's company typically pays for the tuition, which is usually provided by outside parties.

that new employees settle in quickly so they can begin work straight away. The induction process includes welcoming new employees, making them feel accepted, and providing training about company procedures and expectations.

- **On-the-job** – when employees are trained while they are doing their normal job. Often on-the-job training occurs through mentoring, which is when an experienced employee guides the employee being trained. Another common type of on-the-job training is shadowing, when one employee follows ("shadows") another to learn a new skill.

- **Off-the-job** – when the employee is given time off from work to attend training away from the job. That training may be a workshop, conference, or course run by consultants, agencies, or educational institutions. Today, many managers choose to earn an MBA with the support of their employer. In light of the importance of education in contemporary post-industrial economies, many employers pay for courses at local universities, even if the coursework is not otherwise required of the employees. Businesses just want to see their employees gain a better education.

On-the-job training is often led by an experienced employee

Case study

Starbucks

Starbucks is an American coffee shop, or café, that began as one location in Seattle, Washington, USA, and has since grown into a worldwide chain. Starbucks does not franchise as it believes that the customer experience is centrally important to the success of the brand. Starbucks wants to keep quality control over that customer experience.

Starbucks places emphasis on employee training and uses a 70-20-10 model:

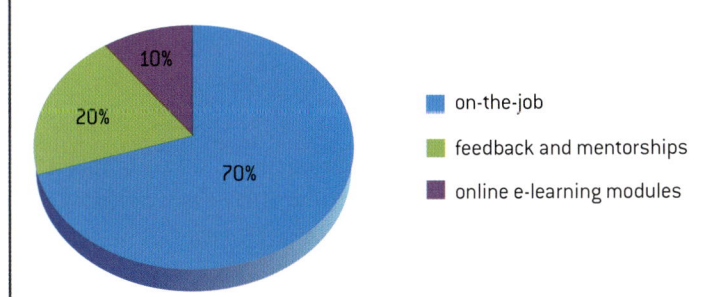

- on-the-job: 70%
- feedback and mentorships: 20%
- online e-learning modules: 10%

Figure 2.4.2 Training at Starbucks for baristas

Starbucks promotes internally, so it has training beyond the barista level. For example, it runs a "shift supervisor training program", "retail management training program" (for store assistant managers and managers), and "district manager training program".

Starbucks is well known for having a motivated workforce. One reason it has earned this reputation is for the training it offers.

Pie chart

A pie chart is a statistical graphic. A circle is divided into slices to illustrate numerical proportion.

This is illustrated in the case study here, in which the different methods of training at Starbucks are shown.

Appraisal (HL only)

Appraisal occurs when the performance of the employee is reviewed.

Appraisal is different from a more traditional form of employee review know as **inspection**. Under a system of inspection, managers review employees' performances and make judgments based on their observations. Communication tends to be one-way (the employee is not given the opportunity to respond) and top-down (from manager to employee).

Often, in a system of inspection, the process focuses on the negative indicators of performance – what the employee has failed to do, or the frequency with which the employee did not meet targets.

Under a system of **appraisal**, employees may respond to or even initiate discussion. Communication is two-way, and managers include constructive feedback in order to foster a positive and inclusive working environment. Appraisal is supposed to be a non-threatening, non-judgmental and supportive process.

For an employee, appraisal can:

- be motivating
- be instructive – employees can learn from past mistakes
- help employees progress along their career path
- lead to a change in career direction.

For the business, appraisal can:

- act as a check on performance
- help to review new initiatives
- be useful to record and document performance
- be motivating as it formally recognizes good performance.

Appraisal systems can be costly and time-consuming, especially when done well. Good appraisal systems tend to have certain characteristics:

- **They are not directly linked to pay or promotion.** Linking appraisal to pay or promotion can lead to mercenary behaviour, "backstabbing" (when people try to sabotage others' positions or performances in order to look better themselves), and a poisonous atmosphere.

- **Appraisal systems are separate from disciplinary systems.** Sometimes employees have to be punished for some failure to perform. Appraisal, on the other hand, is supposed to be positive. Linking appraisal to punishment destroys the whole essence of appraisal.

- **Good appraisal systems require minimal paperwork.** Having employees fill out numerous forms or having line managers excessively documenting their performance is time-consuming. In addition, it puts the focus of the process on discrete accomplishments, many of which may be nominal but nonetheless easily recordable, rather than on more substantive issues.

- **Appraisals provide an honest exchange of views.** Appraisal has to be transparent. Everyone involved should know their role and the role of those around them. Though appraisal should be positive overall,

---

Key terms

Formative appraisal occurs during the training or work of employees. It is ongoing, continuous, and intended to improve employees' performance.

Summative appraisal occurs at the end of the training or at a fixed time during a year. Summative appraisals are the formal, documented evaluation of employees. They attempts to measure employees' performances.

360-degree feedback occurs when an employee receives input from all categories of people (peers, customers, their supervisor, among others) with whom the employee interacts. Because 360-degree feedback is comprehensive and expensive, usually only senior members of an organization receive it.

Self-appraisal occurs when an employee evaluates their own performance. It can be part of formative or summative evaluation.

conversations should be honest, with appropriate discussions about areas of strength and areas that need improvement.

Appraisal systems may include these methods of assessment:

- **Formative** – because appraisal is intended to be a learning process, often it is a continuous approach to evaluate performance during an employee's time at work. Appraisal is typically run on a one- to three-year cycle. The focus is on giving employees feedback when they have done well and also on areas in which they have had difficulties. The idea is to help employees improve. This type of appraisal presumably "forms" the employee, ie it influences their development.

- **Summative** – this measures an employee's performance according to set standards. A summative assessment has an element of making a judgment about whether the employee passed or failed. Summative assessment tests employees' knowledge and skills against clear and explicit markers and then "sums up" (hence it is summative) how an employee has performed against the standards. Summative appraisal is usually conducted at the end of a project, a contract, or a specific goal. Failure should not necessarily lead to termination.

- **360 degree** – this method provides each employee with the opportunity to receive performance appraisal not only from their line manager, but also from between four to eight co-workers, subordinates and even customers or clients. This method involves an element of upward appraisal and is the most complex, having multiple perspectives. The 360-degree appraisal is often used with CEOs and other executives who serve and interact directly with several groups of stakeholders (see Figure 2.4.3).

- **Self-appraisal** – with this method of appraisal, individual employees reflect on their own performance. Usually, this reflection is done with the help of a self-appraisal form on which employees rate themselves on various performance indicators. Typically, employees can also suggest their training needs, and discuss their accomplishments, strengths, weaknesses, and any potential problems faced during the relevant time period.

Motivation in practice

Many organizations devise complex payment systems in an effort to reward and motivate their employees. Unfortunately, no perfect payment system exists. This section identifies some of the major issues of the main financial rewards that need to be considered.

Salary

Employees are paid a sum of money per month.

Motivation factors: the main motivator is likely to be the security of receiving a regular income.

Disadvantages: the employer is typically relying on the professionalism of the staff to provide the quality and quantity expected.

> **Student workpoint 2.7**
>
> ### Be reflective
> "Appraisal" sounds like a neutral term, but to employees the appraisal process can be scary and even threatening. In some parts of the world, people are protected in their jobs and a poor appraisal will not lead to "termination" (getting fired). In other parts of world, a bad appraisal can mean someone loses their job. Everywhere in the world, though, an appraisal means that an employee's performance is being judged.
>
> If you were six months into a new job that you really liked, would you welcome an appraisal? Why or why not? Do you think your views on the appraisal system would change depending on whether your supervisor said you were doing a good or bad job?

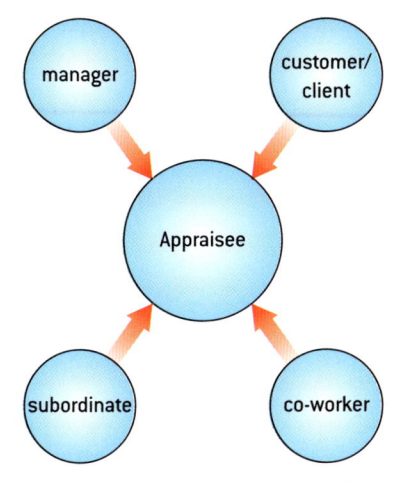

Figure 2.4.3 360-degree appraisal

Human resource management

> **Key terms**
>
> **Financial rewards**
>
> rewards that an employer gives to employees, typically as part of an extrinsic motivation scheme, that have a specific monetary value (pay rise, bonus, commission, employee ownership scheme, etc)
>
> **Salary**
>
> a fixed, regular compensation paid to employees on a periodic basis, usually bi-weekly or monthly. Salaries are typically expressed on an annual basis ("He makes $52,000 a year") and are typically paid to white-collar workers.
>
> **Wages (time and piece rates)**
>
> the monetary compensation paid by employers to workers either on a time basis (eg $22 per hour) or on a piece basis (eg $8 for every item completed). Blue-collar workers typically receive wages rather than a salary.
>
> **Commission**
>
> payment to an employee when they complete a sale. The commission amount is usually a percentage of the sale value.

Wages (time rates)

Employees are paid an hourly rate, or paid for a number of hours per week. It is possible that overtime rates of pay are used too.

Motivation factors: the main motivator is likely to be the security of receiving a regular income and the opportunity to receive overtime pay.

Disadvantages: it is possible that employees will work slowly since their pay is not based on output. If overtime rates apply then employees could benefit financially from ensuring that they extend their work to cover time beyond the usual hours of the working day.

Wages (piece rates)

Employees are paid for each unit (or batch) produced.

Motivation factors: the main motivator is likely to be the fact that increased output will bring a measurable benefit.

Disadvantages: this might involve tedious and repetitive work, and employees may not have control over their results if they rely on others (for example to supply materials).

Employees may work quickly to get as much money as possible. It may be that a system of checks will have to be put in place to ensure that quality standards have been met. There may be an emphasis on quantity rather than quality.

Commission

Employees are paid by results, for example, a flat fee or a percentage for each item sold.

Motivation factors: the main motivator is likely to be the fact that employees will be rewarded by results.

Disadvantages: employees may not have control over results (and thus income). For example, during a recession, sales commission will fall in many industries.

Employees may be tempted to sell products that are not in the best interests of the customer or business and this could create problems for the organization. For example, a bank employee who sells a mortgage to a customer will receive the commission, but the bank may suffer financially if the customer subsequently defaults on the loan.

Profit-related pay

The amount an employee receives is linked to the amount of profit the business makes.

Motivation factors: sharing the financial rewards of a business may encourage a sense of belonging and a desire to contribute to its success.

Disadvantages: productivity may be a consequence of the profitability of the business rather than the cause. If profits fall then employees could experience a demoralizing loss through no fault of their own.

Performance-related pay (PRP)

PRP is usually a bonus paid in addition to the employee's ordinary compensation.

Motivation factors: PRP is ordinarily used with those employees whose productivity or output cannot be measured precisely. However, the pay is based upon pre-established performance targets.

Ordinarily, in a PRP system, employees receive a salary and are expected to reach certain targets. Employees exceeding the targets are then paid an additional amount. The assumption is that employees will be motivated by the opportunity to make extra money by performing better than the targets.

Disadvantages: as long as the tasks are repetitive and involve physical skills, PRP can enhance performance. However, when cognitive tasks are involved, PRP may actually reduce productivity. In addition, PRP can cause divisions in a business if the evaluation of employees' performance is based on subjective factors.

Employee share-ownership schemes

These come in two forms. The first is as some type of bonus where the payment is shares in the business rather than cash. The second is some type of employee savings plan where employees are allowed to purchase shares through a payroll deduction (typically a fixed amount per pay period) without having to pay brokerage fees.

Some employers will also offer a "match" programme (for example, for every $1 the employee invests in shares the company will give (or "match") the employee's contribution with $0.50).

Motivation factors: when offered as a bonus, employee share schemes can motivate in the same ways that other types of bonuses do. Even when an employee share-ownership scheme is simply a savings plan, a benefit is that employees become partial owners of the business, which is thought to provide an incentive for employees to work harder (as they now have a "stake" in the business).

Disadvantages: when offered as a bonus, the basis for awarding the bonus must be clear and, ideally, measurable to avoid accusations of "favouritism" in granting them. Also, if employees have all their savings in a company match plan, both their salaries and their savings are tied to the viability of the business.

Fringe payments (perks)

Fringe payments, or perks, are the many types of extras that businesses offer to their employees. They can include medical insurance, a car, and private pension plans, among other forms of payment. They often include perks related to the nature of the business (for example, a hotel chain may offer discounted rates at its hotels to employees).

> **Key terms**
>
> **Performance-related pay**
>
> compensation that is based upon performance of an individual, a unit, or even an entire company. In performance-related pay schemes, management establishes measurable goals. When an individual, a unit, or the company exceeds the goals, employees receive compensation in addition to their regular wages or salary.
>
> **Employee share-ownership schemes**
>
> award employees shares in the company, permit employees to purchase shares in the company at a below-market price, or match employees' purchases of shares (eg for every share that employees purchase, the company buys 0.5 shares for them)
>
> **Fringe payments**
>
> forms of compensation that an employee receives other than their salary, such as life insurance coverage or use of a company car

Gym membership is one type of fringe payment

2 Human resource management

Motivation factors: employees like fringe benefits as they often have substantial value. While employees may have to declare some fringe benefits for tax purposes, many do not have to be declared. This provides the employee with an additional benefit: the business paying for fringe benefits on a pre-tax basis is much cheaper than employees paying for these items with after-tax salary. Thus, the business is able to give more value to employees than if it paid them the equivalent amount in additional salary.

Disadvantages: if fringe benefits are not given equally to all employees or on a clear, fair basis, division among the staff can result. In addition, employees can come to expect certain fringe benefits and may become angry if some perks are taken away.

> **Concept**
>
> **CHANGE**
>
> Organizations sometimes have to change how they motivate their workers, for example with increases in salary or wages, or through new opportunities for job enlargement and teamwork.
>
> What factors may lead to those changes in financial and non-financial rewards? You may want to distinguish between internal factors and external factors.

Case study

Salaries of hospitality workers in Slovenia

Hospitality industry	Salary (€ per month)
Hotel receptionist	850
Cleaner (hotel, restaurant)	700
Cook/chef	1,200
Waiter	900
Restaurant/hotel manager	1,900

Based upon categories of workers (not actual numbers of workers), the **mean income** of people in the hospitality industry in Ljubljana is €1,110, which is calculated as follows:

$$\frac{(850 + 700 + 1{,}200 + 900 + 1{,}900)}{5} = 1{,}110$$

However, the pay of restaurant/hotel managers is substantially greater than that of the other categories of hospitality workers. This inclusion of restaurant/hotel managers' pay skews the data.

Perhaps a better way to consider the pay of hospitality workers in Ljubljana is to consider the **median**, which requires we reorder the data from lowest pay to highest pay and then find the midpoint. The median pay of hospitality workers by category is €900:

Hospitality industry	Salary (€ per month)
Cleaner (hotel, restaurant)	700
Hotel receptionist	850
Waiter	**900**
Cook/chef	1,200
Restaurant/hotel manager	1,900

Though we do not know exactly how many workers fall into each category, we can be confident that restaurants and hotels have fewer managers and chefs than cleaners, receptionists, and waiters. Thus, the median figure of €900 probably better represents "typical" earnings of a hospitality worker in Ljubljana than the mean of €1,110 does.

> **Descriptive statistics**
>
> Descriptive statistics describe or summarize characteristics of a set of data. The two most basic aims of descriptive statistics are to measure the central tendency of a set of data, and to characterize the dispersion of data within the set. This dispersion is also referred to as variability.
>
> Consider the case study here about hospitality workers in Ljubljana, Slovenia.

2.4 Motivation and demotivation

Examples of non-financial rewards

Job enrichment

Job enrichment makes an employee's job "richer" (more meaningful and rewarding) by allowing employees to use the full range of their abilities. It typically involves supervising employees less and making their responsibilities more challenging. Often enrichment will mean that an employee does the entirety of a production process in order to have a greater sense of ownership and responsibility in what they produce.

Motivation factors: employees typically prefer to have responsibilities that are challenging. Employees who are more satisfied are typically more motivated to work hard.

Disadvantages: job enrichment cannot be applied in all situations, either because of the type of work involved or because of the calibre of the workers.

Job rotation

Job rotation involves rotating an employee through different divisions in a business over a period of time. It is often used with young employees as a form of training, but can be used at many different stages of a career.

Motivation factors: job rotation benefits companies as it gives them employees who have a better sense of the business as a whole. For employees, rotation provides additional training and the acquisition of new skills and knowledge, which can lead to new opportunities with the business (or with other organizations).

Disadvantages: job rotation means employees go through periodic productivity dips as they begin in a new division and must go through a training phase before they fully understand the new position.

Job enlargement

Job enlargement may include job rotation or job enrichment. It may involve giving employees more tasks to do, sometimes because of a shortage of staff.

Motivation factors: in general, employees prefer some variation in the tasks they must do.

Disadvantages: if job enlargement is nothing more than giving employees additional duties, it may increase employee dissatisfaction.

Empowerment

Empowerment involves giving individuals access to resources and information to do their jobs and giving them the power to make decisions. In an employment context, empowerment means giving employees considerable control over how their jobs should be done.

Motivation factors: empowered employees generally believe that they can be instrumental in changing things and find this rewarding.

Key terms

Non-financial rewards

rewards that an employer gives to employees, typically as part of an extrinsic motivation scheme, that do not have precise monetary value but which employees nonetheless value, such as a better job title or some type of recognition ("employee of the month")

Job enrichment

when an employee is given additional tasks that are challenging and usually done by managers. These extra tasks lead to professional growth and improve motivation.

Job rotation

occurs when employees rotate positions in an organization

Job enlargement

occurs when additional tasks associated with a job are added to the job description. Differs from job enrichment in that the additional tasks do not generally require additional skill or are more difficult.

Assessment advice ✓

Though they sound similar, job enrichment and job enlargement are not the same thing. With job enrichment, an employee is given additional tasks of greater complexity and challenge. With job enlargement, an employee is given additional duties that do not require additional skill.

Disadvantages: businesses run some risk that the empowered employees will not be able to manage the responsibility they have been given. Employees may make decisions that are not fully productive or that cost the business unnecessarily.

Purpose or opportunity to make a difference

Purpose or the opportunity to make a difference in the world refers to the ability of businesses or other organizations to connect employees to the aims of the organization other than profit. Non-profit organizations have this advantage, as they typically exist to meet some social or environmental need. Many for-profit businesses today, however, have also adopted other-than-profit aims into their objectives.

Motivation factors: many individuals want to do more than merely make money. They want to know that they are making a difference in the world and are connected to purposes larger than themselves or their organization. People tend to find these purposes intrinsically motivating.

Disadvantages: if for-profit organizations overemphasize social or environmental aims, employees may lose focus on the profit-making objectives.

Teamwork

Teamwork involves working cooperatively with a group of people to achieve a goal.

Motivation factors: the success of teams can be crucial to an organization's performance, so an organization will strive to have high-performance teams. Individuals tend to be energized by working in teams, which creates a sense of group cohesion and common purpose.

Disadvantages: when successful, teamwork can have great yields for organizations. However, team failures can amplify dissatisfaction and, thus, weaken employees' productivity.

All of the above financial and non-financial rewards have differing degrees of effectiveness in different countries and cultures. In general, in developing countries, many people are unaccustomed to making significant incomes. For many, work tends to be a contemporary version of traditional industrial production: a series of simple, uninteresting tasks. In addition, many traditional forms of social cohesion (family, village, labour association, etc) remain strong. In these contexts, financial rewards tend to be important. Wages based upon piece rates can be especially motivating.

In developed countries, circumstances have changed significantly since the 1970s. Individuals are accustomed to (and in many developed countries virtually guaranteed) high standards of living. Economies have largely shifted to the tertiary and quaternary sectors, where work tasks tend to be more complex and require cognitive processes. Finally, traditional forms of social cohesion have weakened. In these contexts, people are increasingly interested in non-financial rewards. Personally satisfying work, teamwork and making a difference in the world are of considerable importance to workers.

> **Assessment advice** ✓
>
> Remember that salaries are typically paid to white-collar workers, and wages (either time or piece rates) are paid to blue-collar workers.

However, remember that generalizations such as these can be misleading. In all economies, some people are mostly interested in making money, while others are mostly interested in non-financial objectives.

Revision checklist

- ✓ Many theorists have offered explanations about what motivates individuals. Early theorists included:
  - ✓ Frederick Winslow Taylor, who believed that the standardization of working practices and enforced adoption of the most efficient ways of working were the key to ensuring maximum output.
  - ✓ Abraham Maslow, who argued that human needs can be categorized into levels of importance. The more needs an employer can satisfy, the more motivated a worker will be.
  - ✓ Frederick Herzberg, who distinguished between "hygiene needs" and "motivational needs". Motivational needs are the ones which truly motivate workers.
- ✓ As the business landscape changed and modern industrial society in the West matured, new theorists offered new insights into human motivation. Some of these theorists include:
  - ✓ David McClelland, whose acquired needs theory states that people are motivated by achievement, affiliation or power. What motivates them has considerable bearing on the types of organizations they work in and the types of roles they do. **(HL only)**
  - ✓ Edward Deci and Richard Ryan, whose self-determination theory maintains that individuals' autonomous motivation increases when their needs for autonomy, competence, and relatedness are met. **(HL only)**
  - ✓ John S. Adams, whose equity theory maintains that individuals are motivated when they feel they are being treated fairly: that what they get out of the work arrangement (outputs) is worth what they had to put into it (inputs), and that they are treated comparably to other employees. **(HL only)**
- ✓ Labour turnover is the movement of employees into and out of a business in a given time period (usually a year). It is an indicator of how stable a business is. **(HL only)**
- ✓ Businesses evaluate employees using formative and summative assessment, 360-degree feedback, and self-appraisal. **(HL only)**
- ✓ Businesses can recruit employees internally and externally, and there are merits to both approaches. **(HL only)**
- ✓ Financial rewards include salary, time and piece rate wages, commission, profit-related pay, performance-related pay, share-ownership schemes, and fringe payments.
- ✓ Non-financial rewards include job enrichment, job rotation, job enlargement, empowerment, purpose, and teamwork.
- ✓ Many businesses offer training for employees, and training can come in many forms.

> **TOK discussion**
> 1. When we refer to "motivation theory", is the word "theory" the same as in mathematics?
> 2. Can we ever really know what motivates (or demotivates) an employee?
> 3. Can financial rewards always be measured and quantified, and thus are they more precise and meaningful than non-financial rewards?

2 Human resource management

Practice question

To answer the questions below effectively, see Unit 6 pages 398–402.

Fish Packaging Ltd

The firm *Fish Packaging Ltd* owns a fish packaging plant in Reykjavik, Iceland, and sells frozen fish to the domestic market. Workers in the plant are paid €10 per hour to pack fish into boxes.

Workers are expected to pack approximately 13 kg per hour. When local fishing boats do not go out fishing, workers have nothing to pack. When this happens, the workers stay at home and are still paid €4 per hour.

The workers are concerned about several issues, including:

- poor weather has led to the local boats fishing less, so workers are staying home more often
- an autocratic leadership style
- a lack of involvement in day-to-day decision-making
- a shortage of protective clothing
- insufficient rest breaks during the working day.

Management complains that workers seldom exceed the target of 13 kg per hour and are also concerned about the possible imposition of fishing quotas by governments. Furthermore, the fish packaging industry has been badly hit by the competition from Russian factory ships. Management feels it has to make some changes and is considering the introduction of a piece rate payment system.

a) State **two** features of a time rate payment system. [2 marks]

b) Explain **one** disadvantage and **one** advantage to the workers of a piece rate payment system at *Fish Packaging Ltd*. [4 marks]

c) Explain **two** external factors that could influence *Fish Packaging Ltd*. [4 marks]

d) Using an appropriate motivation theory, evaluate possible changes that *Fish Packaging Ltd* management could introduce to improve the motivation of the workforce. [10 marks]

Source: Adapted from IB examination paper, May 2008

2.5 Organizational (corporate) culture (HL only)

By the end of this chapter, you should be able to:
- Define **organizational culture**
- Explain several **different types** of organizational culture
- Discuss the nature of **cultural clashes**, including why they occur

Key terms

Culture

the achievements, arts, attitudes, customs, norms, social institutions, and values of a particular nation, people, or other social group. Organizations can have their own culture, which in business is referred to as corporate culture.

Organizational culture

similar to corporate culture. It is the achievements, arts, attitudes, customs, norms, social institutions, and values of a particular organization. An organization's culture will often reflect some of the cultural practices of its host country, although two organizations within the same country could also have different cultures.

Organizational culture (HL only)

The term organizational culture (or "corporate culture") refers to the attitudes, experiences, beliefs, and values of an organization. These are generally considered to make up the elements of corporate culture. The ways that individuals in an organization dress or treat each other and those outside the organization often reflect the culture of the organization.

If an individual joins an organization and does not share its values and beliefs, it is highly likely that person will not stay there long. This situation is described as a culture clash.

Managers may try to influence the culture of an organization. Doing so, however, is difficult, especially at established and old institutions with low staff turnover (institutions with a strong corporate culture). Nonetheless, setting the values and the way things get done is a role of managers. New managers will spell out their beliefs and values to staff, and expect staff to behave in a manner that reflects the beliefs that managers have set.

Different cultural norms will exist in different departments of an organization. The factors that influence these will be the head of department, the members of the team, the senior managers, the culture of the country in which the organization is operating in, and the culture of the nationality of the department members.

Types of organizational culture (HL only)

Charles Handy

The management scholar and theorist Charles Handy introduced a highly memorable way of viewing organizational culture when he described four distinct organizational cultures: power culture, role culture, task culture, and person culture. In his book *Gods of Management: The Changing Work of Organizations*, Handy chose four Greek gods, each of which reflected the constellation of values corresponding to the four types of organizational culture.

2 Human resource management

Power culture   Role culture   Task culture   Person culture

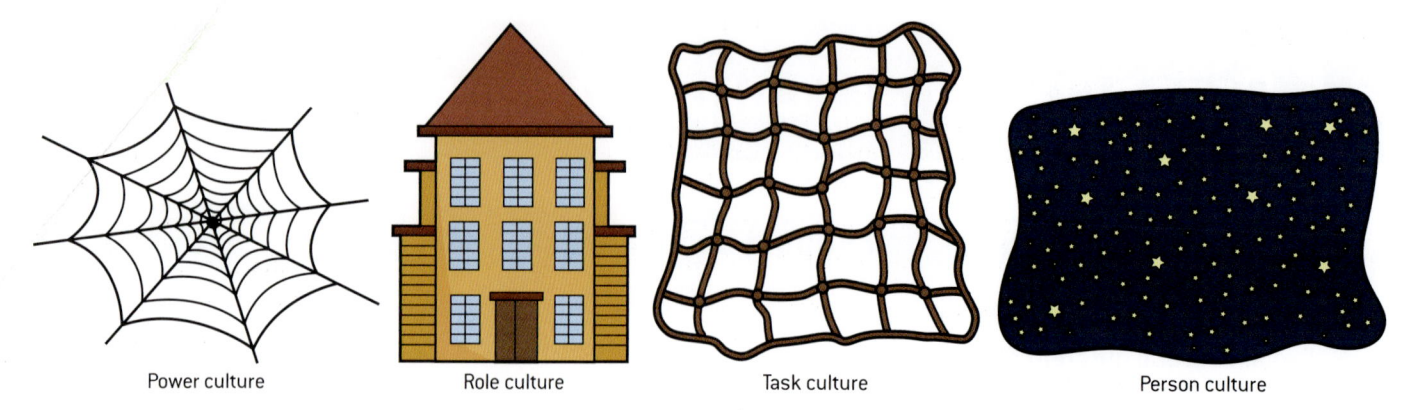

Figure 2.5.1 Handy's organizational culture

> **Key terms**
>
> **Power culture**
> exists when a few individuals retain the essential power in an organization. Power cultures have few rules and procedures, and decision-making tends to be swift.
>
> **Role culture**
> refers to organizations where employees have clearly defined roles and operate in a highly controlled and precise organizational structure. Organizations with a role culture are usually hierarchical bureaucracies.

Power culture

A power culture exists when a few individuals retain the essential power. Control comes from these individuals and spreads out across the organization. This type of culture corresponds to the Greek god Zeus, who ruled as king of the gods on Mount Olympus.

Power cultures have few rules and procedures. People are usually judged by their results rather than how those results are achieved, since ends are more important than means. Swift decision-making can result, but the decisions may not be in the long-term interests of the organization.

The collapses of the US energy-trading giant Enron and the family-owned merchant bank Barings Bank are attributed to dominant power cultures. Family businesses and merchant banks often have power cultures.

Handy represented a power culture as a spider's web. The power comes from the spider; a web with no spider has no strength. The spider can reward or punish. In a power culture, individuals who do not fit in are unlikely to work there for long.

Role culture

In a role culture, employees have clearly defined roles and operate in a highly controlled and precise organizational structure. These organizations are usually tall hierarchical bureaucracies with a long chain of command. Power stems from a person's position. Position and a "rule book" (corporate procedures) play dominant roles in decision-making, which is often slow and detailed. This type of culture corresponds to the Greek god Apollo, who represented a harmonious combination of bodily, moral and spiritual virtues.

In role cultures, people avoid taking risks. Civil services, military organizations, and nationalized industries often have role cultures.

Handy uses the symbol of a temple or building to describe a role culture. Temples or buildings are old and exist in stable environments. The oldest buildings in a town traditionally house organizations with role cultures, such as government offices and the main post office.

2.5 Organizational (corporate) culture (HL only)

Task culture

The task culture describes a situation in which short-term teams address specific problems. Power within a task culture shifts from person to person, since different people with different skills can lead the team at different times. The task culture often features the crossing lines of a matrix structure. This type of culture corresponds to the Greek god Athena, who represented wisdom, war, and crafts. She was the god who got things done.

Many people like the idea of a task culture because they like to work in a rapidly changing environment. A strong team spirit with a great deal of emotional energy can emerge. However, divisive decisions can seriously damage the team. This passion for a team can be highly constructive, but the reverse can also be true.

A task culture is often found in management consultancies, where a team enters an organization to work on projects. Once a project is completed, the team will break up and a new team will form for another project. In schools, drama departments may resemble a task culture. One team produces a major theatrical production and then a new team emerges for the next one.

Handy used the image of a net to describe the task culture. The strength of a net is its different strands.

Person culture

A person culture exists where individuals believe themselves to be superior to the organization and just want to do their own thing. These organizations are where employees simply go to work; they see themselves as separate from the organization (as "free spirits"). Some professional partnerships, such as architecture firms and some university departments, can be predominantly person cultures. There, each specialist brings a particular expertise to the organization. This type of culture corresponds to the Greek god Dionysus (known as Bacchus to the ancient Romans), who was the god of wine and viticulture, fertility, religious ecstasy, and other human passions.

Handy represents the person culture as a constellation of stars. Each star (or person) is unique and different, and individuals operate on their own. Person cultures are difficult to manage. Individuals preferring this culture will often find working in organizations difficult because the constraints they impose on these individuals seem unbearable.

Edgar Schein

Edgar Schein described three levels of organizational culture.

Organizational attributes

You sense organizational attributes when you walk into an organization. When entering a government building in a communist country, stern signs or warnings are everywhere. Often visible is a picture or statue of a dominant leader. People may speak in hushed tones and dress in a conformist fashion. Outsiders are viewed with suspicion. What is seen, heard, and felt reflects the culture.

Key terms

Task culture

refers to an organizational culture focused on specific problems. In this context, power shifts from person to person as different people are suited to different tasks or issues.

Person culture

exists where individuals believe themselves to be superior to the organization. Some professional partnerships, such as architecture firms and some university departments, can be predominantly person cultures.

Culture clash

when two different cultures come into conflict. In a business setting, a culture clash occurs when one organization has to work with another organization, often because of a merger or acquisition, and the two organizations have very different cultures.

Student workpoint 2.8

Be a thinker

For each of the following, suggest one type of business organization that would suit it.

a) A power culture
b) A role culture
c) A task culture
d) A person culture

Professed culture

Some organizations "profess" their culture with slogans, statements, or images that project a certain image. These slogans, statements, or images give clues to how the organization operates. Websites of most large organizations give clear statements of what the business professes to believe or value. These sites contain statements about commitment to employees, customers, charities, and other stakeholders. These are what Schein classified as elements of professed culture.

Organizational assumptions

People who have been with an organization for a long time will often talk about "how things really get done" as opposed to the "official" channels. These people are referring to the organizational assumptions. This aspect of the organization is the most difficult to understand.

People are often afraid to talk about organizational assumptions or are not really able to articulate them. The people who understand organizational assumptions best are those who have been there the longest. They know how things really get done – even if the "official" organizational structure and literature state otherwise.

This insight helps Schein to explain the difficulty that people new to an organization often have. The best way to understand organizational assumptions is to work closely with someone who has been with the organization for some time. (Although even if that person knows how things "really work", the truth may be unmentionable.) The existence of organizational assumptions helps explain why some managers new to an organization may find it difficult to initiate change.

Case study

Corporate culture and Godrej Consumer Products

Godrej Consumer Products (GCP) was founded in 2001 and is a subsidiary of Godrej Group, an Indian conglomerate that began making locks in 1897 and has since expanded into numerous industries. GCP is noted for its dynamic and uplifting corporate culture which is based on two ideas: always demanding excellence of employees, and always giving them as mush support and flexibility as possible.

According to Prachi Kulkarni, HR General Manager at GCP, "What gets noticed here is the quality of your work, not the number of hours you put in. There's flexibility, a very open and approachable leadership team, as well as an environment that keeps challenging you."

Vivek Gambhir, Managing Director of GCP, says that his organization is a great place to work and an inspiring one. GCP recruits high-quality talent. The work environment is energizing, and GCP develops employees by stretching them beyond what they thought they could do, and by rewarding strong performance.

GCP works hard to create a work environment with the kind of culture and values that are uplifting to its employees. So, despite being a demanding organization that expects excellence out of everyone, GCP has low labour turnover. People want to work there.

2.5 Organizational (corporate) culture (HL only)

Cultural clashes (HL only)

Reasons for culture clashes

When individuals enter an organization or when two or more organizations merge together, "culture clashes" can occur. Reasons for these clashes include the following:

- **Different comfort levels with diversity** – some organizations are used to diversity; others are ethnocentric.
- **Different degrees of formality** – some organizations are highly formal whereas others are informal.
- **Different languages** – organizations typically have a language that is the norm. Individuals who do not speak the language well often experience difficulties. Misunderstanding can also occur if differences exist in modes of non-verbal communication.
- **Different leadership styles** – when two organizations merge, individuals can experience changes in leadership styles. For example, if an organization with an authoritarian leadership style acquires a company accustomed to democratic leadership, both leaders and employees will find the situation difficult.
- **Different orientations to tasks and to people** – some organizations are task-orientated, and others are relationship-orientated.
- **Different practices** – all organizations, even those from the same country, have some differences in practices compared to other organizations. These differences can be greater when organizations are from different countries or cultures.
- **Different senses of time** – in some cultures, time is fixed: exact appointment times and schedules are taken very seriously. Other cultures have a more fluid sense of time.

A bank is likely to have a very different culture than a small creative start-up

Consequences of culture clashes

Businesses combine for different reasons. In a merger, the owners and management of the two firms anticipate achieving benefits (such as economies of scale or increased market share) from combining the resources of the organizations. In an acquisition or takeover, the acquiring organization has similar goals. However, sometimes when businesses combine, culture clashes occur for the reasons noted above. The overarching consequence of a culture clash when two or more companies combine is that the new organization does not achieve the expected benefits.

The consequences of a culture clash can be significant. Leaders of the business should develop a strategic plan for managing the merger, including harmonization of the two cultures. Similarly, when a change in leadership occurs at an organization, managers need to anticipate that employees may struggle with the new leadership style.

The most severe consequences of a failure to harmonize cultures or prepare for new leadership can include the failure of the business. However, the signs of such a serious consequence may take several years to reveal themselves – typically when final accounts are prepared after the first several years of the new, larger organization. Evidence of problems as significant as potential failure may take a long time to appear, so managers must be acutely sensitive to the early indicators of a culture clash. Those early indicators include:

- **Lack of focus** – employees may not understand the values and aims of the new organization or the new leader and, thus, are not focused on organizational aims.
- **Preoccupation with the merger** – employees focus their attention and energy on the fact of the merger or the fact of a new leader, rather than on their own jobs. Productivity and job performance suffer.
- **Sense of division** – employees focus on their differences rather than on their common purpose and their many similarities. Or, in the case of a new leader and new leadership styles, some employees may think that they have fallen out of favour.
- **Sense of isolation** – while managers focus on the strategy of the new organization, employees feel isolated and ignorant of what is happening.
- **Unresponsive management** – employees feel that managers are not concerned for their well-being.

If these early indicators go unaddressed, the organization can then experience more serious problems, including the following:

- **Lower productivity** – workers in the new organization do not produce the expected efficiencies but actually find working in the new organization more difficult because they are unfamiliar with norms and procedures.
- **Higher labour turnover** – dissatisfied with the new organization and fearful that they may not have a place in it, many employees may seek new jobs. Increased labour turnover is especially troublesome when a primary purpose of the merger is to form greater human capital.
- **Various types of conflict in the workplace** – when differences between cultures occur, conflict is likely to increase. The stress of a merger can bring out the worst in people.
- **Decreased profitability** – if workers are less productive, labour turnover increases, and conflict in the workplace increases, the business will have to devote important resources to these problems, which is likely to reduce profits.
- **Bankruptcy or failure** – if the problems from a merger are severe enough and profitability falls too much, the organization runs the risk of bankruptcy or failure.

Organizational culture and individuals (HL only)

Individuals influence organizational culture, and organizational culture influences individuals.

Culture is a very tricky issue to address in organizations, as it is simultaneously everything and, paradoxically, nothing. Culture is everything because it is the sum of values, attitudes, beliefs, practices, and norms of an organization. It is the sum total of the organization, and so it can influence everything that happens in a business.

2.5 Organizational (corporate) culture (HL only)

Even though businesses with high-performing cultures typically attract high-performing individuals, such businesses usually also *transform* people into high-performing individuals. New employees can "feel" the energy of the organization and intuitively sense the hierarchy of values in the business. Employees will then strive to fit in by shaping their values, attitudes, beliefs, practices, and norms to the organization. Most respected business leaders know the power of organizational culture over individuals, and they deliberately make issues of culture a high priority.

On the other hand, although individuals often remark that they can "feel" the culture of an organization, in a literal sense they cannot. Culture cannot be seen, heard, tasted, smelt, or touched. Culture derives from values, attitudes, beliefs, practices, and norms of individual employees and groups of employees. When someone asserts "We need to change the culture of our organization", they actually mean that values, attitudes, beliefs, practices, and norms must change. In other words, what changes is not "culture", but rather what individuals think, value, and do.

From this perspective, individuals can influence organizational culture significantly. For example, imagine that an individual joins an organization where the practices of employees include long, unauthorized breaks and spending too much time sending personal emails. If the new employee decides not to follow these practices and only takes authorized breaks and sends only the occasional personal email, that person is starting to influence the culture of the organization.

In this scenario, it is possible that fellow employees will grumble that they will be made to look bad. They may be hostile to the new employee for violating unofficial company practice. Possibly fellow employees will think the person is odd and not care; they are not going to change their behaviours regardless of what any new employee does. Possibly, however, the new person will inspire others. For example, other employees may start to feel guilty about taking long breaks and sending numerous emails, but they may lack the courage to break with the culture of the organization.

TOK discussion

1. If culture cannot be heard, seen, smelt, tasted, or touched, is it appropriate to speak about "culture" at all in a business context?
2. Who has the best perspective to describe the culture of an organization? The managers or the workers?
3. As an external person, is it possible to really know about the culture of an organization, or can only internal stakeholders access that knowledge?

Revision checklist

- ✓ Organizational culture is the attitudes, beliefs and values of an organization.
- ✓ A power culture exists when a few individuals retain most of the power.
- ✓ In a role culture, each employee has a clearly defined role and operates within a highly controlled structure.
- ✓ In a task culture, teams address specific problems within a defined timeframe.
- ✓ A person culture exists where individuals believe that they are superior to the organization and just do their own thing.
- ✓ Reasons for culture clashes include different degrees of formality, different leadership styles, different languages, and different senses of time and urgency.

2 Human resource management

Practice question

To answer the question below effectively, see Unit 6 pages 398–402.

Fourth Wave Econometrics Inc (FWE)

Fourth Wave Econometrics Inc (FWE) is a private limited company operating in the quaternary sector. *FWE* specializes in the new field of data analytics and general econometric services for health, housing, and community development organizations. *FWE* is a young organization, founded only 10 years ago, by four graduate students working in data analytics.

FWE's organizational chart is flat, the leadership style is laissez-faire, and the company prides itself on its nimbleness and flexibility. Despite the youth of the organization and its four founders, *FWE* has grown rapidly and has expanded its workforce by almost 10% per year for the past five years. Labour turnover is low.

As part of its 10-year strategic review, *FWE* has identified the American healthcare sector as a great opportunity. The American health sector is market-driven, decentralized, very expensive (American healthcare is the most expensive in the world) and, because of demographic changes (especially an aging American population), it is growing rapidly. Thus, it presents a great business opportunity. A major concern, however, is the organizational culture of most healthcare companies. Unlike *FWE*, hospital chains and other large healthcare companies are bureaucratic and decision-making is slow.

Two of *FWE's* founders fear that, in working with healthcare companies, culture clashes might become an issue. The other two founders are less concerned. They observe that *FWE* is not the organization it was 10 years ago. The four founders are older, they now manage a large work force, and some bureaucratic procedures have had to be put into place now that *FWE* is a much larger organization.

a) Define the term *quaternary sector*. [2 marks]

b) Explain **two** possible reasons why labour turnover at *FWE* is low. [4 marks]

c) With reference to *FWE*, explain **two** ways that demographic change could influence human resource planning. [4 marks]

d) With reference to *FWE*, discuss the issue of culture clash. [10 marks]

2.6 Communication

By the end of this chapter, you should be able to:

→ Evaluate **formal and informal methods of communication** for an organization in a given situation

→ Explain **barriers to communication**

An important element of the organizational structure is how a business communicates with its stakeholders. Communication is integral to how a business functions. Successful businesses communicate effectively with both their internal and external stakeholders.

Communication can take two routes: formal communication, which is channelled through the organizational structure, and informal communication outside the "proper" channels. The communication loop in Figure 2.6.1 shows the process by which a message is communicated.

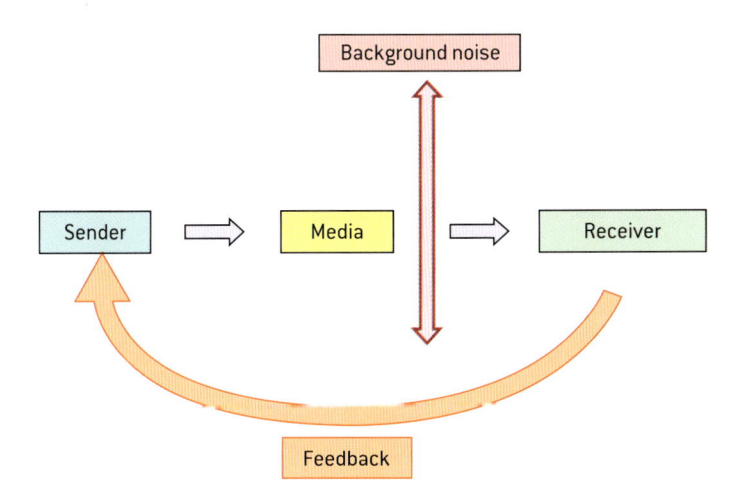

Figure 2.6.1 The process of communicating a message

The sender of the message is said to "encode" the message by deciding what form the message should take. The sender chooses what they consider to be the appropriate media through which to deliver the message. The receiver is the person who gets the message and "decodes" it.

If the message has been delivered successfully then the sender should receive some form of feedback to show that the message has been understood and acted upon successfully. However, the message may not get through clearly because of so-called "background noise". This can be anything from the wrong choice of media to something outside the control of either party. Background noise can even be due to deliberate interference.

Communication can take several forms using a variety of different media, which increases the likelihood that the message will get across. Sometimes, different methods of communication are combined. The most common forms of communication include the following.

Key terms

Formal communication

refers to the official and formally recognized methods of communication in an organization. Traditionally, formal communication was often through paper memos and meetings. Today, formal communication occurs more commonly through group or individual emails, some type of electronic announcement system, and, for natural disaster and emergency communication, via text.

Informal communication

refers to the various ways in which information is casually disseminated. A manager might "get the word out" by dropping by people's offices or sharing information with a few key, highly connected individuals who then share the information with others in the department. Informal communication also includes gossip and rumours.

Barriers to communication

the various impediments that prevent communication from happening when and how it should. Sometimes these barriers are linguistic (people do not all speak the same language). Sometimes they are psychological (people do not "hear" the message as it was communicated). Sometimes they are structural (because of organizational structure management has limited opportunities or windows to communicate).

Verbal

This communication relies on the spoken word. Formal verbal communication occurs in:

- Interviews
- Meetings
- Lectures
- Presentations
- Telephone conversations (recorded)

Informal verbal communication might include:

- Face-to-face conversations
- Gossiping
- Telephone conversations (unrecorded)

Verbal communication can be quick, direct and effective, especially if combined with other forms of communication. It also allows for immediate feedback. However, the message can be misunderstood if the sender uses the wrong language, does not speak clearly, or does not allow for feedback.

Visual

This form of communication relies on sight. Formal visual communication can take place through:

- Presentations
- Videos
- Noticeboards
- Signs
- Sign language
- Symbols
- Maps

Many employees at work shift between the different models of communication constantly

Informal visual communication might include:

- Body language
- Gestures

Visual communication can be effective as it can be permanent, recognizable, and immediate. However, this type of communication can be difficult, especially for those who have limited sight or if the communication is not in a position where it can be seen easily. It can also be less effective if the image or picture requires interpretation, as some cultures may respond differently to the same image.

Written

Written communication relies on the written word. Formal written communication is found in:

- Reports
- Letters

- Notices
- Bulletins
- Forms
- Press releases

Informal written communication might include:

- Memos*
- Emails*
- Texts
- Blogs

(*In some organizations, memos and emails would be considered formal communication.)

Written communication can be effective. Records of the message may be kept, and written communication can be amended or revised. However, written communication can be considered impersonal and often the "tone" of the message may be lost. In addition, feedback is not immediate.

> **Student workpoint 2.9**
>
> **Be reflective**
>
> What would be the most appropriate method of communication in these situations?
>
> a) Your manager needs to tell all staff that the office will be closed tomorrow for emergency maintenance.
>
> b) You want to persuade your managers that your new product idea is a good one. You have done lots of research and have figures and data to back up your arguments.
>
> c) A new product is launching globally in two months' time. It will be the first of its kind and you want it to sell well.
>
> You might choose more than one method for each scenario. Think about what influences your choices so that you can justify your decision.

> **Concept**
>
> **CREATIVITY**
>
> When communicating with both internal and external stakeholders, creativity can be important. It can help in ensuring that the recipient pays attention to the message. However, creativity could also become an obstacle to good communication.
>
> How can organizations communicate creatively to their stakeholders? Research some examples of successful creative communication, and also some examples of less successful creative communication.

Barriers to communication

Many barriers to communication exist. For reasons explained below, disconnects often exist between the person trying to communicate and those for whom the message is intended.

These barriers can be costly. The Society for Human Resources Management (SHRM) conducted a study of 400 American companies with over 10,000 employees. According to the SHRM's findings, each company lost an average of $62.4 million per year in revenue due to poor communication. If you multiply $62.4 million by 400 companies, that is more than $24 billion dollars a year.[2]

---

[2] Willkomm, A C. July 2018. "6 Barriers to Effective Communication". https://drexel.edu/goodwin/professional-studies-blog/overview/2018/July/6-barriers-to-effective-communication/

2 Human resource management

> ### TOK links
>
> 1. "Between what I think, what I want to say, what I believe I say, what I say, what you want to hear, what you believe to hear, what you hear, what you want to understand, what you think you understand, what you understand... They are ten possibilities that we might have some problem communicating" (Bernard Werber). What are the implications of this in a business context?
> 2. Is the difference between formal and informal methods of communication a difference of degree or a difference of kind?
> 3. Does "communication" mean the same internally (within the organization) and externally (with stakeholders such as customers)?

The main barriers to communication include:

- **Communication styles** – people communicate differently. Some people are chatty while others are quiet. Some people speak very directly: they are candid and honest. Others approach communication with greater subtly, preferring suggestion and indirectness.

- **Conflicts in the workplace** – there are often conflicts between people within organizations, and when that occurs communication becomes more difficult. People may stop talking altogether or, when they are communicating, they may not be open to hearing the message that is being conveyed.

- **Cultural differences and language** – in our increasingly diverse world, groups of people living in the same area or working for the same organization may not speak the same language. In the business world English is typically spoken, but the speakers of English may have varying proficiency in the language.

  Cultural differences also play a major role in communication. For example, some people come from low-context cultures (where communication is very direct and based upon the words spoken). Other people come from high-context cultures (where the words spoken are embedded in a host of other communication cues).

- **Dissatisfaction or disinterest with one's job** – many people in the workplace are not happy to be there, or at least they are not happy to be in the job they are in. In this situation, the unhappy employee often communicates ineffectively (which probably makes their dissatisfaction worse). Unhappy employees often do not communicate with their colleagues and supervisors, and they may not hear what others are trying to communicate to them.

- **Inability to listen to others** – listening is a skill which many people have never fully developed. Effective listening requires active listening: paying attention to what is being said rather than making assumptions about what the speaker intends (which is easier than active listening).

- **Lack of transparency and trust** – few organizations are 100% transparent, and for good reasons. Managers may still be reviewing options before they make a decision. Employees have the right to privacy in certain areas. Some information may be sensitive and needs to be closely guarded. However, whenever there is a lack of transparency, people tend to make assumptions, and that hinders communication.

Revision checklist

✓ Communication within businesses and between stakeholders comes in many forms, including formal and informal, and written and not written.

✓ Many barriers to communication exist, and they can be very costly to businesses.

2.6 Communication

Practice question

To answer the question below effectively, see Unit 6 pages 398–402.

Get Going (GG)

Get Going (GG) is a non-profit social enterprise that provides wheelchairs to disabled people. Many of the positions at *GG* involve mostly manual work, and many of the workers are recent immigrants with limited proficiency in English (the language of the country where *GG* is located).

After a successful start, the business experienced financial problems, which has led to low motivation among employees. Some employees are considering leaving *GG*. Rumours have been circulating about the cause of the financial problems. Rumours have also started about job losses, and that is increasing employee dissatisfaction.

Recently, the management of *GG* delayered the organization in order to cut costs. The change from a tall organizational structure to a flat structure, however, led to communication problems. The chief executive officer sent out a memorandum to all employees explaining the reasons for the restructuring. She also promised to start sending out a weekly memorandum.

a) State **two** examples of a non-profit social enterprise other than *GG*. [2 marks]

b) Explain **two** barriers to communication at *GG*. [4 marks]

c) Explain **one** example of formal communication and **one** example of informal communication at *GG*. [4 marks]

Source: Adapted from IB examination paper, May 2005

2 Human resource management

2.7 Industrial/employee relations (HL only)

> **By the end of this chapter, you should be able to:**
> → Explain **sources of conflict** in the workplace
> → Evaluate **approaches to conflict** in the workplace, including:
>   - approaches of **employees**, such as collective bargaining, work-to-rule, and strike action
>   - approaches of **employers**, such as collective bargaining, threats of redundancies, changes of contract, closure and lockouts
> → Evaluate approaches to **conflict resolution**, including conciliation and arbitration, employee participation and industrial democracy, no-strike agreement, and single-union agreement

This chapter discusses employer and employee relations. As with any aspect of business that is governed or influenced by the laws of a country, situations can differ from country to country. Nevertheless, what follows is generally applicable in many countries.

Sources of conflict (HL only)

The primary causes of conflict between workers and the management team in the workplace include the following:

- **Change** – this can be driven by either internal or external factors. Either way, change can cause stress. Not all employees will respond well to the introduction of new technology, for example. When employees adapt poorly to change, the likelihood of conflict in the workplace increases.

- **Different interests** – workers, who in certain respects have a lesser stake in the business than managers or shareholders, focus on their individual goals (such as more flexibility in the workplace or higher wages). Managers sometimes believe that workers do not sufficiently consider the goals of the business.

- **Different values** – individuals see the world differently. A lack of acceptance and understanding of these differences can cause conflict. Often, workers have a culture that differs from that of the management team.

- **External factors** – any number of external factors can disrupt the workplace: changes in the economic environment can affect the resources available to the business, migration of labour can bring in new workers unaccustomed to an organization's traditional culture, and political changes can lead to new laws and regulations that workers or managers do not like.

2.7 Industrial/employee relations (HL only)

- **Insufficient resources** – no organization has unlimited resources. Managers must decide how resources are allocated. Frequently, employees think that they have to compete for available resources just to do their jobs. Having insufficient resources also affects employees' pay. Conflict often arises when workers or managers demand more pay.
- **Poor communication** – sometimes managers and workers clash because a lack of communication has created misunderstanding. Even when managers or workers have tried to communicate, misunderstandings can occur.
- **Poor performance** – sometimes people do not do their jobs properly, and this is a situation that can happen at all levels of an organization. People not doing their jobs properly, whether they are managers or workers, has an impact on others and can lead to conflict. If the problem is addressed (the non-performing employee is reprimanded, demoted, or even sacked), that too can cause conflict.

Approaches by employees to conflict in the workplace (HL only)

Collective bargaining

When the management team and workers have representatives who negotiate on the terms and conditions of employment, this is called collective bargaining. Large organizations do not have the time to negotiate with individual employees. For both workers and managers, having employer and employee representatives to negotiate makes better sense.

Work-to-rule

Sometimes the collective bargaining system may not work, and an industrial dispute may arise. Workers may start a "go slow", which means they deliberately work below their potential. Alternatively, they may "work-to-rule", which involves working strictly by the company rulebook – and following every rule in the organization would probably bring it to a standstill.

An overtime ban occurs when employees refuse to work overtime. In this case, the organization may find it very difficult to operate.

Strike action

Perhaps the most drastic step that workers can legally take is to take strike action or "go on strike". A strike is when employees stop working to force an employer to meet their demands. During strikes, employers do not pay their workers, who are not working. If the workers are unionized, they may receive strike pay from the union for a period of time.

As part of a strike, employees typically try to raise awareness and sympathy for their demands in the hope that this will pressure management into accepting them

> **Key terms**
>
> **Conflict in the workplace**
> most commonly refers to conflict between management and organized groups of workers. Disputes usually occur over pay, benefits, and control over the work.
>
> **Collective bargaining**
> occurs when employees of an organization work together when bargaining with management about wages and work conditions. Typically, collective bargaining occurs at organizations where the employees are unionized, and union representatives assist with the bargaining process.
>
> **Work-to-rule**
> occurs when employees precisely follow the rules of their existing contract. In this way, they do the minimum required. They meticulously follow every single regulation, which may slow down work or decrease productivity. During work-to-rule, workers typically will not work overtime or beyond their contracted hours.
>
> **Strike action**
> when workers stop working because they are dissatisfied with work conditions or compensation. When workers "go on strike", the work stoppage provides leverage against the employer to discuss pay and conditions.

2 Human resource management

Key terms

Threats of redundancies

when management threatens to eliminate employment positions if workers do not accept terms in an industrial dispute. Were those positions to be made redundant, the workers in them would lose their jobs.

Changes of contract

when agreement is reached over new contract terms in collective bargaining and negotiation. Changes are made in the existing contract between management and labour, and typically relate to pay, benefits, and control over the work.

Lockout

when, as part of the negotiating process, management locks up the company or factories, preventing workers from entering them. During a lockout, workers can no longer can work and so they do not receive any pay.

Closure

refers to the permanent or temporary shutting down of a site, such as a factory, a plant, or an office. Many countries have national laws, which vary from country to country, stipulating various conditions and consequences of closure.

Conciliation

occurs when a third-party conciliator mediates between management and labour and offers ideas that may help the two sides come to an agreement

Approaches by employers to conflict in the workplace (HL only)

Collective bargaining

The collective bargaining process involves both worker representatives and management (or someone representing management). The aim of the collective bargaining process is to find common ground between the two sides and arrive at a resolution to the conflict.

Threats of redundancies

A redundancy occurs when an employer determines that a position or job in the business no longer needs to be performed, and thus the position is made redundant. In colloquial English, the term is often used in reference to people ("He was made redundant"). Employers can threaten redundancies as a way to put pressure on employees to be more willing to agree with management.

Changes of contract

In most developed countries, the right of one party in a contract to make unilateral changes to the contract is severely limited by law. However, depending on the laws of country where the dispute is occurring, the employer may be permitted to make certain changes to an employment contract if all the correct legal considerations are followed. If those possible changes to the contract are objectionable to employees, even the threat of changes might give some bargaining power to the employer.

Lockouts

A lockout is a work stoppage that, unlike a strike, is initiated by management. Employees are locked out of the work premises and therefore they are unable to work. Like a strike, during a lockout workers are not paid because they are not working. Depending on where they live, workers may be entitled to some compensation from the government during the period of the lockout.

Closure

Closure is the most drastic action that the employer can take during a conflict in the workplace, as it may mean the permanent closure of the business itself.

Approaches to conflict resolution (HL only)

Conciliation and arbitration

Conciliation and arbitration are two ways to resolve a conflict between management and labour. Both approaches involve bringing in an outside party – a conciliator or an arbitrator – to help resolve the conflict.

In **conciliation**, a conciliator will offer ideas to management and labour with the hope that these ideas may form the pathway to a resolution, but any final decisions are made by management and labour. In **arbitration**, the third-party arbitrator has the authority to settle the disagreement.

2.7 Industrial/employee relations (HL only)

With either conciliation or arbitration, an assumption is that the conciliator or the arbitrator, as an outside party, can look at the dispute objectively and arrive at a settlement that is fair to both sides.

Employee participation and industrial democracy

Employee participation and industrial democracy are used to described situations where workers make decisions or share responsibility and authority in the workplace. In some countries, traditionally it is rare for workers to participate in decision-making. In other countries, however, workers are viewed differently. Though the shareholders own the company, the company (and therefore the shareholders) could not make a profit without the workers, so the workers ought to have some say. Generalizations about employee participation and industrial democracy are difficult, because circumstances vary from company to company and country to country.

Employee participation and industrial democracy have a bearing on the nature of conflict resolution. In countries where a tradition exists of employee participation and industrial democracy, an assumption is that workers have a right to some voice in decision-making. In countries without such a tradition, the assumption is that the shareholders alone (through their designated agents: management) have the right to make decisions.

No-strike agreement

A **no-strike agreement** is a stipulation in the collective bargaining agreement that, during the lifetime of the contract, workers will not go on strike. Workers will typically agree to a no-strike stipulation in exchange for some concession made by management during the collective bargaining process.

Single-union agreement

A single-union agreement occurs when workers agree that one union will represent the workers' interests in the collective bargaining process.

Revision checklist

- ✓ Employee and employer representatives act on behalf of employees and employers in negotiations.
- ✓ Collective bargaining is a negotiation between employees (usually through a trade union) and their employers to agree wages and/or working conditions.
- ✓ If in collective bargaining employees are not getting the outcomes that they seek, they can take stronger action to improve their bargaining position, eg work-to-rule or going on strike.
- ✓ When employees work-to-rule, they follow every rule and regulation exactly, which often means slowing down production. When workers strike, they refuse to work and may also protest outside their workplace.
- ✓ Employers may negotiate by threatening redundancies or changing the terms of employees' contracts. This would put pressure on workers and might persuade them to agree to a settlement.
- ✓ A lockout involves closing the business for a short time, preventing employees from working and being paid.

Key term

Arbitration occurs when a third-party arbitrator mediates between management and labour. Unlike in conciliation, the arbitrator has the authority to decide how the conflict between management and labour will be resolved.

Student workpoint 2.10

Be a researcher

Use the internet to research an industrial dispute that has occurred in your country.

- What caused the dispute? Was it one or a combination of many factors?
- What strategies were adopted by a) the employees and b) the employers?
- What was the outcome of the dispute? Was there a clear "winner"?

TOK links

1. In what ways can language be both a source of conflict in the workplace and the main vehicle of conflict resolution?
2. Are conflicts always about a difference between stakeholders' perspectives?
3. Should good managers anticipate and therefore prevent all conflicts?

2 Human resource management

Practice question

To answer the questions below effectively, see Unit 6 pages 398–402.

Gabriel de Solages

In 1752, Gabriel de Solages received the right to open a coal mine and glass factory in Carmaux, France, and thus began a long history of profitable mines and glassmaking in the southern French city. The glassmaking factory required considerable amounts of coal to make the glass, and coal could be sold to other users as well for other purposes. As for the glass, the Solages factory made bottles for wine.

The work at the glass factory was different than most other types of secondary sector employment at the time. For one thing, the on-the-job training period was very long: 14 years. The work was also very dangerous, and master glassblowers – those who reached the pinnacle of the trade – often suffered lung ailments, and the average age of death was low compared to other vocations (including mine workers, whose occupation was also dangerous).

Despite these risks, glassworkers took great pride in their profession. They were well paid – the best-paid industrial workers in France in the late 19th century. Moreover, the glassworkers had considerable control over the workplace. During the 18th century and most of the 19th century, glassworkers controlled their craft more like a medieval guild than a modern industrial workforce. The glassworkers determined who was admitted as an apprentice and who advanced, and they controlled the shop floor, as long as they met quality and production targets.

In the late 19th century, new owners and new management took over the glassworks factory. The new owners instituted many changes, including a high degree of automation (for the day). Operating the new machinery required far less skill than traditional glassblowing, and workers' pay soon got cut. Management also took over the shop floor and determined the new rhythms and practices of work.

Soon, the glassworkers of Carmaux took strike action. The workers had many complaints. Management responded by arguing that, without these changes, the glassworks factory in Carmaux would no longer be competitive. Despite efforts by both sides at collective bargaining, workers and management threatened various types of action in response to the conflict.

Source: Adapted from Scott, J W. 1980. *The Glassworkers of Carmaux, French Craftsmen and Political Action in a Nineteenth-Century City.*

a) Define the term *on-the-job training*. [2 marks]

b) With reference to the Solages glassworks, explain the term *secondary sector*. [2 marks]

c) Explain **one** advantage and **one** disadvantage to the Solages glassworks of offering the highest industrial wages in France. [4 marks]

d) Discuss **one** approach that management could take and **one** approach that workers could take in trying to resolve the industrial conflict. [10 marks]

3 FINANCE AND ACCOUNTS

3.1 Introduction to finance

> **By the end of this chapter, you should be able to:**
> → Explain the role of finance for businesses in terms of **capital expenditure** and **revenue expenditure**

Introduction

All forms of business organization need funding or finance for the various activities they undertake. The money could be required for a variety of reasons, including starting a business, for its day-to-day operations, or for its future growth and expansion. As a result, businesses need to be clear on the exact role finance plays in their business operations.

The role of finance for businesses can be categorised as either **capital expenditure** or **revenue expenditure**.

Capital expenditure

This is money spent to acquire items in a business that will last for more than a year and may be used over and over again. Such items are known as **fixed assets** and include machinery, land, buildings, vehicles, and equipment. These fixed assets are needed for the purpose of generating income for the business over the longer term.

Due to their high initial cost, most fixed assets can be used as **collateral** (financial security pledged for repayment of a particular source of finance, such as bank loans). Capital expenditures are therefore

> **Key terms**
>
> **Capital expenditure**
> money spent to acquire fixed assets in a business
>
> **Revenue expenditure**
> money used in the day-to-day running of a business

3 Finance and accounts

> **Student workpoint 3.1**
>
> **Be a researcher**
>
> Choose any two multinational companies that you are interested in. Using the internet or any other available resource, find out for each company what its main capital and revenue expenditures are. Separately list each company's expenditures in a table.

> **TOK discussion**
>
> 1. What role does intuition play in financial decision-making?
> 2. As finance is largely about mathematics, how different is knowledge about finance from knowledge in other areas of business management, such as human resource management?
> 3. Is finance "value free"?

long-term investments intended to assist businesses to succeed and grow. For example, when a business purchases a van, this is seen as capital expenditure because the benefits accrued to the business from this will be spread over the long term.

Revenue expenditure

This is money spent on the day-to-day running of a business. These payments or expenses include rent, wages, raw materials, insurance, and fuel. They do not involve the purchase of longer-term, fixed assets. Funds for revenue expenditure need to be available immediately to keep the business operational and should therefore provide instant benefits, unlike capital expenditure which has a long-term focus.

Businesses need to be cautious not to have consistently high revenue expenditure as this makes it difficult for them to build sufficient capital required to make long-term investments. In addition, it makes it extremely difficult for them to get out of a sudden crisis situation. For example, if a school is spending most of its money paying salaries and bonuses to teachers or paying food suppliers, and these costs are not checked, it may be unable to build new classrooms to accommodate any increases in student demand. In a business, a high level of expenses may also erode the profits.

Revision checklist

✓ Capital expenditure is money spent to acquire fixed assets in a business, which include machinery, land, buildings, vehicles and equipment.

✓ Revenue expenditure is money spent on the day-to-day running of a business, such as rent, wages, raw materials, insurance and fuel.

3.1 Introduction to finance

Practice question

To answer the question below effectively, see Unit 6 pages 398–402.

Peter Dee is an agricultural consultant and has worked with farmers in South-East Asia for over 15 years. He has been heavily involved in developing their capital expenditure plans, helping them with purchasing decisions about farm inputs that would last for a longer period of time.

Over the years he has been tracking progress to assess how useful the plans have been to the farmers. Now he also wants to help the farmers with their revenue expenditure plans because most farmers have not been able to track their expenses (such as wages and fertilizer costs) sustainably. He believes having a balanced approach to these two types of plans will lead to better growth prospects for the farmers.

a) Explain why an understanding of both capital expenditure and revenue expenditure would be beneficial to the farmers in South-East Asia. [4 marks]

3.2 Sources of finance

> **By the end of this chapter, you should be able to:**
> → Comment on the following internal sources of finance: **personal funds**, **retained profit** and **sale of assets**
> → Comment on the following external sources of finance: **share capital**, **loan capital**, **overdrafts**, **trade credit**, **crowdfunding**, **leasing**, **microfinance providers** and **business angels**
> → Examine the appropriateness of **short-** or **long-term** sources of finance for a given situation

The sources of finance for a business can be either internal or external.

Internal sources of finance

Internal finance is money obtained from within the business and is easier to access by businesses that are already established. Some of these internal sources include the following.

Personal funds

This is a key source of finance for sole traders and it comes mostly from their own personal savings. By investing using their personal savings, sole traders maximize their control over the business. In addition, the sole trader shows a personal commitment to the business by investing in this way. This is also a good signal to other investors or financial institutions should the sole trader need to approach them for additional sources of finance.

> **Key term**
>
> **Personal funds**
>
> a source of finance for sole traders that comes mostly from their own personal savings

Advantages

- The sole trader knows exactly how much money is available to run the business.
- It provides the sole trader with much more control over the finances than other finance options. It also means that the sole trader does not need to pay the funds back or rely on outside investors or lenders, who could decide to withdraw their support at any time.

Disadvantages

- It poses a large risk to the owners or sole traders because they could be investing their life's savings, hence putting a strain on family or personal life.
- If the savings are not sufficient it may prove difficult to start or maintain a business, especially if this is the only source of funding.

Retained profit

This is the profit that remains after a business (a profit-making entity) has paid out dividends to its shareholders. It is also known as **ploughed-back profit** and may be reinvested back into the business for growth purposes. It is considered to be one of the most important long-term sources of finance for a business.

Advantages

- It is cheap because it does not incur interest charges (like bank loans do).
- It is a permanent source of finance as it does not have to be repaid.
- It is flexible as it can be used in a way the business deems fit.
- The owners have control over their retained profits without interference from other financial institutions such as banks.

Disadvantages

- Start-up businesses will not have any retained profit as they are new ventures.
- If retained profit is too low, it may not be sufficient for business growth or expansion.
- A high retained profit may mean that either very little or nothing was paid out to shareholders as dividends. This could be less attractive to stock buyers than a similar profitable business that distributes dividends generously to its shareholders.

For non-profit businesses or entities, the money remaining at the end of a financial year is referred to as "retained surplus".

Sale of assets

This is when a business sells off its unwanted or unused assets to raise funds. These assets that are no longer required by the business include obsolete machinery or redundant buildings. To raise cash, businesses could also sell off any excess land or equipment they may not be using.

Advantages

- This is a good way of raising cash from capital that is tied up in assets which are not being used.
- No interest or borrowing costs are incurred.

Disadvantages

- This option is only available to established businesses as new businesses may lack excess assets to sell.
- It can be time-consuming to find a buyer for the assets, especially for obsolete machinery.

In some cases, businesses adopt a sale and leaseback approach, which involves selling an asset that the business still needs to use. For example, the business can sell an asset to a specialist firm and then lease it back.

Key terms

Retained profit

profit that remains after a business (a profit-making entity) has paid out dividends to its shareholders

Sale of assets

when a business sells off its unwanted or unused assets to raise funds

---

Student workpoint 3.2

Be a researcher

Using an internet search engine such as Google, find at least five organizations that rely to a large extent on internal sources of finance to operate. What are the main internal sources they use, and why?

3 Finance and accounts

External sources of finance

External finance is money obtained from sources outside the business, usually from financial institutions or individuals. Some of these external sources include the following.

Share capital

This is money raised from the sale of shares of a limited company and is also known as **equity capital**. Buyers of these shares are known as **shareholders** and may be entitled to dividends when profits are made. The term **authorized share capital** is the maximum amount the shareholders of a company intend to raise.

Unlike private limited company shares that are not sold to the public, the shares of public limited companies are sold in a special share market known as the **stock exchange**. This is a regulated and organized market where securities (for example shares and bonds) are purchased and sold to willing investors. The oldest stock exchange in the world is the London Stock Exchange. Other global exchanges include Bombay, Tokyo, Nairobi, Johannesburg, and New York stock exchanges.

The trading floor of the Tokyo stock exchange

Key terms

Share capital

money raised from the sale of shares of a limited company

Loan capital

money sourced from financial institutions such as banks, with interest charged on the loan to be repaid

Advantages

- It is a permanent source of capital as it will not need to be redeemed (repaid by the business). If shareholders want to get their money back they have to find a buyer for their shares.
- There are no interest payments and this relieves the business from additional expenses.

Disadvantages

- Shareholders will expect to be paid dividends when the business makes a profit.
- For public limited companies, the ownership of the company may be diluted or change hands from the original shareholders to new ones via the stock exchange.

Loan capital

Also known as **debt capital**, this is money sourced from financial institutions such as banks. Interest is charged on the loan to be repaid; however, these repayments (installments) are usually spread evenly until the full loan amount (principal plus interest) is paid. The interest rates may be either fixed or variable. A **fixed interest rate** is one that does not fluctuate and remains fixed for the entire term of the loan repayment. A **variable interest rate** changes periodically based on the prevailing market conditions.

Advantages

- Loan capital is accessible and can be arranged quickly for a firm's specific purpose.
- Its repayment is spread out over a predetermined period of time, reducing the burden to the business of having to pay it in a lump sum.

- Large organizations can negotiate for lower interest charges depending on the amount they want to borrow.
- The owners still have full control of the business if no shares are issued to dilute their ownership.

Disadvantages

- The capital will have to be redeemed even if the business is making a loss.
- In some cases, collateral (security) will be required before any funds are lent.
- Failure to repay the loan may lead to the seizure of a firm's assets.
- If variable interest rates increase, a firm that has a variable rate loan may be faced with a high debt repayment burden.

Overdrafts

This is when a lending institution allows a firm to withdraw more money than it currently has in its account, also called **overdrawing from the account**. In most cases, the overdrawn amount is an agreed amount that has a limit placed on it. Interest is charged only on the amount overdrawn. Exceeding the limit set may attract higher additional costs.

Advantages

- It provides an opportunity for firms to spend more money than they have in their account (even in situations where there is no money in the account), which greatly helps in settling short-term debts such as paying suppliers or wages for their staff.
- It is a flexible form of finance as its demand will depend on the needs of the business at a particular point in time.
- Charging interest only on the amount overdrawn can make it a cheaper option than loan capital.

Disadvantages

- Banks can request for the overdraft to be paid back at very short notice.
- Due to the variable nature of an overdraft, the bank can at times charge high interest rates.

Trade credit

This is an agreement between businesses that allows the buyer of goods or services to pay the seller at a later date. No immediate cash transaction occurs at the time of trading. The credit period offered by most creditors or suppliers (trade credit providers) usually lasts from 30 to 90 days; jewelry businesses are known to extend it to at least 180 days.

Advantages

- By delaying payments to suppliers, businesses are left in a better cash flow position than if they paid cash immediately.
- It is an interest-free means of raising funds for the length of the credit period.

> **Key terms**
>
> **Overdraft**
> when a lending institution allows a firm to withdraw more money than it currently has in its account
>
> **Trade credit**
> an agreement between businesses that allows the buyer of goods or services to pay the seller at a later date

Disadvantages

- Debtors (trade credit receivers) lose out on the possibility of getting discounts had they purchased by paying cash.
- Delaying payment to creditors or suppliers after the agreed period may lead to poor relations between the debtors and suppliers, with the latter refusing to engage in future transactions with the former.

Crowdfunding

> **Key term**
>
> **Crowdfunding**
>
> when a business venture or project is funded by a large number of people each contributing a small amount of money

This is where a business venture or project is funded by a large number of people each contributing a small amount of money. Crowdfunding makes use of the vast networks of people who can be accessed primarily online through crowdfunding websites or social media. Its success relies upon the ability to appeal to a sufficiently large group of potential contributors in order to reach a specified financial target.

Examples of crowdfunding platforms include Indiegogo, Kickstarter, 40Billion, Funding4Learning and Fundable.

Advantages

- Crowdfunding provides access to thousands of investors who can see, interact with and share a project's fundraising campaign.
- It is a valuable form of marketing because pitching a project or business through the online platform can result in media attention that publicises the business.
- It provides an opportunity for feedback and expert guidance. By sharing the business idea, suggestions about how to improve it can be provided by a team of experts.
- The business still maintains full control and won't have to forfeit control when raising funds. It can decide how to structure the campaign, including how much to ask for, and then choose how to operate once it gets the funding.
- It is a good alternative finance option as it provides another pathway for businesses that have struggled to get bank loans or traditional funding.

Crowdfunding is a popular strategy used by businesses to raise funds

Disadvantages

- Businesses seeking crowdfunding have strong competition. As crowdfunding is quite popular because of its advantages and accessibility, there are numerous projects on the major platforms at any given time. So businesses need a detailed plan of attack, and a clever way to differentiate themselves from their competitors.
- The business is subject to thorough scrutiny and rejection. Having a solid idea does not mean it is going to be accepted by the crowdfunding platform of choice. Some popular platforms (like Kickstarter) have very detailed rules about what is allowed and what is not, and if all requirements are not met then the campaign might never be seen.
- Fees need to be paid. Many crowdfunding platforms take a percentage of the contributions raised. The fees are usually minimal, but they still reduce the amount of money a project may otherwise get.

- There is a potential risk of failure. If the crowdfunding campaign fails, it can be hard to recover. A failed crowdfunding campaign is a sign that the business plan is not good enough to the majority of investors. In addition, most crowdfunding platforms will not allow you to list the same project twice. Hence, the consequences of failure are severe.

Leasing

This is where a business (lessee) enters into a contract with a leasing company (lessor) to acquire or use particular assets such as machinery, equipment or property. This allows a firm to use an asset without having to purchase it with cash. Periodic or monthly leasing payments are made by agreement between the lessor and lessee. In some cases, businesses may get into a **finance lease** agreement, where at the end of the leasing period (which usually lasts for more than three years) they are given the option of purchasing the asset. Large organizations such as airlines, electronics and car companies are known to lease their assets.

Key terms

Leasing
a source of finance that allows a firm to use an asset without having to purchase it with cash

Microfinance providers
institutions that provide banking services to low-income or unemployed individuals or groups who would otherwise have no other access to financial services

Advantages

- A firm does not need to have a high initial capital outlay to purchase the asset.
- The lessor takes on the responsibility of repair and maintenance of the asset.
- Leasing is useful when particular assets are required only occasionally or for short periods of time.

Disadvantages

- Leasing can turn out to be more expensive than the outright purchase of an asset due to the accumulated total costs of the leasing charges.
- A leased asset cannot act as collateral for a business seeking a loan as an additional source of finance.

Microfinance providers

A microfinance provider offers banking services to low-income or unemployed individuals or groups who would otherwise have no other access to financial services. These include small businesses that lack access to conventional banking services. Microfinance services include microcredit, which is the provision of small loans to poor clients; microinsurance; and savings and current accounts (also known as checking accounts), among other services. The ultimate goal of microfinance is to reach excluded customers and provide them with an opportunity to become self-sufficient. Examples of microfinance providers include 51Give, Bank Rakyat Indonesia, Faulu Kenya DTM, Grameen Bank and Kiva.

Advantages

- Most microfinance institutions do not seek any collateral for providing financial credit.
- They provide or disburse loans quickly and with less formalities to individuals, groups or small businesses, so they can meet any financial emergency.

Microfinance can transform lives and provide hope to many

- They have an extensive portfolio of loans, including working capital loans, housing loans, etc.
- They promote self-sufficiency and entrepreneurship. They do this by providing funds to individuals to set up a business that may need minimal investment but will provide a sustainable profit.

Disadvantages

- Microfinance institutions can adopt harsh recovery methods in the event of a default if the customer does not have legal representation.
- They offer smaller loan amounts or financial capital than other financial institutions that provide much larger amounts.
- The interest rates on their loans are high and they find it difficult to offer lower rates. This is partly because they do not operate in the same way as traditional banks that find it easy to accumulate funds. In addition, they borrow money from these banks in order to execute their functions. Hence, their operating cost per transaction is quite high despite the large volume of transactions every day.

Business angels

Also known as **angel investors**, these are affluent individuals who provide financial capital to small start-ups or entrepreneurs in return for ownership equity in their businesses. They invest in high-risk businesses that show good potential for high returns or future growth. They may provide a one-time initial capital injection or continually support the businesses through their lifetime.

> **Key term**
>
> **Business angels**
>
> highly affluent individuals who provide financial capital to small start-ups or entrepreneurs in return for ownership equity in their businesses

Advantages

- Business angels are more open to negotiation than other institutions or lenders to small or start-up businesses. This is because they are usually successful entrepreneurs who understand the amount of risk involved with establishing a business. Their flexibility and risk-taking attitude make them one of the best sources of finance in this situation.
- No repayment or interest is required. Angel investors fund the business and in exchange get an ownership stake in the business. If the business succeeds, both the business and angel investor benefit; if not, the angel does not get paid back.
- They offer valuable knowledge and they focus on helping a business succeed by using their extensive business experience coupled with good financial capital.

Disadvantages

- Business angels may assume a large degree of control or ownership in the businesses they invest in, therefore diluting the ownership of the entrepreneur.
- They may expect a substantial return on their investment within the first few years, sometimes equal to 10 times their original investment. This can create additional pressure on the business.

Case study

The story of microfinance in India

Microfinance is a type of banking service provided to those who have difficulty accessing formal financial services. It is targeted at low-income and unemployed people. The institutions supporting microfinance offer services such as lending, setting up bank accounts, and providing microinsurance products. In developing countries such as India, financial services through formal channels do not meet the demands of the rural poor, so microfinance can help small-scale businesses flourish by providing greater financial stability.

Microfinancing was introduced in India in the 1970s as a solution to poverty and as a way to empower women. Despite its strong potential, the microfinance sector faces various challenges related to accessibility in rural India.

The main reason formal banking institutions fail to lend to the large rural population in India is that these people are unable to provide proof of income or employment or collateral. The high risk and high transaction costs of small loans create problems for the banks as well. This leaves the poor with no alternative but to borrow money from local moneylenders at high interest rates.

Microfinance in India aims to promote socio-economic development at the grassroots level through a community-based approach, empowering women and increasing the household income.

How microfinance started in India

The first initiative to introduce microfinance in India was the Self Employed Women's Association (SEWA) in Gujarat, which established the SEWA Bank in 1974. Since then, this bank has been providing financial services to individuals in rural areas who want to grow their own businesses.

Kudumbashree, the Kerala state's Poverty Eradication Mission, was launched in 1998. This female-led community organization of Neighbourhood Groups (NHGs) brings women from rural and urban areas together to fight for their rights, and it helps to empower them. Through these NHGs, women work on a variety of issues like health, nutrition and agriculture. The scheme allows them to earn an income at the same time as seeking microcredit. Such small-scale initiatives are promoting financial independence in underprivileged areas.

Challenges

As with implementing any transformative initiative, running a microfinance programme in rural India comes with some challenges:

Schemes do not reach those who need them

The microfinance delivery models fail to focus on people who are below the poverty level as they are deemed to be too risky.

3 Finance and accounts

There is a bias when selecting those who qualify for the schemes – the operators of the schemes look for people who are economically stable. This allows the programme to run successfully and to attain higher repayment rates. Most of the poor are too risk-averse to consider borrowing in order to invest in their future. So they are less likely to benefit from the microfinance schemes.

Limited spread in the poorer states

There are few microfinance schemes in those states where a large percentage of the population lives in poverty. States such as Orissa, Bihar, Chhattisgarh, Jharkhand, Madhya Pradesh and Uttar Pradesh lag behind in implementing microfinance schemes. The successful distribution of microfinance schemes depends on the support extended by the respective state governments, the local culture and practice, and concentration of microfinance institutions (MFIs) in these states.

High interest rates

Borrowers are interest sensitive, so the capacity to borrow reduces as interest rates increase. Thus, high interest rates are counterproductive and weaken the economic status of poor clients. It is also exploitative to charge very high interest rates for poor clients. Generally, interest rates are not well regulated in the microfinance sector. Those MFIs that have regulated interest tend to impose transaction costs, which increases the burden that comes with borrowing and makes it less attractive. Whereas the banking sector charges a 9–10% annual interest rate, MFIs may charge 11–24%. However, these rates of interest vary according to the lending conditions and policies of the MFI.

Low uptake

The microfinance programme is expanding but the number of loans taken remains small. Often the loans are too small to really make a difference to the situation of poorer people. The insufficient loan size and the short loan term (rarely more than a year) restrict borrowers from using the loans for productive purposes. They generally use these small loans to address liquidity issues, rather than borrowing to invest.

The next steps in implementing microfinance in India

The microfinance programme has witnessed phenomenal growth in India. However, the focus of most of the microfinance service providers is still on expanding uptake with little attention to the quality and viability of the financial services. In addition to removing these problems, there needs to be a proper structure to let microfinance empower rural India.

Adapted from: https://www.bridgeindia.org.uk/the-story-of-microfinance-in-india

Student workpoint 3.3

Be a researcher

Find out how the various sources of finance for private sector organizations compare with the sources for public sector organizations.

Short- and long-term finance

In determining whether to classify a source of finance as short or long term, it is important to consider the investor's preference or the type of asset to be financed. The type of finance should therefore be matched to the type of asset being financed. Thus, a long-term asset should be financed with long-term finance and a short-term asset with short-term finance.

There is no uniformly agreed way of determining the exact duration of a source of finance, but most financial literature uses the following definitions.

Short-term finance

This is money needed for the day-to-day running of a business and therefore provides the required working capital. External short-term financing is usually expected to be paid back within 12 months or less. Examples of short-term finance include bank overdrafts, short-term loans and trade credit.

Long-term finance

This is funding obtained for the purpose of purchasing long-term fixed assets or other expansion requirements of a business. It is normally used for the overall improvement of the business. Businesses that take up external long-term financing usually have a time span of more than one financial year to pay it back. Long-term finance sources include long-term bank loans and share capital.

Factors influencing the choice of a source of finance

In determining the appropriateness of using a particular source of finance for a given situation, firms need to consider a number of factors which can influence their decision. Some of these factors are explored below.

Purpose or use of funds

Businesses will need to match the source of finance carefully to their specific requirements. What exactly will the finance be used for? Will it be used for the purchase of long-term fixed assets or for the short-term day-to-day running of the business? Long-term loan capital may be appropriate when purchasing a fixed asset, while trade credit may be suitable if raw materials are needed urgently for the business.

Cost

Businesses will need to consider thoroughly all of the costs associated with obtaining a source of finance. Such costs include interest payments, administration costs, and costs associated with a share issue. In addition, the **opportunity cost** (the lost benefit that would have been derived from an alternative) is an important consideration when deciding on the most appropriate source of finance.

Status and size

Public limited companies have more options in obtaining finance compared to sole traders. This is because sole traders are less well known and smaller in size than public limited companies. For example, issuing shares is a source of finance that is only possible for public limited companies and not sole traders. In addition, large organizations have added collateral that they can use to negotiate lower interest rates from financial institutions.

Student workpoint 3.4

Be knowledgeable

Prepare and complete a table that classifies the following sources of finance into short or long term:

- retained profit
- trade credit
- leasing
- sale of assets
- crowdfunding
- share capital
- overdrafts
- loan capital
- microfinance

Amount required

For small amounts, firms may consider mostly short-term sources of finance such as bank overdrafts, while for larger amounts, long-term bank loans or the issuing of shares are available options. Therefore, varying sources will be used depending on the amount required.

Flexibility

This considers the ease with which a business can switch from requiring one form or source of finance to another. Businesses may need additional finance at particular points during the trading period. This could be influenced by, for example, unexpected seasonal changes in demand that may require additional financing. The availability of these funds in such a short period depends on how flexible the business is in adapting to change.

State of the external environment

This involves factors that the business has no control over. For example, increases in interest rates or inflation (persistent increases in average prices in an economy) will greatly affect the purchasing decisions of both consumers and producers. Consequently, this will affect the choices businesses make in sourcing their finance. Taking up a bank loan with rising interest rates may not be the best choice for a firm because of the increased cost involved.

Gearing

This refers to the relationship between share capital and loan capital. If a company has a large proportion of loan capital to share capital it is said to be **high geared**, while a company that is **low geared** has a smaller proportion of loan capital to share capital.

For example, assume there are two companies, company A and company B, each with a total capital of $60 million. Company A may have a loan capital of $10 million and share capital of $50 million, while company B may have a loan capital of $40 million and share capital of $20 million. Company A is therefore low geared compared to company B, which is high geared. High-geared businesses are viewed as risky by financial institutions, and they will be reluctant to lend money to such firms. These businesses will therefore need to seek alternative sources of finance. One way of measuring gearing is by calculating the gearing ratio (see Chapter 3.6).

> **Concept**
>
> **CREATIVITY**
>
> Creativity is about coming up with new ideas or developing innovative solutions to existing problems. The case study below explains how M-Pesa revolutionised the banking sector in Kenya.
>
> Carry out some research on two or more organizations that have creatively developed solutions to existing problems.

> **Case study**
>
> ## How Kenya created the world's most successful mobile-payments service
>
> M-Pesa has transformed the everyday lives of most Kenyans, disrupting the traditional banking system and capturing the previously unbanked market. Allowing whole businesses to be run from a mobile phone, the secret to M-Pesa's impressive performance can be found backstage.

3.2 Sources of finance

What's this M-Pesa thing all about?

The word *pesa* means "money" in Swahili, which is the most widely spoken language in Southeast Africa. M-Pesa is a mobile-payment service developed by Kenya's largest mobile-network operator, Safaricom. Launched in 2007, M-Pesa was originally developed to allow for payments on microloans to be easily collected. However, it was found that M-Pesa users were also using the service to transfer money to one another. In response, the M-Pesa platform was built out around an e-wallet, allowing for deposits and withdrawals of cash, bank account transfers, the payment of bills from electricity to school fees, loan and savings transactions, and the receipt of salaries.

Today, M-Pesa has captured roughly 70% of households in Kenya, and over 50% of lower-income households, demonstrating its contribution to financial inclusion. Kenyans benefit from the following advantages of M-Pesa:

- A fast and convenient money-transfer system, available throughout the country and accessible to everyone with a mobile phone.
- A secure and trusted service, removing the need to carry cash and the consequent risk of theft or loss.
- Time savings for users by removing the need to travel to banks and wait in queues.
- Cheap rates that reduce the costs of financial products, eg lower rates on microloans.

Taking advantage of a range of contextual factors, M-Pesa has reaped the dividend of network effects (the more people using M-Pesa, the more value it offers). In fact, the introduction of M-Pesa has spurred a host of Kenyan start-ups who run their businesses wholly on mobile phones. But few of the ideas spawned from M-Pesa and implemented elsewhere have managed to replicate its unique success.

So what's the big secret?

M-Pesa has met all of the critical success factors of a high-performing mobile-payments service – great technology, simple marketing, sound partnerships with banks, and support from the regulator. But one factor outshines the rest in terms of the proficiency with which it has been structured and maintained: M-Pesa's distribution system. As effortless as it may seem, transferring money via mobile requires a robust backstage set-up.

Customers who wish to deposit or withdraw cash from their M-Pesa e-wallet, in exchange for mobile money, can do so at one of Kenya's 40,000-plus registered M-Pesa agents. Compared to the 840 bank branches found countrywide, the superior convenience of M-Pesa is evident, especially in rural areas.

To appreciate the strength of the distribution system though, we must understand the challenges it faces. A large proportion of the population is employed in cities and sends money home to family in rural areas using M-Pesa. As a result, M-Pesa agents in cities mostly receive

3 Finance and accounts

deposits of cash, while agents in rural areas mostly pay out withdrawals. Therefore, the reliability of the system rests heavily on active liquidity management; rural agents need to have an efficient system of replenishing their cash resources once these have been swapped out for mobile money via customer withdrawals. M-Pesa has achieved this through "pooling" and "layering" within the distribution system.

M-Pesa agents pool the net mobile money they receive from customers and travel a short distance to exchange this for cash from a registered M-Pesa intermediary. These intermediaries, in turn, pool the cash and mobile money received from agents, and arrange the logistics between affiliated banks.

The pooling in the system aims to increase efficiency by reducing the number of players that need to ferry cash at each stage. Meanwhile, the layering in the system acts as a cushion against clearing delays in the banking system, allowing for the speed of M-Pesa transfers. Because the availability of liquidity is core to any payment service, Safaricom visits all agents on a bi-monthly basis to check on the quality of this process, and how agents are handling the growth in volumes of transactions.

What's the headline?

In summary, if money transfers made through M-Pesa were not immediately available, or if cash could not be reliably obtained from an agent, the M-Pesa system would be of little value to its users. M-Pesa's carefully orchestrated distribution network enables the required customer service levels.

Source: Adapted from https://digital.hbs.edu/platform-rctom/submission/how-kenya-created-the-worlds-most-successful-mobile-payments-service

Concept

CHANGE

Due to increasing competition and unexpected changes in consumer behaviour, businesses are forced to adapt in order to remain relevant and succeed. These adaptations come with frequent changes to organizational objectives, including decisions regarding the best source of finance to choose to achieve the set objectives.

How flexible in terms of finance should businesses be in adapting to change? Carry out research on how various global businesses are adapting to change in respect of their financial requirements.

TOK links

1. Are objective facts or appeals to emotion more effective when applying for an external source of finance such as crowdfunding?
2. Is there a moral obligation for financial institutions to lend to every start-up business?
3. Is it ever possible to know what the best source of finance is?

Revision checklist

✓ Internal sources of finance, which are obtained within the business, include personal loans, retained profits and sale of assets.

✓ External sources of finance that are obtained outside the business include share capital, loan capital, overdrafts, trade credit, crowdfunding, leasing, microfinance providers and business angels.

✓ Short-term finance which lasts for one year or less provides a business with the working capital that it needs. Long-term finance with a duration of more than one year is funding obtained for the purpose of purchasing long-term fixed assets or other expansion requirements of a business.

✓ In deciding on the appropriate source of finance to use, businesses need to consider the purpose of the funds, cost, flexibility, their status and size, amount required, gearing, and the state of the external environment.

3.2 Sources of finance

Practice question

To answer the question below effectively, see Unit 6 pages 398–402.

Three Hills Driving School (THDS)

Three Hills Driving School (THDS) provides driving instruction for people interested in obtaining a licence to drive a car. They target people aged 18 to 25 who are mostly students who have finished high school, and/or university students.

THDS is owned by Maria who set it up two years ago using her personal funds. Maria took a long time to save up for this and was determined to get the business started. This included selling some of her household items in order to generate the necessary funds.

Her capital expenditure was about $90,000 in the first year, while her revenue expenditure was half that amount in the same year. She plans to sell her business after five years to a business angel who has shown interest in buying it.

Currently, due to increased demand, she is planning to buy more cars and employ more instructors. She will need to seek external sources of finance to fund this. She is considering whether to take up a long-term loan or a bank overdraft. Maria is worried that the interest rates charged by banks can be quite high if funds are borrowed for a short period of time. She is also not sure if she has enough security to acquire a long-term loan. However, the fact that she has a reasonable amount of money in her account and has been in business for two years could work to her advantage.

a) Define the term *business angel*. [2 marks]

b) Explain **two** benefits to Maria of raising money using personal funds. [4 marks]

c) Evaluate the view that taking up a long-term loan would be preferable to getting a bank overdraft for Maria's business expansion plans. [10 marks]

3.3 Costs and revenues

> **By the end of this chapter, you should be able to:**
> → Explain the different **types of costs** (fixed, variable, direct and indirect/overhead), using examples
> → Comment on the meaning of the term **revenue** and, using examples, suggest various **revenue streams** available to organizations

Introduction

Costs and revenues are very important factors that determine the success of any business. Businesses therefore need accurate and reliable information on these elements to enable effective decision-making.

- **Cost** is an expenditure or amount paid to produce or sell a good or service, including the acquisition of business resources.
- **Revenue** is income earned or money generated from the sale of goods or services.
- **Profit** is calculated by subtracting costs from revenue. A high positive difference (where revenue is higher than costs) is a good indicator of business success.

Types of costs

Fixed costs

These are costs that do not change or vary with the amount of goods or services produced. They are expenses that have to be paid regardless of any business activity the firm engages in.

They are mostly time related and are usually paid per month, per quarter, bi-annually, or per year. They remain fixed in the short run. The short run is defined as a period of time when at least one factor of production (resource needed to produce goods or services) does not change.

Examples of fixed costs include rent, insurance, salaries, and interest payments. For instance, if a firm usually pays rent of $5,000 per month and decides to take a week's holiday, this rent will still need to be paid despite the holiday. It is therefore important to note that fixed costs do not change due to a change in output in the short run.

Variable costs

These are costs that vary or change according to the number of goods or services produced. They are expenses that change in proportion to business activity. Variable costs are volume related as they are paid per quantity produced.

Key terms

Fixed costs
costs that do not change with the amount of goods or services produced

Variable costs
costs that change with the number of goods or services produced

Direct costs
costs that can be identified with the production of specific goods or services

Indirect costs
costs that are not clearly identified with the production of specific goods or services

3.3 Costs and revenues

These are costs that can be incurred both in the short run or in the long run (a period of time when all factors of production are variable). They are also pegged to sales, in that an increase in sales or output sold leads to an increase in variable costs. If no units are produced, then no variable costs are incurred. Examples of variable costs include raw material costs, sales commissions, packaging, and energy usage costs.

All fixed costs (total fixed costs) added to all variable costs (total variable costs) gives us the total costs. Hence, total costs (TC) = total fixed costs (TFC) + total variable costs (TVC).

Direct costs

These are costs that can be identified with or clearly attributed to the production of specific goods or services. They are expenses that can be traced directly to a particular product, department, or process (known as cost centres). Some examples of direct costs include the cost of flour used in making bread in a bakery, the cost of labour used in car production in a manufacturing firm, and the cost of chicken in a fast-food restaurant selling only chicken products. Generally, direct costs include raw materials, direct labour, and packaging costs.

Raw materials are a direct cost

Indirect costs

These are costs that are not clearly identified with the production of specific goods or services. They are expenses that are not directly traceable to a given cost centre such as a product, activity, or department. As a result, they are difficult to assign to particular cost centres. They are also known as **overheads** or **overhead costs**. Examples include rent, office staff salaries, audit fees, legal expenses, insurance, advertising expenditure, security, interest on loans, and warehouse costs.

Rent on business premises is an indirect cost

Student workpoint 3.5

Be a researcher

Research the following organizations and identify the various costs they incur.

- An airline
- A mobile phone company
- A college
- A hospital
- A bank

Classify the costs as either fixed or variable. Which of these costs can also be categorised as direct or indirect?

Assessment advice

In most cases, indirect costs are fixed costs while direct costs are variable costs. However, both indirect and direct costs can be either fixed or variable depending on the specific nature of the business activity.

Total revenue

This is the total amount of money a firm receives from its sales. It is calculated by multiplying the price per unit by the number of units sold:

$$\text{total revenue} = \text{price per unit} \times \text{quantity sold}$$

167

3 Finance and accounts

> **Key terms**
>
> **Revenue**
> a measure of the money generated from the sale of goods and services
>
> **Total revenue**
> the total amount of money a firm receives from the sale of goods or services, found by multiplying the price per unit by the number of units sold

Abbreviated as TR = P × Q, where TR is total revenue, P is price per unit and Q is the quantity sold.

For example, if a toy-producing firm charges $8 per toy and sells 200,000 toys a month, then its total revenue for the month will be ($8 × 200,000) = $1,600,000 or $1.6 million.

Total revenue (also known as sales revenue or turnover) should not be confused with profit, which takes costs or expenses into account. In addition, total revenue includes all income received, whether the goods or services were sold on credit or for cash. However, a firm's revenue is obtained not only from its trading activities. Other revenue streams include the following:

- **Rental income** – a business could receive income from rent it collects from property it has invested in. A seasonal business could also hire out its office or factory space during times when demand for its products is low.
- **Sale of fixed assets** – this could be from the sale of unused or underutilized assets in a business.
- **Dividends** – a business could be a shareholder in other businesses and is entitled to a share of the profits, also known as dividends.
- **Interest on deposits** – holding substantial amounts of cash in the bank can lead to a business earning good levels of accumulated interest on the money if the interest rates are favourable.
- **Donations** – these could be cash gifts made by an individual or organization targeting mostly charitable organizations.

Contribution: absorption costing (HL only)

As a contribution tool, absorption costing aids in business decision-making by providing a platform where various cost situations are analysed and evaluated. Absorption costing (also called full costing) is a managerial accounting method that captures all costs associated with producing a given product. The direct and indirect costs, including direct materials, direct labour, rent, and insurance, are accounted for using this method.

Research the following.

- How does absorption costing differ from variable costing?
- What are the advantages and disadvantages of using absorption costing in accounting?

Find two company examples that use this method.

> **TOK links**
>
> 1. When calculating the costs and revenue streams of a business, is it always objective, or is there scope for subjectivity?
> 2. Could it sometimes be arbitrary to decide if a cost is fixed or variable, or if it is direct or indirect?
> 3. We can know retrospectively about previous costs, but how we can know about future costs?

Descriptive statistics

Descriptive statistics involve the use of statistical data and they help to present large amounts of data in simplified and manageable forms.

To what extent would the use of mean, mode and median be useful when analysing financial data for businesses? How would this information be visually presented?

3.3 Costs and revenues

Revision checklist

- ✓ Fixed costs are costs that do not change with the amount of goods or services produced and are paid regardless of any business activity the firm engages in.
- ✓ Variable costs are costs that vary with the number of goods or services produced or that change in proportion to business activity.
- ✓ Total cost is the summation of all fixed and variable costs.
- ✓ Direct costs are expenses that can be directly traced to a particular product, department or cost centre, while indirect costs are not clearly identified with the production of specific goods or services.
- ✓ Total revenue is the total income gained from the sale of goods and services. It is also known as sales revenue or sales turnover.
- ✓ Available revenue streams to businesses include rental income, sale of fixed assets, dividends, interests on deposits, donations, grants and subsidies.
- ✓ Descriptive statistics involve the use of statistical data and help to present large amounts of data in simplified and manageable forms.

Practice question

To answer the question below effectively, see Unit 6 pages 398–402.

TAK

TAK is a sole proprietorship business set up by Tom that focuses on providing tour and travel services to tourists. He obtained the funds to set up the business from selling part of his shares in another company.

The set-up costs included a large amount spent on fixed costs. *TAK* owns a three-storey building with sufficient office space where all employees are housed. However, during low tourist seasons, most offices are not used. As he operated his business, Tom became aware of the increasing direct costs that had an impact on his total costs.

Tom has three drivers working for him who are paid based on the number of trips they make, driving tourists using *TAK's* tourist vans. Tom currently owns three newly acquired tourist vehicles and two five-year-old vehicles. The fuel consumption per vehicle is monitored based on the number of trips each vehicle makes.

In his first year Tom did not make any profit because his revenue was quite insignificant, especially due to the downturn in the economy. He has therefore cut down on his costs and is seeking more revenue streams in order to guarantee a profit by the close of next year. He has approached a financial consultant to help him improve the performance of his business.

a) Define the following terms:

    (i) fixed costs   *[2 marks]*

    (ii) revenue   *[2 marks]*

    (iii) profit   *[2 marks]*

b) Using examples from *TAK*, explain the term *direct costs*.   *[4 marks]*

c) Explain **three** ways the financial consultant could advise Tom about ways to improve his revenue streams.   *[6 marks]*

3.4 Final accounts

> **By the end of this chapter, you should be able to:**
> → Discuss the **purpose of accounts to different stakeholders**
> → Prepare and interpret final accounts, namely the **profit and loss account** and the **balance sheet**
> → Describe the different types of **intangible assets**
> → Calculate and distinguish between the **straight-line** and **units of use** depreciation methods **(HL only)**
> → Examine the appropriateness of the **straight-line** and **units of use** depreciation methods **(HL only)**

Purpose of accounts to different stakeholders

Final accounts are financial statements compiled by businesses at the end of a particular accounting period, such as at the end of a fiscal or trading year. These records of accounts – including transactions, revenues, and expenses – help to inform internal and external stakeholders about the financial position and performance of an organization.

Internal stakeholders include shareholders, managers, and employees, while examples of external stakeholders are customers, suppliers, the government, competitors, financiers, and the local community. The purpose of accounts to each of these stakeholders is explored below.

Shareholders

Shareholders are interested in knowing how valuable the business has become throughout its financial year. They are keen to establish how profitable the business is in order to assess the safety of their investment. They check on how efficiently the business is investing capital in an attempt to make a worthwhile return on their investment. The performance of the directors is also of interest to them: shareholders want to see whether the directors need to be motivated further or replaced.

Managers

Final accounts are used by managers to set targets, which they can use to judge and compare their performance within a particular financial year or number of years. These will help them in setting budgets, which will then help in monitoring and controlling expenditure patterns in various departments. Knowing the financial records will therefore greatly assist managers in strategic planning for more effective decision-making in the businesses.

Employees

A profitable business could signal to employees that their jobs are secure. This may also indicate that they could get pay rises. The potential for business growth could help to strengthen these two aspects of job security and salary increases. However, an increase in profitability does not necessarily lead to pay increases for employees, leading them to involve trade unions to negotiate further on their behalf.

Customers

Customers are interested in knowing whether there will be a constant supply of a firm's products in the future. This will determine how dependent they should be on the business. If a firm lacks security, perhaps due to low profitability, customers will go elsewhere where supply is reliable and guaranteed.

Suppliers

Suppliers can use final accounts to negotiate better cash or credit terms with firms. They can either extend the trade credit period or demand immediate cash payments. The security of the business and thus its ability to pay off its debts will be a key concern for suppliers.

The government

The government and tax authorities will check on whether the business is abiding by the law regarding accounting regulations. They will be interested in the profitability of the business to see how much tax it pays. A loss-making business will be of grave concern to the government because it could mean an increase in unemployment, which could be detrimental to a country's economy.

Competitors

Businesses will want to compare their financial statements with those of other firms to see how well they are performing financially. They will look for the answers to key questions such as:

- Are their competitors' profitability levels higher than theirs or are the competitors struggling financially?
- How do the competitors' sales revenues compare with theirs?

Financiers

These include banks who check on the creditworthiness of the business to establish how much money they can lend it. This will also depend on the gearing of the business, because a high-geared business will have problems soliciting funding from financial institutions (see Chapter 3.2). Banks will thoroughly assess the accounts of a business in order to be confident that it will be able to pay back its loan with interest.

The local community

Residents living around a particular business will want to know its profitability and expansion potential. This is because it may create job opportunities for them and lead to growth in the community. However, the residents will also be concerned about whether the business will be environmentally friendly and whether its accounts consider costs for minimizing air or noise pollution.

3 Finance and accounts

Case study

Ethics and the code of conduct

Ethics and ethical behaviour refer more to general principles such as honesty, integrity, and morals. The code of professional conduct, however, is a specific set of rules set by the governing bodies of certified public accountants. Although the rules set out by different bodies around the world are unique, some rules are universal. Let's take a closer look at some of these important rules.

Is it ethical to give suppliers expensive gifts like luxury watches or holidays abroad?

Rules and guidance

One of the key rules set out by professional accounting bodies in North America is the idea of independence. This is the idea that, as an auditor, you must be totally objective and must be without ties to or relationships with the client, since that could potentially impair your judgment and impair the overall course of the audit work.

There are two forms of independence:

- Independence in **fact**
- Independence in **appearance**

Independence in fact refers to any factual information, such as whether you, as an auditor, own any shares or other investments in the client firm. These facts are usually easy to determine.

Independence in appearance, however, is more subjective. Let's say, for example, that as an auditor you were invited to a year-end party at the client firm. The party turns out to be extremely luxurious and you also receive a nice watch as a gift. In appearance, would the auditor, who was invited to the party and who also received a gift, be able to maintain independence in the audit? In order to solve a potential conflict of interest, a reasonable observer's test is used (ie what would a reasonable observer say about the situation?).

Threats to independence

There are always threats and situations that can reduce the level of independence. Let's take a look at examples of some of these threats:

1. Familiarity threat: If the auditor has a long relationship with the client or they are close friends/relatives.

2. Intimidation threat: If the auditor changes the financial statements, the client threatens to switch auditors.

3. Self-interest threat: If the auditor has a direct financial interest through shares or a large fee outstanding from the client.

4. Self-review threat: If the auditor performs both audit and bookkeeping services, it is a review of the auditor's own work.

Concept

ETHICS

Ethics in accounting is the study of moral values and judgments as applied in the accounting process. A code of ethics is therefore a set of principles, usually based on the firm's core values, that guide accountants on the standards that need to be upheld. A code spells out the "rules" for behaviour with respective pre-emptive warnings. The case study here provides a deeper understanding of some of the important rules set by professional accounting bodies.

Research how ethics has influenced the finance and accounting practices of one or more organizations.

> **Other important rules**
>
> Some other rules outlined by professional accounting bodies include the following:
>
> - Contingent fees are not allowed. For example, audit fees that are based on a percentage of the net income figure or a percentage of a bank loan received.
>
> - Integrity and due care. Audit work must be done thoroughly, diligently, and in a timely manner.
>
> - Professional competence. Auditors must be competent, which means they must have both the necessary academic knowledge and experience in the relevant industry.
>
> - Duty to report a breach of rules. This rule is commonly referred to as the whistleblower rule. If an auditor observes a fellow auditor violating any of these rules, they have a responsibility to report it.
>
> - Confidentiality. Auditors must not disclose any information regarding the client to outsiders.
>
> Source: Adapted from https://corporatefinanceinstitute.com/resources/knowledge/accounting/accounting-ethics/

The main final accounts

The profit and loss account

This is also known as the **income statement** and shows the records of income and expenditure flows of a business over a given time period. It therefore establishes whether a business has made a profit or a loss and how this was distributed at the end of that period. It is divided into three parts: the **trading account**, the **profit and loss account**, and the **appropriation account**.

The trading account

The trading account shows the difference between the sales revenue and the cost to the business of those sales. It is shown as the top part of the income statement that establishes the gross profit of the business (see Table 3.4.1). In calculating gross profit, the following formula is used:

$$\text{gross profit} = \text{sales revenue} - \text{cost of sales}$$

Sales revenue is the income earned from selling goods or services over a given period. Cost of sales or cost of goods sold (COGS) is the direct cost of producing or purchasing the goods that were sold during that period. The formula for cost of sales is as follows:

$$\text{cost of sales} = \text{opening stock} + \text{purchases} - \text{closing stock}$$

3 Finance and accounts

Key terms

Profit and loss account
also known as the income statement, this is the record of income and expenditure flows of a business over a given time period

Cost of sales
the direct cost of producing or purchasing the goods that were sold during that period

Gross profit
found by deducting cost of sales from sales revenue

Profit before interest and tax
the difference between gross profit and expenses

Profit before tax
found by subtracting interest from profit before interest and tax

Profit for period
equal to profit before tax less tax

Dividends
a sum of money paid to shareholders, which is decided by the board of directors of a company

Retained profit
the amount of earnings left after dividends and other deductions have been made

---

For example, a firm at the beginning of a trading period had $500 worth of stock. It then bought more stock during this period valued at $800. It then closed this period with stock valued at $200. What is its COGS during the period?

$$COGS = \$500 + \$800 - \$200$$
$$= \$1,100$$

What would the firm's gross profit be if it sold 400 units of a product at $10 each?

$$\text{Sales revenue} = \$10 \times 400 = \$4,000$$
$$\text{Gross profit} = \$4,000 - \$1,100$$
$$= \$2,900$$

The profit and loss account

This is the second part of the income statement that shows the profit before interest and tax, profit before tax, and profit for period (see Table 3.4.1).

To find out profit before interest and tax, expenses are subtracted from the gross profit shown in the trading account. These expenses comprise indirect costs or overheads which are not directly linked to the units sold. Examples include advertising costs, administration charges, rent, and insurance costs. Therefore:

$$\boxed{\text{profit before interest and tax} = \text{gross profit} - \text{expenses}}$$

Profit before tax is calculated by subtracting interest payable on loans from the profit before interest and tax:

$$\boxed{\text{profit before tax} = \text{profit before interest and tax} - \text{interest}}$$

Then, the profit for period is found by deducting corporation tax (tax on company profits) from profit before tax:

$$\boxed{\text{profit for period} = \text{profit before tax} - \text{corporation tax}}$$

The appropriation account

This is the final part of the profit and loss account that shows how the company's profit for period is distributed (see Table 3.4.1). This distribution is in two forms: either as dividends to shareholders or as retained profit (ploughed-back profit). Retained profit is calculated using the following formula:

$$\boxed{\text{retained profit} = \text{profit for period} - \text{dividends}}$$

3.4 Final accounts

Table 3.4.1 Profit and loss account for XYZ Ltd (profit-making entity)

XYZ Ltd (profit-making entity) Statement of profit or loss for the year ended 30 June 2021		
	US$ million	
Sales revenue	800	
Cost of sales	(250)	Trading account
Gross profit	550	
Expenses	(300)	
Profit before interest and tax	250	
Interest	(20)	Profit and loss account
Profit before tax	230	
Tax	(40)	
Profit for period	190	
Dividends	(50)	Appropriation account
Retained profit	140	

It is important to note that for non-profit entities, the term "surplus" is used instead of "profit" in the statement of profit or loss. As noted in Table 3.4.2, the organization is exempt from corporation tax and hence nothing is deducted from the surplus before tax to get surplus for period. In addition, no dividends are paid and therefore the surplus for period is also the retained surplus.

Table 3.4.2 Profit and loss account for XYZ (non-profit entity)

XYZ Ltd (non-profit entity) Statement of profit or loss for the year ended 30 June 2021	
	US$ million
Sales revenue	800
Cost of sales	(250)
Gross surplus	550
Expenses	(300)
Surplus before interest	250
Interest	(20)
Surplus before tax	230
Tax	(0)
Surplus for period	230
Retained surplus	230

Student workpoint 3.6

Be a thinker

Profit and loss account for BTW Ltd for the year ended 31 December 2021

	$000
Sales revenue	950
Cost of goods sold	?
Gross profit	650
Expenses	?
Profit before interest and tax	350
Interest	10
Profit before tax	?
Tax	40
Profit for period	?
Dividends	50
Retained profit	?

a) Complete the above profit and loss account by filling in the missing numbers (indicated by question marks).

b) Identify **four** stakeholders who would be interested in the profit and loss account for BTW Ltd.

c) Explain how the above stakeholders would use the information in this account.

3 Finance and accounts

> **Key terms**
>
> **Balance sheet**
> a financial statement that outlines the assets, liabilities and equity of a firm at a specific point in time
>
> **Assets**
> resources of value that a business owns or that are owed to it
>
> **Liabilities**
> a firm's legal debts or what it owes to other firms, institutions or individuals
>
> **Net assets**
> found by subtracting total liabilities from total assets

The balance sheet

Also known as the statement of financial position, this outlines the assets, liabilities, and equity of a firm at a specific point in time. It is a snapshot of the financial position of a firm and is used to calculate a firm's net worth. It gives the firm an idea of what it owns and owes, including how much shareholders have invested in it.

The basic requirement of a balance sheet is that what a business owns (total assets) must equal what it owes (total liabilities) plus how the assets are financed (equity). This is what makes the balance sheet balance. The three main components of assets, liabilities, and equity are explored below.

Assets

These are resources of value that a business owns or that are owed to it. They include fixed assets and current assets.

Non-current assets, also called fixed assets, are long-term assets that last in a business for more than 12 months. Tangible examples that are physical in nature include buildings, equipment, vehicles, and machinery.

Some of these assets, such as machinery, usually depreciate (lose value) over time. In this case, the accumulated depreciation is deducted from the non-current asset. Intangible assets that are non-physical in nature tend to be difficult to value. (These will be looked at later in the unit.)

Current assets are short-term assets that last in a business for up to 12 months. They include cash, debtors, and stock.

- Cash is money received from the sale of goods and services, which could be held either at the bank or by the business.
- Debtors are individuals or other firms that have bought goods on credit and owe the business money.
- Stock, also known as inventory, includes raw materials, semi-finished goods, and finished goods.

> total assets = non-current assets + current assets

Liabilities

These are a firm's legal debts or what it owes to other firms, institutions, or individuals. They arise during the course of business operation and are usually a source of funding for the firm. They are classified into non-current liabilities and current liabilities.

Non-current liabilities, also known as long-term liabilities, are long-term debts or borrowings payable after 12 months by the business. They include long-term bank loans and mortgages.

Current liabilities are short-term debts that are payable by the business within 12 months. These include creditors (unpaid suppliers who sold goods on credit to the firm), a bank overdraft (see Chapter 3.2), and tax (money owed to the government, such as corporation tax).

> total liabilities = current liabilities + non-current liabilities

To work out net assets, total liabilities is subtracted from total assets:

> net assets = total assets − total liabilities

Having calculated the net assets of the business, we then need to find out how they were financed.

Equity

This refers to the amount of money that would be returned to a business if all of the assets were liquidated. **Liquidation** is a situation where all of a firm's assets are sold off to pay any funds owing. For profit-making entities there are two aspects to equity: share capital and retained earnings. However, for non-profit entities there is only one aspect of equity (retained earnings).

Share capital

This refers to the original capital invested into the business through shares bought by shareholders. It is a permanent source of capital and does not include the daily buying and selling of shares in a stock exchange market or the current market value of shares.

Retained earnings

This includes all current and prior period retained profits (profit-making entities) or retained surpluses (non-profit entities).

Hence, for profit-making businesses, equity is the combination of share capital and retained earnings:

> equity = share capital + retained earnings

For non-profit-making businesses, equity is equal to retained earnings:

> equity = retained earnings

In both profit-making and non-profit entities, equity helps to finance the net assets of the business and enables the balance sheet to balance:

> net assets = equity

Tables 3.4.3 and 3.4.4 are examples of balance sheets that incorporate what has been discussed above and use the required IB format.

Key terms

Equity
refers to the amount of money that would be returned to a business if all of the assets were liquidated

Liquidation
a situation where all of a firm's assets are sold off to pay any funds owing

Table 3.4.3 A statement of financial position for a profit-making entity

XYZ Ltd (profit-making entity) Statement of financial position as at 30 June 2021		
	$m	$m
Non-current assets		
Property, plant and equipment	600	
Accumulated depreciation	(30)	
Non-current assets		570
Current assets		
Cash	20	
Debtors	15	
Stock	55	
Current assets		90
Total assets		660
Current liabilities		
Bank overdraft	10	
Trade creditors	20	
Short-term loans	15	
Current liabilities		45
Non-current liabilities		
Borrowings – long term	250	
Non-current liabilities		250
Total liabilities		295
Net assets		365
Equity		
Share capital	220	
Retained earnings	145	
Total equity		365

Assessment advice ✓

The formats for the profit and loss account and balance sheet used in this chapter are the recommended ones that are indicated in the IB *Business Management Guide*.

3.4 Final accounts

Table 3.4.4 A statement of financial position for a non-profit entity

XYZ (non-profit entity) Statement of financial position as at 30 June 2021	$m	$m
Non-current assets		
Property, plant and equipment	600	
Accumulated depreciation	(30)	
Non-current assets		570
Current assets		
Cash	20	
Debtors	15	
Stock	55	
Current assets		90
Total assets		660
Current liabilities		
Bank overdraft	10	
Trade creditors	20	
Short-term loans	15	
Current liabilities		45
Non-current liabilities		
Borrowings – long term	250	
Non-current liabilities		250
Total liabilities		295
Net assets		365
Equity		
Retained earnings	365	
Total equity		365

3 Finance and accounts

> **Student workpoint 3.7**
>
> **Be a thinker**
>
> 1. Using Table 3.4.3, prepare another balance sheet for the year ended 30 June 2022 after the following adjustments occurred:
>   - Cash increased by US$10 million.
>   - Trade creditors rose by US$15 million.
>   - Stock decreased by US$5 million.
>   - A long-term loan increased by 10%.
>   - Debtors rose by US$5 million.
>   - Retained earnings fell by US$26 million.
>   - The bank overdraft reduced by US$4 million.
>   - Non-current assets, share capital and short-term loans remained the same.
>
> 2. Explain **two** uses and **two** limitations of the balance sheet.

Intangible assets

These are assets that are non-physical in nature. However, even though they do not have a physical value, they can prove to be very valuable to a firm's long-term success. Some of them are explained below.

Patents

These provide inventors with the exclusive rights to manufacture, use, sell, or control their invention of a product. The inventors are provided with legal protection that prevents others from copying their ideas. Anyone wishing to use the patent holder's idea must apply and pay a fee to be granted permission to use it. The legal life for most patents is about 20 years, although this depends on the useful life of the patent. Interesting patents include a pen with a scanner, steel kidneys and rubber shoes for horses' health.

Goodwill

This refers to the value of positive or favourable attributes that relate to a business. It includes a good customer base and relations, a strong brand name, highly skilled employees, a desirable location and the good reputation a firm enjoys with its clients. Goodwill usually arises when one firm is purchased by another. During an acquisition, goodwill is valued as the amount paid by the purchasing firm over and above the book value of the firm being bought.

Copyright laws

These are laws that provide a creator with the exclusive right to protect the production and sale of their artistic or literary work. Creators include musicians, authors, and film producers. Copyright laws will only apply if the original ideas are put to use, such as in the creation of a published novel, a music album or developed computer software. Most copyright

---

Key terms

Intangible assets
assets that are non-physical in nature

Patents
provide inventors with the exclusive rights to manufacture, use, sell or control the product or process they invented

Goodwill
the value of positive or favourable attributes that relate to a business

Copyright laws
legislation that provides creators with the exclusive right to protect the production and sale of their artistic or literary work

Trademark
a recognizable symbol, word, phrase or design that is officially registered and that identifies a product or business

lasts for between 50 and 100 years after the death of the creator. As with patents, anyone wishing to use a copyright holder's works must seek permission to do so.

Trademarks

These are a recognizable symbol, word, phrase or design that is officially registered and that identifies a product or business. Trademarks also help to distinguish one firm's products from another's. Anyone who infringes the trademarks of others can be sued by the trademark owners. Trademarks can be sold for a fee and most last for a 15-year renewable period, depending on their use. Examples of popular trademarks include Apple, Coca-Cola, the Nike "swoosh", the McDonald's golden arches symbol, and slogans like Capital One's "What's in your wallet?"

Intangible assets are difficult to value due to their subjective nature, and in many cases they will not be shown in the balance sheet. Their value can fluctuate over time and simple changes in the reputation of an organization can either inflate or deflate a firm's value. As a result, intangible assets can be used to "window dress" or artificially increase the value of a firm just before a purchase. The setting of specific parameters to be used to quantify an intangible asset just serves to increase the complexity and inaccuracy of including it in the balance sheet.

The diamond retailer De Beers has trademarked the famous slogan "A diamond is forever"

Depreciation (HL only)

This is the decrease in the value of a non-current asset over time. It is a non-cash expense that is recorded in the profit and loss account in order to determine the profit before interest and tax. Two reasons why assets depreciate are:

- Wear and tear – the repeated use of non-current assets such as cars or machinery causes them to fall in value and more money is needed to maintain them.
- Obsolescence – existing non-current assets fall in value when new or improved versions are introduced in the market. With time these "old" assets become obsolete or out of date and are eventually withdrawn.

Two methods for calculating depreciation are the **straight-line method** and the **units of production method**, as explained below.

Straight-line method

This is a commonly used method that spreads out the cost of an asset equally over its lifetime by deducting a given constant amount of depreciation of the asset's value each year. It requires the following elements in its calculation:

- The expected useful life of the asset, which is the length of time it intends to be used before replacement.
- The original cost of the asset, which is its purchase or historical cost.
- The residual, scrap or salvage value of the asset, which is an estimation of its worth or value over its useful life.

> **Key terms**
>
> **Depreciation**
> the decrease in the value of a fixed asset over time
>
> **Straight-line depreciation**
> a method that spreads out the cost of an asset equally over its lifetime by deducting a given constant amount of depreciation of the asset's value per annum
>
> **Units of production depreciation**
> also called units of activity method, it calculates the depreciation of the value of an asset based on usage

181

Incorporating the above, the annual depreciation can be calculated as:

$$\text{annual depreciation} = \frac{\text{original cost} - \text{residual value}}{\text{expected useful life of asset}}$$

Example 1: On 1 January 2021, ABC Company purchased a vehicle costing $30,000. It is expected to have a value of $6,000 at the end of four years. Calculate the depreciation expense on the vehicle for the year ended 31 December 2021.

First, it is important to identify the key elements: the original cost is $30,000, the residual value is $6,000, and the expected useful life is four years. Then apply the annual depreciation formula:

$$\text{annual depreciation} = \frac{\$30{,}000 - \$6{,}000}{4 \text{ years}} = \$6{,}000$$

The above information can be presented in a table to show the net book value over four years.

Table 3.4.5 Straight-line depreciation at $6,000 per annum

Year	Annual depreciation expense ($)	Net book value on vehicle ($)
0 (present)	0	30,000
1	6,000	24,000
2	6,000	18,000
3	6,000	12,000
4	6,000	6,000

Example 2: Calculate the depreciation expense of the above vehicle if it was purchased on 1 July 2021 with the year ending on 31 December 2021.

In such a case we will be required to charge depreciation for half the year as follows:

$$\text{depreciation expense} = \left(\frac{6 \text{ months}}{12 \text{ months}}\right) \times \left[\frac{(\$30{,}000 - \$6{,}000)}{4}\right] = \$3{,}000$$

Advantages of using straight-line depreciation

- It is simple to calculate as it is a predictable expense that is spread over a number of years.
- It is most suitable for less expensive items, such as furniture, that can be written off within the asset's estimated useful life.

Disadvantages of using straight-line depreciation

- It is not suitable for expensive assets such as plant and machinery, as it does not cater for the loss in efficiency or increase in repair expenses over the useful life of the asset.
- It can inflate the value of some assets which may have lost the greatest amount of value in their first or second years (eg motor vehicles).
- It does not take into account the fast-changing technological environment that may render certain fixed assets obsolete very quickly.

Key term

Residual value

an estimation of an asset's worth or value over its useful life, also known as scrap or salvage value

Units of production method

Also called the units of activity method, this depreciation method calculates the depreciation of the value of an asset based on usage. It assumes that an asset's useful life is more closely related to its usage than just the passage of time. In this method, depreciation will be higher when there is a greater volume of activity during the year when an asset is used a lot, and lower during times when an asset is used less.

The following information is required to calculate depreciation using the units of production method:

- The cost basis of the asset. The cost basis of a non-current asset is the total amount paid to acquire the asset for use in the business. This is the original value of the asset.
- The salvage value of the asset. This is the estimated value of the asset if it were to be sold at the end of its useful life.
- The estimated total number of units to be produced. The wear and tear on the machinery is the result of the number of units it is expected to produce over its useful life. This figure is usually based on production estimates and historical information.
- Estimated useful life. This is the length of time an asset is expected to be used before it wears out and needs to be replaced.
- Actual units produced. The number of units the asset produced during the current year.

Based on the above, the units of production depreciation formula is:

$$\left[\frac{\text{(cost basis of asset} - \text{salvage value)}}{\text{estimated total units to be produced over estimated useful life}}\right] \times \text{actual units produced} = \text{depreciation expense}$$

Note that:

$$\left[\frac{\text{(cost basis of asset} - \text{salvage value)}}{\text{estimated total units to be produced over estimated useful life}}\right] = \text{units of production rate}$$

Hence, the units of production depreciation formula can also be written as:

$$\text{units of production rate} \times \text{actual units produced} = \text{depreciation expense}$$

Example: Use Table 3.4.6 to calculate the depreciation for two non-current assets using the units of production method.

Table 3.4.6 Information required for units of production depreciation calculation

Non-current asset	Cost basis	Salvage	Useful life (years)	Total estimated units produced over useful life	Actual units produced for period
Photocopier	$4,000	$500	5	200,000	40,000
Tractor	$8,000	$800	8	96,000	12,000

Photocopier annual depreciation expense calculation

To calculate the annual depreciation expenses for the photocopier, the units of production rate will be calculated first. Once that is complete, the depreciation expense will be calculated.

The steps used in calculating the unit of production depreciation expense for the photocopier in year one are as follows:

1. **Calculate the units of production rate for the photocopier**

$$\frac{\text{(cost basis - salvage value)}}{\text{estimated units produced over useful life}} = \text{units of production rate}$$

$$\frac{\$4,000 - \$500}{200,000} = 0.0175$$

2. **Calculate the photocopier depreciation expense**

Actual units produced × units of production rate = depreciation expense for Year 1

$40,000 \times 0.0175 = \$700$

Tractor annual depreciation expense calculation

To calculate the annual depreciation expenses for the tractor, the units of production rate will be calculated first. Once that is complete, the depreciation expense will be calculated.

The steps used in calculating the unit of production depreciation expense for the tractor in year one are as follows:

1. **Calculate the units of production rate for the tractor**

$$\frac{\text{(cost basis - salvage value)}}{\text{estimated units produced over useful life}} = \text{units of production rate}$$

$$\frac{\$8,000 - \$800}{96,000} = 0.075$$

2. **Calculate the tractor depreciation expense**

Actual units produced × units of production rate = depreciation expense for Year 1

$12,000 \times 0.075 = \$900$

Advantages of using units of production depreciation

- As the depreciation expense is directly tied to the wear and tear on the asset, this method writes down an asset based on its usage as opposed to time. This is a more accurate reflection of the declining physical value of the asset.

- It accurately matches revenues and expenses. As this method is based on asset usage, it is important to note that the expenses fluctuate with customer demand. This allows revenues generated to be matched to expenses when producing financial statements, hence providing a more realistic view of what is taking place in the business.

Student workpoint 3.8

Be knowledgeable

Suppose a business has an asset that had an original cost of $2,000, a salvage value of $200, and five years of useful life.

1. Use the straight-line method to determine its annual depreciation expense.
2. If the estimated units produced over the useful life is 100,000, calculate the depreciation expense using the units of production method.

Disadvantages of using units of production depreciation

- It is only useful to manufacturers or producers. It makes little sense to tie depreciation to asset usage if a business does not manufacture or produce a product.
- This method is not allowed for tax purposes. It cannot be used when a business computes its tax returns at the end of the year.
- It can be complicated to compute the units of depreciation. Also, measuring output can be tricky and depreciation expense must be recalculated each period.

By assessing the advantages and disadvantages of each depreciation method above, a business can determine which method is most appropriate for it over a given period. As noted, key factors to consider include whether the asset is cheap or expensive, whether the asset depreciates by use or by passage of time, and what the tax considerations are in the choice of depreciation method.

Revision checklist

- ✓ Final accounts are financial statements compiled by businesses at the end of an accounting period that inform internal and external stakeholders about the financial position and performance of an organization. Internal stakeholders include shareholders, managers and employees, while examples of external stakeholders are customers, suppliers, government, competitors, financiers and local community.
- ✓ A profit and loss account shows the records of income and expenditure flows of a business over a given time period and is also known as an income statement.
- ✓ A balance sheet is a snapshot of the financial position of a firm and is used to calculate a firm's net worth. It gives the firm an idea of what it owns (assets) and owes (liabilities), including how much shareholders have invested in it (equity).
- ✓ Current assets last up to a year while non-current assets last for more than a year.
- ✓ Non-current liabilities are payable after a year, while current liabilities are payable within a year.
- ✓ For a balance sheet to balance, a firm's net assets should equal its equity.
- ✓ Intangible assets are non-physical in nature and can be very valuable to a firm's long-term success. These include patents, copyrights, trademarks and goodwill.
- ✓ The straight-line depreciation method spreads out the cost of an asset equally over its lifetime by deducting a given constant amount of depreciation of the asset's value per annum. The units of production depreciation method calculates the depreciation of the value of an asset based on usage. **(HL only)**

Concept

ETHICS

The Sarbanes–Oxley Act was passed in 2002 by the United States Congress to protect investors from fraudulent financial reporting by organizations and hence deter unethical accounting. This came in response to financial scandals in the early 2000s that involved companies such as Enron Corporation, Tyco International plc, and WorldCom.

Are there any other global examples of unethical behaviour in accounting that come to mind? How did the firms concerned handle the situation?

TOK links

1. Do final accounts reflect "the truth" about a business?
2. Financial information is sometimes presented to the wider audience in tabular, graphical or another form of quantitative summary. Do such simplifying representations limit our knowledge of accounts?
3. Is it possible to know the value of intangible assets?

3 Finance and accounts

Practice question

To answer the question below effectively, see Unit 6 pages 398–402.

BPT Ltd

BPT Ltd is a small, private limited company owned by Mary Davis that specialises in providing online education. The business has enjoyed many years of expansion.

Mary owns the copyright for her patented software. However, the copyright will expire in the near future. Moreover, several rival companies have recently established a presence in the online education market.

Mary said, "Due to the rapidly changing technology industry it is important to get the valuation of your non-current assets right." She recently started using a units of production method to calculate the depreciation expenses for her non-current assets. Prior to that she was using the straight-line method. She believes the units of production method will give a more accurate reflection of the wear and tear on her non-current assets (consisting mostly of computer hardware). She is also looking for an easier way to track her revenues and increasing expenses.

Mary's accountant has just presented the financial information shown in Table 1 for *BPT Ltd* as of 31 October 2021.

Table 1 Extract from the balance sheet for *BPT Ltd* for the year ended 31 October 2021

	US$
Cash	2,000
Cost of sales	3,000
Creditors	X
Debtors	28,000
Depreciation	1,500
Expenses	25,000
Long-term loan	0
Net assets	Y
Non-current assets	30,000
Retained earnings	8,500
Share capital	2,000
Short-term borrowing	0
Stock	0
Total (current assets)	30,000
Total (current liabilities)	48,000
Total equity	10,500

a) Define the term *copyright*. [2 marks]

b) Using Table 1:

   (i) calculate the missing figures X and Y [4 marks]

   (ii) construct a complete balance sheet for *BPT Ltd* for 2021. [4 marks]

c) Explain **two** benefits to Mary of using the units of production method for calculating depreciation. [4 marks]

3.5 Profitability and liquidity ratio analysis

> **By the end of this chapter, you should be able to:**
> → Calculate and comment on the profitability ratios: **gross profit margin**, **profit margin**, and **return on capital employed (ROCE)**
> → Examine possible strategies to **improve profitability ratios**
> → Calculate and comment on the liquidity ratios: **current ratio** and **acid test (quick) ratio**
> → Discuss possible strategies to **improve liquidity ratios**

Ratio analysis

This is a financial analysis tool used in the interpretation and assessment of a firm's financial statements. It helps in evaluating a firm's financial performance by determining certain trends and exposing its various strengths and weaknesses. It aids in decision-making by making meaningful historical and inter-firm comparisons through analysing past ratios and ratios of other businesses in the same or different industries.

The following types of ratios are explored below: **profitability ratios** and **liquidity ratios**.

Profitability ratios

These ratios assess the performance of a firm in terms of its profit-generating ability. Other variables are used in interpreting this profitability. Two types of profitability ratios are **gross profit margin** and **profit margin**.

Gross profit margin

This is found by dividing the gross profit by the sales revenue, expressed as a percentage, as follows:

$$\text{gross profit margin} = \frac{\text{gross profit}}{\text{sales revenue}} \times 100$$

Example: A business has sales revenue of US$100 million and gross profit of US$70 million. Calculate its gross profit margin, using the above formula:

$$\text{gross profit margin} = \frac{\text{US\$70 million}}{\text{US\$100 million}} \times 100 = 70\%$$

The business generates a gross profit margin of 70%. This is interpreted to mean that for every $100 of sales, the business makes $70 as its gross profit. That is, every $1 of sales revenue brings in 70 cents as gross profit. Businesses aim for higher gross profits to help them pay their expenses.

> **Key terms**
>
> **Gross profit margin**
> calculated by dividing the gross profit by the sales revenue, expressed as a percentage
>
> **Profit margin**
> calculated by dividing the net profit before interest and tax by the sales revenue, expressed as a percentage

Possible strategies to improve gross profit margin

- A firm can increase prices for products in markets where there is less competition or markets where consumers are less sensitive to price changes. Raising prices here could increase sales revenue because the quantity purchased may not alter significantly when the price changes. In this case the market may have very few if any substitutes. The drawback is that this could damage the image of the business with loyal consumers if they perceive it as a way of charging them too much in order to make higher profits.

- A business can source cheaper suppliers of materials in order to cut down on its purchase costs. This will help reduce the cost of sales and help increase the gross profit margin. The business will need to be careful not to compromise on the quality of the materials bought, which could lead to customer resentment.

- A firm can adopt more aggressive promotional strategies that could persuade customers to buy its products (see Chapter 4.5). Businesses need to ensure that they do not use expensive campaigns that will lead to increased costs.

- A business can aim to reduce direct labour costs by ensuring that its staff are more productive or are able to sell more units of the goods produced. Unproductive staff may need to be shed. However, care should be taken not to demotivate or reduce the morale of the remaining staff.

Profit margin

This is a measure of the profit that remains after deducting all costs from the sales revenue. It is calculated by dividing the profit before interest and tax by the sales revenue, expressed as a percentage:

$$\text{profit margin} = \frac{\text{profit before interest and tax}}{\text{sales revenue}} \times 100$$

Example: A firm has sales revenue of US$150 million and a profit before interest and tax of US$75 million. Calculate its profit margin, using the above formula:

$$\text{profit margin} = \frac{\text{US\$75 million}}{\text{US\$150 million}} \times 100 = 50\%$$

The firm therefore makes a profit margin of 50%. This means that for every $100 of sales revenue made, the business generates a profit margin of $50. That is, every $1 of sales brings in 50 cents as profit margin.

A high profit margin could mean that a firm is meeting its expenses very well; a low profit margin could indicate difficulties in controlling its overall costs. Businesses should therefore look for ways to improve their profit margin for better financial performance. In addition to the strategies used to increase gross profit margin, the following can help to boost profit margin.

3.5 Profitability and liquidity ratio analysis

Additional strategies to improve profit margin

- A firm can carefully check the indirect costs to see where unnecessary expenses may be avoided. For example, reducing expenditure on expensive holiday packages for senior managers. However, this could demoralize the managers who have been used to expensive holidays.

- A firm could negotiate with key stakeholders with the aim of cutting costs. For example, with landlords for cheaper rent or with suppliers for product discounts. However, negotiating cheaper rent could lead to a firm moving to another location that is less than ideal. Customers might see the move as detrimental and the firm could lose some of its prestige.

It is important to note that measures to increase revenues and cut costs should be used collectively in an effort to raise both gross profit margin and profit margin.

Return on capital employed (ROCE)

This ratio measures the profitability of a firm's invested capital. It assesses the returns a firm is making from its capital employed. Capital employed is found by adding a firm's non-current liabilities to its equity, as shown below:

$$\text{capital employed} = \text{non-current liabilities} + \text{equity}$$

This is then used in calculating the return on capital employed as follows:

$$\text{ROCE} = \frac{\text{profit before interest and tax}}{\text{capital employed}} \times 100$$

> **Key term**
>
> **Return on capital employed** assesses the returns a firm is making from its capital employed

Example: Suppose a business has share capital of US$1 million, retained profit of US$0.5 million and non-current liabilities of US$2 million. It generated a profit before interest and tax of US$700,000. Calculate its ROCE.

First, the capital employed will need to be calculated by adding non-current liabilities (US$2 million) and equity (share capital US$1 million + retained profit US$0.5 million) as follows:

Capital employed = US$2 million + US$1 million + US$0.5 million = US$3.5 million

Then, ROCE is calculated as follows:

$$\text{ROCE} = \frac{\text{US\$0.7 million}}{\text{US\$3.5 million}} \times 100 = 20\%$$

The business is making an ROCE of 20%. This means that for every $100 of capital invested, the firm generates $20 as profit before interest and tax. Generally, the higher the ROCE, the greater the returns businesses get from their capital employed. This acts as an incentive for business owners to inject more money into their businesses for higher returns.

ROCE is an important ratio because it analyses and judges how well a firm is able to generate profit from its key sources of finance. Comparisons should also be made on the ROCE of past years, together with those of other firms, to get a better assessment of the performance of a firm.

Possible strategies to improve ROCE

In addition to the strategies above on improving gross profit margin and profit margin, the following could be used to improve ROCE:

- A firm should try to reduce the amount of long-term loans while still ensuring that profit before interest and tax remains unchanged or does not fall. The problem with this is that the long-term loans may be needed to purchase essential fixed assets such as machinery, which will aid in the further production of goods that could be sold to generate more profit.

- A firm could declare and pay additional dividends to shareholders. This will have the effect of reducing the retained profit, and hence raising the ROCE, assuming profit before interest and tax remains unchanged or does not decrease. The drawback is that reducing retained profit leads to less ploughed-back profit for future investment.

Liquidity ratios

These ratios measure the ability of a firm to pay off its short-term debt obligations. Businesses need sufficient levels of liquid assets to help them pay their day-to-day bills. Liquidity is a measure of how quickly an asset can be converted into cash. Liquid assets include cash and others such as stock and debtors that can be quickly turned into cash. Two important liquidity ratios are the **current ratio** and the **acid test ratio**.

Current ratio

This ratio compares a firm's current assets to its current liabilities. It is calculated using the following formula:

$$\text{current ratio} = \frac{\text{current assets}}{\text{current liabilities}}$$

Example: A business has current assets totalling $500,000 while its current liabilities amount to $250,000. What is its current ratio?

$$\text{current ratio} = \frac{\$500,000}{\$250,000} = 2$$

The above firm's current ratio is 2, which can also be expressed as 2:1. This is interpreted to mean that for every $1 of current liabilities, the firm has $2 of current assets.

Accountants differ on the acceptable range of the current ratio, but many recommend a range of 1.5:2. This range will allow for the availability of sufficient working capital to pay off the short-term debts of the business. A current ratio of below 1:1 means that the current assets are less than the current liabilities, which could put the firm in financial difficulties when it comes to paying its creditors. This depends on the industry the firm operates in. A high current ratio should also be avoided. A high current ratio could mean any of the following:

Key terms

Current ratio

a ratio that compares a firm's current assets to its current liabilities

Acid test ratio

a stringent ratio that subtracts stock from the current assets and compares this to the firm's current liabilities

- There is too much cash being held and not being invested. This could be used in purchasing non-current assets.
- There are many debtors, increasing the possibility of bad debts.
- Too much stock is being held, leading to high warehouse storage costs.

Possible strategies to improve the current ratio

- A firm could reduce bank overdrafts and choose instead to seek long-term loans. This helps to reduce the current liabilities and hence improve the current ratio. However, increasing long-term loans could increase the interest payable and the gearing ratio of the business (see Chapter 3.6), thereby affecting its efficiency and future liquidity position.
- Another strategy would be to sell existing long-term assets for cash. This increases the available working capital for the business. The disadvantage is that if the same long-term assets are needed back, the business will have to lease them, which can be costly.

Acid test (quick) ratio

This is a more stringent indicator of how well a firm is able to meet its short-term obligations. This is because it removes stock as part of the current assets. It is calculated using the following formula:

$$\text{acid test ratio} = \frac{\text{current assets} - \text{stock}}{\text{current liabilities}}$$

Example: Using the current ratio example above, suppose the same business has stock worth US$150,000. What is its acid test ratio?

$$\text{acid test ratio} = \frac{\text{US\$500,000 - US\$150,000}}{\text{US\$250,000}} = 1.4$$

In the above case, for every $1 of current liabilities, the business has $1.4 of current assets less stock. By removing stock, the business gets rid of the least liquid of current assets to focus on the most liquid ones. In some cases, there is no guarantee that stock can be sold, eventually leading to obsolete items.

This ratio indicates to creditors how much of a firm's short-term debts can be met by selling its liquid assets at short notice. As with the current ratio, an acid test ratio of less than 1:1 could mean that the business is not in sound financial health. It may be facing a liquidity crisis (the inability to pay its short-term debts) and should therefore be scrutinized with extreme caution by financial institutions. However, as with the current ratio, the variation of acid test ratios in different industries needs to be considered. A high acid test ratio has the same implications as a high current ratio except that there is no stock to be considered.

Possible strategies to improve the acid test ratio

In addition to the strategies to improve the current ratio, the following can help with the acid test ratio:

Student workpoint 3.9

Be a thinker

1. Referring to Tables 3.4.1 and 3.4.3, calculate and comment on:
   a) **three** profitability ratios
   b) **two** liquidity ratios.
2. Which of the ratios from (a) and (b) are in need of further improvement? Evaluate possible strategies to improve each of those ratios.

- A firm could sell off stock at a discount for cash. This will help to improve the liquidity position of the business and make more working capital available to pay off its short-term debts. However, selling stock at a discount could reduce the revenue generated from the sold stock, thereby reducing the firm's profits.

- A firm could increase the credit period for debtors to enable them to purchase more stock on credit. The problem here is that it may lead to increased bad debts in the business if the debtors do not pay.

SWOT analysis

The internal and external attributes that impact on Apple are explored below using a financial lens.

Strengths	Weaknesses
• Great revenue streams from its iPhone sales and service provision. • High retained earnings with an ability to finance its own investment and research.	• Due to the high prices of products, no source of revenue from low-income market segments.

Opportunities	Threats
• Develop products that target low-income market segments for increased revenue potential.	• The US government imposed higher tariffs on imports from China. The overall cost of the products increased as a consequence, and gross margin on the products was adversely affected. • Intense competition may reduce revenues and profitability.

TOK links

1. How do our expectations and assumptions have an impact on how we interpret financial ratios?
2. Do liquidity ratios represent a financial reality?
3. What role do reason and emotion play when analysing financial performance?

Revision checklist

✓ Ratio analysis is a financial analysis tool that assesses a firm's financial statements and aids its decision-making. It makes meaningful historical and inter-firm comparisons through analysing past ratios and ratios of other businesses in the same or different industries.

✓ Profitability ratios that assess a firm's ability to generate profit include gross profit margin, profit margin and return on capital employed (ROCE).

✓ Liquidity ratios measure the ability of a firm to pay off its short-term debt obligations. Two examples are current ratio and acid test (quick) ratio.

3.5 Profitability and liquidity ratio analysis

Practice question

To answer the question below effectively, see Unit 6 pages 398–402.

WAW

WAW manufactures energy-efficient windows for houses. The windows are sold to suppliers of building materials in Canada. The WAW brand is widely recognized in the residential construction industry in Canada.

Because of the housing crisis in North America, WAW has seen its sales fall and its financial position deteriorate.

WAW manufactures only standard-sized windows. WAW offers trade credit with payment in 30 days. However, WAW is considering taking "special orders", that is, to manufacture windows that are not standard-sizes. Doing so could be profitable if the minimum number of windows per special order was 100. For special orders, the buyer would pay 50% upon placing the order and the remainder upon delivery. The disadvantage is that an additional employee would have to be employed to plan the production process for each special order. WAW is not certain that special-order sales will be sufficient to improve its financial position.

a) Using the information from **Table 1** and showing all your working, calculate:

   (i) the long-term loan (X) [1 mark]

   (ii) the current ratio [2 marks]

   (iii) the acid test (quick) ratio. [2 marks]

b) Using the information from **Table 2** and showing all your working, calculate:

   (i) the profit before interest and tax [2 marks]

   (ii) the gross profit margin [1 mark]

   (iii) the profit margin. [1 mark]

c) Using the information from **Tables 1 and 2** and showing all your working, calculate the return on capital employed (ROCE). [2 marks]

d) Examine WAW's decision to start producing special order windows. [10 marks]

Table 1 Selected items from WAW's balance sheet as at 31 May 2021 (all figures in $ thousands)

Cash	150
Creditors	515
Debtors	850
Long-term loan	X
Short-term borrowing	285
Retained earnings	1,300
Share capital	300
Stock	400
Total (non-current assets)	1,800

Table 2 Selected items from WAW's profit and loss account for the year ended 31 May 2021 (all figures in $ thousands)

Cost of sales	4,700
Expenses	2,150
Gross profit	2,195
Sales revenue	6,895

3.6 Debt/equity ratio analysis (HL only)

> **By the end of this chapter, you should be able to:**
> → Calculate and comment on the efficiency ratios: **stock turnover, debtor days, creditor days** and **gearing ratio**
> → Evaluate possible strategies to **improve efficiency ratios**
> → Distinguish between **insolvency** and **bankruptcy**

Key terms

Stock turnover ratio
measures how quickly a firm's stock is sold and replaced over a given period

Debtor days ratio
measures the average number of days a firm takes to collect its debts

Creditor days ratio
measures the average number of days a firm takes to pay its creditors

Gearing ratio
measures the extent to which the capital employed by a firm is financed from loan capital

Efficiency ratios (HL only)

These ratios assess how well a firm internally utilizes its assets and liabilities. They also help to analyse the performance of a firm. In this chapter, the following efficiency ratios will be explored: stock turnover, debtor days, creditor days and gearing ratio.

Stock turnover ratio

This ratio measures how quickly a firm's stock is sold and replaced over a given period. It considers the number of times stock is sold and replenished. It can be calculated using two approaches.

One approach looks at how many times in a given period (usually a year) a firm sells its stock. The formula is:

$$\text{stock turnover ratio (number of times)} = \frac{\text{cost of sales}}{\text{average stock}}$$

Average stock is calculated by finding the average value of the stock at the beginning of the year and at the end of the year:

$$\text{average stock} = \frac{(\text{opening stock} + \text{closing stock})}{2}$$

Example: Suppose a firm has a cost of sales totalling $400,000. It started the year with goods worth $150,000 and closed the year with goods worth $50,000. Calculate its stock turnover ratio.

Average stock is first calculated:

$$\text{average stock} = \frac{\$150{,}000 + \$50{,}000}{2} = \frac{\$200{,}000}{2} = \$100{,}000$$

$$\text{stock turnover ratio} = \frac{\$400{,}000}{\$100{,}000} = 4 \text{ times}$$

Another approach in calculating stock turnover is to consider the number of days it takes to sell the stock. The following formula can be used:

$$\text{stock turnover ratio (number of days)} = \frac{\text{average stock}}{\text{cost of goods sold}} \times 365$$

Using the above example, stock turnover ratio in the number of days is calculated as:

$$\text{stock turnover ratio} = \frac{\$100{,}000}{\$400{,}000} \times 365 = 91.25 \text{ days}$$

The above business turns over its stock four times a year, or every 91 days, on average. A higher stock turnover in terms of number of times is preferred by a business – or a lower stock turnover ratio (in number of days).

In considering the first approach to stock turnover (number of times), a high stock turnover ratio means that the firm sells stock quickly, thereby earning more profit from its sales. This also means that goods do not become obsolete quickly and perishable goods do not expire, showing that the firm has good control over its purchasing decisions.

It is important to note, however, that stock turnover differs significantly between different industries. For example, manufacturing companies such as luxury car producers may have on average lower stock turnover times than retail businesses such as supermarkets. This ratio is not very relevant to service industries that do not hold "tangible" products as their stock.

Stock turnover ratio is a good instrument for assessing the effectiveness of working capital management. Working capital management is an assessment of the way the current assets and current liabilities are being administered. Generally, the faster a business turns over its stock, the better. However, it is important that this is done profitably, rather than selling stock at low gross profit margins or, worse still, at a loss.

A supermarket has a high stock turnover ratio

A luxury car dealer like Tesla is likely to have a low stock turnover ratio

Possible strategies to improve stock turnover ratio

- Slow-moving or obsolete goods should be disposed of. This will help reduce the firm's level of stock. The downside is that it could lead to losses due to the lost sales revenue that these goods could have generated.

- Firms with a wide range of products may need to offer a narrower, better-selling range of products. The disadvantage is that this may minimize the variety of products offered to consumers.

- Keeping low levels of stock has the added benefit of reducing the costs of holding stock. However, during sudden increases in demand for goods by customers, businesses with low levels of stock may not have sufficient amounts to sustain the market.

- Some firms are able to adopt the just-in-time (JIT) production method, where stocks of raw materials are ordered only when they are needed (see Chapter 5.3). The major drawback is that if there are any delays in the delivery of the raw materials to producers then it could negatively affect production and eventually sales.

Debtor days

This ratio measures the number of days it takes on average for a firm to collect its debts from customers it has sold goods to on credit. These customers who owe the business money are known as debtors, and the ratio is also referred to as the **debt collection period**. It assesses how efficient a business is in its credit control systems. It is calculated using the following formula:

$$\text{debtor days ratio (number of days)} = \frac{\text{debtors}}{\text{total sales revenue}} \times 365$$

Example: A firm's total sales revenue amounts to $16 million, while the total number of debtors equals $2 million. What is its debtor days ratio?

$$\text{debtor days ratio} = \frac{\$2 \text{ million}}{\$16 \text{ million}} \times 365 = 45.625 \text{ days}$$

It therefore takes the business an average of 46 days to collect debts. The shorter the debtor days, the better it is for the business. This is because this provides the business with working capital to run its day-to-day operations, and it can also invest this money in other projects.

The credit period given to customers varies from business to business and could range from 30 days to as many as 120 days. However, allowing too long a credit period could lead to serious cash-flow problems for the business and a liquidity crisis.

Possible strategies to improve debtor days ratio

- A firm can provide discounts or other incentives to encourage debtors to pay their debts earlier. The drawback here is that the business receives less income from these customers than was originally agreed.
- A firm could impose stiff penalties, such as fines for late payers. However, the firm might lose long-time loyal customers.
- A firm could stop any further transactions with overdue debtors until payment is finalized. This still does not guarantee payment though, and some debtors may opt to seek alternative suppliers for their goods.
- A business can resort to legal means, such as court action for consistently late payers. This may harm the reputation that a business has with its customers.

Creditor days

This ratio measures the average number of days a firm takes to pay its creditors. It assesses how quickly a firm is able to pay its suppliers. The ratio is calculated using the following formula:

$$\text{creditor days ratio (number of days)} = \frac{\text{creditors}}{\text{cost of sales}} \times 365$$

Example: A business owes its creditors $700,000, with a cost of sales of $7 million. Calculate its creditor days ratio.

$$\text{creditor days ratio} = \frac{\$700{,}000}{\$7 \text{ million}} \times 365 = 36.5 \text{ days}$$

This means that the firm has about 37 days to pay its creditors. A high creditor days ratio enables the firm to use available cash to fulfil its short-term obligations. However, allowing this period to extend too long may strain the firm's relations with its suppliers, leading to future financial problems. In addition, other stakeholders such as investors may perceive this as a firm in financial trouble and may reconsider investing in it.

The creditor days period will vary according to a firm's relationship with its suppliers or other creditors.

Possible strategies to improve creditor days ratio

- Having good relationships with creditors such as suppliers may enable a firm to negotiate for an extended credit period. However, some suppliers could object to the extension and refuse to support the business in the future (when it might be in dire need of assistance).

- Effective credit control will improve the creditor days ratio. Managers will need to assess the risks of paying creditors early versus how long they should delay in making their payment. This may not be an easy task and will depend on the cash flow position and needs of the business at that time.

Gearing ratio

This measures the extent to which the capital employed by a firm is financed from loan capital. Loan capital is a non-current liability in the business, while capital employed includes loan capital, share capital and retained profits.

The commonly used gearing ratio formula is:

$$\text{gearing ratio} = \frac{\text{loan capital}}{\text{capital employed}} \times 100$$

Example: A business has a long-term loan of US$10 million with a capital employed of US$25 million. What is its gearing ratio?

$$\text{gearing ratio} = \frac{\text{US\$10 million}}{\text{US\$25 million}} \times 100 = 40\%$$

The business has a gearing ratio of 40%, which means that two fifths of the capital requirements of the business come from long-term loans. A gearing ratio can help assess the level of debt a business is burdened with.

A business is seen as high geared if it has a gearing ratio above 50% and low geared if below 50%. A high gearing ratio could be viewed as risky by financiers, who may be reluctant to lend to businesses in such a situation due to the large debt burden. Shareholders and potential investors will be concerned about high-geared businesses. They may not foresee any future dividend payments due to the fact that the main obligation of these firms is to pay their long-term loans. In addition, any sudden interest rate increases will worsen the loan repayment position of such businesses.

3 Finance and accounts

On the other hand, low-geared businesses that might be viewed as "safe" may in fact not be borrowing enough to fund future growth and expansion initiatives. Shareholders may therefore see low-geared businesses as offering minimal returns. They may even prefer high-geared businesses with good growth strategies promising higher future returns on investment.

Possible strategies to improve the gearing ratio

Businesses that are very highly geared can find themselves in a difficult financial position. This ratio could be reduced using the following measures:

- A business can seek alternative sources of funding that are not "loan related", for example issuing more shares. The drawbacks are that it may take a long time to issue shares and it may go against the objective of any existing shareholders who do not want to lose ownership of the business.

- A firm could decide not to issue dividends to shareholders so as to increase the amount of retained profit. But this may lead to resentment among shareholders, especially if the reasons for doing so are not well explained.

Insolvency and bankruptcy (HL only)

Insolvency is a financial state where a person or firm cannot meet their debt payments on time. The person or firm no longer has the money to pay off their debt obligations, and their debts exceed their assets. Naturally, people or firms that become insolvent will take certain steps towards a resolution. One of the most common solutions for insolvency is declaring bankruptcy.

Bankruptcy is a legal process that happens when a person or firm declares that they can no longer pay back their debts to creditors. It is a legal process for liquidating the property and assets a debtor owns in order to pay off their debts. This process can provide protection and relief for people or firms that are unable to pay off their debts.

In some cases when a firm files for bankruptcy, a Licensed Insolvency Trustee is assigned to liquidate their assets, contact their creditors, and investigate their affairs. The firm will have to comply with bankruptcy duties, which include attending credit counselling sessions. Once all necessary tasks are completed, the firm can be released from bankruptcy and become solvent again. The process usually takes 9 to 21 months.

Insolvency does not mean bankruptcy. Insolvency is a financial state, whereas bankruptcy is a legal declaration and process. Insolvency is a state of economic distress that an organization may be able to work through, while bankruptcy usually leads to a court order dictating how debts will be covered.

> **Student workpoint 3.10**
>
> **Be a thinker**
>
> Referring to Tables 3.4.1 and 3.4.3 in Chapter 3.4, calculate and comment on the following ratios:
>
> a) stock turnover
> b) debtor days
> c) creditor days
> d) gearing ratio

> **Key terms**
>
> **Insolvency**
> a financial state where a person or firm cannot meet their debt payments on time
>
> **Bankruptcy**
> a legal process that happens when a person or firm declares that they can no longer pay their debts to creditors

3.6 Debt/equity ratio analysis (HL only)

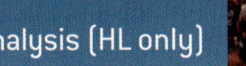

Case study

Future of staff and residents secured as care home sold out of liquidation

Yellow Homes is a small, independent residential care home based in Vancouver. It houses the elderly and is registered with the Quality Life Commission for up to 25 residents.

The problem

Lifecare Ltd, which traded as Yellow Homes, had amassed substantial tax arrears and after consistent non-payment, the Revenue Agency issued the company with a winding-up petition. This petition would have seen the care home forced out of business and closed down with immediate effect.

The solution

Following advice from Secure Inc, the business and assets of Lifecare Ltd were sold out of liquidation to Yellow Homes in an attempt to safeguard the futures of 20 residents and 21 staff.

The result

The sale ensured that the care home remained open and its residents could continue living there without disruption. All 21 jobs were also saved.

James Smith, partner at Secure Inc., said: "We only became involved after the petition had been filed; that meant we had very little time to find a sale and plan a future for the business before the bankers froze its account.

"Initially we tried to secure a company voluntary arrangement or place the company into administration. But the tight timescale and the financial constraints placed on the business by the presence of the winding-up petition meant we were left with no alternative – we had to pursue a creditors' voluntary liquidation. Then we were able to sell the business out of liquidation."

Source: Adapted from https://www.realbusinessrescue.co.uk/case-studies/future-of-residents-and-staff-secured-as-care-home-is-sold-out-of-liquidation

Revision checklist

- ✓ Efficiency ratios assess how firms utilize their resources in terms of assets and liabilities. These ratios include stock turnover ratio, debtor days, creditor days and gearing ratios.
- ✓ Stock turnover ratio measures how fast a firm's stock is sold and replenished over a given period. It can be measured in two ways. Firstly it assesses how many times in a given period a firm sells its stock, and secondly it considers the number of days it takes for a firm to sell its stock.
- ✓ Debtor days measures the average number of days it takes for a firm to collect money from its debtors. It is also known as the debt collection period.
- ✓ Creditor days assesses how fast in a number of days within a year a firm is able to pay its creditors.
- ✓ Gearing ratio measures the percentage to which the capital employed by a firm is financed from loan capital, to establish whether it is high geared or low geared.
- ✓ Insolvency is a financial state where a person or firm cannot meet their debt payments on time, while bankruptcy is a legal process that happens when a person or firm declares that they can no longer pay their debts to creditors.

TOK links

1. What role does today's financial evidence play in making judgments about an organization's future performance?
2. Are the results of some types of ratio analysis less open to interpretation than others?
3. Is it ethical for businesses to insist on early payments from debtors while they delay payments to creditors?

Practice question

To answer the question below effectively, see Unit 6 pages 398–402.

CB Ltd

CB Ltd started up in business ten years ago producing web cameras for computers. It has developed a reputation among its customers for high quality and reliability. At first, the company grew rapidly and was initially valued at $75 million at the height of the technology boom.

However, despite slow but consistent sales growth, *CB Ltd* has faced significant financial problems up to the point where it is facing insolvency. The cost of raw materials to produce the web cameras has increased rapidly, which has negatively impacted their cost of sales and hence profitability. *CB Ltd* has also had to increase their advertising expenses for their newly designed web cameras. The financial director has been looking at a range of solutions, one of which is that *CB Ltd* declares for bankruptcy.

The profit and loss account and balance sheet for 2020 and 2021 are given below.

Balance sheet as at 31 December 2020 and 2021 ($000)

Year		2020		2021
Non-current assets		1,500		1,400
Current assets				
Cash	10		5	
Debtors	550		650	
Stock	910		1,220	
Current assets		1,470		1,875
Total assets		2,970		3,275
Current liabilities				
Overdraft	350		475	
Trade creditors	300		250	
Current liabilities		650		725
Non-current liabilities				
Long-term loan	1,750		1,950	
Non-current liabilities		1,750		1,950
Total liabilities		2,400		2,675
Net assets		570		600
Equity				
Share capital		250		250
Retained earnings		320		350
Total equity		570		600

3.6 Debt/equity ratio analysis (HL only)

Profit and loss account for the year ended 31 December 2021 ($000)

Year	2020	2021
Sales revenue	5,750	6,100
Cost of sales	(4,175)	(4,750)
Gross profit	1,575	1,350
Expenses	(1,250)	(1,300)
Profit before interest and tax	325	50
Interest	(175)	(225)
Profit before tax	150	(175)
Tax	(100)	(10)
Profit for period	50	(185)
Dividends	20	0
Retained profit	30	(185)

a) Define the term *insolvency*. [2 marks]

b) Recommend whether *CB Ltd* should declare for bankruptcy. [10 marks]

3.7 Cash flow

By the end of this chapter, you should be able to:
- Distinguish between **profit** and **cash flow**
- Construct and comment on **cash-flow forecasts**
- Explain the relationship between **investment**, **profit** and **cash flow**
- Evaluate the strategies for dealing with **cash-flow problems**

Key terms

Cash flow
money that flows in and out of a business over a given period of time

Profit
the positive difference between sales revenue and total costs

Cash is generated by selling goods or services

The difference between profit and cash flow

Cash is money that a business obtains through either the sale of its goods or services, borrowing from financial institutions, or investment by shareholders. It is the most liquid asset in a business and is placed under current assets in the balance sheet. This cash is essential to the smooth running of any business and a lack of it could result in business failure or bankruptcy.

Cash flow is the money that flows in and out of a business over a given period of time. **Cash inflows** are the monies received by a business over a period of time, while **cash outflows** are the monies paid out by a business over a period of time.

Cash flow is a key indicator of a firm's ability to meet its financial obligations. A positive cash flow (where cash inflows exceed cash outflows) will enable businesses to meet their day-to-day running costs.

Profit is obtained by subtracting total costs from total revenue. It is profit if the difference is positive and it is a loss if the difference is negative. Profit is a great indicator of the financial success of a firm.

Profit and cash flow are different. When buying goods or services, customers can either use cash or they can buy on credit. If either of the two methods is used, this will still count as part of the sales revenue of a business. If the sales revenue exceeds the total costs, a business is said to have earned a profit. However, if most of the purchases were credit purchases, then the cash-flow position at that point in time for the business will be different from its profitability.

Example: During a particular month, a business sold $10,000 worth of goods, incurring a total cost of $4,000. The business offered customers one month's credit of 50% of sales. What was the profit and cash flow for that month?

profit = sales revenue − total costs

profit = $10,000 − $4,000 = $6,000

net cash flow = cash inflow − cash outflow

net cash flow = (50% of 10,000) − $4,000 = $1,000

In the above example, during the month in question the business incurred a profit of $6,000 but had a positive cash flow of only $1,000. The cash-flow figure is lower than the profit figure because even though the goods were sold, 50% of the money was not received in that month. However, the sold goods counted as sales revenue for the month.

Two possibilities can arise in differentiating between profit and cash flow.

a) A business can be profitable but have little or no cash. This is also known as insolvency (see Chapter 3.6) and it may be brought about by:
- poor collection of funds, possibly by allowing customers a very long credit period
- paying suppliers too early and leaving little or no cash for operations
- purchasing capital equipment or many non-current assets at the same time
- overtrading – purchasing too much stock with cash that is eventually tied up in the business
- servicing loans with cash.

b) A business can have a positive cash flow but be unprofitable. It can achieve a positive cash flow in the following ways:
- sourcing cash from bank loans
- gaining cash from the sale of a firm's fixed assets
- obtaining cash from shareholders' funds.

Cash flow forecasts

These are future predictions of a firm's cash inflows and cash outflows over a given period of time. The forecast is a financial document that shows the expected month-by-month receipts and payments of a business that have not yet occurred.

Examples of likely cash inflows include cash sales from selling goods or business assets, payments from debtors, cash investments from shareholders, and borrowing from banks. Cash outflows include purchasing materials or fixed assets for cash; cash expenses such as rent, wages and salaries; paying creditors; repaying loan; and making dividend payments to shareholders.

> **Key term**
>
> **Cash flow forecast**
>
> the future prediction of a firm's cash inflows and outflows over a given period of time

Constructing cash flow forecasts

In constructing a cash flow forecast, it is important to know the following terms:

- **Opening cash balance** – this is the cash that a business starts with every month. It is also the cash held by a business at the start of a trading year.
- **Total cash inflows** – this is a summation of all cash inflows during a particular month.
- **Total cash outflows** – this is a summation of all cash outflows during a particular month.

- **Net cash flow** – this is the difference between the total cash inflows and the total cash outflows.
- **Closing cash balance** – this is the estimated cash available at the end of the month. It is found by adding the net cash flow of one month to the opening balance of the same month.

Table 3.7.1 shows how the above terms are applied.

Table 3.7.1 Cash flow forecast for XYZ Ltd for the first five months of trading

All figures in $	January	February	March	April	May
Opening balance	2,000	4,500	5,600	4,650	3,250
Cash inflows					
Cash sales revenue	10,000	9,000	8,000	9,500	7,500
Payment from debtors	6,000	5,000	4,500	4,000	4,750
Rental income	4,000	4,000	4,000	4,000	4,000
Total cash inflows	20,000	18,000	16,500	17,500	16,250
Cash outflows					
Electricity	1,500	1,800	1,750	2,000	1,900
Raw materials	5,000	4,000	4,500	5,500	6,000
Rent	3,000	3,000	3,000	3,000	3,000
Wages	5,000	5,000	5,000	5,000	5,000
Telephone	500	600	700	900	450
Loan repayments	2,500	2,500	2,500	2,500	2,500
Total cash outflows	17,500	16,900	17,450	18,900	18,850
Net cash flow	2,500	1,100	(950)	(1,400)	(2,600)
Closing balance	4,500	5,600	4,650	3,250	650

> **Assessment advice** ✓
>
> The format for the cash flow forecast used in this chapter is the recommended one as indicated in the IB *Business Management Guide*.

In the above example, XYZ Ltd shows a positive closing balance at the end of May. However, this amount has been reducing since March. This can be attributed to the negative net cash flows in March, April and May. Can you identify the specific reasons for this? Assuming the cash sales revenue in December of the previous year was $12,000, what does this tell you about the credit period offered to customers?

It is important to note that cash-flow forecasts are based on estimates. Hence, the accuracy of the figures depends on how well the business is able to predict its future cash inflows and cash outflows.

Benefits of cash flow forecasts

- A cash flow forecast is a useful planning document for anyone wishing to start a business. This is because it helps to clarify the purpose of the business and provides estimated projections for future performance.
- Cash flow forecasts provide a good support base for businesses intending to apply for funding from financial institutions. This is because they enable the banks to check on the businesses' solvency and creditworthiness.
- Predicting cash flow can help managers identify in advance periods when the business may need cash, and therefore plan accordingly to source it.

- A cash flow forecast can help with monitoring and managing cash flow. By making comparisons between the estimated cash flow figures and its actual figures, a business should be able to assess where the problem lies and seek the respective solutions to solve it.

The relationship between investment, profit, and cash flow

Investment generally refers to the act or state of investing. In finance or business, investing is spending money on purchasing an asset with the expectation of future earnings. Investing involves wealth creation, including hoping that the bought asset appreciates in value over time. Examples of financial investments include buying bonds, stocks, or property. All forms of investment come with risks, especially risks brought about by unexpected changes in the market conditions in an economy.

The relationship between investment, profit, and cash flow can be linked to the different stages of growth in a business. This is noted in Table 3.7.2.

> **Key term**
>
> **Investment**
>
> the act of spending money on purchasing an asset with the expectation of future earnings

Table 3.7.2 The relationship between investment, profit, and cash flow, using various stages in a business

Business stage	Investment (owner's funds)	Profit	Cash flow
Start-up	This involves very high investment due to the purchase of initial assets or set-up costs	There is no profit because costs are not yet met	Cash flow is negative – cash outflow is significantly higher than cash inflow
Growing	Investment could still be high because the business is not yet fully established	There is a small profit, as more revenue starts to be generated to cover costs	Cash flow may be positive (ie cash inflow is higher than cash outflow) but low until cash inflows increase, especially from sales revenue
Established – thriving	Investment may be minimal as the business can plough back profits	High profit is achieved	Cash flow is positive – cash inflow is higher than cash outflow

Table 3.7.2 provides a simplified model of how investment in terms of the owner's injection of capital into the business relates to profit and cash flow. However, it is important to note that the above features could be affected by qualitative attributes that are beyond the control of the business. (A more detailed explanation of the difference between profit and cash flow has been covered earlier in this chapter.)

Strategies for dealing with cash flow problems

As noted earlier, a business can be profitable yet insolvent, which means it is facing a liquidity crisis and is having difficulties in sustaining its working capital to run its day-to-day operations. The major causes of cash flow problems in a business are a lack of effective planning and poor credit control. The following strategies can be used to deal with these problems.

Reducing cash outflows

The following methods aim to decrease the amount of cash leaving a business:

- A business can negotiate with suppliers or creditors to delay payment. This helps it to have working capital for its short-term needs. The drawbacks with this are that negotiations may be time-consuming, and delaying payment to suppliers could affect future relationships – suppliers may refuse to supply in the future.

- Purchases of fixed assets can be delayed. Assets such as machinery and equipment may take up a lot of the business's cash, and delaying purchases of them helps to avail cash in the business. However, if the machines or equipment are becoming obsolete or outdated, delaying the purchase of replacements may lead to decreased efficiency and higher costs in the long term.

- A business can decrease specific expenses that will not affect production capacity, such as advertising costs. If not well checked, though, this may reduce future demand for a business's products.

- A business could look into sourcing cheaper suppliers. This will help to reduce costs for materials or essential stock, decreasing the outflow of funds. A possible danger of this is that the quality of the finished product may be compromised, affecting future customer relationships.

Improving cash inflows

- A business can insist that customers pay with cash only when buying goods. This avoids the problem of delayed payments from debtors, which ties up cash. The disadvantage is that the business may lose customers who prefer to buy goods on credit.

- Offering discounts or incentives can encourage debtors to pay early. This will reduce the debt burden on debtors as they will pay less than earlier agreed. The limitation here is that, after the discount, businesses will receive less cash than previously expected.

- A firm may diversify its product offering. This will help to increase the variety of goods on offer to customers, potentially increasing sales. It is worth remembering that diversification comes with higher costs and with no clear guarantee of sales.

Looking for additional finance sources

These additional finance sources were discussed in Chapter 3.2 and they include the following:

- **Sale of assets** – the focus should be on selling obsolete fixed assets to generate cash. Selling assets that are still needed could lead to reduced production.

- **Arranging a bank overdraft** – this is a short-term loan facility that allows firms to overdraw from their accounts. It is a great help during times of immediate cash setbacks. However, there will be interest payments on the overdraft, which are usually high.

- **Sale and leaseback** – assets can be sold to generate cash and these assets can then be hired back by the business for use in production.

The disadvantage is that leasing can prove costly in the long run, and this also denies the business the use of the asset as collateral when seeking future loans.

Limitations of cash flow forecasting

A cash flow forecast is generally a prediction, and inaccuracies are bound to occur that limit the forecast's effectiveness. Some of the causes of these inaccuracies include the following:

- **Unexpected changes in the economy** – for example, fluctuating interest rates could affect borrowing by firms and have a negative impact on their cash flow needs.
- **Poor market research** – improperly done sales forecasts due to poor demand predictions can have a negative effect on future cash sales, thereby affecting cash inflows.
- **Difficulty in predicting competitors' behaviour** – competitors may change their strategies often and make it hard for other businesses to predict their actions and compete with them. This can negatively affect the cash flow of a struggling business.
- **Unforeseen machine or equipment failure** – breakdown of machinery is difficult to predict, and it can drastically affect the cash position in a business.
- **Demotivated employees** – being demotivated can negatively affect the productivity of workers, reducing output or sales and leading to less cash inflow.

> ### Student workpoint 3.11
>
> #### Be knowledgeable
>
> Juma plans to open a restaurant next year beginning in January. Use the following information to answer the questions below:
>
> - He has $4,000 of his own money to inject into the business.
> - He has secured a bank loan of $6,000 to add to his capital requirements.
> - He estimates the cash sales revenue for the first five months of trading to be as follows: $2,000, $4,000, $5,000, $5,500, $6,000.
> - Material expenses are 50% of cash sales revenue per month and paid in cash every month.
> - Wages and salaries are a constant figure of $5,000 every month.
> - Total advertising costs of $6,000 are paid in two installments, one in February and the other in April.
> - A loan repayment is $500 each month.
> - Rent is $6,000 every month.
>
> 1. Using the format shown in Table 3.7.1, construct a cash flow forecast for Juma's restaurant business for the first five months of trading.
> 2. Comment on the cash flow position faced by Juma's business and recommend a way forward for him.

Concept

CHANGE

The cash flow statement will only change if the inflows and outflows impact on cash and cash equivalents. The net change in cash position is the difference between the total amount of money brought in by the business and the total amount that it expended over the reporting period.

The cash flow statement therefore provides information on an organization's liquidity and solvency and its ability to change cash flows in future circumstances. In addition, it provides additional information for evaluating changes in assets, liabilities and equity.

Using the internet, do some research on the various cash-flow statements of different organizations. How do the changes in the other financial documents influence their cash-flow statements?

TOK discussion

1. How do our assumptions have an impact on the way that we analyse cash flow forecasts?
2. As cash flow forecasting is about imagining the future, to what extent is it reliable?
3. Is it ethical for a business to seek finance by using a cash flow forecast that is knowingly too optimistic?

Revision checklist

✓ Profit is the positive difference between total revenue and total costs when both cash and credit transactions are considered. Cash flow, on the other hand, is the flow of money in and out of the business, and only considers cash transactions.

✓ A cash-flow forecast is a financial document that shows the expected month-by-month cash receipts (cash inflows) and payments (cash outflows) of a business that have not yet occurred. Cash inflows include: cash sales from selling goods or business assets, payments from debtors and borrowing from banks. Cash outflows include: purchasing materials or fixed assets for cash, cash expenses such as rent, wages and salaries, and dividend payments to shareholders.

✓ When constructing cash-flow forecasts, the following need to be included: opening cash balance, total cash inflows, total cash outflows, net cash flows and closing cash balance.

✓ Some strategies to reduce cash outflows include: negotiating with creditors to reduce payments, and delaying the purchase of fixed assets. Some strategies to improve cash inflows include: insisting on cash purchases, and offering incentives to encourage debtors to pay early.

3.7 Cash flow

Practice question

To answer the question below effectively, see Unit 6 pages 398–402.

NPF

Steve Dawes founded *NPF* in 2015. It was set up with a very generous donation from a retired businessman. It is an online non-profit organization, financing educational opportunities for children in developing countries. Steve has been looking at his financial statements and is getting worried about *NPF's* liquidity situation. *NPF's* cash reserves are being used up quickly and in the current poor economic climate, *NPF's* main source of finance – online donations – is falling.

In 2020, *NPF* has no debt but also no non-current assets. *NPF's* expenses are an internet usage fee, a maintenance fee for servers and computers, and a web designer's fee for regularly updating the *NPF* website. Steve is thinking of engaging in some investment projects.

NPF has volunteers from all over the world running the organization. An online community of social networking websites connects them with Steve as the chief website administrator. All funds to finance educational projects are transferred electronically and only email communication is allowed. *NPF* aims to become the first paperless charity.

Steve has been asked by a very popular rock band to sponsor a reunion concert, which will be broadcast only over the internet. The opportunity would generate substantial public relations opportunities, but some volunteers on the *NPF* forums are not convinced. They argue that the money spent sponsoring the concert should be used to provide further educational opportunities for children. They also believe that many people watching the concert may be frustrated if global broadband connections become too slow or fail.

Steve is preparing a cash flow forecast for the next four months (all figures refer to 2020) based on the following:

- Donations are transferred to the educational projects **one month after** the money has been received.
- Educational projects receive 95% of all donations.

a) Define the term *investment*. [2 marks]

b) (i) Using Steve's forecast figures, prepare a cash flow forecast for NPF from June to September 2020, clearly showing the opening and closing monthly cash flow forecast balances. [6 marks]

   (ii) Comment on your results from part (i). [4 marks]

   (iii) Explain **two** possible solutions to the liquidity problems highlighted in parts (i) and (ii). [6 marks]

Forecast	Donations (millions of US$)
June	40
July	30
August	30
September	20

	Millions of US$
Opening balance in June 2020	1
Donations received in May 2020	50
Internet usage fee	1 to be paid in June and September
Maintenance fee for servers and computers	0.25 per month
Web designer's fee	0.5 per month
Concert sponsoring fee	5 to be paid in September

209

3.8 Investment appraisal

> **By the end of this chapter, you should be able to:**
> → Calculate and evaluate the **payback period** as an investment appraisal method
> → Calculate and examine the **average rate of return** (ARR) as an investment appraisal method
> → Calculate and discuss the **net present value** (NPV) as an investment appraisal method **(HL only)**

Key terms

Investment appraisal
the quantitative techniques used in evaluating the viability or attractiveness of an investment proposal

Payback period
the length of time required for an investment project to pay back its initial cost outlay

Introduction

Investment appraisal refers to the quantitative techniques used in evaluating the viability or attractiveness of an investment proposal. It assesses and justifies the capital expenditure allocated to a particular project. It therefore aims to establish whether a particular business venture is worth pursuing and whether it will be profitable. Investment appraisal also assists businesses in comparing different investment projects.

In this chapter, we look at three methods of investment appraisal: **payback period**, **average rate of return**, and **net present value**.

Payback period

This method estimates the length of time required for an investment project to pay back its initial cost outlay. It looks at how long a business takes to recover its principal investment amount from its net cash flows. It can be calculated using the following formula:

$$\text{payback period} = \frac{\text{initial investment cost}}{\text{annual cash flow from investment}}$$

Example 1: A construction engineer plans on investing $200,000 in a new cement-mixing machine and estimates that it will generate about $50,000 in annual cash flow. Calculate the payback period for the machine.

$$\text{payback period} = \frac{\$200{,}000}{\$50{,}000} = 4 \text{ years}$$

Hence the payback period for the new machine would be four years.

Example 2: Another construction engineer aims to invest $300,000 in a new timber-cutting machine. The machine is expected to generate the following cash flows in the first four years: $60,000, $80,000, $100,000 and $120,000.

The payback period for this machine can be found by first calculating the cumulative cash flows over the four years, as shown in the table below.

Table 3.8.1 Expected cash flows of a new machine

Year	Annual net cash flows ($)	Cumulative cash flows ($)
0	(300,000)	(300,000)
1	60,000	(240,000)
2	80,000	(160,000)
3	100,000	(60,000)
4	120,000	60,000

The initial investment outlay will be paid back sometime in year four – but in which month exactly? This can be calculated using the following formula:

$$\frac{\text{extra cash inflow required}}{\text{annual cash flow in year 4}} \times 12 \text{ months}$$

The extra cash inflow shown in Table 3.8.1 is $60,000. This is because in year 3, it has been calculated that only $60,000 needs to be paid in year 4 to pay off the initial investment. The annual cash flow in year 4 is $120,000. Applying this information to the formula, we get:

$$\frac{\$60,000}{\$120,000} \times 12 \text{ months} = 6 \text{ months}$$

It therefore takes three years and six months to pay back the initial investment of $300,000.

The results in examples 1 and 2 can be compared with results from other projects to help decision-making. As a general rule, the shorter the payback period of the project, the better it is for the investing business.

The business may have also decided on an internal payback period or "cut-off" that an investment should not go below, such as four years. In example 1 above, the investment project just meets this criterion (it pays back in four years), while the project in example 2 is better off by six months (it pays back in three years and six months).

Advantages of payback period

- It is simple and fast to calculate.
- It is a useful method in rapidly changing industries such as technology. It helps to estimate how fast the initial investment will be recovered before another machine, for example, can be purchased.
- It helps firms with cash flow problems because they can choose the investment projects that can pay back more quickly than others.
- Since it is a short-term measure of quick returns on investment, it is less prone to the inaccuracies of long-term forecasting.
- Business managers can easily understand and use the results obtained.

Disadvantages of payback period

- It does not consider the cash earned after the payback period, which could influence major investment decisions.
- It ignores the overall profitability of an investment project by focusing only on how fast it will pay back.
- The annual cash flows could be affected by unexpected external changes in demand, which could negatively affect the payback period.

Average rate of return

> **Key term**
>
> **Average rate of return (ARR)** measures the annual net return on an investment as a percentage of its capital cost

This method measures the annual net return on an investment as a percentage of its capital cost. It assesses the profitability per annum generated by a project over a period of time. It is also known as the accounting rate of return. It can be calculated using the following formula:

$$\text{average rate of return (ARR)} = \frac{\frac{(\text{total returns} - \text{capital cost})}{\text{years of usage}}}{\text{capital cost}} \times 100$$

Example: A business is considering purchasing a new commercial photocopier at a cost of $150,000. It expects the following revenue streams for the next five years: $30,000, $50,000, $75,000, $90,000 and $100,000 respectively. Calculate its ARR.

total returns = $30,000 + $50,000 + $75,000 + $90,000 + $100,000
= $345,000

$$\text{payback period} = \frac{(\$345{,}000 - \$150{,}000)}{5} = \$39{,}000$$

$$\text{ARR} = \frac{\$39{,}000}{\$150{,}000} \times 100 = 26\%$$

The business therefore expects an ARR of 26% on its investment. A business can compare this figure with the ARR of other projects and choose the project showing the highest rate of return.

The ARR can also be compared with banks' interest rates on loans to assess the level of risk. For example, in the above case, if banks offer an interest rate of 15%, businesses may find it worthwhile to pursue investment projects with a return of 11% higher than the base lending rate.

Other businesses set criterion rates or a minimum rate that an investment project should not go below if it is to be selected. For example, if the criterion rate was 20% for the above business, the ARR is 6% above this rate and this would still be considered a desirable project to pursue.

Advantages of average rate of return

- It shows the profitability of an investment project over a given period of time.
- Unlike the payback period, it makes use of all the cash flows in a business.
- It allows for easy comparisons with other competing projects for better allocation of investment funds.

3.8 Investment appraisal

- A business can use its own criterion rate and check this with the ARR for a project to assess the viability of the venture.

Disadvantages of average rate of return

- Since it considers a longer time period or useful life of the project, there are likely to be forecasting errors. Long-term forecasts reduce the accuracy of results.
- It does not consider the timing of cash inflows. Two projects might have the same ARR but one could pay back more quickly compared to the other due to faster cash inflows.
- The effects on the time value of money are not considered.

Net present value (HL only)

This is defined as the difference in the summation of present values of future cash inflows or returns and the original cost of investment. Present value is today's value of an amount of money available in future. For example, $100 invested at the beginning of the year in a bank account offering 10% interest would be worth $110 at the end of the year:

$$\left(\frac{10}{100} \times \$100\right) + \$100$$

Hence, $110 in one year's time is worth $100 today. In other words, $100 is the present value of $110 in a year's time.

If $110 is invested for another year, it amounts to $121 and in a further year to $133. What do you observe? If $100 invested in a bank account at 10% over three years grows to $133, then $100 received over a three-year period will be less than a $100 received today, ie a fixed amount of money paid in the future is worth less than a fixed amount paid today. How do we get to the present value of $100 invested over three years at 10% interest?

To do this we use what is called the **discounted cash flow method**. This is a technique that considers how interest rates affect the present value of future cash flows. It uses a discount factor that converts these future cash flows to their present value today. This discount factor is usually calculated using interest rates and time.

> **Key terms**
>
> **Net present value (NPV)**
> the difference in the summation of present values of future returns and the original cost of investment
>
> **Discounted cash flow**
> uses a discount factor that converts future cash flows to their present value

Table 3.8.2 Discount factors

Years	Discount rate				
	4%	6%	8%	10%	20%
1	0.9615	0.9434	0.9259	0.9091	0.8333
2	0.9246	0.8900	0.8573	0.8264	0.6944
3	0.8890	0.8396	0.7938	0.7513	0.5787
4	0.8548	0.7921	0.7350	0.6830	0.4823
5	0.8219	0.7473	0.6806	0.6209	0.4019
6	0.7903	0.7050	0.6302	0.5645	0.3349
7	0.7599	0.6651	0.5835	0.5132	0.2791
8	0.7307	0.6271	0.5403	0.4665	0.2326
9	0.7026	0.5919	0.5002	0.4241	0.1938
10	0.6756	0.5584	0.4632	0.3855	0.1615

> **Assessment advice** ✓
>
> Discount factors, as shown in Table 3.8.2, are provided in the IB *Business Management Guide*.

To get the present value of future cash flows, the appropriate discount factor is multiplied by the net cash flow in the given year. In the earlier example, the present value of $100 invested over three years at 10% will be:

Present value = 0.7513 (taken from Table 3.8.2) × $100 = $75.13. This means that $100 received in three years' time is worth only $75.13 today.

Example: Consider an investment project that costs $500,000 and produces net cash flows over the next four years as follows:

- Year 1: $100,000
- Year 2: $200,000
- Year 3: $300,000
- Year 4: $250,000

Calculate the net present value (NVP) at a discount factor of 8%.

The working is shown in the following table:

Table 3.8.3 Calculating net present value

Year	Net cash flow ($)	Discount factor at 8%	Present value in $
0	(500,000)	1	(500,000)
1	100,000	0.9259	92,590
2	200,000	0.8573	171,460
3	300,000	0.7938	238,140
4	250,000	0.7350	183,750

> **NPV = total present values − original cost**

NPV = $685,940 - $500,000 = $185,940

The NPV in this example is a positive value of $185,940, signifying that this is a viable project that should go ahead. If the value was negative, then the viability of the project would be in question and it should not be pursued. An increase in the discount rate reduces the NPV because future cash flows will be worth less when discounted at higher rates.

Advantages of net present value

- The opportunity cost and time value of money is put into consideration in its calculation.
- All cash flows, including their timing, are included in its computation.
- The discount rate can be changed to suit any expected changes in economic variables, such as interest rate variations.

Disadvantages of net present value

- It is more complicated to calculate than the payback period or ARR.
- It can only be used to compare investment projects with the same initial cost outlay.
- The discount rate greatly influences the final NPV result obtained, which may be affected by inaccurate interest rate predictions.

3.8 Investment appraisal

Student workpoint 3.12

Be knowledgeable

A large retail business has the following forecasted net cash flows for a major project:

Year	Net cash flows ($)
0	(40,000)
1	15,000
2	30,000
3	10,000
4	5,000

1. Calculate the payback period.
2. Calculate the ARR.
3. Calculate the NPV at a discount rate of 6% (use the discount factors in Table 3.8.2). **(HL only)**

BCG matrix

The BCG matrix is a planning and decision-making tool that uses graphical representations of a firm's goods or services in order to help the firm to decide what to keep, sell or invest more in.

How can the knowledge of this tool help businesses to improve their financial decision-making?

Case study: What is sustainable finance?

Sustainable finance generally refers to the process of taking due account of **environmental, social and governance (ESG) considerations** when making investment decisions in the financial sector, leading to increased longer-term investments into sustainable economic activities and projects.

More specifically, **environmental considerations** may refer to climate-change mitigation and adaptation, as well as the environment more broadly, such as the preservation of biodiversity, pollution prevention and circular economy.

Social considerations may refer to issues of inequality, inclusiveness, labour relations, investment in human capital and communities, as well as human rights issues.

The **governance** of public and private institutions, including management structures, employee relations and executive remuneration, plays a fundamental role in ensuring the inclusion of social and environmental considerations in the decision-making process.

In the EU's policy context, sustainable finance is understood as finance to support economic growth while reducing pressures on the environment and taking into account social and governance aspects. Sustainable finance also encompasses transparency on risks related to ESG factors that may impact the financial system, and the mitigation of such risks through the appropriate governance of financial and corporate actors.

Sustainable finance at EU level aims to support the delivery of the objectives of the European Green Deal by channelling private investment into the transition to a climate-neutral, climate-resilient, resource-efficient and just economy, as a complement to public money.

Concept: SUSTAINABILITY

Sustainability is about finding ways to efficiently use resources today (including finances) while considering the needs of future generations. The case study here discusses what sustainable finance is and why it is important, and it provides the European Union's perspective as a context.

Research on how one or more organizations are sustainable in their financial practices.

3 Finance and accounts

Why is sustainable finance important?

Sustainable finance has a key role to play in mobilising the necessary capital to deliver on the policy objectives of the European Green Deal, as well as the EU's international commitments on climate and sustainability objectives. It helps ensure that investments support a resilient economy and a sustainable recovery from the impacts of the Covid-19 pandemic.

The EU is strongly supporting the transition to a low-carbon, more resource-efficient and sustainable economy and it has been at the forefront of efforts to build a financial system that supports sustainable growth.

In 2015, landmark international agreements were concluded with the adoption of the UN 2030 agenda and sustainable development goals and the Paris climate agreement. The Paris climate agreement, in particular, includes the commitment to align financial flows with a pathway towards low-carbon and climate-resilient development.

On 11 December 2019, the Commission presented the European Green Deal, a growth strategy aiming to make Europe the first climate-neutral continent by 2050.

As part of the Green Deal, the Commission presented on 14 January 2020 the European Green Deal investment plan, which will mobilise at least €1 trillion of sustainable investments over the next decade. It will enable a framework to facilitate public and private investments needed for the transition to a climate-neutral, green, competitive and inclusive economy.

Reaching the current 2030 climate and energy targets alone would already require additional investments of approximately €260 billion a year by 2030. The EU is already providing impetus to help attract the required investments with the European Fund for Strategic Investments and other initiatives. However, the scale of the investment challenge is beyond the capacity of the public sector alone. The financial sector has a key role to play in reaching those goals. It can:

- re-orient investments towards more sustainable technologies and businesses
- finance growth in a sustainable manner over the long term
- contribute to the creation of a low-carbon, climate-resilient and circular economy.

To this end, the Commission has developed a comprehensive policy agenda on sustainable finance since 2018, comprising the action plan on financing sustainable growth and the development of a renewed sustainable finance strategy in the framework of the European Green Deal. The Commission is also coordinating international efforts through its international platform on sustainable finance.

Source: Adapted from https://ec.europa.eu/info/business-economy-euro/banking-and-finance/sustainable-finance/overview-sustainable-finance_en

Sustainable finance supports investment in renewable energy

Revision checklist

✓ Investment appraisal is the quantitative assessment of the viability of an investment proposal. It establishes whether a particular business venture is worth pursuing or profitable, as well as assisting businesses in making comparisons with other investment projects. Investment appraisal techniques include payback period, average rate of return and net present value.

✓ Payback period looks at how long a business will take to recover its principal investment or initial cash outlay from its net cash flows. It is simple to calculate and a useful method in rapidly changing industries. However, it does not consider the cash earned after the payback period and ignores the overall profitability of an investment project.

✓ Average rate of return assesses the profitability per annum generated by a project over a period of time and is also known as accounting rate of return. It makes use of all the cash flows in a business and shows the profitability of an investment project over a given period of time. However, it does not consider the timing of cash inflows and effects on the time value of money.

✓ Net present value is the difference in the summation of present values of future cash inflows or returns and the original cost of investment. It makes use of the discounted cash flow method in its calculation. It includes all cash flows in its computation as well as the opportunity cost and time value of money. However, it is more complex to calculate and can only be used to compare investment projects with the same initial cost outlay. **(HL only)**

TOK links

1. To what extent are the methods used to gain knowledge in investment appraisal scientific?

2. The discount factors (given in discount tables) are arbitrarily decided, so how reliable are the NPVs calculated using those numbers?

3. Can we really know in advance whether an investment will be successful?

3 Finance and accounts

Practice question

To answer the question below effectively, see Unit 6 pages 398–402.

EEB

EEB is a small, well-known, reputable and financially stable online hotel reservation service. *EEB* employees are highly motivated and take great pride in their work. *EEB* has received recognition for its high-quality customer service. Due to an increase in global demand, greater competition and changes in technology, the finance director, Maia, has decided to upgrade *EEB*'s computers and/or software.

Maia has two options:

Option A: purchase new software called "Book-Fast" from a local software designer.

Option B: purchase new computers, with installed software called "Global Reach", from a manufacturer abroad.

	Option A	Option B
Cost	$20,000	$40,000
Technical support	24 hours onsite at *EEB*	24 hours online
Further payments payable:		
Employees	No change	At the end of their contract 15% of employees to be made redundant, cost: $15,000 in year 2
Training cost	On-the-job: free	Intensive: $12,000 in year 1
Maintenance cost	Free	$1,000 per year
Insurance cost	$500 per year	$1,000 per year

The estimated return/total revenue in $ per year is shown below. Each option will last for four years.

	Option A	Option B
Year 1	10,000	14,000
Year 2	12,000	16,800
Year 3	17,000	23,800
Year 4	20,000	28,000

The average rate of return (ARR) of Option A is 46.25%.

Maia is considering carrying out an investment appraisal on each option.

EEB employees favour Option A, even though some of their competitors using Book-Fast have reported problems with the software, including security issues. However, Maia has chosen Option B, which will provide more up-to-date, sophisticated and secure reservation system software. It will also give *EEB* a competitive advantage and an ability to handle a large global volume of hotel reservations.

a) Define the term *investment appraisal*. [2 marks]

b) Calculate the payback period for Option A (show all your working). [2 marks]

c) Calculate the average rate of return (ARR) for Option B (show all your working). [2 marks]

d) For **both** Option A **and** Option B, calculate the net present value (NPV) using a discount rate of 4% (show all your working). [4 marks]

e) Explain **one** advantage and **one** disadvantage for *EEB* of using the NPV method of investment appraisal. [4 marks]

f) Examine Maia's choice of Option B. [10 marks]

3.9 Budgets (HL only)

> **By the end of this chapter, you should be able to:**
> → Explain the **difference between cost and profit centres**
> → Analyse **the role of cost and profit centres**
> → Construct and comment on a **budget**
> → Calculate and analyse **variances**
> → Explain the **importance of budgets and variances in decision-making**

A **budget** is a quantitative financial plan that estimates revenue and expenditure over a specified future time period. Budgets can be prepared for individuals, for governments, or for any type of organization.

Budgets help in setting targets and are aligned with the main objectives of the organization. They enable the efficient allocation of resources within the specified time period.

The person involved in the formulation and achievement of a budget is known as the **budget holder**. The budget holder is responsible for ensuring that the specified budget allocations are being met. Commonly used budgets are sales revenue budgets and cost budgets.

Cost and profit centres (HL only)

To be able to account for the revenues generated and costs incurred, different parts of a business are divided into **cost centres** or **profit centres**.

Cost centres

This is a part or section of a business where costs are incurred and recorded. Cost centres can help managers to collect and use cost data effectively. Examples of costs collected and recorded in these sections include electricity, wages, advertising, and insurance, among other costs. Businesses can be divided into cost centres in some of the following ways:

- **By department** – examples include finance, production, marketing, and human resources, where each department is a specific cost centre.
- **By product** – a business producing several products could ensure that each product is a cost centre. For example, Samsung produces mobile phones, televisions, computers, and many more products. Each of these products could be cost centres because costs are incurred in their production.
- **By geographical location** – businesses such as KFC or The Coca-Cola Company are located in different parts of the world. Each of the geographic areas that they are located in could be cost centres.

Key terms

Budget
a quantitative financial plan that estimates the revenue and expenditure over a specified future time period

Budget holder
a person involved in the formulation and achievement of a budget

Cost centre
a section of a business where costs are incurred and recorded

Profit centre
a section of a business where both costs and revenues are identified and recorded

KFC has outlets all round the world (these two are in the Netherlands and Thailand) – each geographical area could be treated as a cost centre

Profit centres

This is a part or section of a business where both costs and revenues are identified and recorded. These sections allow businesses to calculate how much profit each centre makes.

Profit centres enable comparisons to be made so as to judge the performance in the various sections of the business. For example, Toyota can identify the most profitable car models in the market by comparing the profit each product makes or by comparing which geographical location is most profitable.

Just like cost centres, profit centres can be divided according to product, department or geographical location, as long as in addition to cost, revenue is also generated.

The role of cost and profit centres

- **Aiding decision-making.** Cost and profit centres help in providing managers with financial information about the different parts of a business. This information can assist them in deciding whether to continue or discontinue producing a particular product. With such information, the production of high-cost and least profitable products can be stopped to make way for new, lower-cost but more profitable products.

- **Better accountability.** Cost and profit centres help to hold specific business sections accountable. For example, managers who perform poorly in their department can be identified and held accountable for their inefficiency.

- **Tracking problem areas.** Cost and profit centres enable particular problem areas in a business to be detected. For example, if in one store there are a lot of customer complaints resulting in a high number of costly product replacements, this can be checked by the use of a cost centre, and quick solutions can be sought.

- **Increasing motivation.** Providing departmental managers and staff with incentives (such as promotion or bonuses) to enable them to achieve set targets helps to increase their morale within cost and profit centres. Empowering staff and delegating control to the managers in charge of these centres also helps to improve motivation.

- **Benchmarking.** Comparing the performance in the various cost and profit centres in a business can help to find the areas that are most or least efficient. This monitoring of individual parts of a business can help to improve overall efficiency in the business.

Problems of cost and profit centres

- **Indirect cost allocation.** Indirect costs such as advertising, rent or insurance are difficult to allocate specifically to particular cost centres. They may be allocated unfairly, distorting the overall business performance.

- **External factors.** Factors beyond the control of the business may affect specific cost and profit centres differently. There may be more competition in one centre than in another, thereby negatively influencing the performance of the centres experiencing greater levels of competition.

- **Centre conflicts.** Staff and managers could consider the performance in their own centres to be superior to the overall performance of the organization. This could lead to unhealthy competition between the centres for the firm's resources and a lack of sharing of vital information.
- **Staff stress.** The pressure of managing a cost and profit centre may be very high for some staff, especially if they lack the right skills. This could lead to staff demotivation.

Constructing a budget (HL only)

The following terms (some of which have been used in earlier chapters) are important when constructing a budget:

- **Total income** – this is a summation of all income or money received by a business. Common income sources include sales revenue and interest earned.
- **Total expenses** – this is a summation of all expenses or cost of operations incurred by a business. Common expenses include material costs, salaries and wages, rent, and advertising costs.
- **Net income** – this is the difference between the total income and total expenses.
- **Budgeted figure** – this is the estimated amount of money to be received or spent as set out in the budget.
- **Actual figure** – this is the amount of money that is definitely received or spent as a result of business activity.
- **Variance** – this is the difference between the budgeted figure and the actual figure.

Table 3.9.1 shows how the above terms are applied.

Table 3.9.1 Budget for PQR Ltd for the period ended 2021 ($m).
F – favourable, A – adverse

	Budgeted figures	Actual figures	Variance
Income			
Sales revenue	600	650	50 (F)
Interest earned	50	45	5 (A)
Total income	650	695	45 (F)
Expenses			
Salaries and wages	180	200	20 (A)
Materials	90	85	5 (F)
Rent	10	10	0
Advertising	7	10	3 (A)
Electricity	14	11	3 (F)
Total expenses	301	316	15 (A)
Net income	349	379	30 (F)

Assessment advice

The format for the budget shown in Table 3.9.1 is the recommended one as indicated in the IB *Business Management Guide*.

In Table 3.9.1, PQR Ltd obtained a positive balance on its total income of $45 million, while it got a negative balance on its total expenses of $15 million. Overall, it had a positive net income of $30 million. The analysis of (F) (which means favourable variance) and (A) (which means adverse variance) is discussed below.

Variance analysis (HL only)

In budgeting, as noted above, a **variance** is the difference between the budgeted figure and the actual figure. This variance is usually calculated at the end of a budget period once the actual amounts are determined.

Variance analysis is a budgetary control process of assessing the differences between the budgeted amount and the actual amount. This analysis can be done for both cost and sales revenue budgets.

Variances can either be **favourable** or **adverse**.

A **favourable variance** is when the difference between the budgeted and actual figure is financially beneficial to the firm.

For example, if the budgeted sales revenue in one month was $30,000 and the actual sales revenue was $40,000, then the firm has a favourable variance of $10,000. If the budgeted marketing costs were $80,000 in a month and the actual figure turned out to be $65,000, then the firm has a favourable variance of $15,000.

An **adverse variance** occurs when the difference between the budgeted and actual amount is financially costly to the firm.

For example, if the actual sales revenue amount was lower than the budgeted figure or the actual costs were higher than the budgeted costs, then the firm has an adverse or unfavourable variance.

In Table 3.9.2, the positive total income is termed as a favourable variance as the actual income received is more than the budgeted income by $45 million. However, the total expenses are an adverse variance because actual expenses exceed the budgeted expenses by $15 million. But PQR Ltd makes a favourable variance of $30 million as the favourable total income exceeds the adverse total expenses.

Example: Table 3.9.2 shows some of the budgeted and actual amounts taken from Mr Kamau's business. The third column shows the amount and nature of the variance obtained, where F = favourable and A = adverse.

Table 3.9.2 Variance in Mr Kamau's business

Particulars	Budgeted figure ($)	Actual figure ($)	Variance
Sales of televisions	10,000	12,500	2,500 (F)
Cost of materials	4,000	3,800	200 (F)
Sales of laptops	15,000	13,900	1,100 (A)
Cost of labour	5,000	5,700	700 (A)
Cost of rent	3,000	3,000	0

Key terms

Variance
the difference between the budgeted figure and the actual figure

Favourable variance
when the difference between the budgeted and actual figure is financially beneficial to the firm

Adverse variance
when the difference between the budgeted and actual figure is financially costly to the firm

The above example shows that:

- Favourable variances were experienced in the sale of televisions and cost of materials. Here, both presented a financial benefit to the business, one with an actual sales figure that is higher than expected (by $2,500) and the other with lower actual costs (by $200).

- Adverse variances were experienced in the sales of laptops and the cost of labour, which proved financially costly to the firm. Expected laptop sales declined by $1,100, while the cost of labour increased by $700.

The importance of budgets and variances in decision-making (HL only)

Decision-making is a process that involves selecting a course of action from various possible alternatives with the aim of providing a solution to a given problem. Choices are made by identifying the problem, gathering relevant data or information, and assessing alternative resolutions.

A business is always faced with decision-making opportunities as it aims to define its future direction and decide on how to allocate its resources effectively in order to fulfil its vision and mission.

In defining its future position, it first needs to know its current position and the opportunities available before pursuing its desired course of action. The course of action involves formulating key goals or objectives derived from the vision and putting in place a series of steps to achieve them. Budgeting and carrying out variance analysis is one of those steps, and both play an important role in decision-making. This role is further explored in the following points.

Benefits of using budgets and variances in decision-making

- **Planning:** by setting targets, managers ensure that budgets help to provide a sense of direction or purpose for organizations. These should be realistic targets that are clearly understood by all internal stakeholders to help in the attainment of an organization's goals. A budget as a planning document should also assist in anticipating future problems and devising possible solutions.

- **Motivation**: budget holders who are responsible for budgetary control (modalities taken that ensure the budgeted performance is in line with actual performance) feel empowered and trusted, which boosts their morale. In addition, staff who are involved in the budgetary process feel recognized as part of the organizational team, which could even lead to increased productivity.

- **Resource allocation:** budgets help to prioritise how resources will be used in the organization. Since the demands for financial resources could be very high, budgets set certain boundaries that ensure that available resources are not overstretched but are used for specified purposes based on designated needs.

> **Key term**
>
> **Decision-making**
>
> a process that involves selecting a course of action from various possible alternatives with the aim of providing a solution to a given problem

- **Coordination:** budgets help to bring people from different departments together to work for a common purpose. This helps in improving the flow of communication and ensuring a sense of collaboration between the people working together. Coordination helps all departments to reach uniform budget agreements for a more effective achievement of the set targets.

- **Control:** budgets act as monitoring and evaluation tools to check how funds are being spent in each department. Budgets help to control revenue and expenditure by regulating how money is spent to minimize losses and wastage of resources. Budget holders need to ensure that they are within the budget in their spending patterns and especially ensure that they do not exceed the budget, as this could lead to serious financial debt problems in the organization.

- **SMART goals:** budgets should be set based on the SMART criteria – specific, measurable, agreed, realistic and time-bound – and should all be in line with the organization's objectives.

- **Comparison:** variance analysis aims to compare actual performance to budgeted performance, thereby helping to assess organizational performance.

- **Detecting deviations:** variance analysis helps in detecting the causes of any deviations in the budget so that corrective measures can be taken to rectify them.

- **Objective appraisal:** variance analysis provides an objective way of appraising the budget holders responsible for their various departments.

However, in an attempt to fulfil the vision and mission of an organization, budgeting brings with it some of the following limitations.

Limitations of budgets in decision-making

- Inflexible budgets that do not consider any unforeseen changes in the external environment, such as increases in raw material costs, may be too difficult to stay within and therefore be unrealistic.

- Significant differences between the budgeted and actual results could make the budget lose its importance as a decision-making tool.

- Since most budgets are based on the short term, long-term future gains (such as increased sales potential due to unexpected increases in demand) could be lost by looking only at the current budgeted amount.

- Highly underspent budgets towards the end of the year could result in unjustified wasteful expenditure by managers.

- Setting budgets without involving some people could make them feel resentful and affect their motivation levels.

Despite these limitations, budgets and variance analysis do play an important role in decision-making. They are vital financial planning documents or processes that help to monitor and control income and expenditure so that the specified organizational objectives are attained.

> **TOK links**
>
> 1. How can we know if a budget is realistic, or if it is too optimistic or too pessimistic?
> 2. What assumptions underlie the techniques used when budgeting?
> 3. Could it be said that variance analysis is both objective (with the mathematic calculation of the variances) and subjective (with the interpretation of the variances)?

3.9 Budgets (HL only)

> **Student workpoint 3.13**
>
> **Be a thinker**
>
> The following information refers to XAV Ltd.
>
> | Particulars | Budgeted figure ($) | Actual figure ($) | Variance ($) |
> |---|---|---|---|
> | Material costs | 12,000 | 18,500 | |
> | Direct labour costs | 9,000 | 7,800 | |
> | Sales of radios | 25,000 | 25,600 | |
> | Sales of Apple iPad | 15,000 | 12,750 | |
> | Advertising costs | 6,000 | 7,100 | |
>
> 1. Calculate the missing figures in the table above and note whether the variance is favourable (F) or adverse (A).
> 2. Comment on the material costs variance and suggest possible reasons for your answer.
> 3. What do the overall variance figures tell you about the business?

Revision checklist

- ✓ A budget is a financial plan that helps in target setting by estimating the revenue and expenditure of a business over a specified future time period.

- ✓ Cost centres are sections of a business where costs are incurred and recorded, which helps to collect and effectively use cost data. Profit centres are sections of a business where both costs and revenues are identified and recorded, which allows businesses to calculate how much profit each centre makes.

- ✓ Cost and profit centres are important in aiding decision-making, improving accountability, tracking problem areas, increasing motivation, and benchmarking. However, some challenges faced include difficulties in allocating indirect costs to particular cost centres, and external factors beyond the firm's control.

- ✓ Budgets are important for planning, motivation, resource allocation, coordination, and control.

- ✓ Variance analysis is a budgetary control process of assessing the differences between the budgeted amount and the actual amount. If the difference between the budgeted figure and actual figure is beneficial to the firm, it is known as a favourable variance. On the other hand, if the difference between the budgeted and actual figure is financially costly, it is known as an adverse variance.

3 Finance and accounts

Practice question

To answer the question below effectively, see Unit 6 pages 398–402.

KJC Ltd

KJC Ltd specialises in making pots of all sizes and shapes. Over the years it has developed a good reputation for high-quality products. *KJC Ltd* has a well-developed distribution network both nationally and overseas. For the first half of this year they have experienced significant growth in the sales of their products. However, for the second half of the year their sales have slowed down drastically. Some stakeholders attribute this to the recession that the country is experiencing, while others feel that increased competition is the cause.

The company's financial manager, Mr Jon Liu, has been tasked with carrying out a variance analysis to ascertain how the company performed over the year. He may have to carry out strict budgetary controls and monitor each cost centre and profit centre closely so that he can track the specific problem areas. On his part, Mr Liu feels that this will make him more accountable and efficient as a finance manager. He can also advise the other managers about which sections of the business could have caused the decrease in sales of the pots in the second half of the year.

The table below shows the budgeted figures and actual figures for *KJC Ltd* for this year.

$000	Budgeted figures	Actual figures	Variance
Sales revenue	500	400	
Interest earned	100	80	
Direct labour costs	90	75	
Direct material costs	80	90	
Advertising	20	10	
Rent	15	15	
Electricity	30	40	

a) Define the term *cost centre*. [2 marks]

b) Construct a complete budget for *KJC Ltd* using the information from the table above. [6 marks]

c) Comment on **two** variances from the complete budget completed in question (b). [4 marks]

d) Explain **two** roles of profit centres to *KJC Ltd*. [4 marks]

4 MARKETING

4.1 Introduction to marketing

By the end of this chapter, you should be able to:
- → Define **marketing**
- → Distinguish between **market orientation** and **product orientation**
- → Distinguish between **market share** and **market growth**
- → Calculate market share
- → Calculate market growth
- → Discuss **the importance of market share and market leadership** (HL only)

Introduction

Marketing is essential to the success of any business. However, marketing is not just about selling or advertising, as many people think. It is much more than that: it is more of a business philosophy of how best to think about satisfying consumer needs or demands.

There are many globally acceptable definitions of marketing. Some common ones include the following:

"Marketing is the management process involved in identifying, anticipating and satisfying consumer needs profitably."

The Chartered Institute of Marketing

4 Marketing

> "Marketing is the activity, set of institutions, and processes for creating, communicating, delivering, and exchanging offerings that have value for customers, clients, partners, and society at large."
>
> *American Marketing Association*

Kotler (1994) summarized it well when he said, "Marketing is meeting the needs of your customer at a profit."[1] Ultimately, marketing is about getting the right product to the right customers at the right price at the right time. This means that marketing involves a number of activities that every marketing department should aim to satisfy, all centred on the consumer.

Market orientation versus product orientation

There are two distinct approaches that businesses can use to market their products. They can either use a **product-orientated** approach or a **market-orientated** approach. These two approaches are shown in the table below.

Table 4.1.1 Differences between a product-orientated approach and a market-orientated approach

Product-orientated approach	Market-orientated approach
Inward looking; focused on making the product first and then trying to sell it.	Outward looking; focused on carrying out market research first and then making products that can sell.
Product-led and assumes that supply creates its own demand (Say's law). Here, businesses produce innovative products and tempt customers to buy them.	Market-led and focused on establishing consumer demand in order to supply products that meet consumers' needs and wants.

Organizations that have adopted a product-orientated approach to their products include Bosch, Siemens, Microsoft, Ferrari and Dyson. However, many organizations are now market-orientated businesses, including Amazon, Google, Facebook, Uber and Airbnb.

Benefits of a market-orientated business

- Due to market research, firms have increased confidence that their products will sell, which reduces the risk of failure.
- Access to market information means that firms can anticipate and respond quickly to changes in the market.
- As a result of regular feedback from consumers due to market research, firms are in a strong position to meet the challenges of new competitors entering the market.

> **Key terms**
>
> **Marketing**
>
> the management process of getting the right product to the right customer at the right price, the right place and the right time
>
> **Product orientation**
>
> a business approach that focuses on making the product first before attempting to sell it
>
> **Market orientation**
>
> a business approach of first establishing consumer demand through market research before producing and selling a product

> **Student workpoint 4.1**
>
> *Be a thinker*
>
> 1. Explain what you understand by the term "marketing".
> 2. Using specific organizational examples, comment on the benefits of market orientation.

---

[1] Kotler, P. 1994. *Marketing Management: Analysis, planning, implementation and control*. Englewood Cliffs, NJ. Prentice Hall.

Limitations of a market-orientated business

- Conducting market research can be costly and therefore weigh heavily on a firm's budget.
- Due to frequently changing consumer tastes, firms may find it difficult to meet every consumer's needs with its available resources.
- Uncertainty about the future could have a negative influence on the market-planning strategy.

Product-orientated businesses place a lot of emphasis on the production process rather than on their potential customers. They focus mostly on the firm's internal capabilities.

Benefits of a product-orientated business

- It is associated with the production of high-quality products such as luxury sports cars, or safety products like crash helmets.
- It can succeed in industries where the speed of change is slow and the firm has already built a good reputation.
- It has control over its activities, with a strong belief that consumers will purchase its products.

Limitations of a product-orientated business

- Since the firm ignores the needs of the market, it takes risks that may lead to eventual business failure or closure.
- Spending money on research and development without considering consumer needs could be costly and not yield any promising results.

Dyson takes a product-orientated approach to marketing

Google uses a market-orientated approach to marketing

Market share

Market share is the percentage of total sales that a business has within an industry. It is the percentage of one firm's share of the total sales in the market, and is calculated by using the following formula:

$$\text{market share percentage} = \frac{\text{firm's sales}}{\text{total sales in the market}} \times 100$$

Market share can be measured by volume (units) or value (revenue):

- **By volume:** this measures the number of goods bought by customers. It is a quantitative measure of the units sold by businesses, for example the number of bags of maize.
- **By value:** this measures the amount spent by customers on the total number of goods sold by businesses. It is the total revenue expressed in monetary terms, such as Kenyan shillings (KSh), US dollars (US$), or Indian rupees.

4 Marketing

Calculating market share

Assume PQR Electronics sold €8 million worth of computers in Sweden, and €100 million worth of computers were sold during the same period in the total market.

Using the market share formula:

$$\text{market share percentage} = \frac{\text{firm's sales}}{\text{total sales in the market}} \times 100$$

$$= \frac{€8 \text{ million}}{€100 \text{ million}} \times 100$$

market share = 8%

The market share for PQR Electronics is 8%.

An increase in market share could mean that a business has adopted effective marketing strategies so that it sells more products and takes business away from its competitors. This could lead to increased profits and it may result in the business being a key player in the industry.

Market growth

Market growth is the increase in the number of consumers who buy a good or service. It is the percentage change in the market size over a given period of time, usually a year.

Market size represents the total sales made by all businesses in a given market. Market size can be measured by value or volume.

Calculating market size

Assume there are three firms in a given market. In the last two years:

- the sales revenue in Firm A was $20 million in the first year, and it experienced a 10% increase in sales revenue to $22 million in the second year
- Firm B had a sales revenue of $28 million in the first year and $32 million in the second year
- Firm C's sales revenue was $14 million in the first year and it increased by $2 million in the second year to $16 million.

Adding up the sales revenue figures for each year results in market sizes of $62 million for year one and $70 million for year two.

Table 4.1.2 Calculation of market size

	Sales revenue ($) – year 1	Sales revenue ($) – year 2
Firm A	20 million	22 million
Firm B	28 million	32 million
Firm C	14 million	16 million
Market size (Firm A + Firm B + Firm C)	62 million	70 million

> **Key terms**
>
> **Market size**
>
> the total sales of all firms in a market
>
> **Market growth**
>
> the percentage change in the total market size over a period of time

Calculating market growth

Market growth is first calculated by subtracting the market size in the first year from the market size in the second year. The result is then divided by the market size in the first year and multiplied by 100 to convert it to a percentage.

$$\text{market growth percentage} = \frac{\text{market size (second year)} - \text{market size (first year)}}{\text{market size (first year)}} \times 100$$

Example 1: in Table 4.1.2, the market size for the first year was $62 million and the market size for the second year was $70 million. Using the formula:

$$\text{market growth percentage} = \frac{\$70 \text{ million} - \$62 \text{ million}}{\$62 \text{ million}} \times 100$$

$$= \frac{\$8 \text{ million}}{\$62 \text{ million}} \times 100$$

market growth = 12.9%

Example 2: the sales revenue from televisions sales increased from US$50 million in year one to US$80 million in year two. What is the market growth?

$$\text{market growth percentage} = \frac{\$80 \text{ million} - \$50 \text{ million}}{\$50 \text{ million}} \times 100$$

$$= \frac{\$30 \text{ million}}{\$50 \text{ million}} \times 100$$

market growth = 60%

An example of market growth is the sale of smartphones, which has seen increasing growth worldwide, with many consumers finding multiple uses for them. This has attracted many smartphone suppliers because of the high profit potential. However, such growth does not happen in isolation. There are several external factors influencing the growth of the smartphone market, such as economic growth patterns, technological changes, and changes in consumer tastes and income, among others.

> **Assessment advice** ✓
>
> It is important to remember that the calculations for market share and for market growth are different.

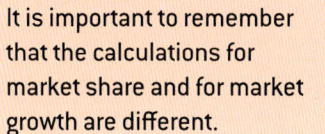

Student workpoint 4.2

Be a thinker

In its second quarter 2020 results, The Coca-Cola Company announced that it had experienced a decrease in market share in its total non-alcoholic ready-to-drink (NARTD) beverages.

Do you think that publishing such information can be a marketing tool for businesses?

> **Key terms**
>
> **Market share**
> the percentage of one firm's share of the total sales in the market
>
> **Market leader**
> a firm with the largest market share in a given market

Importance of market share and market leadership (HL only)

Even though market share does not show exactly how profitable a firm is, it does provide useful insights into the firm's revenues, growth and profit margins.

This is because of economies of scale (a decrease in the average costs of production as a result of increasing a firm's scale of operation). The bigger the firm, the better it can serve greater numbers of consumers in a more cost-efficient manner. This is because goods can be bought for greater discounts due to larger wholesale orders.

Hence, even when a larger firm is selling its goods for the same price as its competitors, with a greater market share and economies of scale it can attain higher profit margins, making it a stronger firm overall in the given market. As a result, it can offer more promotions, thereby driving market share even higher, as it captures new consumers from its competitors.

Firms that have a compounding effect tend to use market share as a driving force. This means that the larger the firm, the more efficiently it can provide goods or services, and hence the more effective the firm is at capturing market share. The more market share it captures, the more efficiently it can provide goods or services, and so the cycle continues.

However, when calculating and interpreting market share, careful thought is needed:

- Since market share can be measured in different ways, by value and volume, different results may be obtained in the same time period.
- Changes in the time period and market can influence market share results.
- The type of products included may also influence the calculation of market share.

Measuring market share is important because it can indicate that a firm is a market leader. A market leader is the firm with the largest market share in a particular industry.

The market leader can use its dominance in the market to influence other businesses or competitors to follow it. This influence could extend to winning over consumers, pricing decisions, distribution coverage, etc. Increasingly, the internet age has provided huge scope for businesses to become market leaders.

Benefits of being a market leader

- The market leader often has first-mover advantages in new markets. Microsoft with its operating system (Windows) and Apple with the idea of a portable computer with a touch-screen display (the iPad) are examples of companies that have leveraged this advantage.
- The market leader enjoys increased sales revenue that translates to higher profits.
- The business is be able to gain economies of scale.

Microsoft is a market leader known for its Windows operating system

- Since the market leader could also be the brand leader (providing the product with the highest market share), the leading brand can act as a good promotional tool for consumers who would like to be associated with popular brands.
- Market leaders manage to attract the highest-quality development partners and adopt innovative technologies and processes which help them continue to outperform their competition.

However, market leaders need to be cautious about how they use and obtain their market share. Businesses that become too dominant in the market or seem to be abusing their position may be subject to anti-trust lawsuits. For example, Microsoft was once a target of regulators.

In addition, a market leader may not necessarily be the most profitable business for an investor. Even though it may have a high market share, the firm's total expenses (including manufacturing costs, research and development (R&D) costs and marketing costs) may be too high to make it the most profitable firm among its competitors in the industry.

Student workpoint 4.3

Be knowledgeable

Table 4.1.3 Different sales volumes and values from different companies

Company	XYZ		ABC		PQR	
Year	2020	2021	2020	2021	2020	2021
Sales of toys (million units)	550	580	700	740	620	650
Sales of toys ($ million)	25	28	45	48	32	30

Use Table 4.1.3 to calculate the following:

1. Market share for company XYZ by volume in 2020
2. Market share for company ABC by value in 2021
3. Market share for company PQR by volume in 2020
4. Market growth for the whole industry by value from 2020 to 2021

TOK links

1. Why would all businesses need to know their market share and their market growth?
2. As market share and market growth can be calculated and expressed as percentages, does that mean that they are necessarily true?
3. To what extent are marketing practices a reflection of the values of a given time and culture?

Revision checklist

✓ Marketing is essentially about getting the right product to the right customers at the right price and at the right time. It involves working with other business functions to satisfy the needs of the customer.

✓ Product orientation focuses on producing the product first before selling it, while market orientation involves carrying out market research before producing and selling the product.

✓ Market size looks at the total sales of all firms in a market, while market growth is the percentage change in market size over a period of time.

✓ Market share is the percentage of one firm's share of the total sales in the market. A firm is a market leader if it has the highest market share in a given market.

4 Marketing

Practice question

To answer the question below effectively, see Unit 6 pages 398–402.

Bak

Bak is a market leader in motorbike manufacturing. Recently, its market share in the motorbike industry has been increasing. There are two other companies that produce motorbikes in a market that is growing in size due to the high demand for motorbikes. *Bak* is market orientated and offers 10 different models to satisfy the needs of its consumers. The other two companies are product orientated and offer fewer models in the market. These two companies believe they know what is right for the market without the need to approach consumers for insights. *Bak*, on the other hand, relies a lot on consumer feedback.

Market size information for the motorbike companies is given below.

Motorbike company	Sales revenue (rupees) – 2020	Sales revenue (rupees) – 2021
Bak	100 million	145 million
Jia	70 million	95 million
Ter	40 million	68 million

a) Explain the difference between market orientation and product orientation. [4 marks]

b) Calculate the market share for *Bak* in 2021. [2 marks]

c) Comment on the importance of market share and market leadership for *Bak*. [4 marks]

4.2 Marketing planning

> **By the end of this chapter, you should be able to:**
> - Explain the role of **marketing planning**
> - Distinguish between **segmentation**, **targeting** and **positioning**
> - Distinguish between **niche market** and **mass market**
> - Explain the importance of having a **unique selling point/proposition (USP)**
> - Evaluate how organizations can **differentiate** themselves and their products from competitors

The role of marketing planning

Marketing planning is a process that involves an organization deciding on the marketing strategies that would be most effective in attaining its overall strategic objectives. To facilitate this, it is essential to draw up a comprehensive marketing plan.

A marketing plan is a detailed document about the marketing strategies that are developed in order to achieve an organization's marketing objectives. Marketing departments need to plan adequately and prepare themselves to face the competition in the market. The marketing plan includes some of the following components:

- **Marketing objectives** that are SMART (specific, measurable, achievable, relevant (or realistic), and time-specific). For example, increasing sales by 6% in the next year.
- **Key strategic plans**, which are steps that provide an overview of how the marketing objectives will be achieved. For example, plans on how to sell new products in existing markets.
- **Detailed marketing actions** providing information on the specific marketing activities that are to be carried out. For example, which pricing strategies will be used and how the products will be distributed.
- **The marketing budget**, including the finance required to fund the overall marketing strategy.

Benefits of marketing planning

- Marketing planning helps a firm to identify potential problems and seek solutions to them.
- Setting SMART objectives improves the chance of success for a firm's marketing strategy.
- Sharing the marketing plan with other business departments improves coordination and provides the whole organization with a clearer picture or sense of where it is heading.

> **Key term**
>
> **Marketing planning**
>
> the process of formulating marketing objectives and devising appropriate marketing strategies to meet those objectives

235

4 Marketing

- Devising a marketing budget ensures that resources are not wasted on unprofitable activities.
- A clearly spelled-out plan could improve employees' motivation and inspire confidence about the organization's future.

Limitations of marketing planning

- Marketing plans may become outdated if organizations are not quick to consider changes in market conditions.
- The process may consume considerable resources in terms of time, expertise, and money in designing the plans.
- Failure to prioritize marketing objectives may make it difficult for firms to tell whether they are meeting them.

To be effective, marketing planning needs to be a reflective exercise where organizations constantly review and evaluate their marketing policies. They need to do this if they are to survive in today's competitive business environment.

Segmentation, targeting and positioning
Market segmentation

A **market segment** refers to a sub-group of consumers with similar characteristics in a given market. **Market segmentation** is the process of dividing the market into smaller or distinct groups of consumers in order to meet their desired needs and wants.

Markets can be segmented in the following ways.

Demographic segmentation – this considers the varying characteristics of the human population in a market, which include:

- **age** – babies will need diapers while teenagers will want smartphones
- **gender** – there is a higher demand for personal care products for women than for men
- **religion** – businesses will find it difficult to sell certain animal products in a country where people are discouraged from eating them
- **family characteristics** – some businesses have used creative acronyms to segment their markets; for example, OINK (one income, no kids) targets young singles, while DINKY (double income, no kids yet) targets young married couples
- **ethnic grouping** – radio stations in many African countries broadcast in languages that are geared towards a particular ethnic group.

Geographic segmentation – this is where the market is divided into different geographical sectors and considers factors including:

- **regions in a country where consumers reside** – for example, there may be more demand for office products in the city and agricultural products in rural areas
- **climatic conditions** – for example, there will be greater demand for thick jackets in Tibet than in Botswana, which is usually quite hot throughout the year.

Student workpoint 4.4
Be a thinker
1. Using an organization of your choice, explain how it would go about creating a marketing plan.
2. Explain the limitations of a marketing plan.

Key terms

Market segment

a sub-group of consumers with similar characteristics in a given market

Market segmentation

the process of dividing the market into distinct groups of consumers so as to meet their desired needs and wants

Psychographic segmentation – this divides the market based on people's lifestyle choices or personality characteristics, such as:

- **social and economic status** – some high-income-earning individuals belong to luxury clubs that exclude people who have not attained a specified wealth status
- **values** – people's morals and beliefs are considered here, for example customer values regarding recycling of products or animal testing.

Advantages of segmentation

- Segmentation helps businesses to identify existing gaps and new opportunities in domestic as well as international markets.
- Designing products for a specific group of consumers can increase sales and hence profitability.
- Segmentation minimizes the waste of resources by businesses through identifying the right consumers for their products.
- By differentiating their products, businesses can diversify and spread their risks in the market and so increase market share.

However, market segmentation can be expensive in terms of research and development, production, and promotion, as a firm attempts to reach a large segment of actual and potential consumers.

Geographic segmentation could lead a winter clothing retailer to target colder climates

Case study

Real-world examples of effective market segmentation

Market segmentation groups customers based on their needs. Businesses can adapt their products and services so that they more closely correspond to what particular groups of customers expect. Such segmentation helps a business satisfy those expectations in a differentiated and more effective manner. Many companies use segmentation to customize products for particular markets. You can see how companies carry out such customization based on real-world examples.

Demographics

Segmenting your market based on demographics means grouping your customers by age, gender or similar characteristics.

McDonald's segments by age, and directs different ads to different segments. The Ronald McDonald ads target children with products aimed at younger age groups. Ads for a quick breakfast before work are aimed at the adult segment.

Procter & Gamble segments by gender, and offers the "Secret" brand deodorant to women while marketing the Rogaine treatment for hair loss to men.

Income

Income is an effective segmenting technique, because you can target expensive items to customers who can afford them.

237

Department store Neiman Marcus, Rolex watches and Rolls-Royce cars target the upper-income market segments of their respective industries.

If you target lower-income segments, you can carry reduced-price items or value products. Walmart is a successful example for retailing. The store emphasizes low pricing in its ads and emphasizes the message that customers can get more for their money. Hyundai follows a similar strategy for car sales.

Purchases

Businesses may also segment their existing customers to encourage them to buy more. Companies carry out such segmentation based on the purchase history of each customer.

The adventure travel firm Backroads studied what trips customers took, where they went, what season they preferred and whether they travelled with children. The company then proposed personalized packages to their customers and were able to substantially increase revenue. Such detailed segmentation is based on studying customers and giving them exactly what they want.

Causes

Cause-based marketing lets companies segment their markets by what causes customer support. Typical examples are environmentalism, animal rights and fair trade.

Patagonia, a company selling high-end outdoor clothing, targets a high-income, environmentally aware market segment. It emphasizes quality and responsible production, appealing to outdoor enthusiasts and environmentalists. The company makes donations to small environmental groups and innovates to produce high-performing products while favoring environmentally sound raw materials such as organically grown cotton. This targeting has allowed the company to develop high brand loyalty and achieve high margins.

Key terms

Target market

a group of consumers with common needs or wants that a business decides to serve or sell to

Targeting

the process of marketing to a specific market segment

Mass market

a large or broad market that ignores specific market segments

Targeting

After segmenting its market, a firm must then decide on its **target market**. A target market is a group of consumers with common needs or wants that a business serves or sells to. Targeting is the process of marketing to a specific market segment.

Targeting strategies

Undifferentiated marketing or **mass marketing** – a strategy where a firm ignores the differences in the specific market segments and targets the entire market. Here, businesses consider the common needs or wants of consumers in the market and aim to sell their products to many customers in order to maximize their sales. Examples of companies that do this are Samsung, Walmart, LG, Levi Strauss, Dell, HP, Coca-Cola and Zoom.

4.2 Marketing planning

Differentiated marketing or **segmented marketing** – a strategy that targets several market segments and develops appropriate marketing mixes for each of these segments. For example, Toyota designs cars for the different socio-economic status of people in the world. With segmented marketing, firms can gain a stronger position in each of their segments, thereby increasing sales and market share.

Concentrated marketing or **niche marketing** – a strategy that appeals to smaller and more specific market segments. It is a good strategy for smaller firms that have limited resources. These small firms can serve market niches where there are few competitors and take advantage of opportunities that have been overlooked by larger firms. Products provided by businesses that operate in niche markets include Apple's iTunes and Rolls-Royce cars. Targeting specific consumers in these segments enables businesses to market their products more efficiently and effectively.

Understanding consumer profiles is key to effective targeting. A **consumer profile** is a description of the characteristics of consumers of a particular product in different markets. These characteristics include gender, age, social status, and income levels. Consumer profiles can also consist of consumer spending patterns in terms of the number and frequency of products bought.

For segmentation and targeting to be successful, it is very important that firms have good knowledge of who their consumers are. This will enable them to target their products effectively to the right consumers, using appropriate marketing strategies. In addition, a firm that is aware of its target market can cut its costs and utilize more cost-effective promotional techniques.

Zoom is a video conferencing service targeted at the mass market

Key terms

Niche market

a narrow, smaller or more specific market segment

Consumer profile

the characteristics of consumers of a particular product in different markets based on their gender, age, and income levels, among other characteristics

Case study

Identity marketing: a modern approach to market segmentation

Identity marketing rises above the shortcomings of traditional market segmentation. Rather than using costly, limited methods of data collection to build a market segment, identity marketing is based on a consumer tribe that aligns with a brand's values – the ultimate market segmentation!

These consumer tribes share deep-seated identity attributes such as their life stage (students, seniors), occupation (teachers, nurses, first responders), or affiliation (the military community).

Identity marketing campaigns boost customer acquisition by helping brands harness the networking power of consumer tribes to make an offer go viral. Unlike traditional market segments, consumer tribes are socially connected, which greatly enhances sharing. For example, 83% of Gen Z would share a gated (personalized, exclusive) offer with friends.

Identity marketing success stories

Leading brands in retail, streaming, software, hospitality, and finance use identity marketing to acquire high-value consumer tribes:

> **CheapCaribbean brings 8,000 nurses into its travel club**
>
> CheapCaribbean wanted to create a promotion for its nurses – a consumer tribe that pairs well with the brand. The brand's personalized offer brought 8,000 nurses into its "ER&R Club," reduced fraud by 36%, and saved more than 100 hours of staff time.
>
> **Targus uses identity-driven offers to increase orders by 389%**
>
> Targus wanted to generate greater brand awareness and loyalty while rewarding key consumer tribes and corporate clients. After running the identity-driven offers for a year, it decided to ramp things up. The new programmes generated a 389% increase in the number of orders and a 413% increase in revenue, year over year.
>
> **Headspace acquired 25,000 new subscribers**
>
> Headspace, the popular subscription-based meditation app, wanted to honour educators with a personalized offer that gave them free access to the app and classroom support. Headspace acquired 25,000 new educator subscribers in three new markets, reduced fraud by 41%, and boosted engagement.
>
> Source: Adapted from https://www.sheerid.com/blog/how-top-brands-use-market-segmentation-to-reach-customers/

Positioning

Product positioning involves analysing how consumers define or perceive a product compared to other products in the market. As consumers are sometimes faced with an overload of information, to simplify their purchasing process they categorize products and position them accordingly. Marketers must therefore plan positions that will give their products a competitive advantage in the market.

An effective tool they could use is a **position map** or **perception map**. This is a visual representation of how consumers perceive a product in relation to other competing products.

> **Key term**
>
> **Product position map/ perception map**
>
> a visual representation of how consumers perceive a product in relation to other competing products

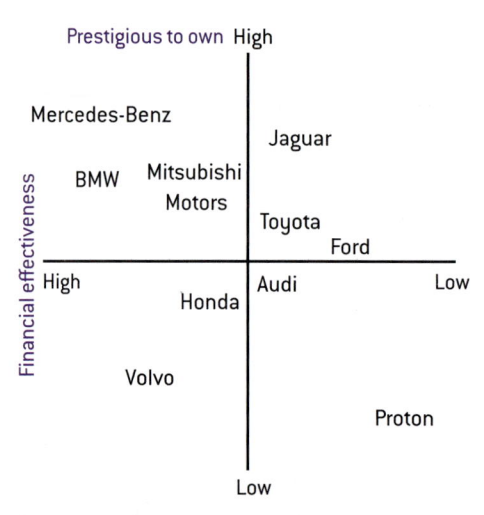

Figure 4.2.1 A position map for cars

4.2 Marketing planning

The first step in positioning requires marketers to identify product features that consumers find important, such as quality, price, and image. In the second step, the firm chooses the key features to use to develop its positioning strategy. Finally, the firm communicates its desired position to its target customers with the support of its marketing mix.

The importance of a position map

- It can help a firm to establish who its close competitors or threats are in the market.
- It helps to identify important gaps or opportunities in the market that the firm could fill by creating or offering new products.
- It is a simple and quick way of presenting usually sophisticated research data.
- It helps a firm in targeting specific market segments to best satisfy consumer needs and wants.

The difference between niche market and mass market

A **niche market** focuses on a small group of people or consumers who have interests that align with the product or service of a specific organization.

In niche marketing, it is important that an organization establishes the niche appeal of its product or service. For example, instead of providing plumbing as a service in general, an organization can specialize in offering plumbing services targeted to old buildings only, hence pursuing a niche market that may be under-served.

A niche market aims to capture a moderate number of buyers in the market. The niche marketer targets a specific market and is aware of the consumer group the product is aimed at.

A **mass market** is aimed at a large or broad market segment. A mass marketing strategy would involve communicating to the largest possible audience. For example, using a TV commercial or a huge flyer printing and distribution campaign.

In mass marketing, restrictions in an organization's marketing strategy are limited as it focuses on capturing a wide customer base with the aim of finding the highest number of potential customers for its needs. Coca-Cola, for example, is a brand that employs mass marketing techniques, with the goal of capturing as many consumers as possible.

Many organizations have been able to move from niche market success to targeting a mass market. For example, the skate shoe company Airwalk found its identity by catering to the needs of skaters in Southern California in the USA. Once it dominated this niche market, the business then expanded to a larger mass market with great success.

In another example, Henry Ford realized that before he created the Model T, the automobile was viewed as a niche product only for the wealthy. However, the Model T was aimed at the mass market and later gained him huge success in the automobile industry.

> **Student workpoint 4.5**
>
> **Be a thinker**
>
> Suggest the possible consumer profile for someone who buys the following:
>
> a) Louis Vuitton handbag
> b) Yamaha motorbike
> c) Nintendo Wii game console

Airwalk first aimed at a niche market selling skate shoes

How niche brands create social media sales in China

The bag and accessories label BY FAR took Chinese social media by storm despite the Covid-19 pandemic. As Chinese fashion influencers brought the Instagram darling to China's Weibo, WeChat, and Little Red Book platforms, more millennial and Gen-Z customers have become loyal fans of the niche Bulgarian brand.

BY FAR is known for its unique designs and vintage details. Every season, the brand always offers customers some classic IT bags and leads trends on fashion-featured social media. According to the brand's founder, BY FAR's aesthetic is inspired by styles from the late 1980s, the 1990s, and the early 2000s. For example, its Mini Rachel bag, which is now one of the most popular bags by the brand, was smartly based on the style of the character Rachel from the 90s sitcom *Friends*.

Recently, BY FAR launched a WeChat Mini Program in China that serves as a shopping space on the social messaging app WeChat. It is currently one of the most effective tools for brands to set up e-commerce functions (ie trading over the internet), as it directs their WeChat followers to buy products and make payments.

For niche brands, WeChat and other social media will be the top battlefield of luxury marketing in the foreseeable future. High-end luxury brands like Cartier, Bulgari, and Dior already have a heavy presence on WeChat, yet BY FAR's social marketing in China has shown the best path to converting online traffic – a quick way to expand a customer base.

As the top social media app for Chinese consumers, WeChat accumulated more than 1.15 billion monthly active users in 2019 and has become the most strategically important space for marketing campaigns. Much in the way many emerging designer brands use a "mood" to succeed on Instagram, brands can use WeChat Mini Program to mimic that success. The social DNA of brands like BY FAR is useful for winning over young customers, creating purchasing motives, and enhancing brand consistency via images.

BY FAR's ambitious commercialization can also be seen in its naming of celebrity KOL Grace Chow as its new face. The influencer had an affair with a famous Chinese singer months ago but then found fame among younger women. The constant news about Chow has helped BY FAR win over some new followers, but the controversy might be problematic for the brand in the future.

"BY FAR has got this era's social media DNA," said Martha Tu, a fashion researcher at Central Saint Martin's College. She said the brand knows how to connect with the local social atmosphere, such as with the branding of its "armpit bag" on e-commerce platforms in China.

Luxury brands love to collaborate with high-profile stars and bloggers in China, but controversial influencers usually aren't a top choice. Some fashion critics believe that after seeing huge potential on Chinese social media and catering to the country's mass market, BY FAR could lose its niche positioning.

Yet the company's founders – Ignatova, her twin sister Sabina Gyosheva, and their lifelong friend Denitsa Bumbarov – still plan to expand the brand's physical presence in China. When asked about their future vision, Ignatova stated, "We believe this is just a start, and the future will show our true potential."

For brands like BY FAR, signature products are good, but they aren't enough for achieving long-term success in China. For a niche brand, its designs should be worth the money and have customers raving about them. "Chinese consumers are the early adopters of the e-market and can have a big impact on a brand's growth and success in the longer term," said Marble Xia, a senior fashion editor at Elle. "After all, niche brands' value will be judged by online traffic and sales profits here in China."

Source: Adapted from https://jingdaily.com/how-niche-brands-create-social-media-sales-in-china/

The unique selling point or proposition (USP)

This is a feature of a product that differentiates it from other competing products in the market. The differentiating factor is what makes a product unique and helps to explain why consumers choose one product over another.

The importance of having a USP

A USP:

- Helps to establish a firm's competitive advantage in its product offering and, as a result, helps to attract more customers.
- Leads to customer loyalty as customers can identify something special about the product in comparison to rival products.
- Leads to improved revenue as customers buy a product or service that best meets their needs. Some customers can pay top prices for a reputable brand that they view as being high quality.
- Makes the product or service easy to sell. Sale representatives who see value in the product or even use the product will find it easier to passionately and persuasively sell the product to customers.

> **Key term**
>
> **Unique selling point/ proposition (USP)**
>
> a product's feature that differentiates it from other competing products in the market

> **Concept**
>
> **CREATIVITY**
>
> Creativity involves considering existing ideas from new perspectives in addition to generating new ideas. To be successful, businesses create unique features that differentiate them from the competition. The case study here gives three examples of businesses that have thought creatively about their USPs.
>
> Research one more business that uses their USP creatively.

Case study: How three businesses creatively use their unique selling points (USPs)

1. **Love with Food (lovewithfood.com)**

   Love with Food sells organic snack-boxes which are delivered directly to customers each month. For every box sold, the company donates a meal to a food bank to feed hungry children. This creates a unique buying experience for their customers that they wouldn't get anywhere else. Love with Food offers something different, while still selling exactly what their customers want.

2. **BridgeU (bridge-u.com)**

   BridgeU aims to help students discover and explore the best career pathways available to them worldwide. It uses data to assist in identifying opportunities for students wherever they may be. It focuses on empowering secondary schools and universities, with software and solutions designed to help them meet global challenges.

3. **Hear and Play (hearandplay.com)**

   Many websites and businesses help people learn music. Hear and Play focuses specifically on learning to play the piano by ear, making it ideal for people who don't want to, or can't, read sheet music.

> **Student workpoint 4.6**
>
> *Be an inquirer*
>
> 1. Draw a position map of an industry of your choice and identify the products or brands on offer.
> 2. Using the information in question 1, why is it important for the organizations offering those products and brands to have a USP?

How organizations can differentiate themselves and their products from competitors

Differentiation enables an organization to provide superior value to its customers and can boost its overall profitability and viability. There are several differentiation strategies. However, not all are equally effective, and the choice of strategy will depend on the type of organization. To stand out from the competition, organizations need to invest in those differentiation strategies that best suit them. These strategies could include any of the following.

Product differentiation

This is the physical or perceived difference in a product. It can take the form of product features such as durability, performance, reliability, or other criteria. Due to its tangible nature, most marketers spend their time on this type of differentiation when pursuing customers.

However, product differentiation can be a short-term strategy, as many product innovations can be easily duplicated. Despite the existence of intellectual property rights like patents and copyrights, in several cases these do not present practical challenges. Some businesses choose not to patent as this reveals to their competitors how to duplicate their product. However, a patent at least protects the product for the life of the patent, unlike when there is none and any competitor with capital can quickly produce a similar product.

Service differentiation

This includes customer service, delivery, and supporting business elements like installation and training. HubSpot is a good example of an organization that differentiates on service. It ensures that its employees are provided with the right information and processes needed to better know their customers and understand their specific needs, which leads to great customer service.

Some organizations, however, view this as a simple component of a business not requiring any level of sophistication.

Price differentiation

A successful price differentiation strategy recognizes that every customer is willing to pay a different price for a product. Through segmentation and differentiation, a business can maximize its potential revenue by offering a differentiated product at a different price in each of its market segments.

For example, the mobile network operator Safaricom has always managed to offer affordable prices to its consumers in the Kenyan market despite the existing competition, and the company has still managed to post very high after-tax profits.

Importantly, in price differentiation (or discrimination) the value of the goods can be subjective and vary by consumer, use and operating environment. In the world of business, most prices are subject to some form of negotiation and customers exist who are prepared to pay more for a product or service than the prevailing market price.

Distribution differentiation

The channel of distribution or path through which a good or service passes until it reaches the end consumer is an effective means of differentiation. This could be through providing immediate access to expertise, greater ease when ordering goods or services, or high levels of technical service.

For many manufacturing organizations facing an unequal market (in which consumers demand different products in the same market), it is not possible to reach the end consumer without the distribution function. Where a supportive relationship exists between the distributor and manufacturer, it can be very time-consuming and expensive for a competitor to duplicate this level of differentiation.

For example, PepsiCo has managed to differentiate itself well globally by having a wide range of retail outlets providing its product close to its consumers.

Relationship differentiation

This is differentiation through the organization's personnel, including employees or team members with customer links. They are responsible for the day-to-day communication with customers, and are an important link between the product and the customer. If this link is broken then the business can be ruined.

A closer relationship between the personnel and the customer builds trust, leading to better business performance. This type of differentiation is closely related to service, but its main focus is on the people. Even though building this relationship takes time, it establishes a highly differentiated position for any organization.

Image/reputation differentiation

This is usually created through other forms of differentiation (such as high product quality, great service, or superior performance), although a business can control and manage its image with the means of communication it uses with its customers.

New entrants to a given market can find it difficult to establish themselves in markets dominated by reputable businesses with exemplary images. For example, DuPont has the strong image of being a technical powerhouse in the market in which it participates.

It is important to note that a brand does not automatically differentiate an organization from its competitors. For effective differentiation, a brand must stand for something, it needs to be recognized by the target audience, and it must communicate something unique and different from the existing competition. To be successful in this, an organization requires a large marketing budget.

4 Marketing

> ## Porter's generic strategies (HL only)
>
> Michael Porter came up with generic strategies that are applicable to products and services in all organizations and industries regardless of their size. These are "cost leadership" (a no-frills approach), "differentiation" (involving the creation of uniquely desirable products and services), and "focus" (offering a specialized service in a niche market).
>
> The focus strategy is subdivided into two parts: "cost focus", which emphasizes cost-minimization within a focused market, and "differentiation focus", which involves pursuing strategic differentiation within a focused market.
>
> The case study below focuses on the "differentiation" strategy by having uniquely desirable products and services that stand out from the competition.

Case study

Five examples of organizations that use a differentiation strategy

Emirates

While airlines like Ryanair and Wizz Air have chosen the approach of cost leadership as a competitive advantage strategy, other companies within the airline industry are looking for ways to differentiate themselves.

Based in Dubai, Emirates is the state-owned airline and flag carrier of the United Arab Emirates. The company operates about 3,600 flights per week to more than 150 cities in 80 countries.

However, what really differentiates them is not the number of flights or countries that they fly to. The elements that make them stand out are as follows.

Exceptional customer service

The company provides exceptional service and commodities to their passengers throughout the whole flight.

Economy class, for example, includes:

- High-quality, regionally inspired dishes from the flight destination
- In-flight digital entertainment with over 4,500 movies to choose from
- Excellent customer service and catering
- Complementary beverages
- On-board wifi

Latest technology

An important aspect of Emirates' differentiation strategy is investing in the latest technologies available on the market.

From using advanced navigation technology for their airplanes to ensuring the best entertainment on board, their dedication to innovation is a fundamental part of the customer-centric experience that they aim to provide.

Tesla

With a mission to accelerate the world to sustainable energy, this American electric vehicle company initially entered the market with the idea of targeting affluent customers in the luxury sector. They were then to move into larger markets at lower price points at a later point.

But what makes the company stand out and differentiate itself from its competitors?

Product innovation

The first and most important point is product innovation. Tesla entered the automotive industry offering market-disruptive electric vehicles that people liked.

Their cars are not only environmentally friendly and extremely high tech, but also have a very distinctive and beautiful aesthetic. Over the years, many companies have tried building electric or hybrid cars, but none of them with the detail and elegant design that Tesla achieved.

But these are not the only aspects of Tesla's product differentiation. Some others include:

- The possibility to customize your car
- Regular software updates
- Solar panels and supercharging compatibility
- Self-driving features

From the tech functionalities to the materials the cars are built from, it is no surprise that Tesla really managed to differentiate from its competitors.

Marketing strategy

Another point of differentiation for Tesla is their marketing strategy.

According to Forbes, the company focuses more on referrals and word-of-mouth advertising than traditional TV advertisements and pushing their products onto the target audience.

Shopify

Shopify is a Canadian multinational e-commerce platform that provides the necessary tools so that people can build their own business online. But what makes it so different from its competitors?

Customer service

The company is known for its excellent customer service. From 24/7 support to a live chat and a help centre, Shopify has got its clients covered in case they need to contact them, no matter the time of the day.

However, Shopify also identified the communication and social media channels that their customers most often frequent and took their support even further. The company actually made a Twitter account dedicated entirely to providing help to their customers.

In this account, people can tweet their issues and problems to Shopify, and they will receive responses providing immediate assistance.

Lush

This company has managed to stand out in a saturated cosmetics market.

Lush is a UK-based cosmetics retailer that has grown to operate in 49 countries and is quickly building its way in the highly competitive industry. Here is what makes the company stand out.

Handmade quality

The first differentiation point for Lush is quality – not only in terms of ingredients, but also when it comes to the production of the final product.

All Lush products are 100% vegetarian, and about 85% are also vegan, often containing fruits and vegetables such as grapefruit juice, fresh papaya, vanilla beans, avocado butter, and aloe vera. Their products are also handmade, which is highly valued by their customers.

Ethics

The company's values are also aligned with those of their target customers in terms of ethics and social responsibility. Instead of testing on animals, the company actually tests on human volunteers before selling their products to the public.

They are also involved in a series of donation and charity campaigns, such as the Charity Pot campaign. Launched in 2007, the campaign generated over $33,000,000 in profits, of which 100% were donated to small organizations in the areas of human rights, animal welfare, and environmental conservation.

Nespresso

Nespresso, a Swiss-based operating unit of the Nestlé Group, provides premium-priced coffee, and it is mostly known for its single-use coffee capsules.

Product differentiation

The capsules, offered in elegant boxes, are made of aluminium and hermetically sealed, preventing the coffee aroma from degrading over time (as opposed to a pack that has been opened).

The company is currently offering a huge variety of options on the market, selling 28 different Original Line arabica and robusta capsules. They also release limited editions occasionally, allowing their customers to select from a wide range of carefully selected flavours.

Additionally, the beautiful, elegant packaging gives a sense of luxury and premium quality.

Physical locations

Another way Nespresso differentiates from its competitors is the company's physical shop locations. The majority of its competitors don't have stores exclusively for their capsules, and you are only able to purchase them in conventional stores and supermarkets.

Additionally, the company's shops are designed to create an experience once you are there, and you feel that you are purchasing a premium product.

The way their capsule boxes are ordered by colour and flavour only adds up to the high-end experience. You can also try their coffee right there in the shop, which is something that competitors are not able to offer in a conventional store unless they do a specific campaign within the store.

Source: Adapted from https://mktoolboxsuite.com/differentiation-strategy-examples/

TOK links

1. As a two-dimensional diagram, is a positioning map a true representation of the market?
2. Can a USP be only partly unique?
3. How much knowledge (of the market, of the customers, of the competitors) is necessary to ensure successful marketing planning?

Revision checklist

- ✓ A marketing plan is an essential document that concerns the development of marketing strategies that help in achieving an organization's marketing objectives.
- ✓ A target market is a group of consumers with common needs or wants that a business decides to sell to, while a market segment is a sub-group of consumers with similar characteristics in a given market.
- ✓ A mass market is a broad market that ignores specific market segments, while a niche market focuses on a narrow market segment.
- ✓ The primary focus of product positioning is to analyse how consumers perceive a firm's product compared to other products in the market, in an effort for the firm to gain a competitive advantage in the market.
- ✓ There are various ways organizations can differentiate themselves from the competition, including by product, service, price, distribution, relationship, and image/reputation.

Marketing

Practice question

To answer the question below effectively, see Unit 6 pages 398–402.

TX

TX, a huge company with a global focus on the automobile business, is an excellent niche marketer. It was one of the first companies to realize there was a group of car buyers who would be very interested in environmentally friendly cars. *TX* answered this need with the development of Tyb, one of the first mass-produced hybrid cars.

Where other car manufacturers that focused only on the mass market saw *TX* as taking a huge risk, *TX* saw it as an opportunity to identify a new niche and establish its brand in that niche.

In marketing, often the first brand to market (provided it is done successfully) can own the niche market with their brand.

Once *TX* took the plunge, it pursued an effective niche marketing plan. It didn't promote Tyb in just any media. It focused on media outlets that were watched, read or listened to by people concerned about the environment. For example, it heavily promoted the car through environmental groups and their publications. In doing this, *TX* not only dominated the niche – it *was* the niche.

Despite growing competition from other hybrid cars, so far Tyb is a success and is regarded as a niche leading brand. However, *TX* will need to think about how long it can depend on Tyb as its main brand in this niche market.

a) Define the term *mass market*. [2 marks]

b) Explain the statement "*TX* not only dominated the niche – it *was* the niche." [2 marks]

c) Discuss the likely reasons for the success of Tyb. [10 marks]

4.3 Sales forecasting (HL only)

> **By the end of this chapter, you should be able to:**
> - Define **sales forecasting**
> - Explain the **terminology associated with sales forecasting**
> - Comment on **sales forecasting data**
> - Examine **the benefits and limitations of sales forecasting**

Introduction

Sales forecasting is the process of predicting what a firm's future sales will be. It uses quantitative methods to estimate the future sales levels and trends over a specified period of time.

Accurately predicting the future reduces uncertainty, helps in the management of stock and cash flow, and ensures better planning for growth. Businesses need sales forecasting information to help them make intelligent business decisions. However, making accurate predictions is a complex process and can be affected by numerous external factors.

Sales forecasting terminology (HL only)

Time series analysis

This is a quantitative sales forecasting method that predicts future sales levels from past sales data. It relies on time series data, which is sales information that businesses have kept over a given period of time. The businesses rely on this past data to predict the future.

Below are key aspects that need to be identified in time series data.

- **The trend** – this is the visible pattern seen after inputting the past sales data. It can indicate the rise and fall of sales over a given period.
- **Seasonal fluctuations** – these are changes in demand due to the varying seasons in the year. An example of seasonal variation is when a business experiences an increase in sales of clothing at the beginning of a new year but these sales decline in the middle of the year. Seasonal variations are usually repeated and occur within one year or less.
- **Cyclical fluctuations** – these are variations tied to the business cycle in an economy. For example, sales could rise during the growth phase but decline during a recession. Cyclical variations can extend for more than one year.
- **Random fluctuations** – these are notable changes or fluctuations that stand out from a given trend. For example, a sudden increase in the demand for ice-cream during a rare warm day in winter. Random variations are unpredictable and can occur at any time.

> **Key terms**
>
> **Sales forecasting**
> the process of predicting the future sales of a firm
>
> **Time series analysis**
> a quantitative sales forecasting method that predicts future sales levels from past sales data

4 Marketing

> **Key terms**
>
> **Moving average**
> sales forecasting method that identifies and emphasizes the direction of a trend
>
> **Extrapolation**
> an extension of a trend line to predict future sales
>
> **Variation**
> difference between actual sales and trend values

Moving averages (HL only)

This is a useful indicator in sales forecasting for identifying and emphasizing the direction of a trend. It is a more accurate and complex method than simply predicting future sales from actual sales data. This is because it helps to smooth out any fluctuations from sales data.

Calculating a three-year moving average

Table 4.3.1 Yearly sales of a calculator manufacturer

Year	1	2	3	4	5	6	7	8
Sales (US$000)	400	600	800	650	700	850	950	1,200

Using Table 4.3.1, the following steps can be used to calculate the three-year moving average:

1. Calculate the mean sales for the first three years. For example, the mean from years 1, 2 and 3 is

$$US\$ \frac{(400,000 + 600,000 + 800,000)}{3} = 600,000.$$

2. Do the same for the next three sets of data:

$$US\$ \frac{(600,000 + 800,000 + 650,000)}{3} = 683,333 \text{ for years 2, 3 and 4.}$$

3. The same process should be used for the following sets of threes:

Years 3, 4, 5: $US\$ \frac{(800,000 + 650,000 + 700,000)}{3} = 716,667$

Years 4, 5, 6: $US\$ \frac{(650,000 + 700,000 + 850,000)}{3} = 733,333$

Years 5, 6, 7: $US\$ \frac{(700,000 + 850,000 + 950,000)}{3} = 833,333$

The above data is summarized in Table 4.3.2 and Figure 4.3.1.

Table 4.3.2 Sales revenue with three-year moving average (trend)

Year	1	2	3	4	5	6	7	8
Sales (US$000)	400	600	800	650	700	850	950	1,200
Trend (three-year moving average) (US$000)		600	683.333	716.667	733.333	833.333		

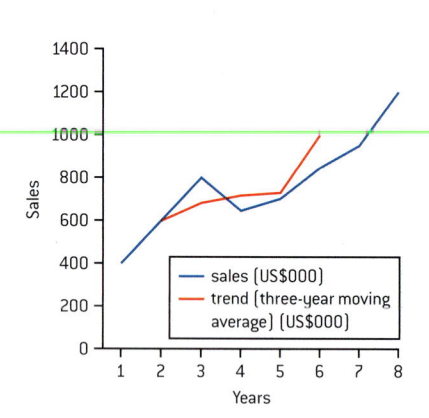

Figure 4.3.1 Actual sales and the three-year moving average trend for the calculator manufacturer

4.3 Sales forecasting (HL only)

Extrapolation

Once the trend line has been drawn, this line can be extended using a "line of best fit", shown by a dotted line, to predict future sales. This is known as **extrapolation**. The trend line from Figure 4.3.1 can be extrapolated to provide an estimated sales value for future years. Figure 4.3.2 shows how a trend line can be extrapolated.

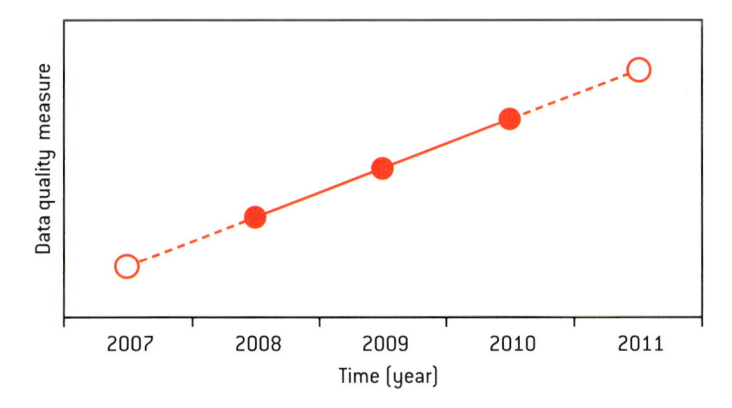

Figure 4.3.2 Example of an extrapolated trend line

Variation

Variation is the difference between actual sales and the trend values. This is shown in Table 4.3.3.

Table 4.3.3 Sales revenue with variations in each year

Year	1	2	3	4	5	6	7	8
Sales (US$000)	400	600	800	650	700	850	950	1,200
Trend (three-year moving average) (US$000)		600	683.333	716.667	733.333	833.333		
Variation		0	116.667	−66.667	−33.333	16.667		

> **Assessment advice**
>
> Calculation of moving averages and variations is not required in the examination. However, to gain a better understanding of sales forecasting, it is important to know how it is done.

Benefits of sales forecasting

- Alignment of an organization strategy for better results. When sales forecasting aligns with an organization's strategy, it enables the right resources to be allocated at the right time. An organization with a goal of increasing its customer base by 20%, for example, could base this on its sales forecasts and allocate the necessary resources to its personnel to seek potential customers.
- Better cash-flow management. By considering cyclical and seasonal variation factors, financial managers can better plan to improve the liquidity position of a business.
- Increased efficiency. Sales forecasting helps the production department to know the number of goods to produce and to plan for stock required in the future.

253

- Better workforce planning. Accurate sales forecasting can help the human resources department in succession planning regarding the number of staff required in the future.

- Improved marketing planning. Marketers will gain greater awareness of future trends and be able to adjust their marketing strategies accordingly to increase their market share.

Limitations of sales forecasting

- Sales forecasting is time-consuming. It takes a long time to calculate because of its complex nature, especially when considering the calculation of average seasonal variations in each quarter over a number of years.

- Sales forecasting ignores qualitative external factors. Political, social, and economic factors can influence the accuracy of sales forecast predictions, for example political instability, changes in consumer tastes and preferences, and exchange rate fluctuations.

- In sales forecasting, the entry of competitors into a market may be unforeseen. This can significantly change an organization's dynamic and influence its sales position. For example, a firm that is enjoying a monopoly status in the present can lose that position if the consumers decide to switch to buying the competitors' products.

- Sales forecasting may be based on present technology which can be rendered obsolete due to technological progress. Hence, products which may currently be enjoying good sales may lose their market to products made with the latest technology. An example is the market for electronic products and computers.

> **Simple linear regression (HL only)**
>
> Simple linear regression comprises tools that predict or describe the relationship between two variables. These tools include scatter diagrams and correlation.
>
> How would a business or marketing department benefit from understanding and applying these tools?

TOK links

1. To what extent does knowing help us in predicting?
2. How do we know that our sales predictions are reliable?
3. Is it ethical to knowingly overpredict?

Revision checklist

✓ Sales forecasting is a quantitative process of estimating a firm's future sales levels and trends over a specified period of time.

✓ Seasonal variations are caused by changes in demand due to the varying seasons in the year. Cyclical variations, on the other hand, are tied to the business cycle in an economy, while random variations are notable changes that stand out from a given trend.

✓ Moving averages greatly assist in developing trend lines that help to smooth out any fluctuations from sales data.

✓ Extrapolation is the use of a line of best fit drawn to predict future sales.

4.3 Sales forecasting (HL only)

Practice question

To answer the question below effectively, see Unit 6 pages 398–402.

B-Games

B-Games is a well-known private limited company, which prides itself on its innovative computer games and dedicated workforce. A recession is predicted for the coming three years in the domestic economy, so the managers of *B-Games* are considering revising their product portfolio. The preferred option is to increase their product offering.

While accepting the need for a growth strategy, the marketing director is worried about *B-Games'* sales of a new product during a recession. The financial director is worried about lack of funds to produce a new product range. The managers of *B-Games* are considering the best option for the company. They intend to use sales trend data from the previous seven years to carry out sales forecasting to help them decide.

B-Games computer games sales record: 2015–2021

Financial year	Sales (units)
2015	5,000
2016	5,500
2017	4,500
2018	8,600
2019	9,100
2020	9,300
2021	11,000

a) Define the term *sales forecasting*. [2 marks]

b) Discuss the benefits and limitations to *B-Games* of using sales forecasting in aiding their decision to increase their product portfolio. [10 marks]

4.4 Market research

> **By the end of this chapter, you should be able to:**
> → Examine why and how organizations carry out **market research**
> → Analyse the **primary market research methods**
> → Comment on the **secondary market research methods**
> → Distinguish between **qualitative** and **quantitative research**
> → Explain the various **sampling methods**

Market research is the process of collecting, analysing, and reporting data related to a particular market. This includes data on consumption of goods and services and on competitors' behaviour. Importantly, businesses use market research information to make key decisions.

The purposes of market research

- To identify consumer needs and wants, as well as to understand consumer satisfaction levels and patterns in purchasing behaviour. For example, a beverage company may want to find out the type of customers buying their sodas and the sales trends over a given period.

- To assist a business in predicting what is likely to happen in the future. For example, an upcoming recession may signal firms to be prepared for decreases in overall spending patterns because of a possible decline in consumer income levels.

- To reduce the risk of product failure (especially of new products) by effectively carrying out market research that establishes the likes and dislikes of consumers.

- To measure the effectiveness of a marketing strategy. This can be done by assessing or evaluating how a firm implements its marketing mix activities in specific market segments.

- To provide the latest information on activities happening in the market. For example, most large technological companies have huge research and development budgets to keep up to date with developments in the market and benefit from first-mover advantages.

Conducting market research means analysing all the information about the market in an effort to investigate possible ways for the business to operate successfully in the market, increase sales, attract its target audience, and gain competitive advantages.

Market research methods

Market research can broadly be carried out in two ways: **primary** and **secondary research**.

> **Key terms**
>
> **Market research**
> the process of collecting, analysing, and reporting data related to a particular market
>
> **Primary research**
> the collection of first-hand information from the market
>
> **Secondary research**
> the collection of second-hand information from the market

Primary market research

This is also known as "field research" and involves the collection of first-hand information from the market.

Most organizations will conduct this research to find out specific buying patterns of consumers and attempt to anticipate any changes in their spending behaviour over a given period of time. Firms may decide to carry out this research themselves or seek the help of a market research agency.

A key advantage of primary research is that the organization can gain information directly from its customers, which gives it an advantage over its rivals. For example, a hotel may discover through primary research that a particular airline is prone to flight cancellations. It can use this information to attract customers who may be waiting for many hours and possibly days for their connecting flights. However, field research is expensive because the research process takes time and requires specialist researchers.

Asking customers to complete surveys is one form of primary market research

Secondary market research

This is the collection of second-hand information from the market. Also known as "desk research", it involves analysing data that already exists in some form.

Organizations should first carry out secondary research to get an overall background picture, and then conduct primary research as a gap-filling measure. Desk research is a quicker and cheaper method than field research and most of the information involved is readily available. However, the information collected may be out of date and it might have been collected for purposes other than the specific needs of the researching organization. In some cases, the source of the data may be unreliable.

Primary market research methods
Surveys

These are questionnaires sent out to a particular target audience to enable the researcher to gather useful information. The questionnaire may contain different types of questions, such as closed questions needing "yes" or "no" answers, and open-ended questions which require a lengthier response. A consumer survey can focus on getting specific information from consumers by seeking their opinion on a particular product or issue.

Surveys can be implemented in different ways. Some of the most common ways to administer surveys include:

- **by mail** – for example, an alumni survey distributed via direct mail by the development office in a school, seeking opinions from past students about an issue
- **by telephone** – for example, a researcher calling consumers to elicit their opinion about using a certain product or service

- **online** – for example, workshop leaders can use online surveys as an evaluation tool to seek participants' opinions of the workshop.

Advantages	Disadvantages
• They enable researchers to collect a large amount of data in a relatively short period of time. • If designed well, surveys can be administered and completed easily by the respondents. • Surveys can be used to collect information on a wide range of aspects, including attitudes, preferences, and opinions.	• Surveys that are poorly constructed and administered can undermine otherwise well-intended research. • The answers provided by respondents to a survey may not be an accurate reflection of how they feel, with some results also being biased. • As large samples are normally used, surveys can be costly and take a long time to construct and administer. While random sampling is generally used to select participants, response rates can bias the results of a survey.

Interviews

An interview is a conversation during which the interviewer asks the interviewee questions in order to gain information. Interviews can be conducted one on one, face to face, by telephone or online.

Advantages	Disadvantages
• They can provide detailed information about the perceptions and opinions of consumers through in-depth questioning. • They usually achieve a high response rate because of the one-on-one attention provided. • Precise wording can be tailored to the respondent and the meaning of questions clarified during the interview process.	• The whole process can be very time-consuming as it involves setting up the interview, carrying it out, analysing responses, gathering feedback, and reporting. • Some interviewers may be biased, therefore influencing interviewees' responses.

Focus groups

Focus groups consist of a small number of people brought together to discuss a specific product or idea. The group comprises individuals who are representative of the customers of the business or of a specific segment of customers.

In the discussion, participants respond to questions prepared by market researchers. Participants share their opinions, ideas, and reactions freely. They can also be asked to try a new product. Usually, all participant responses are viewed and studied to help researchers predict the reaction of the larger market population.

4.4 Market research

Advantages	Disadvantages
• As focus groups consist of a small group of individuals, using them is a cheap and easy way of gathering market research. • They can be used to measure the reaction of customers to a firm's new product or to the firm's strategies. • They help identify key product requirements as well as other needs not addressed by the business and its competitors. • They provide insights on the current position of the firm's competitors in the mind of the customer.	• A business could be seeking information about the entire market; however, the opinions of a small number of individuals may not reflect this. • It is possible that some members of the group may not express their honest and personal opinions on the discussion topic. They may be hesitant to express their own views, especially when their opinions differ from those of another participant. • Focus groups are more costly to set up than surveys as each participant is usually compensated in cash or in kind.

Observation

Observation is a fundamental and basic method of getting information by carefully watching and trying to understand certain things or people's behaviour. Some observations are scientific in nature, but not all are.

Observation can be used by supermarkets to check how quickly consumers notice their displays or how long they may spend queuing to pay. It can also be used by a government's traffic department to observe the flow of traffic in certain areas and help provide recommendations for improvement.

Advantages	Disadvantage
• It is a direct method of collecting data or information when studying actual human behaviour, as the researcher can see exactly how people behave in a given situation. • A large number of individuals can be surveyed in a short space of time. • Observation is usually a cost-effective way of gathering data.	• Complete answers to any problem or issue cannot be obtained by observation alone, so market researchers need to combine this with other methods (such as issuing questionnaires).

Secondary market research methods

Academic journals

These are publications of scholarly articles written by experts. The articles should be well referenced to provide the exact source of the information given. The experts usually include professors, graduate students, or others with first-hand experience in a particular subject.

Academic journals are written for the sole purpose of providing and distributing knowledge and not as a money-making opportunity.

Advantages	Disadvantages
• Academic journals undergo a peer-review process where they are checked by academics and other experts. This increases the reliability of the information. • Most academic journals include reports, reviews of current research, and topic-specific information. They are therefore good sources when a firm needs original research on a topic. • They take less time to publish than books.	• Since they contain information of very specific academic interest, they may not be the best source for general-interest topics. • The peer-review process can be time-consuming, which may also affect the provision of the latest or current event information.

Media articles

These include texts written and submitted for publication. Some examples are newspapers and magazines.

A newspaper is a printed publication containing news, feature articles, advertisements, and correspondence. Once viewed as the dominant means of communicating world events, newspapers have declined in readership since television and the internet have become more widespread.

Advantages	Disadvantages
• Communicating via a newspaper is cheaper than communicating via television. • Most serious newspaper articles have been well researched, written using reliable sources, and edited for accuracy, which is not the case for some internet resources. • They are widely available and can be found in many retail stores.	• It is difficult to communicate events in real time. As the process of producing content, printing, and distributing the finished paper is time-consuming, articles that were written may be out of date by the time they are delivered to the customer. • Newspapers can be biased, depending on the type of organization that owns them. • The process of producing newspapers could be considered a waste of paper and energy resources.

Government publications

These are documents produced by the government that provide an official record of government activities and cover a wide variety of topics. They can be issued by local, regional, or national governments or by their respective agencies.

4.4 Market research

Advantages	Disadvantages
• They provide details about any changes in government policy or governance in a country. • They provide information that in most cases would only be undertaken by the government, such as a population census in a country. • They provide useful statistical information on a wide range of activities such as education, trade, and social trends. • The information that the government collects to inform its activities is up to date as it is collected on an ongoing basis.	• It can be difficult to gain access to some official government data.

Market analyses

These include commercial publications or market intelligence reports that gather data about particular markets. The highly detailed reports are usually carried out by specialist market research agents. They can be sourced at various local business libraries. Organizations that provide such reports include Dun, Mintel and Verdict.

Advantage	Disadvantage
• The information provided is usually accurate and recent as it is carried out by specialist research agents.	• Obtaining information this way can be quite costly as some organizations charge a lot for this service.

Online content

This involves gathering information from the internet or websites. The internet provides access to an abundance of data. Both published and unpublished secondary data can be found on the internet.

Advantages	Disadvantages
• Many websites provide up to date news and information about current events, trends and interesting topics. • Information is provided quickly and most of it is easy to access.	• As anyone can publish on the web, information can be inaccurate or biased, and even outdated. • A limited amount of scholarly research or information is openly available on the internet.

> **Concept**
>
> **ETHICS**
>
> Ethics involves moral philosophies or guidelines that influence the way businesses conduct themselves. This includes how they conduct their market research. The case study on the next page provides a deeper understanding of the ethical considerations in market research.
>
> Carry out research on any two organizations that consider ethical implications in their market research practices.

Case study

Ethical considerations of market research

Market research has experienced a resurgence with the widespread use of the internet and the popularity of social networking. It is easier than ever before for companies to connect directly with customers and collect individual information that goes into a computer database to be matched with other pieces of data collected during unrelated transactions.

The way a company conducts its market research can have serious ethical repercussions, impacting the lives of consumers in ways that have yet to be fully understood. Further, companies can be faced with a public backlash if their market research practices are perceived as unethical.

The use of deceptive practices

Any action that uses lies and deceit to find out about consumer opinions falls under the category of deceptive practices.

The ease with which a company can access and gather data about its customers can lead to deceptive practices and dishonesty in the company's research methods. This type of ethical problem can range from not telling customers that information is being collected when they visit a website, to misrepresenting research results by using faulty data. At no time should a researcher ever coerce or pressure a respondent to give a particular answer.

Another deceptive technique is known as "sugging", the practice of selling under the guise of research. With this method, a salesman contacts an individual by phone posing as a market researcher. As they ask questions, supposedly in the name of research, they are in fact gaining information about a potential sales lead or even leading the person towards developing a bias for a particular product.

Invasion of privacy

One of the most serious ethical considerations involved in market research is invasion of privacy. Companies have an unprecedented ability to collect, store and match information relating to customers that can infringe on a person's right to privacy. In many instances, the customer does not know or understand the extent of the company's infiltration into their life.

The company uses this information to reach the customer with targeted advertising, but the process of targeting can have a chilling effect on personal freedom. Laws such as the EU's GDPR (General Data Protection Regulation) have increased punishments and fines for data privacy violations. Similarly, California has adopted a new law granting greater protections to resident consumers.

Breaches of confidentiality

Another significant ethical consideration involved in market research involves breaches of confidentiality. Companies regularly share information about customers with partners and affiliates, requiring the customer to opt-out of the sharing if they don't want to be involved. (The US and EU have different standards.) Some companies sell information they have gathered on customers to outside companies.

Ethically, any unauthorized disclosure of customer information is problematic.

Undertaking objective market research

Marketing and advertising have a significant impact on public perceptions. Market researchers have an ethical obligation to conduct research objectively, so that available data allows for the development of a balanced or reality-based picture.

Researchers who allow their own prejudices to skew their work tend to contribute to the perpetuation of stereotypes in advertising, the development of destructive social constructs, and the enabling of unjust profiting from poverty. For example, a market researcher with a one-dimensional view of minorities could do a lot of harm if allowed to shape an advertising campaign based on skewed data collection.

Source: Adapted from http://smallbusiness.chron.com/ethical-considerations-marketing-research-43621.html

4.4 Market research

The differences between qualitative and quantitative research

Primary research or secondary research can be either qualitative or quantitative in nature.

Table 4.4.1 shows the differences between qualitative and quantitative research.

Table 4.4.1 Differences between qualitative and quantitative research

Qualitative research	Quantitative research
This involves the collection of data about opinions, attitudes or beliefs.	This involves the collection of numerical data or data that can be measured.
Information is open to a high degree of interpretation.	Information is less open to interpretation.
It is subjective.	It is objective.
Key research questions would include "Why?"	Key research questions would include "How many"?
The researcher is part of the process.	The researcher is separate.
It provides multiple realities, ie the focus is complex and broad.	It provides one reality, ie the focus is concise and narrow.

Generally, qualitative research is collecting, analysing, and interpreting data by observing what people do and say. Quantitative research refers to counts and measures of things, whereas qualitative research refers to the meanings, definitions, characteristics, and descriptions of things.

For example, quantitative research may seek answers to the question: How many customers bought the company's sports shoes in the month of May 2020? Qualitative research may seek answers to the question: Why do customers like the company's sports shoes?

Common methods used in collecting qualitative data include the use of focus groups and in-depth interviews. Surveys and government publications are the methods normally used to collect quantitative data.

Key terms

Qualitative research
the collection, analysis, and interpretation of data about consumer opinions, attitudes, or beliefs

Quantitative research
the collection, analysis and interpretation of numerical data or data that can be measured

Case study

How Safaricom adopts market research to overcome competition

Safaricom is the leading telecommunications company operating in Kenya. It provides a host of products and services for telephony, GPRS, 3G, EDGE and data and fax.

It has been faced with a number of problems, one of which is the entry of many other telecommunications companies into the market over the years. These companies include Telkom, Yu and Zain. The problem caused by the entry of other companies is that they bring about unwanted competition (and a decrease in market share). This problem can be solved by conducting marketing research.

The **first step** in the market research process is identifying and defining the problem. "Defining the problem" would mean expanding on it and explaining why it should be seen as a problem. In this case, Safaricom has identified a number of competitors, and the threat is that they could lose customers and market share. This would lead to lower profit margins, and growth at the end of the year that is less than they want.

Step two is to develop an approach. Generally speaking, the approach should be developed almost exclusively around a defined set of objectives. Clearly identifying and defining the problem in step one will lead to a better approach development. Developing the approach should involve an honest assessment of the team's market research skills, establishing a budget, understanding the business's environment and its influencing factors, and formulating hypotheses.

Safaricom has to find an approach to counter the problem they are facing, which is increased competition. A special team at Safaricom has come up with a number of possible solutions.

The first proposed solution is to introduce lower call rates for subscribers, and introduce a competition in which only Safaricom subscribers can participate. The second solution is for Safaricom to have a charity event where the money they make goes to a special cause, for example food aid, tree planting etc. This would affect the market socially. And the final solution is supremacy – to control the telephony industry by outmatching other operators by being the first to launch Apple's iPhone 3G.

After carrying out extensive research, Safaricom has decided to be the first to launch Apple's iPhone 3G, increasing the competitor advantage.

The **third step** is to do market research to enable the firm to make an appropriate decision on all the elements of the marketing mix, as well as to reduce the risk of investing in an unprofitable marketing venture.

Safaricom has decided to launch Apple's iPhone 3G in a limited geographical area where demand is observed. The price will be high as it is a unique product, but it will attract non-price-sensitive consumers who see new products as a novelty. After the product has been around for a while, the price will be reduced to attract the more price-sensitive consumer. It will be launched in Westlands, Nairobi, next to two shopping malls, and extensive advertising will be launched to ensure consumers receive information about the new and exciting product.

Step four is called data collection or survey fielding. Generally, data collection is concerned with collecting, editing and presenting the raw material in a form suitable for solving the research problem and making decisions. The data collected from the test market research includes diagrams, sales, etc.

Safaricom will evaluate the data collected and decide whether to launch the product officially in the whole of Kenya.

Step five is the analysis of the collected information. Data presentation methods should allow for easy interpretation of the research findings by the analyst. Charts and diagrams can be used to plot the data to show trends and relationships between variables. Test marketing provides first-hand information about the market, and revenues are also received during the collection of data. For example, the analyst can use a graph that shows the trend of the sales to help in making decisions.

Step six involves the market research report. The report must provide the readers (the sponsor) with the information they require in a format they are able to understand and appreciate. The vocabulary, presentations, and analysis methods used should match the readers' level of understanding and requirements. Also, the report should show any threats of launching the product.

In this case, Safaricom has decided to launch the iPhone 3G as their research in this area was positive. However, this was a test on a small group that may not effectively represent the behaviour of the whole market.

Source: Adapted from http://www.123helpme.com/marketing-research--view.asp?id=166275

Sampling methods

The population comprises all potential consumers in a market. There is simply not enough time, energy, money, labour, or equipment to carry out a survey of the whole population. However, to gather adequate primary research and still have a clear idea of consumers' views, it is necessary to take a sample of the population.

A **sample** is a small group of people selected to represent the population or target market under research. For example, a small group of consumers could be selected out of a large number of potential buyers of a product. **Sampling** is simply the process of selecting the appropriate sample.

Below are a number of commonly used sampling methods and the advantages and disadvantages of each.

Quota sampling

This involves segmenting a given population into a number of groups that share certain characteristics (mutually exclusive sub-groups) such as age or gender. Targets are then set for the number of people who must be interviewed in each segment. For example, in a school of 500 students offering the IB diploma programme, a researcher may target 15 males and 20 females to interview regarding their perception of the programme.

Advantages	Disadvantages
• This is a quick and cost-effective sampling method, especially where the proportions of the different groups in the population are known. • Findings obtained are usually more reliable than those of random sampling.	• Results obtained are not always statistically representative of the population as random sampling (see below) is not done; this also leads to statistical errors. • The interviewer may be biased in the selection of interviewees and choose those who will be the most cooperative in the process.

Random sampling

Every member in the population has an equal chance of being selected as part of the sample, as the sample of respondents is selected randomly (for example, by using a computer to generate a list of random numbers from a target population). An example of selecting a random sample is choosing any 50 people from a telephone directory containing the names of 1,000 people.

Advantages	Disadvantage
• Random sampling reduces bias as everyone has an equal chance of being chosen. • It is a relatively easy way of obtaining a sample.	• The sample chosen may be too small and/or it may not consist of the target population; a larger, more representative sample may have to be selected.

Key terms

Sample

a group of people selected to represent the population or target market under research

Sampling

the process of selecting an appropriate sample

Assessment advice ✓

In determining the best sampling method to use, it is important to analyse the strengths and weaknesses of each method. A key consideration is the level of bias in the sample and how cost-effective the method is. This could also be influenced by factors such as financial resources, business size, and rationale of the research.

4 Marketing

> **Concept: CHANGE**
>
> Technological innovation has transformed the way market research is done. Social media has expanded the landscape and is transforming research in exciting new ways. It allows unfiltered feedback but requires new research skills. With new technology, researchers can precisely target what to measure and who their focus will be. Using the most recent social media and online survey methods, businesses can collect data about all sorts of things. They can do it faster, better and cheaper than ever.
>
> What do you think are the major drawbacks in conducting market research given the recent changes in technology? How do you think these drawbacks can be addressed?

Convenience sampling

This is a sampling technique where research groups are selected based on their easy access and proximity to the researcher. For example, a teacher doing research on the school canteen could conduct a study by being physically present and directly interviewing students purchasing items from the canteen at break time or lunchtime.

Another example would be a researcher using the first 10 names in the patient list to select a sample when conducting research in a hospital.

Advantage	Disadvantage
• It is a fast, easy and cheap method of sampling because the research groups are readily available.	• The sample may be biased and not representative of the entire population.

Importance of properly collected data

Businesses are interested in the range of results they get from carrying out research. It is therefore very important that they ensure their data collection methods are appropriate and offer a high degree of accuracy. Whether using quantitative or qualitative data, or a combination of both, it is essential to maintain integrity in the research process.

Selecting the appropriate data collection instruments and providing clear instructions for their correct use reduces the likelihood of sampling errors occurring.

Benefits of properly collected data include:

- the ability of the research to accurately answer the research questions posed
- the ability to repeat and validate a particular study where needed
- increased accuracy of findings resulting in an efficient use of resources
- good opportunities for other researchers to pursue areas needing further investigation.

The main aim of research is to gather reliable information about an issue or intervention and analyse it to determine the significance of the sample results. Collecting and analysing quantitative data can help to highlight connections (correlations) among variables and address other factors the researcher may not have considered. Collecting and analysing qualitative data can provide insight into the varying participant experiences, including what may need to be improved or changed.

On gaining the required knowledge from the research information provided, a researcher should continue evaluating the whole process to obtain even better results in the next research round.

> **Concept: CHANGE**
>
> There are several different reasons why companies use market research, and these reasons change according to the organization's objectives.
>
> Before a product is introduced, a company uses market research to establish the needs of the targeted consumers. The case study on the next page describes how companies have changed and succeeded as a result of using market research.
>
> Research two more organizations that have changed and succeeded as a result of carrying out market research.

4.4 Market research

Case study: How five massive companies changed using market research

Cargill

Customers turn to Cargill for their scientific expertise, whether it involves enhancing an existing product, improving process efficiencies, or uncovering a solution that helps them launch a first-to-market innovation. To achieve this status, Cargill leverages its extensive market research capabilities to generate distinctive value through new, improved products and innovative ways to reduce costs.

Due to Cargill's strong regional presence, they are able to easily reach out to customers to enquire on how they can improve their systems and processes to serve their customers even better. Based on customer feedback, this enables Cargill to provide their customers with the latest applications and technical services support so they can create products tailored to meet local tastes and cultures.

Apple

Apple has been the largest name in technology for years. This is not necessarily because they appear to be the most innovative. Instead, it is because they use market research to find out exactly what their customers want from their devices; they then figure out how to make those wants a reality.

Their "Apple Customer Pulse" research group is a prime example. Because these are online surveys, the company is able to compile and analyse the data faster, and the surveys are easy to administer. This makes the market research more appealing to those that participate, as well as to the company.

These surveys have led to different designs and modifications of Apple products. Such modifications include having bigger screens to view videos and games more clearly.

Google Nest

Google Nest is trying to reinvent several products normally found in the home. They use Google Consumer Surveys for their marketing research.

Their surveys include questions about how their current products are functioning and what needs to be done to improve them. This allows any customer to give their feedback on Nest's services and products. The surveys open up opportunities for Google Nest to quickly gain information from thousands of people on whatever they want.

One question they have asked their customers is, "How high is your ceiling?" They asked this in order to get an average height so they could judge how large to make a certain appliance.

By incorporating the feedback that they are receiving from online marketing research, Google Nest is able to improve its products and, in turn, improve sales.

McDonald's

McDonald's is one of the largest fast-food chains in the world. In order to continue this trend, McDonald's uses ongoing market research.

In their market research, they have narrowed their focus to four different questions:

1. Which products are well received?
2. What prices are consumers willing to pay?
3. What TV programmes, websites and advertising do consumers read and view?
4. Which restaurants are most visited?

By answering these questions, McDonald's is able to determine whether the pool of their target customers is growing.

One of the problems addressed by such research was whether McDonald's was serving healthy or organic food. As a result, the company launched a campaign to prove that their meat patties and chicken nuggets are real. They also changed part of their menu to include healthier alternatives, such as apple slices.

Tyson Foods

Tyson Foods recognizes that many demographic factors drive customer preferences and consumption patterns, making marketing even more personal to the consumer. Consumers have unique preferences and triggers that motivate them to buy.

To predict diet preferences and consumption patterns, the company carries out market research into how age groups use media, even segmenting within those demographics, such as distinguishing between millennials who use Twitter and those who use Instagram. This had kept Tyson informed on the latest consumption trends, enabling them to change their food processes to suit market demands.

Conclusion

In order to keep on the leading edge of consumerism, businesses must be willing to listen to customers. Whether it is over the phone, through direct mail, online, or using focus groups, there is no excuse for companies to ignore market research. Technology is making online market research not only possible, but also a cheaper and more accurate way to conduct research. Not only can businesses provide services, but they can now know exactly which of their services are wanted and why.

Source: Adapted from https://www.surveypolice.com/blog/how-5-massive-companies-changed-using-market-research/

TOK links

1. To what extent is market research information reliable?
2. How does the language used in questionnaires influence consumers' and businesses' conclusions when doing market research?
3. Could companies know us better than we know ourselves?

Student workpoint 4.7

Be an inquirer

Investigate an organization of your choice that carries out market research. In the process, consider the following:

1. What are the primary and secondary research methods that it uses?
2. Does it use qualitative or quantitative research, or both?
3. Comment on the sampling method or methods that it uses.

Revision checklist

✓ Market research helps in business decision-making by collecting, analysing and reporting data related to a particular market.

✓ Primary research (field research) and secondary research (desk research) are the two ways in which market research can be carried out.

✓ Primary research methods include surveys, interviews, focus groups, and observations.

✓ Secondary research methods include academic journals, media articles, government publications, and market analyses.

✓ Quantitative research concerns the collection, analysis and interpretation of numerical data, as compared to qualitative research, which collects, analyses and interprets data about consumer opinions, attitudes or beliefs.

✓ In conducting market research, it is important that the data collection methods businesses use are appropriate and offer a high degree of accuracy while maintaining integrity in the research process.

4.4 Market research

Practice question

To answer the question below effectively, see Unit 6 pages 398–402.

Technology and research

Recently, when Professor Lin spoke to a large audience of company chief executives, she argued that rapid changes in technology was one of the factors that influenced how businesses were conducting themselves. She said that if businesses are to remain competitive, they should increase their market research budgets and target the right customers.

The professor continued, "It is no accident that the companies with the biggest market research budgets have produced products that are very well recognized globally. These companies use a combination of quantitative and qualitative research. This means that consumer opinions about a given product or the number of consumers using a particular product is very important information for a business to have." The professor added that such companies use both primary and secondary research methods to ensure that they are effectively targeting existing and potential customers.

She gave an example of how company X, which produces cellphones, relied a lot on gathering information directly from consumers in order to seek their views on the type of cellphone they would like to see in the future. On the other hand, she said that company Y, producing children's toys, collected data that already existed in the market and used these data to influence their next toy production decisions.

In conclusion, the professor noted that because of technological advancements, conducting market research was enabling researchers to reach a wider audience, especially using online platforms.

a) Define the term *market research*. [2 marks]

b) Distinguish between quantitative and qualitative research. [4 marks]

c) Explain **two** primary research methods that companies can use "to ensure that they are effectively targeting existing and potential customers". [4 marks]

4.5 The seven Ps of the marketing mix

> **By the end of this chapter, you should be able to:**
> → Explain the stages in a **product life cycle**
> → Examine various **extension strategies** that could be used by firms
> → Analyse the relationship between the **product life cycle, product portfolio and the marketing mix**
> → Comment on the relationship between the **product life cycle, investment, profit and cash flow**
> → Explain the various aspects of **branding**
> → Comment on the **importance of branding**
> → Justify the appropriateness of using particular **pricing methods**
> → Explain the **main forms of promotion**
> → Discuss the role of **social media marketing** as a promotional strategy
> → Examine the importance of different types of **distribution channel**
> → Discuss the importance of **employee–customer relationships** in marketing a service and **cultural variation** in these relationships
> → Evaluate the importance of **delivery processes** in marketing a service and changes in these processes
> → Examine the importance of **tangible physical evidence** in marketing a service
> → Evaluate the **appropriate marketing mixes** for particular products or businesses

The marketing mix – an introduction

Central to marketing planning is the development of a firm's **marketing mix**. This is a collective term that includes the key elements that ensure the successful marketing of a product. In this section, the seven Ps of the marketing mix (**product, price, promotion**, **place, people, processes** and **physical evidence**) are briefly introduced and explained.

- **Product** – this is a good or service that is offered in a market. A good such as a television is tangible, while a service such as health insurance is intangible. Products should aim to satisfy the needs and wants of consumers. Whether providing a new or existing product, firms need to ensure that the consumer's interests are taken into consideration.

4.5 The seven Ps of the marketing mix

- **Price** – this is the amount consumers are charged when they buy a product. It indicates the value consumers perceive the product to have. For example, when the Samsung special edition Galaxy Smartwatch was launched, consumers paid a high price for it because of its perceived quality. On the other hand, second-hand clothes are priced lower than brand new ones because they are perceived as having a lower value. Setting an appropriate price can be difficult for businesses because of the sensitive nature of consumer purchasing behaviour and the various internal and external factors that influence these behaviours.

- **Promotion** – this refers to the various ways consumers are informed about and persuaded to purchase a product. The communication methods used to attract the consumer to buy the product are very important. A firm could use television advertising, sales promotions or a combination of both in order to convince consumers to buy the product.

- **Place** – this refers to a product's location or channels of distribution used to get the product to the consumer. Products can be purchased in shops or over the internet. Intermediaries, including wholesalers, retailers, and agents, are also used to get products to where consumers need them. For example, large supermarkets such as Shoprite or Giant have many retail outlets distributed countrywide to ensure that their products are available to as many consumers as possible.

- **People** – many businesses work very hard on the other elements of the marketing mix and pay little attention to the people in the business who are involved in decision-making on a regular basis. A firm's ability to select, recruit, hire, and retain the best people, with the right skills and abilities to do the job, is a crucial aspect of any business. Collins (2001) found that an important factor present in the best companies was that they first "got the right people on the bus and the wrong people off the bus". After hiring the right people they then "got the right people in the right seats on the bus".[1] Successful businesses think in terms of getting the right people to carry out specific tasks and responsibilities.

- **Processes** – This refers to the procedures and policies related to how an organization's product is provided and delivered. It should inform customers on "how easy it is to do business" with a particular organization. Examples of processes that don't function well and need urgent attention include, for example, call centre staff who do not answer customers' questions, and products in supermarkets with barcodes that are not recognized when customers are ready to pay. The more intangible the product, the more important it is to get the process right.

- **Physical evidence** – This refers to all the tangible or visible touch points that are observable to customers in a business. Unlike businesses offering tangible products where consumers can try, touch, or smell the product before purchasing it, service businesses usually depend on customers' recommendations or testimonials, which are usually based on trust. As a result, businesses need to ensure that they are providing adequate evidence of quality throughout. Examples of good-quality

> **Key terms**
>
> **Marketing mix**
> the key elements of a marketing strategy that ensure the successful marketing of a product
>
> **Product**
> any good or service that is offered to the market with the aim of satisfying consumer needs or wants
>
> **Price**
> what consumers pay to acquire a product
>
> **Promotion**
> ways of convincing consumers why they need a product and why they should buy it
>
> **Place**
> this concerns where the product will be sold and how it will be delivered to the market
>
> **People**
> the human capital in terms of skills, attitudes, and abilities necessary in the production of goods or the provision of services
>
> **Processes**
> the procedures and policies pertaining to how an organization's product is provided and delivered
>
> **Physical evidence**
> the tangible or visible touch points that are observable to customers in a business

---

[1] Collins, J. 2001. *Good to Great: Why Some Companies Make the Leap ... and Others Don't*. London. HarperBusiness.

evidence include well-dressed staff, a well-organized reception area, ambient lighting with pleasant music in a restaurant, and offices located in a prime location. To create a good customer experience, tangible aspects must therefore be delivered with the service.

The seven Ps are explored in more detail below.

Product

A **product** is any good (tangible item) or service (intangible offering) that is offered to the market with the aim of satisfying consumer needs or wants.

A **product life cycle** shows the course that a product takes from its development to its decline in the market. Most products go through six stages in their life cycle: development, introduction, growth, maturity, saturation, and decline.

> **Key term**
>
> **Product life cycle**
>
> the course a product passes through from its development to its decline in the market

Stage 1: Development

In this stage, the product is designed following a series of steps.

1. **Generating ideas** – this is a brainstorming session where a number of stakeholders are consulted to come up with anything that may help satisfy consumer needs and wants. These stakeholders may include employees, department managers, and customers, among others. Conducting market research also helps to identify any potential gaps in the market.

2. **Screening ideas** – this involves deciding which ideas to leave out (poor ideas) and which ones to research further (good ideas). Some product ideas may not be practical or sell well, while others may be too expensive to produce.

3. **Creating a prototype** – a prototype is a first or trial form of a product. It allows for visualization or physical examination of the product, especially by the production department. A select group of customers can be given the prototype so they can provide feedback that will help in making changes to the product if necessary.

4. **Carrying out test marketing** – after making the necessary changes to the product, samples of the developed product are launched in a small but representative part of the market to assess the potential demand for or sales of the product. At this stage, if the product does not sell well, it can be changed or removed without costing the business too much.

5. **Commercialization** – after successful test marketing, a full launch of the product to the market takes place. This will involve using all of the elements of the marketing mix.

At this first stage, the research and development costs are high as a lot of time, money, and effort is invested in developing the product. There are no sales yet and therefore no profit is earned. Cash flow is also negative.

Stage 2: Introduction

This is the launch stage of the product on to the market. Sales are low because most consumers are not yet aware of the product's existence. Costs incurred in the launch are high, so it is likely that the product is not profitable. Moreover, the cash flow is negative as the cash outflow is still greater than the cash inflow.

High prices or **price skimming** may be used for brand-new technological products (such as personal computers or smartphones), especially where there are few or no competitors. Where there are many competitors, a **penetration pricing** strategy could be adopted, where low prices are initially charged.

To increase awareness of the product, informative advertising can be used. Expensive products could be sold in restricted retail outlets targeting high-income consumers.

Stage 3: Growth

Once the product has been well received by the market, the sales volumes and hence revenues start to increase significantly. This translates to rising profits, especially with the possibility of economies of scale or lowering of unit costs. Cash flow now becomes positive.

After a successful launch, prices that were initially low (through penetration pricing) can be increased to maximize profits. Products that started at high prices (through price skimming) may need to have their prices reduced slightly because of the increased competition from other businesses attracted by the profits.

Advertising convinces consumers to buy more products and establish brand loyalty. A larger number of distribution outlets are used to push the product to different consumers in various locations. To maintain consumer demand, discussions begin on issues regarding product improvements and developments.

Stage 4: Maturity

At this stage, sales continue to rise, but they do so slowly. The product is well established, with a stable and significant market share resulting in a positive cash flow. Sales revenue is at its peak and profit is high, but there is little growth as competitors have entered the market to take advantage of these profits. A **promotional pricing** strategy is preferred to keep competitors at bay.

Promotion assumes a reminding role, to maintain sales growth and emphasize brand loyalty. A wide range of distribution outlets for the product has been established.

Plans for new product developments are at an advanced stage, with some firms introducing extension strategies to extend the life of their products. (This is discussed further below.)

Stage 5: Saturation

By this point, many competitors have entered the market and saturated it. Sales are at their highest point and begin to fall. However, cash flow is still positive. Some businesses are forced out of the market as a result of the stiff competition. Prices will have to be reduced, so promotional pricing is used.

Many firms use extension strategies to stabilize their market share, and they use high levels of promotional activities such as aggressive advertising in an effort to maintain sales. The widest range of geographical distribution outlets has been established to get the products to consumers. Profits are high and mostly stable.

Apple use price skimming when introducing most of their new products

Key terms

Price skimming

setting a high price when introducing a new product to the market

Penetration pricing

setting a low initial price for a product with the aim of attracting a large number of customers quickly and gaining a high market share

Promotional pricing

temporarily reducing the price of a good or service to attract customers

Stage 6: Decline

This stage signifies the steady drop in sales and, as a result, decreased profits. In addition, cash flow begins to fall but is still positive.

The product may have lost its appeal to consumers because new models have been introduced. If sales fall too low, the product is slowly withdrawn from the market.

Promotional activities are reduced and kept at a minimum. Prices are reduced in most cases to sell off any existing stock. Distribution outlets that are not profitable are closed.

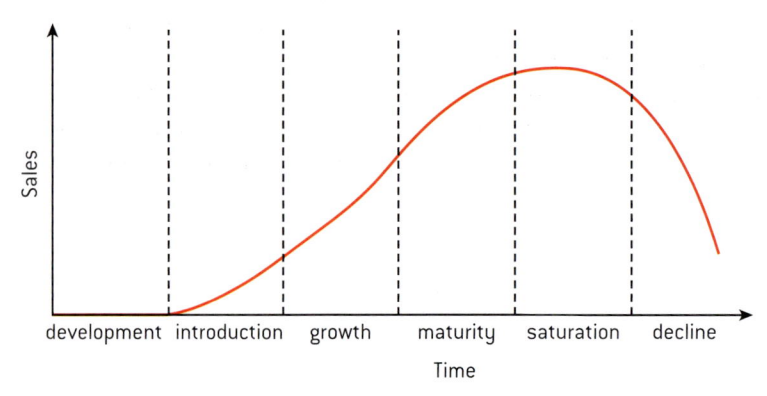

Figure 4.5.1 The product life cycle

> **Key term**
>
> **Extension strategies**
>
> plans by firms to stop sales from falling by lengthening the product's life cycle

Extension strategies

Extension strategies are an attempt by firms to stop sales from falling by lengthening or extending the product's life cycle. This is done at the maturity or saturation stages of a product's life cycle.

Common methods that businesses use to extend their products' life cycles include:

- Selling existing products into new markets. For example, selling products in other regions within a country and/or exporting them.
- Finding new uses for the product. For example, the cellphone was first introduced as a basic communication device but now the smartphone has a much wider variety of uses, including offering banking and other online services.
- Changing the product's packaging. This could include changing the design, appearance, and colour of the package to stimulate consumers' interest and persuade them to buy the product. For example, the washing detergent Omo has been repackaged many times, which has helped to sustain demand for it for a long time.
- Targeting different market segments. One example is banks having different accounts that customers may open based on their income levels. Some banks have also accommodated customers with various religious beliefs and have special accounts for them. For example, in Kenya, Barclays bank opened a sharia account to appeal to customers of the Muslim faith.
- Developing new promotional strategies. For example, firms could create new advertising campaigns to encourage consumers to continue using their products, thereby helping to revive demand for their product.

4.5 The seven Ps of the marketing mix

Extension strategies are important to the long-term success of a product as the market becomes saturated and sales begin to drop. For businesses, it would be better to extend the life of a mature product *before* this decline in sales starts. However, it is not always easy to determine where exactly a product is in its life cycle.

Some businesses use sales forecasting to help with this. However, since forecasting is based on predicting trends, the results obtained may not always be entirely accurate. Moreover, unexpected external factors may have a strong influence on any future sales.

For example, a recession could have a negative effect on the demand for a firm's existing products as well as any new products that it may have introduced as part of its extension strategy. In this situation, it would be critical for the firm to know where its products lie in the life cycle in order to manage its resources efficiently. Spending money on a terminally declining product is a waste of resources – one example would be spending money on marketing DVD players today.

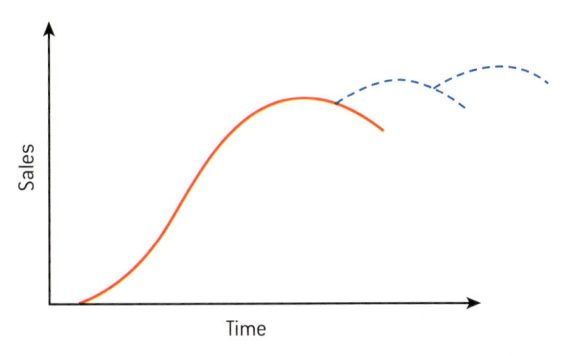

Figure 4.5.2 Extension strategies in a product life cycle

Product life extension models

Product life extension models extend the use period of existing products. They slow the flow of constituent materials through the economy, and help to reduce the rate of resource extraction and the generation of waste. The case study below gives an example of an organization that uses a product life extension model.

Case study

Better World Fashion

The aim of Better World Fashion is to offer high-quality, durable goods with a business model that embraces changing styles and preferences.

For Better World Fashion, the decision to specialize in leather – and initially leather jackets – was important for three main reasons. Firstly, rearing cattle for food or leather production is very energy and resource intensive under today's traditional methods. Secondly, it enables the company to explore the inner loops of a circular economy, focusing on the higher value re-use activities. Finally, leather is one of few clothing materials that actually gets better the more it's used, improving the look and feel of the garment. These factors led Better World Fashion to seek to prevent old or "unfashionable" leather products from being disposed of or sitting unused in closets.

The jackets available today are made from reused leather collected from NGOs across Denmark and as much reused polyester and aluminium as possible. Customers obtain one of the jackets either through a monthly lease arrangement, or an outright purchase with buyback option. The customer can hang onto the jacket for as long as they like, but when they're done with it, the onwards phase is clearly in place. Those that purchased a jacket can send it back to Better World Fashion receiving a 50% discount on a new garment. Alternatively, the customer can transfer the lease to a friend or relative.

The patina of the material isn't the only thing that develops over time. Owners can share the story of their jacket, which is also passed on to the next user (something the founder describes as a "family tree" for clothing). Each garment has a unique ID and profile to give customers a better understanding of the story of the product. This works in conjunction with any scars or blemishes the jacket has picked up during its use. The repairs are taken care of by Better World Fashion, with the imperfections and the story behind them harnessed as a unique design element, giving the jacket a one-off appeal for subsequent customers. At the point when a jacket can no longer be repaired, as much of the leather as possible is reused in new jackets or in the manufacture of bags, gloves, and other smaller accessories.

Source: Adapted from https://www.ellenmacarthurfoundation.org/case-studies/a-model-for-fast-fashion-that-lasts

> **Key term**
>
> **Boston Consulting Group matrix**
>
> an analysis method of a firm's product portfolio regarding its market share and market growth

Product portfolio analysis

A **product portfolio** includes all the products or services provided by an organization. Product portfolio analysis is the process of evaluating these products. Portfolio analysis uses various models to help the business make decisions regarding its overall product offering and business portfolios. A business will want to invest more resources into its profitable products and phase out those that are not doing well.

A common product portfolio analysis method is the **Boston Consulting Group (BCG) matrix** (also known as the **Boston matrix**), which was developed by the management consulting firm Boston Consulting Group.

The BCG matrix is a growth–share matrix that measures the market growth rate on the vertical axis and relative market share on the horizontal axis. The market growth rate shows how attractive a product is in the market, while relative market share looks at how much of the market a product has captured – its strength in the market. This growth–share matrix is classified into the following four categories:

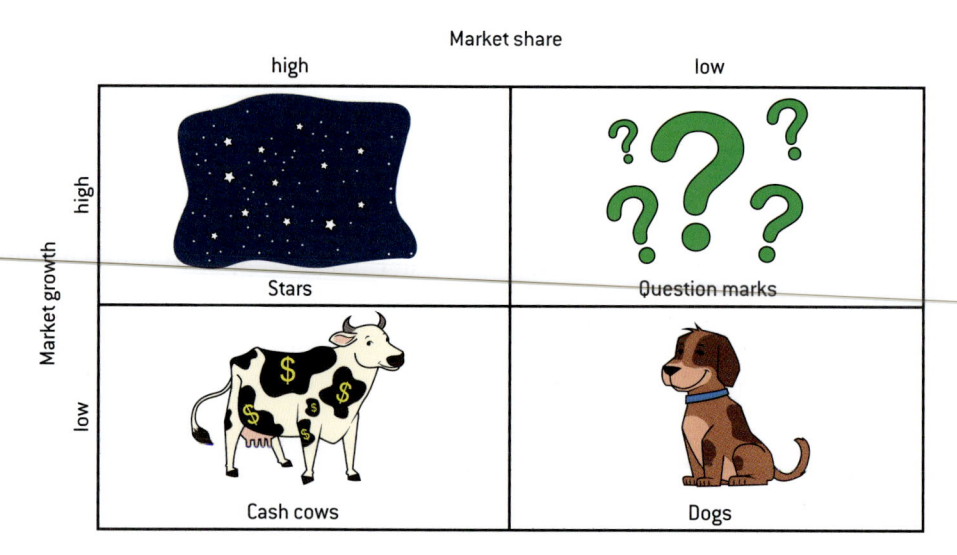

Figure 4.5.3 The BCG matrix

- **Stars.** These are products with high market growth and high market share. They are successful products in the market and generate high amounts of income for the business. However, they need high levels of investment to sustain their rapid growth and status in the market, especially in a fast-growing market where competing firms can easily gain market share by attracting new customers. With time, as these products mature and their market growth slows down, they eventually turn into cash cows.

- **Cash cows.** These are products that have low market growth and high market share. They comprise well-established products in a mature market and, as a result, businesses will invest less to hold on to their market share. The product sales are high and very profitable, so they generate a reasonable amount of cash for the business. As the products have a strong presence in the market, businesses can even charge slightly higher prices to increase their profit margins.
- **Problem children or question marks.** These are products with high market growth and low market share. They are a concern to businesses because of the large amount of money needed to increase their share in the market. Moreover, the high market growth could mean that the products are operating in a fiercely competitive market and need a strong marketing strategy if they are to succeed. Businesses need to think carefully and be very selective about which problem children they should develop into stars and which ones should be eliminated.
- **Dogs.** These are products that have low market share and low market growth. They operate in markets that are not growing or in declining markets and therefore generate little income for the business. They offer poor future prospects for the firm and may need to be replaced. Businesses with many of these products may be faced with cash flow problems if they continue sustaining them.

BCG matrix strategies

- **Holding strategy** – the focus here is on products with a high market share, to ensure that they maintain their current position in the market. Some investment will be needed to ensure sustained consumer demand.
- **Building strategy** – this focuses on turning problem children into stars. Money from the cash cows could be invested in promoting or distributing these products to increase market share.
- **Harvesting strategy** – the focus here is on milking the benefits of products with a positive cash flow. These products provide the necessary finance, which can be invested in the other portfolio products.
- **Divesting strategy** – this is where the poor-performing dogs are phased out or sold off. The resources freed up from this will need to be used effectively to boost the performance of the other products in the portfolio.

A product portfolio that has a good number of stars and cash cows (finance generators) will be able to invest in the other (high market growth) products, such as problem children. However, a relatively large number of dogs and problem children can seriously drain any positive cash flow from the business if this is not well managed.

The limitations of the BCG matrix

- It focuses on the current market position of the firm's products, with little advice or information for future planning.
- It may be a time-consuming and complex exercise for businesses to define or classify their products according to market share and market growth.

4 Marketing

- High market share does not necessarily equate to high profits. This is because sales revenue could be gained using promotional pricing, which may drive down a firm's profitability.

Table 4.5.1 Summary of the relationship between the product life cycle, product portfolio and the marketing mix (using only the first four Ps)

Strategies	Development	Introduction	Growth	Maturity	Saturation	Decline
Product	In the planning phase. The product has not yet launched in the market.	The basic product is marketed. Most products released into the market start as stars or question marks.	Product improvements or new product development plans start. Products are stars or question marks due to high growth.	New product development is at an advanced stage. Extension strategies are introduced in some cases. The product becomes a cash cow as growth stabilizes.	Extension strategies are critical to maintain sales. Products are cash cows due to high market share.	Weak products are withdrawn from the market. The product becomes a dog due to low market share and no opportunity for growth.
Price	Research is ongoing on the appropriate pricing methods to use.	Cost-plus, price skimming or penetration pricing can be used.	Penetration prices slightly increase.	Promotional pricing can be used.	Promotional pricing can be used.	Price cuts are made.
Promotion	Research is ongoing on the appropriate promotion strategies to use.	Informative advertising is used.	Persuasive advertising is used.	There is extensive advertising to remind customers of the product.	Aggressive advertising is carried out to emphasize the brand's benefits and differences.	Advertising is reduced to a minimum.
Place	Research is ongoing on appropriate distribution channels to use.	Selective or restricted distribution takes place.	Intensive distribution or more distribution outlets are used.	There is more intensive distribution or a wide range of distribution outlets.	The widest range of geographical distribution outlets is used.	There is selective distribution and unprofitable outlets are eliminated.

Table 4.5.2 Summary of the relationship between the product life cycle, investment, profit, and cash flow

Product life cycle stage	Development	Introduction	Growth	Maturity	Saturation	Decline
Investment level	High research and development costs	High costs on promotion	Average to high costs on promotion	Lower costs on promotion	Cost focus is on extension strategies	Very low costs on promotion
Profit	None	None or negative	Some profit and rising	High profit; reaches its peak	High and mostly stable profit	Decreasing profit
Cash flow	Negative	Negative but improves with sales	Positive	Positive	Positive	Positive but decreasing cash flow

4.5 The seven Ps of the marketing mix

> **Student workpoint 4.8**
>
> *Be a thinker*
>
> 1. Analyse the relationship between the product life cycle, product portfolio and the marketing mix.
>
> 2. Why are extension strategies important to a business?
>
> 3. Using the BCG matrix, evaluate the product offering of a business of your choice.

Case study

Facebook – BCG matrix

Facebook's Star — Instagram

Besides its high market share, Instagram is also currently the highest growing strategic business unit (SBU) owned by Facebook, and has doubled its user base to 700 million monthly active users in two years. This is largely due to Instagram's features "Direct" and "Stories". By sticking to its roots of visual communication while shrewdly adapting to new trends by investing in product development, Instagram has managed to stay on top of the game.

Facebook's Question Mark — Oculus

Oculus specializes in virtual reality (VR) hardware and software products. Large investments are required in research and development efforts, yet there is no guarantee that Oculus will be successful or whether people have a desire for VR. *NY Times* reports that Zuckerberg plans to invest $3 billion over the next decade to bring VR to millions of users, signalling Facebook's intentions to turn Oculus into a Star.

Facebook's Cash Cow — WhatsApp

WhatsApp's growth rate has been more or less maximized, with few competitors. Investment in WhatsApp is hence deemed unnecessary. Their market share, however, is very high, making WhatsApp a money-generating cash cow.

Facebook's Dog — Messenger

Since almost everyone uses WhatsApp, an additional app like Messenger seems unnecessary. Facebook can consider divesting Messenger due to its low growth rate and low market share, making it a dog.

Source: Adapted from https://medium.com/pitchspot/an-in-depth-analysis-of-the-bcg-growth-share-matrix-with-examples-82d17b092b8

BCG matrix

The case study here examines Facebook's product portfolio based on its relative market share and industry growth rate. The BCG matrix assists Facebook in making decisions regarding what it should invest in, discontinue or develop in the future.

Key terms

Brand

a name, symbol, sign, or design that differentiates a firm's product from those of its competitors

Branding

the process of distinguishing one firm's product from another

Branding

A **brand** is defined as a name, symbol, sign, or design that differentiates a firm's product from that of its competitors. **Branding** is the process of distinguishing one business's product from another business's, and can add great value to a product. Branding can have a strong influence on how consumers view or perceive a product.

4 Marketing

> **Key terms**
>
> **Brand awareness**
> the ability of consumers to recognize the existence and availability of a firm's good or service
>
> **Brand loyalty**
> when consumers become committed to a firm's brand and are willing to make repeat purchases over time
>
> **Brand value**
> how much a brand is worth in terms of its reputation, potential income, and market value

Examples of well-known global brands include Nike, Samsung, Apple, Coca-Cola, Google, and KFC, among many others.

Aspects of branding

Brand awareness

This refers to the ability of consumers to recognize the existence and availability of a firm's good or service. Creating brand awareness is a major step businesses should take to effectively promote a product.

In addition, brand awareness is important when promoting related products because there is usually very little difference between one firm's product and its competitors' products. As a result, the product with the greatest brand awareness will sell more. For example, in the beverage industry there are numerous soft drinks available in the market. However, the name "Coca-Cola" is easily recognized by most consumers, clearly showing the strong image it portrays in their minds.

A high level of brand awareness often leads to higher sales, and can serve as a strong indicator to competitors of the amount of market share a product commands.

Brand development

This is any plan to improve or strengthen the image of a product in the market. Brand development is a way of enhancing the brand awareness of a product by increasing the power of its name, symbol, or sign, ultimately leading to higher sales and market share.

Businesses may have to invest more in promotional campaigns such as sales promotions and advertising to persuade consumers to purchase their products and therefore further develop their brands. Offering free samples is a common way that businesses producing consumables (such as Cadbury's) use to give consumers a chance to taste or try their products in an effort to tempt them into buying their brands.

Brand loyalty

This is when consumers become committed to a firm's brand and are willing to make repeat purchases over time. Brand loyalty is a result of brand preference, where consumers prefer one brand over another. Customers with brand loyalty will consistently purchase products from their preferred brands, despite the high prices of some products, because they feel the added value the brand carries justifies its price.

Successful businesses will often employ a variety of marketing strategies to cultivate loyal customers. In so doing, these businesses develop **brand ambassadors**. These are consumers who will market a particular brand by talking positively about it among their colleagues, friends, or relatives. They help to provide free marketing by word of mouth, which is very effective in enhancing the image and reputation of a business. Samsung is a name that is establishing strong brand loyalty in the electronics industry and benefiting significantly from consumer recommendations or marketing by word of mouth.

Brand value

This refers to how much a brand is worth in terms of its reputation, potential income, and market value. Brand value is the extra money a business can make from its products because of its brand name.

Brands that have a high value are regarded as considerable assets to a business. This is because consumers are willing to pay a high price to obtain such brands. One example is a consumer purchasing a higher-priced coffee at Starbucks instead of a coffee at another café. Such brands increase the overall value of a business.

Brand values are an expression of a brand's "personality" and act as a code by which a particular brand lives. Brand values are also those things that cause customers to buy a firm's product rather than its competitor's product. They help in differentiating a business and making it seem in some way special and better than its competitors. Emphasizing a firm's brand value is therefore at the heart of successful branding.

The importance of branding

Branding is one of the most important tasks of marketers. Despite the heavy initial investment required in ensuring that a brand is widely known and recognized, it is an essential factor for any type of business – from the start-up to the large, well-established companies.

For start-ups, branding is about giving customers a clear image with which they can associate the business. As the business grows, it can work on customer perceptions of its image, and try to establish its brand so that it can be recognized immediately. Initially, it is critical that the brand complements the market and meets the expectations of the target audience. Branding that does not meet the expectations of its target audience is bound to result in decreased sales.

Businesses with well-known brands can use premium pricing or charge high prices for their products because of the image the brand has in the minds of consumers. Consumers will associate such brands with consistently high quality, enabling the businesses to make good sales and earn high profit margins on a regular basis. For example, Mercedes-Benz and BMW have consistently provided good-quality cars to the global market and their brands have been viewed as representing good quality by most consumers.

Customers make judgments about certain products and services based on the way they are presented to them. Something as simple as choosing the right colour for a firm's brand can have a massive impact on the way it is perceived by the general public. For example, some men may not particularly like their gym being painted pink.

A firm's brand name can provide legal protection to a product's specific features to prevent the product being copied by competitors. Branding provides the product with a unique name that makes it different from its competitors, therefore enabling the business to have a sense of ownership over its products. For example, companies such as Nike, Nestlé, and Toyota have been able to distinguish themselves well in their respective industries.

The values associated with Starbucks keep many customers coming back, even though cheaper alternatives are available

Concept

ETHICS AND SUSTAINABILITY

Ethics and sustainability have had a major impact on the way businesses brand themselves and their products. This includes an assessment of their code of conduct and their conservation of resources for future generations. The case study on the next page on the energy and resource exploitation industry provides a clear example of this.

Research two more examples of how ethics and sustainability help to enhance an organization's image.

4 Marketing

Effective branding can enable a sense of personal identification and emotional connection among consumers. The key is the impression that branding leaves on potential customers. If the impression is positive, the chances of having repeat customers are high. Good brands communicate messages that ensure that their target customers respond positively. There is a saying that "the first impression is the lasting impression". Therefore, to succeed, businesses need to use enough resources to build a good brand reputation.

Case study: How companies rebrand to keep their corporate image

Two major events have reshaped the consumer's perception of oil companies since the 1980s. These are the Exxon Valdes oil spill in 1989 and the BP Deep Water Horizon spill in 2010.

Each incident caused a great deal of damage to the corporate images of not only BP and Exxon but to all oil companies around the world. As a result, most have rebranded themselves to enhance their corporate images and improve their stakeholder relations – without which they could not be profitable.

For example, Chevron (formerly Texaco) now has "protecting the environment" as one of its core values and "sustainability" as one of its visions. In terms of its marketing mix, particularly its promotional techniques, Chevron has branded itself as a socially responsible organization interested in the well-being of ordinary people and innovating energy technologies to solve social issues such as poverty.

BP similarly rebranded by promoting on Twitter and other social media its compensation efforts after the oil spill. It also promoted its new safety regulations and policies online to reach as many customers as possible to avoid major losses.

This shift in marketing techniques paid off. A year after reporting a loss, BP declared a US$3.3 billion net profit in 2012 and it continues to record strong results, with $10 billion net profit recorded in 2019.

BP and Chevron recognize the value of their corporate image and have attempted to ensure that this image is not damaged. If consumers dislike an organization, they often boycott that organization, causing it to lose revenue and possibly even causing it to close down.

However, many of the oil companies' shifts in marketing practices and strategies have resulted in fiercer opposition from the public and other stakeholders. Companies such as Royal Dutch Shell and Chevron have been accused of "double standards" by environmental groups like Greenpeace because while they market themselves as socially responsible, their extraction processes continue to damage the environment. This causes regular fluctuations in their share prices.

In addition, shareholders are uncertain about their long-term profitability due to fears around new legislation that would hugely increase the costs of production. However, the adoption of new marketing strategies has largely helped to mitigate the effects of such market uncertainties.

Price

Price plays a significant role in the marketing mix because it is the only "P" that generates revenue for a business. The other aspects of the marketing mix are associated with costs.

Price refers to the money customers pay or give up for having or using a good or service. To meet their marketing objectives, businesses need to set the appropriate pricing strategies for new and existing products.

Cost-plus pricing (mark-up pricing)

Cost-plus pricing refers to adding a mark-up to the average cost of producing a product. The mark-up is a percentage of the profit a firm wishes to gain for every product that it sells. The average cost is the cost per unit or the total cost divided by the number of products produced.

For example, imagine the total cost of producing 10,000 packets of biscuits is US$20,000. The business wants to calculate how much it would sell each packet for and get a 50% mark-up on each packet. To do that, it would use the following cost-plus pricing method:

- First, it would calculate the average cost, which is US$2 (US$20,000/10,000).

- Second, it would work out the mark-up profit, which is $1 (50% of US$2).

- Finally, it would add the average cost to the mark-up to get US$3 as the selling price.

> **Key term**
>
> **Cost-plus pricing**
>
> refers to adding a mark-up to the average cost of producing a product

Advantages	Disadvantages
• It is a simple and quick method of calculating the selling price of a product.	• It fails to consider market needs or customer value when setting prices.
• It is a good way to ensure that a business covers its costs and makes a profit.	• Since competitors' prices are not considered, a firm could lose sales if it sets a selling price that is higher than its competitors'

Penetration pricing

Setting a low initial price for a product with the aim of attracting a large number of customers quickly and gaining a high market share is known as penetration pricing. This could be used by businesses either introducing a new product to an existing market or entering new markets with existing products. This is a strategy used in mass marketing. Then as a firm gains market share, it can start to increase its price slowly. For example, IKEA is known to have entered the Chinese market by using this strategy.

Advantages	Disadvantages
• As the prices are low, consumers are encouraged to buy the products and this leads to high sales volume and market share for the business. • The high sales volume can lead to decreases in the costs of production and increases in stock turnover.	• Gaining a high sales volume does not necessarily mean achieving high profits, especially where the prices are too low. • Customers may perceive the product to be of low quality if the price is kept too low. • Penetration pricing is only suitable for use in markets that are very price sensitive. Therefore, as businesses increase their prices over time, they risk losing potential customers, who may seek lower-priced products from rival firms.

The loss leader

Businesses that charge a low price for a product, usually below its average cost, refer to that product as a loss leader. The aim of this strategy is to attract many customers. Large supermarkets use this strategy by selling some products at a loss with the view that customers will also buy other higher-priced (profitable) products and therefore compensate for any losses made.

> **Key terms**
>
> **Loss leader**
>
> charging a low price for a product, usually below its average cost, to attract consumers to buy other higher-priced products
>
> **Predatory pricing**
>
> when a firm deliberately sets a very low price on its good or service with the aim of driving its competitors out of the market

Advantages	Disadvantage
• Businesses selling a large number of frequently purchased products may attract many customers and benefit from higher overall profits. • Businesses may use loss leaders as a promotional strategy to encourage consumers to switch to their brand instead of buying the competitors' brands.	• Firms using this strategy may be accused by competitors of undercutting them by using unfair business practices.

Predatory pricing

Predatory pricing is when a firm deliberately sets a very low price on its good or service with the aim of driving its competitors out of the market. A predatory pricing strategy restricts new competitors from entering the market and hence acts as a barrier to entry. After a certain period of time when there is no competition left in the market, the firm increases its prices and recoups its profits. Organizations that have employed this strategy include ABC Food Ltd and Amazon.

Advantages	Disadvantages
• The firm can gain a dominant position in the market using this strategy. • Competition is minimized, as financially weaker competitors that are unable to bear the loss will be driven out of the market. • New entrants are deterred from entering the market, cutting out any potential competition.	• Predatory pricing is a form of anti-competitive behaviour and is illegal in many countries because it is used to restrict competition. • This strategy may work in the short term but it will be difficult to sustain in the long term as new competitors may enter the market.

Premium pricing

Premium pricing is a strategy where a firm sets a high price for its product. This is usually substantially higher than the competitors' products to give the impression that the firm's product is superior. The firm expects that customers will purchase its product as they perceive it to be of better quality than the competitors' products. This strategy is also known as image pricing or prestige pricing.

Premium pricing is different to price skimming, where a high price is initially set for a new (sometimes low-quality) product and then reduced. In premium pricing, as the product is of high quality, the high price is sustained for a long time. Examples of premium-priced products include Gucci bags, Rolls-Royce cars and Rolex watches.

Gucci is known for its premium-priced products

Advantages	Disadvantages
• As customers are convinced of the high quality of the product, they do not try to buy it for less. This leaves the firm to concentrate on improving the product's quality or features without worrying about consumer purchases. • When a firm can set a high price for its product but still manage to sell it, there is the potential to maximize its profit margin. • A high price on a product can increase the brand value of a firm. The product then becomes exclusive, where not everyone is able to afford it. Loyal customers continue to enjoy and buy the product, further increasing the brand value. • Premium-priced products can gain a high status in a society. These products become status symbols or a symbol of luxury. Their owners tend to show them off to others, thereby providing free advertising for the firm.	• The firm misses out on price conscious consumers who find the price too high. • High marketing costs are incurred as a firm will need to create brand awareness of its product to convince customers that its high price equates to a high-quality product. • Premium pricing cannot be applied to all products, especially those that face stiff competition.

Dynamic pricing (HL only)

Dynamic pricing is a strategy where firms charge different prices for their products depending on which customers are buying them or when the products sell. Dynamic pricing involves tailoring the prices of goods or services based on specific customer preferences. It is also known as surge pricing, demand pricing or time-based pricing.

This strategy considers factors such as demand and supply, competition, and other market conditions. Here, product prices are continuously adjusting in response to real-time demand and supply. Dynamic pricing examples include:

- Increases in airline prices due to high demand.
- Hotels offering discounts on their rooms during off seasons.
- Ridesharing services charging twice the normal amount during high traffic periods.

Some firms that use this strategy include Uber and Amazon.

> **Key terms**
>
> **Premium pricing**
> where a firm sets a high price for a high-quality product
>
> **Dynamic pricing**
> where firms charge different prices for their products depending on which customers are buying them or when the products sell

Advantages	Disadvantages
• There is the potential for high sales and profits, as product prices can be increased when demand rises. • A firm can beat its competition easily by adjusting to customer preferences and providing a better experience at a cheaper price compared to its competition. • If a business has a product that is producing a good profit, it gives them the flexibility and freedom to focus on other business areas or different sources of revenue while still breaking even during the difficult times. • It helps with better stock management. Discounts can be provided for overstocked products and higher prices charged for items in high demand, helping to maintain the flow of stock.	• Can lead to customer dissatisfaction as some customers end up paying a higher price for the same product. Those who pay a higher price tend to become hostile towards the firm, reducing its brand image, while those who paid a lower price may become loyal to the firm's brand. • It could lead to the loss of sales if customers are knowledgeable about the prices of products in the market. If a customer comes across the same product which is priced significantly lower by another firm, they may opt to buy the lower-priced product from the competitor. • Some customers can play the system and have worked out methods and tools to help them beat the changing prices. These tools provide customers with a list of prices for the same product from different sellers. This helps them to find cheaper deals for products and means they do not need to worry about a firm's brand any more but can focus on pricing only, thereby spending less. • Dynamic pricing is not applicable to all industries and works better in certain areas than others. Some businesses prioritize customer satisfaction to attain a better brand image than aiming purely for high profit margins. • Can lead to significant price fluctuations in the market, which will disadvantage the firm practising it. For example, if the firm increases its price then a competitor may immediately reduce its price. Alternatively, the firm may lower its price and the competitor lowers their price even further. In such scenarios the firm's revenue can be negatively impacted.

Key terms

Competitive pricing

where a firm sets the price of its product relative to the competitors' prices

Contribution pricing

the calculation of the variable cost of production of a firm's product, after which the product's price is set

Competitive pricing (HL only)

Competitive pricing (also known as a market-orientated strategy) is where a firm sets the price of its product relative to its competitors' prices. Instead of pricing based on consumer demands, the prices of competitor products are used for comparison before the firm arrives at its own pricing strategy.

Competitive pricing requires in-depth research or detailed market analysis of competitor behaviour to determine their product offerings, including the prices they charge for their products.

Advantages	Disadvantages
• Can prevent a firm from losing customers and market share to its competitors. With adequate intelligence on the competition, a firm can control the competition and respond to their every move. • As online shoppers depend on pricing before making their final purchase, adopting a competitive pricing strategy helps to keep a stable customer base and aids business growth. • It is a low-risk strategy as the competitors are usually well-known players in the market who have been in existence for some time. Hence, using their pricing as a starting point has a high probability of success. • It can be used in combination with other pricing strategies to make it more efficient. For example, competitive pricing can be used in conjunction with cost-plus pricing to decide on the target profit margins based on the competitor pricing model.	• Competitive pricing is not sustainable in the long term. It can work in the initial stages of market entry, but in the long term competitors might improvise based on pricing data and change their pricing strategy entirely to focus on a different market segment. • A firm focusing purely on competing with the other players in the market may miss out on other important aspects, like covering their production or overhead costs. This can lead to lower future revenue and profit. • A firm will find it difficult to differentiate itself from other competitors in the market as its pricing strategy is solely based on the co-market players. The firm's brand may not stand out as customers view the products as being similar to other competitors' products in the market.

Contribution pricing (HL only)

Contribution pricing involves calculating the variable cost of production of a firm's product, after which the product's price is set (usually at a higher level). Contribution per unit is the difference between the variable cost per unit and the price per unit. Note that it is not profit but the contribution that goes towards covering the unpaid fixed costs of production.

For example, let us assume that JCD Cars Ltd has fixed costs of $300,000 with the following scenario:

Product (type of car)	Sales	Variable cost per unit ($)	Price per unit ($)	Contribution per unit ($)	Total contribution ($)
A	20	8,000	10,000	2,000	40,000
B	17	12,000	16,000	4,000	68,000
C	15	18,000	24,000	6,000	90,000
D	12	25,000	30,000	5,000	60,000
E	10	35,000	43,000	8,000	80,000
					$338,000

As the fixed costs are only $300,000, JCD's total contribution of $338,000 will be able to cover these costs and generate a profit of $38,000 ($338,000 – $300,000).

Advantages	Disadvantages
• The contribution per unit measure is useful as it enables the firm to know how much profit it will earn for every unit sold beyond the point where the firm breaks even. • It is conducted using existing information that the firm already has or is calculating for other purposes. For example, sales revenue and cost information. It can therefore be used without much additional cost. • It is a useful strategy for a firm to use if it wants to determine the price to charge for a special order.	• The price set for each product using this approach may not be competitive in the market. It is important for firms to check what competitors are charging before finalising the price. • Allocating costs appropriately across the whole range of a firm's products can be difficult, which may lead to inaccurate pricing.

Price elasticity of demand (HL only)

A firm's pricing strategy will directly impact on its revenue. Therefore, it is essential for the firm to understand its products' price elasticity of demand to help determine whether a change in price will have a positive or negative impact on its revenue.

Price elasticity of demand (PED) is a measurement of how the quantity demanded of a good is affected by changes in its price. In other words, it is a quantitative measure of the responsiveness of consumers to fluctuations in the price of a good.

PED is calculated as follows:

$$\text{price elasticity of demand} = \frac{\text{percentage change in quantity demanded } (\%\Delta QD)}{\text{percentage change in price } (\%\Delta P)}$$

> **Key terms**
>
> **Price elasticity of demand**
> a measurement of how the quantity demanded of a good is affected by changes in its price
>
> **Price discrimination**
> charging different prices to different groups of consumers for the same product

The calculated price elasticity (provided in absolute values) will always be greater than 0, and is usually separated into the following ranges:

0–1: Markets in this range are classified as **inelastic**. Here, a large change in price results in a small change in the quantity demanded. In these markets, consumers find it difficult to switch away from the product despite its higher price. Examples of such products include those that are a necessity for consumers, such as insulin for diabetics, salt, tap water, petrol, or cigarettes (due to consumers' addiction to this product).

=1: A price elasticity of 1 is defined as **unit elastic** and represents a situation where a percentage change in price is matched by an equal percentage change in quantity demanded.

1+: Elasticities greater than 1 are known as **elastic**, where a small change in price will result in a large change in the quantity demanded. In highly elastic markets, the products generally have many substitutes, such as bottled water, chocolate bars, and products where consumers are not affiliated to a particular brand.

In extreme cases, if the PED is zero then this is called **perfectly inelastic demand**, and if it is infinite it is called **perfectly elastic demand**.

Examples of calculating PED

Example 1: When the price of lamps increased from $10 to $12, the quantity of lamps demanded reduced from 100 to 65.

What is the price elasticity of demand for lamps?

- The price increased from $10 to $12. Therefore the percentage change = 2/10 = 0.2 = 20%.
- Quantity demanded fell by 35/100 = −0.35 = 35%.
- PED = 35/−20.
- Therefore PED = −1.75 = **1.75** (in absolute values).

Hence the demand for lamps is **price elastic**.

The price change has the following impact on the firm's revenue:

- With the original price of $10, the revenue earned is $1,000 ($10 × 100).
- With a new price of $12, the revenue earned is $599.04 ($12 × 65).
- Evidently, in this example the increased price has led to reduced revenue.

Example 2: When the price of milk increased from $2 to $4, the quantity of milk demanded decreased from 200 to 170.

What is the price elasticity of demand for milk?

- The price rose from $2 to $4 (100% rise in price).
- Quantity fell from 200 to 170 (15% fall).
- PED = −15/100.
- Therefore PED = −0.15 = **0.15** (in absolute values).

Hence the demand for milk is **price inelastic**.

The price change has the following impact on the firm's revenue:

- With the original price of $2, the revenue earned is $400 ($2 × 200).
- With the new price of $4, the revenue earned is $680 ($4 × 170).
- In this example, an increase in price has led to an increase in revenue.

Therefore, if a firm has information on the PED that its product commands in the market, it can change its price accordingly and influence its revenue. PED also allows a firm to keep track of how competitive its product is in the marketplace. For example, a product may become more elastic if a competitor starts offering persuasive substitutes in the market, or consumers' incomes decrease and they become more sensitive or conscious to price.

A pricing strategy that makes use of PED is price discrimination.

Price discrimination

Charging different prices to different groups of consumers for the same product is referred to as price discrimination. For effective price discrimination, certain conditions must be satisfied.

First, the business must have price-setting ability. This means that a firm can vary its prices and charge higher prices in a market that is not very competitive. Second, consumers should have different price sensitivities or elasticities of demand. This is the measure of how consumers respond in their buying patterns as a result of changes in the price of a product.

As noted above in the section on PED, if the change in price leads to a greater than proportional change in the quantity demanded, we say that consumers have price elastic demand, ie they are very sensitive to changes in price. Sellers will reduce the price of their products if the demand is elastic as there is a possibility of getting a higher total revenue.

On the other hand, if a change in price leads to a less than proportional change in demand, we say that consumers have price inelastic demand, ie they are less sensitive to changes in price.

The third condition for effective price discrimination is that the markets should be separated to ensure that the product is not easily traded. For example, the prices for children's and adults' tickets may differ for the same music concert, but an adult cannot gain access with a child's ticket and vice versa.

> **Student workpoint 4.9**
>
> *Be knowledgeable*
> 1. Analyse the importance of branding for a start-up business.
> 2. Examine the most appropriate pricing strategies needed when introducing a new product to the market.

Advantage	Disadvantage
• Time-based price discrimination can be of benefit to either consumers or producers. For example, during peak times, phone companies charge high prices and so generate higher revenues, while during off-peak times consumers benefit from the lower prices charged.	• Businesses need to be certain about the type of elasticity of demand of their consumers. For example, charging higher prices in a market with elastic demand could lead to lower sales revenue. If firms were to charge a lower price in the elastic market, they should ensure that the extra cost of producing and selling more products does not exceed the extra revenue.

Promotion

Promotion is concerned with communicating information about a firm's products to consumers. The main aim of promotion is to obtain new customers or to retain existing ones. Promotional activities should be communicated clearly to consumers and provide useful information to enable them to purchase a firm's product.

Some promotional objectives include:

- creating awareness or informing consumers of a new or improved product in the market
- convincing or persuading consumers to purchase a firm's products instead of its competitors' products
- reminding consumers of the existence of a product in order to retain existing customers or gain new customers for a product
- enhancing the brand image of the product as well as the corporate image of the business.

Promotion can be categorized into three forms: above-the-line, below-the-line and through-the-line promotion.

> **Key terms**
>
> **Above-the-line promotion**
> a paid form of communication that uses independent mass media to promote a firm's products
>
> **Below-the-line promotion**
> a form of communication that gives a business direct control over its promotional activities so that it is not reliant on the use of independent media
>
> **Through-the-line promotion**
> a form of promotion that uses an integrated approach of combining both above-the-line and below-the-line promotion strategies

Above-the-line promotion

This is a paid form of communication that uses independent mass media to promote a firm's products. It includes advertising via television, radio, or newspapers to reach a wide target audience. In this case the control or responsibility for advertising is passed to another organization.

Advertising

Advertising plays a central role globally in passing on information about a product to a particular target audience. Choosing the right media for advertising is important in ensuring a successful promotional campaign. Advertising can be categorized as follows:

- **Informative advertising** – the focus here is to provide information about a product's features, price, or other specifications to consumers. It increases consumers' awareness of a firm's product to enable them to make rational decisions about what to buy. It is useful when businesses want to introduce a new product to the market. Examples of informative advertising include classified advertisements in newspapers and government campaigns to discourage drink-driving.

- **Persuasive advertising** – this aims to convince customers to buy one firm's product instead of a competitor's product. It persuades consumers to think that they really need the product and should buy it. It convinces consumers to make unplanned purchases of a product – an act known as impulse buying. It also helps in enhancing a product's brand image.

  For example, when advertising a slimming product, firms may use pictures of how people looked before they bought the product and how they looked after they consumed the product. In this case, they show the picture of a slim and healthy-looking individual based on the idea that most people would want to look like that.

- **Reassuring advertising** – the focus here is on existing customers, to remind them that they made the right purchasing decisions when they chose to buy the firm's product and that they should continue to purchase it. Coca-Cola's promotional campaigns are well-known examples of this strategy.

The main forms of advertising media include television, newspapers, magazines, cinema, radio, posters, billboards, and the internet.

Below-the-line promotion

This is a form of communication where the business has direct control over its promotional activities. Unlike above-the-line promotion, it does not depend on the use of independent media. Below-the-line promotion can focus the promotional activities on consumers the business knows or on those who are interested in their products.

Forms of below-the-line promotion include:

- **Direct marketing** – this ensures that the product is aimed directly at the consumers. It eliminates the use of intermediaries and therefore can save the business money. Direct mail, which is a form of direct marketing, refers to sending information about a product through the

---

Concept

ETHICS

The primary concern of most businesses is to make a profit. A business's marketing strategy is therefore designed to make the service or product on offer seem as attractive as possible.

However, businesses should consider their ethical responsibility to promote their products accurately. Many countries have a regulating body to monitor advertising (such as the Advertising Standards Authority in the UK). Ethical advertising is not only a moral choice but also a pragmatic business decision – the reputation and sales of a business can be severely affected if advertising methods are found to be misleading or offensive.

Do some internet research to find examples of unethical advertising. Can you find widespread press coverage? What sort of criticisms are made, and how might these affect the reputation of the businesses?

post or via email. Businesses that commonly use this method include restaurants sending out their menus or property developers sending out their catalogues.

A limitation of this method is that most consumers regard the information as junk and may not pay any attention to it.

- **Personal selling** – this involves the sale of a firm's product through personal contact. It makes use of sales representatives and can be done face to face or over the telephone. It is commonly used when selling expensive products such as cars, or technically complex products such as specialized machinery. In these cases, customers will need to be reassured that they are making the right purchasing decision. They can then be given personal and individualised attention.

  A major disadvantage of this method is the cost involved. It may be expensive to retain a team of sales representatives for this type of selling, especially if they are also paid commission.

- **Public relations** – these are promotional activities aimed at enhancing the image of the business and its products. It includes the use of publicity or sponsorships. For publicity purposes, a business could hold a press conference where it invites the media and provides information about a social responsibility project it would like to launch. In the process, the business could showcase its products and gain free publicity for them. Through sponsorship, a business may provide financial support to an organization, team or event. Examples include Three sponsoring Chelsea football club in the UK, and Twenty First Century Media sponsoring the Asia Cup tournaments.

- **Sales promotions** – these are short-term incentives provided by a business with the aim of increasing or boosting its sales. Some examples are given below.

  - **Money-off coupons** – discounts provided to customers when a product is purchased. The coupons are often found in newspapers, leaflets, or magazines.

  - **Point-of-sale displays** – can be used for the attractive arrangement or display of products at the location where the business sells the items. The main objective is to draw the attention of consumers and encourage impulse buying. It is commonly used by supermarkets when selling confectionary products such as sweets, chocolates, and other snacks, which are placed near the checkouts.

  - **Free offers or free gifts** – for example, offering a free charger to customers when they buy a smartphone. Giving free samples (such as through food tasting sessions outside supermarkets) can also help encourage sales.

  - **Competitions** – after purchasing a product, customers can enter a draw where they stand a chance to win a prize in the competition. This method is commonly used during festive seasons to attract customers.

  - **"BOGOF"** (buy one get one free) – a promotional strategy that can be used to attract new customers or help in eliminating excess stock. It is often used in the maturity or saturation stages of a product's life cycle.

Many businesses sponsor sporting teams or events in return for advertising space

Through-the-line promotion

This form of promotion uses an integrated approach of combining both above-the-line and below-the-line promotion strategies. In this approach, a business aims to get a holistic view of the market and reach out to their customers in as many ways as possible. An important outcome of this strategy is that it leads to improved brand awareness and visibility.

A drawback of this approach is the cost involved in implementing the promotional campaigns. Hence, only well-established and financially secure businesses can afford to carry out through-the-line promotional activities successfully.

Examples of through-the-line promotions include:

- **360 degree marketing** – this is marketing carried out by integrating both above-the-line and below-the-line activities to gain a maximum advantage. For example, supplementing a television advertisement with pamphlets of the advertised product attached to newspapers.

- **Digital marketing** – this involves offering above-the-line marketing benefits while at the same time acting as a below-the-line communication to the consumer. It uses a cookie-based type of advertising or targeting method. Cookie-based targeting is where pieces of data ("cookies") are used to target small audiences based on their web browser behaviour. It allows businesses to display advertisements throughout a user's browsing experience once the user has shown interest in the business's website. Consumers are thereby provided with highly personalized communication that targets their needs or wants.

  For the business, this strategy has a higher return on investment (ROI), and it is a method driven by consumer preferences. Examples of digital marketing methods include social media posts and online banners.

Choosing a promotional method

Overall, there is no one-size-fits-all approach when it comes to choosing the type of promotional method to use. Some businesses would like to use above-the-line activities only, while others want to supplement these with below-the-line methods. However, certain factors will need to be considered when deciding on the promotional method to use:

- **Cost** – does the marketing budget support the use of a particular promotional method?

- **Legal framework** – has the law been considered when deciding on the various promotional methods to use?

- **Target market** – what specific segment of the market is the product aimed at?

- **Stage in the product life cycle** – which promotional methods will be most appropriate at the different product life cycle stages?

- **Type of product** – has the promotional method considered the nature of the product and how it would be successfully sold to customers?

The strategy to adopt depends a lot on how well the marketing department in a business can read the market, and whether there is a good fit between the consumer and the communication method used. The business will need to be flexible in their choice and decide on the best method or combination needed to succeed in achieving their marketing objectives.

Social media marketing (SMM) as a promotional strategy

SMM is a marketing approach that uses social networking websites to market a firm's products. It is a marketing tool that incorporates the use of technological concepts and techniques with the aim of growing a business through different media. This technology is used to build relationships, drive repeat business, and attract new customers through individuals sharing with other individuals. SMM is the process of gaining website traffic or attention through social media sites.

SMM usually centres on creating content that attracts attention and encourages readers to share it with their social networks. A corporate message spreads from user to user and presumably resonates because it appears to come from a trusted, third-party source, as opposed to the brand or company itself. In essence, SMM is promotion through word of mouth powered by technology.

SMM has increased in popularity with the development of websites such as Instagram, Facebook, Twitter, LinkedIn, YouTube and WeChat.

Benefits of SMM

- **Wide reach** – the internet has enabled firms to reach out to more consumers at a more personal and interactive level. A large percentage of the internet's total population uses social networking sites such as Facebook, Twitter, and YouTube, and time spent in social media far exceeds time spent on emails.

- **Engagement** – in most cases, customers and other key stakeholders are participants rather than passive viewers. This means that a firm can find out what challenges customers are facing and what they like or dislike about the firm's product offerings. These interactions provide customers with the opportunity to ask questions and voice their complaints. This is known as social customer relationship management. Engaging in ongoing dialogue can be more valuable than any kind of paid market research, and it helps to create a sense of community.

- **Market information** – SMM provides useful and valuable measurable data on trends, consumer interaction, feedback, public opinion, brand activity, and customers' buying habits.

- **Cost savings** – using SMM is less expensive than using traditional methods such as television advertising.

- **Brand recognition** – the sharing and spreading of information, especially due to repeat exposure, can increase consumers' awareness of particular brands, leading to brand loyalty and an enhanced brand image.

- **Speed** – coupled with high internet speed, advertisements can reach a wide audience in a short space of time.

> **Key term**
>
> **Social media marketing**
>
> a marketing approach that uses social networking websites to market a firm's products

Social media can be a powerful way to reach lots of customers quickly

Limitations of SMM

- **Accessibility problems** – regions with no computers or internet, or areas with poor internet connectivity will miss out on any ongoing promotional campaign that uses this tool.
- **Lurkers** – these are individuals who merely absorb information online rather than promote or share it. According to TopRank Marketing, 34% of social media users are lurkers, while others are newcomers who have not quite honed their online social skills. These are individuals who may not be active in helping a firm promote its product.
- **Used as a supplement** – most businesses will use SMM as a supplement to other marketing methods and not as a replacement for them. Since it is easy for any business to join a social networking website, it can be difficult for businesses to stand out from the crowd, hence the need to also have other marketing techniques.

Despite these limitations of SMM, the benefits in many ways outweigh the drawbacks and, most importantly, SMM provides a great way for a firm to drive repeat business and attract new customers.

Place

Place is about how the product reaches the intended user. It is concerned with how the product is distributed to make it available to consumers. The distribution system includes getting the right product to the right place at the right time. Distribution is a crucial element in the marketing mix for businesses of any size.

Place in the marketing mix

- This refers not only to the location of the business but also to the location of the customers. Businesses should therefore develop strategies to get goods from their present location to their consumers' location.
- It enables businesses to come up with the best ways to distribute their products efficiently and effectively to consumers.
- The use of intermediaries, such as wholesalers and retailers, helps businesses to store and market their products and enhance their brand image.
- The growing global use of the internet is making it easier for businesses to reach a wide range of consumers directly with their products.

The importance of different types of distribution channels

A distribution channel or channel of distribution is the path taken by a product from the producer to the consumer. Some distribution channels make use of intermediaries. These are middle people such as wholesalers, agents, and retailers that lie in the product's path from the producer to the consumer. The common distribution channels are described below.

> **Student workpoint 4.10**
>
> *Be a thinker*
>
> 1. Distinguish between above-the-line, below-the-line and through-the-line promotional strategies.
> 2. Using a business of your choice, evaluate how new technologies are having an impact on its promotional strategies.

> **Key term**
>
> **Channel of distribution**
>
> the path taken by a product from the producer or manufacturer to the final consumer

Zero intermediary channel

This is where a product is sold directly from the producer to the consumer. For example, perishable products such as lettuce or milk can be sold using this method. Other examples include the use of mail order catalogues and e-commerce. In the service sector, airline ticket bookings can be made via this method.

One intermediary channel

This involves the use of one intermediary (such as a retailer or an agent) to sell the products from the producer to the consumer. In most cases, it is used where the retailer is operating on a large scale or where the products are expensive. Examples include selling expensive furniture or jewelry through retailers. Two other examples are Volkswagen using retail car dealerships, and large supermarket chains (such as Walmart) being used to sell various household products.

Two intermediaries channel

In this case, two intermediaries (usually wholesalers and retailers) are used by producers to sell the product to the consumer. The wholesalers are important in this channel and act as an additional intermediary between the producer and the consumer. This channel is particularly useful when selling goods over large geographical distances.

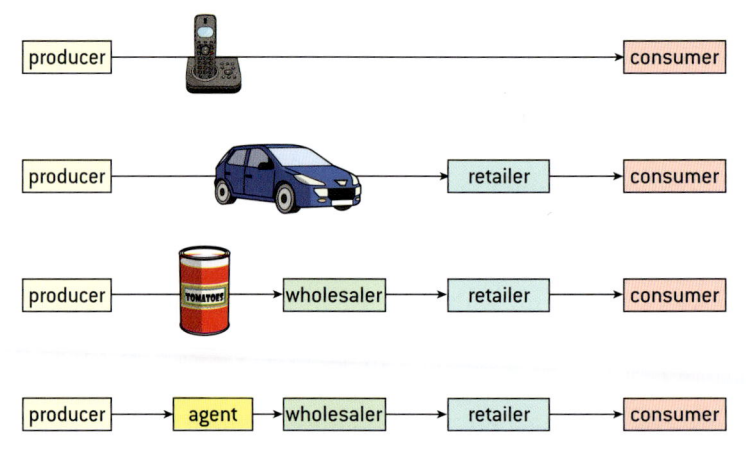

Figure 4.5.4 Channels of distribution

Table 4.5.3 Advantages and disadvantages of different distribution channels

Distribution channel	Advantages	Disadvantages
Zero intermediary channel	• Low cost. • Fast. • Ideal for perishable products. • The producer is the key decision-maker in the distribution process.	• Promotion is done by the producer, which could be time-consuming and expensive. • The producer incurs all storage and delivery costs.

4.5 The seven Ps of the marketing mix

Distribution channel	Advantages	Disadvantages
One intermediary channel	• Promotion and customer service are done by the retailer. • The costs of holding stock are incurred by the retailer. • The retailer assists in selling the product at convenient places to consumers.	• As the retailer's profit mark-up is included in the selling price, the product may be expensive for consumers. • The producer may not be aware of the promotional strategy used by the retailer.
Two intermediaries channel	• The wholesaler incurs storage costs, therefore reducing these costs for the producer. • The wholesaler breaks the bulk for the retailer by providing large quantitates in smaller batches. • This is an appropriate channel when selling over long distances.	• Two profit mark-ups could lead to a more expensive product offered to consumers. • This channel further reduces the producer's responsibility for promoting products.

Case study: Ansoff matrix – some organization examples

Market penetration

The Android operating system is a good example of a market penetration strategy. Apple and Blackberry dominated the US smartphone industry in the early 2000s. But today Android is the market leader, with a greater market share than Apple.

Product development

An example of product development in the Ansoff matrix is smartphone companies like Apple and Samsung putting out new phone models every few years.

Market development

A good example of a market development strategy is PayPal. They initially started their service in the US and expanded to other countries.

Diversification

Alphabet Inc exemplifies this. They started on the internet with Google search but gradually moved into different markets, including the oil sector.

Ansoff matrix

This case study gives some examples of how the Ansoff matrix provides businesses with a framework with which to analyse and plan their growth strategies.

Student workpoint 4.11

Be an inquirer

Using specific organizational examples, explain which distribution channels are likely to be most effective for each of these industries:

a) clothing
b) jewelry
c) bakery

People

People are the most important element of any service business. Services are produced and consumed at the same moment, and the specific customer experience can be changed to meet the needs of the person consuming it. People usually buy from people they like, so businesses should ensure that their staff have the right attitude, skills, and appearance at all times. For example, restaurants should encourage their waiters and waitresses to dress appropriately, to be courteous, and to smile when serving customers.

Offering customers an opportunity to provide feedback to staff can help to assess how effective customer service is. Examples of how to collect feedback include banks providing brief questionnaires asking customers if they waited too long to be served, or questioning cinema goers on the service experience as they queue to book a ticket.

People have an important role to play in service delivery and maintaining good customer relationships. Behind key events such as hosting the FIFA World Cup, there are many people (including managers, engineers, chefs, and security guards) who ensure that the service is appropriately delivered to the customers.

Another important factor is that people form a transactional link between the organization and its customers. For example, people deliver the service and they collect money, ie they get paid on behalf of the organization for the service. When you go to a restaurant, in most cases there will be a waiter or waitress who greets you on arrival, takes your order and serves you what you requested. After you eat, you pay them money for what you consumed, completing the contractual transaction.

Therefore, the person's role in the customer relationship between the business and the consumer is vital. Customer relationship management (CRM), which ensures that staff are trained to deliver good customer service, is important in developing a long-term employee–customer relationship.

All organizations need to deal with the various cultural settings they are faced with. Culture includes the way employees perceive or behave in the organization. Undoubtedly, some cultures may dominate others in the same organization, with groups of employees having differing beliefs and opinions, leading to the formation of a cultural gap.

It is the organization's responsibility to close this gap and foster a sense of unity among its employees. This will help to improve teamworking and will motivate employees to work to achieve the organization's goals. Consequently, a motivated workforce will treat customers well, further strengthening the employee–customer relationship. In addition, marketers need to learn and understand the cultural dimensions of customers to be able to satisfy the customers' needs fully.

Processes

Processes not only relate to the procedures and policies involved in providing and delivering an organization's products. They also involve how the product is delivered to the consumer.

DHL, for example, is known for its fast and efficient delivery of parcels or documents, and prides itself on having the right systems and processes to facilitate this. It also ensures that utmost care is taken by doing a security check on documents before they are sent to the recipient. This ensures that the product is delivered in its exact state and form, as required by the sender, maintaining optimal quality standards throughout. In addition, the sender receives a tracking number that they can use to track the document's path and enquire about any delay in delivery if necessary.

At the outset, businesses need to clearly define the shape their processes will take so that all stakeholders are fully aware of what to do. For marketing to be effective, there are a number of processes that businesses need to consider, including processes for identifying customer requirements, handling customer complaints, and handling orders, among others. If these are tackled well, they can go a long way towards developing customer loyalty and ensuring repeat customers.

Some ways a business can improve on its processes include:

- providing easy and varied payment methods for customers, such as paying over the internet, paying cash, or paying on credit
- providing after-sales services, such as technical support that reduces the time a customer spends solving problems when using a product
- informing customers how long it will take to prepare their meal in a restaurant, which adds to customer service
- exploring and taking measures to speed up the delivery of products to customers.

Ensuring the right process is in place can be time-consuming, complex, and expensive, especially for start-up businesses which lack the experience and capital that larger businesses may have.

A business like DHL puts many processes in place to operate efficiently

Physical evidence

Physical evidence is an important differentiator in service marketing. For example, managers of a private school may pay more attention to providing well-designed and well-equipped classrooms and spacious offices for their teaching staff than managers in public schools, clearly bringing out the differentiating element of physical evidence.

However, the intangible nature of products with a service element makes it difficult for consumers to evaluate the service being offered before deciding to buy, especially with regard to its quality and value for money. Also, it is difficult for a business to position new products with a service element because of their intangible nature. Effectively focusing on the tangible aspects of the service offering will enable the business to remain competitive in the market.

Physical evidence should therefore enable customers to "see" what is on offer prior to purchasing the service offering. Businesses should also ensure that the testimonials customers pass on to others about their product are good and lead to an enhanced image and increased sales.

Appropriate marketing mixes for particular products or businesses

An appropriate marketing mix ensures that consumers' needs and wants are adequately met. This requires businesses to produce the right product, sell it for the right price, make it available at the right place, and communicate through the right promotion channels.

Concept

CREATIVITY

Today, creative thinking is rated as one of the most in-demand skills by leading organizations. Creativity is a way of thinking that motivates and challenges people to generate innovative solutions to problems. Creativity is more than just artistic value.

How can organizations effectively incorporate creativity in their marketing strategies? To what extent does creative marketing lead to business success?

In addition, businesses should consider hiring the right people, adopting efficient procedures to ensure effective delivery of their products to consumers, and paying attention to any visible touch points that are observable to customers.

Benefits of a seven Ps marketing mix model

- It brings together marketing ideas and concepts in a simple manner, making it easier for a business to market its products or services.
- It assists a business in strategy formulation all the way to strategy implementation.
- The model allows a business to vary its marketing activities based on customer needs, resource availability and market conditions.

Drawbacks of a seven Ps marketing mix model

- The incorporation of three extra Ps (people, processes, physical evidence) in the seven Ps may be viewed as complicated by some businesses that are used to the four Ps model (product, price, promotion, place).
- The seven Ps model misses out on addressing issues related to business productivity.
- As product is mentioned in the singular, this could mean that businesses that produce more than one product sell these in isolation, which is not necessarily the case.

It is important to note that if the message of the marketing mix is not clear and focused, a firm could risk a potential loss in sales, which will affect its long-term profitability. Consumers may not identify with the product and therefore may not buy it.

Examples of inappropriate marketing mixes include:

- advertising an expensive car in a colourful children's magazine
- selling an exclusive perfume at a stall where second-hand clothes are sold
- a real-estate agent attempting to sell houses in a vegetable market.

To be effective, and in order to achieve its marketing objectives, an appropriate marketing mix for a business will need to:

- be well coordinated so that the elements consistently complement each other
- be clear and focused, not abstract or ambiguous
- consider the market it is aiming to sell the product to
- look into the degree of competition that the product faces
- target the right consumer.

4.5 The seven Ps of the marketing mix

Business plan

A business plan is the blueprint for taking an idea for a product or service and turning it into a commercially viable reality.

The marketing portion of a business plan addresses how to get people to buy the product or service in sufficient quantities to make the business profitable. It consists of the following:

- **Market analysis**, which assesses the market environment in which the business competes, identifies its competitors and analyses their strengths and weaknesses, and identifies and quantifies the target market.

- **Marketing strategy**, which explains how the business will differentiate itself from its competitors' businesses, and what approach it will take to get customers to buy from it.

- **Marketing and sales plans**, which specify the nature and timing of promotional and other advertising activities that will support specific sales targets.

Using an organization of your choice, devise a marketing plan (with seven Ps) that would be part of the wider business plan.

Product
- design
- technology
- perceived usefulness
- convenience of use
- quality
- packaging
- brand utility
- accessories
- warranties

Price
- skimming
- penetration
- value based
- cost plus
- cost leadership

People
- employees
- management
- organization culture
- customer services
- orientation

Place
- retail
- wholesale
- mail order
- Internet
- direct sales
- peer to peer
- multi-channel

Marketing mix

Physical evidence
- facilities
- infrastructure
- service delivery

Promotion
- special offers
- advertisements
- endorsements
- user trials
- campaigns
- joint ventures

Processes
- uniformity of offering
- service delivery
- service consumption

Figure 4.5.5 Summary of the seven Ps relevant to a business in the service sector providing intangible products

4 Marketing

Case study: Apple's seven Ps marketing mix

This is how Apple uses the seven Ps method to achieve success.

Product

Apple was founded as a computer company in 1976 in the United States, but since then has launched a wide range of electronic products, adapting well to customer needs. Based on its sales history, the iPhone has been the most sold product.

Price

Since the beginning, Apple has opted for innovation and prestige; something that has, from a business aspect, defined how their pricing and sales strategy evolves. The first Apple product was sold for £666.66 and since then Apple has managed to keep charging high prices. Despite the relatively high prices compared to some competitors, one of the main strengths of Apple is the UX or User Experience. Apple can tailor its products depending on the user's requirements.

Apple's pricing strategy has always acknowledged consumer feedback, giving its audience what they need to become potential customers. To cater for another segment of consumers who found its products too expensive, the brand later released the iPhone SE for a lower price so that everyone could join Apple's community and enjoy its services.

Apple uses a price skimming strategy, which means it sets a high initial price for a product, then once the main consumers have bought it, Apple will drastically reduce the price to capture the low-end buyers. The objective here is to obtain as much revenue as possible before other new products arrive on the market.

Place

Apple stores sell only Apple products.

Apple's products and services are available in physical stores situated mostly on high streets and at strategic locations. They are also available on Apple's website, who also use other distributors such as telephone companies to sell their products.

Promotion

Apple uses most of the main marketing communication channels to promote its products and services. These include Twitter, Instagram, Facebook, TV, print, and billboards. Apple thus makes good use of social media marketing and through-the-line promotional strategies.

People

Since its launch, Apple has hired more than 75,000 people worldwide. The giant tech company seeks to employ the best staff and spends a lot of time on professional development and training to help its staff deliver the best outcomes for its customers.

Processes

In the processes stage, product designers are especially important for Apple and are actually isolated from other departments. Once the design of the product has begun, the Executive Team meets every Monday to review and check the product's design. Then the Engineering Program Manager and the Global Supply Manager will work alongside each other, making decisions that aim to produce the best product.

Once Apple has built a product, it redesigns the product and sends it through the manufacturing process again. This is a rigorous 4 to 6 week process.

The product is then packaged. Apple has special designers who work only on the packaging in an effort to communicate the right message to the consumer: simplicity, sophistication, and premium products.

The next stage is to launch the product and ensure that staff are well trained on the new features or services it provides.

Physical evidence

Apple has online and physical stores and, as with its products, they focus on simplicity, minimalism, and sophistication, which leads to an attractive physical evidence. Every effort is made to improve customer experience.

Source: Adapted from https://www.kevinvejo.com/post/applemarketingmix

4.5 The seven Ps of the marketing mix

SWOT analysis

The internal and external attributes influencing Apple are provided below from a marketing perspective.

Strengths	Weaknesses
• Most valuable brand in the market, with a brand value of over $300 billion. • A brand of choice in corporate offices. • Millions of loyal customers whose numbers are steadily increasing.	• High-priced products due to their premium pricing. • Limited advertising and promotions that rely heavily on their retail stores. • Narrow product line.
Opportunities	**Threats**
• Consistent customer growth, with the power to tap into the internet for future opportunities to gain new customers and form new alliances. • Expansion of its distribution network for greater market growth. • Expansion of its music streaming services due to a growing youthful population and rapid economic growth in emerging economies.	• Increasing competition from brands like Samsung, Google and Dell. • Android commands a greater market share globally in the software smartphone market. • Lawsuits were filed when it announced that it deliberately controls CPU performance on iPhone models that have older and degraded batteries.

TOK discussion

1. The seven Ps frameworks suggest that marketing has seven aspects, all of which can be described with a word that starts with the letter "P" in the English language. If this model had been created by speakers of another language, would the marketing mix be different?

2. Some advertisements use scientific and technical terms, for example about cosmetics. Why is that? What does this tell us about the hierarchy of different areas of knowledge?

3. What role do logic and emotion play in marketing? Is there room for both?

Case study

How two companies shifted their marketing strategy to stay competitive
BMW

BMW operates across the globe in a highly competitive industry – the automotive industry. As a result, BMW invests heavily in its marketing mix to maintain its customer base and brand loyalty. However, competitors Mercedes-Benz and Jaguar are similarly well invested in marketing campaigns to increase their market shares while maintaining their brand loyalties.

Previously, BMW used its unique selling point or proposition (USP) of building high-performance, high-quality sports cars with unique handling characteristics to gain customers' attention and loyalty. Slogans such as "Pure driving pleasure" and "Perfection perfected" featured in BMW's marketing campaigns around the world. In the context of the Ansoff matrix, BMW began with a market-extension strategy into markets such as China and India, but later switched to product development as its key strategy.

This shift in marketing strategies came about because a new market segment became the largest single market in which BMW operated. Customers have developed a new preference since 2000 that continues to grow in strength and popularity – high fuel efficiency. Due to dramatic increases in oil prices in all but the OPEC nations (a STEEPLE factor), customers have sought out vehicles that use less fuel to travel further. For example, Toyota and Tesla have thrived with their cars that are environmentally friendly and have low fuel consumption – a result of focused differentiation. In response to this development, BMW instituted a raft of changes to its marketing strategy.

First, as part of product changes in the marketing mix, BMW began designing and showcasing "vision" concept cars at the largest automotive expos in the world. None was more definitive than the BMW i8, which was branded the "efficient dynamics" concept car. Essentially, it showcased BMW's latest fuel-efficiency technology to the world's media and immediately positioned BMW towards consumers' new preferences.

BMW also changed many of its promotion techniques to fit this new brand image. Below-the-line methods (including slogans such as "Exhilaration without excess") became BMW's new focus, and efficient dynamics became its USP and major product-differentiation tool.

The new products in BMW's marketing strategy were paired with new promotion strategies. BMW began to emphasize the fuel efficiency of its existing models (which it had previously neglected to publicise), and products such as the BMW X Series cars were rebranded by taking part in the gruelling Dakar Rally. The rally is known as a race that requires participants to have vehicles with extraordinary fuel efficiencies.

However, BMW's shift in market strategy has not been a complete success. In an attempt to please the majority of customers who want fuel-efficient cars, BMW has lost some of its most loyal customers to competitors. This has largely been a result of changes to the product element of its marketing mix. In order to increase fuel efficiency and to lower carbon emissions, BMW ceased using V10 engines in its 5 Series cars in favour of V8 engines that use less fuel. As a result, BMW lost many loyal, high-income customers who preferred the more powerful V10.

In short, BMW's pivot towards a new customer preference caused its profitability to be damaged to some extent. However, with increased market shares in Africa, North America, and Asia, BMW's medium-risk strategy appears to have paid off.

The MultiChoice Group

The MultiChoice Group has also shifted its marketing mix and strategy to meet customers' preferences. In particular, the arrival of high-definition (HD) technology in a variety of fields, ranging from smartphones to cameras and televisions, has attracted a great deal of attention from its customers.

Unlike BMW, it is apparent that MultiChoice does not operate in a highly competitive market. In fact, DStv (owned by MultiChoice) could be considered a monopoly as it benefited heavily from the first-mover advantage. But Multichoice has still changed to meet customer preferences to ensure that there is no market gap for new entrants to exploit.

MultiChoice's marketing mix has been refocused in terms of the techniques used to reach customers. For example, DStv's premium subscribers (those who pay the highest rates) form part of the demographic in Southern Africa that has the highest income. As a result, they are the most technologically aware demographic in Southern Africa, and because of this DStv has placed a greater emphasis on online advertising on websites and social media.

DStv now has Twitter and Facebook pages for customers to follow and prospective customers to view. These provide the latest information on new products brought to market. For example, the arrival of HD channels such as Discovery Showcase HD and M-Net HD were first promoted online to their premium customers (those most likely to purchase these products) before reaching other customers via television advertisements (a result of market segmentation).

However, the implementation of this strategy has not come without some drawbacks – the largest of which is the increased cost to customers. As a result of expensive technological upgrades to DStv's broadcasting system to support HD television, customers have suffered a price increase to pay for both the new systems and the marketing campaign to promote it. This increase in price also priced out prospective customers who could have increased DStv's market share. This demonstrates how responding to customer preferences can have a negative effect on the customers themselves.

4.5 The seven Ps of the marketing mix

Revision checklist

✓ The seven Ps of the marketing mix are product, price, promotion, place, people, processes and physical evidence.

✓ A product life cycle illustrates the six life cycle stages that a product passes through: its development, introduction, growth, maturity, saturation and decline in the market.

✓ Extension strategies are implemented at the maturity or saturation stages of a product's life cycle to stop a firm's sales from falling by lengthening the product's life cycle.

✓ The Boston Consulting Group (BCG) matrix is a growth–share matrix that measures the market growth rate and relative market share of a firm's product portfolio by classifying the products as stars, problem children (or question marks), cash cows or dogs.

✓ BCG matrix strategies include harvesting, holding, building and divesting.

✓ Branding is concerned with distinguishing one business's product from that of another, and it has a strong influence on how consumers perceive a product.

✓ Price, as one of the marketing mix elements, is essential in generating revenue for a business and refers to the money customers give up for using a good or service.

✓ Appropriate pricing strategies include cost-plus pricing, penetration pricing, loss leader, predatory pricing, premium pricing, dynamic pricing, competitive pricing and contribution pricing.

✓ Promotion's main aim is to obtain new customers or retain existing ones by communicating information about a firm's products to consumers. It can be categorized as either above-the-line, below-the-line or through-the-line.

✓ Above-the-line promotion uses independent mass media to promote a firm's products, including advertising through the television, radio or newspapers.

✓ Below-the-line promotion does not depend on the use of independent media. Instead, firms focus their direct control on promotional activities aimed at consumers they know or those who are interested in their products, eg through direct marketing, personal selling, public relations and sales promotions.

✓ Through-the-line promotion uses an integrated approach of combining both above-the-line and below-the-line promotion strategies. The aim is to get a holistic view of the market and reach out to customers in as many ways as possible.

✓ Social media marketing is a way of building relationships, driving repeat business and attracting new customers through social media sites.

✓ Place is about how a firm's product is distributed to make it available to consumers by getting the right product to the right place at the right time.

> **Assessment advice**
>
> Researching how different organizations market their products provides a good insight into how marketing works in the real world.

- ✓ Distribution channels include the zero intermediary channel, one intermediary channel and two intermediaries channel.

- ✓ People comprise an essential element of any service business, so businesses should ensure that their employees have the right attitude, skills, and appearance at all times as they are the face of the organization. These people also form a transactional link between the organization and its customers due to their vital role in the long-term relationship between the business and the consumer.

- ✓ Processes are the procedures and policies pertaining to how an organization's product is provided and delivered to the consumer. They inform customers on the ease of doing business with a particular organization.

- ✓ Physical evidence includes the visible touch points that are observable to customers in a business. It is an important differentiator in service marketing.

- ✓ An appropriate marketing mix for a business ensures that consumers' needs and wants are sufficiently met by producing the right product at the right price, available at the right place and communicated through the right promotion channels. In addition to hiring the right people, this involves adopting efficient procedures and paying attention to any visible touch points that are observable to customers.

4.5 The seven Ps of the marketing mix

Practice question

To answer the question below effectively, see Unit 6 pages 398–402.

Quick Bite

Quick Bite, a fast-food restaurant company that started in 2010, has always placed a lot of emphasis on branding, and until 2020 it had always made a profit. From 2020, sales in Europe (the company's biggest market) started to decline. The following table gives information on *Quick Bite's* current portfolio:

Date of launch	Product	Market information	Other information
2010	burger rolls	high market share but beginning to fall, very low sales growth	very profitable, core product but profitability is beginning to fall
2010	fried potatoes	high market share but beginning to fall, very low sales growth	very profitable, core product but profitability is falling rapidly
2015	toasted cheese sandwich	high market share, low market growth	very successful product
2020	chicken roll	falling sales, low market share in a low growth market	not a commercial success
2020	cheese and tomato pizza	falling sales, low market share in a low growth market	not a commercial success

Between 2012 and 2017, *Quick Bite* opened restaurants worldwide at the rate of 250 a year. However, by 2020 *Quick Bite* was closing restaurants and concentrating on attracting more customers into existing outlets. Industry analysts suggest that the trend towards healthier food is affecting the popularity of the chain. So *Quick Bite* is proposing the introduction of a new product to cater for the market. Newly established health-food stores are becoming major competitors. *Quick Bite* is caught in a marketing war with aggressive rivals. In addition, economic downturn in its major markets is affecting demand.

a) Define the term *branding*. [2 marks]

b) (i) Applying the Ansoff matrix, explain *Quick Bite's* past and current growth strategies. [4 marks]

   (ii) Applying the Boston Consulting Group matrix, analyse *Quick Bite's* product portfolio. [4 marks]

c) With reference to the seven Ps of the marketing mix, recommend a new product for *Quick Bite*. [10 marks]

4.6 International marketing (HL only)

> **By the end of this chapter, you should be able to:**
> → Explain how businesses **enter international markets**
> → Examine the **opportunities** and **threats** posed by entry into international markets

International marketing refers to the marketing of goods and services across national boundaries: products from one country are marketed to another country. Unlike global marketing, where firms use a standardized approach to market their products in other countries, in international marketing firms have the flexibility to differ in their marketing approach to other countries. Increasing worldwide competition, also known as **globalization**, is the main cause of the rise in international marketing.

How businesses enter international markets (HL only)

Businesses use various methods or modes to enter an international market. Some of the channels or strategies businesses use to enter international markets are considered below.

- **The internet** – many businesses are increasingly using the internet to market their products because of its global reach. New internet businesses are being set up to take advantage of the low costs involved in marketing their products abroad. Existing businesses are using the internet as an additional channel to enhance their current marketing methods. Trading over the internet, also known as **e-commerce**, has become popular as an entry strategy for many businesses.

- **Exporting** – this can be done both directly and indirectly. In direct exporting, a country commits to marketing its product abroad on its own behalf. The main advantage here is that the business has control over its products and operations abroad. Indirect exporting involves hiring an export intermediary or agent in the home country to market the domestic firm's product abroad. A common form of indirect exporting is **piggybacking**, where already existing distribution channels of one domestic business are used by another home country business trying to sell a new product overseas.

- **Direct investment** – also known as foreign direct investment, this is where a business sets up production plants abroad. One benefit of investing in production plants in a foreign country is that a business gains access to the local market, making products easily available to

---

Key terms

International marketing
the marketing of goods and services across national boundaries

Globalization
the increasing worldwide competition leading to a rise in international marketing

E-commerce
trading over the internet

Piggybacking
the use of the existing distribution channels of one domestic business by another home country business trying to sell a new product overseas

4.6 International marketing (HL only)

customers. It also gains local market knowledge, so that it can adapt its products accordingly to suit consumer needs and wants. Many companies have followed this route, including Coca-Cola, Nike, Samsung, and Toyota.

- **Joint venture** – this is a business arrangement where two or more parties agree to invest in a business project. These parties share their resources, with each being responsible for the costs, profits, and losses incurred. However, the participants keep their independent business interests separate from the newly formed joint venture. For example, in order to enter international markets, the joint venture Virgin Mobile India, which is a cellphone service provider company, was formed from Tata Teleservices and Richard Branson's Service Group. The company (joint venture) makes use of Tata's CDMA network to offer its services under the Virgin Mobile brand name.

- **International franchising** – this is a business arrangement where the franchisor (a business in one country) grants the franchisee (a business in another country) permission to use its brand, trademark, concepts, and expertise in exchange for a franchise fee and a percentage of the sales revenue as royalty. Examples of businesses that have used this as an international marketing strategy include Ocean Basket, Steers, Wimpy and Nando's. See Chapter 1.5 for more on franchising.

Virgin Mobile India is an example of a joint venture

Opportunities as a result of entering and operating internationally (HL only)

- **A larger market** – introducing a company's products to a new market provides a greater reach for those products, which increases the customer base. This enables the business to gain higher sales and profitability. This is also an effective extension strategy when an existing product is in the saturation stage of its product life cycle in the home country but enters a new market to begin its life cycle afresh.

- **Diversification** – this provides an opportunity for businesses to spread their risks by investing in other countries. Diversification reduces dependence on gaining sales revenue from just the home market in case of key risks such as an economic downturn.

- **Enhanced brand image** – the global reach brought about by international marketing means that the businesses involved can be perceived as more "successful" than those that operate only in the domestic market. This creates greater brand prestige that can drive brand loyalty.

- **Gaining economies of scale** – a business can increase its scale of operations through international marketing by selling more products abroad. As a result, this can reduce the average costs of production and so make the business more competitive. The business can then take advantage by increasing its profit mark-up and gaining higher profits.

- **Forming new business relationships** – marketing overseas can enable a business to make new contacts with various stakeholders. Such suppliers may offer better prices for inputs like raw materials compared to suppliers in the home market. These contacts can therefore provide opportunities for increased efficiency and profitability for home businesses.

Threats as a result of entering and operating internationally (HL only)

- **Economic challenges** – the inequitable distribution of income in many countries can pose a major problem for countries wanting to market overseas. Many developing countries have very low per-capita incomes or purchasing power and therefore may lack the income to buy the products being marketed. Fluctuating exchange rates and differing interest rates also pose planning problems for businesses willing to market abroad.

- **Political challenges** – due to the volatile nature of the political arena, unstable political regimes pose a threat to domestic businesses that are willing to operate in foreign markets. The ease with which governments can change regulations also increases the political risk of doing international business. The increased threats of global terrorism and civil unrest have also heightened awareness regarding which countries businesses should trade with. The instability in the Middle East and the invasions of Afghanistan and Somalia are some examples.

- **Legal challenges** – different countries have different laws that businesses need to abide by if they are to market overseas. For example, the EU is known for its strict policies on anti-competitive behaviour, advertising and product standards. International marketers must also adhere to the various consumer protection laws and intellectual property rights that exist in other countries.

- **Social challenges** – differences in the demographic or population structures of different countries should be a key consideration for international marketers. In a number of countries in Europe there is an increasing older population, while in many African countries there is a growing younger population. Marketers need to be aware of this disparity and segment the markets accordingly if they are to reap any benefits.

- **Technological challenges** – the growing use of the internet has increased the speed at which businesses operate on a global scale. However, a number of developing countries still lack access to this vital resource. This, coupled with limited infrastructure and poor communication systems, can have a drastic impact on how businesses operate.

4.6 International marketing (HL only)

Hofstede's cultural dimensions (HL only)

Hofstede's cultural dimensions help businesses to understand the cultural similarities and differences across borders in order to assess the different ways they can conduct business in those countries. Hence, when businesses market their products and services across international boundaries, they need to understand each local market individually.

Using Hofstede's cultural dimensions, carry out research on how culture influences international marketing.

Student workpoint 4.12

Be a thinker

1. Examine the implications of increased worldwide competition on international marketing.
2. Discuss how firms can adapt their international marketing strategies to suit the changing global business environment.

TOK discussion

1. Is the difference between national (domestic) marketing and international marketing a difference of degree or a difference of kind?
2. Could it be easier to know about customers in other countries than in the home country?
3. Regarding international marketing, what is an opportunity and what is a threat? Is it only a matter of perspective?

Revision checklist

✓ International marketing is the marketing of goods and services from one country to another. It provides businesses with the flexibility to differ in their marketing approach to other countries. Globalization is the main causal factor in the rise of international marketing.

✓ Modes of entry into international markets include the internet, exporting, direct investment, joint ventures and international franchising.

✓ The opportunities of international marketing include a larger market share, diversification, enhanced brand image, economies of scale, and the formation of new business relationships.

✓ The threats of international marketing include political, economic, social, legal, and technological challenges.

Practice question

To answer the question below effectively, see Unit 6 pages 398–402.

FT Blue

In 2020, the low-cost airline *FT Blue* entered the South African market with an initial offer to sell 50,000 tickets at low prices on flights between Johannesburg and Cape Town. Almost half of the $50 tickets were booked online within hours. Chief executive Brian Kan expressed his surprise: "It almost caused our website to crash."

The other two competing airlines were quick to respond to the new competitor by cutting prices to $80. A director of the leading airline SA Air doubted whether *FT Blue* could sustain these prices as part of its long-term strategy to enter the South African market.

Brian Kan accepted that *FT Blue* might run at a loss initially, but he was confident about the international marketing strategy they adopted: "We have done this before in India and we have money in the bank to survive. We hope to offer more routes, subject to government approval and the support of the South African public."

The other two airlines promised to remain competitive.

a) Define the term *international marketing*. [2 marks]

b) Explain **one** opportunity and **one** threat that *FT Blue* faced when entering the South African market. [4 marks]

5 OPERATIONS MANAGEMENT

5.1 Introduction to operations management

> **By the end of this chapter, you should be able to:**
> → Define **operations** and describe their **relationship with other business functions**
> → Explain the **role of operations management**

What are "operations"?

"Operations" refer to the fundamental activities of organizations: what they do and what they deliver, ie how they produce goods and services to meet consumers' needs and wants. Every organization is a producer of something. When we think of production processes, we tend to imagine a large factory with long lines of sophisticated machines, but production can take a variety of forms. There are the large-scale, capital-intensive production lines such as oil refineries or car plants, but a small bakery, a restaurant, and a school are also all organizations with an end product. The art of managing production to get the best end product is called **operations management**.

5 Operations management

Case study: The first factory

The historical text *Rites of Zhou* states that in ancient China, imperial and private workshops, mills and small manufactories had been employed since the Eastern Zhou Dynasty (771–221 BC). In Europe, large mills and manufactories were established in ancient Rome. The Venice Arsenal provides one of the first examples of a factory in the modern sense of the word. Founded in 1104 in Venice, Italy, several hundred years before the Industrial Revolution, it mass-produced ships on assembly lines using manufactured parts. The Venice Arsenal apparently produced nearly one ship every day and, at its height, employed 16,000 people.

Operations may be easier to understand in the case of the secondary sector, with the image of a modern factory and its semi-automated machines. However, operations are found in all sectors, for example:

- in the primary sector, mining or harvesting
- in the secondary sector, industrial manufacturing
- in the tertiary sector, open-heart surgery
- in the quaternary sector, business consultancy.

The study of operations provides the opportunity to investigate how products are made, at a very basic level. Look around you – at this book, your phone, your clothes, the furniture in your school and in your house. They are all manufactured using raw materials (eg cellulose pulp extracted from wood for a book) that go through a process of transformation. A simple input–output model can show how operations are the result of this transformational process (see Figure 5.1.1).

The finished product can then be packaged, transported, maybe exported or imported, and then commercialized, sold and bought.

Student workpoint 5.1
Be a thinker

1. List 10 organizations that you know. Try to cover a range of types (eg sole trader, charity) and sectors (eg primary, quaternary), as studied in Chapters 1.1 and 1.2.
2. Identify the main operations of those organizations. Are they always straightforward? Why is that?

Student workpoint 5.2
Be a thinker

1. Apply the input–output model to an organization that you have studied, for example the organization you chose for your IA. How useful is that model?
2. Apply the input–output model to your school; what corresponds to "the input", "the process" and "the output"? What conclusions can you draw from this?

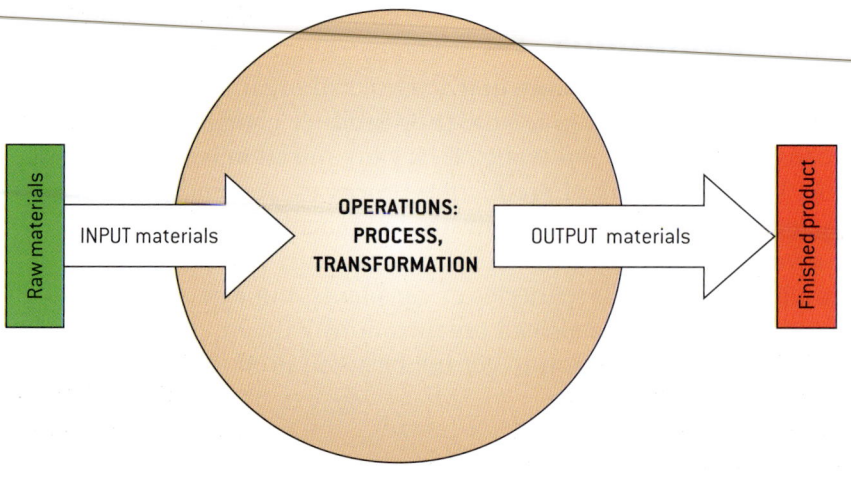

Figure 5.1.1 Input–output model

Raw materials → INPUT materials → OPERATIONS: PROCESS, TRANSFORMATION → OUTPUT materials → Finished product

5.1 Introduction to operations management

Operations and the other business functions

Operations can be described as the "what" of business management. Operations are closely linked to the other functions:

- Operations deliver the "what" question of an organization's objectives (see Unit 1), for example manufacturing cars or cutting someone's hair.

- Operations are done by people (see Unit 2), directly in the case of the hairdresser or indirectly in the case of the car factory worker who programs and controls the manufacturer's machines.

- Operations need funding (see Unit 3) and all financial aspects must be carefully budgeted and monitored, for example to pay the car factory worker's salary or to ensure that the hairdressing salon breaks even.

- Operations produce goods and services that must be marketed (see Unit 4), promoted and sold at the right price to the right audience, so that both the hairdressing salon and the car manufacturer are profitable and successful.

In the hairdressing salon, operations are carried out directly by employees

The relationship between operations and the other business functions is easy to understand: all business functions depend on one another and are part of a system. So the operations manager of a large company is in a good position to work with the other departments and make valuable recommendations. Here are some examples:

- The operations manager has direct experience of the economies of scale or diseconomies of scale that may take place on the factory floor (Chapter 1.5), and can identify some of the strengths and weaknesses of the organization that other departments would not necessarily know about, such as machinery obsolescence or likely costs of maintenance in the foreseeable future.

- The operations manager can suggest which forms of non-financial rewards (such as job rotation or teamwork) may be suitable (or not) for the organization (see Chapter 2.4). For example, the HR manager may not realize that some forms of motivation may be very good in theory, but not in practice.

- The operations manager may know which production costs (such as some semi-variable energy costs) could be cut (Chapter 3.3), which would in turn have an impact on the break-even point and the organization's margin of safety (Chapter 5.5).

- The operations manager can advise on which product extension strategies (Chapter 4.5) may be easily implemented (and those that may not). However, the marketing manager may have interesting ideas that would result in diseconomies of scale.

It is important that you understand that operations is not just about "doing and delivering" (despite the negative image that operations may sometimes have). Operations management is an integral part of the organization and its decision-making process.

> **Student workpoint 5.3**
>
> **Be a thinker**
>
> 1. Find an organizational chart of an organization showing the relationships between workers, with levels of hierarchy and chains of command.
>
> 2. On that organizational chart, identify the department and the workers responsible for operations. How are they linked to the workers in the other business functions? What can you conclude?

5 Operations management

A plane journey is a service which includes some physical elements

Operations and the production of goods or services

Production is usually defined as the creation of physical products (goods) or non-physical products (services). Although some products can be either purely goods or services, there are also a range of products that are a combination of both, and there can be an overlap in definitions, as shown in Table 5.1.1.

Table 5.1.1 Range of goods and services

Goods	High physical content but with some services	High service content but with some physical products	Services
Mobile phone, smartphone	Cosmetic surgery	Airline travel	Music concert
Consumer gets the product but there may also be after-sales service (for example in cases of malfunction or when updates are needed)	Consumer gets the "new" nose or a wrinkle-free face but there is extensive treatment before and after the operation	Customers travel from A to B but they may have a meal and watch a film, all part of the experience that the airline offers	Assuming that consumers don't buy the T-shirt or the CD or even the sponsor's soft drink, they only pay for the pleasure of the music

This may also be represented through a continuum, as shown in Figure 5.1.2.

Pure goods ⟵ Combination of goods and services ⟶ Pure services

Figure 5.1.2 Continuum of goods and services

There could not be a business without some form of operations, even if in the tertiary and quaternary sectors it is not always easy to identify exactly where the operations take place. Think of a book author, for example. Where did the operations take place? In the author's mind, as they thought about the text? On their computer, as they wrote the sentences? In their home office? Or when they were walking their dog, thinking about the chapters they would write? And ultimately, does it matter?

For both goods and services, operations are essential, but the definition must be adapted to the context. The secondary sector and the manufacturing of goods still provide the best situations in which to examine the operations of a business.

Student workpoint 5.4

Be a thinker

1. Consider the continuum between "pure goods" and "pure services". Place some examples of products on this continuum.

2. How useful do you find this visual representation between the two extremes?

Operations management and sustainability

In our typical example of a large factory, operations management is about planning, organizing, and controlling the different elements and stages of the production process, from choosing the most appropriate raw materials and equipment, to ensuring that the finished product is of the standard required.

5.1 Introduction to operations management

The input–output model (Figure 5.1.1) reminds us of the responsibilities of an operations manager. If the finished product is not of the standard required (for example it is defective), the operations manager will need to identify where in the process an error occurred. The role of the operations manager, however, is wider than just ensuring that production is correctly planned and executed; operations managers also have to take several other factors into account. These factors fall into three categories:

- Economic factors
- Social factors
- Ecological (also called "environmental") factors

Economic factors refer to the fact that budgets must be respected; wastage must be kept to a minimum and, whenever possible, further savings should be made, for example through greater efficiency. This is usually measured in monetary terms. For example, in some cases it may be possible to cut some unnecessary costs, such as energy costs.

The aim is to use the available resources and raw materials to their best advantage – ultimately ensuring profitability over the long term (as a profitable organization is more likely to continue to operate from one year to the next). This is also called **economic sustainability**.

Social factors refer to the fact that more and more organizations are becoming aware of their responsibility towards their workers, as internal stakeholders, and towards local communities, as external stakeholders. As a consequence, they seek to ensure that all employees are fairly treated, that their working conditions are acceptable, and that the quality of life for local people is not negatively affected by the decisions taken by the organization (for example in the case of expansion or relocation). This is also called **social sustainability**.

Ecological (or "environmental") factors refer to the fact that more and more managers understand the negative impact that their organization may have on the natural environment, especially different forms of pollution, such as air pollution (from carbon monoxide and CFCs), water pollution (industrial waste near factories, mills, and mines), or noise pollution (industrial noise that can also affect the workers themselves, for example in a noisy environment such as ship building). This is also called **ecological sustainability** (or **environmental sustainability**).

Economic sustainability, social sustainability and ecological sustainability are also known as "the three pillars of sustainable development". They are sometimes referred to as "the 3 Ps": **P**rofit, **P**eople and **P**lanet. Together they are called the "triple bottom line", which is often represented in a Venn diagram, as shown in Figure 5.1.3.

The triple bottom line stresses the fact that business decisions should not only consider financial aspects (such as breaking even and making money for shareholders), but also the well-being of local communities and the natural environment. Although this is relevant for all business functions, it is particularly relevant for operations, as manufacturing activities may have more negative impacts than

> **Key terms**
>
> **Economic sustainability**
> the need to use available resources and raw materials to their best advantage, ultimately ensuring profitability and financial performance
>
> **Social sustainability**
> the need to take human factors into account, both internally (eg workers) and externally (eg local communities), when making business decisions
>
> **Ecological sustainability**
> the need to take environmental factors into account when making business decisions (especially about nature and ecosystems)
>
> **Triple bottom line**
> the need to take economic, social, and ecological factors into account when making business decisions (the 3Ps)

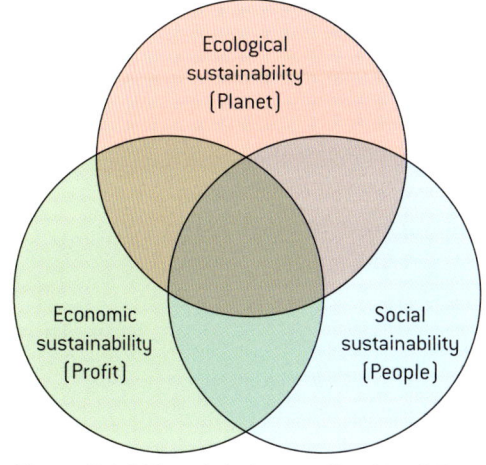

Figure 5.1.3 The triple bottom line/the 3 Ps

317

5 Operations management

marketing campaigns or financial transactions. In many cases, though, the triple bottom line remains an ideal rather than a reality, as economic aspects largely drive most commercial organizations.

> **Circular business model**
>
> The notion of a circular business model is one of the key tools of sustainable development. A circular business model shows how an organization creates, offers and delivers value to its stakeholders, while minimizing social and environmental costs.
>
> 1. There are many ways to develop circular business models (ie to make business operations more sustainable). For example, by making better use of raw materials, or by making products last longer. Can you think of some others?
> 2. How can you link the circular business model and the triple bottom line?

> **Student workpoint 5.5**
>
> *Be a thinker*
>
> 1. How can you link sustainability and the triple bottom line to concepts you studied in Unit 1, such as corporate social responsibility (CSR) and social enterprise?
> 2. Consider one organization that you have studied. How important is the triple bottom line in the decisions made by senior managers? Why?
> 3. Can you think of examples of situations of conflict between different types of sustainability (economic, social, and ecological)?

> **TOK links**
>
> 1. Does the difference between "goods" and "services" really matter? Why/why not?
> 2. Is it possible to measure sustainability?
> 3. As operations are what the business actually does, is it more important than the other functions (marketing, finance, human resources)?

> **Concept**
>
> **SUSTAINABILITY**
>
> The Practice Question on the next page about Luis Pacheco Muñoz and his Casa Blanca Eco-lodge is a good example of a business that places sustainability at its core.
>
> Can you find another example? You could decide to write your IA about that organization.

Revision checklist

✓ Operations are the fundamental activities of organizations.

✓ Operations are done by people – human resources.

✓ Operations need to be funded – accounts and finance.

✓ Operations produce goods and services which need to be promoted and sold at the right price – marketing and sales.

✓ Operations management is influenced by economic, social and environmental factors.

✓ Operations should aim to be sustainable in all three areas: the 3Ps of profit, planet and people.

5.1 Introduction to operations management

Practice question

To answer the question below effectively, see Unit 6 pages 398–402.

The Casa Blanca Eco-lodge

The word "eco-lodge" is used to describe a type of accommodation (lodge) that is environmentally friendly (eco-friendly). Eco-lodges aim to minimize their negative impacts on the environment and they make this very clear in all of their promotional materials. They often receive official certificates confirming that they fulfill the criteria of sustainable development.

The Casa Blanca Eco-lodge is a small business and it has strategies and practices for economic, social, and ecological sustainability. It is located in the Mayan mountains of Belize in Central America. The eco-lodge targets three types of visitor: rich tourists and jet-setters who seek an exotic, nature-based holiday experience; young backpackers keen to see non-coastal parts of Belize; and environmental scientists working on research or conservation projects.

The rainforest around the eco-lodge offers many opportunities for exploration and adventure. Visitors can go horse riding or hiking up the many canyon trails with a local guide, or they may prefer to canoe down the nearby rivers. The abundant bio-diversity of fauna and flora contributes to the tourist appeal of the area, from its butterflies to its jaguars, and from its iguanas to its toucans, not to mention the rare black orchids unique to that environment.

Luis Pacheco Muñoz opened The Casa Blanca Eco-lodge in 2016. Here is an extract from an interview with Luis that was published on the website Eco-tourism Today in 2019:

> Luis, why did you set up this business venture?
>
> *Of course I realized that there was a market opportunity, but I also wanted to do something for the local community. You see, I grew up here before I moved to Belize City where I worked in the hospitality industry. I am very attached to this area which has so much to offer. With the eco-lodge, we want to give tourists the chance to discover the beauty of the area, yet without destroying what we have. We are totally embracing the principles of eco-tourism and the UN Sustainable Development Goals.*
>
> Luis, can you give us some examples of what that means?
>
> *For example, all our electricity is produced from solar power, and all our water is supplied by a nearby mountain spring. We make sure that we stay in harmony with the natural environment.*
>
> So the eco-lodge is all about integrating the accommodation in its environment, is that correct?
>
> *Yes, this is true, although we go further than that. We are fully integrated in the local economy; for example we only employ local people and we only use food produced from local suppliers.*

a) Analyse the actions that Luis has already taken to ensure the sustainability of the Eco-lodge. [6 marks]

The Casa Blanca Eco-lodge merges well with its surrounding environment

Concept

SUSTAINABILITY

The 17 SDGs (Sustainable Development Goals) were adopted by the United Nations in 2015 as a universal call to action to end poverty, protect the planet, and ensure that by 2030 all people enjoy peace and prosperity.

Can you find examples of how business activities can positively contribute to each goal?

5.2 Operations methods

By the end of this chapter, you should be able to:

→ Define and explain the following **operations methods**:
- job production
- batch production
- mass/flow production
- mass customization

→ Recommend the most **appropriate method of production** for a given situation

A business organization, such as a factory manufacturing cars or cakes, may use a range of production/operations methods. The main methods of production are defined in Table 5.2.1, which also provides some typical examples for large, complex products (cars) and smaller, simpler ones (cakes or cookies).

Table 5.2.1 The main methods of production

Type	Definition	Example
Job production	Production of a special "one-off" product made to a specific order (for one individual customer).	The design of a space shuttle. A personalized wedding cake following the bride and groom's own design, favourite colours and required size: it is unique and follows particular specifications.
Batch production	Production of a group of identical products (the word "batch" refers to the fact that the items in each group go together from one stage of production to the next).	Car models with differing features for each model. A series of cookies in different flavours: chocolate chip, peanut, and coconut.
Mass/flow standardized production	Production of a high volume (hence the word "mass") of identical, standardized products. Flow production, process production, and line production are alternative terms that stress one particular aspect of the mass-production process.	Cars that are made to a standard design. Identical, undifferentiated cookies produced for a mass market.
Mass individualized customization	This manufacturing technique combines mass production with the personalization of custom-made products. It is particularly important for marketing purposes, as customers can personalize the goods they order and make them unique, hence the alternative names of "made-to-order" or "built-to-order".	Flat-pack furniture with many options of components or configurations chosen by the customer (colours, fabric, elements, sizes, etc).

Job production

Job production is a production method normally associated with the highest end of the market, where the emphasis is on quality, uniqueness and originality; the producer can charge premium prices. Production is market-orientated, with the client deciding precisely what the product should be. This is also called "customized production", which means that the order is made for a specific customer.

Job production requires clear objectives and careful planning, so there may be a longer development phase of the product life cycle. The client may require and expect greater consultation during the process and even after the product has been created. It is likely that the same format would be inappropriate another time. This can add to the time taken to produce the product, as there may not be a "blueprint" to use.

Advantages

- The mark-up is likely to be high.
- Clients get exactly what they want.
- This production method is likely to motivate skilled workers focusing on individual projects.
- It can be flexible.

Disadvantages

- This production method can be expensive, requiring skilled workers and non-standardized materials.
- It is likely to be time-consuming, as there is much more consultation with the client than for other production methods.
- The product might fail because of the lack of knowledge of the client. This may reflect badly on the business.
- This method can be very labour-intensive and reliant on skilled workers.

Batch production

Batch production is normally associated with the middle of the market, where the emphasis is on both quality and affordability. Products are still market-orientated; customers are offered customized products, but using a range of standardized options.

This method of production requires careful planning, as the components for the products need to be interchangeable. There will have to be some consultation with customers, as their needs have to be taken into account, although the exact options may be limited. Market research can replace the individual consultation.

Advantages

- Businesses can achieve economies of scale (for example when a small manufacturer makes savings by bulk buying, or when a group of operators pools resources).

> **Key terms**
>
> **Job production**
> production of a special "one-off" product made to a specific order (for one individual customer)
>
> **Batch production**
> production of a group of identical products (the word "batch" refers to the fact that the items in each group go together from one stage of production to the next)
>
> **Mass production**
> production of a high volume (hence the word "mass") of identical, standardized products
>
> **Mass customization**
> combines mass production with the personalization of custom-made products for marketing purposes

- Batch production allows customers more choice than mass production – and so captures more market share.
- It may be useful for trialling products, especially with smaller quantities.
- It may help deal with unexpected orders.

Disadvantages

- Businesses may lose production time as machines are recalibrated and/or retooled (this is known as "down time").
- Businesses may need to hold large stocks (in case of unexpected orders).
- The sizes of batches depend on the capacity of the machinery (or of labour) allocated to them.

All wedding ceremonies are unique (a feature of job production)

Bakeries often use batch production

In mass production, most process are automated (in this factory, bottles are transported from one machine to another)

Mass production

As its name indicates, mass production is all about quantity: it refers to the production of a high volume of standardized products, typically by using a continuous flow of raw materials along an assembly line. Labour is usually unskilled; its main role may be one of quality control. This method of production tends to be automated, as machines do not need regular breaks and can be relied on to produce to the same standard every time.

Mass production, however, requires careful planning in order to synchronize all the stages of the production process. For the process to be viable, the production must rely on large, reliable orders of the final product. Setting up this method may be expensive, and this investment must be recouped by selling a high volume. The product is therefore sold at the low end of the market and in large quantities.

The term "flow production" is sometimes used instead of "mass production". This term uses the image of a continuous flow of materials along an assembly line. This is the common image of a Taylorist factory with long conveyor belts routing the product through the different stages of production without any pause. Likewise, the terms "line production" and "process production" are sometimes used too, stressing the idea of a line (where the end product is gradually created, step by step) and of a process (ie a progression through different stages in a particular order).

Advantages

- Once set up, the system may need little maintenance.
- The business can cater for large orders, thereby achieving considerable economies of scale.
- Labour costs may be low as the jobs required are relatively unskilled; with a fully automated process, the need for workers is reduced.
- The business can respond to an increase in orders very quickly, as the process has already been set up.

Disadvantages

- Set-up costs are usually high.
- Breakdowns are costly, as the whole assembly line may have to stop.

- The business is dependent on a steady demand from a large segment of the market.
- The system is inflexible. For example, if there is any sudden drop in demand, the factory may well be left holding large stocks of unwanted products.
- The production process can be demotivating for workers who are doing repetitive activities.

Comparison of the main production methods

The three main methods of production may be compared according to different criteria (such as set-up time or labour), as shown in Table 5.2.2.

Table 5.2.2 Comparison of the main production methods

	Job production	**Batch production**	**Mass production**
Set-up time	There is a long set-up time as there is a new set-up for every new job	As set-up is usually a modification of an existing process, set-up time can be reasonably fast	There is a very long set-up as it takes time to synchronize the whole process
Cost per unit	High	Medium	Low
Capital (machinery)	This can be flexible as it depends on specific use	A mixture of machines is used, but this method is based on general-purpose machines	This can involve large numbers of general-purpose machines designed for a specific function
Labour	Highly skilled workers are needed – and they may be craft workers	Workers are semi-skilled and need to be flexible	Workers are unskilled and need minimum training
Production time	This is likely to be long	Once set up, production can be swift	Production is swift
Stock	This involves low quantities of raw materials and finished stock but a high amount of work in progress	High quantities of raw materials are needed (buffer stocks) – there will be medium amounts of work in progress and finished stock	There will be high quantities of raw materials and finished stock, and a low amount of work in progress

Mass individualized customization shares most features of mass production; the main difference is that finished stock cannot be prepared in advance but is rapidly finalized.

Case study

American Leather

Located in Dallas, Texas, American Leather is one of the most luxurious furniture brands in the United States. It uses mass customization to produce sofas, chairs and recliners to customer specifications within a few weeks.

At the start of the manufacturing process, all of the basic frames of the furniture are the same: this follows a mass production model. Afterwards, in the final production stages, automated cutting machinery ensures that each piece of furniture is personalized for each customer, according to the colour, fabric type and leather of their choice. There are many options and alternatives, for example a choice of texture (pebbled or smooth) and choice of protection (heavy, light or medium), so there are thousands of possible combinations, all entirely personalized.

This is a good illustration of how mass production and customization can be successfully integrated, hence the name mass individualized customization.

5 Operations management

> **Student workpoint 5.6**
>
> *Be an inquirer*
>
> Consider organizations around you, and identify:
>
> a) three that use job production
>
> b) three that use batch production
>
> c) three that use mass production

> **Business plan**
>
> A business plan is a comprehensive document in which an entrepreneur outlines all of the key aspects of the proposed business project. It covers the four business functions (human resources; marketing; operations; and finance, especially information regarding start-up costs and the break-even point). It also includes information about the business idea itself, as well as the business's organization, aims and objectives.
>
> For new enterprises in the secondary and tertiary sectors of the economy, should business plans mention production methods? Why/why not?

Changing the production method

Once a business has chosen and implemented a particular production method, it can be difficult and costly to change. At the very least, this may involve retooling machines, redeploying human resources and refinancing the new system. At its most drastic, a business could decide to re-engineer itself. This means that the company completely reorganizes itself, not only by changing the production process, but also the entire structure of the business. Business re-engineering was a fashionable management tool in the 1990s, but it is not so popular now.

Changing the production method would have implications for all of the business functions.

These are some of the implications for **HR**:

- Some workers may have to be redeployed, retrained, or even let go, so human resources would need to be managed carefully.
- Refining the roles and responsibilities of workers and middle managers would require careful planning.

These are some of the implications for **marketing**:

- Production runs can reflect the orientation of a business as well as the choice of product available to the consumer, so the image or perception of the business may be altered.
- Distribution channels may be affected, which may lead to differing response times.
- Changes in costs of production could be passed on to the consumer through changes to prices (which are likely to mean an increase, at least in a short term, to pay for the transition costs).

These are some of the implications for **finance**:

- Changing the production method will have an impact on stock control, which affects costs.
- Changes may take time and could interrupt current production, causing delays in the working capital cycle.
- Any change will need financing, whether it is short term or for significant developments that may require major long-term funding.

What is the most appropriate method of production for a given situation?

The most appropriate method will vary from business to business – there is no one correct method. Factors affecting the decision include:

- **The target market** – for example, the business may be producing high volumes of a low-cost product for a large market with little disposable income.
- **The state of existing technology** – this can limit how flexible production can be.
- **The availability of resources** – fixed capital, working capital, and human capital.
- **Government regulations** – for example, a business may have to meet certain targets for recycling or waste emissions.

As noted above, once a business has a particular production method in place, it is not easy to change it, and there will be opportunity costs. However, it may be possible to combine different production methods. This may result in the advantages of each different model being integrated so that the business's production becomes more efficient.

For example, Apple might mass produce its popular iPhones and iPads, but it could also have limited editions of luxury gold-plated $30,000 models. In this way, Apple could achieve economies of scale from the mass-produced products, while satisfying the need for changes in demand for more customized and higher-market-value products. There is no rule stating that a particular business should adopt a particular production method; all of the advantages and disadvantages should be compared and contrasted before a recommendation is made.

Revision checklist

✓ Job production is market-orientated, meaning that the customer or client decides what the product should be. This is often production of a special, one-off product.

✓ Batch production creates a group of identical products, which can be customized.

✓ Mass production creates a high volume of identical, standardized products.

✓ Mass customization combines mass production with the personalization of custom-made products for marketing purposes.

TOK links

1. What evidence and whose experiences should be considered when deciding on the production method?
2. Should the choice of production method be based on quantitative or on qualitative data?
3. Is "mass customization" a distinct production method, or it is mainly a marketing technique?

5 Operations management

Practice question

To answer the question below effectively, see Unit 6 pages 398–402.

Au Bon Chocolat (ABC)

Au Bon Chocolat (*ABC*) owns a small chocolate factory located in Bayonne, a French city near the Spanish border. *ABC* is a family business founded in 1996 by Jerome Lagarde, who operated it as a sole trader. Since 2015, *ABC* has been a private limited company. All shareholders are members of the Lagarde family.

ABC manufactures most of its chocolates in a mass (flow) production process. Some special orders, however, are made through batch production, such as sugar-free Christmas chocolates, or egg-shaped Easter chocolates.

a) With reference to *ABC*, contrast mass (flow) production and batch production. [6 marks]

5.3 Lean production and quality management (HL only)

> **By the end of this chapter, you should be able to:**
> → Outline the following **features of lean production**:
> - less waste
> - greater efficiency
>
> → Distinguish between the following **methods of lean production**:
> - continuous improvement (kaizen)
> - just-in-time (JIT)
>
> → Explain the features of **cradle-to-cradle design and manufacturing**
> → Outline the features of **quality control and quality assurance**
> → Explain the following **methods of managing quality**:
> - quality circle
> - benchmarking
> - total quality management (TQM)
>
> → Examine the **impact of lean production and TQM** on an organization
> → Explain the importance of **national and international quality standards**

What is lean production? (HL only)

"Lean production" (also called "lean manufacturing" or just "lean") is an approach to operations management that focuses on cutting all types of waste in the production process (such as waste of time) with one aim: greater efficiency.

Lean production originated in Japan (it was first developed by the car manufacturer Toyota) and became popular in other countries in the 1990s. The word "lean" refers to the fact that, as with a healthy piece of lean meat without much fat (if you are a meat eater), the production process gets rid of all the elements that do not directly add value.

This is not a new idea: Taylorist manufacturing in the early 20th century was already based on the idea of cutting waste, with assembly lines and factory workers specialized in one task (see Chapter 2.4). But it was only in the late 20th century that management researchers started writing books conceptualizing lean production and studying how this approach might be applied in other companies, in other industries, and in other sectors.

The principles of lean production have now spread all around the world, especially in the automobile industry, but they can also be adopted and applied to other industries, from logistics to distribution and from

5 Operations management

Lean production was first developed by Toyota to improve the efficiency of its car assembly lines

Student workpoint 5.7

Be an thinker

Can you link lean production to topics from other parts of the course?

Key terms

Lean production
a Japanese approach to operations management focusing on less waste and greater efficiency

Kaizen
a method of lean production based on continuous improvement

JIT (just-in-time)
a method of stock control which means avoiding holding stock by getting supplies only when necessary and producing only when ordered

JIC (just-in-case)
holding reserves of both raw materials and finished products in case of a sudden increase in demand

construction to retail. Even some government agencies and services such as education and healthcare now use the principles of lean production.

The starting point for lean production is to identify the values desired by the customer (such as a long battery life, the possibility for customization, or easy after-sales service), then all the stages of the production process that do not add value are eliminated. This elimination of waste is a key goal of lean manufacturing, and the word "waste" must be interpreted in a broad sense. It can include waste of:

- **Time** (eg waiting for the next stage of production, or waiting for some elements to arrive from a different location).
- **Transportation** (eg the movement of half-constructed cars in a factory may not add anything to the production process itself).
- **Products** (eg defects that need to be reworked or scrapped).
- **Space** (eg when too much stock is being produced and stored; this is called "overproduction").
- **Stock** (eg too many raw materials being purchased and stored before they are used).
- **Energy** (eg by under-utilizing some machines, which at full capacity would not require proportionally more power).
- **Talents** (eg not optimally using workers' skills and knowledge).

As this list shows, in the context of lean production the meaning of "waste" is very broad. It is not just about the disposal of substances or objects such as scrap metal or papers; it is about all other aspects of the production process.

Cutting waste is directly linked to greater efficiency: with less waste, the organization's resources (such as physical resources, human resources, and financial resources) will be better used.

- **Physical resources** can be used more efficiently, and the amount of space for storage is reduced (which is doubly expensive, because of both the unused stock and the storage space itself, such as rent, lighting, and heating of a warehouse).
- **Human resources** can be deployed more efficiently, for example to reduce unproductive travel times between venues (which is also expensive and not environmentally friendly).
- **Financial resources** can be used more efficiently. For example, holding stock ties up working capital (which means that this money cannot be used elsewhere in the organization).

Methods of lean production (HL only)

Over the years, several methods of lean production have been created and implemented. If the managers of an organization decide to adopt lean production, they will choose the method that best suits their context. The following two methods are particularly important:

- Continuous improvement (*kaizen*)
- Just-in-time (JIT)

5.3 Lean production and quality management (HL only)

Continuous improvement (*kaizen*)

The word *kaizen* (which means "continuous improvement") is a Japanese term as this method originates from Japan. Like lean production as a whole, the idea of *kaizen* was developed by Toyota.

The emphasis is on continuous change, as opposed to just occasional changes. In its simplest form, this process may involve suggestion boxes or competitions to find suitable areas for improvements, as often the workers themselves may have very good ideas based on what they observe or experience directly on the shop floor. However, *kaizen* can be more sophisticated, requiring certain key principles:

- It must be inclusive of all levels of the hierarchy (ie the whole organization must adopt this management philosophy, not just a group of managers or one department).
- No blame should be attached to any problem or issues raised (otherwise some employees may hesitate to make comments and suggestions).
- Systems thinking is needed in order to consider the whole production process, and not just some parts of it.
- *Kaizen* focuses on the process and not on the end product.

The main problem with *kaizen* is the fact that it is difficult to maintain the necessary momentum over a long period of time. To do so would require high levels of commitment and a sense of loyalty among the employees. The culture of the organization may influence this, and so will the leadership style: *kaizen* is unlikely to work under an autocratic leadership or bureaucratic corporate culture (see Chapter 2.5).

Just-in-time (JIT)

A business may hold stock (inventory) for many reasons, for example to ensure that it can respond to any sudden, unexpected demand (this is called "buffer stock"), or to take advantage of bulk purchasing of raw materials. Holding stock, however, may incur several costs: not only storage costs, but also insurance costs and even the payroll costs of staff who look after the stock. Controlling stock levels is very important for a business, and this function is called **stock control**. Stock control is based on a balance between:

- JIC, which stands for "just-in-case": holding reserves of both raw materials and finished products in case of a sudden increase in demand (or of a problem in production or in the supply chain).
- JIT, which stands for "just-in-time": avoiding holding stock by getting supplies only when necessary, and producing only when ordered.

The difference between JIT and JIC and the factors affecting stock control and optimal stock levels are explored in Chapter 5.6.

JIC is the traditional method of stock control. However, in terms of lean production, JIT means that the company will not hold buffer stock, which contributes to the two pillars of less waste (there is no waste of space in storage facilities) and greater efficiency (not having money tied up in stock).

Large warehouses like this one keep a lot of stock and use JIC

5 Operations management

> **Key term**
>
> **Cradle-to-cradle design and manufacturing**
>
> a recent approach to design and manufacturing based on principles of sustainable development, especially recycling

> **Student workpoint 5.8**
>
> *Be a thinker*
>
> How can you link cradle-to-cradle design and manufacturing to other parts of the course?

Cradle-to-cradle design and manufacturing (HL only)

Cradle-to-cradle design and manufacturing refers to a recent approach to design and manufacturing based on principles of sustainable development, especially recycling.

The term "cradle" refers to the production phase, ie the creation of a product such as a book or a car. The term "cradle-to-cradle" comes from the expression "cradle-to-grave". It suggests that products, once they have been used, should be entirely recycled to create new products that are either the same or different.

At the moment, this is only the case for a small number of products from a small number of companies, for example some clothes or office furniture. But the current socio-cultural momentum towards environmental sustainability will put pressure on companies to design and manufacture more and more products that are partly, if not entirely, recycled and recyclable.

To receive the official "cradle-to-cradle (C2C) certification", products need to fulfill several criteria, for example regarding:

- the reutilization of the material itself (recycling, strictly speaking)
- the amount of energy necessary for the recycling process (ideally renewable energy)
- the amount of water needed as part of the recycling process
- the corporate social responsibility (CSR) of the company, for instance with regard to fair labour practices.

Cradle-to-cradle design and manufacturing is still in its infancy. The independent non-profit organization called The Cradle to Cradle Products Innovation Institute was launched in 2012. This means that the criteria and features will become more defined and refined over time.

As part of their research and development, many companies are exploring what cradle-to-cradle design and manufacturing could mean in practice. For example, in 2003 Ford proposed a concept car called "Ford Model U", a car for the 21st century based on recycling and eco-friendliness. It uses sunflower-seed engine oil and hemp and soy in its construction. However, the Ford U only exists as a prototype and as a theoretical example of what cradle-to-cradle could do.

> **Case study**
>
> ## Fat Llama
>
> Fat Llama is based on the concept: "Borrow stuff you need. Lend stuff you don't." Anyone can create an account on Fat Llama's website and begin to list items, or rent other people's belongings for a day or more. It's free to list and browse, and Fat Llama takes a cut on each instance of lending and borrowing.
>
> A lot goes on in the background to create a thriving network and to ensure it all runs smoothly. As well as customer support, messaging services and ratings and reviews for lenders, every item is covered by a £25,000 insurance policy. So if an item is lost, stolen or damaged during the rental, lenders can be reimbursed through Fat Llama.

5.3 Lean production and quality management (HL only)

> This is a major reason why this start-up is succeeding, as having an insurance policy massively opens up the pool of items people are willing to rent. The items found on the website are often high-end, technical equipment with an average value of £1,500.
>
> While Fat Llama's lending marketplace has categories in sports, electronics, clothing and much more, an early trend has been the rental of equipment for creatives. Professional cameras are popular, as are drones, studio lighting and DJ equipment, offered not only by individuals but also businesses who have assets sitting idle. Users posting items like these for others to use are seeing a real financial benefit. The 30-day leaderboard found on the Fat Llama homepage frequently shows individuals earning £3,000 or more. This shows how innovative business models that redefine their relationship with "stuff" can also open up new ways for people to participate in the economy.
>
> It's hard to judge precisely how this impacts resource use. Fat Llama is proud to say that some users purchase items specifically to list them on the platform, which could sound contrary to the ethos of a circular economy. However, if one person rents out a camera to multiple borrowers, who consequently don't need to purchase cameras themselves, then there's a significant resource saving on offer. In addition, lenders are much more likely to buy a quality product that is durable and can be repaired, so they can lend it again and again. That's how Fat Llama is encouraging people to move away from take, make and dispose.
>
> Source: Adapted from https://www.ellenmacarthurfoundation.org/case-studies/borrow-stuff-you-need-lend-stuff-you-dont

Sharing models

Sharing models facilitate the sharing of underutilized products. This reduces the demand for new products and their associated raw materials. The case study here gives an example of an organization that is based on a sharing model.

Quality control and quality assurance (HL only)

A key component of operations management is the issue of quality. In the past this was very much a matter of quality control but, thanks to the quality revolution that has sprung from Japan since 1945, there has been a move towards quality assurance. This change in quality management came about largely due to the work of one man: the American management theorist W. Edwards Deming, whose ideas about how to produce quality products are still influential today.

Quality is important for a producer as it can lead to:

- increased sales
- repeat customers (brand loyalty, see Chapter 4.5)
- reduced costs (see Chapter 3.3)
- premium pricing (see Chapter 4.5).

From a marketing viewpoint, a product does not need not be high-quality in order to bring all of these rewards; as long as the consumer perception is one of quality, this can be enough. League tables showing "top" business schools, airlines, or smartphones can be hugely important for businesses, even if the product voted "the best" is not actually the best!

5 Operations management

> **Student workpoint 5.9**
>
> ### Be a researcher
> An IB class did some research to find the best-quality tablet. They initially did a survey of all the students, then used the website of a professional magazine for an external, reliable judgment.
>
> Then they created a product positioning map, with the two axes of price and quality (similar to Figure 5.3.1). They concluded that quality is not always reflected in the price.
>
> Try the same exercise for a product of your choice.

The term **quality** suggests that a product is:

- reliable – it is not going to break down and fail
- safe – it is not dangerous for its users
- durable – it is going to last
- innovative – it is leading the way in terms of functionality or design
- value for money – you get what you pay for.

The quality revolution has shown that even businesses not at the top end of the range can benefit from producing good-quality products. For example, while a Honda car may not have the same brand image as a BMW, there is still a lot to be gained by producing good-quality, cheaper cars.

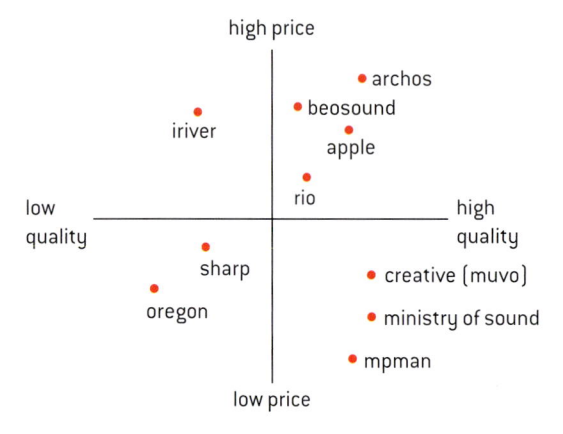

Figure 5.3.1 A way of mapping products based on scales of quality and price

The move from "quality control" to "quality assurance" is summarized in Table 5.3.1, which shows the major difference between the two systems.

Table 5.3.1 Quality control versus quality assurance

	Quality control	Quality assurance
Concept	• Quality is "controlled" by one person carrying out an inspection after the production run has been completed	• Quality is "assured" through the organization; no one person is in control of quality – instead the whole business focuses on it
Costs	• A maximum percentage of rejects is set, for example 2% of products are allowed to fail • Wasteful production	• Zero rejects are expected – every product is expected to pass inspection • Lean production
Processes	• It is rare to halt production as it is costly to do so • Quality stops with the job; the focus is only on the job at hand	• The company expects to halt production to fix errors • Quality includes suppliers and after-sales servicing
People	• Quality is the responsibility of one person • "Role culture" • Autocratic leadership • Top-down, one-way communication	• Quality is the responsibility of the team (quality circles) • Total quality culture • Democratic consultative leadership • 360-degree communication

5.3 Lean production and quality management (HL only)

Methods of managing quality (HL only)

In order for quality assurance to work effectively, the whole business has to embrace a total quality cultural shift. As with a *kaizen* approach, this is difficult and costly to achieve in the short term, but it may prove beneficial to the business in the long run.

Several methods are possible to manage quality; the following three are particularly important:

- Quality circle
- Benchmarking
- Total quality management (TQM)

Quality circles

A quality circle is a formal group of employees (from different departments and from all levels of hierarchy) who meet regularly to discuss and suggest ways of improving quality. The meetings are facilitated by a team leader (who needs to be trained in leadership and group facilitation). This is comparable to a focus group for market research, although a focus group would not necessarily meet several times, whereas a quality circle needs continuity to be successful.

Quality circles may operate in different ways: they could choose any topic they want to discuss, or they may be working on specific issues. The underlying principle is the idea that, coming from a range of perspectives on the company, the members of the quality circle will be able to improve the overall quality of the company.

For example, when discussing an issue of staff turnover, the members of the quality circle may present different views. This enables the company, as a learning organization, to understand the problem and to come up with solutions, such as reducing safety hazards and giving workers more flexibility. This is not the same as managers doing a consultation exercise: the focus here is on generating solutions that are about quality.

Quality circles were first established in Japan in 1962. This illustrates again how the quality revolution came from Japan after the Second World War. Quality circles are now very common in some countries (such as Japan and China), though less so in Anglo-Saxon countries and Western Europe, where the method did not spread and did not prove that successful.

Benchmarking

Benchmarking is about comparing yourself to your competitors. Benchmarking is a tool that many businesses use. As a point of reference, some benchmarks are established – and the businesses can then compare their practices and standards with those of their competitors.

A well-known example of benchmarking is the number of stars used to classify hotels: a five-star hotel has a different quality standard than a three-star hotel. This is useful for consumers, who know what they can expect, but it is also very useful for business managers, as the benchmarks help them identify how they could improve the quality of their products and services, should they wish to do so.

> **Assessment advice** ✓
>
> You do not need to memorize all details of Table 5.3.1. What matters is that you understand the difference between quality control and quality assurance.

> **Key terms**
>
> **Quality circle**
>
> a formal group of employees who meet regularly to discuss and suggest ways of improving quality in their organization
>
> **Benchmarking**
>
> a tool for businesses to compare themselves to their competitors in order to identify how they can improve their own operations and practices
>
> **Total quality management (TQM)**
>
> an approach to quality enhancement that permeates the whole organization (TQM can include quality circles and benchmarking)

> **Student workpoint 5.10**
>
> *Be a thinker*
>
> 1. What skills may facilitators of quality circles need? What could their training require?
>
> 2. Quality circles are very common in some regions of the world (such as South-East Asia) but not others (such as Europe). Why could that be?

5 Operations management

Businesses look at the market leaders in their industry and follow those organizations' "best practices". It is less about copying the rivals' products than learning from their practices and processes in order to improve quality.

Benchmarking can be done in several ways. Some companies may use the benchmarks that already exist in their industry (such as hotel standards). Or a company that has a specific quality issue (such as communicating on quality and innovation) may study another company that they identify as the model they want to follow and emulate. Benchmarking can also be done in a collaborative way, with competing businesses acting together to keep up to date.

In all cases, the success of benchmarking relies on the business's readiness to "think outside the box", ie to try to be creative and innovative. But what works for one organization may not necessarily work for another, so benchmarking has its limitations.

In many countries the hotel industry uses a star rating system to rank hotels

Total quality management (TQM)

As indicated by its name, total quality management is an approach to quality enhancement that permeates the whole organization, like *kaizen*. TQM can include quality circles and benchmarking. These quality tools are not mutually exclusive; they may be combined and integrated in a wider framework of TQM.

Some other possible features of TQM are outlined in Table 5.3.2.

Table 5.3.2 Other features of TQM

Feature	Purpose
Quality chain	As the quality of a business depends on the quality of its suppliers and after-sales service, all stages of the production process must be taken into account.
Statistical process control (SPC)	All stages of production are monitored and information is given to all parties, usually in the form of easy-to-understand diagrams, charts, and messages.
Mobilized workforce	All employees (at all levels of seniority and in all departments, even the ones not directly in contact with products or customers) are expected to embrace TQM. Everyone is encouraged to take pride in their work, and they are given responsibilities and recognition (for example through "employee of the month" schemes). Everyone is included in the quality decision-making process.
Market-orientated production	By focusing on what the customer wants, the business can make sure that it is innovating and continually reinventing its products. This can lead to improved sales and brand loyalty.

Student workpoint 5.11

Be a researcher

Brands and shops occasionally have to recall products that they have sold, often for safety reasons.

1. Research recent examples of such product recalls.
2. In your opinion, are product recalls a good idea? Why/why not?

5.3 Lean production and quality management (HL only)

The impact of lean production and TQM on an organization

Lean production and TQM are closely linked. Lean production focuses on less waste and greater efficiency, TQM focuses on quality assurance and quality enhancement. For a company, implementing lean production and TQM has many advantages:

- It can create closer working relationships with all stakeholders (including suppliers and customers).
- It can motivate the workforce.
- It can reduce costs (especially long-term costs).
- It can improve the design and production of quality products.
- It can enhance the reputation of the company.

However, implementing lean production and TQM has some disadvantages too:

- It is costly (especially in the short term).
- Staff may need significant training.
- It may take time to change a corporate culture.
- It can create a lot of stress on formal relationships in the business.
- It is difficult to maintain over a long period of time.

TQM and lean production are more commonly used by businesses that are new or looking to make significant changes to retain their competitive advantage. However, many long-established businesses now also understand that their traditional approaches to operations (including production and quality control) may be too costly, and that they need to make changes to ensure their economic sustainability.

> **Concept**
>
> **CHANGE**
>
> As we learned in Chapter 5.2, changing production methods can be costly and time-consuming. However, that has not deterred many businesses from making the change towards leaner production.

National and international quality standards (HL only)

An excellent way for businesses to assure the consumer of the quality of their products is by gaining certification for recognized quality standards. At a national or (even better) international level, a certificate is a mark of assurance that the product has met certain minimum requirements.

International standards are set by organizations such as the IOS (International Organization for Standardization) or the EU (European Union). The most common standards published by the IOS are the ISO9000 family, which certifies quality management systems in organizations.

Meeting recognized standards can help a business because it can:

- enable exports (market development abroad)
- give a competitive edge
- enhance the image and reputation of the business
- save on the costs of withdrawing products
- act as an insurance
- lead to higher profit margins.

5 Operations management

Case study

ISO and ISO 9001

The acronym ISO stands for "International Organization for Standardization", an NGO (non-governmental organization) formed in 1947 and based in Geneva, Switzerland. It is the world's largest developer of voluntary international standards. It helps countries and businesses trade together by setting common international standards across all sectors of the economy, from agriculture and food safety to healthcare, manufacturing and technology.

The standard called "ISO 9001" sets out the criteria for a quality management system. It can be used by any organization, irrespective of their size or field of activity. Over one million companies and organizations in more than 170 countries are ISO 9001 certified.

To be ISO 9001 certified, businesses have to build and implement a quality management system that complies with the latest version of the ISO 9001 standard. An official audit then takes place to ensure that everything is in accordance with the ISO 9001 standard. This standard is based on several principles, such as customer focus and a commitment to quality throughout the organization.

To internal and external stakeholders, the certification ISO 9001 is a sign that an organization is committed to quality and quality management, so organizations are usually proud to display this certification.

TOK links

1. Can quality be measured objectively?
2. Is the notion of "good quality" universal, or does it change over time or over place?
3. Is a quality product always more expensive (to manufacture or to buy) than a mediocre product?

Revision checklist

✓ Lean production is an approach to operations management which aims to cut waste and promote maximum efficiency.

✓ The continuous improvement method of lean production involves constant changes as opposed to occasional changes. This approach must include all levels of hierarchy, focusing on the process rather than the end product.

✓ The just-in-time method (JIT) reduces the amount of stock held by ensuring products are made only when ordered.

✓ Cradle-to-cradle design and manufacturing is the concept that once products are used, they should be entirely recycled to create new products.

✓ Quality control and quality assurance should ensure that products and services are reliable, safe, durable, innovative and offer value for money.

✓ Quality control involves inspecting finished products to check they meet the desired level of quality.

✓ Quality assurance is a system of setting and monitoring quality standards across the whole production process.

✓ A quality circle is a group of employees who meet to discuss ways of improving quality.

✓ Benchmarking involves comparing products or services to the products or services of competitors.

✓ Total quality management (TQM) is an overarching approach to improving quality. It can include a combination of different quality tools.

5.3 Lean production and quality management (HL only)

Practice question

To answer the question below effectively, see Unit 6 pages 398–402.

AMM

AMM is a private limited company that designs, manufactures and sells air conditioners. It is located in Pasig City in the Philippines.

The market and competition for air conditioners are growing rapidly. *AMM* operates at full capacity.

Primary market research revealed that:

- consumers do not differentiate *AMM* air conditioners from those of its competitors; all products are perceived as medium price and medium quality
- *AMM's* customer service is rated as poor, especially when customers have problems with defective air conditioners
- customers increasingly demand energy-efficient products using ecologically sustainable production methods.

To exploit opportunities and overcome weaknesses and threats, *AMM's* CEO Anna Maria Montejo has made two decisions:

- Firstly, *AMM* will change its quality system from quality control to quality assurance.
- Secondly, *AMM* products will be redesigned in order to be more energy efficient. Anna Maria is considering two strategic options:

    - **Option 1:** implement lean production methods and invest in ecologically sustainable machines that will increase capacity by 10%. Total quality management (TQM) will also be implemented. However, the financial manager is worried about *AMM's* ability to meet high initial costs. The forecast payback period is three years and average rate of return (ARR) is 4%.

    - **Option 2:** outsource production to *QS*, a company known for its reliability and high capacity to produce air conditioners of excellent quality using cradle-to-cradle manufacturing principles. However, *QS* refuses to sign an exclusive long-term contract with *AMM*, insisting instead on renegotiating the contract every two years. *AMM* will have to close its production facility and will use the cost savings to improve customer service and to reposition and differentiate its air conditioners.

a) Define the term *Total quality management (TQM)*. [2 marks]

b) With reference to *AMM*, distinguish between quality control and quality assurance. [4 marks]

c) With reference to *QS*, explain **two** features of cradle-to-cradle manufacturing. [4 marks]

d) Recommend to Anna Maria one of the two strategic options. [10 marks]

5 Operations management

5.4 Location

By the end of this chapter, you should be able to:

→ Explain the reasons for a **specific location of production**

→ Discuss the following ways of **reorganizing production**, both nationally and internationally:
  - outsourcing (subcontracting)
  - offshoring
  - insourcing (also called inshoring)
  - reshoring

Location of production

One of the most important decisions a business has to make is where it will be based or, as the business grows, where it should relocate to. Which factors must be taken into account when deciding where to start up or where to move to?

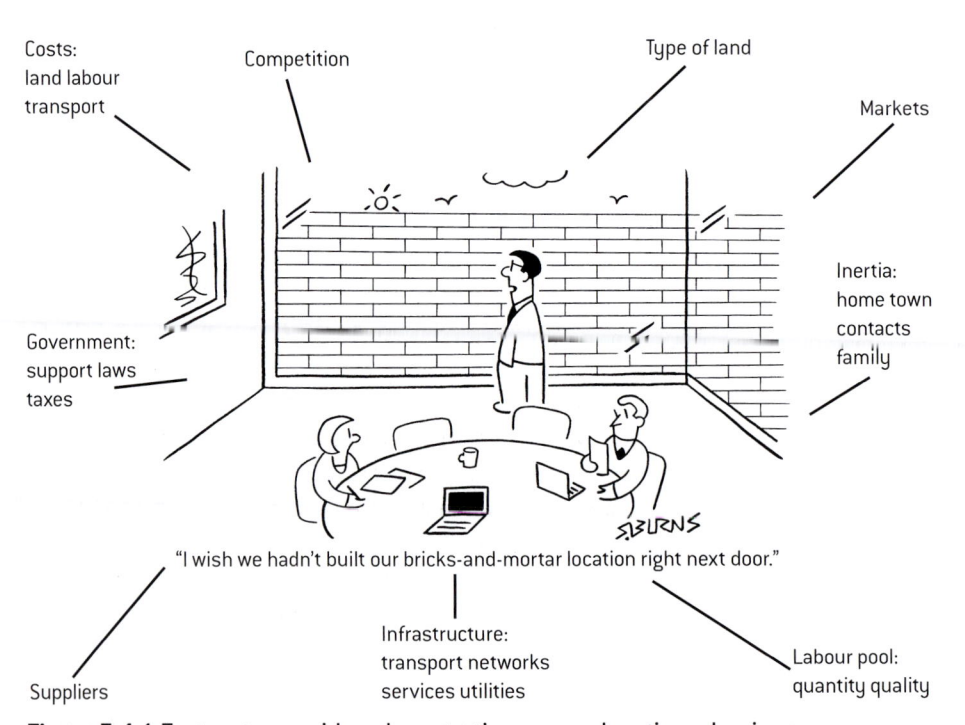

Figure 5.4.1 Factors to consider when starting up or relocating a business

Factors in locating a business

There is a distinction between setting up a business for the first time and moving the business to a new location. However, many of the same factors have a bearing in both cases. The main difference involves the objectives of the company at that particular time. Setting up may be simply to get started, but relocation may be necessary for various reasons, such as expanding or following the market. The business might also go through a merger and need new, larger premises.

Costs

Costs will be a key determining factor and will largely depend on the type of business being started or relocated. Costs may depend on the following:

- **Land** – if the business is a large manufacturer, it may need a large, flat surface area, whereas a small home-based office may only require a spare room.
- **Labour** – if the business is a technical one requiring skilled workers (such as a laboratory), the biggest cost may be labour.
- **Transport** – if the business is producing large quantities of a physical product, transport costs could be crucial. Two options are possible:
  - If the business is "**bulk increasing**" (buying in many components and building something bigger, such as televisions or cars), it may make sense to set up the business close to the market, as transporting the finished items would be more expensive than bringing in lots of small components.
  - If the business is "**bulk decreasing**" (buying in large quantities of raw materials and turning them into smaller end products, as in paper mills or glass foundries), it may make sense to set up the business close to the source of the raw materials.

Competition

Where are competitors located? A balance needs to be made between finding a gap in the market and setting up not far from the direct competitors. Retail outlets, theatres, law firms, and many other businesses often operate close to their rivals, as the chances of getting passing trade increase if the area becomes known for a particular product.

Sometimes, some companies (such as chains of coffee shops) adopt a system called "cannibalistic marketing" in order to stop possible competitors from opening their own outlets and taking some of their market share. Cannibalistic marketing involves setting up more than one branch in a location (such as a shopping mall); they may keep on opening more branches in the same area, even though each new branch eats up some of the profits of the existing outlets (hence the word "cannibalistic"), until eventually there are so many outlets that there is no more possible extra trade to be generated.

Type of land

Different types of land will incur different costs, and their suitability for a given business will vary. For example, some ski resorts may have been popular and successful in the 20th century, but with the onset of climate change and global warming, those locations might not be appropriate any more if there is not enough snow for skiers. Importing artificial snow could be an alternative, though skiers (consumers) may prefer to go elsewhere.

The outer circle is a city. The small circle is the first franchise and its sphere of influence (where its customers come from).

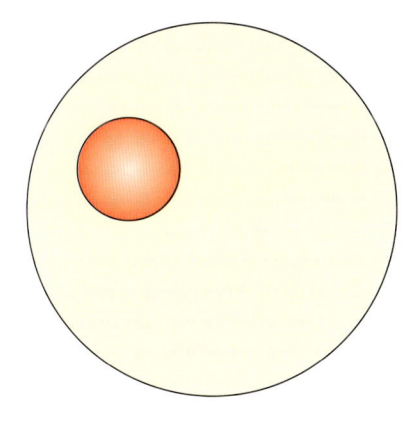

So another outlet is opened and as yet there is no problem—so another outlet is opened…

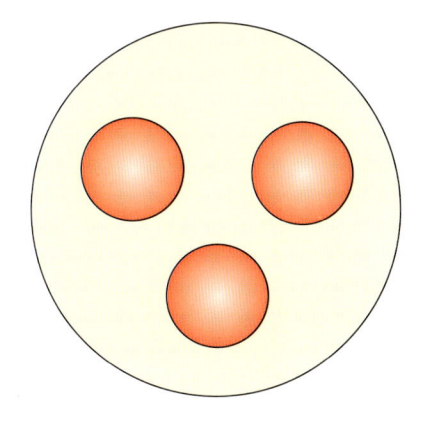

… until eventually although the franchisor (for instance, McDonalds) is doing OK—the company is covering lots of the market—the individual franchisee finds themselves losing custom.

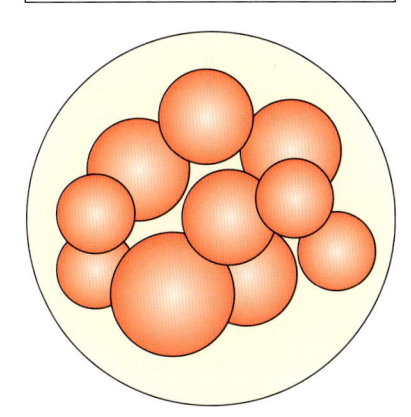

Figure 5.4.2 Cannibalistic marketing is a strategy linked to decisions about location

5 Operations management

The Grand Bazaar, Istanbul – one of the largest and oldest markets in the world

Markets

In the past, many businesses had to set up close to their customers. There were even special markets that were set up for special products, as well as general marketplaces (such as the great bazaars in North Africa and the Middle East, like Damascus, Marrakesh, Aleppo, and Istanbul).

However, the need for a physical marketplace has declined, which can bring considerable advantages to start-up internet companies. Rather than depending on a physical market, they may require only an efficient distribution system. This is a key aspect of e-commerce (see Chapter 5.9).

Familiarity with the area

Often, new businesses are set up in the place that the owners are familiar with. This has advantages and disadvantages. On the one hand, it means the business owners may already have some knowledge of local networks (such as possible suppliers and customers). On the other hand, they may overlook a more appropriate venue in another area (such as one with better access to suppliers or distribution networks). For example, setting up a business in your garage may cut down on costs, but it will also restrict your ability to expand.

Labour pool

Workers are critical to any business. Whether the business requires university graduates or school leavers, most businesses need to take account of the type of workers available locally and balance this with the skills and qualifications needed for all the business operations.

From a more strategic perspective, demographic change could make considerable differences to the type of workers available, not only in the present but also in years to come. For example, the increasing number of women in the workplace – and in senior roles – means that more and more businesses may have to adapt to part-time working, job sharing, flexi-time and the provision of crèche facilities to accommodate those women who choose to have children or who need to look after older family members.

Linked to the labour pool, another point to consider is the level of unemployment in the area. This may be a good indicator of possible savings on salaries: a higher unemployment level could mean that more people want a job, even on a low salary. The increase in teleworking (working from home) is another factor, though it may not be possible for many posts directly involved in production in the primary and secondary sectors. For example, a secretary or an administrator may be able to work from home, but not a farmer, driver, or a factory worker.

Infrastructure

Infrastructure refers not only to the existing transport networks for people and products, but also to electronic networks (for example telephones, computers, the internet, and all forms of digital communication). In a broader sense, other factors and facilities may need to be taken into consideration when choosing a location for the business, for example the provision of services such as education, housing, healthcare, and police, as well as utilities such as power and water.

Access to services is important for the business, as this may affect the welfare and motivation of staff. If staff have to be relocated, this could become a major issue.

Suppliers

The availability of reliable local suppliers may be important for some businesses, especially those using the JIT system of stock control (see chapters 5.3 and 5.6), which requires a greater degree of coordination.

Government

The role of both local and national government can be crucial for a business, especially for a new one or one that is considering locating in a deprived area. In some cases, local authorities may offer financial support, resulting in significant savings. This could be through grants (non-returnable, one-time-only funds), subsidies (funds to be offset against the cost of production), soft loans (loans at preferential rates of interest), or tax rebates (a cut in the tax to be paid).

- **Laws** – these are crucial for all businesses, from labour laws and health and safety regulations, to rules on advertising and restrictions on sales. Businesses have to be particularly careful because laws do change. Even if there is no regime change, there may well be a change in government policy. Even minor local changes (for example to traffic rules or hours of delivery) could have a major impact on a business (especially with a JIT method of stock control, if delivery is only possible during certain restricted hours).

- **Taxes** – the amount of money a business is liable to pay in tax will have a major effect on where a business may wish to locate. Businesses are more highly taxed in some countries (especially developed countries) than in others, and there are different types of taxes. They include national corporation tax and local council taxes for the business itself, income tax for the employees, capital gains tax for the owners and shareholders, and even variable taxes and duties payable by the customers. All of these will have a major impact not only on the amount of business the company can conduct, but also on how much profit can be retained and reinvested – and that, too, may be taxed.

National, regional or international ambition

The improvements in communications since the early 1900s have led to major changes in where businesses set up. In the past, businesses were initially local, serving their immediate community. However, it has become much easier to communicate and transport large volumes of materials across greater distances. Many businesses when locating or relocating must now think beyond their locality.

The increasing importance of regional trading blocs (such as the EU, Mercosur and NAFTA) has also had a major impact on decisions about location. For example, in 1986 the Japanese car manufacturer Nissan opened a giant car factory in Sunderland in the north of England to circumvent the EU import duties. However, as a result of Brexit (the UK leaving the EU), Nissan has had to reconsider this, and at the time of writing no decision had been made. The growth of trading hubs such as

5 Operations management

Hong Kong, Singapore, and Dubai needs to be considered as these can represent good options for a business wanting to set up a regional base or to access global transport networks.

Decision trees

A decision tree is a visual representation of the forecast outcomes of alternative scenarios. This tool can help managers make decisions by mathematically identifying the most suitable outcome (from a financial viewpoint) using estimates and probabilities. Outcomes are usually shown as "succeed" or "fail", with a probability percentage. To interpret a decision tree, you need to do the following:

1. Calculate the expected values (EV) of the different outcomes, by multiplying the estimated financial effect by its probability.
2. Calculate the different net gains (total EV minus cost).
3. Compare the different outcomes.

For example, a business has two options for growth: option 1 is to open a new branch (in country A or in country B, called "sub-option 1a" and "sub-option 1b"); option 2 is to start selling online (e-commerce).

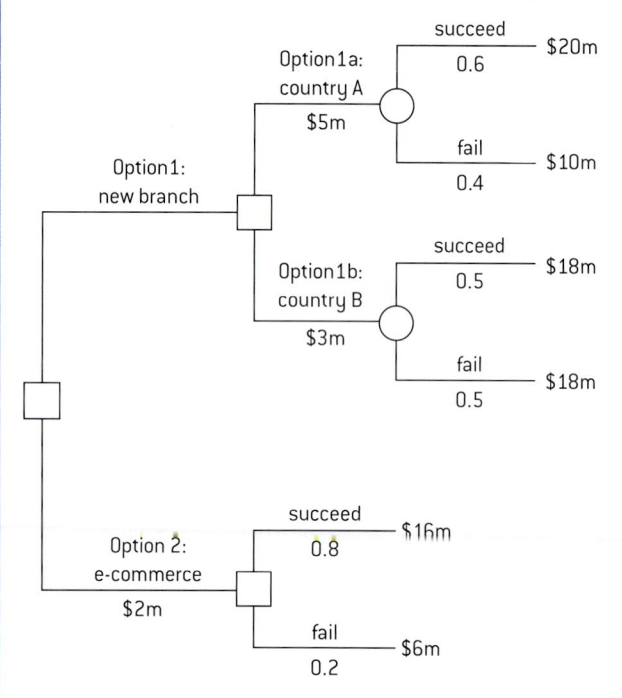

```
Option 1:                Option 1a:        succeed 0.6 — $20m
new branch               country A
                         $5m               fail 0.4 — $10m

                         Option 1b:        succeed 0.5 — $18m
                         country B
                         $3m               fail 0.5 — $18m

Option 2:                                  succeed 0.8 — $16m
e-commerce
$2m                                        fail 0.2 — $6m
```

The decision tree above shows the different probabilities of success/failure rates, and the different outcomes.

The expected values are as follows:
- For option 1a: (60% × $20m) + (40% × $10m) = 12 + 4 = $16m
- For option 1b: (50% × $18m) + (50% × $8m) = 9 + 4 = $13m
- For option 2: (80% × $16m) + (20% × $6m) = 12.8 + 1.2 = $14m

The net gains are as follows:
- For option 1a: $16m − $5m = $11m
- For option 1b: $13m − $3m = $10m
- For option 2: $14m − $2m = $12m

1. Based on these results, which option would you recommend? Why?
2. What are the limitations of a decision tree as a decision-making tool?

342

The impact of globalization on location

The impact of globalization on location decisions is best analysed in terms of "push factors" and "pull factors" affecting the four busines functions, ie the four areas of operations management, marketing, HR and finance.

Pull factors

The following scenarios may make it attractive for a business to set up or relocate abroad:

- Improved communications
- Dismantling of trade barriers
- Deregulation of the world's financial markets
- Increasing size of multinational companies

These are known as "pull factors".

Improved communications

Nowadays, it is far easier to transport products around the world and to communicate with suppliers, customers, or co-workers, irrespective of their own locations and time zones.

Dismantling of trade barriers

More than three-quarters of the world's countries are signatories to the World Trade Organization (WTO). The WTO has a commitment to reduce trade barriers, making it far easier for trade to take place across borders. China became a member of the WTO in 2001 and since then it has exploded onto the world stage. With the money earned, China is now acquiring foreign banks and manufacturers, and it is even sponsoring football teams. The same applies to other countries, such as Qatar, which features heavily in sports sponsorship.

The World Trade Organization was set up in 1995. Its headquarters are in Geneva, Switzerland.

Deregulation of the world's financial markets

The deregulation of the world's financial markets has made the transfer of vast sums of money very easy, which has facilitated quicker start-ups for many businesses. The prevalence of internet banking has made it much easier to keep track of a company's finances and, allied to the digitization of the world's financial markets, it is much more common for investors to invest abroad. This helps to build up collaboration, such as forming joint ventures and strategic alliances, or working with venture capitalists.

Increasing size of multinational companies

The size and consequently the influence of the world's biggest companies (conglomerates) makes it easier for them to persuade countries to allow them to set up new operations there. The enormous power and influence of multinational companies can create momentum for other businesses in the same field. For example, the impressive growth of Chinese influence in Africa may have been driven by China's need for raw materials, but it has generated interests in other areas.

Push factors

As well as the external factors noted above, there are a number of internal factors that may help to push companies (especially those that are already multinational) to operate overseas. By expanding overseas, they may be able to:

- reduce costs
- increase market share
- use extension strategies
- use defensive strategies.

Reducing costs

By setting up production facilities abroad, businesses may be able to reduce costs by moving closer to the raw materials or using cheaper labour, so they may be able to achieve productive economies of scale. They may also be able to take account of more favourable tax regimes and achieve financial economies of scale.

Increasing market share

By opening up a branch in a new country, an organization hopes to tap into a new market (market development in the Ansoff matrix – see Chapter 4.5) and increase its market share. However, there are some risks and disadvantages, such as:

- Language barriers
- Different cultural practices
- Historical tensions between countries
- Lack of knowledge of local or regional networks
- Local law and politics, especially labour law
- Time differences and the challenges of working across many time zones
- Possible challenges in finding reliable, trustworthy partners

The rewards can be very high, especially if the business has the advantage of being the first to enter a large market (known as "first-mover advantage"). This partly explains the rush by many big-name companies to enter China and India, with over 1 billion potential customers in each country.

Using extension strategies

Some businesses may have reached the saturation point for their products and may be looking to extend the life cycle of their products. McDonald's, one of the leading players in the global fast-food industry, has faced increasing competition not only from other burger outlets, but from pizza suppliers, sandwich bars, and other fast-food outlets. This increased competition has had a major impact on McDonald's profits. As a market leader, McDonald's has also been one of the hardest hit by bad publicity and by an increasing awareness of obesity and the dangers of overindulging in fast food.

To counter this, McDonald's has made major strategic changes. The company has introduced healthy food options, diversified into coffee, published its nutritional values, and reduced the fat and salt content in its foods. Besides these general strategies, McDonald's has also targeted areas where people are more likely to appreciate the service it provides. (See Chapter 4.5 for more on extension strategies.)

Using defensive strategies

Many businesses decide to move overseas not because they really need to but because they do not want their competitors to do it first. This is a defensive strategy. Growth and expansion are key drivers for businesses, and the fear that rivals might steal a lead can act as a catalyst for locating overseas. The rush for oil companies to set up in Central Asia to secure oil and gas reserves is an example, and so is the emergence of China as a big player in Africa, as China has felt the need to secure the supply of raw materials to feed its growing industries.

Ways of reorganizing production, both nationally and internationally

Outsourcing (subcontracting)

Outsourcing refers to the practice of using another business (as a third party) to complete a part of the work. That work is "contracted out", hence the term "subcontracting". This can enable the organization to focus on its core activity. A school, for example, would regard teaching as its core activity – and it could then outsource other services, such as:

- Catering
- Transport
- Administrative duties and examination invigilation
- Excursions, visits, and expeditions
- Staff recruitment and training
- Security
- Cleaning and maintenance

Outsourcing can help a business cut costs (and consequently reduce prices) in order to earn a competitive advantage. A business may have a number of activities happening on a day-to-day basis that are not part of its core skillsets. By buying in these peripheral services from external providers (who can achieve economies of scale because they are specialists in that particular service), the main business can reduce costs.

The following activities are commonly outsourced:

- **In marketing** – using an advertising agency
- **In production** – licensing a producer to make part of a product, such as the packaging
- **In HR** – employing an agency to "headhunt" potential staff
- **In finance** – hiring accountants to run an external audit

5 Operations management

Key terms

Outsourcing or subcontracting

the practice of employing another business (as a third party) to perform some peripheral activities (this enables the organization to focus on its core activity)

Offshoring

the practice of subcontracting overseas, ie outsourcing outside the home country

Insourcing

the practice of performing peripheral activities internally, within the company (the opposite of outsourcing)

Reshoring

the practice of bringing back business functions (jobs and operations) to the home country (the opposite of offshoring)

Student workpoint 5.12

Be an inquirer

Does your school outsource (subcontract) some of its services? What are the advantages and disadvantages for your school?

Outsourcing can bring many advantages:

- It can reduce costs.
- It can allow the business to focus on its core activities and what it does best, ensuring improvements in quality.
- It can lead to improved capacity utilization.
- Delivery time can be reduced.
- It can lead to transfer of expertise.

Outsourcing also has disadvantages:

- The business can become dependent on the supplier. Reliability could be an important issue: for example, what if the transporters go on strike?
- The business may have less control of the final product. What if a key component does not meet the expected quality standards?
- Dilution of the brand could be a problem, for example if consumers realize that the company's product is not produced by that company at all.

Offshoring

Offshoring is an extension of outsourcing. In business, "offshore" means abroad or overseas. In the case of offshoring, a business outsources something to an external provider in a location outside the home country.

With improved global communications, offshoring has become more common in the modern business environment. India, for example, saw a massive growth in IT offshore contracts in the early 2000s, such as call centres and help desks signed up with Western businesses.

All of the advantages and disadvantages of outsourcing apply with offshoring, but the international aspect usually intensifies them. In particular:

- There may be cultural differences between the companies, both in terms of national cultures and corporate cultures.
- Communication could sometimes be difficult (especially when people have to deal with different languages and time zones).
- There may be issues of quality and ethics (for example the use of sweatshops).

Insourcing

This is the opposite of outsourcing. It is also called "inhousing" or "inshoring" (meaning "in the house" or "at source"). A trend can be observed in the business world where some companies have now started to reverse outsourcing, ie they are performing peripheral activities internally again. The business decision to stop outsourcing may be motivated by the desire to regain full control, or to reduce the costs of taxes, labour, and transportation.

Reshoring

The word "reshoring" (also known as "backshoring") refers to the practice of bringing production and manufacturing of goods and services back to the organization's home country in order to refocus on the quality end of the market. This is the opposite of offshoring. Unlike insourcing, the business may still use external providers: they are now simply located in the home country. It is too early to evaluate the extent to which reshoring will fully affect manufacturers.

Force field analysis (HL only)

A force field analysis (FFA) is a tool used to compare the driving forces and the restraining forces for and against a specific decision, which is written at the centre of the diagram.

Here is an example of an FFA for a company that is considering outsourcing its social media marketing activities to an outside agency:

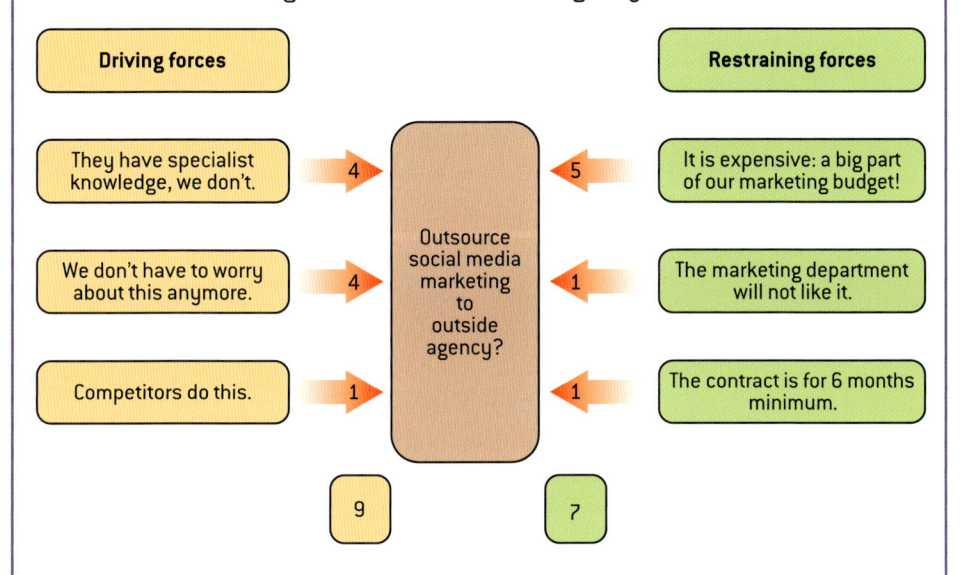

Driving forces
- They have specialist knowledge, we don't. (4)
- We don't have to worry about this anymore. (4)
- Competitors do this. (1)

Total: 9

Outsource social media marketing to outside agency?

Restraining forces
- It is expensive: a big part of our marketing budget! (5)
- The marketing department will not like it. (1)
- The contract is for 6 months minimum. (1)

Total: 7

1. What is the meaning of the numbers here?
2. Would you say that FFA is a quantitative tool, or is it a qualitative one?

Revision checklist

✓ Locating a business depends on multiple factors, including costs, competition, type of land, labour pool, infrastructure, government, and proximity to suppliers.

✓ Outsourcing is the practice of using another business to complete part of the work.

✓ Offshoring is an extension of outsourcing, which involves contracting with a business in another country.

✓ Insourcing is the reverse of outsourcing. It is when organizations choose to bring outsourced activities back into the main business.

✓ Reshoring is the opposite of offshoring. Activities may still be outsourced, but in the home country rather than overseas.

Concept: CHANGE

Decisions to relocate and reorganize production (outsourcing, offshoring, insourcing, reshoring) always lead to many changes and have a range of impacts, especially in terms of human resources. For example, some employees may need to be laid off, while new job opportunities are created for others.

In the media, find recent examples of outsourcing, offshoring, insourcing and reshoring.

TOK links

1. What methods do business leaders use to decide where to locate their production?
2. When business leaders decide to relocate or to offshore, should they consider emotional factors (for example the impacts of staff lay-offs)?
3. Is the shift in the business world to insourcing and reshoring predictable?

5 Operations management

Practice question

To answer the question below effectively, see Unit 6 pages 398–402.

Finn

Finn is an American public limited company. It mass produces jeans that are sold worldwide. Twelve years ago, production was offshored to China and Turkey to reduce manufacturing costs. To benefit from economies of scale, *Finn* sells standardized regular-fit jeans.

Despite the global popularity of American jeans, *Finn* has experienced a significant fall in demand due to:

- customer complaints about poor-quality jeans

- economic recessions in *Finn*'s main markets (although economic forecasts expect improvements within two years)

- increased global competition of mass-produced clothes.

In addition, *Finn*'s management is worried about labour costs in China rising faster than in the United States (US). It also has communication problems with its offshored employees.

Finn's management decided to reshore back to the US and completely change its strategic focus. Recent market research has revealed a niche market: some customers in North America are willing to pay high prices for individually designed and produced jeans. To create a new competitive advantage, *Finn* will aim for different market positioning by using highly skilled, creative fashion designers located in major American cities. Cost-effective production of individually designed jeans requires specialized technology currently available in the US. *Finn* will no longer mass produce jeans.

a) Define the term *offshoring*. [2 marks]

b) Discuss *Finn*'s decisions to reshore back to the US and to produce only individually designed jeans. [10 marks]

5.5 Break-even analysis

By the end of this chapter, you should be able to:

→ Distinguish between **contribution per unit** and **total contribution**

→ Draw a **break-even chart** and calculate the **break-even quantity, profit (or loss) and margin of safety**

→ Calculate **target profit output, target profit** and **target price**

→ Analyse the **effects of changes in price or cost** on break-even quantity, profit and margin of safety, using graphical and quantitative methods

→ Examine the **benefits and limitations of break-even analysis** as a decision-making tool

Organizations usually need to know the minimum quantity of products they must sell in order to start making a profit. This minimum quantity is called the **break-even quantity**. For example, a school play may need to sell at least 100 tickets in order to cover all of the expenses (such as the rental of the costumes, the refreshments for the actors and some marketing expenses like printing posters). If more than 100 tickets are sold, the venture is profitable. In this case, 100 is the **break-even point**.

In the case of a school play, the break-even point may be easy to calculate, as all the costs may be fixed costs, but most situations involve a combination of fixed costs and variable costs (for the difference between variable costs and fixed costs, see Chapter 3.3). Calculating the break-even point is done in several steps. The first one involves the calculation of two contributions: the contribution per unit and the total contribution.

Contribution

The **contribution** shows how much a product contributes to the fixed costs of a business, and thus to its overall profit, after deducting the variable costs. The **contribution per unit** is the difference between the selling price per unit and the variable cost per unit:

> contribution per unit = price per unit − variable cost per unit

For example, if a business manufactures and sells wooden tables for $150 each and the variable cost per table is $60 (the cost of wood as raw material), then the contribution is $90 per table ($150 − $60). In other words, the sale of each table contributes $90 to the fixed costs of the business (cost of salaries, rent, and other overhead costs such as insurance).

The **total contribution** is calculated when more than one unit is sold, by subtracting the total of all variable costs from the total sales revenue:

> total contribution = total sales revenue − total variable costs

Key terms

Contribution per unit

the difference between selling price per unit and variable cost per unit

Total contribution

the difference between total sales revenue and total variable costs

Profit

obtained by subtracting total fixed costs from the total contribution; the positive difference between total revenue and total costs

349

5 Operations management

Following on from the above example, if the business sells 100 tables at the same price of $150 and a variable cost of $60 per table, then:

$$\text{total contribution} = (\$150 \times 100) - (\$60 \times 100) = \$9{,}000$$

This $9,000 will contribute towards the firm's total fixed costs and thus to its profit.

Alternatively, the total contribution can be calculated by multiplying the contribution per unit by the number of units sold:

> **total contribution = contribution per unit × number of units sold**

Still using the above examples:

$$\text{total contribution} = \$90 \times 100 = \$9{,}000$$

Contribution and profit

Knowing the total contribution and the total fixed costs, it is possible to calculate the profit:

> **profit = total contribution − total fixed costs**

If our business sells 100 tables, the total contribution of these sales is $9,000; if the business incurs a total fixed cost of $5,000 then its profit will be:

$$\text{profit} = \$9{,}000 - \$5{,}000 = \$4{,}000$$

Contribution is not the same as profit: it is always much higher, as contribution only subtracts the variable costs from sales revenue, whereas calculating profit also subtracts the fixed costs.

Contribution (HL only)

Contribution is one of the key notions in break-even analysis. It is important to understand what it means, and to know how to calculate it (both "contribution per unit" and "total contribution").

1. What is the link between contribution and the cost-plus pricing strategy (see Chapter 4.5)?
2. Why can it be difficult to calculate contribution?

Breaking even

The **break-even quantity** is the minimum number of items that must be sold so that all costs are covered by the sales revenue. At the **break-even point**, there is no loss, but no profit either. This can be calculated numerically or graphically on a **break-even chart**.

Break-even chart

This is a graphical method that shows the value of a firm's costs (fixed costs, variable costs, total costs) and revenue against a given level of output. The break-even point can be identified by drawing all three cost lines and

---

Assessment advice

There are two ways to calculate profit. You can use the formula **profit = total revenue − total costs** or the formula **profit = total contribution − total fixed costs**. It does not matter which method you use, but once you have obtained your result, it is worth spending a couple of minutes to double check it using the other method. You will be reassured if both answers match, or you will be able to spot that you made a mistake and correct it!

Student workpoint 5.13

Be knowledgeable

A cellphone company sells two phone models. Model A phones each sell for $250 while Model B phones each sell for $180. In the month of January 2020, 1,000 Model A phones were sold while 1,500 Model B phones were sold. Model A's variable cost per unit was $90 and Model B's was $70.

If the total fixed costs incurred by the company that month amounted to $10,000, calculate:

a) the contribution per unit for each model

b) the total contribution for each model

c) the profit for the company that month

5.5 Break-even analysis

the total revenue line on a graph. The horizontal axis (the X-axis) measures the output (the number of units sold), while the vertical axis (the Y-axis) measures the financial values (of the costs and revenue).

When drawing a break-even chart, the following points need to be carefully considered (see Figure 5.5.1).

- **Fixed costs** (FC) are paid whatever the level of output is; as they remain constant, they are represented by a horizontal continuous line.
- With zero output, there will be no **variable costs** (VC), so the VC line starts from zero (origin). The higher the number of units produced, the higher the variable costs will be. In some cases, the VC line is not included in the break-even chart.
- The **total cost** (TC) line begins on the Y-axis at the level of the FC line; it then follows the same trend as the VC line, running parallel to it.
- With no units sold, there will be no revenue, so the **total revenue** (TR) line begins from the origin (zero), like the CV line. The greater the number of units sold, the greater the TR will be.
- The **break-even point** is the point where the TC line intersects the TR line. At this point, the break-even level of output can be read on the horizonal axis.
- The left of the break-even point shows the loss made by a firm, whereas the right of this point shows the profit made.

> **Key terms**
>
> **Break-even chart**
> a graphical method that measures the value of a firm's costs and revenues against a given level of output
>
> **Break-even quantity**
> a measure of output where total revenue equals total costs

> **Assessment advice** ✓
>
> It is important to label the break-even chart fully (including the axes and lines) and to provide an appropriate title or caption. In addition, you should be able to interpret and modify the break-even chart when required.

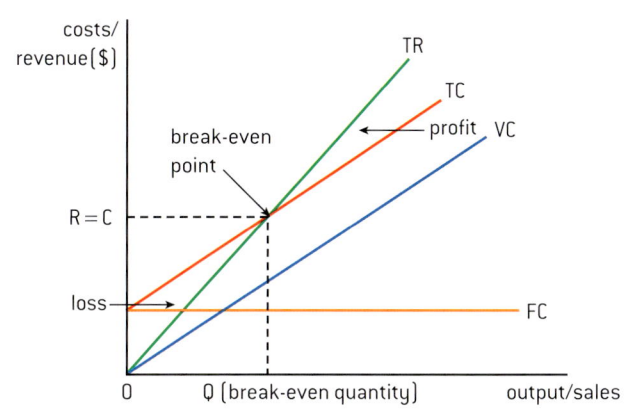

Figure 5.5.1 A break-even chart

Simple linear regression (HL only)

Simple linear regression is a statistical method that shows the relationship between two quantitative variables (x on the horizontal X-axis, and y on the vertical Y-axis) using a straight line. The algebraic relationship is as follows: $y = a + bx$.

Simple linear regression is one of the key notions in break-even analysis.

1. In graphical representations of break-even analysis, where do we see simple linear regression?
2. What are the limitations of simple linear regression for break-even analysis?

5 Operations management

> **Key term**
>
> **Margin of safety**
>
> the output amount that exceeds the break-even quantity

Margin of safety

The difference between the break-even level of output and the actual (current) level of output is known as the margin of safety (or safety margin). It is the range of output over which profit is made. The greater the difference between the break-even quantity and the sales levels, the greater the margin of safety, and so the more profit the firm makes (see Figure 5.5.2).

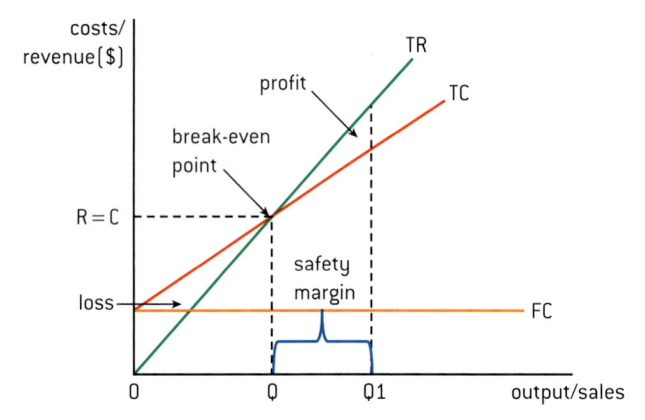

Figure 5.5.2 A break-even chart with margin of safety

$$\text{margin of safety} = \text{current output} - \text{break-even output}$$

For example, if the break-even quantity is 2,500 units and actual output is 4,000 units, then the margin of safety is 1,500 units or 60% above the break-even quantity. As a positive value, this is a favourable position for a firm.

However, a firm producing below the break-even point is making a loss and has a negative margin of safety. For example, if the break-even quantity is 2,500 units and the current output is 1,800 units then the margin of safety will be −700 units. The negative sign denotes that the current output level is below the break-even level.

Calculating break-even quantity

The break-even quantity can be calculated in two ways: using the "contribution per unit" method and using the "total costs = total revenue" method. Both methods give the same result, which can also be checked graphically.

1. Using the "contribution per unit" method

The break-even quantity can be calculated with the following formula:

$$\text{break even quantity} = \frac{\text{fixed costs}}{\text{contribution per unit}}$$

For example, a shirt retailer incurs fixed costs amounting to $3,000 a month. The variable cost per shirt is $12 and the selling price for each shirt is $22. Using the above formula:

$$\text{break even quantity} = \frac{\$3,000}{(\$22 - \$12)} = 300 \text{ shirts}$$

2. Using the "total costs = total revenue" method

The **total revenue** (TR) is the total amount of money a firm receives from its sales (see Chapter 3.3). It is calculated by multiplying the price per unit by the number of units sold:

> **total revenue = price per unit × quantity sold**

This is abbreviated as TR = P × Q where TR is total revenue, P is price per unit and Q is the quantity sold.

The **total costs** (TC) is the addition of the total fixed costs (TFC) and the total variable costs (TVC), where TVC is variable cost per unit (VC) × Q:

> **total costs (TC) = total fixed costs (TFC) + total variable costs (TVC)**

Using the above example of the shirt retailer, the break-even quantity can be calculated like this:

total revenue (TR) = total costs (TC)

P × Q = TFC + TVC

22 × Q = 3,000 + (12 × Q)

(22 × Q) - (12 × Q) = 3,000

10 × Q = 3,000

Q = 300 shirts

Both methods give a break-even quantity of 300 shirts (ie the retailer needs to sell 300 shirts in order to break even).

Profit or loss

The break-even chart showed that the sales that exceed the break-even quantity generate profit for a business, whereas the sales that are below the break-even quantity lead to losses.

Profit can be calculated in two ways.

Profit can be calculated using total contribution, as seen above:

> **profit = total contribution − total fixed costs**

Profit can also be calculated using the following formula:

> **profit = total revenue (TR) − total costs (TC)**

If the shirt retailer sells 1,000 shirts a month, the profit per month is calculated as follows:

profit = TR - TC

profit = [P × Q] - [TFC + TVC]
     = [22 × 1,000] - [3,000 + (12 × 1,000)]
     = $22,000 - $15,000
     = $7,000

5 Operations management

The shirt retailer will therefore make a profit of $7,000 if they sell 1,000 shirts a month.

What would be the profit or loss if in another month only 200 shirts are sold?

Target profit

Target profit output

The break-even chart can be used to determine the level of output needed to earn a given level of profit. Output found this way is known as the **target profit output**, and the expected profit is known as the **target profit**. As shown in Figure 5.5.3, to reach a target profit of $1,500 ($9,600 − $8,100) the bicycle producer will need to sell 80 bicycles.

> **Key term**
>
> **Target profit output**
>
> the level of output that is needed to earn a specified amount of profit

The producer needs to sell 80 bicycles to reach the target profit

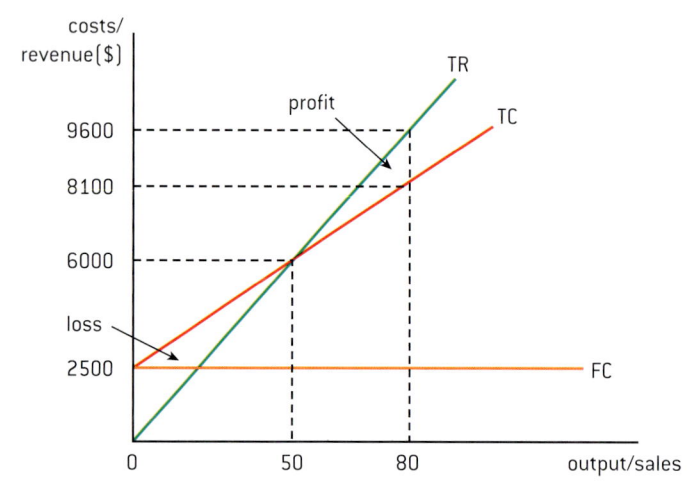

Figure 5.5.3 The break-even chart of a bicycle producer

An alternative method of getting target profit output is by using the following formula, which is based on the break-even formula:

$$\text{target profit output} = \frac{\text{fixed costs} + \text{target profit}}{\text{contribution per unit}}$$

Using the information for the bicycle producer, where fixed costs amount to $2,500, variable cost per unit is $70, price per bicycle is $120, and the target profit is $1,500, the target profit output can be calculated as follows:

$$\text{target profit output} = \frac{2{,}500 + 1{,}500}{120 - 70} = \frac{4{,}000}{50} = 80 \text{ bicycles}$$

The result obtained using the calculation method confirms what was obtained using the break-even chart method.

The above formula can also be used in calculating target profit and target price.

Calculating target profit

Assuming that the bicycle producer's fixed costs remain at $2,500, contribution per unit is $50 and the target profit output is now 100 bicycles, what is the target profit?

This is found as follows, using the target profit output formula:

$$\frac{\$2,500 + \text{target profit}}{\$50} = 100$$

$$\$2,500 + \text{target profit} = 100 \times \$50$$

$$\text{target profit} = \$5,000 - \$2,500$$

$$\text{target profit} = \$2,500$$

Calculating target price

Target price can also be calculated using the same approach. If the fixed costs are $2,500, the variable cost per bicycle is $50, the target profit is $6,500 and the target profit output is 200 bicycles, the target price can be calculated as follows:

$$200 = \frac{\$2,500 + \$6,500}{\text{target price} - \$50}$$

$$200 (\text{target price} - \$50) = \$9,000$$

$$200 (\text{target price}) - \$10,000 = \$9,000$$

$$\text{target price} = \frac{\$19,000}{200} = \$95 \text{ per bicycle}$$

Therefore to reach a profit of $6,500 at a target output of 200 bicycles, the bicycle producer will need to sell each bicycle for $95.

Break-even revenue

The break-even revenue can be determined using a break-even chart, as seen in Figure 5.5.3, which shows a break-even quantity of 50 bicycles, corresponding to $6,000. At this point, the total revenue equals the total costs, ie it is the revenue required to cover both the fixed and variable costs in order for a firm to break even.

It can also be calculated using the following formula:

$$\text{break even revenue} = \frac{\text{fixed costs}}{\text{contribution per unit}} \times \text{price per unit}$$

Using the previous example of a bicycle producer, if the price per bicycle is $120, variable costs are $70 and fixed costs are $2,500, the formula can be applied as follows:

$$\text{break even revenue} = \frac{\$2,500}{50} \times \$120 = \$6,000$$

This calculation shows that the break-even revenue is $6,000 – the same result shown graphically in Figure 5.5.3.

> **Student workpoint 5.14**
>
> **Be a thinker**
>
> XYZ Ltd has the capacity to produce 180,000 units of its key product per month. The fixed costs amount to $600,000 per month, while the variable costs are $15 per unit. The selling price for each product is $20.
>
> 1. Calculate the:
>   a) monthly profits at maximum capacity
>   b) break-even quantity
>   c) break-even revenue
>
> 2. The company has a profit target of $250,000 per month. Calculate the:
>   a) output level needed to reach the target profit
>   b) price it will need to charge to achieve the profit target at a capacity of 150,000 units

Effects of changes in price or costs

The break-even chart can be a helpful decision-making tool as it can show the impact on break-even quantity, profit, and margin of safety that may result from changes in price or cost. The new position after the changes can then be compared with the previous position.

Changes in price

Figure 5.5.4 shows the effect of an increase in price. This leads to a shift of the total revenue line from TR_1 to TR_2. This indicates that the sales revenue has increased at all levels of output. The firm will also break even at a lower level of output; as a consequence, there will be higher profits at every output level. This also leads to an increase in the firm's margin of safety.

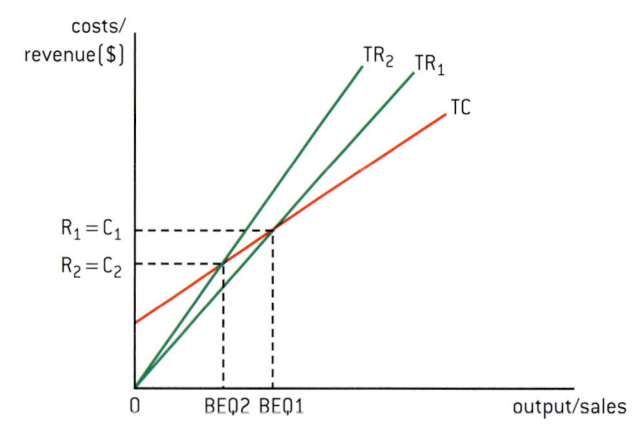

Figure 5.5.4 Break-even chart showing an increase in price

Changes in costs

Increase in fixed costs

Figure 5.5.5 shows the effect of an increase in fixed costs (FC_1 to FC_2), leading to an upward parallel shift of the total cost line from TC_1 to TC_2. An increase in fixed costs leads to an increase in total costs by the same amount at every level of output. Break-even quantity also increases and therefore profit decreases at all levels of output. This also decreases the margin of safety.

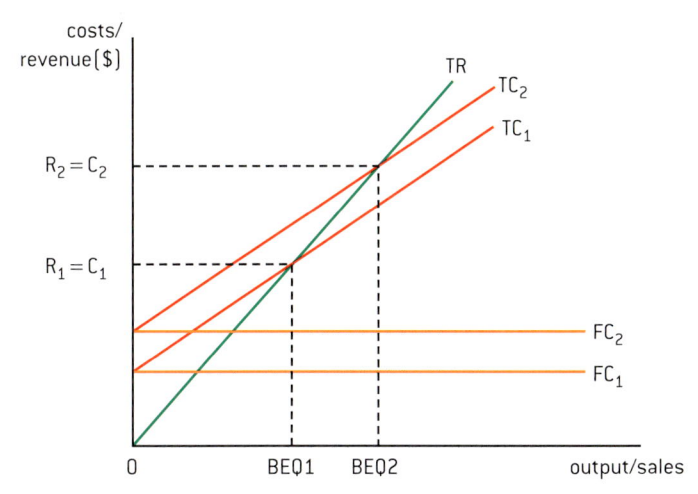

Figure 5.5.5 Break-even chart showing an increase in fixed costs

Increase in variable costs

Figure 5.5.6 shows the effect of an increase in variable costs. Increases in variable costs increase the gradient of the total cost line. This is shown by the shift of the total cost line from TC_1 to TC_2. This leads to a rise in the break-even quantity and reduces the margin of safety.

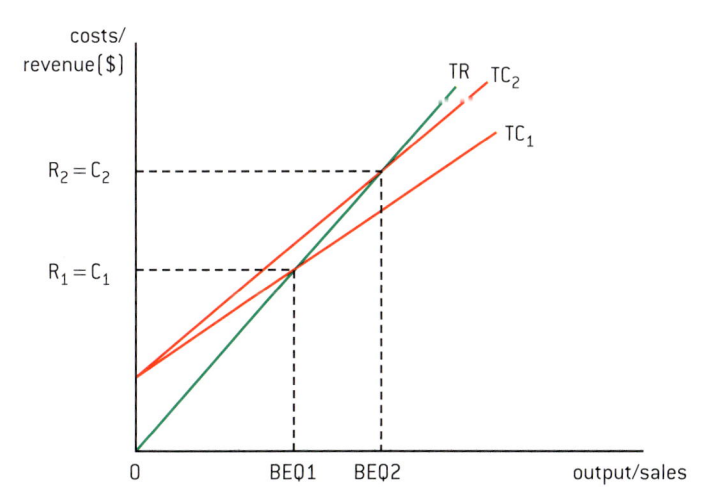

Figure 5.5.6 Break-even chart showing an increase in variable costs

5 Operations management

Student workpoint 5.15

Be a thinker

A chocolate business is considering which of the following three prices to charge its customers per chocolate:

A $1.50 **B** $2.00 **C** $2.50

The following information is useful in its decision-making:

- Fixed costs: $100,000
- Variable cost per chocolate: $1
- Current output: 300,000 chocolates

1. For each price, calculate:
   a) the break-even quantity
   b) the margin of safety
   c) the profit or loss
   d) break-even quantity as a percentage of the current output

2. If the variable costs per chocolate increase to $1.20, recalculate parts (a) to (d) above.

3. Comment on your observations from questions 1 and 2.

Student workpoint 5.16

Be knowledgeable

JTS Ltd produces clocks and sells them to a number of countries globally. The following monthly information is provided:

- Maximum capacity: 200,000 clocks
- Current output and sales: 160,000 clocks
- Selling price: $12
- Fixed costs: $900,000
- Variable cost: $4 per clock

The management propose that a possible reduction in price per unit to $10 would lead to an increase in sales and help them reach their maximum capacity.

1. Construct a break-even chart using the original price and current output level.

2. Use the chart to determine:
   a) the break-even point
   b) the margin of safety
   c) the profit at current output

   Use the calculation method to check your answers.

3. Construct a second break-even chart to show the situation after the price reduction. Repeat the tasks in question 2 above using the new chart.

4. Recommend which of the proposals JTS Ltd should pursue.

Benefits and limitations of break-even analysis

Benefits

- Break-even charts help visualise a firm's profit or loss at various levels of sales.
- By using break-even charts, a manager can determine the margin of safety, break-even quantity, and break-even revenue or cost.
- Formulae and calculations can be used to confirm the break-even charts and to check the results.
- Changes in prices and costs and their impact on profit or loss, the break-even point, and the margin of safety can be compared by using the charts or by calculation.
- Break-even analysis can be used as a strategic decision-making tool to decide on key investment projects, or whether a business should relocate or merge with another one.

Limitations

- Break-even analysis assumes that all the units produced are sold, with no stocks built up or held. In reality, businesses often hold stocks to cater for sudden changes in demand. Stocks may also build up because goods cannot be sold.
- Break-even analysis assumes that all costs and revenue are linear, ie represented by straight lines. This is not always the case as, for example, price reductions or discounts will influence the slope of the revenue line. Similarly, the slope of the variable cost line would change if workers are paid overtime in an effort to increase output. This change will then influence the slope of the total cost line.
- Fixed costs may change at different levels of activity. It would be preferable to represent these fixed costs as a "stepped" line. For example, in order to increase output, a firm may need to double its capacity. This may lead to sharp rises in fixed costs, thereby complicating break-even analysis.
- Semi-variable costs are not usually represented on simple break-even charts, for example if some workers receive a variable commission on top of their regular wages. If they are included, it makes the process more complex.
- A break-even chart may not be very useful in dynamic business environments with sudden changes in prices, costs, or technology.
- The accuracy and quality of the costs and revenue data used determine the effectiveness of break-even analysis. Unreliable or inaccurate data may influence the conclusions reached in the overall analysis, leading to wrong decisions being made.

> **TOK links**
>
> 1. "The most important figures that one needs for management are unknown or unknowable ... but successful management must nevertheless take account of them." (W. Edwards Deming) What does this statement imply for break-even analysis?
> 2. Is it always possible to calculate the break-even quantity both numerically and graphically? What is the difference?
> 3. With reference to break-even analysis and other areas of knowledge, do you think that the results obtained from quantitative methods always outweigh qualitative ones?

5 Operations management

Revision checklist

- ✓ Contribution per unit is the difference between the selling price per unit and the variable cost per unit, whereas total contribution is the difference between the total revenue and the total variable cost.

- ✓ Profit can be obtained by calculating the difference between the total contribution and the total fixed cost, or by subtracting the total costs from the total revenue.

- ✓ A break-even chart is a graphical method that measures the value of a firm's costs and revenues against a given level of output. It helps to identify the break-even point.

- ✓ Margin of safety measures the difference between the break-even level of output and the actual (current) level of output.

- ✓ Break-even quantity can be calculated by dividing the total fixed costs by the contribution per unit.

- ✓ Target profit output formula is $\dfrac{\text{fixed costs} + \text{target profit}}{\text{contribution per unit}}$

- ✓ Break-even revenue formula is $\dfrac{\text{fixed costs}}{\text{contribution per unit}} \times \text{price per unit}$

Practice question

To answer the question below effectively, see Unit 6 pages 398–402.

Dan Electro

Dan Bowen is a sole trader who sells tablet computers directly to consumers. He owns an online business and all sales are processed electronically under the business name *Dan Electro*. The office, storage place and call centre are located together in an expensive and desirable city centre location.

Dan started the business three years ago by borrowing a considerable amount of money from a bank. He used his residential property as collateral for the loan, which means that it was offered to the lender (the bank) as security in case the loan repayments were not made.

The tablets are bought and shipped from a reputable and reliable overseas supplier who charges a high price for good-quality tablets and prompt transportation. Dan has to pay in advance for the tablets. *Dan Electro's* customers are very loyal and see their purchases as good value for money. Repeat purchases comprise a large percentage of *Dan Electro's* sales. Some customers have even indicated that they would pay a higher price for the tablets because of their quality and the good service he provides.

Dan is now worried about the forecast rise in interest rates, inflation and an increase in online competition. *Dan Electro* may face some cash flow difficulties in the coming years. He is considering various strategies in order to prevent these potential cash flow difficulties.

5.5 Break-even analysis

Financial information for 2020 (all figures in US$)			
Fixed costs per year			
Rent	Marketing	Administration	Interest payments
20,000	4,000	5,000	1,000
Variable costs per tablet			
Tablet	Transportation	Direct labour	Price per tablet
135	45	20	250

Dan is expecting to sell 700 tablets in 2020.

a) Define the term *variable costs*. [2 marks]

b) State **two** advantages for Dan of operating as a sole trader. [2 marks]

c) (i) Construct a fully labelled break-even chart for *Dan Electro* for 2020. [4 marks]

    (ii) Calculate the margin of safety. [1 mark]

    (iii) Calculate the projected profit at 700 tablets (show all your working). [2 marks]

d) Calculate the number of tablets *Dan Electro* must sell in order to double the projected profit (show all your working). [2 marks]

e) Calculate the price per tablet that needs to be charged (at expected sales of 700 tablets) in order to double the projected profit (show all your working). [2 marks]

f) Explain **two** possible limitations of the break-even model as a decision tool for *Dan Electro*. [4 marks]

g) Examine **two** possible strategies for *Dan Electro* to prevent cash flow difficulties. [6 marks]

Source: Adapted from IB examination paper, November 2010

5.6 Production planning (HL only)

> **By the end of this chapter, you should be able to:**
> → Explain the **supply chain process**, both locally and globally
> → Compare and contrast **just-in-time** (JIT) and **just-in-case** (JIC) methods of stock control
> → Interpret a **stock control chart** (especially the buffer stock, reorder level, reorder quantity, and lead time)
> → Calculate and interpret the following:
> - capacity utilization rate
> - defect rate
> - productivity rate
> - labour productivity
> - capital productivity
> - degree of operating leverage
> - cost to buy (CTB) and cost to make (CTM)

The supply chain process (HL only)

The supply chain refers to the wide system of connected organizations (for example suppliers), information (such as orders), resources (for example raw materials), and activities (such as manufacturing, storage and transport) needed to produce goods and deliver them to their end customers.

This involves two types of flows that must be managed:

1. The flow from raw materials to finished product that eventually reaches the end customer, via different stages of transformation (for example, from the oranges on trees to the orange juice on the consumer's kitchen table).

2. The flow of information (for example, a factory ordering oranges and specific packages to protect the juice from spoilage and deterioration during distribution and storage).

So the supply chain has two dimensions:

1. **Logistics:** the "hardware" of the supply chain, for example the trucks transporting the oranges to the factory or the cartons of juice from the warehouse.

2. **Information and communication:** the "software" of the supply chain, as illustrated by the databases and spreadsheets used by the administrative staff of the factory.

> **Key term**
>
> **Supply chain**
>
> the system of connected organizations, information, resources, and activities that a business needs to produce goods or provide services to its customers

5.6 Production planning (HL only)

Two flows of the supply chain

Supply chains can be local or global.

A **local supply chain** is characterized by the short distance between producers and consumers. Farmers' market are a typical example: they feature agricultural produce that is grown, bought and consumed locally.

This has many advantages. For example, the food is usually fresher and may have more nutritional quality – you may be eating an orange that was still on the tree 24 hours ago. A local supply chain also involves less transport, less pollution, fewer transactions, and it may benefit the local community more. In many ways, it is more sustainable than the global supply chain.

A **global supply chain** involves international trade, ie exports and imports. For example, you may be buying and eating fruit that was harvested days or even weeks ago on another continent, which was then packaged, stored and transported thousands of miles. In many ways, this is less sustainable than a short supply chain. However, consumer demand means that it can be very profitable to trade internationally. From an economics viewpoint, exports and imports are essential because not every country produces every type of good.

Supply chains are often presented through networks or flowcharts linking the organizations involved, as illustrated by Figure 5.6.1 where some distribution channels have also been included (a wholesaler and a retailer, as studied in Chapter 4.5).

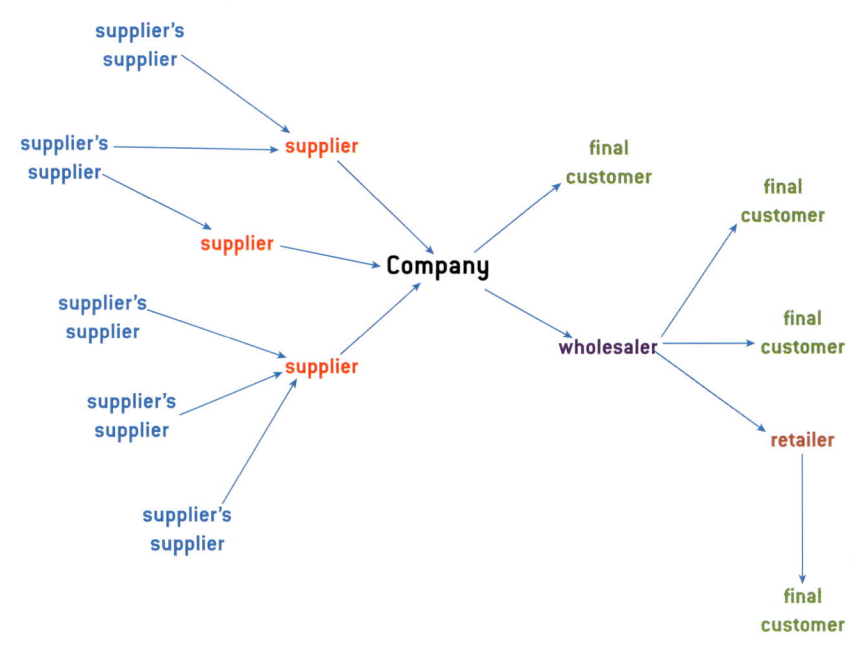

Figure 5.6.1 Simplified representation of networks and relationships in a supply chain

5 Operations management

Figure 5.6.1 is a simplified representation of the complexity of networks and relationships involved. For example, if a supplier is not able to deliver its product, it may block the entire chain. The final customer may be left waiting for the spare part of a good (such as the door seal to repair a washing machine), and becoming increasingly dissatisfied with the manufacturer of the washing machine. Yet the responsibility lies elsewhere, as the manufacturer might well be dependent on its own supplier, or its supplier's supplier.

When considering the whole supply chain process, stock control becomes particularly important. When businesses adopt a just-in-time (JIT) method of stock control, they do not hold much stock, which may create problems in the supply chain.

Just-in-time (JIT) and just-in-case (JIC) (HL only)

Chapter 5.3 introduced JIT as a more modern method of stock control in the perspective of lean production, and its more traditional counterpart JIC.

There are arguments in favour of each method, but the current trend is towards JIT methods. Table 5.6.1 shows the main differences between JIT and JIC.

Table 5.6.1 The main differences between JIT and JIC

JIT	JIC
Stock is only brought in from suppliers as and when required. The aim is to hold low (even zero) levels of stock.	Stock is brought in and stored with a reserve (the buffer stock) in case it is needed.
JIT is beneficial for the working capital – the business can use its money for its day-to-day activities.	JIC reduces pressure on the cash flow.
JIT reduces costs (storage and wastage).	JIC reduces costs (by buying in bulk: economies of scale).
JIT reduces the chance of holding stock that cannot be sold (eg obsolescent stock).	JIC means it is possible to meet sudden changes in demand.
JIT means less chance of damaged or ruined stock.	JIC provides spare parts.
JIT creates more space for alternative production plans.	JIC means that all stock is stored ready to use. There is no delivery issue and no waiting time for customers.
JIT creates a closer relationship with suppliers (they may need to run JIT too).	JIC has the advantage that suppliers will not charge a premium price.

Stock control (HL only)

The question of holding stock raises two issues in terms of cost:

- Holding too much stock is costly (especially in relation to storage and also possible damage).
- Not holding enough stock can be costly too (for example an emergency delivery may be more expensive, or customers may decide to go elsewhere, which means lost orders).

> **Key terms**
>
> **JIC ("just-in-case")**
> the traditional method of stock control, which involves holding reserves of both raw materials and finished products in case of a sudden increase in demand (or a problem in the supply chain)
>
> **JIT ("just-in-time")**
> a modern method of stock control, which involves avoiding holding stock by being able to get supplies only when necessary and to produce just when ordered
>
> **Buffer stock**
> the minimum amount of stock that should be held (to ensure that production is still possible and customers' orders can still be fulfilled)
>
> **Reorder level**
> the level at which stock has to be reordered (a form of trigger or signal)
>
> **Reorder quantity**
> the amount of stock that is reordered
>
> **Lead time**
> the amount of time it takes between ordering new stock and receiving it

5.6 Production planning (HL only)

We can combine these two sets of costs in Figure 5.6.2.

- **Cost of holding stock** – if we do not have any stock, there is no cost, but then the cost rises as we store more and more units.

- **Cost of stock out** – if we have a small amount of stock, then the cost of having a sudden surge in demand could be substantial, but this will reduce as more stock is ordered and bought in.

- **Total cost** – by combining the two sets of costs, we can see the minimum point of the total cost. This is called the "economic order quantity" (EOQ); it is the amount that should be ordered for a given time period. The EOQ is one of the oldest calculations in the area of operations management and stock control.

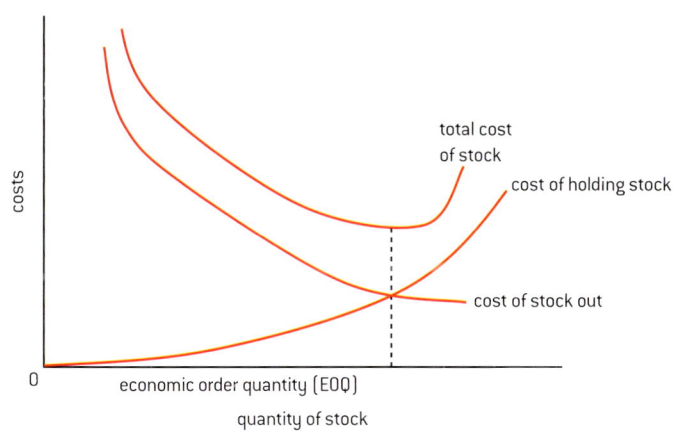

Figure 5.6.2 Costs of holding stock and of stock out

The following seven elements of stock control are important:

- **The initial order:** the first amount of stock delivered.

- **The usage pattern:** how much stock is used over a given time period. Is usage pattern regular or not? Are there some predictable highs and lows (for example for Christmas, Chinese New Year, or school holidays)? In general, the stock is depleted over time and so is shown by a line with a negative slope.

- **The maximum stock level:** the maximum amount of stock held at any one time.

- **The minimum stock level:** the amount of stock that is kept back as a reserve, also called the **buffer stock**. The amount of stock should never go lower than this level (otherwise production of finished goods may not be possible, and customer orders cannot be fulfilled).

- **The reorder level:** the level at which stock has to be reordered (this is always a bit higher than the minimum stock level) as a type of trigger.

- **The reorder quantity:** the amount of stock that is ordered.

- **The lead time:** the amount of time it takes between ordering new stock and receiving it.

A typical stock control diagram will look like Figure 5.6.3.

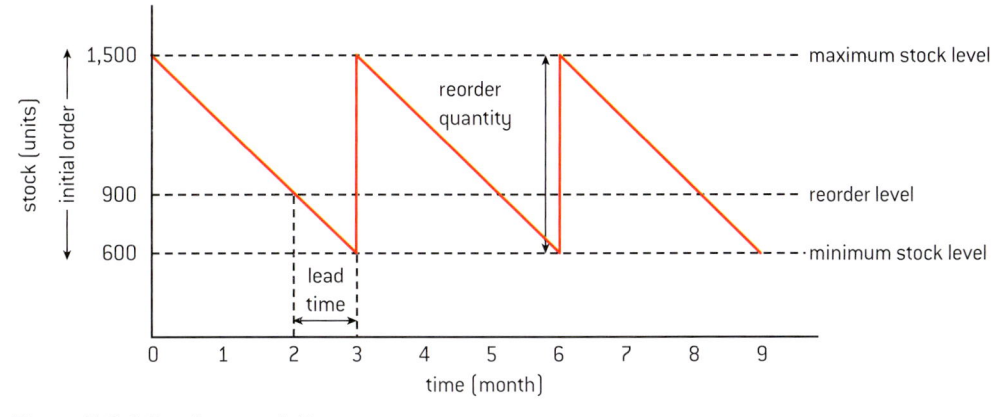

Figure 5.6.3 Stock control diagram

Imagine that the example shown in Figure 5.6.3 is a company selling smartphones online:

- The company may always want to keep a reserve of 600 smartphones (minimum stock) just in case.
- The manager has calculated that, assuming no unforeseen changes in demand, she will sell 900 phones over a three-month period.
- After two months, she knows that stock will go down to 900 phones, which is her reorder level, when she decides to arrange for a new delivery of phones to be made from the suppliers.
- It takes one month for that reorder quantity of 900 phones to arrive (lead time); when they arrive, the whole cycle continues.

This simple example assumes no unforeseen changes in demand, but usage patterns may be forecast to take account of seasonal differences and occasional surges in demand. Nowadays, many businesses have software to make these calculations and establish the optimum reorder level and reorder quantity, but the basic diagram remains as shown in Figure 5.6.3.

Optimal stock levels

In order to calculate the optimal level of stock, a business must take several factors into account:

- **The market** – is it growing? Are there new competitors? Is market share likely to shrink?
- **The final product** – what type of product is it? Is it a cheap, single-use, high-volume product, or is it the opposite? Is it a complex product requiring many individual components? Does its production depend on many suppliers?
- **The stock** – is it perishable? Is it likely to be out of date? How big is it? Will it need much storage space?
- **The infrastructure** – is it reliable, or is there a need to stockpile? Could the weather or other factors influence the ability of suppliers to meet demand?
- **Finance** – does the business have the required money at the right time? What possibilities for credit do the suppliers allow? Could there be significant savings from buying in bulk (economies of scale)?
- **Human resources** – what are the workforce planning implications if the business decides to hold more stock or less stock?

Stock control is particularly important in retail food stores that sell perishable items

Using the EOQ and stock control charts and diagrams, businesses may get some idea of the correct amount of stock to order and when, although overall it is difficult to know precisely. Businesses are aware that many factors can change, which creates more pressure and some uncertainty, depending on the stock control model that they are using.

5.6 Production planning (HL only)

Critical path analysis (HL only)

Critical path analysis (also called the critical path method) is a tool used for project management. Its aim is to identify the minimum duration of a project, when different stages may overlap. In the expression "critical path", the word "critical" does not refer to discussing or arguing (unlike the expression "critical thinking"): it refers to the sequence of tasks that would enable the whole project to be completed in the shortest possible time.

A simple network diagram could look like this:

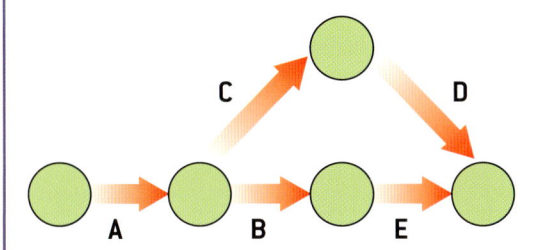

Each stage could have the following duration:

A: 1 week, B: 2 weeks, C: 1 week, D: 2 weeks, E: 2 weeks.

The critical path is A–B–E, as the project needs a minimum of five weeks to be completed.

1. What is the duration of the other path (A–C–D)? Why isn't it the critical path?
2. If C is delayed by one week, does this cause any problem for the overall project? Why/why not?

Capacity utilization rate (HL only)

Operations managers often need to know how efficient their facility is. Is it used to its maximum capacity? For example, a hotel manager may want to know what the occupancy rate of the hotel's rooms is; a factory manager may want to know how often a machine breakdown affects the work done; a school principal may want to know whether there is capacity for more children on the premises.

In theory, it would be possible for a hotel to be full all year round, or a factory to work at full capacity (24 hours a day, 365 days a year), or a school to house a day school and a night school in the same buildings. In reality, though, there will be times when it is neither desirable nor suitable. For example, the hotel may need some quiet time to refurbish the rooms, the factory may need time to upgrade the machines, and the school may need to close on certain holidays when no students would be willing to attend. These simple examples show that it is usually impossible to achieve 100% capacity utilization, though businesses will often aim to get as close as possible to this figure.

Capacity utilization can be calculated using the following equation:

$$\text{capacity utlization rate} = \frac{\text{actual output}}{\text{productive capacity}} \times 100$$

For example, if a hotel has 100 beds (the maximum capacity), and on average 80 are filled (the actual output), the capacity utilization rate is 80%. Similarly, a factory might be able to produce a maximum of 100,000 pairs of shoes in a year, but it only has orders for 40,000. Its capacity utilization rate is 40%. Finally, a school with sufficient space for 3,000 students but with only 2,900 students has a capacity utilization rate of 96.6%.

In sectors where profit margins are low, such as budget aviation or fast-food catering, businesses should aim for a high capacity utilization rate. These businesses cannot afford to lose any opportunity to sell their products and so will need to market them accordingly. In most cases a higher capacity utilization rate is better, though this is not always the case. For example, business-class travel or five-star restaurants will not always need and seek high-volume sales and maximum capacity utilization rates.

Defect rate (HL only)

A defect is a problem or fault in one item gained during its production, such as stains on a new shirt, a protruding nail on a frame, or scratches on a mirror. These items are said to be defective: they cannot be sold and are usually discarded. The defect rate is the percentage of output (units) that fail to meet set quality standards. It is calculated using the following equation:

$$\text{defect rate} = \frac{\text{number of defective units}}{\text{total output}} \times 100$$

The lower the defect rate, the better. The defect rate is an indicator of quality: it shows the operations manager where quality should be monitored and improved, for example to go from a 2% defect rate to a 1% defect rate. One of the principles of lean production is to reduce the defect rate as much to possible, ideally bringing it to zero (see Chapter 5.3).

Productivity rate (HL only)

The productivity rate is another ratio that a manager may be interested in. It is a measure of the efficiency of production. In Chapter 5.1, Figure 5.1.1 showed the input–output model. The productivity rate is the ratio of output to input in production; it refers to the added value of the business. It can be calculated using the following equation:

$$\text{productivity rate} = \frac{\text{total output}}{\text{total input}} \times 100$$

On its own, the productivity rate is very crude; it needs to be contextualized, particularly in connection to the industry in which a business operates, ideally by establishing comparisons and benchmarks with competitors. For example, knowing that a factory's productivity rate is 65% would not help an operations manager much: is this low, or is this high? Only when comparing it with the industry averages can the operations manager make a judgment and possibly take action.

- If the productivity rate is much lower than the industry average, the manager should take remedial action; adopting a lean strategy could help cut down on waste and increase efficiency. Several factors and variables should be considered. Maybe the input is too high, with too many raw materials held in stock that lose value, cannot be used, and are eventually discarded. Maybe the output is too low because of a high defect rate.

- If the productivity rate is higher than the industry average, the manager will be pleased with the efficiency of the company's operations. Nonetheless, the manager may still examine how the plant could be even more productive, using its resources (raw materials, human resources, machines, energy) in a more efficient and sustainable way.

Quartiles

In statistics, a quartile divides the number of data points into four parts (four quarters) of equal size:

- The first quartile corresponds to the lowest 25% of numbers
- The second quartile corresponds to the numbers between 25.1% and 50% (ie up to the median)
- The third quartile corresponds to the numbers between 50.1% to 75%
- The fourth quartile corresponds to the highest 25% of numbers

To calculate each quarter, it is only necessary to know the total number (N) and to do some simple multiplications:

- Lower quartile $(Q1) = (N + 1) \times 0.25$
- Middle quartile $(Q2) = (N + 1) \times 0.5$ (Q2 is the median)
- Upper quartile $(Q3) = (N + 1) \times 0.75$

This can be represented as follows:

0%	25%	50%	75%	100%
1st quartile	2nd quartile	3nd quartile	4th quartile	
	Q1	Q2	Q3	

When a company states that it wants to reach top quartile performance, it means that it wants to be in the top 25% when considering all of its competitors.

1. Company A has a productivity rate of 74%. In its sector, Q1 is 53%, Q2 is 68%, Q3 is 72%. How would you describe the productivity rate of company A, compared to its competitors?

2. Company B has a productivity rate of 74%. In its sector, Q1 is 63%, Q2 is 75%, Q3 is 85%. How would you describe the productivity rate of company B, compared to its competitors?

3. Why is it particularly important to take quartiles into account when examining rates such as the capacity utilization rate, productivity rate and defect rate?

Labour productivity (HL only)

Labour productivity measures the efficiency of a worker. It represents the value of the output produced by a worker per unit of time (usually per hour). It can help compare the efficiency of different workers and identify if one is under-performing compared to the average.

For example, if in a dispatch warehouse the average productivity by worker is 15 boxes per hour but one worker only manages 12 boxes per hour, this worker is less efficient than the others.

Labour productivity can be calculated using the following equation (where in this case, labour productivity is expressed in units per hour):

$$\text{labour productivity} = \frac{\text{total output}}{\text{total hours worked}}$$

Labour productivity can be calculated for a single worker, for a group of workers, for the entire workforce of a company, or even for the whole country to help make international comparisons as part of macroeconomic analysis.

> **Assessment advice** ✓
>
> Remember to include the unit, or the percentage sign, in your answer when calculating productivity rates. You can lose a mark if you forget, even if your calculation is correct!

Capital productivity (HL only)

Capital productivity measures the efficiency of the company's capital, especially its working capital. The working capital is calculated using financial information from the balance sheet, using the following formula:

$$\text{working capital} = \text{current assets} - \text{current liabilities}$$

The productivity of the working capital can then be calculated as follows:

$$\text{working capital productivity} = \frac{\text{sales revenue}}{\text{working capital}}$$

Like other rates, this needs to be contextualized, particularly in connection to the industry in which a business operates, for example by establishing comparisons and benchmarks with competitors, or by analysing trends over a period of time.

Operating leverage (HL only)

Operating leverage measures how total costs are made up of fixed costs and variable costs in an effort to calculate how well a company uses its fixed costs to generate profits. It uses the same financial data as break-even analysis (see Chapter 5.5) as it is based on the relationship between quantity, price and variable cost per unit to fixed costs.

It can be simply described as the ratio of fixed costs to variable costs, and can be calculated using the following formula:

$$\text{operating leverage} = \frac{\text{quantity} \times (\text{price} - \text{variable cost per unit})}{\text{quantity} \times (\text{price} - \text{variable cost per unit}) - \text{fixed costs}}$$

Companies with a high operating leverage must cover a large amount of fixed costs each month, no matter how many units they sell. However, a high operating leverage also means that an incremental increase in sales will result in much more revenue. A business with a low operating leverage may have high costs that vary directly with its sales, but it may have lower fixed costs to cover each month.

Cost to buy (CTB) and cost to make (CTM) (HL only)

One business decision is whether to buy or to make.

In Chapter 5.4 we discussed the decision to outsource (or even offshore) or not. A key factor, as always in business decisions, is costs: it may be cheaper for a business to buy a product made elsewhere, by specialists, rather than making it directly (and this applies to services too). The decision can be supported by using the costs and revenues formulae in Chapter 3.3 to create cost to buy (CTB) and cost to make (CTM) equations:

$$CTB = P \times Q$$
$$CTM = FC + (VC \times Q)$$

Where P = price, Q = quantity, FC = fixed costs, VC = variable costs.

For example, imagine that a small international school in South-East Asia has to decide whether to subcontract the transport of students by bus, or to provide the service itself. If the school requires 20 buses and a company called School Run charges $10,000 per bus for the year, according to the formula CTB = P × Q, this service would cost the school:

$$20 \times \$10,000 = \$200,000$$

If, however, the school decides to buy the 20 buses from Dodgy Dealers Inc for $100,000 but faces variable costs of $10,000 per bus for fuel and the drivers' wages over the year, then the cost to make the service using the equation CTM = FC + (VC × Q) would be:

$$\$100,000 + (\$10,000 \times 20) = \$300,000$$

In this case CTB < CTM, so the school should "buy" (outsource).

This simple example ignores some of the factors that may have an impact on the supply chain. For example, how reliable is the company School Run? How reliable are the buses from Dodgy Dealers? What are the implications of the school employing drivers as opposed to someone else doing so? Are there some legal issues involved? When deciding what action to take, a business would also take qualitative factors such as these into account.

In some countries, transport for school children is organized by the local authorities. In other cases, some schools organize it themselves; they may decide to outsource the service to a specialist bus company.

5 Operations management

Gantt chart (HL only)

A Gantt chart is a tool used to plan a project. It shows the various tasks (which may overlap), when they are scheduled, and the deadlines and milestones.

Here is an example of a Gantt chart for a music producer who wants to plan the production of a new CD:

	Tasks	Jan	Feb	Mar	Apr	May	Jun	Jul	Aug	Sep	Oct	Nov	Dec
1	Band writes the music for 10 songs	■	■										
2	Band writes the lyrics for 10 songs		■	■									
3	Initial recording by the band				■								
4	Full production by the band and other musicians					■	■	■					
5	Creation and design of the cover artwork				■	■							
6	Production of the completed CDs								■				
7	Production of the online version								■				
8	Promotion of individual songs on radio shows								■	■			
9	Promotion by interviews and press releases					■	■		■				
10	Promotion of the music through concerts									■			

1. Can you draw a Gantt chart for your IA?
2. Can you draw a Gantt chart for another project of yours, outside school?

TOK links

1. Is it possible to draw an exhaustive supply chain diagram?
2. In stock control, is the reorder level objective or subjective?
3. Are rates such as capital productivity and labour productivity always open to interpretation?

Revision checklist

✓ The supply chain is the system of connected organizations, information, resources and activities that allow a business to fulfill its operations. It includes suppliers, distributors and customers.

✓ Just-in-case (JIC) is a traditional method of stock control which involves holding a reserve (stock) of raw materials and finished products in case of a sudden increase in demand.

✓ Just-in-time (JIT) is a modern method of stock control which involves getting supplies only when necessary and producing only when an order is made.

✓ The capacity utilization rate is calculated by (actual output/productive capacity) × 100.

✓ The productivity rate is calculated by (total output/total input) × 100.

5.6 Production planning (HL only)

Practice question

To answer the question below effectively, see Unit 6 pages 398–402.

Gisela Fair Coffee (GFC)

Gisela is about to open a small coffee shop, *Gisela Fair Coffee (GFC)*, in the district of Buenos Aires where she lives. On opening day, *GFC* will have a stock level of 500kg of coffee beans. Gisela estimates that the coffee beans will be used at a constant rate for the first six months of operation.

She plans the following stock management figures for the coffee beans:

- Maximum stock level: 500kg
- Minimum stock level: 200kg
- Reorder quantity level: 350kg
- Reorder quantity 300kg
- Quantity used per month: 150kg
- Lead time for delivery of the coffee beans: 1 month.

a) Describe **one** factor that Gisela should take into account to calculate the optimal level of stock. [2 marks]

b) Using the information above, construct a fully labelled stock control chart for *GFC* for the first six months of operation. [4 marks]

c) A delivery of coffee beans was one month late, arriving on the last day of the seventh month rather than the last day of the sixth month. Using figures from the chart you constructed in part (b), explain the effects of:

  (i) the late delivery on *GFC*'s stock level [2 marks]

  (ii) the late arrival delivering **only** 75kg of coffee [2 marks]

5.7 Crisis management and contingency planning (HL only)

> **By the end of this chapter, you should be able to:**
> → Distinguish between **crisis management** and **contingency planning**
> → Explain the factors that ensure **effective crisis management**:
>   - transparency
>   - communication
>   - speed
>   - control
> → Comment on the **impact of contingency planning** for a given situation or organization:
>   - cost
>   - time
>   - risks
>   - safety

Key terms

Crisis management
the systematic steps and efforts by an organization to limit the damage from a sudden crisis

Contingency planning
an organization's attempts to put in place procedures to deal with a crisis, anticipating it through scenario planning, modelling and simulation

Crisis management (HL only)

When a major, unpredictable event occurs and threatens to harm an organization and its stakeholders, the organization faces a crisis. Crisis management refers to the systematic steps and efforts take by the organization to limit the damage from a sudden crisis. Crises may be triggered by:

- Human activity (such as the financial crises of 1929 and 2008).
- Industrial accidents (such as the Bhopal gas tragedy of 1984, the Chernobyl nuclear disaster in 1985 and the BP Gulf of Mexico disaster in 2010).
- Natural disasters (such as the Sichuan earthquake in China in 2008, the tsunami in north-eastern Japan in 2011, and the floods in Thailand in 2011).
- A combination of human, industrial and natural forces (such as the Covid-19 pandemic which began in 2019).

Crises can be global, regional or local. They may affect all countries, some regions or just a local area. On a small local scale, a crisis may be a sudden power cut (preventing the whole factory or someone's home office operating), a failure of the IT system of a company, the illness of a key

5.7 Crisis management and contingency planning (HL only)

member of staff (the only one who knows how to reprogram a machine), an accident on the premises, or a gas leak in a nearby building (with the obligation to evacuate, which means it is impossible to work on that day).

The outcomes of a crisis may be major (such as a plane crash with human casualties) or minor (such as a two-day delay in delivering a book ordered online). Any elements of the supply chain may be affected (a road block or some workers on strike may prevent the delivery of an essential component, thereby stopping the production flow). Crises are unpredictable, and managers must take immediate action to limit the damage for their stakeholders.

Four related factors affect crisis management:

- **Transparency** – stakeholders will want to be kept informed about what is happening. Staff, customers, and local residents will want to be sure, for example, that safety is the priority. Irrespective of its size and share of responsibility in the crisis, the business will need to be honest and tell the truth; this is part of its corporate social responsibility (CSR) and it is linked to ethical practices.

- **Communication** – senior managers will need to communicate in an objective way, despite the temptation to turn this into a media exercise in public relations (PR), with a possible bias and concerns for the reputation of the business rather than for the safety of all involved.

- **Speed** – managers will need to act promptly, both in their actions (for example in the factory or in the workplace) and in their communications (such as through a press conference or media release). This will be a particular challenge, as analysing the problem and evaluating possible solutions before implementing one may require more time than is available. A rushed decision will not always be the best one.

- **Control** – managers need to do their utmost to prevent further damage and keep the situation under control. Depending on the crisis and its nature, this may be more or less feasible. This is about minimizing further impacts, be they environmental, social, or economic.

Major crises like a fire have devastating consequences for any organization, which is why measures are usually in place to prevent such incidents, such as using flame-retardant materials and smoke detectors

Concept
CREATIVITY

When organizations have to react to a sudden crisis, they may need to be creative in their responses and decisions.

Find examples of recent situations of crisis management where organizations displayed creativity and were successful (or not!).

Case study: The Bhopal disaster (India)

The Bhopal gas tragedy is still regarded as one of the world's worst industrial disasters. It occurred on the night of 2 December 1984 at the Union Carbide India Limited (UCIL) pesticide plant in Bhopal (Madhya Pradesh, India).

Over half a million people were suddenly exposed to an escape of toxic gas. Thousands died of suffocation, and hundreds of thousands were injured. Although the exact cause of a gas leak is still disputed, corporate negligence is usually presented as a key factor: poorly maintained facilities, faulty equipment, an undertrained workforce, limited concerns about safety, and little awareness of the risks and dangers are all thought to have contributed.

To start managing the crisis, the factory owners immediately sent international medical experts to assist the medical facilities and began providing aid (including financial aid) to the victims. However, the contamination is ongoing, with long-term effects on the environment and on the health and well-being of the local population.

5 Operations management

Contingency planning (HL only)

Contingency planning refers to an organization's efforts to put in place procedures to deal with a crisis, anticipating it through scenario planning. It is about being prepared should the crisis occur for real. Although it is not possible to imagine all possible crises, the most likely ones (such as a fire or a strike) can be anticipated. Set procedures can be written and rehearsed (such as a fire drill with evacuation of the premises).

Contingency planning is comparable to a list of "what if...?" scenarios, with simulations and procedures in place. Four factors are particularly important for contingency planning:

- **Cost** – contingency planning may be costly, due to both the planning process itself and the need to train staff to deal with a wide range of events and scenarios, from IT failure to accidents at work to a terrorist attack. However, contingency planning is much less expensive than dealing with a crisis without any preparation (not to mention the lawsuits that could follow).

- **Time** – contingency planning may also be time-consuming, again both in terms of planning and training. For example, health and safety legislation may mean some members of staff have to be trained and retrained in first aid and emergency response.

- **Risks** – contingency planning will have to assess a range of possible risks (to the workers, to the machines, to the company, and to other stakeholders too, such as suppliers and customers). The degree and level of risks and hazards are also likely to change, so contingency planners will need to review their plans regularly.

- **Safety** – contingency planning hinges on the notion that safety must be the priority, which is why the number one aim of fire drills is to ensure that everyone is kept safe in the case of a real fire.

The key benefit of having people in a crisis management team who have prepared contingency plans is that the plans can be written when modelling a hypothetical crisis (as opposed to a real one). If a crisis occurs and there is no contingency plan in place, it is likely that decisions will be made under great stress and urgency. In this situation, there is a chance that the wrong decision will be made.

While members of the crisis management team will not be able to anticipate every crisis, the fact that they are a team and have a contingency plan means that they will, at least, be prepared. If the crisis that occurs is similar to one that has been simulated, it is more likely that the damage will be limited.

Revision checklist

✓ Crisis management is a direct response to a specific, unpredictable event. It needs to be well-communicated, controlled and prompt (although not rushed).

✓ Contingency planning refers to an organization's efforts to minimize the negative effects of potential crises.

✓ Contingency planners must take account of cost, time, risks and safety.

Student workpoint 5.17

Be a researcher

Read the abstract of the 2012 article by Floor Rink, Michelle K. Ryan and Janka I. Stoker called *Influence in Times of Crisis: How Social and Financial Resources Affect Men's and Women's Evaluations of Glass-Cliff Positions*. You can find it here: https://journals.sagepub.com/doi/abs/10.1177/0956797612453115.

Why could female leaders be better than male leaders at managing crises? Do some research and list the five female business leaders you admire the most.

TOK links

1. As a business cannot plan for all possible crises, how can different types of crises be prioritized by likelihood? Using what knowledge?

2. Can the hypothetical scenario of contingency planning be the same as a real crisis?

3. Contingency planning uses scenarios – what does that tell us about the role of imagination in business management?

5.7 Crisis management and contingency planning (HL only)

Practice question

To answer the question below effectively, see Unit 6 pages 398–402.

Lloyds

Lloyds is a local charity that supports young adults with autism. It was founded 10 years ago and rapidly became a brand name in the community thanks to its social marketing campaigns, popular events combining sports and concerts, and the support of local personalities. Many people regularly give money to *Lloyds*, either through their website or directly through the *Lloyds* phone app.

Lloyds enjoys a good reputation as a friendly yet professional organization, run by volunteers for the sole benefit of young adults with autism. It is led by a board composed of three directors: a local councillor, a retired journalist and a business management teacher.

In March 2021, a serious crisis occurred: criminals hacked into *Lloyds* computer system and, using ransomware, threatened to erase all the data held by *Lloyds*, including the database of all their donors, in one week's time. The directors were shocked: they had always anticipated possible problems such as power failure during the concerts (with auxiliary generators, just in case) and bad weather (with huge tents and canopies), but they never imagined such malicious actions that could entirely ruin a charity that runs for the benefit of the community.

The charity had just enough surplus (retained profit) to pay the ransom, but it would have had no money left for any activity for the rest of the year. If the news went public, the directors feared that donors would stop trusting *Lloyds'* IT system and would not want to donate to the charity again.

a) With reference to *Lloyds*, contrast crisis management and contingency planning. [4 marks]

b) Comment on the possible courses of action for the directors of *Lloyds*. [6 marks]

5.8 Research and development (HL only)

> **By the end of this chapter, you should be able to:**
> → Discuss the importance of **research and development (R&D)** for a business
> → Explain the importance of **developing goods and services** that address customers' unmet needs
> → Explain **intellectual property protection**, **patents**, **copyrights** and **trademarks**
> → Distinguish between different types of **innovation**, especially:
>   - adaptive innovation
>   - disruptive innovation

The importance of research and development (HL only)

Research and development (R&D) is an essential activity for many businesses. It is a form of innovation directly associated with the technical development of existing products or processes, or the creation of new ones.

Large businesses spend vast sums of money on R&D, typically with a department specializing in R&D that houses engineers and researchers whose creativity is essential for the organization. R&D is important in all industries, from pharmaceuticals to household goods, from electronics to space exploration – and also in sectors that might not be obviously associated with R&D, such as agriculture and fashion.

R&D is important as it can help to extend the product life cycle by developing new ways to use existing products (such as increasing the functionality of a cellphone) or by indicating new strategic directions for the company (such as when Apple branched off from PCs to iPods, iPhones and iPads).

Key term

R&D
a form of innovation directly associated with the technical development of existing products or processes, or the creation of new ones

Student workpoint 5.18

Be a thinker
What other topics in this course can you link R&D to?

Case study: WildType

Well-established companies are not the only ones that invest in R&D. Many new enterprises are also set up based on an innovation that may still be under development.

One such example is WildType, one of the pioneers of cellular agriculture in seafood.

Founded in 2016 in San Francisco (California, USA), WildType has been developing bio-technology to grow seafood directly from cells in laboratories, for human consumption, instead of fish raised in fish farms or caught in nature. The founders' vision is based on the principle of sustainability, while ensuring market success and profitability once their lab-grown fish (synthetic fish) is commercialized.

5.8 Research and development (HL only)

There is no single best way to conduct R&D, but to be at its most effective, R&D requires good planning, teamwork, communication, and leadership. There are a number of stages between thinking of an idea and launching a product. These stages are listed in Figure 5.8.1.

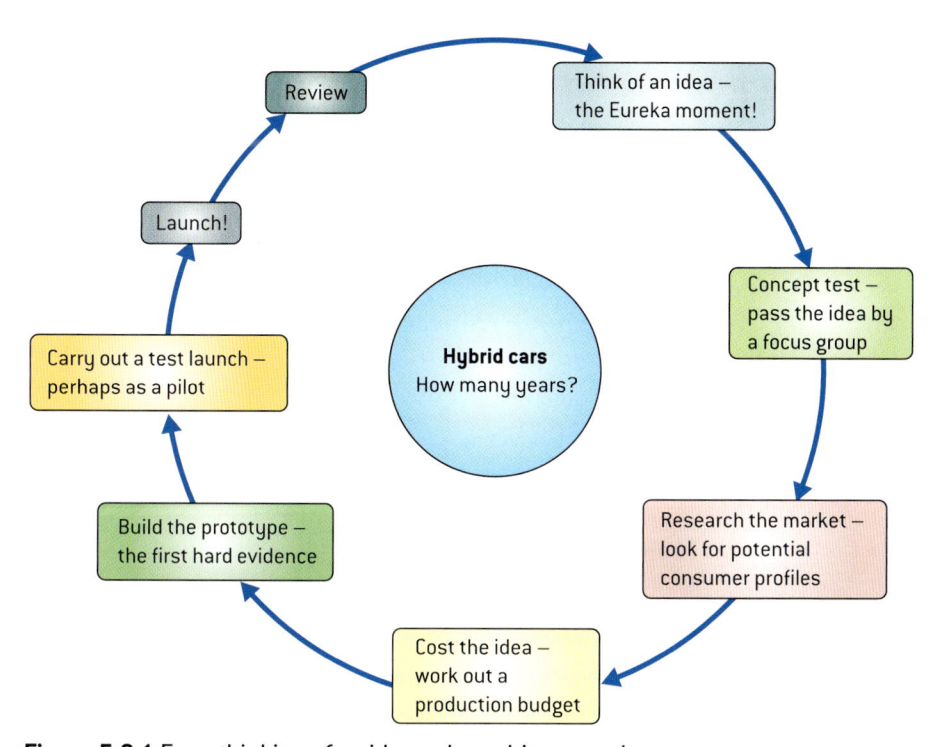

Figure 5.8.1 From thinking of an idea to launching a product

Stages (clockwise): Think of an idea – the Eureka moment! → Concept test – pass the idea by a focus group → Research the market – look for potential consumer profiles → Cost the idea – work out a production budget → Build the prototype – the first hard evidence → Carry out a test launch – perhaps as a pilot → Launch! → Review

Central example: Hybrid cars – How many years?

The process can take a very long time (for example, up to 15 years for a new drug in the pharmaceutical industry, as different stages of testing and authorization are required). Many brilliant ideas do not get to the production stage because the product is deemed too costly, or the market does not seem large enough to make it viable.

Successful R&D can lead to many advantages for a business. It can:

- Give the business a competitive advantage.
- Extend the life of an existing product.
- Open up new markets.
- Enhance the prestige of the company (by being known as an innovator).
- Motivate the workforce (by designing new products and appearing to be at the cutting edge of innovation).
- Lead to improvements in quality.
- Reduce costs.

However, R&D is not without its problems:

- There may be opportunity costs – what else could the money be spent on?
- R&D may head in the wrong direction – a new product does not necessarily mean there is a market for it.
- R&D is time-consuming – the R&D workforce is tied to a project for years, without any ROI (return on investment) for the company during that time.

379

- R&D can be fiercely competitive.
- There may be ethical issues involved – for example with R&D involving genetically modified crops, stem cell research or animal experiments for cosmetics.

Developing goods and services that address customers' unmet needs (HL only)

Innovation is essential for any business. Quality can be improved through methods such as *kaizen* or approaches such as TQM, but most businesses do not simply develop a product and then leave it unchanged for ever. Even Coca-Cola has modified its secret formula, for instance. If businesses fail to innovate, they may lose market share against existing competitors who do innovate, or against new entrants with fresh ideas and new products or services. In the BCG matrix of their product portfolio, their "cash cows" may become "dogs" (see Chapter 4.5).

R&D can also allow the business to find gaps in existing markets, or to open up new markets entirely. It is also important to develop goods and services that address customers' unmet needs, which is why the marketing department and the R&D department should work together.

One of the key functions of market research is to identify customers' unmet needs, ie to spot business opportunities, such as the demand for a new piece of software, a new book, or a new flavour of ice-cream. This information can then help the R&D department develop the items for which there is a market demand. This is a key premise of market orientation (as opposed to product orientation). The absence of a dialogue between the marketing and R&D departments could have unfortunate, costly consequences.

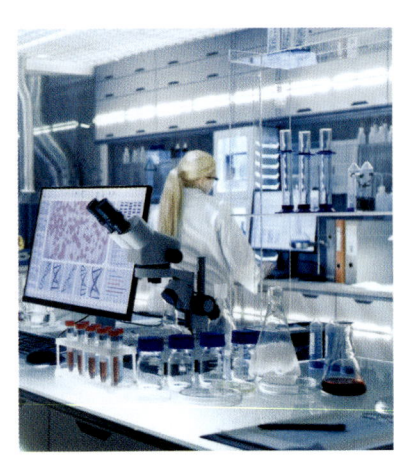

R&D plays a critical role in the innovation process, for example in laboratories in the pharmaceutical industry

> **Student workpoint 5.19**
>
> **Be a thinker**
>
> These products have all been launched in the real world:
>
> - Edible deodorant
> - Canned whole chickens
> - Children's toothpaste in an aerosol
> - Smokeless cigarettes
> - Garlic cake
>
> They didn't sell well. Why do you think this was?

Intellectual property rights (IP rights) (HL only)

Marketing and R&D also overlap on the important issue of intellectual property rights (IP rights). Their ownership by the business constitutes a valuable asset that needs to be protected; without this protection, the business could lose its edge and the competition may be able to develop identical products. The WTO (World Trade Organization) defines intellectual property rights as "the rights given to persons over the creations of their minds". According to the WTO, IP rights fall into two categories:

- **Copyright and rights related to copyright.** Copyright originally applied to written material, hence its name (the right to copy or reproduce written text), but it has now been extended to cover other creative forms such as cartoons, paintings, music, films, and even computer programs.

  The individual author or the business is protected for a period of time (for example 50 years) from the unlawful copying of the material they created. In our digital age, this has become a major source of concern for large record companies, book publishers and film producers, especially with the introduction of file-sharing sites on the internet.

- **Industrial property, especially trademarks and patents.** Industrial property is about the protection of distinctive signs, which distinguish the goods or services of one business from those of its competitors. These distinctive signs (such as a business's name or logo) are protected by law to ensure fair competition and to safeguard consumers.

Patents

When individuals or businesses invent products or production processes, they should take out a patent to protect their idea. Once the patent has been bought, it gives the individuals or businesses undisputed rights to exclude anyone else from making the product exactly to the specifications laid down in the patent, usually for a period of up to 20 years. After that time, the individuals or business can renew their patent.

A patent on one product does not stop anyone producing similar products, but they must not be exactly the same (they must have different features). The patent gives the inventor a "first-mover advantage" in the sector.

Trademarks

Trademarks are another form of IP rights. These are split into two general forms. Conventional trademarks include logos, slogans, designs, and phrases. The name Coca-Cola, for example, is protected by the symbol ™. There are also non-conventional trademarks, which are qualities that are distinctive to the design of something, for example the Coca-Cola label (including the exact colour and shape of the letters).

All of these IP rights help to ensure that the business can:

- have first-mover advantage
- increase profit margins
- safeguard continuity of production
- develop brand loyalty
- have time to develop new products
- financially benefit from its creativity, innovation, and R&D.

Innovation (HL only)

Innovation simply refers to the addition of something new. In business, this may be the incremental or radical improvement of a business idea, product or process in order to be more successful or more competitive. For many business organizations, a key challenge is bringing in "the new" and managing the process of improvement in a sustainable way that does not create conflict.

Although all innovations, by nature, are different, it is possible to distinguish between two main types of innovation:

- **Product innovation** is a type of innovation where new products are created or improvements to existing products are made (for example, producing flat-screen televisions or new models of smartphones). Product innovation refers to what an organization offers.

> **Key terms**
>
> **Product innovation**
> a type of innovation where new products are created or improvements to existing products are made
>
> **Process innovation**
> a type of innovation where some parts of the manufacturing or service delivery are improved
>
> **Adaptive innovation**
> an innovation in existing organizational elements
>
> **Disruptive innovation**
> an innovation so important that it may change the industry itself

5 Operations management

- **Process innovation** is a type of innovation where some parts of the manufacturing or service delivery are improved, for example with the JIT system. Just as product innovation refers to the "what", process innovation refers to the "how".

In the case of services, the notion of "service innovation" may cover aspects pertaining to both product innovation and process innovation (for example, the ability in e-commerce for customers to track online the progress and location of an item they have purchased).

Adaptive innovation

The term "adaptive innovation" is used when the starting point is either an existing product or an existing process, which is then adapted; it is not a radical innovation, but a gradual, incremental one. The phrase "adaptive innovation" is also used to refer to changes in a company's business model or in organizational aspects other than production. For example, during the Covid-19 pandemic, many companies had to adapt and reinvent themselves, letting some staff work from home or developing new ways of operating.

Disruptive innovation

A new product or a new process may have a major impact on the whole industry: this is called "disruptive innovation". It refers to an innovation so important that it changes the industry itself. The focus is on the impacts, both short-term and long-term.

For example, in the 1990s the advent of no-frills airlines and budget air travel created a massive change in thinking (and in travelling practice) by individuals, airports, and established airlines. It also spawned a whole set of new business opportunities, such as buying property in other countries (because travelling to them had become much cheaper), or organizing trips abroad for final-year high-school students.

Factors affecting R&D and innovation

Numerous factors may affect the ability of an individual, team, or business to innovate successfully, which may influence the R&D practices and strategies of an organization.

- **Organizational culture** (see Chapter 2.5) – if an organization has a low-risk, role-based, bureaucratic or autocratic culture, innovation may be very limited, as the fear of failure can outweigh the rewards of success. However, democratic or collaborative organizational cultures may foster risk-taking and view creative input as a valuable resource.

- **Past experience** – a proven track record of innovative practices can help to develop the expectations for future change and can act as an archive of what has worked in the past. This is also called "path dependence". It may shape and frame the R&D strategy of the organization.

- **Technology** – this can play a leading role in the development of ideas, especially with computer-assisted design (CAD) and the use of the internet. For example, the collaborative nature of freeware (such as open-source software) has largely resulted from the ease of sharing ideas and practices in a supportive environment – hence the success of Mozilla Firefox and other freeware.

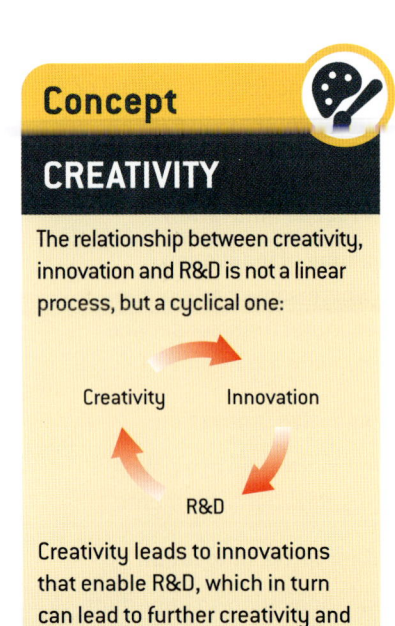

Concept

CREATIVITY

The relationship between creativity, innovation and R&D is not a linear process, but a cyclical one:

Creativity → Innovation → R&D → (back to Creativity)

Creativity leads to innovations that enable R&D, which in turn can lead to further creativity and more innovations.

Consider one organization that you find particularly creative. What makes it so innovative?

5.8 Research and development (HL only)

- **The pace of change** – some industries are more responsive to change than others. In high-tech industries, businesses may be less able to stay ahead of the market for long as the pace of development is so fast. Other markets (for example for local, traditional goods or for services such as organizing weddings) are not affected in the same way.
- **The level of competition** – the more competition there is in a market, the more incentive there is for businesses to create the competitive edge brought about by innovation.
- **Finance** – the amount of finance available (particularly in regards to the R&D budget) can limit the amount of innovation that a business may be able to achieve.
- **HR** – in addition to finance, workers need to be available to innovate. The number of workers, their skillsets, and the amount of time allocated to innovation will all have an impact on their ability to innovate.
- **Legal constraints** – at all stages of a product (such as the development stage or the implementation stage) there are legal concerns that a business must take into account. Taking airlines as an example, the ability to reduce the turnaround time of planes on the ground is dependent on labour law. It will also vary from country to country.
- **Ethical concerns** – even when some innovations are possible legally, some stakeholders may have strong ethical concerns, for example about testing new cosmetic products on animals. Some companies such as The Body Shop and LUSH do not do animal testing of any kind. They use this fact as a marketing tool.

Given all of the above, the ability for businesses to innovate successfully may be restricted. The number of businesses that come up with disruptive inventions is even more limited. However, any business has the capacity to make small-scale adjustments to improve productivity by adopting new techniques and innovative practices, as long as the resistance to change can be addressed.

> **TOK links**
>
> 1. How might the methods used in R&D be limited by ethical considerations?
> 2. Is R&D a topic of business management, or a topic of science, design, and technology? Why?
> 3. *"Imagination is more important than knowledge."* How can Einstein's famous words be interpreted in a business context, especially considering R&D?

Revision checklist

✓ R&D enables organizations to develop new and existing products in an innovative way.

✓ Product innovation is the creation of new products or the improvement of existing ones.

✓ Process innovation improves the manufacturing or service delivery processes.

✓ Adaptive innovation refers to changes to an existing product, process, business model or other organizational element.

✓ Disruptive innovation is a substantial innovation which can change a whole industry.

Practice question

To answer the question below effectively, see Unit 6 pages 398–402.

R&D in the pharmaceutical industry

In the pharmaceutical industry, R&D departments have a critical role in ensuring successful innovation. New product development can lead to competitive advantage, business growth, higher profits and therefore shareholder satisfaction.

However, R&D is a long and expensive process. It could take more than 17 years from the discovery of a new drug to its launch onto the market:

- Basic research: 2–3 years
- Pre-clinical studies: 3–5 years
- Clinical studies: 3–7 years
- Application for approval: 1–2 years

The processes that a new drug has to go through in order to gain approval are subject to full public disclosure. Therefore, it would be relatively easy for other pharmaceutical companies to copy the drug.

When pharmaceutical companies set the prices of their drugs, they must cover not only the costs of production and distribution, but also the costs of past R&D. This explains why new drugs may seem very expensive and why patents are essential.

a) State **two** possible problems with R&D. [2 marks]

b) Explain **two** reasons why patents are essential in the pharmaceutical industry. [4 marks]

c) With reference to the pharmaceutical industry, distinguish between "adaptive innovation" and "disruptive innovation". [4 marks]

5.9 Management information systems (HL only)

> **By the end of this chapter, you should be able to:**
> - Define key terms related to **information systems management**: database, data mining and data analytics
> - Examine how companies use **data mining and data analytics** to inform decision-making, create customer loyalty programmes, and monitor their employees (digital Taylorism)
> - Define **cybercrime** and **cybersecurity**
> - Analyse some of the **critical infrastructures** that are part of advanced computer technologies: artificial neural networks, data centres and cloud computing
> - Distinguish between **big data, virtual reality**, the **internet of things** and **artificial intelligence**
> - Evaluate the **benefits, risks and ethical implications** of advanced computer technologies and technological innovation on business decision-making and stakeholders

Information systems (HL only)

An information system (IS) is a system composed of databases in the form of electronic files used to record information. In a business context, databases are usually about customers and sales transactions. These files may be opened and used by administrators who have the necessary permissions (username and password) in order to ensure that customers' personal details (such as name, address and even bank details) are stored safely.

For example, the owner of a flower shop may have a simple database with the contact details of all previous customers. He may contact them occasionally with special offers before events and celebrations such as Mothers' Day, Valentine's Day or Diwali, when many people buy flowers. The IS could be more sophisticated and linked to an email system, sending those customers automatic reminders a few days before they ordered birthday flowers in previous years.

More advanced IS use software that enable two related practices: data mining and data analytics. These practices are mainly relevant for large companies that collect a lot of data, such as e-commerce websites tracking who has clicked on what link or visited a particular webpage and for how long.

5 Operations management

> **Key terms**
>
> **Database**
> a collection of data that is organized to be easily accessed, managed, explored and updated
>
> **Data mining**
> the process of finding trends, patterns and correlations within large databases
>
> **Date analytics**
> the process of inspecting and modelling data in order to discover useful information
>
> **Digital Taylorism**
> the use of digital technology to monitor workers

Data mining

Data mining is the process of finding trends, patterns and correlations within large datasets. The name comes from the image of a miner digging for gold – but in this case, tools and techniques are used to search through data in order to discover hidden connections and predict future trends. Companies can then use those findings to predict future situations, and thus to increase revenue, improve customer relations, cut costs, and reduce risks.

Data mining is common in many sectors, from manufacturers to telecommunications providers and from e-commerce retailers to banks and insurers. The starting point of data mining is usually a hypothesis to be tested. For example, the marketing team of a company designing, manufacturing and selling running shoes may hypothesize that running shoes in colourful packaging sell more in December than in other months because they are offered as Christmas presents. As this is only a hypothesis, the marketing team will use data mining to examine whether any data can confirm this.

Data analytics

Data analytics shares many similarities with data mining. It can be defined as the process of inspecting and modelling data in order to discover useful information. The aim is not to find any hidden pattern nor to test some hypothesis, as in data mining, but simply to reach conclusions based on the analysis of the raw data collected.

Data analytics can be used in three ways:

- **Descriptive analytics** is about past performance. For example, historical data show the manager of a cinema that the Saturday night 8pm show is the one with the largest audience number. The manager may have thought that was the case, following her anecdotal observations, but now with data analytics she has reliable, objective evidence to show that this is true.

- **Predictive analytics** is about forecasting the future. Following on from her use of descriptive analytics, the manager of the cinema can anticipate that Saturday nights will always be the busiest. So she may decide to hire extra cashiers for the Saturday night shifts in order to reduce queues and improve cinema-goers' experiences.

    Data analytics has helped the manager to draw factual, evidence-based conclusions, and she is using this information in a forward-looking way, as a decision-making tool to help with workforce planning in order to ensure higher customer satisfaction and customer loyalty, which may lead to increased sales and possibly higher revenue.

- **Prescriptive analytics** is the third phase of business analytics, after descriptive analytics and predictive analytics. Using both historical data and external data, prescriptive analytics explores what may happen in the future. To use the same example of the cinema, with prescriptive analytics, the manager could process more data, not only about their cinema, but also about other leisure venues and the impact of seasonal variation on people's behaviour, integrating several variables and comparing scenarios to achieve the best possible outcome. Prescriptive analytics could show that in winter months it is better to schedule the first evening show at 7pm, but in summer months it is better at 9pm, and that the manager should follow specific courses of action in order to maximize sales.

The use of data analytics and data mining (HL only)

Data analytics and data mining are used in different ways to help business managers make informed decisions, for example for market research (to collect data from potential customers), for promotional purposes (targeting certain groups using a selection of criteria), or for credit risk management (profiling how some customers may not creditworthy).

Data mining techniques are also used by many large supermarket chains and grocery stores for customer loyalty programmes. Many offer free loyalty cards that give members access to reduced prices not available to non-members. Thanks to these cards and all the data they generate, the businesses can keep track of who is buying what, when, where and at what price. Data mining and data analytics can help identify patterns to send certain customers offers, vouchers, discounts or coupons, based on their buying habits. They also help managers to decide when to put items on sale or when to sell them at full price.

For customers, there are advantages and disadvantages. Customers may appreciate the offers and discounts, but they may feel uncomfortable knowing that so much personal information is collected, stored and used (not only their contact details, but also what they buy and when, how much they spend on different types of food and drinks, etc).

The use of data to manage and monitor employees

Information systems and data analytics can help make decisions about marketing and operations, as well as about human resources (although this may be more controversial).

Taylor's scientific management was explained in Chapter 2.4. He applied scientific methods (such as observation and experimentation) to find the most efficient production process to increase productivity.

One of Taylor's key principles (known as Taylorism) is that managers should monitor their workers' performance. In the early-20th-century context of Taylor's factories, managers could visually observe their workers; in the 21st century, in our digital era, computer systems enable this, hence the term "digital Taylorism" to describe the practice of monitoring workers through IT systems.

For example, the manager of a team working from home can see when her staff log into the company's computer system and track what they do and when. This can help the manager to spot a worker who underperforms and needs retraining or upskilling, for example because they are not employing the company's software at a satisfactory level, or to spot a worker who logs in but does not appear to do any productive work.

Technology also makes it possible for employers to keep track of all workplace communications by their employees, including reading emails sent from the company's work email accounts. In many countries, cases have gone to court about conflicts linked to the use of data to manage and monitor employees. For example, employees might complain that their work emails were read by their managers (work emails are not normally private, unless the company has a clear privacy policy).

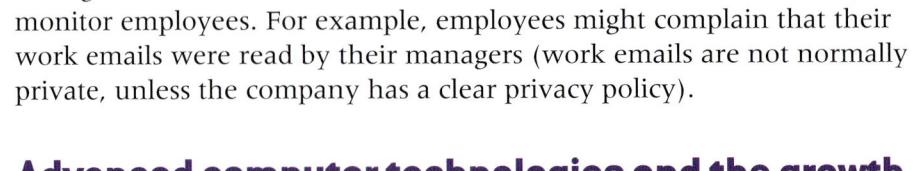

Advanced computer technologies and the growth of e-commerce (HL only)

Advanced computer technologies have enabled the growth of e-commerce, which is now present in most countries. E-commerce can be defined as the buying and selling of goods and services through electronic networks, commonly via the internet.

E-commerce has many **advantages for businesses** selling online:

- They can reach a wide target market, resulting in an increased customer base (which may even be international).
- There is no need for physical spaces such as expensive shops in city centres; instead, warehouses are the main buildings used for storage (Amazon is a well-known example).
- E-commerce platforms make it possible to advertise goods and services in many ways, including text, images and videos, as well as previous customers' reviews.

E-commerce also has many **advantages for customers** purchasing online:

- It is convenient for consumers because they can shop from home, 24/7, without having to visit a shop physically. This is particularly beneficial for people who live in more rural areas or who cannot easily leave their home.
- Consumers can compare the various products on offer before deciding to make a purchase, and they have more choice.
- They can buy from other individuals, for example to purchase second-hand goods. This is called C2C (customer-to-customer) as opposed to B2C (business-to-customer).

E-commerce also has many disadvantages for businesses and consumers. For example, consumers cannot try or feel certain products before buying them, and businesses now have more even competitors.

Cybercrime and cybersecurity

Businesses and consumers share common concerns regarding **cybercrime** (an intentional, malicious attack on an organization or an individual by targeting their computer systems and accessing their data, including confidential data such as banking details). Consumers may fear that internet security related to the payment process is not strong enough, which may reduce the number of sales and the growth potential for firms.

Fraud and ID theft are real risks, which is why companies invest in **cybersecurity** systems designed to protect and defend their networks, computers, and other related electronic systems and devices from any type of cyberattack.

Home delivery has become more common due to the development of e-commerce

5.9 Management information systems (HL only)

Critical infrastructures (HL only)

Critical infrastructures are the systems, networks and assets that are essential for operations – in this case for information systems.

Artificial neural networks (ANN)

Artificial neural networks (ANN) are elements of computing systems designed to simulate how the human brain operates, by processing and analysing information. The name comes from the fact that they are built like a human brain, with its billions of nerve cells that are all connected.

ANN are the foundation of artificial intelligence (AI) as they help to solve problems that are too complicated for humans. ANN can also learn from the data they receive and from the operations they do, hence the expression "machine learning" (a branch of AI).

In a business context, ANN are everywhere, even if we do not realize it. For example:

- E-commerce platforms use ANN to personalize recommendations for their audience, based on previous browsing and purchases, cross-referencing millions of other transactions by other people.

- Email service providers use ANN to detect spam (junk mail).

- Chatbots are developed with ANNs in order to simulate how a human would naturally behave in a conversation (this is called "natural language processing" or NLP).

Data centres

Data centres are the buildings where computer systems and associated components are housed. From simple computer rooms they have now evolved into carefully designed, specialized facilities that are heavily protected again accidents such as fire, power cuts and unauthorized intrusion, either physical (terrorism) or digital (cybercrime, cyberterrorism).

Data centres provide a range of services, such as: data storage, management and recovery; high volume e-commerce transactions; powering online gaming communities; and hosting cloud-based systems.

Nowadays, data centres have become essential for everyone in society: individuals, businesses and also governments.

Key terms

Cybersecurity

the practice of defending computers and IT systems against malicious attacks

Artificial neural network (ANN)

an element of a computing system designed to simulate how the human brain analyses and processes information

Data centre

a building or a room designed to house computer systems and their components

5 Operations management

Cloud computing

Cloud computing refers to the delivery of services through the internet, especially data storage, databases, networking, and software. The name comes from the metaphor of a cloud far away in the sky, suggesting that the data is not stored in personal devices (such as tablets or smartphones) but somewhere distant, eg on a company's server that may well be in another country. Using "the cloud" means that someone can retrieve their data from anywhere whenever they want (hence the phrase "on demand"), as long as they have access to the internet.

The practice of cloud computing has many advantages for businesses:

- Flexibility of work practices: employees can work remotely, from virtual offices in their home.
- IT costs may be reduced (for example there is no need to buy storage equipment and systems); operating costs may be reduced too (for example energy consumption costs may be reduced).
- Business continuity: in case of accidents such as a local fire, power failure, natural disaster or other crisis, all data is stored and protected in a secure and safe location, and can easily be retrieved.

However, cloud computing has some disadvantages:

- Concerns for security, data protection, privacy and confidentiality: could cybercriminals gain access to sensitive data?
- The location of the servers: these may be in another country where security and privacy laws are different.
- Cloud providers may lock businesses into contracts that they may later regret, with less flexibility than anticipated and high service fees.

The difference between big data, virtual reality, the internet of things and artificial intelligence (HL only)

Advances in computer technologies have opened up a very rich and complex field of studies that keep expanding. New terms need to be coined to describe new phenomena, new facts and new realities that did not exist when your grandparents or even your parents were at school. This section covers the following terms:

- Big data
- Virtual reality
- The internet of things
- Artificial intelligence

Big data

"Big data" is a term used to describe extremely large databases. The simplicity of the term does not do justice to the complexity of the tasks around the collection, organization, processing, storage, analysis, utilization, management and interpretation of the data collected.

Key terms

Cloud computing

the delivery of services via the internet, especially data storage, databases, networking, and software

Big data

extremely large databases that can be analysed to show trends and patterns

Virtual reality

the creation of a simulated three-dimensional environment that can be explored by a person who has entered that computer-generated world

The internet of things (IoT)

the network of connected devices that transmit data to one another without human involvement

Artificial intelligence (AI)

the ability of computers (and other machines such as computerized robots) to mimic humans, especially how humans think and process information

5.9 Management information systems (HL only)

The characteristics of big data were initially called "the 3Vs" – volume, variety and velocity. These considered the amount, diversity and speed at which data is created. Other Vs are sometimes added, such as value and veracity (how useful is the data, and how truthful is it?), as well as other parameters such as comprehensiveness (is all data collected, or just a sample?).

Big data comes from many sources, such as the increasing number of devices that are interconnected every second (computer, laptops, smartphones, tablets etc) as well as retail e-commerce databases, social media applications, and transportation information (GPS location), among others. Very large amounts of data are created, which constitute the data sets necessary for data analytics and data mining.

Businesses use big data in many ways, for example:

- To track the performance of equipment or of employees, and to make decisions as a consequence (eg to tell if a worker underperforms compared to others and may need retraining or upskilling).

- To help market research, generating marketing intelligence about the needs and wants of customers, for example by using feedback and comments posted on social media. In this sense, big data is revolutionizing market research.

- To set prices automatically according to fluctuations in demand and level of interest (many airlines and hotels have adopted techniques known as "dynamic pricing" and "yield management" in order to maximize sales revenue).

As with all systems of data collection, there are important socio-ethical concerns. That is why more and more countries are adopting measures to ensure the protection of their citizens' personal data. For example, since 2018, the European Union (EU) has had a law called the General Data Protection Regulation (GDPR) to protect the privacy of EU citizens. And since 2020, California has had a comparable statute called the California Consumer Privacy Act (CCPA). Other countries are gradually passing similar legislation.

Case study: CHEP

CHEP is the shipping and logistics arm of Australian giant Brambles. It calls itself the "invisible backbone" of the global supply chain. Its core business is reusable packaging equipment – providing crates, pallets and boxes to companies around the world to ship their stuff.

CHEP is one of the largest pallet businesses in the world, and at any given moment, it will have 300 million packaging units on the move. The business model has circularity embedded in its core. In contrast to many companies that sell pallets, CHEP rents them to customers and then collects almost every unit back after use to inspect, repair and send back out into the supply chain again. The business is built around the idea of sharing and reusing. Reusing wooden pallets averted the logging of 1.7 million trees in 2020.

But Brambles is no longer content with maintaining a circular model in its own business. Having spotted that the idea of the circular economy is starting to take off in corporate circles, it wants to be at the centre

Product service system models

In cases where services rather than products are marketed, these models improve the incentives for "green" product design and lead to more efficient product use. This promotes a more economical use of natural resources. The case study here gives an example of an organization that uses a product service system model.

5 Operations management

of the business action. Brambles believes that the circular economy is everywhere. As the planet's natural resources are under great pressure, it is a huge opportunity for Brambles to reduce costs and unlock efficiencies in the supply chain.

Brambles has a business programme dubbed "Zero Waste World": a three-pronged scheme that helps customers in the United States and Europe to cut waste and improve efficiency in their own supply chains.

The first pillar of the programme is focused on eliminating waste, from single-use packaging to unsaleable products. Lots of companies have made zero-waste-to-landfill pledges, but in much of their supply chain single-use plastic wrapping and used-once cardboard boxes are proving tricky to eliminate. CHEP is planning to expand its range of reusable supply chain packaging solutions, to help firms slash single-use waste.

The second pillar is transport. In Europe, 30% of freight miles are driven with empty trucks, returning to depot once they have delivered their load. CHEP already teams up with companies to use their empty fleets to transport pallets, for example, but under Zero Waste World, it plans to take this one step further and team firms up with rival companies to share transport miles.

The third pillar is focused on improving traceability in the supply chain. CHEP uses a platform called BXB Digital, which uses "internet of things" technology to collate and analyze the data from CHEP pallets. With that information, companies can spot inefficiencies or bottlenecks in their supply chain that leads to issues such as food waste.

Across the strategy, CHEP is promoting its role as a purveyor of big data, and its position as a "neutral actor" in the supply chain. This privileged position will help corporates develop the trust to try new ways of working.

Source: Adapted from: https://www.greenbiz.com/article/circular-economy-giant-youve-never-heard-planning-major-expansion

Assessment advice

You do not need to memorize specific definitions for the key terms in this chapter (such as "artificial intelligence" or "virtual reality"), but you must be able to explain what they mean in your own words.

Concept

ETHICS

All technological and digital developments have ethical implications, for example regarding data protection, privacy or confidentiality.

Can you find some examples of recent ethical problems or dilemmas linked to IT in the context of business management?

Virtual reality (VR)

Virtual reality (VR) is the creation of a simulated three-dimensional environment that can be explored by a person who then enters that computer-generated world, is immersed within it, and has interactions with other people, characters or objects.

VR is often used for entertainment and leisure, but increasingly for other purposes too, especially educational ones. For example, a surgeon can practise an operation in VR before performing it for real, or a pilot can practise landing in adverse weather conditions in VR before having to do it live.

VR uses many complex technologies to present to the senses a virtual environment that seems genuine. As these technologies keep developing and as they become cheaper and more widespread, new applications of VR are being invented and imagined. For example, one day it may be possible to test-drive different cars before choosing one, or to visit different tourist destinations in VR before choosing one for your next holiday.

5.9 Management information systems (HL only)

The internet of things (IoT)

"The internet of things" (IoT) is an expression that refers to the network of computerized devices transmitting data to one another without human involvement. For example, in a "smart house", a system of "smart windows" could liaise with sensors inside and outside, as well as with the heating, ventilation and air conditioning systems. So if it gets too hot inside, the windows could automatically open (unless it is dark or raining outside, in which case the air conditioning system could switch itself on).

In a business context, IoT has many applications that keep evolving, for example in the following sectors:

- **Retail, shopping and supply chain management:** managers do not need to check the stock themselves, as stock control can be automated and reorder is done via IoT.
- **Health:** wearable devices that monitor heart rate, sleep and activity patterns, communicating with medication dispensers and healthcare providers.
- **Agriculture:** "smart farming" with sensors to monitor natural conditions such as humidity, air temperature and soil quality, connected to automated irrigation and fertilization systems.

A smartwatch is a good example of "the internet of things"

Artificial intelligence (AI)

Artificial intelligence (AI) is a broad term that refers to the ability of computers (and other machines such as computerized robots) to mimic humans, ie to do things normally associated with human beings, such as recognizing objects and situations, learning from examples and experience, and problem solving and decision-making. AI is possible thanks to artificial neural networks (ANN) processing large amounts of data faster and better than humans could do.

In the 20th century, AI was a topic of science fiction, but it is now a part of our daily lives. It encompasses, for example:

- The predictive text function when typing a message.
- The virtual travel assistant on a smartphone that shows alternative routes to a destination, with live information about train or bus times.
- Search engines and social media platforms that also recommend news items you may be interested in.
- Appliances such as a smart vacuum cleaner that scans the room, identifies obstacles, determines the best route and needs no human assistance to clean the floor.

AI keeps developing with new and sometimes controversial features, such as face recognition. It is used in many sectors, including healthcare, finance and e-commerce.

TOK links

1. To what extent is big data changing what it means to know your customers?
2. Are data mining and data analytics leading us to redefine the meaning of the words "research" and "knowledge"?
3. Should all business decisions be made rationally using algorithms and artificial intelligence?

Revision checklist

✓ Organizations increasingly make use of advanced computer technologies, such as cloud computing, artificial neural networks (ANN) and artificial intelligence (AI).

✓ Those innovations have different roles and benefits. For example, data mining and data analytics can help inform decision-making, create customer loyalty programmes, and monitor employees.

✓ Many risks are present, such as cybercrime and breaches of cybersecurity on the one hand, and ethical issues of privacy, confidentiality and anonymity on the other hand.

✓ Some areas are in the growth phase of their lifecycle, for example the use of big data and the internet of things (IoT); others are still in their developmental phase, such as virtual reality (VR) for commercial purposes.

Practice question

To answer the question below effectively, see Unit 6 pages 398–402.

Digital Taylorism in the modern era

Many jobs in the modern economy have been sapped of their humanity. How should we resist the rise of "digital Taylorism"?

Fears about humans becoming like machines go back longer than you might think. The sort of algorithmic management we see in the modern gig economy has its roots in a management theory developed by Frederick Taylor in the early 20th century. As a young man, Taylor worked as a shop foreman for a steel-making corporation in Philadelphia, where he diagnosed inefficiencies he saw as being products of poorly structured incentives, unmotivated and sometimes shirking workers, and a huge knowledge gap that rendered management ineffective. Managers, he proclaimed, knew too little about the workforce, their tasks, capabilities and motivations.

Taylor and his disciples extolled the virtues of breaking down tasks into inputs, outputs, processes and procedures that can be mathematically analysed and transformed into recipes for efficient production. Over decades, and across different industries, his theories have been used to apply time-and-motion studies to workplaces, workers and what they produce.

The assembly line is the most recognized example of Taylorism: unskilled workers engage in repetitive, mindless tasks, attending to semi-finished parts that, in the end, are combined into a whole product. Over time, Taylorism became synonymous with the evils of extracting maximum value from workers while treating them as programmable cogs in machines.

Taylor's approach jump-started debates about data-driven innovation and surveillance that continue today. The modern, digital version of Taylorism is more powerful than he could have ever imagined, and more dehumanizing than his early critics could have predicted. Technological innovations have made it increasingly easy for managers to quickly and cheaply collect, process, evaluate and act upon massive amounts of information. In our age of big data, Taylorism has spread far beyond the factory floor.

5.9 Management information systems (HL only)

Technology also allows much more sophisticated performance management of employees than during Taylor's lifetime. Back then, employee reviews were costly in resource terms. They required face-to-face meetings or documents that took time to pull together. Today, small businesses as well as giants such as Amazon are using digital tools to create continuous streams of data for employee appraisal. Constant monitoring, and the addition of peer review to supervisor feedback, can create overly competitive, and sometimes hostile, dynamics between employees.

It's not just the intensity of the monitoring that is different. Surveillance is increasingly covert. In Taylor's analogue era, workers were acutely aware when they were being observed by management with stopwatches and notebooks. Today management tools are much less visible. A cashier at a fast-food franchise who rings up purchases with a virtual cash register app on her tablet might be unaware of the programs running surreptitiously in the background, logging keystrokes, recording audio or video, transmitting data and continuously rating performance. Workers who might know that their boss monitors calls, texts, and browsing on their employer-issued smartphones might be surprised to learn that the device also communicates geolocation data, allowing tracking of their movement 24/7.

Source: Adapted from Frishmann, B and Selinger, E. September 2017. "Robots have already taken over our work, but they're made of flesh and bone". *The Guardian*.

a) Define the term *gig economy*. [2 marks]

b) Explain the meaning of the sentence "in our age of big data, Taylorism has spread far beyond the factory floor". [4 marks]

c) Analyse how information systems may be used by human resources managers. [4 marks]

d) To what extent are the practices of digital Taylorism ethical? [10 marks]

6 ASSESSMENT

External Assessment

By the end of this chapter, you will know:

→ The basic structure of **external assessment** in IB Business Management (for first examinations in 2024)

→ The meaning, importance, and definitions of examination **command words**

→ How to **prepare** for examination questions

→ How to **answer** examination questions

→ How IB examinations are **marked**

→ The key requirements for the **internal assessment** (IA)

Basic structure

IB Business Management is assessed differently at standard level (SL) and higher level (HL):

	SL		HL	
	Task	Weight	Task	Weight
External assessment	Paper 1	35%	Paper 1	25%
	Paper 2	35%	Paper 2	30%
			Paper 3	25%
Internal assessment	Business research project	30%	Business research project	20%

The structure of the external assessment exams is as follows:

	Paper	Contents	Length	Marks available
SL	Paper 1	Case study	1½ hrs	30
	Paper 2	Data response	1½ hrs	40
HL	Paper 1	Case study	1½ hrs	30
	Paper 2	Data response	1¾ hrs	50
	Paper 3	Case study	1¼ hrs	25

External assessment

Similarities and differences between SL and HL

Two components are the same for SL and HL:

- Paper 1
- The internal assessment task

For Paper 2, the questions are different but the approach is similar, as outlined below.

Paper 3 is only taken by HL students.

Paper 1 overview

Paper 1 is exactly the same for SL and HL. Three months before the examination, the IB will release a statement that specifies the context and background of the examination case study. It will include a short extract from the case study itself (typically the first 200 words), and a list of keywords and business topics on which you should do some preparatory research.

At the start of the examination, you will receive the full case study (of approximately 800 to 1000 words) and the questions. Most questions in Paper 1 are qualitative, although there could be some questions involving calculations too.

Paper 2 overview

Paper 2 is different for SL and HL.

Paper 2 has a quantitative focus. This means that many questions will involve calculations (for example about investment appraisal or break-even analysis). There will also be some qualitative questions.

At the start of the examination, you will receive a booklet with some stimulus material (short texts, charts, tables, infographics, etc) and questions. You will write your answers in the booklet itself.

Paper 3 overview

Paper 3 is based on a case study with a social entrepreneurship focus.

At the start of the examination, you will receive a case study composed of some documents to help you understand the organization and the issues it faces. These documents may include text, infographics, excerpts from emails, online posts, newspaper articles, etc.

You will have to identify and describe a human need and the potential organizational challenges facing the social entrepreneur who wants to meet that need. You will have to propose a plan of action as a decision-making document for the social enterprise, with recommendations about what they should do strategically.

You will be assessed on the following four aspects:

- Your ability to use the documents to support your plan of action (criterion A).
- Your ability to apply appropriate business management tools and theories (criterion B).

- Your ability to evaluate the expected impact of your plan of action on the relevant areas of the business (criterion C).
- Your ability to sequence your ideas and plan of action in a clear and coherent manner (criterion D).

Command terms

A crucial part of doing well in IB Business Management examinations is to understand the meaning, importance and definitions of the command terms. Command terms are the verbs in examination questions that indicate:

- the demand of the question (ie how you should approach it – are you asked to state, to explain, to compare, to recommend, etc?)
- the depth of treatment you should provide.

All command terms have specific meanings that are defined and exemplified in the *IB Business Management Guide*. Knowing what the command terms ask you to do will allow you to provide sufficient depth to your answer, while also preventing you from writing answers that are longer or more detailed than necessary (this is important for your time management in the exam).

The command terms indicate the depth required by your answer. These command terms are organized by assessment objective (AO) level as follows:

- AO1 – knowledge and understanding
- AO2 – application and analysis
- AO3 – synthesis and evaluation
- AO4 – use and application of appropriate skills

The table below, with the main command terms at each assessment objective level, is taken from the subject guide.

	Assessment objective	Command terms	Depth
AO1	Knowledge and understanding	Define Describe Identify List Outline State	These terms require students to learn and comprehend the meaning of information.
AO2	Application and analysis	Analyse Apply Comment Distinguish Explain Suggest	These terms require students to use their knowledge and skills to break down ideas into simpler parts and to see how the parts relate.

Assessment objective	Command terms	Depth
A03 Synthesis and evaluation	Compare Compare and contrast Contrast Discuss Evaluate Examine Justify Recommend To what extent	These terms require students to rearrange component ideas into a new whole and make judgments based on evidence or a set of criteria.
A04 Use and application of appropriate skills	Annotate Calculate Complete Construct Determine Draw/Label Plot Prepare	These terms require students to demonstrate the selection and use of subject-specific skills and techniques.

On the examination papers, the first question to each case study is usually theoretical, whether this is the long case study for Paper 1 of the shorter case studies for Paper 2. This means that candidates have to demonstrate their knowledge but do not have to apply it to the case study (or stimulus).

Here are some sample first questions:

1. Define the term *tertiary sector*. [2]
2. Outline **two** common steps in the process of starting up a business or enterprise. [4]

For these questions, candidates should respond according to the command word, which in these two instances are "Define" and "Outline". According to the *IB Business Management Guide*, when a student is asked to **define**, they should "Give the precise meaning of a word, phrase, concept, or physical quantity." When they are asked to **outline**, they should "Give a brief account or summary."

After the first question, several questions follow that ask more of you and use more demanding command terms, such as "Explain" or "Identify." With these types of command terms, what you are being asked requires more than just demonstrating knowledge. You must also demonstrate understanding and the ability to apply knowledge to a given situation.

Preparing for exams

To prepare for your exams, you should study the syllabus in the context of case studies (ie real or fictitious organizations). This way, you can apply your knowledge. You should also be familiar with the examination format:

both the overall format and what the individual questions look like.

In IB Business Management, a common problem is that candidates sometimes memorize extended responses to certain types of questions (for example, the advantages and disadvantages of franchising). To examiners, it looks like those candidates have regurgitated a memorized response after reading just a few words of the question (for example, they see the word "franchising" and just produce the memorized response). Often, when candidates provide memorized responses without carefully considering the question asked, they get fewer marks than if they had written a shorter yet properly focused answer.

A similar caution must be made about studying from past exams. Using them as practice is a good strategy, as you need to be familiar with examinations (both their overall structure and the various types of questions) so that you know what to expect in terms of format, question type, and command terms.

However, past examinations should not be the only way you prepare for your exams and studying from them can be taken too far. If candidates only learn through past exams, they may not be genuinely learning about business, but rather solely learning examination techniques and strategies to try to score more marks. This shallow preparation may lead to limited answers, especially for longer, more demanding questions. Use past exams to know what to expect and to practise, but do not overuse them.

How to answer examination questions

The five most important points to remember when answering IB examination questions are:

- Answer the question exactly as asked
- Answer the question to the depth expected
- Structure your answers
- Provide balanced answers when required
- Make sure that you understand the meaning of "evaluation" (AO3)

The first two bullet points have already been covered above, and the final three bullet points (structure, balance and evaluation) are discussed below.

Structure

Two common, weaker structures that you should avoid are as follows.

Bullet points: unless the command term used is "identify", "list" or "state", a bulleted response rarely helps an answer as there is not much scope to develop ideas. Too often, bullet points are just lists that do not explain much.

Unstructured responses that read like a "stream of consciousness", ie random thoughts that do not show any planning, logic or coherence. Sometimes, candidates believe that they must write everything they know about a topic; they just start writing without thinking about (a) what they need to say and (b) how they should organize their ideas. In these circumstances, candidates tend to repeat or contradict themselves, make digressions, or include irrelevant information. In such answers, their ideas have less force, meaning and persuasiveness.

You should use structured paragraphs for your longer answers. Each new point deserves a new paragraph – and it will help the examiner to realize that you have mastered the topic!

Balance

Balance is about considering both sides of an answer. It can typically be achieved by providing:

- **Positives and negatives to a situation.** For example, a question such as: "Discuss the decision of Company X to purchase environmentally friendly cars" asks candidates to consider both the positive aspects (they are more sustainable, the company may gain public support for being environmentally friendly, etc) as well as the negatives (the cars cost more to buy, they may be difficult to service if they break down, etc).

- **Two points of view.** It may be suitable to distinguish between different perspectives. For example, the perspective of the business owner versus the perspective of the customers, or of the workers and trade unions. Alternatively, some employees could be in favour of a change, whereas some may be against it.

- **"The extent to which" and the limits.** Some years ago, a standard level Paper 2 (SLP2) question asked candidates to "Examine how branding may have contributed to the success of Zeitim restaurants." Top-mark answers addressed how branding contributed to the success of Zeitim as well as how other factors contributed (which, in effect, says that Zeitim's success was not entirely attributable to branding).

Evaluation

All examination papers will have questions that expect you to evaluate a course of action, which will be asked through an AO3 command term such as "Discuss", "Evaluate", or "Recommend". When you see one of these terms, you should always include a separate concluding paragraph that gives an opinion. Just writing "In conclusion" or "As we can see there are more advantages than disadvantages…" is not a substantial evaluation. A substantial evaluation should take at least one of these points into consideration:

- Short versus long term
- Stakeholders
- Pros and cons
- Priorities

6 Assessment

How IB examinations are marked

All examiners receive training to ensure that they all mark answers in the same way. They all receive the same mark scheme that gives them instructions about how and when they should award marks. This applies to all questions, the short ones (such as "Define the term XXX") and the long ones (such as "Recommend a possible plan of action for XXX"). The IB also has strict quality control and quality assurance methods in place to ensure that all candidates are fairly and equally assessed.

The IB follows what is called "positive marking", which means that examiners will reward you for the relevant business knowledge and the understanding that you show. There is no such as thing as "deducting marks" or "penalising candidates" in IB Busines Management. For example, you will not be penalised for poor English, or for issues of spelling or grammar.

> **Exam advice**
>
> - Answer the question exactly as asked. Do not regurgitate a memorized answer to a question that is similar to the one asked.
> - Do not use bullets, unless responding to the command terms "Identify", "List" or "State".
> - Structure your answer.
> - Know the difference between "Describe" (AO1) and "Explain" (AO2).
> - Provide balance – always think of both sides to a point of view.
> - Look out for AO3 questions – make sure you evaluate.

Internal Assessment

The internal assessment (IA) is an integral and compulsory element of the Business Management programme for both SL and HL students. It accounts for 30% of the final grade for the subject for SL students, and 20% for HL students.

Your IA enables you to demonstrate the application of your business skills and knowledge, and to pursue your personal interests, without the time limitations and other constraints that are associated with written examinations.

The IA requirements for SL and HL are the same. All students are expected to produce a **business research project** about a real issue or problem facing a particular organization, using a conceptual lens. The phrase "conceptual lens" refers to the key concepts that underpin the course: ethics, sustainability, creativity and change. You will have to choose one of those concepts and write your research project focusing on that concept.

Before attempting your IA, you should read the *IB Business Management Guide* carefully to ensure that you understand the task and all of its requirements.

You should refer to the assessment criteria at every stage of your IA, as you will be marked against them. Once you have finished your IA, it is a good idea to consider your work in light of the assessment criteria and ask yourself: *"Have I met the requirements for the higher levels of each criterion in the mark bands?"*

Main features

The main features of your research project are as follows:

- The **title** must be written in the form of a **question** (which could be forward-looking or backward-looking).

- You must select a **real and contemporary issue or problem**, not a fictional one, focusing on a single organization. (You might consider writing about industry-wide issues that impact on that organization, such as increased competition or changing legislation, but your focus should be one single organization.)

- This business issue or problem can relate to **any part of the syllabus**, but it must be clearly linked to the IB DP Business Management syllabus.

- Your research project can be based on **primary and/or secondary research**, selected for its suitability, depth and breadth.

- You must attach to your project **three to five supporting documents** from which the majority of the information for the project has been obtained. You should highlight the parts that relate to your project. You may consult additional sources. They should all be referenced in the body of the commentary and included in your **bibliography**.

- The maximum length of your project is **1,800 words**. It is important that you respect the word count: if your IA exceeds 1,800 words, the marker will stop reading after 1,800 words. This means that your

1800 words maximum

conclusion may not be read and considered, so you could score low marks (or even zero) for criterion E that assesses your conclusion, even if your conclusion was very good.

- You must use **one of the four key concepts** (change, creativity, ethics, sustainability). You will risk losing up to 5 marks for criterion A if do not use one of those four concepts. The concept may or may not be mentioned in your research question itself; however, it must be clearly indicated on the title page.

The research project has no required format, but it should be well-structured, well-presented, and written clearly and concisely.

Introduction	Your introduction should set the context, giving some background information about the business organization, with a clear outline of the issue or problem under investigation and an explanation of your chosen methodology, if you carry out primary research.
Main body	In the main body, you should present the findings of your research from your supporting documents, analysing them with the help of relevant business tools and theories, including integrating the key concept.
	Your findings should be interpreted: What main themes emerge from the analysis of the supporting documents? Why and how are they helpful (or not) to answer the research question?
	You should also evaluate and discuss your findings: What are the strengths and weaknesses of the various positions on the issue or problem? What are their implications?
Conclusion	In your conclusion, you should explicitly answer your research question. You should not introduce new facts or arguments that you have not already mentioned in the main body. However, you can include aspects of the research question that have not been fully answered or that might need further investigation.

A well-presented project includes:

- A title page (cover page) clearly indicating your research question, your chosen concept and the world count of your IA
- A page with an accurate table of contents
- Appropriate headings and sub-headings
- Numbered pages

You must also ensure that you consistently acknowledge your sources, including your supporting documents, and that your bibliography is complete.

For the presentation of references and the bibliography, see the information on acknowledging the ideas and work of another person in the "The Diploma Programme" section of the *IB Business Management Guide*. (The *Guide* also contains important information about what is and is not included in the 1,800 word count.)

Selecting a topic

You should choose an issue that:

- engages your interest
- is realistic and suitable in terms of resources, supporting documents and the conceptual lens
- meets the criteria for assessment.

The title question must be clear and focused, allowing you to investigate the topic within the 1,800-word limit. The following are examples of suitable questions.

- Should company X outsource the service Y to another company?
- How can airline X successfully target segment Y?
- Is producing a range of clothing for male customers a profitable decision for company X?
- Is an increase in wages an effective way to increase productivity and motivation in company X?

Selecting your supporting documents

The selection of supporting documents is very important. You should ensure that they present a range of ideas and views. For example, the selection of three to five documents published by a single company, or three to five surveys of similar populations, would not provide balance or objectivity.

The supporting documents must be contemporary and written within a maximum of three years prior to the submission of the research project to the IB.

One (but not more) of the supporting documents may be a transcript of video or audio material. Only video/audio material published by a reliable organization should be used. Particular attention needs to be paid to referencing the original video/audio file so that it can be traced.

As mentioned above, your project can be based on secondary and/or primary sources.

Examples of secondary sources include:

- Articles from the local, regional, national or international press
- Financial reports
- Business accounts
- Business plans
- Extracts from company websites
- Government reports
- Academic publications
- Transcripts of relevant video/audio files

6 Assessment

Examples of primary data include:

- Responses to questionnaires (you must include a blank copy of the questionnaire and a summary of your results)
- Transcripts of interviews and discussions with focus groups
- Results of surveys you have conducted online or face-to-face

You should choose your documents carefully to ensure they present a range of ideas and views that provide balance and objectivity.

Assessment criteria

Your commentary is assessed against criteria laid out in the *IB Business Management Guide*.

Criterion	Particulars	Marks available
A	Integration of a key concept	5
B	Supporting documents	4
C	Selection and application of tools and theories	4
D	Analysis and evaluation	5
E	Conclusions	3
F	Structure	2
G	Presentation	2
	Total	25

Consult the *IB Business Management Guide* for more details on the level descriptors for each criterion and the markbands.

INDEX

360-degree feedback 122, 123
360-degree marketing 293

above-the-line promotion 290, 291
absorption costing 168
AC *see* average cost
academic journals 259–60
accountability 17–18, 24, 220
accounting, code of conduct 172–3
accounts 4, 25, 150, 170–86
    balance sheet 176, 178–9, 200–1
    depreciation 181–5
    equity 154, 177, 178, 179
    ethical behaviour 172–3
    liabilities 176–7
    purpose of accounts to stakeholders 170–1
    see also assets; finance
acid test (quick) ratio 191–2
acquired needs theory 114–15
acquisitions *see* mergers and acquisitions
Adams, John 116
adaptive innovation 381, 382
adverse variance 222
advertising 291
AI *see* artificial intelligence
airline industry 49, 53–4, 246–7, 382, 383
angel investors 158
ANN *see* artificial neural networks
Ansoff matrix viii, 48–50, 297
Apple Inc. 46–7, 192, 232, 267, 273, 302, 303, 325
appraisal 122–3
appropriation account 174–5
arbitration 146–7
ARR *see* average rate of return
articles of association 23
artificial intelligence (AI) 389, 390, 393
artificial neural networks (ANN) 389, 393
assessment 396–406
    external assessment 396–402
    internal assessment vi, 403–6
assets 176
    depreciation 181–5
    fixed assets 149, 168
    intangible assets 180–1
    sale of assets 153, 206
    short- and long-term 160–1
autonomy 115
average cost (AC) 63, 64
average rate of return (ARR) 212–13

backwards vertical integration 70
balance sheet 176, 178–9, 200–1
banking sector 98, 157–60, 206, 274
bankruptcy 21, 198
batch production 320, 321–2, 323
below-the-line promotion 290, 291–2
benchmarking 220, 333–4
big data 390–1
BMW 303–4
Boston Consulting Group (BCG) matrix vii, viii, 276–8, 279
branding 279–82
    brand ambassadors 280
    brand awareness 280
    brand image 309
    brand loyalty 43, 44, 280
    brand recognition 294
    brand value 280, 281
    rebranding 282
break-even analysis 349–61
    benefits and limitations 359
    break-even chart 350–1, 354, 356, 357
    break-even point 349, 350, 351
    break-even quantity 349, 350, 351, 352–3
    break-even revenue 355–6
    contribution 349–50
    margin of safety 352
    price or cost changes 356–7
    profit or loss 353–4
    target profit output 354–5
budgets 219–26
    budget holders 219
    cost and profit centres 219–21
    decision-making 223–4
    profit centres 219
    variance analysis 222–3
buffer stock 329, 364, 365
bulk increasing/decreasing 339
bureaucracy 95, 96
business angels 158
business ideas 9–10
business objectives 34–51
aims of a business 36, 37
    Ansoff matrix 48–50
    business strategies 38–9, 83
    changes to 39–42
    corporate social responsibility 43–5
    ethical objectives 36, 43–5
    mission statements 34, 35, 36
    operational objectives 36, 37
    SMART objectives 37, 38
    strategic objectives 35, 36, 37–8
    SWOT analysis 45–8
    tactical objectives 35, 36, 37–8
    vision statements 34–5, 36
business plans viii, 10–11, 12, 301, 324
business research project 403–6
business tactics 39
businesses 1–13
    challenges 12
    functions of 3–5
    ownership 21–2, 25
    product outputs 3
    production processes 3
    resource inputs 2–3
    sectors of activity 6–8
    starting up a business 8–11

"cannibalistic marketing" 339
capacity utilization rate 367–8
capital expenditure 149–50
capital-intensive processes 3
capital productivity 370
career breaks 87
Casa Blanca Eco-lodge 319
cash cows (product category) 276, 277, 279
cash flow 202–9, 278
    cash flow forecasts 203–5, 207
    cash inflow/outflow 206
    discounted cash flow 213
    problem-solving strategies 205–7
    profit comparison 202–3
    relationship between investment, profit, and cash flow 205–7
cause-based marketing 238
centralization 96

CEOs *see* chief executive officers
chain of command 95
chain of production 6–7
change
    business objectives 39–42
    definition v
change management 91–2
changes of contract 146
channels of distribution 245, 295–7
charities 30–1
chief executive officers (CEOs) 37, 54, 123
China 242, 314, 343, 345
circular business models viii, 318
closing cash balance 204
closures 146
clothing industry 275–6
cloud computing 389
COGS *see* cost of goods sold
collaboration 28, 77
collateral 149
collective bargaining 145, 146
command terms (assessment) 398–9
commercial organizations *see* profit-based organizations
commission fees 124
communication 91, 139–43, 145, 375
    barriers to 139, 141–2
    formal/informal communication 139
    types of 140–1
communities 29, 32, 44, 171
companies 19–26, 282
    abbreviations 19–20
    initial public offerings 23, 25
    ownership 21–2, 25
    privately held companies 22–3
    public limited companies 22, 23, 161
    registration of 23
    shareholders 20–2, 23, 53, 54, 154, 170
    takeovers 26, 69–71, 135–6
competence 115
competition/competitors 53, 67, 76, 171, 207, 339, 383
competitive advantage 67
competitive pricing 286–7
concepts v–vi, 404
conciliation 146–7
confidentiality 262
conflict in the workplace 136, 142, 144–8
    conflict resolution 146–7
    sources of conflict 144–5
conglomeration (diversification) 50, 70–1, 309
consultants 53
consumers
    consumer profiles 239
    external economies of scale 65
    see also customers
contingency planning 374, 376
continuity 24, 25
continuous improvement (*kaizen*) 328, 329
contracts, changes to 146
contribution ix
    absorption costing 168
    contribution per unit 349
    and profit 349, 350
    total contribution 349
contribution pricing 286, 287–8
control 224, 375
convenience sampling 266

cooperatives 27–8
coordination, budgets 224
copyright laws 180–1, 380
corporate culture *see* organizational culture
corporate image 282
corporate social responsibility (CSR) 43–5
corporations *see* companies
cost centres 219, 220–1
cost of goods sold (COGS) 173–4
cost of sales 173, 174
cost-plus pricing 283
cost to buy (CTB) 371
cost to make (CTM) 371
costs 15, 63–4, 166–7, 339, 344, 357, 364–5, 376
cradle-to-cradle design and manufacturing 330
creditor days ratio 194, 196–7
crisis management 374–5
critical infrastructures 389–90
critical path analysis ix, 367
crowdfunding 156–7
CSR *see* corporate social responsibility
CTB *see* cost to buy
CTM *see* cost to make
cultural differences 88–90, 109, 133, 142, 298
cultural dimensions, Hofstede's 89, 109, 311
culture 78, 131, 136–7
current assets 176, 178, 179
current liabilities 176, 178, 179
current ratio 190–1
customers 43, 171, 388
    brand loyalty 43, 44, 280
    customer relationships 297–9
    see also consumers
cybercrime 388
cybersecurity 388

data analytics 386–8
data centres 389
data collection 266
data mining 386, 387–8
data protection 391
databases 386
debt capital 154
debt collection period 196
debt/equity ratio analysis 194–201
debtor days ratio 194, 196
decentralization 96
decision-making 29, 223–4
decision trees viii, 68, 342
defect rate 368
defensive strategies 48, 345
defusing strategies 48
delayering 96
delegation 95, 96
demographic changes 81, 82
demographic segmentation 236, 237
demotivation 142, 207
depreciation 181–5
deregulation 343
developed and developing economies 7, 128
DHL 298, 299
differentiation strategies 239, 244–9
digital marketing 293
digital Taylorism 386, 387, 394–5
direct action 32
direct costs 166, 167
direct investment 308–9

Index

direct marketing 291–2
disciplinary systems 122
discounted cash flow 213
diseconomies of scale 62–6
distribution channels 245, 295–7
diversification 50, 70–1, 309
dividends 21, 168, 174
dogs (product category) 276, 277, 279
donations 31, 32, 168
downshifting 87
dynamic pricing 285–6

e-commerce 308, 385, 388, 389
ecological issues
    business objectives 42
    sustainability 317
economic issues 41, 82, 207
    international marketing 310
    sustainability 317
economies of scale 62–6, 309
education 82
efficiencies 64, 65
efficiency ratios 194–8
    creditor days ratio 194, 196–7
    debtor days ratio 194, 196
    gearing ratio 194, 197–8
    stock turnover ratio 194–5
elasticities, price 288–9
employees
    business accounts 170–1
    cultural differences 298
    demotivation of 142, 207
    employee participation 147
    external diseconomies of scale 66
    external economies of scale 65
    monitoring of 387–8
    pay rates 54
    resistance to change in the workplace 90–2
    share-ownership schemes 125
    work–life balance 83, 84
    see also industrial/employee relations; motivation; work...
employers, conflict in the workplace 146
employment, changes in 84–5
    see also work...
empowerment 127–8
enterprise 3
entrepreneurs 9–11
environmental issues 215, 317
equity 154, 177, 178, 179
equity theory 116
ethical issues v, xi, 36, 41, 43–5, 248
    accounting 172–3
    big data 391
    HR planning 87–8
    innovation 383
    leadership and management 107–8
    market research 262
ethnic groupings 236
exams 396–402
expansion see growth
expectancy theory 116–17
exporting 308
extension strategies 274–5, 344–5
external environment 40–2, 59–62, 162
external growth 69–74
external stakeholders 52–5
extrapolation 252, 253

failure of start-ups 10, 12

fashion industry 275–6
favourable variance 222
Fayol, Henri 102–3
FC see fixed costs
feedback, marketing 297
FFA see force field analysis
finance 2, 4, 5, 24, 40, 149–226, 324
    amount required 162
    bankruptcy 21, 198
    budgets 219–26
    capital expenditure 149–50
    cash flow 202–9, 278
    costs and revenues 166–9
    debt/equity ratio analysis 194–201
    deregulation of markets 343
    efficiency ratios 194–8
    ethical behaviour 172–3
    and external environment 162
    external sources of 154–60
    flexibility 162
    gearing 162
    HR planning 83
    insolvency 198
    internal diseconomies of scale 66
    internal economies of scale 65
    internal sources of 152–3
    investment appraisal 210–18
    leasing 157, 206–7
    liquidity ratios 190–2
    partnerships 17
    profitability ratios 187–90
    purpose of funds 161
    ratio analysis 187
    revenue expenditure 149, 150
    short- and long-term 160–1
    social enterprises 29–30
    sole traders 14, 15–17
    sources of 152–65
    start-ups 11, 12
    status and size of organization 161
    stock levels 366
    sustainable finance 215–16
    total revenue 167–8
    see also accounts
financial cooperatives 27
financial rewards 124
financiers 171
fixed assets 149, 168
fixed costs (FC) 63, 64, 166, 351, 357
fixed interest rates 154
flexi-time 82, 86
flow production (mass production) 320, 322–3
focus groups 258–9
for-profit social enterprises 26–30
force field analysis (FFA) ix, 347
formative appraisal 122, 123
forwards vertical integration 70
franchises 72–4, 309
fringe payments (perks) 125–6

Gantt charts ix, 372
gearing 162
gearing ratio 194, 197–8
generic strategies, Porter's 246
geographic segmentation 236, 237
geographical mobility 85
gig economy 82, 86
globalization 76–7, 343–5
goods 3, 5, 316
goodwill 180
governance 28–9, 215
government 44, 82, 171, 260–1, 341
gross profit 173, 174
gross profit margin 187–8

growth 25, 48, 59–75
    economies and diseconomies of scale 62–6
    external environment impact 59–62
    internal and external growth 69–74
    multinational companies 77
    reasons to grow or stay small 66–7
    STEEPLE analysis 59–61

Handy, Charles 99, 131–3
Herzberg, Frederick 113–14
hierarchy of needs, Maslow's 113
hierarchy, organizational structure 95, 97
Hofstede, Geert ix, 89, 109, 311
homeworking 86–7
horizontal integration 70
housing cooperatives 27
human resource (HR) management 4, 39, 80–148, 324
    appraisal 122–3
    change management 91–2
    changes in work patterns, practices, and preferences 83–7
    communication 139–43
    cultural differences 88–90
    ethical issues 87–8
    HR planning, internal and external factors 81–3
    industrial/employee relations 144–8
    innovation, impact of 87
    labour turnover 117–18, 136
    leadership and management 102–10
    motivation and demotivation 111–30
    organizational culture 131–8
    organizational structure 94–101
    recruitment methods 118–20
    resistance to change in the workplace 90–2
    training 120–1
hygiene needs, Herzberg's 113, 114

ICT 82, 85
    see also internet; management information systems
identity marketing 239–40
image differentiation 245
immigration 82
income, market segmentation 237–8
income statement 173
India 159–60, 375
indirect costs 166, 167, 220
induction 120–1
industrial democracy 147
industrial/employee relations 83, 144–8
    arbitration and conciliation 146–7
    employee and employer approaches 145, 146
    sources of conflict 144–5
infographics 98
information systems (IS) 385–8
infrastructure 340–1, 366, 389–90
initial public offerings (IPOs) 23, 25
innovation 32, 87, 89–90, 380, 381–3
    adaptive innovation 381, 382
    disruptive innovation 381, 382
    process innovation 381

product innovation 381
input–output model 314, 317
insolvency 198
insourcing 346
inspection 122
intangible assets 180–1
intellectual property rights 380–1
interest 168
interest rates 154, 160
internal environment 39–40
internal growth 69
internal stakeholders 52–5
international marketing 308–12
    entering international markets 308–9
    opportunities/threats 309–10
internet 261, 308, 390
internet of things (IoT) 390, 393
interviews 120, 258
intuitive management 103–4
investment appraisal 210–18
    average rate of return 212–13
    net present value 213–14
    payback period 210–12
investment/investors 24, 278
    angel investors 158
    relationship between investment, profit, and cash flow 205–7
IoT see internet of things
IPOs see initial public offerings
IS see information systems
ISO 9001 standard 336

JIC see just-in-case
JIT see just-in-time
job enlargement 127
job enrichment 127
job losses 55, 146
job production 320, 321, 323
job rotation 127
job shares 87
joint ventures 71, 309
just-in-case (JIC) 328, 329, 364
just-in-time (JIT) 328, 329, 364

kaizen (continuous improvement) 328, 329
Kenya 162–4, 263–4
labour-intensive processes 3

labour mobility 81, 82
labour pool 340
labour productivity 370
labour relations see industrial/employee relations
labour turnover 117–18, 136
land, types of 339
laws 341
    see also legal...
lead time 364, 365
leadership 39, 96, 102–10
    autocratic leadership 105
    cultural differences 109
    democratic leadership 106
    ethical issues 107–8
    laissez-faire leadership 106–7
    paternalistic leadership 105–6
    situational leadership 107
    versus management 104
lean production 327–9
    impact of 335
    just-in-case 328, 329
    just-in-time 328, 329
    kaizen (continuous improvement) 328, 329
leasing 157, 206–7
legal issues 42, 82, 310, 383

Index

legal redress 43
legal requirements 12
   companies 25
   sole traders 16
   start-ups 11
less developed economies 7
liabilities 176–7
limited liability 21, 23, 24
line managers 95
liquidation 177, 199
liquidity ratios 190–2
loan capital 154–5
lobbying 32
location 338–48
   competition 339
   costs 339, 344
   defensive strategies 345
   extension strategies 344–5
   familiarity with area 340
   globalization impact 343–5
   and government 341
   infrastructure 340–1
   insourcing 346
   labour pool 340
   land, types of 339
   market share 344
   markets 340
   national, regional or international locations 341–2
   offshoring 346
   outsourcing 345–6
   push/pull factors 343–5
   reshoring 346–7
   suppliers 341
   see also place, marketing mix
lockouts 146
loss leaders 284
"lurkers" 295

M&As see mergers and acquisitions
M-Pesa 162–4
McClelland, David 114–15
McDonald's 73, 267, 344–5
management information systems 385–95
   artificial intelligence 389, 390, 393
   big data 390–1
   critical infrastructures 389–90
   cybercrime and cybersecurity 388
   information systems 385–7
   internet of things 390, 393
   virtual reality 390, 392
management/managers 102–10
   accounts 170
   cultural differences 109
   ethical issues 107–8
   functions of 102–3
   internal diseconomies of scale 66
   internal economies of scale 65
   organizational structure 95–6
   scientific and intuitive management 103–4
   versus leadership 104
manufacturing see production
margin of safety 352
mark-up pricing 283
market analyses 261
market development 49
market growth 230–1
market leaders 67, 232–3
market orientation 228–9, 286–7
market penetration 49
market position 47–8
market research 10, 12, 207, 256–69
   data collection 266

ethical issues 262
   examples 267–8
   primary research 256, 257–9
   purpose of 256
   qualitative and quantitative research 263
   Safaricom 263–4
   sampling methods 265–6
   secondary research 256, 257, 259–61
market segmentation 236–40
   identity marketing 239–40
   market segments 236
market share 67, 78, 229–30, 232–3, 344
market size 230
market stakeholders 52
market testing 11
marketing 4, 5
   definitions 227–8
   internal diseconomies of scale 66
   internal economies of scale 65
   international marketing 308–12
   market growth 230–1
   market leaders 232–3
   market orientation versus product orientation 228–9
   market share 229–30, 232–3
   production method changes 324
   sales forecasting 251–5
marketing mix, seven Ps of 270–307
   Apple 302
   appropriate marketing mix 299–300
   benefits of 300
   BMW 303–4
   branding 279–82
   drawbacks of 300
   extension strategies 274–5
   people 271, 297–8
   physical evidence 271–2, 299
   place 271, 295–7
   price 271, 283–90
   processes 271, 298–9
   product 270, 272–4
   product portfolio 276–8
   promotion 271, 290–5
   summary of 301
marketing planning 235–50
   benefits of 235–6
   differentiation strategies 239, 244–9
   generic strategies, Porter's 246
   limitations of 236
   market segmentation 236–8, 239–40
   niche market/mass market comparison 241
   product positioning 240–1
   targeting 238–9
   unique selling point 243
markets 309, 340, 343
Maslow, Abraham 113
mass customization 320, 323
mass marketing 238, 241
mass production 320, 322–3
matrix structure 96
memorandum of association 23
mergers and acquisitions (M&As) 69–71, 135–6
microfinance providers 157–60
mission statements 34, 35, 36
MNCs see multinational companies
mobile-payments service 162–4
motivation 67, 111–30, 220

budgets 223
   extrinsic/intrinsic motivation 112
   labour turnover 117–18
   motivators 113–14
   payment systems 123–6
   in practice 123–9
   theories 112–17
moving averages 252–4
multinational companies (MNCs) 76–9, 343
   globalization 76–7
   growth of 77
   host country impact of 78

National Rifle Association 32
Nespresso 248–9
net assets 176, 177, 178, 179
net cash flow 204
net income 221
net present value (NPV) 213–14
Netflix 49
newspapers 260
NGOs see non-governmental organizations
niche brands/markets 67, 239, 241, 242
no-strike agreements 147
non-current assets 176, 178, 179
non-current liabilities 176, 178, 179
non-financial rewards 127–9
non-governmental organizations (NGOs) 30, 31
non-market stakeholders 52
non-profit social enterprises 30–2
NPV see net present value

objectives see business objectives
observation, market research 259
occupational mobility 85
offshoring 346
oil industry 282
on/off-the-job training 120, 121
online content, market research 261
opening cash balance 203
operating leverage 370–1
operational objectives 36, 37, 40
operations management 4, 5, 313–95
   break-even analysis 349–61
   Casa Blanca Eco-lodge 319
   contingency planning 374, 376
   crisis management 374–5
   input–output model 314, 317
   lean production 327–9, 335
   location 338–48
   management information systems 385–95
   operations methods 320–6
   operations and other business functions 315
   production of goods or services 316
   quality management 331–7
   research and development 378–80
   sustainability 316–18
opportunity cost 161
organizational change 40
   see also change management
organizational charts 94–8
organizational culture 131–8, 382
   culture clashes 133, 135–6
   and individuals 136–7
   organizational assumptions 134
   organizational attributes 133
   person culture 133
   power culture 132

professed culture 134
   role culture 132
   task culture 133
organizational structure 25, 94–101
   appropriateness of 100
   changes in 99–100
   organizational charts 94–8
organizational teams, matrix of 99
outsourcing 345–6
overdrafts 155, 206
overhead costs 167
ownership 21–2, 25, 31

packaging 274
partnerships 14, 17–19, 71
   see also cooperatives
patents 180, 381
pay rates 54
payback period 210–12
payment systems 123–6
PDI see power distance index
PED see price elasticity of demand
penetration pricing 273, 283–4
people, marketing mix, 271, 297–8
perception maps 240, 241
performance 145
performance-related pay (PRP) 125
person culture 133
personal funds 152
personal selling 292
PEST/PESTLE analysis 59
physical evidence, marketing mix 271–2, 299
pie charts 121
piggybacking 308
place, marketing mix 271, 295–7
   see also location
planning
   budgets 223
   decision trees viii, 68, 342
   HR planning 81–3
   managers 102
   SWOT analysis viii, 45–8, 83, 192, 303
   see also business plans; marketing planning; production planning
ploughed-back profit 153
point-of-sale displays 292
political factors 41–2, 310
Porter, Michael ix, 246
position maps 240, 241
power culture 132
power distance index (PDI) 89, 90
power–interest model 56–7
price 271, 283–90
   break-even analysis 356
   competitive pricing 286–7
   contribution pricing 286, 287–8
   cost-plus pricing 283
   dynamic pricing 285–6
   elasticity of demand 288–9
   loss leaders 284
   penetration pricing 283–4
   predatory pricing 284
   premium pricing 285
   price discrimination 288, 289–90
   price skimming 273
   share price 21, 26
price differentiation 244
price elasticity of demand (PED) 288–9
primary market research 256, 257–9
primary sector 6, 7
privacy 15–16, 25, 262
private sector 14, 27
privately held companies 22–3

409

Index

process innovation 381
processes, marketing mix 271, 298–9
producer cooperatives 28
product development 49
product differentiation 244
product innovation 381
product life cycle 272, 274, 275, 278
product orientation 228–9
product portfolio 276–8
product positioning 240–1
production 3
    appropriate method of production 325
    batch production 320, 321–2, 323
    changing production method 324
    cradle-to-cradle design and manufacturing 330
    extension strategies 344–5
    insourcing 346
    job production 320, 321, 323
    location 338–42
    mass customization 320, 323
    mass production 320, 322–3
    offshoring 346
    operations management 316
    outsourcing 345–6
    reshoring 346–7
production chain 6–7
production planning 362–73
    capacity utilization rate 367–8
    capital productivity 370
    cost to buy and cost to make 371
    defect rate 368
    just-in-time and just-in-case 364
    labour productivity 370
    operating leverage 370–1
    productivity rate 368–9
    stock control 364–6
    supply chain process 362–4
productivity rate 368–9
products 40, 98, 270, 272–5, 366
profit 18, 20, 44, 153, 278
    cash flow comparison 202–3
    contribution and profit 349, 350
    for-profit social enterprises 26–30
    multinational companies 78
    profit before interest and tax 174
    profit before tax 174
    profit or loss 353–4
    profit margin 187, 188–9
    profit for period 174
    relationship between investment, profit, and cash flow 205–7
    target profit output 354–5
profit and loss account 173–5
profit-based organizations 14–26
profit centres 219
profit-related pay 124–5
profitability 136, 187–90
project-based organizations 99
promotion 271, 290–5
    above-the-line promotion 290, 291
    below-the-line promotion 290, 291–2
    social media marketing 294–5
    through-the-line promotion 290, 293
promotional pricing 273
PRP see performance-related pay
psychographic segmentation 237

public limited companies 22, 23, 161
public relations 292
public sector 14, 27
purchases, market segmentation 238
purchasing, diseconomies of scale 66

qualitative research 263
quality management 331–7
    benchmarking 333–4
    quality assurance 331–2
    quality circles 333
    quality control 331–2
    quality standards 335–6
    total quality management 333, 334–5
quantitative research 263
quartiles 369
quaternary sector 6, 7, 8
question marks (product category) 276, 277, 279
questionnaires 257–8
quota sampling 265

R&D see research and development
random sampling 265
ratio analysis 187
re-orientation strategies 48
receivership 21
recruitment 118–20
    application process 119
    identification process 118
    selection process 120
redundancies 55, 146
registration of companies 23
regulations 82, 171, 341
relationship differentiation 245
rental income 168
reorder level 364, 365
reorder quantity 364, 365
reputation differentiation 245
research and development (R&D) 378–80
    addressing customers' unmet needs 380
    factors affecting 382–3
    innovation 380, 381–3
    intellectual property rights 380–1
reshoring 346–7
residual value 182
resource allocation 32, 223
resource recovery models 42
retained earnings 177
retained profit 153, 174
return on capital employed (ROCE) 189–90
revenue
    break-even revenue 355–6
    sales revenue 15, 173, 252, 253
    surplus revenue 30, 31
revenue expenditure 149, 150
risk 25, 65, 66, 376
ROCE see return on capital employed
role culture 132

salaries 123–4, 126
sale of assets 153, 206
sales forecasting 251–5
    benefits/limitations of 253–4
    extrapolation 252, 253
    moving averages 252–4
    time series analysis 251
sales promotions 292
sales revenue 15, 173, 252, 253
samples/sampling methods 265–6
Schein, Edgar 133–4
scientific management 103–4
secondary market research 256, 257,
259–61
secondary sector 6, 7, 8
sectors of business activity 6–8
segmented marketing 239
self-appraisal 122, 123
self-determination theory 115
service differentiation 244
services 3, 5, 316
seven Ps see marketing mix, seven Ps of
shamrock organizations 99
share capital 154, 177
share-ownership schemes 125
shareholders 20–2, 23, 53, 154
    accounts 170
    conflicting interests of 54
shares 21, 25, 26
simple linear regression ix, 254, 351
single-union agreements 147
skills transfer 77, 78
sleeping partners 17
SMART goals/objectives 37, 38, 224, 235
SMM see social media marketing
social enterprises 26–32
    donations 31, 32
    finance 29–30
    for-profit enterprises 26–30
    non-profit enterprises 30–2
    ownership 31
social issues 40–1, 215, 310, 317
social media marketing (SMM) 242, 294–5
social trends 82, 83
sole traders 14, 15–17
span of control 95
Spaulding, Charles Clinton 103
staff managers 95
stakeholders 52–8
    accounts 170–1
    conflicting interests of 54–5
    internal and external stakeholders 52–5
    stakeholder analysis 55–7
    stakeholder mapping 56–7
Starbucks 13, 49, 121, 281
stars (product category) 276, 279
start-ups 8–12
    branding 281
    business ideas 9–10
    business plans 10–11, 12
    failure of 10, 12
    legal requirements 11, 12
    market testing 11, 12
statistical information viii, ix, 98, 121, 254, 351, 369
STEEPLE analysis viii, 40–2, 59–61, 62
stock control 329, 364–6
    optimal stock levels 366
stock exchange 154
stock market 26
stock turnover ratio 194–5
straight-line depreciation 181–2
strategic alliances 72
strategic objectives 35, 36, 37–8
strike action 145
study leave 87
subcontracting 345–6
"sugging" 262
summative appraisal 122, 123
suppliers 44, 171, 341
supply chain process 362–4
surplus revenue 30, 31
surveys 257–8
sustainability v
    operations management 316–18
    sustainable finance 215–16

SWOT analysis viii, 45–8, 83, 192, 303

tactical objectives 35, 36, 37–8
takeovers 26, 69–71, 135–6
target markets 238
target profit output 354–5
targeting 238–9
task culture 133
taxes 15, 171, 341
Taylor, Frederick Winslow 112
Taylorism, digital 386, 387, 394–5
TC see total cost
teamwork 128–9
technological issues 41, 82, 310, 382
teleworking 86
temporary work 86
tertiary sector 6, 7, 8
test marketing 272
through-the-line promotion 290, 293
time-and-motion studies 112
time series analysis 251
total assets 176, 178, 179
total cash inflows/outflows 203
total contribution 349
total costs (TC) 15, 63, 351, 365
total expenses 221
total income 221
total liabilities 177, 178, 179
total quality management (TQM) 333, 334–5
total revenue (TR) 167–8, 351
trade barriers 343
trade credit 155–6
trademarks 180, 181, 381
trades unions 145, 147
trading account 173–4
training 120–1
triple bottom line 317–18
trust 142
Tyson Foods 268

Uber 61–2
unions 145, 147
unique selling point (USP) 76, 243
United States 84–5
units of production depreciation 181, 183–5
unlimited liability 17
USP see unique selling point

variable costs (VC) 63, 166–7, 351, 357
variable interest rates 154
variance 221, 222
variance analysis 222–3
variation, sales 252
VC see variable costs
vertical integration 70
virtual reality (VR) 390, 392
vision statements 34–5, 36
Vroom, Victor 116

wages (time and piece rates) 54, 124
WFH see working from home
work environment 43
work–life balance 83, 84
work patterns, changes in 84–5
work practices
    changes in 85–7
    resistance to change 90–2
    see also conflict in the workplace
work-to-rule 145
workers' cooperatives 27–8
working capital 370
working from home (WFH) 86–7